Cases on Online Discussion and Interaction:
Experiences and Outcomes

Leonard Shedletsky
University of Southern Maine, USA

Joan E. Aitken
Park University, USA

INFORMATION SCIENCE REFERENCE

Hershey · New York

Director of Editorial Content: Kristin Klinger
Director of Book Publications: Julia Mosemann
Acquisitions Editor: Lindsay Johnston
Development Editor: Christine Bufton
Typesetter: Gregory Snader
Production Editor: Jamie Snavely
Cover Design: Lisa Tosheff
Printed at: Yurchak Printing Inc.

Published in the United States of America by
Information Science Reference (an imprint of IGI Global)
701 E. Chocolate Avenue
Hershey PA 17033
Tel: 717-533-8845
Fax: 717-533-8661
E-mail: cust@igi-global.com
Web site: http://www.igi-global.com/reference

Library of Congress Cataloging-in-Publication Data

Cases on online discussion and interaction : experiences and outcomes /
Leonard Shedletsky and Joan E. Aitken, editors.
    p. cm.
  Includes bibliographical references and index.
  Summary: "This book gives readers a better idea of what is likely to
facilitate discussion online, what is likely to encourage collaborative
meaning-making, what is likely to encourage productive, supportive, engaged
discussion, and what is likely to foster critical thinking"--Provided by
publisher.
  ISBN 978-1-61520-863-0 (hardcover) -- ISBN 978-1-61520-864-7 (ebook) 1.
Forums (Discussion and debate) 2. Information technology. 3. Critical
thinking--Problems, exercises, etc. I. Shedletsky, Leonard, 1944- II. Aitken,
Joan E.
  LC6519.C37 2010
  808.530285'4693--dc22
          2009052434

British Cataloguing in Publication Data
A Cataloguing in Publication record for this book is available from the British Library.

All work contributed to this book is new, previously-unpublished material. The views expressed in this book are those of the authors, but not necessarily of the publisher.

In memory of Lenny's brother, Bernard Sheldon

Editorial Advisory Board

Table of Contents

Section 2
Language and Communication Processes

Detailed Table of Contents

This chapter reviews the literature on critical thinking in online discussion in the context of the online college course. It employs the experimental method to test for the amount of student-to-student interaction and the type of interaction, as defined in critical thinking terms. It presents five experimental studies of instructional media and instructional methods. As the first chapter in the book, it sets a tone for seeking to develop a theory of online discussion. It just begins to open that door, with a hint of understanding what is likely to influence students to collaborate and to do more than just post and flee.

•

Chapter 2 examines student use of critical thinking as students worked on problem solving. The authors looked at three sections of a course over a year and categorized student posts for levels of critical thinking. They speculate on the group dynamics that may lead to disappointing levels of critical thinking or higher levels and take us closer to understanding how it works and what teachers might do to improve online discussions. You may want to read this chapter in close connection with the Shedletsky chapter.

Chapter 3

    Kathy L. Guthrie, Florida State University, USA
    Holly McCracken, University of Illinois at Springfield, USA

This case reports on ways in which course assignments attempt to facilitate community development, trust, interpersonal connectivity, collaboration and experientially-based critical reflection. Students were engaged in service-learning experiences and interacted with peers and instructors in a virtual environment designed to facilitate reflection, support and collective discovery.

Chapter 4

    Lesley A. Withers, Central Michigan University, USA
    Lynnette G. Leonard, University of Nebraska at Omaha, USA
    John C. Sherblom, University of Maine, USA

Three professors report on the use of a virtual classroom project—text or voiced synchronous online discussion with visual three-dimensional space, involving students from three geographically distanced universities, in which students collaborate on an involved project, requiring students " . . .to create an agenda; assign group roles and tasks; research a non-profit organization; describe its goals, multiple audiences, and needs; describe a proposal for assisting the non-profit through some participation in Second Life; and develop a rationale explaining the ways in which this proposal meets the organization's objectives." The chapter reports on both the challenges and successes of the project, offering lessons learned.

Chapter 5

    Stuart Palmer, Deakin University, Australia
    Dale Holt, Deakin University, Australia

This chapter offers a close analysis of the effects of requiring students to reflect on course material and to comment on fellow student postings each week on a course discussion board. Based on a number of behavioral measures and survey data, this study indicates that this simple assignment does produce beneficial effects on student satisfaction and learning.

Chapter 6

    Eleni Sideri, University of Thessaly, Greece

This case chronicles the use of blogs in a college course, Cyberspace and Diasporic Media, with 20 advanced students. The chapter seeks to determine whether or not assigned blogging could foster critical thinking, collaborative knowledge and re-personalization of education. Students wrote on assigned questions or topics. The chapter offers the teacher's observations on how students responded to the media in terms of function, writing, language use, student-to-student dynamics, and assessment. The chapter reflects upon the dynamics of the classroom as it is challenged by new technologies and also the challenges and dynamics of university education in an interconnected world, the relationship of multiliteracies to social-political interconnections .

The authors invite us to think with them about ". . . the potential learning value of a particular technology (affordances). . . ." not solely in terms of how the technology functions but also in terms of the user's imagination and creativity. While the chapter uses Voice Thread as a discussion application, it concentrates on pedagogical affordances of technology. Drawing upon undergraduate and postgraduate students in continuing professional development in education, this chapter reports on the students' experience of online communication, what facilitates discussion online. The chapter points us toward thinking about what students do with technology.

Section 2
Language and Communication Processes

This case furthers our quest for a theory of online discussion by asking two key questions: (1) How does social presence aid in the development of relations between actors in online learning environments? and (2) How is this beneficial to online discussion and interaction? Using an extended interview method, this chapter adds to our understanding of the interpersonal dynamics involved in online discussion, e.g., trust, feelings of safety and respect.

This chapter takes us into the synchronous, multimodal video conference with professionals in the workplace. In part this chapter explores the significance of using naturally occurring language as opposed to, say, experimental data, to study social co-presence. The chapter considers the multimodal conference to face-to-face communication and gives us some appreciation for what is likely to increase the sense of "the other as being perceived as present."

Anna Filipi, Australian Council for Educational Research, Australia
Sophie Lissonnet, Australian Council for Educational Research, Australia

We get to take a close look at the online collaboration of experts developing a test in order to (1) compare the online, asynchronous communication to face-to-face, and (2) uncover how expertise is displayed online. Filipi and Lissonet use the method of conversation analysis to get at matters of structure and identity in the online interactions of experts working together.

Kris M. Markman, University of Memphis, USA

This case employs conversation analysis in an educational context to examine the interaction in synchronous chat during teamwork, with a focus on how coherence is maintained in this fast paced environment. The chapter compares talk online to talk face-to-face in terms of things like turn taking and making sense out of utterances. Markman has useful suggestions for the teacher planning to use chat for online discussions.

Jan Chovanec, Masaryk University, Czech Republic

Chovanec focuses on a type of reporting in which live sports events are reported as the audience engages in online discussion and interaction during the construction of the text. The chapter offers a sociolinguistic approach to this emerging genre, treating closely the use of language, dialogic structure and interpersonal interaction, with attention to the display of identity. The chapter goes a ways towards locating this novel genre against the background of mass media. We see the melding of report of information with interpersonal debate. The chapter does a close reading on ways in which this genre highlights certain features not present in traditional mass media, how layers of meaning reside in the new genre. Humorous and competitive interactions are discussed in gender terms with the notion of 'male gossip.'

Terri Toles Patkin, Eastern Connecticut State University, USA

This case looks at the communication that goes on during an online backgammon game in which the player is extremely limited to four factors: (a) level of play, (b) language selected, (c) chat interface, and (d) and game play. Users select from a list of 27 preloaded comments to discuss with one another and the choice is translated into the language chosen by each receiver. This case is an exercise in discovering just how much is communicated within the framework of a limited system for communicating.

The chapter pays special attention to the attribution of identity under circumstances of highly limited information available.

Chapter 14

This chapter considers the possibility of civic engagement online in the discussion of political issues. Will the Internet promote greater citizen involvement, interaction between citizen's and government, online consultation? Using content analysis, the chapter investigates the degree to which Singapore's online consultation forum reflects the ideals of democratic deliberation. The study employed a set of criteria for democratic deliberation to analyze discussion forum messages. Such criteria as autonomy, transparency, equal participation, privacy and anonymity were applied to the data. Both structure and content were described, with such variables as frequency of posts, interactions among users, post length, date of post, number of users, issues discussed, critical assessment of issues, and tone of message, pro or anti-government. With regard to democratic deliberation, the results are mixed. Some solutions are recommended.

Chapter 15

This chapter chronicles the individual literacy biographies of children five to fifteen years old, collecting data on their online interactivity as they develop. They explore the question of what it means to be literate by viewing the practices and tools of children and adolescents. The children and their parents were interviewed in their homes as they showed the researchers their typical literacy materials and activities, printed and technologically mediated. This study points to the changing nature of literacy and to its individual character, hence the unique digital fingerprints.

Section 3
Support

Chapter 16

This case shows us how people talk to one another in an online cancer support group, documenting (1) content, (2) participants, (3) topics, and (4) and messages that were absent or "silenced." Using a triangulation of methods, this chapter describes support group discussion and offers a good understanding of the importance of these discussions.

Chapter 17

This case uses ethnography of communication to analyze a woman-centered Internet site, focusing on talk about relationship troubles. This chapter describes communication practices women use in an attempt to answer the question, "What are the dominant ways members negotiate relationship troubles?" It takes talk about relationship change as a prominent cultural symbol that allows for insights into rules for communicating. This chapter touches on theoretically promising topics such as self-disclosure online and anonymity.

Chapter 18

Data were gathered on a large number of organizations over a four-year period as the organizatons attempt to network. The focus is on an email list in a non-profit network of organizations dedicated to service for the homeless. The study was interested in the reasons that people used or didn't use the email list; how the email list was used; and the consequences of use or nonuse of the email list. The researchers collected data from recorded logs, an online survey, face-to-face interviews and from attending meetings and events. They report on how the use of technology added to the sense of "we-ness" and connections in the community of users. The attitudes of nonusers were equally significant to understand. Several recommendations for organizational leaders grow out of these findings.

Chapter 19

This case examines how social support is communicated in an online weight loss community website. The chapter compares the communication of social support in the online journals and the discussion forums by analyzing journal entries and discussion forum comments. Interestingly, the nature of support expressed in discussion forums differs from support given in response to journals. Other key differences between discussion in the journals and in the forums are found in how communicators address their audience and the use of double interacts. This chapter gives organizers and site designers for online support groups important ideas to think about.

Foreword

Sitting at an orange-glowing terminal with the harsh prairie wind whistling outside the nearly-empty, drafty computer laboratory in the winter of 1976, I was introduced to computer-mediated communication. I was connected to the PLATO system that interconnected a handful of mainframes and thousands of attached terminals around the world. It wasn't long before I was linking my students at the University of Illinois via this system to those in an analogous class at the University of Hawaii. We used "pnotes, notesfiles, and talkomatic" – among the many early forerunners of what came to be known generically as email, discussion groups, and live group chat.

As I type today, winter is bearing down on the prairie again, but in front of me are dual LCD monitors. The document fills one screen; the other is filled with Google Wave, pulsing with updates creating ever-widening discussion waves every few seconds. From its inception as Arpanet, it was clear that the vibrant, thriving Internet is all about human interaction through forms of discussion. And, it's not just brief emails and 140-character twitter tweets, but deep and broad engagement through synchronous and asynchronous modes; text and video; audio and graphic; small and large groups.

We seem to know very well the architecture, the electronics, the physical aspects of this network of networks that we call the Internet. Yet, even though the first message was sent over the Arpanet on October 29th in 1969 (Kline, 1969), more than 40 years ago, we seem to know far less about the billions of discussions that have ensued in the intervening decades. What works well; what doesn't? What special ways might we consider in using discussions that don't immediately come to mind? What media can enable richer communication, in what situations? How has discussion impacted learning, careers, lives, and societies? The essence of the Internet is not in the electronics; rather it comes from these connections between and among people, and the ways in which people find to efficiently and effectively connect with one another online.

And, that's the genius of this book. The editors, Lenny Shedletsky and Joan Aitkin, have pulled together a mesmerizing collection of case studies of online discussion. The range of these cases is amazing – from college classes to support groups; from the virtual world of Second Life to live text in sports; from gender focused support discussions to chatting in online gaming; from back channeling to deep discussions in the democratic process of Singapore; from text-based to multimedia modes; and much more. These case studies reveal the power of the Internet. They capture the range and passion of social connectedness online. The cases point to the potential to foster public political discourse, pursue deeply meaningful interactions, and, yes, even to be a connected sports fan on the road in smart phone mode.

Those who seek to see the future of the Internet will do well to read these case studies. While the technologies will change over time, the essence will remain the same – people reaching out to people, interacting and engaging one another in an ever-expanding, ever-deepening range of discussion online. And where that leads us, I predict, will be very important in determining our collective future.

REFERENCE

Kline, C.S. (1969). First-arpanet-imp-log.jpg [Web]. Retrieved from http://en.wikipedia.org/wiki/File:First-arpanet-imp-log.jpg

Ray Schroeder directs the Center for Online Learning, Research and Service at the University of Illinois at Springfield. He lives on the prairie of central Illinois where he publishes the very popular Online Learning Update and Educational Technology blogs.

Preface

This book is about discussion. It is largely about discussion on the Internet, but it will also raise to consciousness questions about discussion in person. The book calls us to step back and ask many questions about what we normally see but do not notice in discussion:

- What do we get out of discussion?
- What do we put into discussion?
- When does discussion work?
- What could we mean by discussion working?
- Does discussion online meet our expectations?
- What can we do to improve discussion?

This book should help you to think about the process and the quality of discussion.

Cases on Online Discussion and Interaction: Experiences and Outcomes is filled with examples of online discussions in a variety of contexts and for a variety of purposes. By looking at instances of online discussion, we are better able to speculate about how it works. After reading the case studies, the reader should have a better idea of what is likely to facilitate discussion online, what is likely to encourage collaborative meaning-making, what is likely to encourage productive, supportive, engaged discussion, and what is likely to foster critical thinking. The aim is to draw together in one book, chapters dealing with an array of research methods, online communication media, forms of expression, communication contexts, and philosophical perspectives. The cases observe online discussion in education, the workplace, support groups, politics, social networking, with groups and dyads, in public and private settings. Often, authors will find it useful to compare the online discussion to the more traditional face-to-face discussion. Hence, this book should help us better understand the traditional face-to-face discussion, too. In short, we want to examine discussion with the aim of making it better.

Here is what you will find in each chapter:

TEACHING

Shedletsky's chapter (Does Online Discussion Produce Increased Interaction and Critical Thinking?) reviews the literature on critical thinking in online discussion in the context of the online college course.

It employs the experimental method to test for the amount of student-to-student interaction and the type of interaction, as defined in critical thinking terms. It presents five experimental studies of instructional media and instructional methods. As the first chapter in the book, it sets a tone for seeking to develop a theory of online discussion. It just begins to open that door, with a hint of understanding what is likely to influence students to collaborate and to do more than just post and flee.

Schwartzman and Morrissey (Collaborative Student Groups and Critical Thinking in an Online Basic Communication Course) examine student use of critical thinking as students worked on problem solving. They looked at three sections of a course over a year and categorized student posts for levels of critical thinking. They speculate on the group dynamics that may lead to disappointing levels of critical thinking or higher levels and take us closer to understanding how it works and what teachers might do to improve online discussions. You may want to read this chapter in close connection with the Shedletsky chapter.

Guthrie and McCracken (Promoting Reflective Discourse through Connectivity: Conversations around Service-Learning Experiences) report on ways in which course assignments attempt to facilitate community development, trust, interpersonal connectivity, collaboration and experientially-based critical reflection. Students were engaged in service-learning experiences and interacted with peers and instructors in a virtual environment designed to facilitate reflection, support and collective discovery.

Withers, Leonard & Sherblom (Classrooms Without Walls—Teaching Together in Second Life) report on the use of a virtual classroom project—text or voiced synchronous online discussion with visual three-dimensional space, involving students from three geographically distanced universities, in which students collaborate on an involved project, requiring students " . . .to create an agenda; assign group roles and tasks; research a non-profit organization; describe its goals, multiple audiences, and needs; describe a proposal for assisting the non-profit through some participation in Second Life; and develop a rationale explaining the ways in which this proposal meets the organization's objectives." The chapter reports on both the challenges and successes of the project, offering lessons learned.

Palmer and Holt (Online Discussion in Engineering Education—Student Responses and Learning Outcomes) offer a close analysis of the effects of requiring students to reflect on course material and to comment on fellow student postings each week on a course discussion board. Based on a number of behavioral measures and survey data, this study indicates that this simple assignment does produce beneficial effects on student satisfaction and learning.

Sideri (B-log on Social Change and Educational Reform: The Case of a University Class in Greece) chronicles the use of blogs in a college course, Cyberspace and Diasporic Media, with 20 advanced students. The chapter seeks to determine whether or not assigned blogging could foster critical thinking, collaborative knowledge and re-personalization of education. Students wrote on assigned questions or topics. The chapter offers the teacher's observations on how students responded to the media in terms of function, writing, language use, student-to-student dynamics, and assessment. The chapter reflects upon the dynamics of the classroom as it is challenged by new technologies and also the challenges and dynamics of university education in an interconnected world, the relationship of multiliteracies to social-political interconnections .

Burden and Atkinson ("De-Coupling Groups in Space and Time": Evaluating New Forms of Social Dialogue for Learning) invite us to think with them about ". . . the potential learning value of a particular technology (affordances). . . ." not solely in terms of how the technology functions but also in terms of the user's imagination and creativity. While the chapter uses Voice Thread as a discussion application, it concentrates on pedagogical affordances of technology. Drawing upon undergraduate and postgraduate students in continuing professional development in education, this chapter reports on the students' experience of online communication, what facilitates discussion online. The chapter points us toward thinking about what students do with technology.

LANGUAGE AND COMMUNICATION PROCESSES

Kehrwald (Towards More Productive Online Discussions: Social Presence and the Development of Interpersonal Relations) furthers our quest for a theory of online discussion by asking two key questions: (1) How does social presence aid in the development of relations between actors in online learning environments? and (2) How is this beneficial to online discussion and interaction? Using an extended interview method, this chapter adds to our understanding of the interpersonal dynamics involved in online discussion, e.g., trust, feelings of safety and respect.

Beers Fagersten (Using Discourse Analysis to Assess Social Co-Presence in the Video Conference Environment) takes us into the synchronous, multimodal video conference with professionals in the workplace. In part this chapter explores the significance of using naturally occurring language as opposed to, say, experimental data, to study social co-presence. The chapter considers the multimodal conference to face-to-face communication and gives us some appreciation for what is likely to increase the sense of "the other as being perceived as present."

Filipi and Lissonet (Investigating the Online Interactions of a Team of Test Developers Working in a Wiki Environment) give us a close look at the online collaboration of experts developing a test in order to (1) compare the online, asynchronous communication to face-to-face, and (2) uncover how expertise is displayed online. Filipi and Lissonet use the method of conversation analysis to get at matters of structure and identity in the online interactions of experts working together.

Markman (A Close Look at Online Collaboration: Conversational Structure in Chat and its Implications for Group Work) employs conversation analysis in an educational context to examine the interaction in synchronous chat during teamwork, with a focus on how coherence is maintained in this fast paced environment. The chapter compares talk online to talk face-to-face in terms of things like turn taking and making sense out of utterances. Markman has useful suggestions for the teacher planning to use chat for online discussions.

Chovanec (Online Discussions and Interaction: The Case of Live Text Commentary) focuses on a type of reporting in which live sports events are reported as the audience engages in online discussion and interaction during the construction of the text. The chapter offers a sociolinguistic approach to this emerging genre, treating closely the use of language, dialogic structure and interpersonal interaction, with attention to the display of identity. The chapter goes a ways towards locating this novel genre against the background of mass media. We see the melding of report of information with interpersonal debate. The chapter does a close reading on ways in which this genre highlights certain features not present in traditional mass media, how layers of meaning reside in the new genre. Humorous and competitive interactions are discussed in gender terms with the notion of male "gossip."

Toles Patkin (Online Interpersonal Interactions Utilizing an Extremely Limited Communication Interface) looks at the communication that goes on during an online backgammon game in which the player is extremely limited to four factors: (a) level of play, (b) language selected, (c) chat interface, and (d) and game play. Users select from a list of 27 preloaded comments to discuss with one another and the choice is translated into the language chosen by each receiver. This case is an exercise in discovering just how much is communicated within the framework of a limited system for communicating.

The chapter pays special attention to the attribution of identity under circumstances of highly limited information available.

Wang (Democratic Deliberation in Online Consultation Forums: A Case Study of the Casino Debate in Singapore) considers the possibility of civic engagement online in the discussion of political issues. Will the Internet promote greater citizen involvement, interaction between citizen's and government, online consultation? Using content analysis, the chapter investigates the degree to which Singapore's online consultation forum reflects the ideals of democratic deliberation. The study employed a set of criteria for democratic deliberation to analyze discussion forum messages. Such criteria as autonomy, transparency, equal participation, privacy and anonymity were applied to the data. Both structure and content were described, with such variables as frequency of posts, interactions among users, post length, date of post, number of users, issues discussed, critical assessment of issues, and tone of message, pro or anti-government. With regard to democratic deliberation, the results are mixed. Some solutions are recommended.

Lapadat, Atkinson, & Brown (What We Do Online Everyday: Constructing Electronic Biographies, Constructing Ourselves) chronicle the individual literacy biographies of children five to fifteen years old, collecting data on their online interactivity as they develop. They explore the question of what it means to be literate by viewing the practices and tools of children and adolescents. The children and their parents were interviewed in their homes as they showed the researchers their typical literacy materials and activities, printed and technologically mediated. This study points to the changing nature of literacy and to its individual character, hence the unique digital fingerprints.

SUPPORT

Ginossar ("There's Always Hope:" Content, Participants, and Dynamics in Online Discussion in a Lung Internet Cancer Support Group) shows us how people talk to one another in an online cancer support group, documenting (1) content, (2) participants, (3) topics, and (4) and messages that were absent or "silenced." Using a triangulation of methods, this chapter describes support group discussion and offers a good understanding of the importance of these discussions.

Flanigan ("Change" Talk at iVillage .com) uses ethnography of communication to analyze a woman-centered Internet site, focusing on talk about relationship troubles. This chapter describes communication practices women use in an attempt to answer the question, "What are the dominant ways members negotiate relationship troubles?" It takes talk about relationship change as a prominent cultural symbol that allows for insights into rules for communicating. This chapter touches on theoretically promising topics such as self-disclosure online and anonymity.

Scott, Lewis & D'Urso (Getting on the "E" List: Email List Use in a Community of Service Provider Organizations for People Experiencing Homelessness) gather data on a large number of organizations over a four-year period as they attempt to network. The focus is on an email list in a non-profit network of organizations dedicated to service for the homeless. The study was interested in the reasons that people used or didn't use the email list; how the email list was used; and the consequences of use or nonuse of the email list. The researchers collected data from recorded logs, an online survey, face-to-face interviews and from attending meetings and events. They report on how the use of technology added to the sense of "we-ness" and connections in the community of users. The attitudes of nonusers were equally significant to understand. Several recommendations for organizational leaders grow out of these findings.

Black, Bute, & Russell ("The Secret is Out!" Supporting Weight Loss Through Online Discussion) examine how social support is communicated in an online weight loss community website. The chapter compares the communication of social support in the online journals and the discussion forums by analyzing journal entries and discussion forum comments. Interestingly, the nature of support expressed in discussion forums differs from support given in response to journals. Other key differences between discussion in the journals and in the forums are found in how communicators address their audience and the use of double interacts. This chapter gives organizers and site designers for online support groups important ideas to think about.

As you read each chapter, you will learn about how online discussion was carried out under specific conditions and you will learn of outcomes. It is our hope that these cases will enhance your understanding of online discussion. We believe that the very act of critically focusing on discussion will foster greater understanding and will help us become better at taking part in discussion.

Acknowledgment

As with any project of this type, we wish to thank the many people who supported and contributed to this project. We appreciate the many fine articles submitted to us, including those we were unable to publish. In the review process, the publication rate was 32%.

We thank the members of our editorial board.

Jeremiah P. Conway, *University of Southern Maine*
Charles D. Dziuban, *University of Central Florida*
Em Griffin, *Wheaton College*
Heather Kanuka, *University of Alberta*
Ryan Kelsey, *Columbia University*
Matthew A. Killmeier, *University of Southern Maine*
Judith C. Lapadat, *University of Northern British Columbia*
Lynnett G. Leonard, *University of Nebraska at Omaha*
Raymind E. Schroeder, *University of Illinois at Springfield*
John Sherblom, *University of Maine*
Karen Swan, *Kent State University*
Lesley A. Withers, *Central Michigan University*

We appreciate the review assistance provided by Tamera K. Dirks, Park University amd J. Mark Noe of Park University for their administrative and computer support during this process.

Professor Shedletsky thanks Laura Woods and Alice O. Goodwin for their help in carrying out research with him. Professor John Broida, Department of Psychology, University of Southern Maine has been supportive in every way he could. Thank you Professor Jerry Conway, Department of Philosophy, University of Southern Maine, for challenging my ideas when they ought to be challenged and for always being supportive. Thanks to my wife, Cathie Whittenburg and my children, Noah and Jo Temah, for listening to me, putting up with my writing habits and offering feedback on my ideas. I am indebted to the University of Southern Maine for awarding me the Russell Chair for 2009-2011, which gave me greater opportunity to develop ideas on discussion. Finally, I thank my brother, Bernie Sheldon, who encouraged me to question and to see the humor in our selves.

We appreciate the help from IGI, particularly our editorial staff of Beth Ardner and Christine Bufton.

It is our hope that by laying out these cases on online discussion and interaction, these experiences and outcomes, we are providing the soil in which to grow our understanding of how online discussion works. These cases teach us to pay attention to "who" "speaks," to "whom," "why," "when," "through what channel," with "what level of critical thinking," "against what framework," and with "what intrapersonal and interpersonal dynamics operating."

Leonard Shedletsky, University of Southern Maine
Joan E. Aitken, Park University
Editor

Section 1
Teaching

Chapter 1
Does Online Discussion Produce Increased Interaction and Critical Thinking†?

Leonard Shedletsky
University of Southern Maine, USA

EXECUTIVE SUMMARY

This chapter explores the question: Does online discussion increase critical thinking and interaction? It presents a selective review of the literature concerned with critical thinking and/or interaction during online discussion. It reports a program of 5 studies of the effects of instructional media and instructional methods on critical thinking and interaction. Study 1 tests the influence on critical thinking of online vs. face-to-face discussion, individual vs. group consensus in summarizing discussion, and discussion of examples of concepts vs. discussion of more abstract analysis. Study 2 examines the relationship between the level of critical thinking in discussion and the quality of papers later written by discussants. Study 3 explores the question: Can a teaching assistant (TA) help to facilitate student-to-student interaction and critical thinking? Study 4 asks: Does personal relevance of discussion topic influence student participation and level of critical thinking in discussion online? Study 5 asks: Does the use of rubrics influence the level of student interaction and/or the level of critical thinking in online discussion? The evidence suggests that it is easier to influence students to interact than to think critically. The chapter offers some suggestions on how to increase student-to-student interaction and critical thinking.

BACKGROUND

Whether labeled "discussion," "dialogue" or "conversation," the liveliest interactions are critical. When participants take a critical stance, they are committed to questioning and exploring even the most widely accepted ideas and beliefs. Conversing critically implies an openness to rethinking cherished assumptions and to subjecting those assumptions to a continuous round of questioning, argument, and counterargument. One of the defining characteristics of critical discussion is that participants are willing to enter the conversation with open minds. This requires people to be flexible enough

DOI: 10.4018/978-1-61520-863-0.ch001

to adjust their views in the light of persuasive, well-supported arguments and confident enough to retain their original opinions when rebuttals fall short. Although agreement may sometimes be desirable, it is by no means a necessity (Brookfield and Preskill, p. 7).

After more than 30 years of teaching in the classroom, it was teaching online that really got this teacher to look closely at the nature of discussion. Much of what is called discussion in my online classes has been disappointing. Come to find out, many teachers share that disappointment. That makes me wonder why I didn't notice this let down more in my classroom discussions. Is it because the classroom is a place of highly engaged discussion, the give and take of ideas among equals? In a little book on learning from experience, Edward Cell writes:

Sometimes we learn a lot from our experience of ourselves and our transactions with our world. Friends share their hopes and fears, we test ourselves in difficult times, power reveals itself in unsuspected places. At other times we seem to learn little or nothing at all. We follow routine, talk with echoes of ourselves, cling to comfortable beliefs. As my colleague Bob Zeller put it, "Sometimes someone will say they've had twenty-five years of experience at something when the truth is they've had one year of experience repeated twenty-four times" (Cell, 1984, p. 3).

I am guessing that what I have done in the classroom is pretty much take what I can get, that is, enjoy the give and take with those who will give and take. I have accepted the head nodding onlookers as participants; I have forgiven the reticent students as struggling with speaking up; and I suppose I have been stumped by those who I just can't seem to reach, though I am so busy with the others that maybe I have failed to recognize the real nature of the quality of discussion in the classroom. That is all pure speculation

from one teacher trying to think out loud. But you cannot go very far these days in the teaching world before you bump into the question of online teaching versus classroom teaching as a tug of war between the cold and the warm, the inhuman and human, the asocial and social, the not real and the real. People seem to hold strong views on the value of teaching and learning online versus in the classroom and much of their views are tied to their beliefs about the quality of discussion in those two environments. What is the truth about online discussion?

There are so many questions related to this debate about interaction in an educational course. What do we mean when we speak about participation in a course? What is discussion, conversation, interaction? How important is discussion to learning? Or, how does learning work? What is a good discussion or a good conversation? Does a good discussion aid learning or is it good for other reasons than simply its effects on learning? Do good discussions result in better student papers? Is there more interaction and human connection in the classroom than online? How does human connection relate to learning? What do we mean by more interaction or more human connection? How is the process of meaning-making affected by discussion? Can online discussion be improved by managing the discussion? Are discussions in contexts outside of the classroom influenced by the same factors as educational discussions?

Having asked all these questions about discussion in education, one wonders about other contexts. How does online discussion compare to face-to-face discussion in business, support groups, political discussion, and other contexts?

Not only do people hold positions on many of the questions listed above, they often maintain strongly held views on these questions. Faculty encounter the paradoxical set of views that hold, on the one hand, that online teaching and learning is progressive and innovative, part of the flow of keeping up with the times. But they also encounter the strongly held view, on the other hand, that online teaching, learning, and online scholarship in general, is a lesser form than the traditional means of teaching and learning and publishing scholarship (Shedletsky & Aitken, 2001, July). At the same time, the evidence on learning outcomes does not point to a real difference between online and classroom learning. Benoit, Benoit, Milyo, & Hansen (2006) concluded: " We can be confident at this point in time there is no significant difference in learning between traditional and web-assisted formats. Both a meta-analysis of published research and a new large sample study which includes statistical controls for a wide range of potential covariates support this conclusion" (p. 57).

One argument offered for teaching online is the increased opportunity for discussion and collaboration (Murphy, 2003; Swan, 2006). Meyer (2003), based on her review of over 30 studies comparing web-based and traditional courses, said that "...if there is one strong area where the Web is used to consistent effect, it is by making ample interaction feasible, including students interacting with the course material, faculty or other experts, as well as other students" (para. 4). Gergen (1995) wrote of ongoing exchange as part of the collaborative construction of knowledge, where students are involved in "...engaging, incorporating, and critically exploring the views of others" (p. 34). Curtis and Lawson (2001) wrote: "Interactions among students make positive contributions to students' learning (Laurillard, 1993; Moore, 1993; Ramsden, 1992) (p. 21). The constructivist model is often invoked to argue for the power of online discussion. Lapadat (2002) maintained that discussion promotes critical thinking and that asynchronous online discussion, because it is written, even further enhances the higher order thinking processes. Pena-Shaff and Nicholls (2004) explained that:

Dialogue serves as an instrument for thinking because in the process of explaining, clarifying, elaborating, and defending our ideas and thoughts

we engage in cognitive processes such as integrating, elaborating and structuring (Brown & Palinscar, 1989; Johassen et al., 1995; Norman, 1993). Therefore, it is in the process of articulating, reflecting and negotiating that we engage in a meaning making or knowledge construction process. This process can become even more powerful when communication among peers is done in written form, because writing, done without the immediate feedback of another person as in oral communication, requires a fuller elaboration in order to successfully convey meaning (Koschmann, Kelson, Feltovich, & Barrows, 1996, pp. 244-245).

Time and again we are presented with the idea that discussion is especially well suited for online environments, that students inter-act with one another and the teacher, they debate, they collaborate and offer constructive feedback and engage one another in ideas. At the same time, we hear from teachers that they are disappointed with the level of discussion in their online environments. In discussing just this topic-- online discussions in his courses-- one college professor said that "sometimes they seem to go nowhere/ everywhere." Another concurred with this: "I, too, like the idea of using the Discussion Board to promote thoughtful and organized discussions. However they seem to fall flat for the same reasons that Harry mentioned." And another said: "... often students use these to simply respond to others and/or just complete an assignment. Thoughtful reflections and substantiated arguments are often lacking in the posting. Does anyone have a way of increasing either?"

Numerous teachers have made the same observation: Online discussion is often lifeless. You can add my personal teaching experience to those who have been disappointed with the level of discourse in the online discussions. It would appear that the disappointing level of discourse may be a function of some pervasive influence. Hunt, Simonds and Simonds, (2007), had this to say about first year students' ability to make an argument:

Most first-year students are not information literate, due to poor proficiency in database searches and critical thinking skills (Jacobson & Mark, 2000). Many students, as Jacobson and Mark (2000) note, know how to use the Internet to access needed information; however, most do not know how to build and expand effectively upon this knowledge. Additionally, few students enter college with a firm grasp on how to develop an effective research strategy for a given assignment. The massive proliferation of information resources that we have experienced in the last several years further complicates matters for students (American Association of College and Research Libraries, 2000; Swanson, 2004) (p. 11).

In this chapter, we would like to learn more about the state of online discussion in college classes. Are some models for running a discussion more likely to lead to a better outcome—i.e., more productive, engaged, involved students--than other models. In other chapters, we seek to learn how online discussion works for other contexts.

One experimental study of online discussion set out to discover if managing or designing specific discussion behaviors would improve the level of critical thinking skills displayed by students. Duphorne and Gunawardena (2005) compared three groups of students engaged in online discussion. The students were randomly assigned to either (condition 1) "... a problem-posing, critical inquiry approach to discussion with specific roles supporting critical thinking that were assigned to members" (p. 42); (condition 2) "... a five-step problem-solving approach: (a) formulate the problem, (b) generate or find alternate strategies or explore possible strategies, (c) choose a solution, (d) discuss how one might carry out the solution, and (e) evaluate potential consequences or implications" (Duphorne & Gunawardena, 2005, p. 42). Roles were assigned to individuals, such as Leader, Gatekeeper, Summarizer, and (condition 3) a control group which was not given a specific critical thinking strategy. The dependent measure was the S's use of critical thinking. The results showed no significant difference in critical thinking skills employed in the three conditions.

Garrison, Anderson, & Archer (2001, 2000) found little evidence of any critical discourse in students' online discussion. While there was some brainstorming (42%), there was only 13% Integration (construction of a possible solution) and only 4% of responses in the highest stage of critical discourse, Resolution (assessment of a solution). One review of the literature (Rourke & Kanuka, 2007) reported that "Observers of interaction as it takes shape in computer conferencing rarely report significant instances of critical discourse, dissenting opinion, challenges to others, or expressions of difference" (p. 835). This makes it difficult to assess the relationship between the various models of running online discussion in comparison to running classroom discussion.

Meyer (2003a) performed a content analysis of the threaded discussions of graduate level students. She coded each posting as one of the four cognitive processing categories derived from Garrison, Anderson, & Archer, 2001. Triggering questions refers to posing the problem; Exploration refers to a search for information; Integration refers to construction of a possible solution; and Resolution refers to critical assessment of a solution. She reported the following results: " 18% were triggering questions, 51% were exploration, 22% were integration, and 7% resolution" (para. 1). Clearly, evidence of critical or higher-order thinking was scarce.

What some researchers do report for online discussion is that online students are not the same demographically as in-class students. Online students are more likely to be working at jobs long hours during the week (Dutton, Dutton, & Perry, 2002); more time is spent online in discussion than in the classroom; more voices are expressed online; more convenient times of the day may be chosen to read and respond to online discussion. While some studies suggest that those students who engage in more online interaction achieve more in the course (Picciano, 2002; Spiceland and Hawkins, 2002), it is not clear whether online interaction produces greater levels of satisfaction and achievement or if online discussion simply is something that better students are attracted to take part in. Meyer (2003a) carried out an ethnographic study of graduate students in education who took part in online discussions and face-to-face discussions. The students were in educational leadership and took part in both face-to-face and online discussions. Two separate classes were evaluated. She sought to find out what differences, if any, there were between face-to-face and online discussions from the student's point of view, and whether or not there were higher levels of thinking in online discussion than in face-to-face discussion. Four themes were found in the student comments comparing the two forms of discussion: (1) online discussions went on over a longer period of time, hours and days; and it took lots of time to read others' postings and to take part in the discussion. (2) Students commented on the energy and speed of the face-to-face discussions; they enjoyed the energy, speed and enthusiasm of the face-to-face mode. (3) Some students commented that the in-class discussion moved too quickly and didn't give time for support or for getting back to topics. Some commented that they enjoyed having the time to reflect before speaking, afforded by online discussion. (4) Some expressed missing the nonverbals online, cues that helped them assign meaning.

As for the second question, whether or not there were higher levels of critical thinking online, Meyer reported that a somewhat disappointing body of evidence resulted here if you believed that online discussion produced high levels of critical thinking. Perhaps the most interesting outcome was the idea that different students with different preferences for interacting and learning would have different views on the comparison of online to face-to-face discussion. These findings are tentative. Keep in mind that in Meyer's study, no data were collected on the levels of thinking in

face-to-face discussion. Levels of thinking were collected only in the threaded discussions.

Much of the literature on critical thinking in the online environment seems to be accurately summed up by Rourke and Kanuka (2007), who write:

When studies are conducted, a familiar problem reappears: conference participants rarely engage in anything beyond the lowest levels of interaction (i.e., sharing-and-comparing information). The elements of discussion that are essential to meaning making and knowledge construction—elements such as exploring dissonance and negotiating meaning with peers and the instructor—are absent (p. 836).

Rourke and Kanuka (2007) add this: "Empirical observations of computer conferencing in distance learning consistently find a predominance of monologues, relational communication, or superficial interaction and a meager amount of collaboration and knowledge co-construction" (p. 837).

Some observers of online discussion have likened it to a sequence of soliloquies, where individuals have little influence on each other's thoughts (Marttunen, 1998; Pena-Shaff & Nicholls, 2004). Heckman and Annabi's (2005) study, however, suggests that under some conditions, student-to-student interaction and higher levels of abstract cognitive process are found to a greater extent in the online discussion compared to face-to-face.

There are some notable exceptions to this pattern of disappointing online discussions. Heckman and Annabi (2005) compared 120 seniors in a capstone course in Information Management, using the same facilitator for both online and face-to-face discussions of case studies. The study was careful to make the behaviors of the instructor as consistent across modes as possible, and to randomly assign students to one of 8 groups for comparison, controlling for order effects. An

Table 1. Summary of findings: comparison between FTF and ALN case study discussions

Comparison Between FTF and ALN Case Study Discussions
Teacher presence was much greater in FTF discussions.
Virtually all student utterances in FTF were responses to the teacher. In ALN [asynchronous] discussions nearly two-thirds of student utterances were responses to other students.
FTF discussions used more informal language and active voice.
Student utterances were longer in ALN, while teacher utterances were shorter.
The major interactive operation in ALN was continuing a thread, while in FTF it was asking a question (usually by the teacher).
There was a greater incidence of direct instruction in the FTF discussion. This was true of confirming understanding (a feedback function), presenting content, and focusing the discussion.
There was a greater incidence of drawing in participants, especially through cold calling on students, in the FTF discussions.
More than half of the instances of Teaching Process in the ALN discussion were performed by students rather than the teacher.
In the average FTF discussion there were nearly twice as many instances of Cognitive Process as in the average ALN discussion.
In FTF discussions, the instances of Cognitive Process were predominantly in the lower order exploration category.
In contrast, the ALN discussions contained more high-level Cognitive Process instances, both in absolute and relative terms.
Student-to-student interactions contain a greater proportion of high-level cognitive indicators.

extensive content analysis was done on the transcriptions of the discussions. Numerous categories were applied to the data, such as

- **Cognitive Process:** components of critical thinking (triggering, exploration, integration, & resolution);
- **Social Process:** characteristics of the social interaction, such as cohesiveness;
- **Teaching Process:** design of the learning experience, as well as its delivery and facilitation [either student or teacher behaviors];
- **Discourse Process:** responses between learners and learners and instructors.

Heckman and Annabi reported dramatic differences between the online and face-to-face modes. With regard to critical thinking, they found that the online discussions contained nearly twice as many instances of high level analysis compared to the face-to-face discussions. However, the highest level of cognitive processing, Integration, was identical in both modes. Table 1, taken from Heckman and Annabi (2005), sums up the key findings in their study:

The Heckman and Annabi study gives us reason to be cautious in coming to conclusions on the comparison between online and face-to-face discussion. They report numerous qualitative differences in the process of communication between the two modes. The teacher seeking to facilitate a discussion characterized by student engagement should be encouraged by the active involvement of Heckman and Annabi's online students. Some other studies find the online discussion to generate more critical thinking than the face-to-face discussion (Garrison, Anderson, & Archer, 2003; Vess, 2005). As for critical thinking, Heckman & Annabi's results are a bit mixed as far as which mode is better, although encouraging for the use of online discussion.

Other studies of small groups discussing online versus face-to-face have also produced mixed results. Ocker and Yaverbaum (1999) found that small groups of students online vs. face-to-face produced similar results for learning, quality of solution, solution content and satisfaction with the solution, but that for satisfaction with the process of interaction and the quality of discussion, students preferred the online mode significantly more. Kamin, Glicken, Hall, Quarantillo, and Merenstein

(2001) also compared small groups of students online vs. face-to-face. Kamin et al. found no significant differences in final exam scores. They did find significant differences for participation; face-to-face groups produced greater participation. The asynchronous groups reported putting more thought into comments than face-to-face groups. In a study by Joiner and Jones (2003) on the quality of arguments and the development of argumentative reasoning, which is how they defined critical thinking, the quality of students' arguments was higher in face-to-face than online. Another study that looked at critical thinking, comparing online to face-to-face discussions found similar levels of critical thinking in both modes (Newman, Webb, & Cochrane, 1995). Newman et al. found more new ideas expressed in the face-to-face groups and more important and linked ideas were expressed in the online groups. Guiller, Durndell and Ross (2008) compared small groups of students online vs. face-to-face and found mixed results for critical thinking between the two modes, though they did find that overall the nature of the discourse in the two modes differed. In general, the Guiller et al. findings suggest that the increase in time to reflect online did produce a greater use of "justification with evidence." Students were more likely to expand and elaborate on what others said in face-to-face groups than online.

Most of the studies reviewed, unlike the Heckman and Annabi (2005) study, did not observe the classroom side of discussion, but only reported on levels of critical thinking and other categories for the online discussion. Just how much interaction is in classroom discussion and how high a level of discussion is found in most classroom discussions? One suspects that often we imagine the classroom discussion contains more engaged students than it actually does contain. Heckman & Annabi's results would not support such an optimistic view of classroom discussion.

The teacher-centered climate of the classroom is what Heckman and Annabi find, even with college seniors in a capstone course. To this writer, a classroom teacher with a history of over 30 years of experience, this is not surprising at all. When you stop to think about it, how often are students willing to disagree with one another in the public setting of the classroom, where students challenge one another's statements, seek clarification, or elaboration and ask one another questions? In my experience with undergraduates, students are more likely to back off or possibly roll their eyes than to challenge one another in the classroom. It is unfortunate that so often judgments of online discussion are offered against the backdrop of an imagined classroom discussion, with all its imagined give and take.

We would be remiss if we did not notice what appears to be two different and contradictory stories being told here. On the one hand, it appears that online discussion does not really live up to the promise of engaged students who apply critical thinking to their online discussions. On the other hand, some evidence demonstrates a dramatically more involved student online than in the classroom. How do we resolve this apparent contradiction?

Rourke & Kanuka (2007) offer an important idea that may answer this conundrum. They propose that computer conferencing that results in increased critical thinking takes place in conditions of collaborative meaning making. Features that characterize this design are small group size and purposive collaboration (e.g., case-based learning, problem based learning). The design that produces low levels of interaction and low levels of critical thinking is the open-ended forum of the whole class, with little structure. Pena-Shaff and Nicholls (2004) point to the need for students to reach consensus in the collaborative small group that encourages the interaction. Without this need, disagreements can be ignored. Rovai (2007) reviewed the literature on running effective online discussions, and concluded that "Online courses need to be designed so that they provide motivation for students to engage in productive discussions and clearly describe what is expected, perhaps in the form of a discussion rubric" (p. 77). The studies presented in this chapter attempt to take into account instructional methods and instructional media.

STUDY 1: IS THE LEVEL OF CRITICAL THINKING IN DISCUSSION AFFECTED BY THE MEDIUM AND/OR INSTRUCTIONAL METHODS§?

Setting the Stage‡

The students in a junior/senior level course on discourse analysis, Meaning and Communication, were randomly divided into 4 equal size groups. Over the semester, due to attrition of students, group 1 had 7 students, group 2 had 5 students, group 3 had 5 students, and group 4 had 6 students. To determine the influence of medium (Online vs. Face-to-Face classroom environment), Analysis (abstract or case-based analysis vs. examples of concepts to discuss) and degree of collaborative interdependence or Report (consensus vs. individual posting of the summary of the discussion), the study was designed as shown in Figure 1.

Two students were non-traditional age and were in different groups from each other, but all the rest were traditional college age students. During the 5th week of the course, students got to practice a face-to-face discussion of a transcript and an online discussion of a transcript. The first face-to-face discussion for the purpose of collecting data for this study took place in the classroom 8 weeks into the semester. By then, the students were familiar with course concepts and the idea of analyzing a transcribed conversation. The same week as the first f-to-f discussion, the online discussion started for each group. Students were given 11 days to complete the online discussion. The second f-to-f discussion took place during the 12th week of the course and again the online discussion began the same week and lasted for 11 days.

Case Description

This study was undertaken to determine whether or not online discussion produces a higher level of critical thinking among undergraduate students in a college course than face-to-face discussion [MEDIUM]. In addition, this study sought to determine whether or not having to report on discussion outcomes (a summary) as an individual or a group consensus would influence levels of critical thinking displayed in the discussion [REPORT]. And finally, this study sought to determine whether or not students asked to discuss at the level of finding examples of course concepts versus asked to find a more abstract analysis of course materials (what is going on in a transcribed conversation) would influence levels of critical thinking displayed in the discussion [ANALYSIS].

The three independent variables were:

1. Medium, with two levels, online discussion versus face-to-face discussion;
2. Report, with two levels, subjects are told prior to discussion that each individual will write a summary of the discussion versus one group consensus summary;
3. Analysis, with two levels, subjects are told prior to discussion that they are to find examples of specific concepts in the transcription of a conversation versus they are to discuss broadly what is going on between the communicators in the transcribed conversation.

The dependent variables were four levels of critical thinking and Other:

1. Triggering: messages that evoke thinking about issues, that evoke a response;
2. Exploration: messages that relate and connect with one another but are not supported;
3. Integration: messages that build on previous messages and are supported;

Figure 1.

	CONSENSUS DRIVEN			INDIVIDUAL DRIVEN	
TO DISCUSS:	FACE-to-FACE [4 groups]	ONLINE [4 groups]		FACE-to-FACE [4 groups]	ONLINE [4 groups]
ANALYSIS BASED	Transcript 2, group 1	Transcript 1, group 1		Transcript 2, group 3	Transcript 1, group 3
	Transcript 1, group 2	Transcript 2, group 2		Transcript 1, group 4	Transcript 2, group 4
EXAMPLE BASED	Transcript 4, group 1	Transcript 3, group 1		Transcript 4, group 3	Transcript 3, group 3
	Transcipt 3, group 2	Transcript 4, group 2		Transcript 3, group 4	Transcript 4, grouop 4

Table. Research Design Experimental Groups (2X2X2) Factorial Design

4. Resolution: messages that develop a hypothesis and suggest ways to test and defend the hypothesis;
5. Other: messages that are social in character, such as "Did you watch the game last night?"

The two raters spent several months practicing using the critical thinking coding system taken from Garrison, D. R., Anderson, T., and Archer, W. (2001), and modifying it (see Appendix 1, modifications). They chose an arbitrary discussion from the data to independently code and found substantial inter-rater reliability, using Cohen's Kappa (1960), a chance-adjusted measure of agreement (K =.718), with 81% agreement.

Univariate analysis of variance was performed on the data using SPSS. Main effects were found for the medium of discussion (online versus face-to-face), report (individual summary versus group consensus summary), and analysis (examples discussed versus abstract analysis). In addition, a number of interactions were statistically significant: report * analysis; report * medium; analysis * medium; report * analysis * medium. Interactions will be discussed separately.

Triggering

The medium of discussion had a statistically significant effect on the dependent measure, triggering ($F = 23.986$, df = 1, 50, p <.000). Triggering messages occurred significantly more often in face-to-face discussion (Mean = 2.423) than in online discussion (Mean =.192). The type of analysis (example or abstract) had a statistically significant effect on the dependent measure, triggering ($F = 20.406$, df = 1, 50, p <.000). Triggering messages occurred significantly more often in abstract analyses of the transcript (Mean = 2.337) than in discussion of examples of concepts found in the transcripts (Mean =.278). The type of report (individual or consensus) had a statistically significant effect on the dependent measure, triggering ($F = 12.324$, df = 1, 50, p <.001). Triggering messages occurred significantly more often in consensus summaries of the discussion (Mean = 2.107) than in individual summaries of group discussion (Mean =.508).

Exploration

The medium of discussion had a statistically significant effect on the dependent measure, exploration ($F = 20.310$, df = 1, 51, p <.000). Exploration messages occurred significantly more often in face-to-face discussion (Mean = 9.065) than in online discussion (Mean = 1.141). The type of analysis (example or abstract) did not have a statistically significant effect on the dependent measure, exploration (F = 2.721 df = 1, 51, p >.05). The mean score for exploration messages in abstract analyses of the transcript was 6.554 and the mean for exploration messages during discussions of examples was 3.653. The type of report (individual or consensus) had a statistically significant effect on the dependent measure, exploration (F = 6.665, df = 1, 51, p <.013). Exploration messages occurred significantly more often in discussions leading to consensus summaries (Mean = 7.373) than in discussions leading to individual summaries (Mean = 2.833).

Integration

The medium of discussion did not have a statistically significant effect on the dependent measure, integration (F = 20.310.022, df = 1, 51, p >.05). Integration messages did not occur significantly more often in face-to-face discussion (Mean =.129) than in online discussion (Mean =.111). The type of analysis (example or abstract) did not have a statistically significant effect on the dependent measure, integration (F = 1.612 df = 1, 51, p >.05). The mean score for integration messages in abstract analyses of the transcript was.042 and the mean for integration messages during discussions of examples was.199. The type of report (individual or consensus) did not have a statistically significant effect on the dependent measure, integration (F =.841, df = 1, 51, p >.05). Integration messages did not occur significantly more often in discussions leading to consensus summaries (Mean =.063) than in discussions leading to individual summaries (Mean =.177).

Resolution

The medium of discussion did not have a statistically significant effect on the dependent measure, resolution (F = 0, df = 1, 51, p >.05). Resolution messages did not occur significantly more often in face-to-face discussion (Mean = 0) than in online discussion (Mean = 0). The type of analysis (example or abstract) did not have a statistically significant effect on the dependent measure, resolution (F = 0, df = 1, 51, p >.05). The mean score for resolution messages in abstract analyses of the transcript was 0 and the mean for resolution messages during discussions of examples was 0. The type of report (individual or consensus) did not have a statistically significant effect on the dependent measure, resolution (F = 0, df = 1, 51, p >.05). Resolution messages did not occur significantly more often in consensus summaries of the discussion (Mean = 0) than in individual summaries of group discussion (Mean = 0).

Other

The medium of discussion had a statistically significant effect on the dependent measure, Other (F = 22.449, df = 1, 51, p <.001). Other messages occurred significantly more often in face-to-face discussion (Mean = 6.317) than in online discussion (Mean =.163). The type of analysis (example or abstract) had a statistically significant effect on the dependent measure, Other (F = 7.050, df = 1, 51, p <.011). Other messages occurred significantly more often in abstract analyses of the transcript (Mean = 4.964) than in discussion of examples of concepts found in the transcripts (Mean = 1.515). The type of report (individual or consensus) had a statistically significant effect on the dependent measure, Other (F = 6.921, df = 1, 51, p <.011). Other messages occurred significantly more often in discussions where students were instructed to produce a consensus summary of the discussion

Figure 2. Mean frequency of the triggering response during face-to-face and online discussion

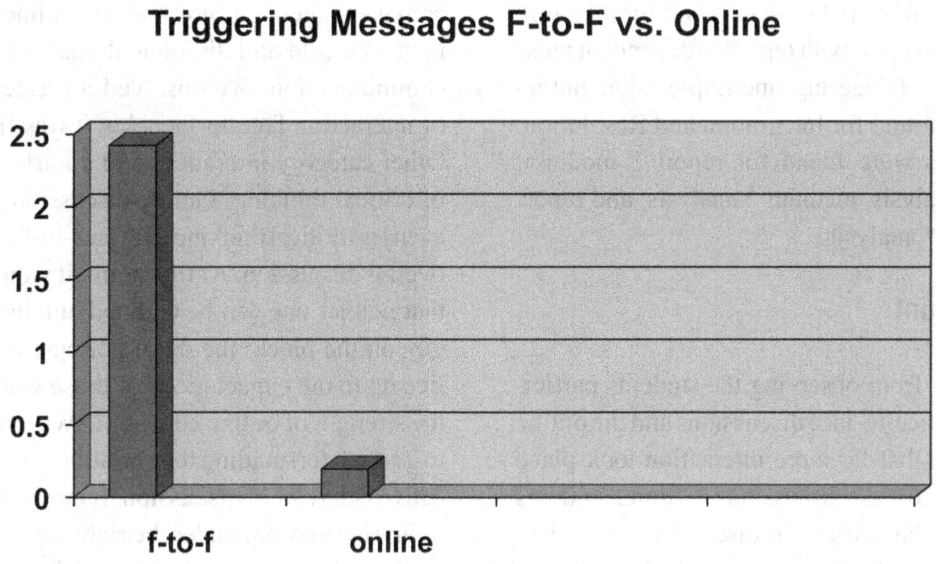

Triggering Messages F-to-F vs. Online

(Mean = 4.948) than in discussions where students were instructed to produce an individual summary of the group's discussion (Mean = 1.531).

Interactions

Report X Analysis

The interaction between type of report (individual or consensus) and type of analysis (example or abstract) had a statistically significant effect on the dependent measure, triggering (F = 12.096, df = 1, 50, p <.001). The level of triggering was highest for the combination of consensus and abstract analysis (M = 3.929).

Report X Medium

The interaction between type of report (individual or consensus) and type of medium (online vs. face-to-face) had a statistically significant effect on the dependent measure, triggering (F = 18.939, df = 1, 50, p <.001). The level of triggering was highest for the combination of consensus and face-to-face (M = 4.214).

Analysis X Medium

The interaction between type of analysis (example or abstract) and type of medium (online vs. face-to-face) had a statistically significant effect on the dependent measure, triggering (F = 16.336, df = 1, 50, p <.001). The level of triggering was highest for the combination of abstract analysis and face-to-face (M = 4.373).

Report X Analysis X Medium

The interaction between type of report (individual or consensus), type of analysis (example or abstract) and medium (face-to-face vs. online) had a statistically significant effect on the dependent measure, triggering (F = 15.630, df = 1, 50, p <.001). The level of triggering was highest for the combination of abstract consensus report, abstract analysis and face to face (M = 4.373).

Multivariate Analysis

The data were entered into a multivariate analysis of variance and the results obtained with the univariate analysis were confirmed. Statistically significant main effects were found for medium, report and analysis with regard to dependent measures, Other, Triggering, and Exploration, but no effect was found for Integration and Resolution. Interactions were found for report * medium, report * analysis, medium * analysis, and report * medium * analysis.

Word Count

It appeared from observing the students participate in the face-to-face discussions and the online discussions that far more interaction took place in the face-to-face discussions. Online, students waited for days after the discussion opened to post anything. It did not appear to be active at all online, nor to be interactive. To verify and document this observation, we took a count of how many words were uttered by each student in each condition. What we found was that online in the two discussions, the average number of words written per student was 262 words. Face-to-face the average number of words spoken by each student in the two discussions was 439 words. The difference between the means was tested with a oneway ANOVA and found to be statistically significantly different (F = 4.194, df = 1,55, p <.05). As stated above, the face-to-face discussions produced significantly more Other talk than the online discussion (F = 22.449, df = 1, 51, p <.001). Other messages occurred significantly more often in face-to-face discussion (Mean = 6.317) than in online discussion (Mean =.163).

Conclusion

Recall the extreme difference of opinion referred to at the outset of this chapter: Some maintain that the classroom is an environment of debate and interaction and immediacy between human beings and that the online environment is a cold and inhuman landscape. It would seem that the research does not support the extreme view that the face-to-face discussion is an environment of active engagement, nor that the online environment is a cold and dissolute domain of inhuman communication. We observed a greater amount of interaction face-to-face, but it was filled with Other category utterances and a fairly low level of critical thinking. Online discussion produced even less critical thinking than face-to-face and less overall discussion. At this point, it would appear that neither one can be counted out, but the new guy on the block, the online discussion, did not live up to the expectations of those who see it as the strength of online education. We have a ways to go in understanding the variations in communicative behavior in discussion. It may turn out that online discussion, under the right conditions, can produce student-to-student interaction but with the conditions studied here, we have not found that to be the case. Keep in mind that in this study the face-to-face groups and the online groups were discussing without the teacher leading. We would like to know more about what sort of outcome derives from these discussions. For instance, do students write better papers after the discussion when the level of critical thinker is higher? Do students write better papers after the discussion when the amount of student-to-student interaction is greater? Study 2 tries to answer these questions.

STUDY 2: THE LEVEL OF CRITICAL THINKING IN DISCUSSION AND THE QUALITY OF STUDENT PAPERS

Setting the Stage

In Study 1, the central question had to do with the level of critical thinking produced during discussion. We also looked at the amount of student-to-student interaction in discussion. It was found that students interacted more in the face-to-face condition compared to the online condition and that the level of critical thinking was higher in the face-to-face condition than online for the two lower levels of the 4 level model of critical thinking we worked with, triggering and exploration.

Recall that in Study 1, with 4 groups of students, 5 to 7 students in each group, in some conditions, all individuals in a group wrote a summary of their group's discussion and in other conditions, groups wrote a consensus summary of their group's discussion, 1 summary for the group. Each of the 4 groups contributed 2 instances of individuals writing a summary and 2 instances of the group consensus producing a summary. Each group contributed 2 discussions in the online medium and 2 discussions in the face-to-face medium, with the first face-to-face discussion followed by an online discussion, then a second face-to-face discussion and the 2nd online discussion. In total, there were 8 online and 8 face-to-face discussions. There was a total of 4 different transcripts used, a random factor. It was thought that where there was a higher level of critical thinking in the discussion, the summaries that came out of those discussions would show an increase in quality as rated by teachers blind to how the summaries were produced. Since the face-to-face discussions produced a statistically significantly higher level of critical thinking in Study 1, we expected to find that the summaries from the face-to-face discussions would be rated higher in quality by the 2 raters. Study 2 was undertaken to test this hypothesis.

Procedure

Two college professors in media studies were asked to read the summaries and rate each on a typical scale from F to A or 50 to 100 as part of our research project on quality of writing. The instructions stated: "By quality what we mean is the level of thinking demonstrated in analyzing the transcript as opposed to writing mechanics, i.e., spelling and grammar, etc. Students in a course on discourse analysis read a transcript of a conversation and then discussed the transcript.

After the discussion, they wrote a summary of the discussion. It is the summaries that we are asking you to rate for the quality of the summary. Your ratings will be used for research purposes and will have no effect on student grades. Please rate each summary on a scale with a maximum of 100, where A quality work is from 90 to 100, B is 80 to 90, C is 70 to 80, D is 60 to 70, and F is 50 to 60. Use numbers to grade each summary."

The raters were given the transcript that was analyzed in each discussion as well as the written student summaries. They were blind as to whether or not the discussions leading to the summaries were conducted face-to-face or online by the students.

Results

The data were entered into SPSS. We entered the ratings two ways, for each rater and an average rating for both raters for each summary. We also entered the ratings in two ways with regard to each subject, one way treated each student in the consensus discussions as having the same grade on the consensus summary and the second way was to only enter the consensus grade once for the group. The grades for the raters were compared and overall there was no difference in their ratings (means were 77.76 and 80.00). Let us start with the analysis for each student having the consensus grade using the average grade of the two raters. There were 27 instances of online summary grades and 30 instances of face-to-face summary grades. The mean grade for the online summaries was 85.00 and the mean grade for the face-to-face summaries was 77.4.

An ANOVA was run with medium as the independent variable (online vs. face-to-face) and the average rating of the summaries as the dependent variable. The medium of discussion had a statistically significant effect on the dependent measure, average rating of the quality of the summaries ($F = 12.787$, $df = 1, 55$, $p < .001$), R squared $= .181$.

When we look at the consensus grade used once per group, again we find the summaries based on the online discussions produced a statistically significantly higher average rating than the summaries based on the face-to-face discussions (F = 5.675, df = 1, 168.8, p <.02).

We also performed a univariate ANOVA with the average rating of the summaries as the dependent variable and all three independent variables, medium, report and analysis. The only variable to have a statistically significant effect on the average rating for the summaries was medium (online discussion vs. face-to-face discussion). Medium produced higher mean ratings for the online discussion summaries (F = 11.863, df = 1, 49, p <.001), R Squared =.250.

These data failed to support our hypothesis that summaries based on discussions that produced higher critical thinking (face-to-face discussions in Study 1) would receive higher grades for quality of the written summary.

In addition, since we know from Study 1 that there was greater student-to-student interaction face-to-face than online, as measured by word count, we can conclude that greater student-to-student interaction did not lead to higher grades for the written summaries.

Discussion

Initially, it is puzzling to find that discussions that consisted of a lower level of critical thinking and interaction would result in summaries written about those discussions that were judged to be of a higher quality than summaries written about discussions with a higher level of critical thinking and a greater amount of interaction. One possible explanation for this outcome is that spoken and written development of ideas are two media that are different enough from one another, such that the writing process introduces its own dynamics of critical thinking. One must ask, though, why should writing about a transcript, whether in terms of examples found in it or an analysis of its underlying

meaning, produce a higher quality summary from online discussion—with a lower level of critical thinking displayed—than from face-to-face discussion? One possibility here is that the less developed discussion online forces the writer to more actively construct an argument about the transcript than the more developed face-to-face discussion, where there were more ideas of a critical nature but not entirely well thought out for each group member (Lapadat, 2002; Pena-Shaff & Nicholls, 2004).

Another possible explanation is simply that the online discussion is accessible for the writer to go back to review when writing their summary. The face-to-face discussion is no longer available verbatim and the student writer must rely on memory if note taking was lax.

STUDY 3: CAN A TEACHING ASSISTANT (TA) HELP TO FACILITATE STUDENT-TO-STUDENT INTERACTION AND CRITICAL THINKING?

Setting the Stage

A senior undergraduate majoring in communication worked as a teaching assistant for this writer's online Introduction to Communication course during the summer of 2008. The course web site was located within Blackboard. The course was taught as a seven-week long online course during summer session. The Introduction to Communication is the first course in the department, required of all majors before they can take any other course in communication. It is also an option for non-majors as part of fulfilling the 6-credit (two 3 credit courses) social science requirement for the core curriculum. Typically, approximately, 90% of the students in this course are taking the course as part of the core curriculum and not to start the major in communication. The course is heavily slanted toward reading the theories in or related to communication, as found in Em Griffin's textbook, Communication: A First Look at Communication Theory. The TA was very comfortable with theories in communication and read the textbook along with the students to be sure to be on top of the readings. She was also well versed in the model of critical thinking used in Study 1 above, consisting of the 4 levels of triggering, exploration, integration and resolution, so that she could try to facilitate discussion in an attempt to raise the level of critical thinking. The teacher (myself) tried to go about his teaching, including responding to discussion posts in his normal manner.

Procedure

The TA was introduced to the class in an announcement on the discussion board in the Blackboard course. The TA was also listed along with the faculty member, picture and all, in an area designated for faculty and staff introductions. The TA posted a greeting message on the discussion board at the start of the course. It read:

"Hi everyone-

I'm Alice Goodwin and the teaching assistant (TA) for this course. I'm a senior majoring in Communication and am here to help. I will be taking part in the blackboard and group discussions and will help to stimulate conversation.

Please feel free to email me at "email address" with any questions you may have. I will be checking my email late afternoons and evenings as I also work part time. I will be checking blackboard throughout the day so will respond to your questions just as quickly as possible."

By design, the TA took part in half of the Discussion Board discussions and stayed out of the other half, so that we could compare any effect her involvement might have on student interac-

tion and level of critical thinking. She responded in a more or less spontaneous style, trying to be pleasant and to encourage additional thinking and posting on topics as she saw fit.

Several studies tried to influence student discussion behavior by design but failed to find an effect on the quality of discussion (Duphorne and Gunawardena, 2005). Nevertheless, we wanted to see if a TA could enhance discussion.

In addition, there were 3 electronic groups in the course, where students responded to exercises on a discussion board. The TA, by design, took part in exercise 1 in one group but not in the other two; she took part in exercise #2 in group 2 but not the other two; and she took part in exercise #3 in group 3, but not the other two. Again, we wanted to compare any effect the TA might have on student interaction and level of critical thinking.

One rater trained to use the modified critical thinking system employed in Study 1, rated student responses in discussions (Garrison, Anderson, & Archer 2001, 2000).

Results

A univariate ANOVA was performed to test the effect of the TA being in or out of a discussion on the number of student to other student interactions. Whether or not the TA took part in a discussion did not have a statistically significant effect on student-to-student interaction ($F = 1.694$, $df = 1$, 17, $p > .05$). The effect of the teacher's involvement in discussion showed a statistically significant effect of the teacher's responding to discussions and student-to-student interactions ($F = 4.002$, $df = 7$, 11, $p < .02$). If the TA's involvement in the discussion is treated as a covariate of the teacher's involvement in the discussion, the teacher still shows a statistically significant effect on student-to-student interaction ($F = 5.178$, $df = 7$, 10, $p < .01$). R Squared was .803.

Whether or not the TA took part in discussion, the level of critical thinking for posts to the TA was not found to be statistically significant for Triggering ($F = .895$, $df = 1$, 17, $p > .05$), but it was statistically significant for Exploration responses to the TA ($F = 6.589$, $df = 1$, 17, $p < .02$), with R Squared $= .279$. There was no statistically significant relationship between the TA's involvement in discussion and Integration or Resolution or Other responses to her.

There was a statistically significant correlation between the teacher's involvement in discussion and the frequency of student-to-student interactions, shown by a Pearson's 1-tailed correlation ($r = .644$, $p < .01$). This relationship between the teacher's response frequency and the student-to-student frequency of interaction held when we controlled for the frequency of the TA's involvement in discussion. When we controlled for the teacher's frequency of response and looked at the correlation between the TA and the student-to-student frequency of response, there was a negative correlation ($r = -.233$) though it was not statistically significant.

In short, we found no evidence for the TA's involvement in discussion to increase the level of critical thinking, except for responses to the TA of an Exploration type, and no evidence of the TA's involvement to facilitate increased student-to-student interaction. It may be noted that Ertmer, Richardson, Belland, and Camin (2007), with graduate students in education giving peer feedback to classmates' discussion postings in an online course, did not find a difference in the quality of postings over a semester, in spite of the fact that the students generally valued the feedback.

To explore these findings a bit further, we went back to data from the same course one summer earlier and looked at the frequency of student-to-student interaction in relation to the frequency of the teacher's involvement in discussions. There was no TA in that course. What we found using the Pearson Correlation, 1-tailed, was that there was no statistically significant correlation between the teacher's frequency of posting and the student-to-student interactions online ($r = -.012$, $p > .05$).

Survey of Student Thoughts about the Online Discussions

We employed the survey function within Blackboard to survey the students in the course about their thoughts on our class's discussions. Blackboard provides an anonymous survey application. The students were informed that the survey was anonymous and would have no effect on their grade. The response rate was 19 out of 20 students. The responses are given in Table 2.

While we recognize that some of the questions are loosely stated and that we cannot treat these survey results as definitive, they do give us a feel for the student reaction. Overall, we read these responses as saying that the discussions were well received and worthwhile, but that the students recognized that the discussions were not as actively undertaken by classmates as they would like to see. There was no clear-cut suggestion for how to make them better, except a wishful, "Gee, I wish more of my classmates took part."

Discussion

We want to caution against interpreting these findings to show that the teacher caused increased student-to-student interactions. Instead, we note that another explanation for the relationship between the teacher's involvement in discussion and the student-to-student increase in interaction is accounted for by recognizing that the teacher tended to join in in animated discussions as a participant. He did not cause the increase in discussion in those instances. He merely took part in them.

But are animated discussions, which seem to be satisfying for many students and often the teacher as well, getting us higher levels of critical thinking?

CASE DESCRIPTION

The Virtual Classroom or Collaboration

During the fall and spring semesters, when the Introduction to Communication course is taught as a hybrid or blended course, that is, ITV plus online (using Blackboard), one meeting is given over to a synchronous online discussion. The discussion lasts for approximately one hour. Blackboard calls this either the Virtual Classroom or Collaboration, depending on the version of Blackboard. During that discussion, the class discusses a movie that each student was asked to view on their own, "You've Got Mail." In advance of the discussion, several questions were posed on the discussion board to get students to think about the movie in relation to our course. As the teacher of the course, I have always taken a back seat and stayed out of the discussion for the most part, introducing a few questions well into the meeting. What has always been striking in this course activity is the difference between the reticence of students in the ITV classroom with the teacher and the high-energy give and take of the online discussion. Many students have expressed a strong enjoyment of this discussion and some have maintained that it is chaotic and unfocused and not enjoyable for them. What stands out more than anything is the high energy and widely dispersed involvement in the discussion.

Setting the Stage

As part of this research program, we went back into one semester's Virtual Classroom discussion and analyzed the archived discussion for critical thinking. The discussion printed out as 50 pages of conversation. We chose to analyze the first 11 pages (the beginning of the discussion) and pages 30–34 (the end of the discussion), at which point, the teacher announced that the discussion was over but people could stay on if they wished to keep talking. Since the discussion went to page 50, you can see that some students continued the interaction. Table 3 shows our findings on levels of critical thinking produced.

It is obvious from Table 3 that the virtual classroom discussion produced an overwhelming percentage of Other talk and very little in the way of critical thinking. What is striking is how many students commented on enjoying the virtual classroom meeting. Many students suggested that we devote more meetings to the virtual classroom. Our observations of critical thinking in the virtual classroom are consistent with Rourke and Kanuka's (2007) conclusions about conferencing online. Summing up what has been found in studies of computer conferencing, their description is "... a predominance of monologues, relational communication, or superficial interaction and a meager amount of knowledge co-construction" (p. 837).

STUDY 4: DOES PERSONAL RELEVANCE OF DISCUSSION TOPIC INFLUENCE STUDENT PARTICIPATION AND LEVEL OF CRITICAL THINKING IN DISCUSSION ONLINE[#]?

Setting the Stage

Hypotheses

1. Personal relevance of discussion topic will produce an increase in student participation.
2. Personal relevance of discussion topic will produce an increase in the level of critical thinking in student posts.
3. Personal relevance of discussion topic will affect students' initial post and response dates to threaded online discussion boards.

Table 2. Survey of student views about our online discussions (summer, 2008)

1. Did you enjoy the course discussions?	2. Did the discussion part of the course add to your learning?	3. Was there any one thing that really helped you get into the discussions or one thing that detracted from your involvement in the discussions? **	4. Did your comfort level in our discussions change over time?	5. Did you find that you posted just to get the job done—to do your homework—or that, at least some of the time, you really got engaged in the discussion?	6. Please write about this one. Is there anything the teacher and/or the teaching assistant could do that would make discussion better?††
YES 84%	YES 79%	Because everyone will be viewing it, I needed to make sure I was perfect with what I said.	YES 58%	JUST TO DO MY HOMEWORK 32%	There was nothing anyone could have done better.
NO 0%	NO 16%	I think you and Alice (TA) helped me to think more about what the discussions were on.	NO 32%	AT LEAST SOME OF THE TIME, I REALLY GOT ENGAGED IN THE DISCUSSION 63%	I don't think there was anything that could have been improved upon by the instructors.
NOT SURE 16%	NOT SURE 5%	One thing that detracted from my involvement was classmates' lack of interest.	NOT SURE 11%	NOT SURE 5%	I do not think there was much you could have done to make the discussions better.
		The major thing that helped with discussions was the participation of others in the group.			Try to make sure everyone participates.

Methodology

Study subjects were college students enrolled in two online communication courses at a University in the Northeast. Courses have been labeled as "Elective Course" and "Required Course" for identification purposes. The Elective Course consisted of 20 students of which 4 were male and 16 were female. In addition 13 were traditional students and 7 were non-traditional students[§§]. The Required Course, a requirement for the major, consisted of 16 students of which 7 were male and 9 were female. In addition 9 were traditional students and 7 were non-traditional students.

The average age of students in the Elective Course was 25 and average age of students in the Required Course was 26. The Required Course did not use strict and specific rubrics about posting but the Elective Course[1] did. The rubrics for the Elective Course specified when to post, when to respond, how often to post, length of posts and indicated that posts were graded each week[2]. We did not set up these variables. One of the researchers in this study was also a student in both courses.

The data for this study were: (1) responses to an online survey to be completed anonymously by Ss in each course (Elective and Required); (2) sex of student; (3) traditional/non-traditional status of student; (4) levels of critical thinking of the S's post; (5) average initial post date during the week; (6) ratings of personal relevance of discussions; (7) early/late posts as well as early/late responses to these posts were counted***. Two early and two late posts from each course

Table 3. Levels of critical thinking in virtual classroom discussion

Level of Critical Thinking	Triggering 12	Exploration 17	Integration 0	Resolution 0	Other 426
Frequency	12 (2.6%)	17 (3.7%)	0	0	(93.4%)

were rated for level of personal relevance by communication students at the same university but not enrolled in these two courses. Authors of posts remained anonymous as did the raters of posts.

1. Anonymous Online Survey

Does personal relevance of discussion topic affect students' participation in the online classroom? During the last week of each course, an online survey was conducted in an attempt to answer this question. The survey consisted of twelve questions and utilized randomization of order of questions asked. Format of questions included Likert Scale, Multiple Choice and Essay. Questions addressed the issues of personal relevance, trust, professor involvement; Ss's comfort level in disagreeing, reasons for participation, and lastly student involvement. It is important to note that 14 of the 20 Ss in the Elective Course completed the survey while 7 of the 16 Ss in the Required Course completed the survey. This survey could only be taken once as multiple attempts were not allowed.

Results of four of the twelve questions asked of each S in the Elective Course and the Required Course are discussed here. Survey results in their entirety can be obtained from this author.

Survey Instructions to Ss were as follows:

The purpose of this survey is to learn more about what makes for good and interactive discussions. It will be used for research purposes only. When you answer the questions think about the discussions in this course. Please answer the following questions as honestly as possible as we are interested in what you really think in regards to discussion. This survey is anonymous and will in no way affect your grade nor will it affect the teacher.

Question 1: Multiple Choice

What is meant by "actively participate" in this question is not simply a one-time "post and flee" response but rather an on-going dialogue.

I am more likely to actively participate in those discussions that are:

- Factual—that is, there is a correct answer expected
- Controversial
- Personally Relevant
- Unanswered

According to the survey results, 71.429% of Ss in the Elective Course were more likely to participate in those discussions that they found to be personally relevant compared to 28.571% in the Required Course. Interestingly, 71.429% of Ss in the Required Course said they were more likely to actively participate in those discussions that were found to be controversial compared to 28.571% of Ss in the Elective Course.

These numbers are a mirror image of one another and as such require closer scrutiny. We will begin by looking at the question asked and perhaps this was not a "good" question. Relevance is defined as "relating to the matter under consideration; pertinent". Controversy is defined as "a conflict of opinion; dispute". It may stand to reason then that the students' interpretation of this question in both the Elective and the Required Course

Figure 3. Controversial and personally relevant discussion vs. factual

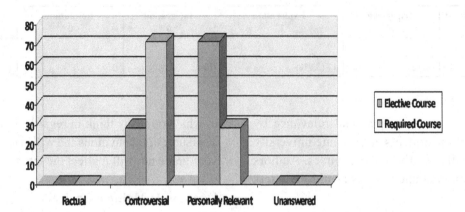

were in fact identical upon closer inspection. A conflict of opinion might very well be thought of as personally relevant by students.

According to the survey, students are 100% more likely to actively participate in those discussions that they find to be personally relevant and controversial. Results also indicate that 100% of students surveyed were not likely to actively participate in those discussions that were factual.

Question 2: Opinion Scale/Likert
I participated in discussion to fulfill the homework assignments as opposed to be being personally engaged.

- Strongly Agree
- Agree
- Neither Agree nor Disagree
- Disagree
- Strongly Disagree
- Not Applicable
- Unanswered

Results for this question have been collapsed as follows: Strongly Agrees/Agrees and Strongly Disagrees/Disagrees responses have been combined.

42.86% of Ss in the Elective Course and 28.57% of Ss in the Required Course agreed with

the statement that "they participated in discussion to fulfill the homework assignments as opposed to being personally engaged." 21.429% of Ss in the Elective Course and 14.286% of Ss in the Required Course disagreed with this statement.

Although it would appear that these results conflict with those in Question 1 this may not be the case at all. Recall that 100% of students surveyed in each course responded that they "actively participated" in those discussions that were both personally relevant and controversial. Why then do students post to threaded online discussion boards?

The answer may be two-fold. Students post because (1) they find the topic of discussion to be personally relevant/controversial; (2) they have a need to satisfy the homework requirements. It would be unrealistic to think that each student would find every discussion topic to be personally relevant. Therefore, if non-relevant topics require student posts as well, it would stand to reason that these posts are made to satisfy individual course requirements.

Question 3: Opinion Scale/Likert
I participated in discussions not just to do the homework but because I was personally engaged in the discussions.

Figure 4. Controversial and personally relevant discussion vs. factual (collapsed)

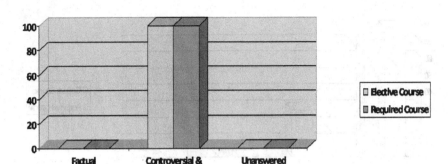

- Strongly Agree
- Agree
- Neither Agree nor Disagree
- Disagree
- Strongly Disagree
- Not Applicable
- Unanswered

Results for this question have also been collapsed as follows: Strongly Agrees/Agrees and Strongly Disagrees/Disagrees responses have been combined. 42.858% of Ss in the Elective Course and 71.429% of Ss in the Required Course agreed with this statement. Again, students post because (1) discussion topics are personally relevant/controversial; (2) they have a need to satisfy course requirements.

Question 4: Multiple Choice
Please select the choice that best describes your reaction to the following statement:

The more personally relevant I find a topic the more likely it is that I will actively participate in an on-going discussion about that topic.

- Almost Always True
- Occasionally True
- Almost Never True
- Unanswered

The overwhelming response for Ss in both courses to this question was "Almost Always True". 78.571% of Ss in the Elective Course compared to 71.429% in the Required Course felt that personal relevance of topic had a direct effect on increased participation in discussion. These results are consistent with those found in question 1. Recall that 100% of Ss in the Elective Course and Required Course responded that they "actively participated" in those discussions that were personally relevant and controversial.

2. Coding of Ss Posts for Levels of Critical Thinking

Does personal relevance of discussion topic affect students' quality of discussion in the online classroom? In order to answer this question Ss discussions in the Elective and Required Courses were coded and measured for levels of critical thinking using Garrison, Anderson, and Archer's (2001) coding system.

The four levels of critical thinking used from lowest to highest respectively were Triggering, Exploration, Integration, and Resolution. "Other" was also included as a category and accounted for those messages that were coded as purely social in nature.

Figure 5. Participation in discussion just to do the homework or personally engaged

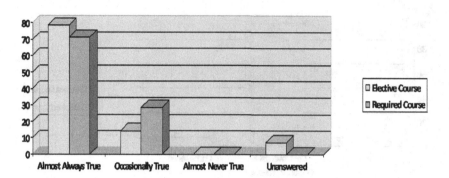

Variables

Let's consider the three independent variables, Course (Required Course, without rubrics vs. Elective Course, with rubrics), Student Status (i.e. Traditional/Non-Traditional), and Gender. What were the effects, if any, of these independent variables on the levels of critical thinking and Other.

Results

A One Way Anova was run using SPSS statistical software to determine whether the independent variables (course, student status, gender) would have any effect on the four levels of critical thinking plus Other. Neither Student Status nor Gender produced statistically significant results with regards to levels of critical thinking. Of the 950 posts that were coded for levels of critical thinking in the Elective Course, 8 were coded as Triggering and account for.01% of discussions. In comparison, of the 706 posts coded for the Required Course, 35 were coded as Triggering and account for.05% of total posts.

Although the numbers themselves are relatively small, statistical significance was found for differences in level of critical thinking in the two courses. The Required Course did produce statistically significantly more Triggering responses than in the Elective Course (p <.05).

Student posts coded as Exploration and Integration did not produce statistically significant differences. Of the 950 posts that were coded for levels

of critical thinking in the Elective Course, 835 were coded as Exploration and account for 88% of discussions. Of the 706 posts that were coded for levels of critical thinking in the Required Course, 564 were coded as Exploration and account for 80% of discussions. Twenty-one Integration responses in the Elective Course accounted for.02% of discussions while 19 Integration responses in the Required Course accounted for.03%. Resolution, the highest level of critical thinking simply did not occur in either course. Lastly, responses coded as Other accounted for.09% of discussion in the Elective Course and.12% in the Required Course and were not statistically significantly different from one another.

3. Early and Late Posts to Threaded Online Discussion Boards

Average initial post dates for each student in the Elective Course and the Required Course were calculated and entered into SPSS. The average initial post date (day of the week) for Ss in the Elective Course was day 3.21 and the average initial post date for Ss in the Required Course was day 4.98 (F = 15.504, df = 1, 34, p <.01). The Elective Course (with rubrics) produced significantly more initial posts during days 1 and 2 of the discussion week than did the Required Course (without rubrics) (F = 5.380, df = 1, 22, p <.05). The Elective Course (with rubrics) produced significantly more initial student-to-student responses during days 1 and 2 of the discussion week than did the Required Course (without rubrics) ($F = 12.256$, $df = 1, 33$, $p < .001$).

What might have brought about this difference in posting behavior between the two courses? One possibility is that in the Elective Course a strict rubric was used. The strict rubric required students to post early in the week, to respond to others and to use thoughtful and substantive writing. Students were motivated via 5 weekly points in the Elective Course to make initial posts to the discussion board on or before day three of each course week. It would appear that there was a connection between average initial post date (day 3.21) for this course and rubrics. Participation in the Required Course was not graded on a weekly basis and day of the week for initial posts was not stipulated. Students were "expected to be active in the course at least 3 days each week". The average initial post date in this course was day 4.98.

4. Rating of Personal Relevance

Are early (day 1 & 2) posts rated as more personally relevant by students than late (day 6 & 7) posts? In an attempt to answer this question, 4 student posts were rated for levels of personal relevance by communication students at the same university but students not in either of these two courses. Authors of posts and raters remained anonymous. Two posts from day 2, Week 7, and two posts from day 6, week 7, were rated for levels of personal relevance. Instructions to raters were as follows:

Instructions to Raters
Thank you so very much for taking the time to rate the enclosed discussions. We are interested in knowing whether or not you find the following discussions to be personally relevant. In other words, would you find yourself inclined to respond?

Please rate each discussion on a scale from 1 to 7 with 1 being not personally relevant and 7 being extremely personally relevant.

Your ratings are anonymous and will be used for research purposes only.

For posts made early in the week (Day 2), the average rating for personal relevance was 5.58 for the Elective Course and 5.50 for the Required Course. These ratings did not produce a difference in statistical significance for personal relevance between the courses.

The average rating for personal relevance for posts made in each course on day 6 were identical at 5.17. Since there were significantly more early posts to the Elective Course than to the Required Course, significantly more responses to early posts in the Elective Course than in the Required Course, significantly more late posts to the Required Course than to the Elective Course, and significantly more late responses to the Required Course than to the Elective Course, it would appear that personal relevance of discussion did not play a role in these posting behaviors.

Earlier posts received more responses ($M = 18.8$) than later ones ($M = 2.9$); however, this was not indicative of personal relevance.

Discussion

Hypothesis 1.
Personal relevance of discussion topic will produce an increase in student participation.

100% of students surveyed indicated that they were, in fact, "more likely to participate in those discussions that were "personally relevant". Students also responded that they would "actively participate in on-going discussions" about those topics that they found to be personally relevant. However, does personal relevance of discussion topic truly motivate students to engage in increased discussion? Are students posting to threaded online discussion boards to simply get the job done?

Survey Question 2 asked students if they "participated in discussion to fulfill the homework assignments as opposed to being personally engaged." 42.86% of students in the Elective Course and 28.57% of students in the Required Course agreed with this statement.

Can an increase in discussion be attributed solely to personal relevance of discussion topic? We don't think so. Recall that the Elective Course used rubrics that specified when to post and respond and the posts were graded each week. Rubrics will continue to remain a critical factor in student participation. Perhaps then it is a combination of personal relevance of discussion topic and rubrics that truly motivate a student to post and participate in on-going discussions.

Hypothesis 2.

Personal relevance of discussion topic will produce an increase in quality of student posts.

Triggering responses, those messages that evoke thinking about issues and evoke responses, include asking questions such as "What do you think?", "What do you mean?" etc. Could it be possible that students enrolled in courses required for their major ask these questions of one another to merely satisfy their weekly posting requirements? Once again, we cannot ignore the role that Rubrics plays.

Coding of these discussions did not produce statistically significant results as pertains to Exploration, Integration, and Resolution, the higher levels of critical thinking. No correlation can be made between personal relevance and these levels of critical thinking.

Hypothesis 3.

Personal relevance of discussion topic will affect students' initial post and response dates to threaded online discussion boards.

Do early posts and responses occur because students find topics of discussion personally relevant or because specific rubrics have been stated?

We had determined that late posts did not receive as many responses as did earlier posts. Was this due to lack of personal relevance or simply due to time of the course week?

Furthermore, are those discussions that occur earlier in the week deemed more personally relevant by students than those occurring later in the week? Was the average initial post date in each course due to personal relevance of discussion topic and a desire to initiate quality discussion or were students simply following their professor's instructions?

The rubrics for the Elective Course and the Required Course were somewhat similar in scope. However, an important distinction existed between the two; that of weekly discussion grading based on date of initial posts and responses in the Elective Course.

Student posts from day 2 and 6 were rated on a scale from 1 to 7 for personal relevance. The average rating for posts made on day 2 was 5.58 for the Elective Course and 5.50 for the Required Course. The average rating for posts made on day 6 was 5.17 for each course. The level of personal relevance did not differ between early and late posts.

Conclusion

This study was a preliminary probe into the effects of personal relevance on discussion. Personal relevance of discussion did not seem to produce an increase in critical thinking or student-to-student interaction.

We speculate that rubrics can be credited with creating earlier discussion but not necessarily better discussion (higher level of critical thinking). Rubrics may have prompted students to make their initial posts earlier in the week in the Elective Course but these earlier postings were not rated significantly more relevant than those posts made later in the week. It appears that rubrics did increase student interaction in discussion.

Does the average student post to an online discussion board to simply get the job done and satisfy course requirements? The answer is undoubtedly "Yes" and this can be seen in the high numbers of posts coded as Exploration in this study. The majority of students' posts included personal narratives and reiteration of material found in the course textbooks. Students indicated in response to the survey that personal relevance of discussion topic was important to them, and that it motivated them to participate more frequently in discussion. How much? The answer to this question remains unclear and therefore Study 5 attempts to test further the effects of rubrics on discussion.

STUDY 5: DOES THE USE OF RUBRICS INFLUENCE LEVEL OF STUDENT INTERACTION AND/OR LEVEL OF CRITICAL THINKING IN ONLINE DISCUSSION?

Setting the Stage

In Study 4 above, where we collected data on two online courses (with two different teachers) for Personal Relevance in relation to amount of interaction and level of critical thinking, we noted that one teacher used strict rubrics concerning when to post and how long posts ought to be and the other did not. But neither course provided students with a demonstration of what is meant by levels of critical thinking, going from low level of critical thinking to a higher level, from opinion or non-text-related or even not related to the other's post, to evidence-based and connected to previous posts. Points were laid out for posts to be graded, with 1 being low and 5 being high. Students were told when in the week to post and how many posts to respond to minimally. Students received a 0 if they posted after the week was over.

In this study we used rubrics that not only specified when to post but also offered examples of what is meant by levels of critical thinking (see Appendix 2). The course is a seven-week, summer class, Introduction to Communication, summer of 2009. The same Introduction to Communication course was taught the summer before, 2008, with the same teacher, but without the strict rubrics in 2008. In 2008 the teacher merely suggested that students post across the week and participation—generally—was used toward a participation grade. We wanted to learn whether or not the strict rubrics would get students to post earlier in the week, post more often and if the rubrics would produce a higher level of critical thinking.

Procedure

On the discussion board, 18 discussion forums were marked to indicate that they would be graded at the end of the week that that discussion was assigned. Each unit of the course ran from Monday until Sunday night, and discussion grades were put into the online grade book on Sunday evening, a grade of 0 to 5, with 0 for the student who had not posted on time. Students received 2 points for posting an initial post by Wednesday evening and for responding to 2 other posts by Friday evening. The remaining 3 points came from the quality of the post according to the rubrics (Appendix 2). Students were informed of the rubrics for the course in a step-by-step announcement at the beginning of the course and in an email after the first week of the course. Data from sixteen forums were used in this study. Two forums were not used because they indicated to students that it was optional to respond to those two. Two forums from the first two weeks of class in 2009 were dropped from grading when students were adjusting to the requirements in the rubrics, but they were included in the research study.

Using the same model for critical thinking we used in the earlier studies (Garrison, Anderson and Archer, 2001), the students' posts were scored for level of critical thinking. In addition, data were collected on the day in the week when students posted their initial post and the day in the week when they responded to other students, as well as the frequency of responding to other students' posts.

Finally, students were asked to respond to a survey almost identical to the one used in 2008, trying to get at their perception of personal relevance, trust, teacher involvement in discussion and checking on their awareness of being graded for rubrics.

Results

Critical Thinking

The 2009 class (with strict rubrics and graded posts) had a statistically significant effect on the dependent measure, triggering (F = 5.947, df = 1, 526, p <.01) compared to the 2008 class without strict rubrics and graded posts. Triggering messages occurred significantly more often in the course with rubrics (Mean =.039) than in the course without strict rubrics (Mean =.004). Exploration messages occurred more often in the course with rubrics (Mean = 1.797) than in the course without strict rubrics (Mean =.688; F = 137.725, df = 1, 527, p <.01). Integration messages occurred significantly more often in the course with rubrics (F = 8.190, df = 1, 527, p <.01). Integration messages occurred more often in the course with rubrics (Mean =.039) than in the course without strict rubrics (Mean =.004). Resolution messages did not occur at all in either class. Other messages occurred significantly more often in the course with rubrics (F = 34.498, df = 1, 526, p <.001). Other messages occurred more often in the course with rubrics (Mean =.289) than in the course without strict rubrics (Mean =.026).

Posting Activity

There were 19 students in the 2008 class and 16 in 2009. Data were collected on day in the week

for initial posts and day in the week for initial responses to posts for the 2008 class (without strict rubrics) and the 2009 class (with strict rubrics and grading of posts). Each post was scored from 1 to 7, depending on the day of the week. If a student did not post or posted after the 7 days were up, an 8 was entered. Also, total frequency of student-to-student responses was taken as data. The difference in posting behavior is quite dramatic for frequency of posting behavior, both for initial posts and initial responding to posts. There were far more initial posts in 2009 than 2008. In 2009, there were 186 initial posts and in 2008 there were 118 initial posts. An ANOVA for frequency of posts showed a statistically significant difference for the two classes (F = 62.094, df = 1, 527, p <.01). When we look at when students posted in each course, there does appear to be a difference in the average day of initially posting (Course 1, 2009, M = 5.09; Course 2, 2008, M = 6.67). Students posted statistically significantly earlier in the 2009 course (with rubrics) than in the 2008 course (without rubrics) (F = 67.763, df = 1, 528, p <.01). Far more students posted an initial response to other students in Course 1 (with rubrics, 120 students) than in Course 2 (without rubrics, 15 students). Clearly, many more students responded to other students in Course 1 than in Course 2. An ANOVA test showed the difference in day of initial responding to be statistically significant (F = 119.802, df = 1, 558, p <.01), with students in 2009 responding earlier in the week than students in 2008. The frequency of students responding to other students was tested with a univariate ANOVA, comparing posting in the 2008 class to posting in the 2009 class. The frequency of student to student responding was statistically greater in 2009, with rubrics, than in 2008, without rubrics (F = 129.571, df = 1, 526, p <.01). In short, there was more student-to-student interaction with rubrics than without.

Survey of Student Thoughts about the Online Discussions

We employed the survey function within Blackboard to survey the students in the 2009 course about their thoughts on our class's discussions. Blackboard provides an anonymous survey application. Questions were randomly ordered for each student. The students were informed that the survey was anonymous and would have no effect on their grade. The response rate was 11 out of 16 students (68% return rate).

Thirteen questions were asked but we will only highlight a few notable ones since the results are similar to the 2008 survey. Overall, students reported that they were more inclined to take part in discussions where the question did not require a factual response and was both personally relevant and controversial. For instance, 0% responded that they would take part in discussions that are controversial, but 27% would take part in personally relevant discussions and 64% would take part in discussions that are both personally relevant and controversial. Approximately a third of respondents said they participated to fulfill homework assignments. Approximately a third of respondents said that trust played a role in their willingness to participate in discussions. And approximately 90% of students said that the professor's active role in facilitating discussions was important to them. In an open ended question, students seem to think that disagreement is important to discussion but in another question, approximately one third indicated that they are not comfortable disagreeing in discussions. Finally, when asked if they were aware that their posts were graded, approximately 80% said they were aware.

While these survey results are not hard evidence, they do fit well with the survey results from the 2008 class and they give us another look at the discussion experience.

Discussion

In short, this study found that strict rubrics and grading posts did bring about an increase in posting and an increase in the level of critical thinking displayed in posts, as well as an increase in student responses to other student posts. We were somewhat surprised by part of the results. We expected an increase in posting, with earlier posts leading the way, due to the demand placed on students by the rubrics and weekly grading of posts. We did not expect the level of critical thinking to show any difference and it did. However, in spite of an increase in level of critical thinking we should note that in practical terms the amount of increased use of higher levels of critical thinking is still a very tiny percentage of total posts. And at the same time, there was a fair amount of student distress in accepting the weekly grades for postings. There seemed to be a price to pay for the demand. Note too that grading weekly posts is labor intensive. In this case, a teaching assistant graded posts and posted weekly grades for posts.

Interestingly, these findings are compatible with findings reported by Bai (2009). Bai compared graduate students' critical thinking displayed in online discussion in two sections of the same course. In one section, students were given *suggestions* on how to discuss online, including deadlines for participation, minimum number of postings, and general information on the quality of postings. In the other section, students were introduced to the Garrison et al. (2001) model for critical thinking. In this section, critical analysis was emphasized, students got to see explicit examples of what is meant by levels of critical thinking. The instructor stayed out of the actual discussions. In Bai's study, posts were not graded. Without explicit instruction on critical thinking, the majority of postings (87%) represented the category Exploration. With instruction, the distribution of levels of critical thinking shifted to higher categories. With instruction, the percentage of Triggering responses rose, Exploration fell, Integration rose, and there were no instances of Resolution. Bai's results are similar to the findings in Study 5 here.

It is noteworthy that in Study 4 presented above, where two online courses were compared for critical thinking, one course merely suggested that students post during the week and the other laid out specific rubrics about posting; while the course with more specific rubrics produced greater interaction, it did not produce greater levels of critical thinking. While it was specific about posting and it graded for posts, it did not display specific guidelines on what is meant by levels of critical thinking.

CURRENT CHALLENGES FACING OUR UNDERSTANDING OF DISCUSSION

This chapter began with a question: Does online discussion produce increased interaction and critical thinking? The main purpose in asking this question was to try to learn what we can to help the teacher in facilitating discussions. Keep in mind that all the studies we ran were with undergraduates. So, what can we report?

To begin with, there is no evidence here for saying that online discussion per se produced increased critical thinking. In fact, in Study 1 we saw that there was a statistically significant difference between the online and face-to-face discussions, with the face-to-face discussions showing a higher level of critical thinking. But perhaps more importantly, neither environment, online or face-to-face produced very high levels of critical thinking, and this was consistent with other studies reviewed. Recall the levels of critical thinking demonstrated in the virtual classroom discussion. There was essentially no critical thinking there. There was, however, a good deal of interaction in the virtual classroom. And that takes us to the

second part of the question: Is there increased interaction in online discussion?

In Study 1, where online discussion was compared to face-to-face discussion with 4 groups of students compared across these 2 environments, face-to-face produced a greater amount of interaction and a higher level of critical thinking. To our surprise, in Study 2 it turned out that the summaries written by students in these (Study 1) groups were rated as higher quality if the papers came from the online discussions. When we looked at the part played by the teacher or the teaching assistant, we found that the teaching assistant did not show a correlation between the frequency of their posting and the frequency of student-to-student postings in the online course discussions (Study 3). The teacher did, however, show a fairly high correlation between his postings and student-to-student interactions. In Study 4 we sought to discover if the personal relevance of a discussion topic predicted student involvement in discussion. While students said in responding to survey questions that personally relevant and controversial topics did attract them to post, we did not find empirical support for this claim. Initial posts that were independently rated for personal relevance and compared for amount of interaction did not support the claim, namely, that personal relevance predicts number of posts in response. Instead, it appeared that day in the week (early versus late) had more to do with how much interaction took place. It did appear that in comparing two online courses, where one used strict rubrics and the other did not, that requirements of what to post and by when, produced earlier posts and more interaction (Study 5). Strict rubrics did improve on the level of critical thinking displayed in the posts, though in practical terms, the amount of improvement is not very large. What sense can we make of all this and what advice might we offer the teacher?

Study 1 did show that instructional methods (type of analysis and type of reporting out) can have an effect upon two of the levels of critical thinking, triggering and exploration, and upon the relational communication (other). Study 1 suggested that *the need for students to reach consensus* (the motivation for collaborative meaning making) can influence critical thinking. Instructional media also showed an effect on the first two levels of critical thinking. Instructional media also showed an effect on relational communication. Stated cautiously, we can at least take these findings to suggest that levels of critical thinking are sensitive to some teacher decisions.

Study 2 failed to support our hypothesis that written summaries based on discussions that evidenced higher critical thinking (face-to-face discussions in Study 1) would receive higher grades for quality of the written summary. Admittedly, this is initially puzzling. We can only speculate. Several possible explanations come to mind and some were mentioned earlier. It is possible that we use different criteria in judging a written piece for quality than we use to categorize levels of critical thinking in spoken discourse. It is possible that the link between critical thinking in discussion and quality in essay writing is not a simple one. Alternatively, it may be that having to write about a case (as opposed to talking about it) sets in motion higher levels of thinking that reach fruition in writing following the discussion.

Study 3 suggested that the teacher's responding to discussions was associated with increased student-to-student interactions. However, the teaching assistant had little to no effect on student-to-student interactions and only a small influence on critical thinking.

Study 4 explored personal relevance of topics to learn more about whether or not personal relevance influences level of interaction and level of critical thinking. Generally, the outcome based on survey questions suggested that personally relevant *and* controversial issues would produce greater interaction. However we did not find that forums rated for personal relevance varied between ones with greater and lesser interaction.

Instead, what appeared to be going on was that where students posted early in the week we found greater interaction than where they waited later in the week to post initially. Neither sex of student nor traditional/non-traditional status seemed to play a role in these findings. As it happened one of the two courses studied in Study 4 used strict rubrics and the other did not. The course with strict rubrics resulted in earlier posts and more triggering posts but no other difference in level of critical thinking.

Study 5 was undertaken to explore further the idea that strict rubrics plus grading of posts would influence the amount of interaction and the level of critical thinking. We did in fact find some evidence to support the claim that rubrics (plus grading) did influence posting behavior, both posting activity and level of critical thinking. The use of rubrics did bring about earlier posts, greater interaction between students and higher levels of critical thinking. It is very important to point out that the rubrics included explicit demonstration of what is meant by each level of critical thinking. However, again, in practical terms, the actual amount of increased critical thinking is still very low, really negligible.

SOLUTIONS AND RECOMMENDATIONS

Our overall interpretation of the data we gathered, based on a variety of methods, experimental, quasi-experimental, survey, and observational is that the level of student-to-student interaction in the online course discussions can be dramatically affected by teaching methods and medium. However, affecting the level of critical thinking is more difficult to do.

When we looked more closely at the actual threads, to see when the teacher or TA got into a discussion and which topics seemed to generate the most (interactive) discussion and the most animated discussion, we believe the data show the strong impact of some qualitative variables that beg for further analysis.

It appears that a student will respond to the teacher or the TA when asked a direct question, but this does not increase the student-to-student interactions. Where student-to-student interactions are more frequent, it appears that the teacher joined in to on-going interactions, hence the positive correlation between teacher postings and student-to-student postings. The teacher didn't create the discussion, but instead took part. Furthermore, those discussions that stood out as especially animated and showing a higher level of interaction than most, seemed to be characterized by topics that carried great personal interest for the students. For instance, one such topic that appeared during the discussion of the movie, "You've Got Mail," was about cheating in romantic relationships. There was a great deal of self-disclosure going on in this discussion and a much greater amount of interaction than normally found, although, even here, it is just a few students who are involved in the discussion. The major characteristic of this discussion was the personal importance of the topic being discussed. We do not know if the online nature of the discussion facilitated this discussion, but the psychological anonymity that students speak about in describing the online experience may have played a role. We speculate that psychological anonymity did play a role in self disclosure (i.e., the reduced immediacy and reduced social cues). The teacher raised the question about cheating, but then got out of the way. In their chapter titled, "Getting Discussion Started," Brookfield and Preskill (2005) assert:

One of the chief reasons people don't speak up in groups is their sense that the topic of the discussion is removed from their experience, that it has no meaning or relevance to their lives. Their prereading may convince them that the topic is one about which only experts have knowledge and opinions. Or they may feel that they are being

asked to talk about a theory or concept that exists only as an abstraction. A useful way to combat this sense of distance is to start a discussion by getting students to talk about a memorable experience in their lives that somehow connects to the topic. Because most students think they are experts on their own experience, starting out with personal stories is often much less intimidating for them than launching straight into a discussion of the strengths and weaknesses of a theory (pp. 73-74).

If Brookfield and Preskill (2005) are correct that students are inclined to talk about their own experience, then we shouldn't be surprised that student discourse so often is at the level of Exploration.

What seems to apply in the discussion about cheating in romantic relationships is a convergence of personal relevance, need to collaboratively make meaning, personal experience, psychological anonymity, and confidence about what one is talking about. What we think we need to look at more closely are the following sorts of concepts: personal significance of the topic and its degree of controversy, perceived anonymity, trust, motivation to learn, motivation to reach consensus, confidence about one's knowledge of the topic under discussion, and of course, critical thinking.

In Study 5, we saw that with strict rubrics and grading, we could increase both the amount of interaction and the level of critical thinking. But it was a battle to push the students into posting early in the week and into aiming for higher levels of critical thinking. Some expressed their negative attitude toward this process during the first round or two of being graded. In addition, it was labor intensive to grade all the posts, a task that fell upon the teaching assistant. Not all teachers will be willing to track posts this closely. In future courses, this teacher is going to try to have students rate one another's posts using the strict rubrics from this study, though these will not count as grades. Note that Bai (2009) found evidence for increased critical thinking in discussion by instructing students in the Garrison et al. model used in these studies, and importantly, Bai did not grade posts.

It is looking like it is easier to get the students to talk than to get them to think. We haven't found the magic bullet to move most students to the highest levels of critical thinking and maybe there isn't one. It appears that a promising route to increased interaction and increased critical thinking is explicit instruction in critical thinking and the requirement that students respond to one another's posts.

ACKNOWLEDGMENT

I am in debt to two wonderful students who worked closely with me on this research project. I owe thanks to Laura Woods and Alice O. Goodwin for their many hours of collecting data and talking with me as we worked through these studies.

REFERENCES

Bai, H. (2009). Facilitating students' critical thinking in online discussion: An instructor's experience. *Journal of Interactive Online Learning, 8*(2), 156–164.

Benoit, P. J., Benoit, W., Milyo, J., & Hansen, G. (2006). *The effects of traditional vs. web-assisted instruction on student learning and satisfaction. Report published by the University of Missouri. Brookfield, S. D., & Preskill, S. (2005). Discussion as a way of teaching* (2nd ed.). San Francisco, CA: Jossey-Bass.

Cell, E. (1984). *Learning to learn from experience.* Albany, NY: State University of New York Press.

Cohen, J. (1960). A coefficient of agreement for nominal scales. *Educational and Psychological Measurement, 20*, 37–46. doi:10.1177/001316446002000104

Curtis, D. D., & Lawson, M. J. (2001, February). Exploring collaborative online learning. *JALN, 5*(1), 21–34.

Duphorne, P. L., & Gunawardena, C. N. (2005, March). The effect of three computer conferencing designs on critical thinking skills of nursing students. *American Journal of Distance Education, 19*(1), 37–50. doi:10.1207/s15389286ajde1901_4

Dutton, J., Dutton, M., & Perry, J. (2002). How do online students differ from lecture students? *JALN, 6*(1). Retrieved from http://www.sloan-c.org/publications/jaln/v6n1/index.asp

Ertmer, P. A., Richardson, J. C., Belland, B., & Camin, D. (2007). Using peer feedback to enhance the quality of student online postings: An exploratory study. *Journal of Computer-Mediated Communication, 12*, 78–99. doi:10.1111/j.1083-6101.2007.00331.x

Garrison, D. R., Anderson, T., & Archer, W. (2001). Critical thinking, cognitive presence, and computer conferencing in distance education. *American Journal of Distance Education, 15*(1), 7–23. doi:10.1080/08923640109527071

Garrison, D. R., Anderson, T., & Archer, W. (2003). Critical thinking, cognitive presence, and computer conferencing in distance education. *American Journal of Distance Education, 15*(1), 7–23. doi:10.1080/08923640109527071

Gergen, K. (1995). Social construction and the educational process. In Steffe, L., & Gale, J. (Eds.), *Constructivism in education* (pp. 17–39). Hillsdale, NJ: Erlbaum.

Griffin, E. (2006). *Communication: A first look at communication theory* (6th ed.). Boston: McGraw-Hill.

Guiller, J., Durndell, A., & Ross, A. (2008). Peer interaction and critical thinking: Face-to-face or online discussion? *Learning and Instruction, 18*(2), 187–200. doi:10.1016/j.learninstruc.2007.03.001

Heckman, R., & Annabi, H. (2005). A content analytic comparison of learning processes in online and face-to-face case study discussions. *Journal of Computer-Mediated Communication, 10*(2), article 7. Retrieved from http://jcmc.indiana.edu/vol10/issue2/heckman.html

Hunt, S., Simonds, C., & Simonds, B. (2007, November) Uniquely qualified, distinctively competent: Delivering 21st century skills in the Basic Course. *93rd annual convention, National Communication Association* (pp. 1-24) (AN 35506038).

Joiner, R., & Jones, S. (2003). The effects of communication medium on argumentation and the development of critical thinking. *International Journal of Educational Research, 39*(8), 861–871. doi:10.1016/j.ijer.2004.11.008

Kamin, C., Glicken, A., Hall, M., Quarantillo, B., & Merenstein, G. (2001). Evaluation of electronic discussion groups as a teaching/learning strategy in an evidence-based medicine course: A pilot study. *Education for Health, 14*(1), 21–32. doi:10.1080/13576280010015380

Lapadat, J. (July, 2002, July). Written interaction: A key component in online learning. *Journal of Computer Mediated Communication, 7*(4). Retrieved July 12, 2007 from http://jcmc.indiana.edu/vol7/issue4/lapadat.html

Marttunen, M. (1998). Electronic mail as a forum for argumentative interaction in higher education studies. *Journal of Educational Computing Research, 18*(4), 387–405. doi:10.2190/AAJK-01XK-WDMV-8M0P

Meyer, K. (2003a). Face-to-face versus threaded discussion: The role of time and higher-order thinking. *JALN, 7*(3), 55–65.

Meyer, K. (2003b). The web's impact on student learning. *T.H.E. Journal, 30*(10).

Murphy, E. (2003). Moving from theory to practice in the design of web-based learning from the perspective of constructivism, Murphy, E. (2003). *The Journal of Interactive Online Learning, 1*(4). Retrieved October 30, 2006 from http://www.ncolr.org/jiol/archives/2003/spring/4/MS02028.pdf

Newman, G., Webb, B., & Cochrane, C. (1995). A content analysis method to measure critical thinking in face-to-face and computer supported group learning. Interpersonal Computing and Technology, 3(2), 56-77. Retrieved from http://www.helsinki.fi/science/optek/1995/n2/newman.txt

Pena-Shaff, J., & Nicholls, C. (2004). Analyzing student interactions and meaning construction in Computer Bulletin Board (BBS) discussions. *Computers & Education, 42*, 243–265. doi:10.1016/j.compedu.2003.08.003

Picciano, A. G. Beyond student perceptions: Issues of interaction, presence, and performance in an online course. *JALN, 6*(1). Retrieved from http://www.sloan-c.org/publications/jaln/v6n1/v6n1_picciano.asp

Rourke, L., & Kanuka, H. (2007). Computer Conferencing and Distance Learning. In Bidgoli, H. (Ed.), *The Handbook of Computer Networks* (*Vol. 3*, pp. 831–842). Hoboken, NJ: John Wiley & Sons.

Rovai, A. P. (2007). Facilitating online discussions effectively. *The Internet and Higher Education, 10*(1), 77–88. doi:10.1016/j.iheduc.2006.10.001

Shedletsky, L. (2000). The online double bind: mixed messages about online teaching & scholarship. *The Maine Scholar, 13*, 163–173.

Shedletsky, L., & Aitken, J. E. (2001, July). The paradoxes of online academic work. *Communication Education, 50*(3), 206–217. doi:10.1080/03634520109379248

Spiceland, J. D., & Hawkins, C. P. (2002). The impact on learning of an asynchronous course format. *JALN, 6*(1).

Swan, K. (2006, February). Online Collaboration: Introduction to the Special Issue. *JALN, 10*(1). Retrieved from http://www.sloan-c.org/publications/JALN/v10n1/v10n1_1swan_member.asp

Vess, D. L. (2005, October). Asynchronous discussion and communication patterns in online and hybrid history courses. *Communication Education, 54*(4), 355–364. doi:10.1080/03634520500442210

ADDITIONAL READING

Angeli, C., Valanides, N., & Bonk, C. J. (2003). Communication in a web-based conferencing system: the quality of computer-mediated interactions. *British Journal of Educational Technology, 34*, 31-43.

Black, A. (2005). The use of asynchronous discussion: Creating a text of talk. *Contemporary Issues in Technology and Teacher Education, 5*, 5-24.

Dixson, M., Kuhlhorst, M., & Reiff, A. (2006). Creating effective online discussions: Optimal instructor and student roles. *Journal of Asynchronous Learning Networks, 10*. Retrieved March 6, 2008, from http://www.sloanc.org/publications/jaln/v10n4/v10n4_dixson.asp

Ertmer, P. A., Richardson, J. C., Belland, B., Camin, D., Connolly, P., Coulthard, et al. (2007). Using peer feedback to enhance the quality of student online postings: An exploratory study. *Journal of Computer-Mediated Communication, 12*(2). Retrieved December 16, 2007, from http://jcmc.indiana.edu/vol12/issue2/ertmer.html

Farrell, T. S. C. (2009). *Talking, Listening, and Teaching: A Guide to Classroom Communication.* Thousand Oaks, CA: Corwin.

Garrison, D. R., & Cleveland-Innes, M. (2005). Facilitating cognitive presence in online learning: Interaction is not enough. *The American Journal of Distance Education, 19*, 133-148.

Hale, M. S., and City, E. A. (2006). *The teacher's guide to leading student-centered discussions.* Thousand Oaks, CA: Corwin Press.

Rourke, L. and Anderson, T. (2002). Using peer teams to lead online discussions. *Journal of Interactive Media in Education, 2002,* (1).

Shedletsky, L. and Aitken, J. (2004). *Human Communication on the Internet.* Boston, MA: Allyn & Bacon/Longman.

Shedletsky, L. J. (2009). How Am I Doing? Anonymity, Contingent Teaching, and Discussion. In *The Proceedings of The Inaugural Conference on Classroom Response Systems: Innovations and Best Practices.* University of Louisville, Louisville, KY, November, 2008. Available online at: http://www.iclicker.com/dnn/UserCommunity/ConferencePapers/tabid/171/Default.aspx

Swan, K., Schenker, J., Arnold, S., & Kuo, C. (2007). Shaping online discussion: Assessment matters. *E-mentor, 1*(18). Retrieved March 6, 2008, from http://ementor.edu.pl/_xml/wydania/18/390.pdf

Topper, A. (2005). Facilitating student interactions through discursive moves. *The Quarterly Review of Distance Education, 6*, 55-67.

Walther, J. B., & Bunz, U. (2005). The rules of virtual groups: Trust, liking, and performance in computer-mediated communication. *Journal of Communication, 55*, 828-846.

ENDNOTES

† With permission from IGI Global, an earlier version of this review of literature and Study

1 was previously published as Shedletsky, L. (2010). Critical thinking in discussion: Online versus face-to-face. In D. Russell (Ed.), *Cases on collaboration in virtual environments: Processes and interactions*. Hershey, PA: Information Science Reference.

§ I must thank Professor John Broida for helping me with SPSS (though I did not always take his advice and I cannot hold him responsible for my errors), for listening to me as I worked through this research and for being supportive all the way.

** The responses took up a number of pages, so we abbreviate a few here in the table. The full body of data can be found at: http://media.usm.maine.edu/~lenny/discuss_survey.ppt

†† Again, a few responses that were representative of the student views were selected.

‡‡ This study was carried out with Alice Goodwin as my research assistant. Alice gets at least equal credit for this study.

§§ Traditional students were those students who attended college directly after high school and non-traditional students were those individuals who did not. The age of traditional students was 18-22 and 23-45 for non-traditional students.

*** The distinction between early/late was as follows. Ss early (initial) posts and responses that occurred during the first two days of each course week were coded as early. Those posts and responses that occurred during the last two days of each course week were coded as late.

1 The Required Course made a suggestion about posts: "You are expected to be active in the course at least 3 days each week."

2 The Elective Course stated: **REMINDER ABOUT WEEKLY DISCUSSIONS:** As a guideline your initial post should be around 150 to 200 words. Subsequent posts when responding to others in class should be around 75-100 words in length. Please try and avoid responses such as "I agree" or "I was thinking the same thing," as they add little to the discussion. Frequent and substantive posts to discussion boards are crucial in an online course since they are the correlate to an in-class discussion in traditional classroom settings. These discussions are your opportunity to reflect what you have learned, and to interact with your course facilitator and colleagues. In order to receive full credit (5 pts. each week) for the discussion questions, you must submit them by: Original Post on the Discussion Questions: Due by day 3 (Friday midnight) of each week. Additional participation: Anytime in the week. Each Discussion Board assignment is worth 5 points, and is awarded as follows: First contribution before or on Day 3 (Friday midnight) - 1 point At least 2 responses to other posts before or on Day 7 (Monday midnight) - 1 point All posts are substantive and advance discussion (**note**: to advance discussion, you must post your responses to others before Day 7) - 1 point Thoughts expressed clearly and succinctly - 1 point Posts reflect reading assignments and outside research - 1 point

APPENDIX 1

Table 4. Triggering events

Descriptor	Indicators	Sociocognitive Processes	Modifications
EVOCATIVE	Recognizing the problem Sense of puzzlement	Presenting background information that culminates in a question Asking questions Messages that take discussion in a new direction	*Asking questions does not necessarily indicate triggering. If the person is using questions to try and evoke a response, triggering may be the appropriate code. If the questions are asked in an assertive or rhetorical way, coding up might be more appropriate.

Example: It has been argued that the only way to deliver effective distance education is through a systems approach. However, this approach is rarely used. Why do you think that is?

Example: One reason I think it is seldom used is that it is too complicated to get cooperation. Another may be that the mind-sets of those in charge to change practices.

Example: We also had trouble getting cooperation. Often the use of new tools requires new organizational structures. We addressed these issues when we implemented a systems approach, and I think that's why we were successful.

Example: A good test of this solution would be to… and then assess how…

Table 5. Exploration

Descriptor	Indicators	Sociocognitive Processes	Modifications
INQUISITIVE	Divergence – within the online community Divergence – within a single message Information exchange Suggestions for consideration Brainstorming Leaps to conclusions	Unsubstantiated contradiction of Previous ideas Many different ideas/themes presented in one message Personal narratives/descriptions/ facts (not used as evidence to support a conclusion) Author explicitly characterizes Messages as exploration – e.g., "Does that seem about right?" or "Am I way off the mark?" Adds to established points but Does not systematically defend/ justify/develop addition Offers unsupported opinions	*If the multiple ideas/themes presented in one message relate and connect with one another and are laid out in a logical, flowing manner the message should not be coded down solely due to divergence. *Personal narratives are utterances about one's personal life that could easily be omitted without altering the message being sent. Personal narratives alone, without the support of other exploration indicators, should not be coded as exploration. *Indicators of brainstorming include Messages such as: "I think" "Maybe" "Might be" "We could.." *Author can support their own opinions with additional opinions if they develop a justifiable and defendable argument. Otherwise, additional information from various sources are needed. Look for terms such as "I believe" "I think" "My opinion"

Table 6. Integration

Descriptor	Indicators	Sociocognitive Processes	Modifications
TENTATIVE	Convergence – among group members Convergence – within a single message Connecting ideas, synthesis Creating solutions	Reference to previous message Followed by substantiated agreement, e.g., "I agree because...." Building on, adding to others' ideas Justified, developed, defensible, yet tentative hypotheses Integrating information from various sources – textbooks, articles, personal experience Explicit characterization of message as a solution by participant	*Agreeing/disagreeing with a previous message applies if, and only if, it is followed by substantiated and developed reasoning as to why they have come to that conclusion. If simply disagreeing or agreeing the student must justify as to why they are taking that stance. *Re-phrasing what another student has said does not fall under this category (even if the unit being re-phrased did) unless there is a clear and developed addition *Simply referencing a source does not qualify unless there is a developed connection *Personal experience is something that the student has gone through that has a clear and distinct connection to the content being discussed. *The student should be using at least 2 sources. For personal experience to count as a source it must be clearly related to a theory, idea or subject that relates to the assignment and also be accompanied by a different source. *The main factors used to distinguish between exploration and integration were unsupported vs. supported statements/opinions.

OTHER: An "other" category was developed in order to provide coding criteria for utterances made that do not fit into any other category. These include messages that are social in context; "Did you watch the game"; message that are vague, e.g., "very thought provoking, thanks" and messages that are mechanical or organizational, "I'll type the summary."

APPENDIX 2

See rubrics at: http://media.usm.maine.edu/%7Elenny/discussion%20rubric.htm

Table 7. Resolution

Descriptor	Indicators	Sociocognitive Processes	Modifications
COMMITTED	Vicarious applications to real world Testing solutions Defending solutions	None Coded	*Resolution mimics the research process. Participants must first develop hypothesis, test their given solutions and then defend and explain the results.

Assessment for Online Discussion

DISCUSSION BOARD POSTS WILL BE GRADED AS WE GO:
Here is a table describing what will earn you points for posts.
Look in the grade book each week to see the points you are getting for your posts.
The grade for posts will make up 10% of your grade:
http://media.usm.maine.edu/~lenny/discussion%20rubric.htm.html

DISCUSSION BOARD POSTS WILL BE RATED AS WE GO:
Here is a table describing what makes for lower to higher level quality posts:
http://media.usm.maine.edu/~lenny/discussion%20rubric.htm.html

WHEN TO POST

Post early each week--an initial post by Wednesday evening-- so discussion can occur and each week respond to at least one other student's post.

WHAT TO POST

Try to respond in a way that reflects high quality, critical thinking (SEE THE LINK ABOVE).

There is need to help make clear what leads to good grades in participation. Below are some suggestions (rubrics) to help you assess your own work:

Read and write to the Discussion Board/Group at least three times/week (you may do more).
Try to engage other's in their postings, to carry on discussion rather than monologues.
Be reflective in your posts (and writing more is not necessarily better). Each piece is to: make clear connections to the question, discussion, and readings; include supporting details and examples.
Be thoughtful and reflective — building from examples to greater insights when possible.
Be supportive but don't be afraid to challenge ideas.
Use correct spelling, punctuation, and grammar.
Your participation in each discussion must also occur within the time frame noted on the Assignments with "talk" over six days or more rather than posted at the last minute.
My objective is for us to function as a community of learners, offering help to one another and also challenging each other's ideas, with the objective of approaching clear and accurate representations of our subject matter.

Here are some criteria for online discussion suggested by Rovai (2004):
http://media.usm.maine.edu/~lenny/rovai.doc.

APPENDIX 3

Questions

1. *What is critical thinking?*

In this chapter, critical thinking is operationalized as 4 categories or levels of thought as evidenced in a variety of behaviors, including triggering or evoking a response to a question, exploring ideas or sharing opinions and experiences or unsubstantiated ideas, integration or making reference to previous messages with substantiated and developed reasoning offered in support of a conclusion, and resolution or testing solutions and defending the solutions.

2. *Think of the last time you were in a great discussion. In your own words, why did you select this particular discussion—what made it great?*
3. *Based on what you have read in this chapter, what could a teacher or discussion facilitator do to try to improve the quality of discussion?*

A few suggestions are: ask questions that do not require factual answers, but instead, may touch on personally important and controversial issues; specifically require students to post early in the unit and require students to respond to one another; offer explicit models of what is meant by levels of critical thinking; grade posts.

4. *Based on the research presented in this chapter, what are some key variables that you think need further study for us to understand the nature of discussion online?*

We still need to test the effects of rubrics and grading; we need to understand more about bringing about motivated collaboration; we need to learn more about trust, personal relevance and the part played by social interaction.

A key speculation that comes out of this chapter is that discussion is more likely to be interactive and open to debate when the participants need to (must) collaborate to perform a task. What evidence do you find in the chapter for or against this position?

On one level, we see in the chapter that when students are forced to interact (use of rubrics and grading) more interaction goes on, though the level of critical thinking is not really affected. Where the topic of discussion is personal and important to the individual and others reciprocate (e.g., the discussion of cheating), it appears that intense discussion can occur.

Chapter 2
Collaborative Student Groups and Critical Thinking in an Online Basic Communication Course

Roy Schwartzman
The University of North Carolina at Greensboro, USA

Megan Morrissey
The University of Colorado at Boulder, USA

EXECUTIVE SUMMARY

This chapter examines discussion board postings of ten undergraduate student groups (n = 45 students) who participated in collaborative problem-solving in a fully online, introductory communication course. Postings during a full academic year—three sections offered during three consecutive 15-week trimesters—reveal that student usage of the online format did not exhibit progressive development of critical thinking. Few student posts exhibited qualities of interrogation, exploration, convergence, or application that constitute the reflective thought process. Instead, students used threaded discussions primarily as forums for personal assertions, relational maintenance, and summaries of research. The study suggests that concepts of critical thinking require adaptation to an online environment that diverges from the linear cognitive process assumed in traditional approaches to critical inquiry. The online learning environment must reconcile the strong need to establish group cohesion with the impetus toward groupthink that limits critical thinking.

INTRODUCTION

Despite the proliferation of fully online and web-augmented academic courses, many opportunities remain to expand the empirical knowledge and theoretical understanding of how students utilize online course components and how to optimize course design. These opportunities are especially intriguing within oral communication instruction in higher education. Although introductory oral communication courses (either public speaking or "comprehensive" courses that also cover interpersonal and group communication) garner large

DOI: 10.4018/978-1-61520-863-0.ch002

enrollments, questions persist regarding the relationship between online peer interactions and critical thinking skills. Studies regarding online communication education express the need for more empirical research documenting "the influence of technology use on student outcomes such as cognitive, behavioral, and affective learning" (Turman & Schrodt, 2005, p. 110).

Threaded discussion boards appear ubiquitously in online course management systems, although how students actually use this learning tool deserves further documentation and analysis (Jeong, 2003). Harman and Koohang (2005) observe that discussion boards potentially improve interactivity and sharing of third-party resources (such as hyperlinked instructional materials). Threaded discussions can intensify group interactions because the transparency of the medium readily exposes lurkers and uncooperative group members (Shedletsky & Aitken, 2004; Schwartzman, 2006). These observations invite further investigation of how to optimize incorporation of threaded discussions into online courses. Studying online instruction in an undergraduate communication course also may improve the representativeness of research regarding discussion boards. A review of the literature on threaded discussions observes: "Current research is predominated by examination of education and graduate level online classes. The typical online student is not a graduate student and does not take education classes" (San Millan Maurino, 2006, p. 14).

Student discussion board posts can provide valuable data for understanding how peer interactions relate to learning in the online environment. Indeed, "the written records of threaded discussions may be a boon to researchers desiring to study the online environment for evidence that students gain the intellectual skills that higher education values" (Meyer, 2003, p. 64). Such studies gain importance given the wide availability of online course offerings in communication studies. Since the implementation of online communication education has rapidly outpaced knowledge of online

instructional techniques (Schwartzman, 2007a), closer exploration of actual student behaviors in online communication courses seems warranted.

Conducting group problem-solving projects via threaded discussions presents many challenges (Schwartzman, 2006). Administering and monitoring online discussions can prove daunting when the medium does not easily capture the energy and mutual supportiveness that personal meetings can generate. To understand how threaded discussions operate, this study examines student postings in collaborative problem-solving groups within an introductory oral communication course that included public speaking, interviewing, interpersonal communication, and group dynamics. Close analysis of the patterns and contents of student discussion board posts reveals how students actually employ online discussion boards and how to improve their use. Although online instruction offers unique opportunities to reach isolated or overlooked student populations (Schwartzman, 2007c), the benefits of such instruction will be offset if the instructional tools are misused.

To understand how students use online threaded discussions, this study addresses the following research questions:

- **RQ1:** To what extent do students develop dialogues that demonstrate higher-order, critical thinking skills and encourage others to employ those skills?
- **RQ2:** What communication patterns among students in threaded discussions facilitate or inhibit collaborative problem-solving?
- **RQ3:** How can instructors utilize online threaded discussions and similar tools to increase the quality of collaborative group work?

LITERATURE REVIEW

A growing body of research specifically addresses online delivery of speech communication courses in higher education. Meyer (2002) observes that too many studies of online instruction attribute results to instructional technology per se without reflecting on how the technology is used in ways that might inhibit or enhance learning. In some studies of online oral communication instruction, disappointing pedagogical outcomes resulted from online instruction that merely migrated course lectures to an electronic medium. Misconceptions persist regarding exactly how online pedagogy differs from the conventional classroom. Simply placing text or lectures online offers no distinct pedagogical advantages (Benyon, Stone, & Woodroffe, 1997). As Twigg (1999) notes, merely shifting traditional lectures to an online format fails to utilize the electronic medium effectively. She adds that instructors should expect no improvement in learning without a transformation of instructional techniques to engage learners in a virtual classroom. Not surprisingly, studies that structure online course work as simply transmitting lectures online as "talking heads" or as hypertextualized notes find no improvement over traditional classroom instruction.

Despite these points that should inform the theory and practice of online education, some important studies dealing with communication education continue to define online academic work as the presentation of the same material via an electronic medium. Research by Carrell and Menzel (2001), for example, judges a distance version of communication instruction inferior to a live counterpart. The study compares a live lecture to a video simulcast and a PowerPoint presentation of the same lecture, with student exposure totaling fifteen minutes to one of the three conditions. Online instruction, however, should not be equated to a brief video simulcast of a "talking head," especially when distance learning relies heavily on interactive tools such as chats, threaded discussions, and electronic exercises. The study's design reflects an assumption that online education represents only a different instructional *medium*, when in reality it requires

different instructional *methods* as adaptations to the medium. The study also did not control for subjects' previous experience with distance education, which could predispose them to have low expectations for instructional formats that did not match their prior educational experience.

Several meticulous studies (Schrodt & Turman, 2005; Turman & Schrodt, 2005; Schrodt & Witt, 2006) manipulate the level of instructional technology use to determine the relationship between technology and initial student perceptions of an instructor's credibility, sex of students, and the type of course (large, introductory lecture versus small, upper-division theory class). The Schrodt and Turman (2005) study uses various written scenarios as the stimulus material, with students answering questions based solely on their perceptions of instructors whose courses were described in the documents. The same methodology is employed in another study by the same authors, this time examining how the variable of technology use relates to student biological sex and affective learning (Turman & Schrodt, 2005). Instead of measuring the reactions of students to the use of educational technology, the study collected student reactions to verbal labels of technological techniques. The scenarios employed a one-paragraph description of the technological tools the instructor used (e.g., PowerPoint, chat rooms, administering tests online, allowing assignment submittals as e-mail attachments) without providing concrete examples of the technology or direct exposure to these instructional resources.

An important intervening variable with such studies, even when they do actually measure reactions to instructional technology itself, is that end-user experiences with specific technological resources may shape perceptions of instructional technology as a whole. For example, if the electronic course delivery platform students use is plagued with problems, then that discontent may become manifest as dissatisfaction with all electronic resources for instruction. Furthermore, the quality of student computer experience and exposure (hardware or software limitations such as screen size; security settings that may block or inactivate course content) can determine the perceived effectiveness of a course or of computer-mediated technology per se (Benyon, Stone, & Woodroffe, 1997).

None of the subjects in these studies actually experienced an online course or online course components as stimulus materials. Such research, while methodologically sound and theoretically useful, may have limited value in assessing the actual outcomes of online instruction. Problems arise if one assumes that measuring student attitudes about online instruction offers insight about how students employ the technology. While the studies measure student attitudes about online coursework, questions about their actual utilization of online course components remain unanswered. To their credit, the researchers do acknowledge the limitations of using hypothetical scenarios. The limitations they discuss, however, remain focused on whether the subjects were affected by the wording of the scenarios, bypassing the larger issue of the validity of written hypothetical scenarios in gauging student experience of online course components. Such studies may be measuring pre-existing attitudes toward electronically supplemented or fully online instruction. More important, Schrodt and Turman (2005) recommend a useful direction for further research concerning online learning by noting that "what is needed is research that examines how instructors actually use technology to achieve educational objectives and to communicate credibility in the classroom" (p. 194).

Another conundrum confronts studies on online instruction that do not gather empirical data regarding how students actually experience computer-mediated formats. A frequent observation of such studies is that students learn by doing, so online course delivery must maximize opportunities for interactivity, both with the delivery system (via learning objects) and with peers (via chats, discussion boards, and collaborative activities). For example, the most recent national survey of faculty teaching introductory courses in speech communication (Morreale, Hugenberg, & Worley, 2006) revealed that the greatest challenges for online learning included achieving sufficient levels of teacher-to-student and student-to-student interaction. It seems puzzling, therefore, that studies would note the centrality of interaction in distance learning, yet not incorporate interactive components in their simulations of an online learning environment. As a result, these studies do not capture how students actually experience online learning. While useful, the findings capture student attitudes rather than behaviors, generating few observations about the relationship between online course design and its usage by the learners.

Ample scholarly literature examines student or instructor attitudes regarding computer-mediated communication. An and Frick (2006), for example, found that two-thirds of their undergraduate student subject pool, all of whom had experience with computer-mediated instructional communication, preferred face-to-face communication for almost all but the simplest kinds of tasks. This research suggests that as tasks become more complex, students prefer that electronic modes of instruction at least be supplemented and not supplanted by direct interpersonal interaction. Perceptions of instructor immediacy, defined as a sense of availability, involvement, and caring about the student as an individual, may heavily influence student attitudes toward online instruction (Arbaugh, 2001). To the extent that instructor variables affect student perceptions of online learning, studies should control for instructors by comparing sections of the same course taught by the same instructor. For example, Arbaugh's (2001) important study on instructor immediacy in online courses did not compare sections of the same course taught by the same instructor in online versus on-ground formats. Student reactions to instructional technology may be mediated by their perceptions of the instructor's credibility (Schrodt & Witt, 2006). Studies that measure reactions to course delivery methods, therefore, must control for the instructor to account for the intervening variable of perceived credibility, which could reduce validity of results. Without correlating student evaluations of online instruction with the evaluation of the instructor, studies might confuse reactions to the instructor with reactions to the online medium. Some criticisms of online communication courses may actually reflect problematic design and administration of the courses rather than limitations inherent to the online delivery mode (Schwartzman, 2007a).

Overall, several concerns about the research regarding online oral communication instruction have emerged. First, the literature does not always clearly distinguish findings based on student attitudes about online delivery from reports of actual student performance. Generalizing from student attitudes to student behaviors may not be warranted in some cases. Second, experimental simulations of online coursework may not capture the interactive nature of much distance education, especially if the simulations include no tools such as learning objects or discussion forums. Third, studies that do not control for instructor may measure student reactions to the instructor more than to the online format.

Beyond the field of communication studies, the Discussion Analysis Tool (DAT), first employed by Jeong (2003), was the first quantitative content analysis tool applied specifically to sequences of online discussion board interactions. The study evaluated two-event sequences (discussion board posts and their responses) to divulge signs of critical thinking in these interactions. Jeong's (2003) study found few instances of disagreement, although cases of disagreement and conflict provided the most thorough examples of critical thinking. This finding corresponds to Schwartzman's (2006) qualitative study wherein collaborative problem-solving groups exhibited substantial groupthink and tended to avoid questioning, challenging, or disagreeing with other group members. The present study differs from the DAT and similar quantitative content analysis

research in several respects. First, the DAT uses sequential interactions as its unit of analysis, which requires that participants' posts clearly engage one another and be identifiable as a stimulus and a response. Unless the respondent posts an item as a direct response or verbally addresses another posting directly, a sequence may prove difficult to identify. Second, the DAT and similar tools do not address the parallels between critical thinking and the process of collaborative problem solving. The current study tracks how students engaged in critical thinking as they progressed through the steps of reflective thinking associated with accomplishing a task.

Finally, while quantitative content analysis furnishes powerful tools for examining online interactions, a qualitative study can provide additional illumination of how individual students' verbal expressions manifest their intellectual progress. The pattern of extant research on threaded discussions also justifies engaging in more qualitative research. "The preponderance of the research is also of a quantitative nature. Class databases are counted, summarized, categorized and graphed. There is a need for rich, in depth data which would call for research of a qualitative nature, particularly from the point of view of the online instructor" (San Millan Maurino, 2006, p. 14).

BACKGROUND AND THEORETICAL FRAMEWORK

This study examines the threaded discussion board posts of 10 groups of undergraduate students ($n = 45$) at a small midwestern U.S. university (enrollment 6,000) enrolled in a fully online, required general education course in oral communication. The duration of the study was one full academic year: three online sections, one in each 15-week trimester, with all sections taught by the same instructor. The course did not require any face-to-face meetings among students or between students and the instructor. Content included a group problem-solving task, which fulfilled a general education mandate to develop problem-solving skills. Each group of 4-6 students was assigned randomly by the instructor. Groups were given a general topic area dealing with current events (example: how to improve education) and completed a preliminary assignment to collaboratively develop a problem statement in that topic area. The preliminary assignment not only generated each group's specific topic (after suitable refinement by the instructor), but also familiarized students with using threaded discussions to complete a collaborative task.

The problem-solving task required each student to post contributions to six threaded discussions, each corresponding to a step in a problem-solving process that paralleled the reflective thinking method developed by John Dewey (1910/1991). The six threaded discussions were:

- Define and Analyze the Problem
- Establish Criteria for Evaluating Solutions
- Identify Possible Solutions
- Evaluate Solutions
- Select the Best Solution(s)
- Implement and Test the Solution(s).

Each step was accompanied by a series of several questions that served as prompts for the content of posts. For example, suggested topics under "implement and test solutions" included:

1. How is success defined?
2. When will the effects be realized?
3. How often should the solution be monitored and assessed?
4. Who ultimately determines whether the solution has succeeded?
5. What alternatives exist if this solution fails?

Students were instructed to make at least three posts for each step. At least one post had to consist of an original idea, another replied to the post of another student and engaged that student's

ideas, and another post evaluated the quality of a researched source on the topic under discussion. The specific content requirement of posts was adapted to each step, and an evaluation rubric showed students how they could earn points for participating in each step. For example, the evaluation rubric established the following standards for selecting the best solution(s):

- Proposed a best solution or combination of solutions
- Explained how solution(s) satisfy practical & value standards
- Described decision-making method (consensus, majority, etc.)
- Contributed at least 3 threaded discussion posts, including:
  - At least 1 original post expressing a clearly justified preference among the solutions discussed in preceding step
  - At least 1 original post connecting a proposed solution to the criteria the group developed in step 2 (Establish criteria for evaluating solutions)
  - Research: discuss & actually use the content (with a link or a complete APA format cite) of a reliable source of outside information (see Research Component of Group Project Guidelines) relevant to this step.

Students had six weeks to post on the discussion boards. Due dates for posting on each discussion board were staggered so that each step would be completed sequentially. The instructions for the assignment as a whole and the prompts for discussion board content in each step were available to students throughout the project.

This study operationalizes critical thinking in terms suggested by the practical inquiry model developed and refined by Garrison, Anderson, and Archer (2000, 2001). The practical inquiry model traces the development of inquiry beginning with recognition of an event that triggers personal exploration. This private exploration leads to personal reflection, integrating the triggering event with other knowledge and experience. Finally, the learner translates deliberation into action by attempting to address the issues raised by the triggering event.

The practical inquiry conceptualization of critical thinking is especially appropriate for research on collaborative groups interacting through threaded discussions. First, the concept arose specifically from examining text-based, computer-mediated communication in group settings, precisely the type of environment created by threaded discussion boards. Second, practical inquiry proves suitable for problem solving because the model tracks the phases of individual resolutions of puzzles or problems, a process that parallels the group's identification and resolution of its challenge.

Practical inquiry begins with a triggering event that the learner recognizes as an exigency that deserves cognitive attention. The triggering event provides a motivational challenge for the learner to progress toward a solution. A triggering event leads to the second phase: exploration. During exploration, private recognition of the problem expands to seeking external resources through asking questions, conducting research, exchanging ideas, and providing context for the triggering event. Exploration leads to a definition of the nature of the issue, which enables the next phase to begin. Integration calls for interpreting and evaluating the information gathered through exploration. Learners still move freely between private reflection and public discourse. The fourth phase, resolution, translates the integrated information into (real or hypothetical) action. Resolution is equivalent to reaching and testing solutions in Dewey's (1910/1991) reflective thinking model. Clearly this four-phase process does not always progress linearly, but the ability to engage in all four phases of inquiry does reflect higher-order thinking skills (Garrison, Anderson, & Archer, 2001).

METHOD

The practical inquiry model was chosen as an operational definition of the degree of critical thinking because previous studies had established its validity and ease of use in classifying the depth of critical thinking exhibited in online discussions (Garrison, Anderson, & Archer, 2000, 2001; Meyer, 2003). By identifying the process of higher order thinking as collaborative, this model easily applies to the development of collaborative skills within a group setting. More specifically, the practical inquiry model aligns well with the collaborative problem-solving steps employed in the group assignment. If students were progressively developing their critical thinking skills during the group activity, then that process might mirror the progress toward accomplishing the group's tasks. Recognition of the task as significant and urgent would enable the identification of the problem to serve as a triggering event. As students ponder the nature of the problem, criteria for solutions, and suggest potential solutions, they should engage in exploration. Integration then would occur as different suggestions coalesce into solutions that the group collectively selects. Resolution concludes with an understanding of how the group's decisions would be implemented and evaluated to determine success. Table 1, adapted from Garrison, Anderson, and Archer (2001, pp. 15-16), describes the necessary and sufficient conditions for posts to qualify as exhibiting the various levels of critical thinking.

This study focuses on the discourse of the students themselves, analyzing content by classifying posts according to the necessary and sufficient conditions for qualifying a post as fitting within a category of critical thinking. This analysis of content permits evaluation of the students' own insights and thoughts in their purest, most unadulterated form rather than relying on a survey conducted outside of the actual course. By avoiding self-reports, the study bypasses potential distortions that might arise from social desirability bias and the Hawthorne effect.

Table 1. Levels of critical thinking according to the practical inquiry model

Critical Thinking Level	Necessary and Sufficient Conditions for Post to Qualify	Example of Qualifying Post
Level 1: Triggering Events	• Acknowledges and recognizes the problem • A question or invitation occurs somewhere in the post • Calls for responses from others that engage the issue at hand	"Do we need to prepare for every possible disaster contingency?"
Level 2: Exploration	• Multiple ideas and themes present in a single message • Adds to or challenges established points but does not defend, justify, or substantiate ideas • Offers unsupported assertions • Self-identifies as tentative or exploratory	"I believe we should leave [North Korea] alone for the time being. Lots of countries have nuclear weapons and I do realize that nuclear weapons are a threat. But right now I don't see them getting mad enough to use them, plus we need to finish one war before getting into another. Last time we tried that with N. Korea we lost."
Level 3: Integration	• Synthesizes different viewpoints and ideas • Seeks or demonstrates convergence among members • Posts explicitly reference or respond to other students' posts • Suggestions justified with evidence, defended, not asserted dogmatically • Attempts to create a solution • Integrates multiple kinds of sources into tentative conclusions	"I agree with Anne and believe that the intercultural course should be a required course for graduation, but I believe that there should be more emphasis on the course. I believe that we have made it very clear that there is a great need for students to learn about other cultures; therefore, I believe that it should be a 3 credit course and if students are greatly interested there should be an additional course."
Level 4: Resolution	• Demonstrates application to the real world • Attempts to test proposed solutions and monitor outcomes • Defends solutions by rationally evaluating them • States commitment to a definite position	"I think we must consider the time constraints for our new ideas. There is no immediate threat right now. How long would our idea take to implement, and does it need to be done right away or do we have time to take?"

A total of 894 student posts were examined and evaluated for the extent that they demonstrated various levels of critical thinking. Each post was categorized into one of the four levels of critical thinking identified by the practical inquiry model plus a residual category of posts that did not fit the category scheme. Category assignment was conducted independently by two coders. Classification differences were resolved by discussions that yielded consensual assignment of each post to a unique category.

As the levels of critical thinking increase, so should the depth and quality of the thinking process. In the context of the reflective thinking process, each level builds cumulatively on the others. Fully developed resolutions to problems become possible only by recognizing a need to deliberate (triggering event), exploring relevant options thoroughly (exploration), crafting solutions as a group while taking into account diverse views (integration), and testing the viability of solutions (resolution).

According to Garrison, Anderson, and Archer (2001), for a post to be considered level one thinking, it had to acknowledge the problem and demonstrate evocativeness. Such comments typically took the form of questions. For example, one student from a group in the fall term writes: "To help keep our focus this is our topic: What should a major U.S. city (Washington D.C.) do to plan and respond effectively to an electrical power outage? There are two components: planning for the outage and responding to its effects. We need to have solutions for planning and for responding."

For a comment to qualify as level two, it needed to display divergence, inquisitiveness, and common characteristics of brainstorming as well as "add to established points but not systematically defend/justify/develop" such (Garrison, Anderson, & Archer, 2001, p. 15). An example of such a post comes from a discussion one group had surrounding how to address bullying in schools. One student commented, "We have decided that our 'problem' that we are researching is bullying, correct? We have done some research and located useful information. Is our scope adolescents and teenagers (school aged), or adults (teachers and faculty) too? And are we just sticking with the emotional trauma of bullying, or the physical too?"

A level three comment should integrate information from various sources as well as offer a "justified, developed, defensible, yet tentative hypothesis" (Garrison, Anderson, & Archer, 2001, p. 16). Many of the posts appear to reach this level, though for many students, this is the highest level of critical thinking that they are able to achieve. An example of one such comment can be found in the dialogue that took place surrounding what to do in the event of power outage in a major American city. One student integrated, developed, and defended her hypothesis when she wrote, "To support the proposed solution of having a comprehensive emergency preparedness plan, I located a testimony of a Hospital Association that was directly involved in and influenced by the 2003 blackout in New York."

Finally, for a comment to be characterized as level four thinking, it needed to commit to a solution and demonstrate "vicarious application to the real world" (Garrison, Anderson, & Archer, 2001, p. 16). One student clearly considered the testability of a proposed solution when he wrote, "Any form of military action would be unfortunate and, I believe in the long run, will make the U.S. less secure and hurt its influential position in the world. Preemptive strikes targeted at known and suspected nuclear power plants may release radiation in the atmosphere that will kill and injure innocent civilians and make the areas contaminated with radiation uninhabitable for many years. Many nations, including some of America's allies, have economic interests in Iran that may be impacted by missile strikes or an invasion. Some of these nations may ally themselves with Iran in a war against America."

RESULTS

A total of 233 of the 894 total posts (24.94 percent) qualified as fulfilling any of the four critical thinking levels. As for the progression of critical thinking, Table 2 shows the distribution of posts exhibiting the different levels of critical thinking. The levels in the practical inquiry model mirror the logical progression of groups from (1) impetus to inquire, to (2) brainstorming ideas, to (3) synthesis and convergence of different views, and finally (4) rational application of a solution and commitment to it. Given this correspondence between the levels of critical thinking and the steps in the group deliberative process, one would expect that posts exhibiting integration and resolution to increase as the group selected preferred solutions. In fact, the testing component of level four (resolution) directly corresponded with the requirement to test solutions and establish criteria for success in the final step of the problem-solving method.

As Table 2 indicates, triggering (level one) posts by the students averaged slightly more than one per group during the first step. Direct calls for other group members to act shrank and remained less than one per group for the remaining five steps of the projects. Exploratory (level two) posts appeared where one might predict: at the first step when all ideas were potentially on the table for consideration and at step three when the groups identified prospective solutions. The integrative (level three) posts occurred most frequently when proposed solutions were being evaluated and selected (steps four and five). The resolution (level four) posts occurred most frequently in the final step, which established the means for testing the success of solutions. Level four posts were by far the least frequent, demonstrating lack of collective engagement with the means for applying and testing solutions in "real world" scenarios.

When examined as clusters rather than as discrete levels of critical thinking, the patterns of student posts demonstrate progressively higher

Table 2. Numbers of posts corresponding to problem-solving steps and critical thinking levels

	Level 1: Triggering	Level 2: Exploration	Level 3: Integration	Level 4: Resolution	Cumulative Totals
Step 1: Define & Analyze Problem	12	35	7	0	54
Step 2: Establish Criteria for Solutions	7	11	9	5	32
Step 3: Identify Possible Solutions	8	25	13	2	48
Step 4: Evaluate Solutions	6	8	20	4	38
Step 5: Select Best Solutions	5	5	21	3	34
Step 6: Test Solutions	1	5	2	9	17
Cumulative Totals	39	89	72	23	223

frequency toward higher levels of critical thinking as the projects moved toward the later steps. While triggering and exploration (levels one and two) posts were most frequent in steps one through three, steps four through six demonstrate a shift toward integration and resolution (levels three and four) posts.

In each group, most content was posted by only a few group members; rarely did any student exceed the minimum number of required posts (three) per step in the assignment. To fulfill the minimum posting requirement, each student was required to make three posts to each of the six discussion boards corresponding to the steps in the problem-solving process. The cumulative number of posts for each group ranged from a low of 47 to a high of 148, with a mean of 99.67 posts. The mean number of posts per student was 19.87, only slightly higher than the minimum number of posts (18) required to complete the assignment.

In addition to the low quantity of posts, the timing of posts was noteworthy. Frequency of posts increased dramatically in the final 48 hours before due dates. Frequently the instructor had to intervene by urging groups to make posts as the due date approached for completion of a step in the task. The relative infrequency of posts may reflect some lack of buy-in to problems such as nuclear proliferation and federal policymaking, where students would have few chances to influence actual solutions. The geographic separation of students (ranging from California to Missouri to Florida and many points between, plus other nations) reduced the opportunity to select topics that had immediate connection to all group members. Thus the apparent paucity of posts may be an artifact of the assignment rather than an effect of the online medium.

ONLINE GROUP DYNAMICS

Given that one quarter of all posts demonstrated any level of critical thinking as described by the practical inquiry model, what factors might contribute to the observed distribution of posts? The results invite deeper inquiry into factors that might have enabled or constrained posts that exhibited critical thinking. If the practical inquiry model accounts for approximately one quarter of the posts, what were students posting for the other 75 percent of their input? Answering this question requires two caveats. First, it remains difficult to judge whether the proportion of critical thinking posts qualifies as high or low without direct comparisons to face-to-face analogues. In the absence of a baseline for what qualifies as a "normal" number or proportion of posts under certain conditions, the proportion of posts that exhibit various levels of critical thinking may not be the only or best way to judge intellectual engagement.

Second, factors other than the online medium may have intervened. For example, if group members need to issue many procedural clarifications or want to encourage reluctant participants, the content of many posts might deviate from critical thinking and constitute organizational tasks or reassurances.

What, then, might account for the observed patterns of discussion board usage? The following sections propose explanations from the perspective of group dynamics. Since the practical inquiry categories had been validated in previous research and the classification in this study was conducted via consensus, the posts probably did not arise as an artifact of the classification scheme itself. Instead, a deeper issue may have surfaced: tensions in relationships between the conventional models of critical thinking and the modes of collaborative problem solving that students employ in online discussions.

Social Loafing Online

Aside from the paucity of input, often posts would sit for days without any response from other group members. The reticence to post and the long lag time for responses may demonstrate how online discussion boards can invite or inhibit students' engagement with each other's ideas. Social loafing describes the lower effort individuals exert in group work compared to the same work performed individually. Observable across many types of activities (Hart et al., 2004), social loafing apparently occurs because the inactive group members believe others will cover or compensate for their own lack of participation. Theoretically, the transparency of threaded discussions should counteract social loafing because each participant's input is uniquely identified with the authorship of each post. In practice, however, lurkers become the social loafers in online collaborative work. The social loafers may not even be lurkers. Course usage statistics showed that non-participants usually did not even visit the discussion board section of the course (although they might have logged in to the course site) during their absence. The literature on social loafing illuminates several factors that may contribute to passivity in online collaborations.

Participation in groups should increase when each member can make and get credit for a unique contribution (Levine & Moreland, 1990). Supposedly threaded discussions do identify each member's contribution, but simply authoring a post seems to provide insufficient recognition and motivation to contribute ideas. If only a few contributors' names appear constantly as authors of posts, it may encourage social loafing by reinforcing the assumption that the more active members will complete everything regardless of cohort input.

Social loafing decreases when group members can produce something that they can claim as theirs, but this becomes challenging on text-based threaded discussions where contributions are visually distinct only by their length. Threaded discussions may need to be combined with other online tools that allow for more individualistic expression, especially since visual and tactile learners may find it tedious to sift through several screens of pure text. Courseware could restructure threaded discussions to look and function in ways that resemble social networking sites. Instead of scrolling through texts organized by abstract topics, users could be greeted by avatars of their cohorts with accompanying summaries of what, where, and when they have been posting. Updates on the whereabouts of people, as with Twitter and Facebook, may engage students more than textual reminders to meet the required numbers of posts. Users would be visible in the discussions more as people than as disembodied textual posts.

Blackboard's RSS feed feature alerts all group members via e-mail whenever a new post appears on a discussion board. Although each user must manually subscribe to the RSS feed for each discussion board, this feature helps make the group's activities more apparent and could add to group participation. This discussion board feature was not available to students during the course of the present study.

The research on social loafing leads to an important point: lack of personal accountability and group cohesiveness is not inherent to the online medium per se, but the online medium also does not automatically invite high participation. As groups become more cohesive, specifically if members consider themselves accountable to each other and responsible for the welfare of the group as a whole, social loafing should decrease (Liden et al., 2004).

Group Cohesiveness and Critical Thinking

Social loafing and group cohesiveness present any group with an ongoing dialectical tension. The more cohesive a group becomes, the less likely social loafing will occur. Excessive cohesiveness, however, can plunge a group into groupthink (a topic discussed at length later) by encouraging unconditional acceptance of ideas simply because the group committed to them. Between these extremes of non-participation and passive agreement lies isolationist behavior. Many posts exhibited some, but not all, characteristics of critical thinking at one of the four levels specified in the practical inquiry model. The most common reason why posts were excluded was that they did not engage the ideas of other group members directly.

Isolationism describes the posting of comments that are self-contained, without reference to other posts or themes of discussion. Isolationist posts constitute the dangling threads of discourse that remain unwoven into any dialogical pattern. Each strand develops independently of the others, so these posts escape synthesis into a unified group position. Applied to threaded discussions, the resolution and application (level four) category of critical thinking describes a group's attempt to "tie up loose ends," to gather the various threads of discussion and account for them even if they are not endorsed collectively. What factors might lead to dangling threads instead of intricately braided syntheses of ideas?

Isolationist posts became especially apparent when group members identified possible solutions. With few exceptions, each student posted one discrete idea at a time without playing off other proposals. Instead of suggesting variations on a previous theme and thereby multiplying the solutions, each plan emerged independently from the others. Aside from generating fewer ideas for the group to consider, isolationist posting demonstrated a withdrawal from the collaborative nature of critical thinking and online discussion forums.

Isolationist posts embody an individualistic view of knowledge, whereby each student proves achievement by offering a distinctive contribution. In the traditional classroom environment, students often have been conditioned to "do their own work," avoid informal collaborations, and "keep their eyes on their own paper." Each student's corpus of knowledge is their property and theirs alone, a scarce resource to be guarded as a personal possession. Students socialized into this protective view of knowledge naturally would display the same tendencies in the online environment. The prevalence of isolationism in online discussions may reflect less a refusal to interact than a manifestation of an educational approach at odds with the collaborative, open access to information in cyberspace.

LEVELS OF CRITICAL THINKING

More detailed examination of the posts reveals the roles the different levels of critical thinking played in group deliberations. This exploration also probes the features of posts that did not qualify for each category and what that exclusion says about the process of critical thinking online.

Level 1: Triggering Events

Triggering events call the group to action by making a direct request that invites others to engage in discussion. This category of posts should evoke responses by initiating and extending calls to address the issue at hand. Posing questions should trigger participation, since every (non-rhetorical) question demands an answer. Triggering posts ordinarily should appear most frequently in the early stages of the discussion when uncertainty about the group's course of action is highest. Triggers initiate discussions by raising issues for the group to confront. When cohorts accept the invitation to respond, triggers can play an important role in productively brainstorming problems and solutions. One student whose group dealt with disaster recovery in New Orleans posted a polemical trigger that revealed the conflicting priorities the group would need to reconcile.

To be blunt about it, are we going to have to purposefully screw over poor (basically, read: black) people because rebuilding their areas of New Orleans will cost more than they will likely contribute back in taxes? Are we going to show preferential [treatment] towards restoring areas for richer (read: white) people who are going to contribute more tax money to make that restoration investment worthwhile? Should political correctness have any say here? Should the goal of racial equality? Should pure and simple economics and likely rates of return?

As was so often the case, the invitation to respond was not accepted; this triggering post generated no direct response. Instead of generating answers, triggering posts degenerated into rhetorical questions because they rarely received any direct response. Triggers usually did not serve as discussion catalysts, even when they were as polemical as the example cited.

The low impact of triggers may indicate something more profound than sheer apathy. If students have been acculturated into an authoritarian educational system, they enact the role of passive recipients of knowledge or spectators who provide an audience for instructional performance (Freire, 1970). As a result, such students may not initiate discussions, deeming it the instructor's role to trigger student participation. For students conditioned to be "received knowers" who deferentially execute an authority figure's instructions (Belenky et al., 1997), triggering discussion may qualify as challenging authority or usurping the role of the instructor. These students may find the sudden shift of responsibility to them for stimulating discussion as confusing and inappropriate.

Student posts on the discussion boards showed signs of received knower behavior. The instructor's posts, which numbered from 14 to 28 (mean = 17.89) per group, repeatedly posed direct questions designed to trigger responses from the group. Students dutifully answered the triggers. The responses, however, replied directly to the instructor instead of inviting other opinions, extending the instructor's question, or connecting the questions to posts by other group members. Even when group members offered drastically different or conflicting responses, they did not weigh the merits or implications of the divergent answers. Instead, the posts demonstrated good behavior by received knower standards. The professor asked a question, and each student answered individually, analogous to raising one's hand in class and giving the answer.

Level 2: Inquisitive Exploration

For the received knower, "giving the answer," defined as an individual's re-production of a response authorized as the correct solution, qualifies as the penultimate demonstration of knowledge (Belenky et al., 1997). The interrogative mode indicates uncertainty, which explains why the traditional authoritarian educational system approaches instructional discourse in the declarative mode, with the "lecture" as its modus operandi. If the student's role is to replicate an already determined answer that lurks in a textbook or in the instructor's mind, exploration has limited value. Instead of exploration empowering each student to investigate new possibilities and unfamiliar ideas, received knowers await revelation and validation of the correct response. The received knower attitude directly contrasts with the intellectual empowerment that accompanies critical thinking.

The main feature that prevented more posts from fitting into the category of exploration was their failure to exhibit their tentative or exploratory nature. Indicators of tentativeness include conditionality (expressed by verb tense or mood, such as subjunctive rather than indicative), qualifiers (terms limiting an assertion's force, such as "perhaps," "maybe"), or presentation of more than one alternative for a position or claim. Far from stimulating exchange of ideas, posts that fulfilled some of the level two criteria demonstrated assertive rather than inquisitive characteristics. By offering dogmatically stated assertions, posts moved to close discussion rather than opening participatory opportunities for cohorts.

A contrast between an exploratory and an assertive post illustrates how students could make strong claims while still encouraging further discussion. A student whose group was devising policies to deal with nuclear weaponry in Russia offered several hypotheses to clarify the group's focus.

This is what I have been able to come up with for defining and analyzing the problem:

The problem as I understand it is threefold:

a. There is fear that due to the financial constraints of Russia, proper maintenance is not being performed on aging satellites and communication links. This could lead to an ambiguous [sic] event causing the launch of nuclear weapons.

b. There may be missing warheads.

c. The safety and security of the storage facilities may not be up to standards due to financial constraints.

This student's post identified threads from several other students' posts, but offered her list as "what I have been able to come up with" for defining the "problem as I understand it" rather than as a definitive answer. Her enumeration of the problem appeared as suggestions, not categorical claims or final assertions. The phrasing "could lead," "may be missing," and "may not be up to" classify her statements as testable and contestable hypotheses.

The contestability of exploratory posts can guide groups toward a variety of options and perspectives, permitting investigation of more nuanced positions. One important function, perhaps qualifying as a sub-category, of exploratory posts, is divergence from established opinions. These disruptive posts offer alternative viewpoints that interrupt the momentum toward groupthink and open the group to other possibilities. For example, one group considering how to complete the recovery from Hurricane Katrina had decided quickly that reinforcing the levees in New Orleans would be their top priority. A student intervened by noting additional dimensions to the problem, posing a question and offering several alternatives.

Are we just focused on New Orleans and its levee system or are we focused on the entire region? Granted that because the levees failed there was massive destruction in New Orleans, but Mississippi and Alabama were hit too and that had nothing to do with levees. I think the problem(s) are obviously the levee system in New Orleans being strong each [sic] to handle a hurricane of that magnitude as well as not building the proper housing structures to accommodate that particular region. For example, you wouldn't build a house without a basement in Tornado Alley or at the very least an underground shelter, or would you?

This student's exploration called attention to housing construction but offered it as a response to a question instead of as a conflicting proposal.

Posts that failed to qualify as exploratory shared opinions and ideas, but expressed them as conclusive statements rather than as hypotheses. One student, whose group was deliberating on what U.S. anti-terrorism policy should be, posted an assertion which she then defended dogmatically.

I believe 1 problem with the Patriot Act dealing with terrorism is the fact that the United States dominates on issues and then those issues also affect other countries. This then makes other countries mad, therefore starting a disagreement.

The student, despite the incoherence of the post, presented the problem as a "fact" but offered no evidence. The same student posted a follow-up that included a hyperlink to an uncredentialed web page, noting that "they also agree." When the instructor requested the credentials of the source, the student simply reasserted that the source was qualified without exploring other viewpoints: "My summary of why the source is highly qualified on the topic for my research post includes the fact that my resource…is not a personal website of someone instead it is a website by *CounterPunch*." The tautologous defense of the "fact" of

the source's credentials simply stated the identity of the source in an attempt to bolster the original claim. The challenge to explore the background of the source went unheeded.

A cohort's response, however, directly engaged the previous student's claim and offered a tentative hypothesis.

I kind of shudder at the comparison of Bush to Hitler in the CounterPunch article. I'm not really sure this article is as much about the Patriot Act as it is against the war in Iraq. I guess my question about the article would be, "Do we want to consider what other countries are going to think of us or how they are going to be affected" when we think about the provisions of the Act? Initially I say no, because it is a foreign terrorist group that launched the 9/11 attack. What does anyone else think?

The post directly challenged the legitimacy of the source while displaying lingering uncertainty: "I'm not really sure," "I guess," "Do we want…?" The student then offered a preliminary "initial" position that addressed the rest of the group as partners in inquiry, while the other student approached the group as an audience to persuade toward her viewpoint.

Level 3: Integration and Tentative Convergence

The third level of critical thinking in the practical inquiry model shows a group synthesizing ideas, reconciling different perspectives by rationally evaluating alternatives. This kind of activity corresponds to the collective process of proposing, evaluating, and selecting possible solutions (steps 3 through 5) in group problem solving. The highest number of level three posts appears in the three corresponding steps of the problem-solving process. The total of 72 level three posts accounts for slightly more than eight percent of the overall number of posts. What might account for the relatively low number of level three posts compared to the other levels?

One answer may lie in the substitution of passive agreement for rationally justified convergence. As the deadlines for completing the projects drew closer, the pressure to reach decisions intensified. The fastest way to render a decision was for group members to agree uncritically, lending support to whatever proposals seem the most expedient to endorse. This premature agreement signifies groupthink, a phenomenon that has not been examined in reference to online group discussions. The classic psychological research on groupthink essentially treats it as a suspension of critical thinking that might generate self-reflection and dissent (Janis, 1972). In online group discussion, however, groupthink might have other dimensions.

One perspective would attribute low cohesion to the online medium itself. Members of online groups that include no opportunities for face-to-face interaction may find that the group lacks adequate means for establishing the bonds between cohorts that can build an *ésprit de corps*. Group cohesiveness, the sense of partnership and collective contribution to a shared goal, may not arise readily in groups that have little history of interaction or opportunity to develop group norms (Tuckman, 1965). Without the conventional means to build cohesiveness, such as regular face-to-face phatic interactions with classmates or group social activities that serve as a prelude to task-oriented meetings, agreement may create a way for group members to acknowledge each other and forge interpersonal bonds. By praising cohort posts instead of modifying, challenging, or building on them, students did not risk the conflict that often accompanies deep dialogical engagement (Baxter & Montgomery, 1996).

The cohesion issue, however, may have more complexity than the familiar and controversial claims about the interpersonal impoverishment of the online medium. First, many other variables

aside from the technology could have intervened to influence cohesiveness. The relatively short time frame for the assignment (less than two months), the fact that the assignment was the only sustained group collaboration, the zero-history nature of the groups and the fact that they were assigned by the instructor could have slowed the development of group cohesion independently of the online medium itself.

Next, the observed patterns of posts may not signify lack of cohesion, but rather different means of utilizing online discussions—methods not captured by interpretive tools that focus purely on task-related content of posts. While many of the student posts did not qualify as critical thinking per se, they may have contributed to creating an interpersonal environment conducive to deeper intellectual engagement and collaboration. Supportive messages classified in this study as passive agreement may function similarly to personal support messages in online health information groups, creating a sense of homophily among group members that invites participation (Wang, Walther, Pingree, & Hawkins, 2008). The rush to agreement in student groups could reinforce peer confidence their own posts, thereby creating an atmosphere where members feel competent to challenge and question ideas. The fact that few such challenges occurred may signify only that the "safe zone" for active disagreement requires more time than the several weeks allotted to the group projects.

What on first glance might appear as a low level of group involvement might, in light of social information processing theory, indicate that students engage in threaded discussions by finding ways to enrich the interactive communication environment (Walther & Parks, 2002). These techniques may extend to making posts that do not themselves embody critical thinking, but establish the conditions within which critical thinking might arise more readily.

Many posts did not qualify as level three because they achieved convergence only by arguing that the group should adopt a single position without assessing alternative or competing claims. By contrast, level three posts enabled groups to modify previous positions, as with this post regarding how to teach cultural diversity in public schools:

I agree with Anne and believe that the intercultural course should be a required course for graduation, but I believe there should be more emphasis on the course. ...I believe that it should be a 3 credit course and if students are greatly interested there should be additional courses, such as integrating the initial intercultural course with the study abroad course. Doing this would be a good way for the schools to as well offer more diverse foreign language courses other than the standard Spanish and French.

When students did engage in integrative thinking, they moved their groups toward ranking the value of different ideas and understanding their interrelationships. Deliberating the issue of how to teach cultural diversity, one student interlaced several salient issues.

I agree very strongly that each school should have the opportunity to have many different programs and classes to help make the students well-rounded. Without giving students the opportunity to experience different activities it is difficult for them to find something that they are interested in and want to proceed in the future. As far as giving each school the same finances and opportunities, I really don't know how you could go about that... you can't control what money comes from outside sources. ...In the end there is only so much money that will be spent on this sort of thing.

This post established the issues of program choice, equity, and financial constraints as relevant to the group's policy decision.

The preference for passive agreement rather than integrating and weighing diverse ideas may represent more than taking the path of least resistance and piggybacking off of cohort ideas rather than generate one's own. Uncritical agreement could serve a productive group maintenance function by acknowledging the value of a cohort's contribution to the group. Some posts deferred to a cohort, implicitly recognizing that student as an opinion leader: "Like Megan suggested, I think it would be wise to have a group of teachers that are always available for students to talk to about bullying." Although such a post does not demonstrate a specified level of critical thinking, it might contribute to clarifying group leadership roles that enable the group to define each member's functions.

Level 4: Resolution and Application

The fourth level in the practical inquiry model treats the group's collective commitment to a position and connection of choices to realistic, practical considerations as the culmination of critical thought. This stage dovetails with the final step of the group problem-solving process, which involved implementing and testing solutions. The assignment instructions posed several questions for students to address in their threaded discussions:

- How is success defined?
- When will the effects be realized?
- How often should the solution be monitored and assessed?
- Who ultimately determines whether the solution has succeeded?
- What alternatives exist if this solution fails?

This final step of the group decision-making process attracted the least student participation. Each group cumulatively made between six and 21 posts, with a mean of 11.67 posts per group. As one might predict, the resolution posts appeared most frequently during the final step, since it corresponds directly to the conditions for level four posts. Yet, nine total posts in the final step qualified as level four, a mean of only one post per group.

Studies of online discussion boards sometimes raise concern that student posts resemble monologues, with each student occupied more with attempting to demonstrate individual contributions than directly addressing or responding to cohorts (Klemm, 2002). While this concern may have merit, it also may oversimplify online group interaction, portraying it as a solipsistic medium that inhibits collaboration. The situation may have greater subtlety.

Many posts in the current investigation did not qualify for inclusion in the practical inquiry model because students rarely called for responses, addressed established points, or synthesized different viewpoints. Posts that cited research typically presented a claim without connecting it to other posts, then summarized the content of a source that backed the claim. The prevailing pattern of research posts challenges the contention that the online medium deindividuates users. As Guiller and Dundell (2007) found in their study of gender patterns in language among students in online discussions, computer-mediated communication may provide a forum for asserting personal opinions more vigorously than in face-to-face environments. Thus what might appear as disengagement with the group's task could reflect a greater willingness to declare a personal position and appear decisive.

Two examples from a group dealing with diversity education in public schools illustrate briefer versions of the overall pattern. One student stated: "Here is a website that gives statistics regarding many aspects of funding and the problems associated with it in schools." He then inserted the citation with a hyperlink and ended the post without contextualizing it in relation to diversity education. The next day, another student in the same group observed: "Here is an interesting paper on maximizing the benefits of student diversity:

lessons from school desegregation research." The post added a hyperlink to the "interesting paper" without connecting its contents to any of the group's discussions. Posts that simply identified research or summarized an external source missed the opportunity to use the research as ways to bridge the group's ideas with proposals and actions that actually had been attempted. The linkage between the group's deliberations and real-world policy deliberations was absent in research-based posts that did not qualify as level four.

When challenged to commit to a decision and consider its application in the real world, practical constraints (a criterion for resolution) on solutions receded as concerns. Lack of attention to contingency plans (which require admitting the possibility of a failed solution) or standards for testing (which again require acknowledging need for improvement) are consistent with discussions characterized by groupthink. A resolution post, however, can add precision to a proposal by explaining how to handle potential exceptions.

Here is a solution that would offer more diversity for students when trying to fulfill cultural education requirements. This would most likely be most successful when implemented in conjunction with a system that has cultural classes available for students. Some students in high school realize early what they're going to major in in college and load their schedules with appropriate classes. Others take dual enrollment classes to out of the gen. ed. classes their first couple of years. Whatever the particular reason, some students just simply do not have time to add more classes to their schedules. An option for these students would be some sort of an outside activity to fulfill obligations. These could be things such as attending cultural rallies and festivals and writing reports or giving presentations over them.

The post sets the parameters within which a solution would achieve greatest success: when a full class can be scheduled. The post establishes the conditions for successful implementation by first noting a condition (lack of time for class scheduling) that might threaten the plan, then making provisions to cope with it. This kind of deliberation enables groups to anticipate and account for possible exceptions to their proposals, thereby improving decisions.

As a group charges headlong toward a quick solution, the act of reaching the decision assumes paramount importance. The more a group becomes committed to a solution, especially if rendering a decision culminates the group's work, the less likely the group will entertain notions that could expose the solution's vulnerability. Thus, contrary to what the practical inquiry model would suggest, a level four post that occurs early in group deliberations may stand a greater chance of successfully introducing practical concerns because the group would not have become steadfastly committed to a solution.

Herein lies the problem with treating convergence as a sign of higher order critical thinking. Once the groups had converged on a solution, they became reluctant to explore any tests that might cast doubt on the solution's viability. Instead of treating practical tests as ways to improve the quality of solutions, the possibility of failure (i.e., that the chosen solutions might not work as planned) signaled regression to the uncertainties that stimulated initial exploration of solutions. Monitoring the quality of solutions requires subjecting them to tests that should initiate the critical thinking process anew, triggering exploration of ways to refine the solutions. The group deliberative process as well as the practical inquiry model drive collaborations toward convergence as an ultimate goal. The lack of challenges or qualifiers attached to solutions may indicate that students embraced an illusory sense of closure once they made the (apparently irrevocable) choice of a solution.

The lack of attention to practical applications or tests may have arisen from the nature of the topics. Because each group's topic had to be broad enough to enable thorough research by group members who were widely dispersed, the assignment may have sacrificed the immediate connection to students that would empower them to feel capable of implementing solutions. In the past the instructor had focused the classroom version of this assignment on campus-wide issues. The focus on current events might have made topics seem too distant for students to feel they had a direct stake in any proposed solution.

IMPLICATIONS AND RECOMMENDATIONS

Analysis of the discussion boards raises several issues that have implications for the ways such forums might be incorporated into online education. The following sections discuss the role discussion forums might play as educational tools, then offer suggestions for further research focusing on critical thinking in online discussions. Finally, limitations of the current study will be addressed.

Pedagogical Considerations

This study offers several insights for online teaching. Instructors who employ online discussion boards for group problem solving need to take an active role in encouraging participation, more so than with face-to-face groups (Levine, 2007). The "out of sight, out of mind" mentality may reduce group member sense of connection with other group members, especially when members are restricted to text-based electronic communication within most course delivery platforms. Some research has noted that high instructor involvement through postings and individual e-mails can help to reduce off-task and disruptive posts (Light, Nesbitt, Light, & Burns, 2000). The present study, however, found that instructor intervention became necessary less to focus content than to generate content in the first place. Regardless of the reason for instructor intervention, one lesson from this study is that the instructor should behave as an ex-officio member of every online group, participating in virtual group meetings through chats and group e-mails as well as posting directly on the discussion boards. This instructor participation can avoid intrusiveness and control if it primarily takes the form of prompting to encourage engagement of group members' ideas and not settling for the simplest answers to problems.

The jury is still out on how much and what type of instructor input best facilitates student postings. A survey by Mandernach, Gonzales, and Garrett (2006) of 96 faculty members who teach online courses finds no clear convergence regarding the frequency or nature of instructor input that proves most effective in maximizing threaded discussion participation. Meyer (2003), for example, suggests that instructors provide concrete tasks to students—such as assigning duties to particular members—that will speed their progress toward accomplishing collective goals.

Threaded discussions might become more viable participatory tools if they include ways of making each group member accountable for particular accomplishments. Social loafing often occurs when group members believe they can lurk in the background without suffering adverse consequences (Hare, 2003). Absence of a student's name as an author of posts may not call sufficient attention to inactivity. Each group member could post a summary of what they contributed to the group—not simply meeting a required number of posts, but fulfilling specific duties and obligations. On the front end of threaded discussions, an initial group task could be to establish definite duties that include visible indicators of progress on the discussion board. Students could establish the division of labor and thereby gain a greater sense of ownership over their collective task. For example, a group member might assume responsibility for locating a designated quantity of research on at least two contrasting positions relevant to the group's topic. Cohorts could monitor each other's progress and offer assistance when needed.

Instructors may attempt to reduce social loafing by structuring discussion boards as more interdependent assignments, perhaps requiring all group members to post at least once before anyone can post again. To reduce time lags or to encourage rapid initiation of posts, incentives could be attached to early or prompt posts. For example, the maximum point value of posts gradually could decrease over time so that the earliest posts can earn the most credit.

Online group collaboration also can improve by incorporating more opportunities for group members to communicate beyond the task-oriented discussion board. In online groups, non-participating members often complain about inadequate contact between group members (Thompson & Ku, 2006). This perceived lack of interaction may prevent online groups from becoming a cohesive, functional unit. Social networks via Facebook, Twitter, or similar tools that facilitate tracking group members and spurring them toward more active posting on discussion boards might provide a fruitful avenue for future investigation. Having a channel for intra-group communication beyond the course allows greater freedom of expression than courseware forums (such as archived chats) that are more susceptible to instructor monitoring.

Considerations for Future Research

What considerations might inform further research on the use of online discussion boards? Although Fahy, Crawford, and Ally (2001) enthusiastically recommend social networking theories for analyzing online group interactions, the present study tempers that recommendation. The interactions among group members in a series of online introductory communication courses may not meet the conditions for a genuine social network wherein members seek and sustain regular contact. To the contrary, many group members required frequent prodding to engage in any interaction whatsoever. Furthermore, the interpersonal contacts via discussion board posts rarely exceeded the minimum required by the assignment guidelines. Fahy, Crawford, and Ally (2001) note that their study of computer-mediated text conferencing in a graduate course raises, but does not answer, the question: "What effects does minimal or unwilling social interaction have on the individuals exhibiting it, and on the network?" (p. 14).

Aside from the dismissive attributions of laziness or insufficient time, what factors might inhibit posting on discussion boards? Research on student use of chats in the Blackboard online course delivery platform reveals an interesting negative peer influence. Apparently students would not engage in chats if they believed other students also would not participate in them (Kirkpatrick, 2005). A similar effect might occur in threaded discussions. Group members may avoid posting if they do not already observe much interaction. Reluctant to shoulder the burden of initiating discussion, each student may assume someone else will—or should—assume the role of initiator (Schwartzman, 2007b).

Another hurdle might be that students feel adrift trying to sustain a discussion they believe might not engage others. During the course of the present study, some students privately e-mailed the instructor asking what they should do when other group members failed to post regularly. One student observed that she didn't want to be responding to her own posts all the time, so she waited until other group members posted a critical mass of content that would enable her to join a dialogue. Unfortunately this mentality becomes pernicious, with each group member awaiting colleagues to post and engage each other's ideas.

Overall, improvement in the administration and usage of threaded discussions seems warranted if this tool will fulfill its potential as a facilitator of critical thinking. In a literature review of 37 studies since 2000 that deal with critical thinking, deep learning, and interaction relating to online threaded discussions, San Millan Maurino (2006) finds little conclusive evidence that shows high levels of critical thinking linked to use of online discussion boards. Such findings, however, may be artifacts of how the definitions of critical thinking may not suit the realities of online learning environments, specifically threaded discussions.

The practical inquiry model portrays critical thinking as progressive movement toward convergence of viewpoints. In the present case study, some group members demonstrated sophisticated critical thinking by disrupting premature convergence. Most groups, pressured by time constraints and inconsistent cohort participation, moved as swiftly as possible toward a solution. Occasionally this pattern was interrupted by students who returned the group to an exploratory stage, inserting divergence by pointing out something the group had neglected to consider carefully. Such divergence was most notable as a "devil's advocate" post that would introduce a drawback or exception to the course of action the group was converging toward. This kind of functional disruption demonstrates how critical thinking includes recursive elements that invoke supposedly "earlier" or "less developed" stages of critical thought (in this case, exploration) to check and improve the group's deliberative process.

Further research should consider technological tools that could more readily facilitate and capture the cyclical aspects of critical thinking. The very nature of the "thread" metaphor in online discussion boards implies a synthesis that misaligns with the realities of most discussion board design. In major courseware discussion boards, such as those on eCollege or Blackboard, students must self-identify the post to which they are posting a reply. The visual relationship among posts is difficult to decipher, since a reply to a person might or might not actually engage the topic that person was discussing. In addition, the linear "threadlike" presentation of discussion discourages parallel development of several different dimensions of a single theme. Reconceiving online discussions more as symphonies with each participant serving a distinctive instrumental role could encourage departure from the solo approach of each student making posts with minimal engagement of cohorts.

Physically constructing discussion boards to accommodate the symphonic approach may present technical challenges, but some simple alterations could move in that direction. One development could provide a tool that would allow students to produce a list of conceptual keywords, each of which would correspond to a color code (much like the categorization tool on Microsoft Outlook for classifying e-mails and tasks). Then each post could be coded by the student as fitting one or more key concepts, or the presence of certain keywords would classify a post automatically. With this kind of categorization tool, students could attach a post to multiple threads and the group could monitor which threads receive the most or least attention.

Limitations

The findings of this study may be artifacts of the assignment design, the practical inquiry model, or the technological tools. The assignment was designed according to the reflective thought process (Dewey, 1910/1991), which introductory communication textbooks commonly employ as a procedural guide to problem solving in groups. This procedure and the structure of the discussion boards did restrict students to a rigidly sequential approach for completing their tasks. The low number of triggering events from the students might be attributable to the guidelines for each step serving as triggers, so students could have understood the triggering events as external stimuli. This interpretation comports well with the perspective of received knowers, who would define their role in discussions primarily as respondents. The frequency of posts that offered encouragement or unqualified agreement, could highlight the need for building more of a "safe zone" to cultivate enough trust and confidence to voice dissent.

The practical inquiry model (Garrison, Anderson, & Archer, 2000, 2001) provides a representative example of the components involved in critical thinking. It is particularly well suited to analyzing group problem solving because the stages of reflective thought described by Dewey (1910/1991) closely parallel the levels enumerated in the practical inquiry model. Still, it does not offer an exhaustive inventory of what constitutes critical thinking. Further research should be conducted with a variety of models and classification schemes to explore whether other approaches to critical thinking offer more robust explanations of discussion forum usage. The practical inquiry model failed to account for a large proportion of posts. This exclusion may indicate the need for some definitions of critical thinking to include relational maintenance components, such as means of building confidence and mutual trust, as preparatory steps that equip group members for critical engagement with each other's ideas.

The results observed in this study likely arose from the threaded discussion interactions themselves rather than from idiosyncrasies in the delivery platform. Since no student ever e-mailed the instructor about any technical difficulties, technological challenges did not seem to pose a problem. Furthermore, all groups already experienced using threaded discussions for the preliminary collaborative group exercise in developing a task within the topic. Aside from occasional inquiries about which discussion threads to review and which chat rooms to visit, students were easily able to navigate the online learning environment. Some students expressed hesitation with some of the available resources, such as one who wrote, "I don't know how well the chat thing will work." That comment, however, could reflect skepticism about willingness of a group member to participate, which several students noted in their posts but more frequently in private e-mails to the instructor. Overall, it appears unlikely that technological challenges intervened as a variable.

CONCLUSION

This analysis of discussion board posts by students in a fully online problem-solving group should lead to reconsideration of how threaded discussions are designed and utilized as collaborative tools. Reticence to participate may reflect differences between the instructional environments of the discussion forum and the lecture hall. Although online discussions have been hailed as means to empower students to participate more actively (Markel, 2001), they also may present an uncomfortable learning environment to received knowers. Accustomed to obeying rather than exercising authority, received knowers may not be prepared to shoulder the responsibility of initiating discussions or questioning the claims made by other students. To meet this challenge, instructors need to build student capacity for embarking on critical thinking. Involving students in constructive team-building through social networking activities and assuring everyone has clearly articulated roles could build a sufficient sense of security to spur participation.

Examination of posts that did not meet the criteria for the four levels critical thinking reveals that students engaged in several kinds of activities. Symptoms of groupthink emerged as groups faced imminent deadlines, but groupthink also represented a way to avoid conflict with cohorts. Passive agreement may have substituted for dialogical engagement, but it also could have built an accepting environment that would tolerate disagreement and perhaps alter the course of discussion. Groupthink avoids the risks of disagreement or challenge, but it also might build cohesiveness, especially in zero-history groups. Engaging in critical thinking requires taking risks, including the risk of reconsidering the group's procedures and decisions. This risk avoidance may explain the infrequency of means to test proposed solutions or devise contingency plans, since both imply the possibility of failure.

A behavior that could threaten group cohesion was the isolationist pattern of staking out a position and dogmatically reasserting it while not engaging with other ideas. Not only does this behavior counteract cohesiveness, but it also reduces exploration of the implications and nuances of each position offered. But the dogmatic assertions or research posts that simply proclaimed discovery of information may exhibit functional adaptations to the online environment. Eager to show some sign of personal achievement, students who posted such proclamations retained the traditional educational focus on the independent learner. The threads of discussion developed more as individual strands dangling individually, rarely interwoven by investigating the relationships among them. The research component of the group assignment became a means for either (a) declaring that the student had found material, or (b) supporting a claim as true. No posts compared the relative quality of sources, which may demonstrate a conception of research as a personal quest for information rather than as a dialogue of different opinions that must be weighed. This declarative, individualistic mode of discourse reflects a view of knowledge as something found rather than created by the students.

Although these behaviors fall through the cracks of the categories employed in the practical inquiry model, future research should take them into account. Instead of dismissing them simply as indicators of skill deficits or as inherent to all online learning environments, researchers should recognize that each of these behaviors appears for a reason. The rationales may reflect interpersonal needs or learning style preferences that online discussion forums need to confront.

REFERENCES

An, Y.-J., & Frick, T. (2006). Student perceptions of asynchronous computer-mediated communication in face-to-face courses. *Journal of Computer-Mediated Communication*, *11*(2), 485–499. doi:10.1111/j.1083-6101.2006.00023.x

Arbaugh, J. B. (2001). How instructor immediacy behaviors affect student satisfaction and learning in web-based courses. *Business Communication Quarterly, 64*(4), 42–54. doi:10.1177/108056990106400405

Baxter, L. A., & Montgomery, B. M. (1996). *Relating: Dialogues and dialectics*. New York: Guilford.

Belenky, M. F., Clinchy, B. M., Goldberger, N. R., & Tarule, J. M. (1997). Women's ways of knowing: The development of self, voice, and mind (10th anniversary ed.). New York: Basic.

Benyon, D., Stone, D., & Woodroffe, M. (1997). Experience with developing multimedia courseware for the World Wide Web: The need for better tools and clear pedagogy. *International Journal of Human-Computer Studies, 47*, 197–218. doi:10.1006/ijhc.1997.0126

Carrell, L. J., & Menzel, K. E. (2001). Variations in learning, motivation, and perceived immediacy between live and distance education classrooms. *Communication Education, 50*, 230–240. doi:10.1080/03634520109379250

Dewey, J. (1991). *How we think*. Buffalo, NY: Prometheus. (Original work published 1910)

Fahy, P. J., Crawford, G., & Ally, M. (2001). Patterns of interaction in a computer conference transcript. *International Review of Research in Open and Distance Learning, 2*(1), 1–24.

Freire, P. (1970). *Pedagogy of the oppressed* (Ramos, M. B., Trans.). New York: Herder & Herder.

Garrison, R. D., Anderson, T., & Archer, W. (2000). Critical inquiry in a text-based environment: Computer conferencing in higher education. *The Internet and Higher Education, 2*(2-3), 1–19.

Garrison, R. D., Anderson, T., & Archer, W. (2001). Critical thinking, cognitive presence, and computer conferencing in distance education. *Distance Education Report, 15*, 7–23. doi:10.1080/08923640109527071

Guiller, J., & Durndell, A. (2007). Students' linguistic behaviour in online discussion groups: Does gender matter? *Computers in Human Behavior, 23*, 2240–2255. doi:10.1016/j.chb.2006.03.004

Hare, A. P. (2003). Roles, relationships, and groups in organizations: Some conclusions and recommendations. *Small Group Research, 34*, 123–154. doi:10.1177/1046496402250430

Harman, K., & Koohang, A. (2005). Discussion board: A learning object. *Interdisciplinary Journal of Knowledge and Learning Objects, 1*, 67–77.

Hart, J. W., Karau, S. J., Stasson, M. K., & Kerr, N. A. (2004). Achievement motivation, expected coworker performance, and collective task motivation: Working hard or hardly working? *Journal of Applied Social Psychology, 34*, 984–1000. doi:10.1111/j.1559-1816.2004.tb02580.x

Janis, I. (1982). *Groupthink: Psychological studies of policy decisions and fiascos* (2nd ed.). Boston: Houghton Mifflin.

Jeong, A. C. (2003). The sequential analysis of group interaction and critical thinking in online threaded discussions. *American Journal of Distance Education, 17*, 25–43. doi:10.1207/S15389286AJDE1701_3

Kirkpatrick, G. (2005). Online "chat" facilities as pedagogic tools. *Active Learning in Higher Education, 6*, 145–159. doi:10.1177/1469787405054239

Klemm, W. R. (2002, September/October). Extending the pedagogy of threaded-topic discussions. *The Technology Source*. Retrieved November 1, 2004 from http://ts.mivu.org/default.asp?show=article&id=1015

Levine, J. M., & Moreland, R. L. (1990). Progress in small group research. *Annual Review of Psychology, 41*, 585–634. doi:10.1146/annurev.ps.41.020190.003101

Levine, S. J. (2007, Spring). The online discussion board. *New Directions for Adult and Continuing Education, 113*, 67–74. doi:10.1002/ace.248

Liden, R. C., Wayne, S. J., Jaworski, R. A., & Bennett, N. (2004). Social loafing: A field investigation. *Journal of Management, 30*, 285–304. doi:10.1016/j.jm.2003.02.002

Light, V., Nesbitt, E., Light, P., & Burns, J. R. (2000). 'Let's you and me have a little discussion': Computer mediated campus-based university courses. *Studies in Higher Education, 25*, 85–96. doi:10.1080/030750700116037

Mandernach, B. J., Gonzales, R. M., & Garrett, A. M. (2006). An examination of online instructor presence via threaded discussion participation. *Journal of Online Learning and Teaching, 2*, 248–260.

Markel, S. (2001). Technology and education online discussion forums: It's in the response. *Online Journal of Distance Learning Administration, 4*(2). Retrieved April 10, 2009 from http://www.westga.edu/~distance/ojdla/summer42/markel42.html

Meyer, K. A. (2002). Quality in distance education: Focus on on-line learning. *ASHE-ERIC Higher Education Report, 29*(4).

Meyer, K. A. (2003). Face-to-face versus threaded discussions: The role of time and higher order thinking. *Journal of Asynchronous Learning Networks, 7*(3), 55–65.

Morreale, S., Hugenberg, L., & Worley, D. (2006). The basic communication course at U.S. colleges and universities in the 21st century: Study VII. *Communication Education, 55*, 415–437. doi:10.1080/03634520600879162

San Millan Maurino, P. (2006). Looking for critical thinking in online threaded discussions. *E-Journal of Instructional Science and Technology, 9*(2), 1–18.

Schrodt, P., & Turman, P. D. (2005). The impact of instructional technology use, course design, and sex differences on students' initial perceptions of instructor credibility. *Communication Quarterly, 53*, 177–196. doi:10.1080/01463370500090399

Schrodt, P., & Witt, P. L. (2006). Students' attributions of instructor credibility as a function of students' expectations of instructional technology use and nonverbal immediacy. *Communication Education, 55*, 1–20. doi:10.1080/03634520500343335

Schwartzman, R. (2006). Virtual group problem solving in the basic communication course: Lessons for online learning. *Journal of Instructional Psychology, 33*, 3–14.

Schwartzman, R. (2007a). Electronifying oral communication: Refining the conceptual framework for online instruction. *College Student Journal, 41*, 37–50.

Schwartzman, R. (2007b). *Fundamentals of oral communication*. Dubuque, IA: Kendall/Hunt.

Schwartzman, R. (2007c). Refining the question: How can online instruction maximize opportunities for all students? *Communication Education, 56*, 113–117. doi:10.1080/03634520601009728

Shedletsky, L. J., & Aitken, J. E. (2001). The paradoxes of online academic work. *Communication Education, 50*, 206–217. doi:10.1080/03634520109379248

Shedletsky, L. J., & Aitken, J. E. (2004). *Human communication on the Internet*. Boston: Allyn and Bacon.

Thompson, L., & Ku, H.-Y. (2006). A case study of online collaborative learning. *Quarterly Review of Distance Education, 7*, 361–375.

Tuckman, B. (1965). Developmental sequence in small groups. *Psychological Bulletin, 63*, 384–399. doi:10.1037/h0022100

Turman, P. D., & Schrodt, P. (2005). The influence of instructional technology use on students' affect: Do course designs and biological sex make a difference? *Communication Studies, 56*, 109–129. doi:10.1080/00089570500078726

Twigg, C. A. (1999). *Improving learning and reducing costs: Redesigning large enrollment courses.* Troy, NY: Rensselaer Polytechnic Institute Center for Academic Transformation.

Walther, J. B., & Parks, M. R. (2002). Cues filtered out, cues filtered in: Computer-mediated communication and relationships. In Knapp, M. L., & Daly, J. A. (Eds.), *Handbook of interpersonal communication* (pp. 529–563). Thousand Oaks, CA: Sage.

Wang, Z., Walther, J. B., Pingree, S., & Hawkins, R. P. (2008). Health information, credibility, homophily, and influence via the Internet: Web sites versus discussion groups. *Health Communication, 23*, 358–368. doi:10.1080/10410230802229738

ADDITIONAL READING

Andreu, R., & Jáuregui, K. (2005). Key factors of e-learning: A case study at a Spanish bank. *Journal of Information Technology Education, 4*, 1–31.

Barnes, S. B. (2003). *Computer-mediated communication: Human-to-human communication across the internet.* Boston: Allyn & Bacon.

Benbunan-Fich, R., & Hiltz, S. R. (1999, March). Educational applications of CMCS: Solving case studies through asynchronous learning networks. *Journal of Computer-Mediated Communication, 4*(3). Retrieved March 8, 2003 from http://www.ascusc.org/jcmc/vol4/issue3/benbunan-fich.html

Clarke, T. D., Human, S. E., Amshoff, H., & Sigg, M. (2001). Getting up to speed on the information highway: Integrating web-based resources into business communication pedagogy. *Business Communication Quarterly, 64*, 38–62. doi:10.1177/108056990106400105

Draves, W. A. (2000). *Teaching online.* River Falls, WI: LERN Books.

Easton, S. S. (2003). Clarifying the instructor's role in online distance learning. *Communication Education, 52*, 87–105. doi:10.1080/03634520302470

Edelstein, S., & Edwards, J. (2002, Spring). If you build it, they will come: Building learning communities through threaded discussions. *Online Journal of Distance Learning Administration, 5*(1). Retrieved July 7, 2005 from http://www.westga.edu/%7Edistance/ojdla/spring51/edelstein51.html

Olaniran, B. A., Grant, T. S., & Sorenson, R. L. (1996). Experimental and experiential approaches to teaching face-to-face and computer-mediated group discussion. *Communication Education, 45*, 244–259. doi:10.1080/03634529609379053

Reeves, B., & Nass, C. (1996). *The media equation: How people treat computers, television, and new media like real people and places.* Cambridge: Cambridge University Press.

Rice, D. J., Davidson, B. D., Dannenhoffer, J. F., & Gay, G. K. (2007). Improving the effectiveness of virtual teams by adapting team processes. *Computer Supported Cooperative Work: The Journal of Collaborative Computing, 16*, 567–594. doi:10.1007/s10606-007-9070-3

Rosenberg, M. J. (2001). *E-learning: Strategies for delivering knowledge in the digital age.* New York: McGraw-Hill.

Russell, T. R. (2001). *The no significant difference phenomenon* (5th ed.). Raleigh: North Carolina State University.

Sauers, D., & Walker, R. C. (2004). A comparison of traditional and technology-assisted instructional methods in the business communication classroom. *Business Communication Quarterly*, *67*, 430–442. doi:10.1177/1080569904271030

Simon, H. A. (2002). Cooperation between educational technology and learning theory to advance higher education. In Goodman, P. S. (Ed.), *Technology enhanced learning: Opportunities for change* (pp. 61–74). Mahwah, NJ: Lawrence Erlbaum.

Warschauer, M. (1999). *Electronic literacies: Language, culture, and power in online education.* Mahwah, NJ: Lawrence Erlbaum.

Web-Based Training Information Center. (2002). *What constitutes quality in web-based training?* Retrieved September 14, 2006 from http://www.webbasedtraining.com/primer_quality.aspx

Wulff, S., Hanor, J., & Bulik, R. J. (2000). The roles and interrelationships of presence, reflection, and self-directed learning in effective World Wide Web-based pedagogy. In Cole, R. A. (Ed.), *Issues in web-based pedagogy: A critical primer* (pp. 143–160). Westport, CT: Greenwood Press.

KEY TERMS AND DEFINITIONS

Cohesiveness: The sense of bonding between group members so they consider the group a unified whole.

Exploration: Tentative suggestions and proposals that invite further examination and testing by group cohorts; an early stage of critical thinking.

Groupthink: The tendency of group members to agree with each other's viewpoints, with minimal reservations or rationale.

Integration: Synthesis of different viewpoints, based on weighing available evidence, that moves a group toward convergence.

Received Knowers: Passive, obedient recipients of information delivered by authority figures who are thought to convey definitive truths.

Resolution: A rationally justified collective position formulated with attention to real-world outcomes and consequences.

Social Loafing: Non-participation by a group member under the assumption that others will do the needed work.

Triggering Event: A discussion board post that prods the group toward action or further inquiry.

Chapter 3
Promoting Reflective Discourse through Connectivity:
Conversations around Service–Learning Experiences

Kathy L. Guthrie
Florida State University, USA

Holly McCracken
University of Illinois at Springfield, USA

EXECUTIVE SUMMARY

Connectivity is vital to the creation of virtual spaces in Web-based academic courses which allow for students to reflect on curricular content and personal experiences. This chapter provides a case study of online service-learning courses utilizing technology to promote reflective conversations and the development of emotional bandwidth.

BACKGROUND

Dialogue and discourse are critical to students' successful participation in applied learning experiences. It is through these processes that they develop capacities for reflection, autonomy and critical thought, essential to the process of learning situated in outreach and service. The creation of secure intellectual and emotional spaces within such academic contexts promote the development of a connectedness that enables both cognitive and personal transformation as well as directly impacts positive social change on local levels. Facilitating the development of "emotional bandwidth," the capacity to learn through

structured and reflective interactions, assists in creating such a connectedness among all stakeholders in the service-learning process. These stakeholders include the student, the instructor, and the placement staff and service recipients. The web-based courses presented in this case study were structured in such ways as to provide both the technical and interpersonal means to create such a capacity that extends throughout students' service-learning experiences and beyond. To better understand the case presented background information related to service-learning theory and practice, emotional bandwidth, and a range of pedagogical approaches, including the facilitation of reflective dialogue and the construction of learning communities, will be explored.

DOI: 10.4018/978-1-61520-863-0.ch003

Service-Learning

Waterman (1997) defined service-learning as "an experiential approach to education that involves students in a wide range of activities that are of benefit to others, and uses the experiences generated to advance the curricula goals" (p. xi). Stanton, Giles and Cruz (1999) defined service-learning as education through active service using the structure of courses and field seminars attached to curriculum and a grading system. While definitions vary slightly, both authors identified service-learning as tied to academic curricula and credit generation. This connection to academic curriculum and graded requirements make it different from co-curricular community service, often seen in institutions of higher education. Co-curricular community service is completed outside of the classroom, perhaps with a group of friends or a student organization. However, service-learning is completed within a course structure and attached to credit generation.

Service-learning joins two complex concepts of knowledge and community action. Creating true service-learning experiences can prove to be difficult; finding appropriate community service experiences that complement specific academic learning is difficult because of the ever changing needs and demands of the community. The service component, community action, when combined with learning is truly service-learning. The learning in this context is connecting the development that occurs in the service experience to already existing knowledge (Stanton, Giles & Cruz, 1999). This service-learning pedagogy is typically achieved through a structure of courses, field seminars and critical reflection workshops. Structured reflection is vital for learning to be connected to service in this pedagogical framework.

Emotional Bandwidth

Emotional bandwidth is inherent to community service as well as online instructional environments, expressed in unique and interesting ways that impact both individual and collective learning. Emotional bandwidth refers, in the simplest terms, to the development of trust among individuals whom the instructor is teaching online (Hoefling, 2003). Promoting the development of group trust in a virtual learning environment requires a particularly complex methodology. Hoefling (2003) suggested that trust was established with virtual groups through logically occurring phenomena, such as the formation of first impressions, as well as by more intentional methods such as identifying early-established patterns that became embedded in classroom culture. Emotional bandwidth can be developed in many ways; however, the optimal approach is through the facilitation of simple conversations using a variety of available technical tools. As the case study illustrates, interpersonal connectedness is promoted through a "high touch" approach to the use of relatively mainstream media-based applications such as e-mail, synchronous instant message/chat, asynchronous discussion, and audio-video conferencing.

Meyerson, Weick, and Kramer (1996) identified "swift trust" in groups as a trust building strategy. This type of trust is initially based on social structures. For example, trust is automatically given to the instructor and fellow students of an online class because of the integrity of the roles each person plays. However, swift trust is only temporary and may not continue. Developing strong relationships and connecting with peers and the instructor on several levels expands swift trust to a new confidence which leads to longer lasting relationships.

Reflection

The cultivation and exploration of emotional bandwidth within experientially-based courses is facilitated through the implementation of learning objectives, activities, and resources that rely heavily on a reflective process. The methods by which reflection is taught to students within the contexts of life-long learning and service-learning have been of specific focus over the last several decades. Boud, Keogh and Walker (1985) suggested that structured reflection was the key to learning from experiences. Daudlin (1996) observed "Reflection is the process of stepping back from an experience to ponder, carefully and persistently, its meaning to the self through the development of inferences; learning is the creation of meaning from past or current events that serves as a guide for future behavior" (p. 39). Eyler, Giles, and Scmiede (1996) found that structured reflection was critical to students' learning.

McCarthy (1987) suggested that learning involved two dimensions of perception and processing. Human perception referred to the ways people took in new information, typically through experience. Human processing referred to the ways people integrated new information, typically through reflection and action. In the field of experiential learning, human perception has been investigated extensively; however, human processing has not been as well-researched. Boud, et al. (1985) suggested that structured reflection is the key to learning from experiences and in essence to human processing.

Stepping away from an experience and carefully, but persistently pondering its meaning serves as a guide for future behavior (Daudlin, 1996). Eyler, Giles, and Schmiede (1996) found that reflection needs to be continuous, connected, challenging and contextualized. Both continuous self- dialogue and collaborative inquiry involves reflection before, during and after the experience. Connected reflection emphasizes the importance of integrating the experience with class work and academic learning. Challenging reflection pushes students to think in new ways and produced new understand and new ways of problem-solving. Contextualized reflection should be appropriate for the particular context and setting the experience is taking place in. Eyler, Giles and Schmeide (1996) also stated that communication with peers provided an interactive way of reflecting and this was often missing in classes.

While service-learning has been practiced for decades (Stanton, Giles and Cruz, 1999), its facilitation in a web-based environment is a new concept. Literature exploring service-learning pedagogy, emotional bandwidth, and reflection provides a strong foundation for further exploring reflective connectivity in web-based service-learning courses.

INSTRUCTIONAL METHODS UTILIZED IN THE CASE STUDY

Strait and Sauer (2004) found that service-learning experiences allowed students to both "…sharpen the focus of their own instruction and learning [as well as] deepen their level of inquiry through questioning, making connections, and honoring multiple perspectives" (section 5). In order for learning to be significant, several aspects of instruction were found to be essential in facilitating meaningful learning within an experiential context using multiple media. These include the creation of a virtual environment that enabled ongoing communication, interaction and relationship building and a teaching approach that fostered both autonomy and collaboration. Additionally, the design and implementation of methodologies that afforded opportunities to integrate critical reflection and inquiry and the selection and consistent delivery of universally accessible technologies that supported both primary learning goals and development of secondary skills (for example, mastering the use of individual applications, software and hardware) are also essential in facilitating meaningful learning.

Creating a Robust Virtual Environment to Support Inquiry and Collaboration

In order to actualize instructional objectives, it is critical to construct a virtual learning environment in which opportunities for continuous communication and interaction can be explored, cultivated and, ultimately, reinforced. The initial charge required the creation of a secure web-based environment in which technologies were utilized to support applied collaborative learning experiences within a context of both individual and collective discovery. Jonassen, Davidson, Collins, Campbell, and Bannan Haag (1995) indicated that the use of varied media enabled communication and interaction that often surpassed what was typically found in face-to-face classrooms. Jonassen (in Huang, 2002) noted that the role of technology within virtual learning environments was so significant as to actually become an "intellectual partner" with students as they pursued learning goals. Indeed, Meyers (2008) emphasized that when used in conjunction with instructional methods that promoted inquiry and collaboration, technological solutions were capable of facilitating transformative learning experiences.

Because stable and secure technologies are critical to enabling interpersonal exchange, applications were chosen based on their capacities to support instructional goals, facilitating interaction (for example, one-to-one and one-to-many communications); minimizing geographic differences (through the use of synchronous and asynchronous activities); promoting access (implementing uniform minimum requirements for software, hardware, bandwidth, etc.); and advancing functionality (promoting skill development related to general use, navigation, and the applications themselves).

A web-based course management system, Blackboard, Inc.®, is used as the infrastructure for the online courses presented in the case study. This system features mechanisms that broadly enable ongoing interaction among peers, instructors, community service contacts, instructional content, and the learning environment itself. Such a system provides structures that promote collaboration (utilizing threaded asynchronous discussions), communication (through email and chat functions), interaction (using a range of conferencing platforms that enables the synchronous use of video, audio or text, and allows archived communications), and information sharing (through the use of text-based lectures, podcasts, and streaming video) (Van de Pol, 2001; Hall, 2003). Additionally, this learning management system enables the coordination of a range of administrative functions that accompany instruction, such as generating and recording assessment data and records and enabling the distribution and management of course content (Hall, 2003; Ullman & Rabinowitz, 2004). Finally, Web 2.0 technologies were integrated as relevant to curricular goals and manageable by course participants. For example, the use of internet-based video sharing sites such as YouTube® facilitate the delivery of students' culminating action research projects and presentations, and delivering lectures via podcasts allow on-demand access to course information and assignments.

Instructional Approaches Facilitating Inquiry and Collaboration

Strait and Sauer (2004) adopted the term "e-service" to describe a media-based distributed approach to facilitating collaborative virtual partnerships between coordinating institutions, students, and their service-learning placements and associates. Such collaborations extend beyond technological connections, dependent upon effectively supporting the development of relationships between members of the learning community, their peers and the instructor, among learners and their placements, and to the technology itself. When collaboration is the center around which instructional design and delivery is based, it is possible to create a cohesive approach to curricular implementation, maintain the integrity of the environment, and deliver educational experiences that are fluid and flexible, meeting the needs of all stakeholders in the e-service system.

Instructional activities are implemented that facilitate the development of practice-based competencies as specifically required by local community service sites. For example, the cultivation of web development skills would be critical if designing a website for the organization. Additionally, skills uniquely learned in collaboration with community members promote critical inquiry and a level of knowledge building that contributed to the environment's capacity for collective learning (Driscoll & Gilbert, 2002). Methods are selected that capitalize on features of the learning management system. Instructional goals are extended to areas for secondary skill building, for example, the development of abilities to interact in meaningful ways in virtual learning environments, and the capacity to analyze personal experiences and communicate in relevant ways using various media. Moreover, strategies are implemented that enable explorations of broader issues such as socio-economic advantage and privilege and their relationship to accessing information technology. Developing skills in information literacy, and the role of culture in individual participation and communication continue to be critical to ensure curricular goals and instructional methods, including the selection and utilization of technologies, are congruent with the larger academic field, pedagogical priorities and social realities. Meyers (2008) remarked that the exploration of such important social concerns extended beyond one dimensional information sharing; this level of dialogue, he found, was particularly effective when migrated to media-rich learning environments (p. 24).

Cooperative Teaching to Promote Learning Autonomy

While the technologies themselves afford frameworks within which to promote ongoing dialogue and discourse, the actual opportunities that generate participation and collaboration are facilitated through reflective pedagogy. Such approaches enable a natural environment in which to facilitate, interpret and analyze meaningful applied experiences. Many of these approaches are constructivist in nature, prioritizing a "... change in focus from individual knowledge constructed singly to public knowledge jointly constructed by students" (Gilbert & Driscoll, 2002, p. 59). Crotty (in Jonassen, et al., 1995) wrote that the deliberate integration of technology enables constructivist educators to create environments where learners "...[were] required to examine thinking and learning processes; collect, record, and analyze data; formulate and test hypotheses; reflect on previous understandings; and construct their own meaning" (p. 30). Meyers (2008) added that such learning environments advance meaning and engagement, leading to personally and academically relevant experiences.

A cooperative teaching approach that encourages challenging questions and dialogues, facilitates critical thinking, promotes conflict resolution and negotiation, and advances consensus building fosters intellectual, as well as cognitive and affective growth. This approach, then, extends to students' community service experiences, as they apply transferable skills learned in the courses' virtual communities in their service experiences. Such a process is facilitated by an instructor who relinquishes traditional classroom direction in favor of a facilitative style to classroom management; responds positively to inquiry, opinion, and information-seeking; is comfortable with collaboration as well as autonomy; and, allows students responsibility for their own learning processes and outcomes. To maximize the effectiveness of instruction the skills, abilities, and experiences of the collective learning community are consistently valued and recognized, all-the-while drawing on individual student interests, competencies, and experiences, and included:

- A valuing and active utilization of experiences, skills, resources and knowledge brought to the classroom by both traditional and non-traditional students.

- The integration of students' expectations and priorities into instructional goals.
- A cohesive yet flexible curriculum that includes opportunities to experiment with developing concepts and original areas of knowledge.
- The utilization of instructional methods and associated media, the use of which evolves based on changing student needs.
- Access to relevant support materials, manuals, guides, etc., that reinforces curricular content, assists in the development of networks, and provides resources for consultation following the course conclusion.
- Ongoing feedback related to individual and group assessment and evaluation throughout the courses.

Using Targeted Discussions to Reinforce Critical Reflection and Inquiry

Shea's research (2006) indicated that distant students reported a strong sense of learning through community in those online classes in which instructors create open environments for discussion, mediation, and resolution of difficult dialogues that ultimately reinforced complex understanding. A primary instructional method that generates individual reflection and collective interaction as well as facilitated skill development and knowledge construction includes the use of intentionally-constructed discussions (Brookfield & Preskill, 1999). Meyers (2008) recognized that discussions addressing difficult dialogues were particularly effective when facilitated in a virtual environment. He emphasized that methods promoting explorations of, for example, social justice issues, were portable, easily migrated to use in web-based classrooms (p. 222). For example, discussion questions, such as "On the most basic level, integrity is defined as having a commitment to your values and matching those values with your actions consistently. Some situ-

ations require some type of value judgment: for example, do you think actions, such as speeding in a school zone, turning in a friend for cheating on an exam, or lying to get medicine for an ill relative are examples of living with integrity?" (Guthrie, 2009) provide opportunities for both private reflection and discourse within the context of individual placements as well as collective exploration within the learning community. By integrating these approaches with practiced facilitation, targeted discussions conducted in virtual classrooms ensure powerful, diverse and interactive learning experiences and enabled communities to evolve, as demonstrated through relationship-building, shared goals, mutual feedback, and the achievement of both individual and collective learning outcomes.

Encouraging Collaboration through Community to Further Knowledge-Building

Generally believed critical to facilitating multi-dimensional experiences for participants in a range of educational environments, the use of learning communities as an important instructional method has been widely recognized across academic disciplines, teaching approaches, and delivery media. Both wide-scale anecdotal feedback and more formal research indicated that the importance of community development to learning is particularly essential to student satisfaction, motivation, and retention in web-based classrooms in which students may never physically come into contact with peers and instructors (Collison, Elbaum, Haavind, & Tinker, 2000; McCracken, 2005; Palloff & Pratt, 1999, 2001; Rovai, 2002; Shea, 2006). Walther and Bunz (2005) indicated that the degree to which trust is formed in learning communities ultimately impacts not only relational dynamics but also the overall performance of the membership, and its collective capacity for problem solving and information sharing (p. 830). Communities that develop in online instructional environments are particularly important to the facilitation of meaningful learning experiences, enabling the exploration of foundational tenets inherent in providing community-based outreach and service. Communities that develop in online instructional environments significantly impact research generation, self-assessment, and critical thought development, as well as important to furthering advising/consulting relationships, social networks, and professional affiliations. Positive community development is indicated by high levels of engagement, social presence, and participation (Walther & Bunz, 2005, p. 831-832). By structuring instructional activities, such that the groups' capacity for affiliation and unity is developed and promoted (for example, through opportunities for teamwork), community formation and involvement ultimately further curricular intent. Beyond interpersonal development, individual and collective learning goals are reinforced (through the promotion of collaborative projects); knowledge acquisition is furthered (through the integration of lectures by subject matter experts or guest speakers); and skill development is fostered creating opportunities for students to take active roles in directing their own learning (by participating in organized teams and study groups to deliver presentations or structure research projects).

Instructional Methods to Facilitate Personal and Academic Development

The previously described learner-centered approaches included a range of techniques utilized to involve students directly in the learning process, providing a variety of opportunities for them to experiment with experientially-based concepts. Several specific methods were implemented to facilitate the broad instructional goal of promoting experientially-based critical reflection and collaborative inquiry.

Action or advocacy based community service projects planned with and implemented at local and regional service organizations enable students to design self directed learning experiences that both are personally meaningful as well as directly related to curricular goals. Many educators, notably Knowles (1984), Tough, (1967) and Houle (1972) identified the importance of constructing instructional environments that recognize and integrate experiential knowledge as students pursue educational goals. Individual participation in action or advocacy based community service placements within students' local and regional communities enable a combined learner- and service-centered focus to be integrated throughout the placement, recognizing the value of and actively utilizing students' experiences, skills, and knowledge. Allowing students to visibly apply expectations and priorities to current learning opportunities and engaging them as peers and resources throughout community membership creates greater learning opportunities. Parameters of such participation are negotiated between students, the community service supervisors and the instructor via learning contracts that enable the accomplishment of individualized learning goals, as well as broader collective instructional objectives. Such environments facilitate both ongoing discovery and a personal relationship to learning. They also enable interpersonal connections, emphasize the application of previous experiences to current learning goals and, promote democratic teaching-learning partnerships, allowing students to develop both collective and individualized perspectives on their evolving knowledge base (Brookfield, 1987, 1999; Daloz, in Taylor, 1995; Taylor, 1995; Palloff and Pratt, 1999).

Online learning is an active process, the strength of which is realized through collaboration between co-learners, facilitators/instructors, and other collateral resources (Palloff & Pratt, 1999). Students are most effectively engaged through active involvement in opportunities for ongoing collaboration that focus on the development of group process and collective knowledge building. Opportunities for ongoing interaction in the courses' virtual communities, the development of which is facilitated through the use of guided questions presented within the framework of asynchronous and synchronous discussions, allow "…students to contribute to each others' learning through social construction of communal knowledge" (Gilbert & Driscoll, 2002, p. 59), not only a best practice within the context of experiential learning but of web-based instruction as well. Rovai (2002) explained that the construction of such active learning environments promote the authentic exploration of involvement in individuals' immediate surroundings (in this instance, students' community placements) within context of their personal world views. Rogo (in Rovai, 2002) emphasized that within this framework learning becomes personally and academically significant, "…[occurring] as a function of all active members of the classroom community, transforming roles and understanding in the activities in which they participate" (p.6). Collaborative learning in community, therefore, provides a foundational context in which experiential learning pursuits and instructional goals merge, enabling a logical connection between academic theory and practical application and development of transferable throughout students' educations (McCracken, 2005).

Acknowledging the important connection between the process of learning and the content of knowledge, Brookfield (cited in Merriam & Cafferella, 1999) observed, "…. the most complete form of self directed learning occur[s] when process and reflection [are] married in the [students'] pursuit of meaning" (p. 291). The development of reflection journals kept throughout the course supports ongoing processes of critical reflection and dialogue related to day-to-day work at students' placements. Journaling also allows them to specifically address issues related to social awareness and personal and collective responsibility. The completion of journals and other targeted reflection assignments allow expanded explorations that incorporate course curriculum material. An individualized, action

research approach enables a foundation for the examination of issues related to social change, democratic citizenship and personal and collective responsibility. Culminating action research papers describe students' discovery processes through illustrating significant reflection points and key experiences within the context of their community-based placements.

CASE DESCRIPTION

At the University of Illinois, Springfield two online service-learning courses have been offered since spring of 2007. These two courses are situated in the Experiential and Service-Learning Programs in the College of Liberal Arts and Sciences, and are designated with the prefix of EXL which refers to "experiential learning". With over 200 undergraduate students having completed these two courses, connectivity among students occurs as a result of using a range of pedagogies, not all of which are media-based. While both these courses have similar structures, they focus on community engagement through slightly different lenses. EXL 200, Learning and Serving in the Community, focuses on community engagement broadly and what that means to students personally. As stated in the course objectives, upon completion of this course students are to have developed a working knowledge and comprehension of: the history and philosophy of American community service; the nature and magnitude of social issues in student's local community; processes, structures and collaboration in community service; basic strategies and tactics utilized by groups and organizations to maintain or improve the quality of life in their communities; activities that lead to development personally, professionally and academically through community service experiences; and, the ability to develop, present and implement an action plan in a community setting. Students are required to participate in 60 hours of community service at a non-profit agency of their choice.

The second offered course, EXL 360, Social Change and Leadership, examines community engagement from a positive social change framework and explores how different leadership styles enact positive social change. As stated in the course objectives, upon completion of this course students are to have developed: an enhanced overall service-learning comprehension by participating in the reflective learning process; recognition of various historical models of leadership in social change; developed core personal values and an ethical framework and apply them in action to civic engagement and leadership issues; identified strategies for social influence/social change in others and self; reflected on the relationship between the individual and society within contemporary American context. In EXL 360, students are required to focus on a community service project where a specific outcome is obtained. To gain a better understanding of the ways these two online service-learning courses promote connectivity among students, course topics, course requirements and guided reflection activities will be further explored.

Course Topics

Included in pedagogical methods are opportunities to address topics that allow students to be connected to the curricula, fellow classmates, and the instructor. Both courses, EXL 200, Learning and Serving in the Community and EXL 360, Social Change and Leadership, require students to examine their personal definitions of community service. While EXL 200 explores this area more in-depth, both courses require students to reflect on what community service personally means to them. For example, students are given a sheet with a list of twenty scenarios, and are asked to rank each scenario on a five-point scale in which they determine levels of community service. These scenarios represent a wide range of behaviors, from, for example, smiling at a stranger to providing soup at a breadline to serving in the

military. Subsequent discussions about the types of activities considered to be service always occur. Encouraging students to contemplate the meaning of and their relationship to community service is important to situate the learning of civic and community engagement in a personal framework. Providing specific scenarios for students to ponder provides some guidance to the conversation.

The history of American community service is also included in both courses. Students are provided an extensive timeline of specific government policies, programs and prominent activists. Educating students about specific policies, programs and activists provides information on how the United States and larger Western world views community service and engagement. Understanding the development of American community service also helps to situate the topic in conversations about current civic engagement. In addition, having knowledge of major leaders and activists helps to develop students' thoughts about appropriate steps toward future change and the differences that one person can make.

In EXL 200, Learning and Serving in the Community, oppression, privilege and social capital are included in course topics. Discussion about the ways these topics contribute to social issues in our world and the means by which one can create positive change by understanding these areas is an important part of community service. Reflecting on the ways privilege and oppression impact the need for community service encourages students to think about service as an exchange rather than simply giving of self to others. In EXL 360, Social Change and Leadership, topics are focused around community organizing and leadership. The framework of leadership as a process in creating positive social change is promoted throughout the course. The work of both famous and obscure activists and leaders are examined. Better understanding of the manner in which these individuals were able to facilitate social change in their communities enables an active process from which students can learn. Often we learn of the outcomes of great leaders, but rarely look at the process they engaged; in these courses this process is examined and often practiced in the community service sites.

Course Requirements

Students enrolled in EXL 200 and EXL 360 at the University of Illinois at Springfield participate in guided reflection assignments throughout the course. This type of structured reflection occurs through course materials, reflective essays, web-based discussions, reflection journals and essays. Requirements for both EXL 200 and EXL 360 include the completion of individual action plans, 60 hours of community service, journals; participation in structured thoughtful discussions; and submission of reflective essays that conclude with a final culminating paper. Each of these requirements facilitates reflection on the course material, student community service experiences and how theory is put into practice.

At the start of each course, students are asked to select a non-profit agency in which their community service will be performed. Once a community service site has been selected and confirmed with an agency representative, students are asked to determine their learning goals for the service experience. Students are required to create service action plans that require three learning outcomes for their service experience. With each outcome, students plan those activities they will complete to accomplish this learning objective, the resources they will use to support their learning and the means by which they will assess that the learning occurred. For example, activities that sustain a learning objective may include specific projects with their community service site or seeking out additional information from an agency employee who assists with their on site experiences. Resources may include individuals with whom they interact during their community service, a professor they have had in class or specific literature. Assessment may refer to reflection journals or providing certain evaluative reports to their community service sites. By putting specific steps in place, students develop accountability for their own learning; this level of forward thinking enables a self determined structure for learning from the community service experience. Moreover, making meaning from their experience is vital to actual learning occurring; such meaning is created through requirements of a reflective nature. These requirements include journals, web-based discussions and papers.

Reflection journals are a required element of both courses. Twenty journal entries, approximately one to two pages in length are required. This is roughly one entry for every three hours of community service provided. The specific assignments are structured to provide guidance to those students who have never utilized a journal format to reflect on experiences. Students are encouraged to focus on a specific situation or learning moment instead of using the journal as a log of what happened during a period of time. For example, students are instructed to discuss the focus of their writing in two or three sentences, and then follow up with those thoughts, feelings and learning moments that occurred in that situation. The written summarization of those feelings and reactions is to be eight to ten sentences in length. This general format allows students to focus more on the learning moments and to be aware of their thoughts and feelings. Having emotional self-awareness in relation to course material and experience adds to the connectivity a student may develop to a course.

Additional requirements include completing original responses to discussion questions as well as responses to peers; such remarks address course materials, experiences and questions posed by instructor. Assignments such as these provide opportunities for students to discuss with classmates and the instructor about important topical areas. Emotional bandwidth is vital to the level of disclosure students provide. The reflection that occurs related to both course topics and community service experiences bring the course material to life allowing the theory learned in class to be applied on a practical level. Trust is built by students reciprocating disclosure of personal histories, thoughts, ideas, and experiences. Instructors who provide personal examples of community service experiences is important to establishing and modeling trust ; such relationships, then, impact the development of the community as well as the quality of both collective and individual learning.

Reflective essays are important requirements of both courses. EXL 200, Learning and Serving in the Community, requires a reflective essay focusing on defining community service. In this essay students write about their historical roots in community service work, influences to their thoughts and actions around community service, the types of community service they have performed and their specific definitions of the term. This reflective essay is an extension of the ranking worksheet covered in the course topics. Since community service is a personal endeavor, it gives a structured opportunity for students to reflect on the meaning of community service and where that definition originates for them.

In EXL 360, Social Change and Leadership, two reflective essays that focus on course readings and experiences are required. One essay asks students to read two excerpts, one from Jane Addams' (1910) "Twenty Years at Hull House" and another excerpt from Andrew Carnegie's (1889) "The Gospel of Wealth" and write a reflective essay comparing and contrasting these two leaders and they ways they created social change differently. Further, they are asked to reflect on their own style of leadership and community engagement, identifying methods of social change that are beneficial to society. The second essay requires students to read Gloria Naylor's (1982) "Women of Brewster Place." This work of fiction provides a story of women in unsuspecting leadership roles. Students reflect on and write about two women in the story and the ways they demonstrated leadership and contributed to social change. Students are asked

to specifically address the manner in which this is or is not related to their personal experiences in community service.

EXL 200 and EXL 360 both require students to develop a final reflective paper that is a culmination of the semester. Students reflect on the course material, community service experiences and personal lessons learned throughout the semester. This final reflective project allows students to see their development in a snapshot of the entire semester. While majority of students write papers, the option to create projects, such as a website or video presentation are also available. Guiding questions such as the following are provided to assist students' reflection on their experiences: How does your community service this semester connect with the readings done throughout the semester? Does it affirm, challenge, and illustrate the concepts and theories presented? What does service mean to you? Has your personal definition of community service change from the beginning of the course to now? What were your struggles and satisfactions with your community service experience? What were your personal learning objectives that you outlined in the action plan? How were your personal learning objectives accomplished?

As previously described, the majority of the course requirements in these two online service-learning courses are reflective in nature. Whether it is foresight or hindsight, reflecting in different ways provides opportunities for students with different learning styles to make meaning out of their experiences and connect it to the course material. The process of reflecting both on course materials and actual experiences from required community service enables a connectivity to the course, classmates and instructor that may not be experienced as typical in other web-based classes.

Reflective Connectivity

A range of reflective pedagogies enables outreach to a variety of students with a wide range of learning styles and processes. Also, allowing for different relationships to build provides space for reflective connectivity to occur in many forms. For example, reflective essays, journals and papers are submitted directly to the instructor; these may provide an additional level of comfort as personal, emotional thoughts and feelings are considered. However, the online discussions are more of an exchange of ideas, thoughts and feelings with several people, often the entire class. These conversations center around specific topics relating to course materials and experiences students have during their community service work.

Students report that they feel extremely connected to their classmates and course materials. Since a significant part of these courses are personal experiences within community service and civic engagement, connectivity occurs through the personal nature of the material. Often intense discussions around global social issues, injustices people deal with and the horrible pain that occurs, enable emotional conversations occur. These emotional conversations cause students to connect on a deeper level than experienced in other courses. Through these emotionally intense conversations, swift trust facilitates long-lasting friendships. Emotional bandwidth is further developed through these conversations. Connectivity to continuance of learning through the course becomes lasting friendships.

Additional feedback received from students is how the topics covered in these online service-learning courses relate to actual situations in the world. In actuality, topics covered in these courses discuss community engagement, lifelong learning and the ways one can make positive change. While it does directly relate to situations occurring in our world, it also relates to students on a person level. Reflection on the ways the course topics relate to each student's individual experience with service enables them to build the confidence to take the course theory and put it into practice in their communities. Reflection becomes the

vehicle for connectivity to the course material, classmates, and instructor.

Students also express gratitude for providing them with opportunities to participate in community service close to their homes related to issues that interest them. The majority of students who enroll in the online service-learning courses at University of Illinois at Springfield are part time students. These students also work part time or full time while pursuing undergraduate degrees. They have expressed a past desire to provide community service, but felt their time was limited. In fact, some state that if it was not for a class requirement they would not have taken the time to do so. Several students initially express concern with time limitations in relation to providing the required number of service hours, however, most are astonished when they exceed their goals. Most not only are able to find the time to participate in activities of interest, but also often include their families. Appreciation for this new connection to the communities they call "home" is often evidenced in course feedback.

In a few cases, connectivity has continued even after the course had ended. Three student networks formed as a result of the bond students made through the course. One network comprised of four students who completed their required community service with a specific population relied on each other beyond course requirements to reflect on their experience. Another network consisted of five students who continued to serve at the agencies for which they provided community service during the course. This group decided to continue their conversations started in class through a Facebook™ group. A third group was formed in one of the service-learning classes because they were interested in taking the second service-learning course together. They requested to be placed in the same discussion group so they could challenge and support each other in future conversations.

CHALLENGES AND NEW DIRECTIONS

Web-based service-learning courses that utilize reflective discussion-based pedagogy have emerged as a structured means for distant students to not only become engaged with their local communities, but also to connect to course materials, instructors, and geographically dispersed peers. However, while there are many successes in these web-based service-learning courses, there are also a range of challenges inherent in developing and teaching curricula that utilize such highly interactive approaches. The establishment of such instructional environments is in and of itself challenging, requiring capturing and nurturing teaching moments that occur both during planned web-based instructional events as well as through spontaneous learning experiences encountered in face-to-face interactions at community service sites. The construction of such instructional experiences is made particularly complex as they occur within virtual learning environments in which students and instructors never come into physical contact with one another. As with all virtual communication, nonverbal body language and unspoken cues are difficult to recognize.

Moreover, while reflective discussions assist in facilitating connectedness, supporting students with a wide range of competencies as they develop essential skills to generate and continue ongoing engagement requires ongoing attention. It is imperative that an instructor facilitating a virtual classroom understand students' developmental levels related to communication proficiency in a highly text-based learning environment, the use of specific technical tools, and the ability to integrate a variety of relationships into a multi-dimensional educational experience. Understanding topics of social responsibility and civic engagement are challenging in that these are complex and highly personal endeavors. Illustrating stories of social responsibility and actually experiencing civic engagement are both steps these courses take in

providing opportunities to understand the concept of being a socially responsible citizen; however, reflective discussions is often where students make meaning of these stories and experiences. Guiding students on these reflective journeys is challenging when interaction is not instantaneously.

The ongoing engagement, examination, analysis and review of students required to instruct courses that prioritize connectedness through reflective conversations is most effectively managed when class size is limited. However, within the context of increased course sizes, growing enrollments pose challenges to managing the relational dynamics inherent in the facilitation of intimate course discussions. While the authors have attempted different formats in creating such highly interactive discussions, it sometimes is at the sacrifice of connectedness of the entire course. For example, one online service-learning course had an enrollment of 34 students, in which online discussions were grouped into two sections of 17. Even with 17 students in each group, meaningful discussions are challenging to facilitate because of the large number of students. At times, students seem reluctant to become vulnerable by sharing emotional stories with such large groups. In addition, in the scenario previously described students realistically were only able to connect to part of the class instead of all participants.

Additionally, the continuous integration of evolving technologies into instruction while meeting curricular goals, monitoring student capabilities, and managing provider needs requires ongoing attention, often necessitating curricular modification as applications are developed and updated. For example, institutional upgrades to new versions of the learning management system are experienced by many students and faculty members as disruptive, distracting from their primary responsibilities of learning and teaching. Certainly, the continued integration of new media in curricula is a priority insofar it facilitates expanded access to the learning environment, enables multiple learning styles and processes, and allows multiple modes of creative expression and responsiveness. However, the integration of media in curricula must correlate directly to the median competencies of enrolled students in order to meet continuing learning goals and outcomes within confines of traditional academic terms. While virtual environments enable increased access to participation, such involvement is dependent upon first mastering secondary skills related to particular applications, hardware and infrastructures.

Finally, explorations of broader issues such as socio-economic advantage and privilege and their relationship to accessing information technology, developing skills in information literacy, and the role culture plays in individual participation and communication continue to be critical to ensure curricular goals and instructional methods, including the selection and utilization of technologies, are congruent with the larger academic field, pedagogical priorities and social realities. Consistent with tenets of experiential education (Brookfield & Preskill, 1999; Cranton, 2006; Merriam & Cafferella, 1999), students' are encouraged to integrate learning occurring in service placements with that obtained in the virtual academic environment as well as within the framework of their general daily existence. While this method promotes critical reflection and dialogue, it functionally requires students attend to restrictions and inequities related to technical access, equipment and applications, and training and technical assistance experienced by those with whom they worked in their communities. Consideration of these types of variables was critical, both for the instructor when planning instructional methodology as well as for students as they provided service to organizations and agencies. While the intellectual examination of such issues as applied in academic, placement, and personal contexts provide a potential for rich reflection, the realities of the disparate use of technologies and participation in associated infrastructures actually detracts students from their primary goal of learning.

The case study provided information on the specific curricular structure and pedagogy of two experientially-based service-learning courses offered online at the University of Illinois Springfield. Examples explored discussion-based pedagogy, instructional approaches characteristic of web-based learning, and challenges to creating and maintaining connectivity through a reflective framework. Variables such as the impact of increased participation of students throughout the world in community service, evolving technologies, ongoing dialogue among those teaching and learning hold exciting promise for the continued development and exploration of reflective pedagogies. It is hoped that ultimately the connectedness generated in courses such as have been discussed, with regard to engagement, community participation and media, can be instrumental in impacting social change that extends beyond geographic boundaries.

REFERENCES

Addams, J. (1910). *Twenty years at hull house*. New York: Signet Classics.

Anderson, B. (2004, June). Dimensions of learning and support in an online community [Electronic version]. *Open Learning, 19*(2), 183–190. doi:10.1080/0268051042000224770

Boud, D., Keogh, R., & Walker, D. (Eds.). (1985). *Reflection turning experience into learning*. London: Kogan Page.

Brookfield, S. D. (1987). *Developing critical thinkers: Challenging adults to explore alternative ways of thinking and acting*. San Francisco: Jossey-Bass Publishers.

Brookfield, S. D., & Preskill, S. (1999). *Discussion as a way of teaching*. San Francisco: Jossey-Bass Publishers.

Carnegie, A. (1889). *The gospel of wealth.* New York: DoubleDay.

Collison, G., Elbaum, B., Haavind, S., & Tinker, R. (2000). *Facilitating online learning: Effective strategies for moderators.* Madison: Atwood Publishers.

Cranton, P. (2006). *Understanding and promoting transformative learning.* San Francisco: John Wiley and Sons, Inc.

Daudelin, M. W. (1996). Learning from experience through reflection. *Organizational Dynamics, 24*(3), 36–48. doi:10.1016/S0090-2616(96)90004-2

Eyler, J., Giles, D. E., & Schmeide. (1996). *A practitioner's guide to reflection in service-learning: Student voices and reflections.* A Technical Assistance Project funded by the Corporation for National Service. Nashville, TN: Vanderbilt University.

Fredericksen, E., Pelz, W., Pickett, A., Shea, P., & Swan, K. (2001). Student satisfaction and perceived learning with online courses: Principles and examples from the SUNY Learning Network. *Journal of Asynchronous Learning Networks, 4*(2). Retrieved March 22, 2009, from http://www.aln.org/publications/jaln/v4n2/pdf/v4n2_fredericksen.pdf

Gilbert, N., & Driscoll, M. (2002). Collaborative knowledge building: A case study. *Educational Technology Research and Development, 50*(1), 59-71. Retrieved June 9, 2009 from http://education.korea.ac.kr/innwoo/edu603/computers_in_education/collaborative%20knowledge%20building.pdf

Guthrie, K. (2009). *Social change and leadership: An undergraduate course developed for the University of Illinois at Springfield.* Springfield, Ill.: University of Illinois at Springfield.

Hall, J. (2003, January). Assessing learning management systems. *Chief Learning Officer.* Retrieved March 15, 2009, from http://www.clomedia.com/features/2003/January/91/index.php?pt=a&aid=91&start=16797&page=6

Harasim, L., Hiltz, R. S., Teles, L., & Turoff, M. (1995). *Learning networks.* Cambridge: MIT Press.

Hoefling, T. (2003). *Working virtually: Managing people for successful virtual teams and organizations.* Sterling, VA: Stylus Publishing.

Houle, C. O. (1972). *The design of education.* San Francisco: Jossey-Bass Publishers.

Huang, H.-M. (2002). Towards constructivism for adult learners in online learning environments. *British Journal of Educational Technology, 33*(1), 27-37. Retrieved May 30, 2009 from http://www.speakeasydesigns.com/SDSU/student/SAGE/compsprep/Constructivism_for_Adults_Online.pdf

Jonassen, D., Davidson, M., Collins, M., Campbell, J., & Bannan Haag, B. (1995). Constructivism and computer-mediated communication in distance education. *American Journal of Distance Education.* Retrieved May 29, 2009 from http://www.c3l.uni-oldenburg.de/cde/media/readings/jonassen95.pdf

Knowles, M. S. (1984). *The adult student: A neglected species* (3rd ed.). Houston: Gulf Publishing Company.

McCarthy, M. D. (1996). *The 4MAT system: Teaching for learning with right/left mode techniques.* Barrington, IL: EXCEL Inc.

McCracken, H. (2005). *Virtual learning communities: Facilitating connected knowing. The Encyclopedia of Distance Learning* (2nd ed.). Hershey, PA: IGI Global.

Merriam, S., & Cafferella, R. (1999). *Learning through adulthood*. San Francisco: Jossey-Bass Publishers.

Meyers, S. (2008, Fall). Using transformative pedagogy when teaching online [Electronic version]. *College Teaching, 56*(4), 219–224. doi:10.3200/CTCH.56.4.219-224

Naylor, G. (1982). *The women of brewster place*. New York: Penguin.

Palloff, R., & Pratt, K. (2001). *Lessons from the virtual classroom*. San Francisco: Jossey-Bass Pfeiffer.

Palloff, R. M., & Pratt, K. (1999). *Building learning communities in cyberspace: Effective strategies for the online classroom*. San Francisco: Jossey-Bass Pfeiffer.

Rovai, A. (2002, April). Building a sense of community at a distance. *International Review of Research in Open and Distance Learning, 2*(1). Retrieved March 22, 2009, from http://www.irrodl.org/index.php/irrodl/article/viewArticle/79/152

Shea, P. (2006, February). A study of students' sense of learning community in online environments. *Journal of Asynchronous Learning Networks, 10*(1). Retrieved March 22, 2009, from http://www.sloan-c.org/publications/jaln/v10n1/v10n1_4shea_member.asp

Stanton, T. K., Giles, D. E., & Cruz, N. I. (1999). *Service-learning: A movement's pioneers reflect on its origins, practice, and future*. San Francisco: Jossey-Bass.

Strait, J., & Sauer, T. (2004). Constructing experiential learning for online courses: The birth of e-Service. *EDUCAUSE Quarterly, 27*(1). Retrieved May 30, 2009 from http://www.educause.edu/EDUCAUSE+Quarterly/EDUCAUSEQuarterlyMagazineVolum/ConstructingExperientialLearni/157274ConstructingExperiential Learning for Online Courses: The Birth of E-ServiceConstructing Experiential Learning for Online Courses: The Birth of E-Service

Taylor, K. (1995). Sitting beside herself: Self-Assessment and women's adult development. In *Learning Environments for Women's Adult Development* (pp. 21–28). San Francisco: Jossey-Bass Publishers.

Tough, A. (1967). *Learning without a teacher. Educational Research Series, 3*. Toronto: Ontario Institute for Studies in Education.

Ullman, C., & Rabinowitz, M. (2004, October). Course management systems and the reinvention of instruction. *T.H.E. Journal*. Retrieved March 15, 2009, from http://thejournal.com/articles/17014

Van de Pol, J. (2001, May/June). A look at course management systems. *IT Times*. Retrieved March 15, 2009 from http://ittimes.ucdavis.edu/june2001/cms.html

Walther, J., & Bunz, U. (2005, December). The rules of virtual groups: Trust, liking and performance in computer-mediated communication. *The Journal of Communication, 55*(4), 828–846. doi:10.1111/j.1460-2466.2005.tb03025.x

Waterman, A. S. (1997). *Service-learning: Applications from the research*. Mahwah, NJ: Lawrence Erlbaum Associates.

KEY TERMS AND DEFINITIONS

Cooperative Teaching: Encourages challenging questions and dialogues, facilitates critical thinking, promotes conflict resolution and negotiation, and advances consensus building fosters intellectual, as well as cognitive and affective growth.

E-Service: A media-based distributed approach to facilitating collaborative virtual partnerships between coordinating institutions, students, and their service-learning placements and associates.

Emotional Bandwidth: Development of trust among individuals in an online course.

Reflection: The process of making meaning from experiences through development of inferences and learning from past or current events which will serve as a guide for future behaviors.

Service-Learning: Service-learning is a method whereby students learn and develop through active participation in thoughtfully organized service that is conducted in and meets the needs of communities.

Social Responsibility: Sustained involvement in community life and acting for the common good.

Search Keywords: Service-Learning, Distance Learning, Reflection.

ADDENDUM #1

EXL 360- Social Change and Leadership

Course Syllabus

This course is designed to promote experiential learning for University of Illinois at Springfield students while advancing the institution's mission of providing a sound basis for informed and concerned citizens. This online course will look at the topics of leadership and social change. Recognizing that social change may be enacted through several means, such as action in the form of community service, advocacy, political work, and many others, it is important that individuals understand leadership is needed to enact change. Students enrolled in this course will be oriented to the concept of social change and leadership through participation in online discussions and a 60 hour semester-long service project. Students will plan and implement a project to meet a community need. Critical reflection on these experiences through online discussion and journaling will enhance the experiential learning.

Course Philosophy

Learning is an active process from the teacher's and from the learner's points of view. The instructor and student have a strong responsibility to one another. My obligation as the instructor include (a) being knowledgeable and current on the subject matter, (b) planning and providing quality learning experiences, (c) evaluating work fairly and promptly, and (d) assisting you to meet the course objectives and to fulfill personal goals. Student obligations include (a) preparing and completing assignments, (b) actively participating in the learning process, and (c) expressing needs to the instructor.

Course Objectives

Upon completion of this course, students should be able to:

- Enhance overall service-learning comprehension by participating in the reflective learning process.
- Recognize various historical models of leadership in social change.
- Develop core personal values and an ethical framework and apply them in action to civic engagement and leadership issues.
- Identify strategies for social influence/social change in others and self.
- Reflect on the relationship between the individual and society within contemporary American context.

Instructor

Kathy Guthrie, Ph.D.

Adjunct Instructor

kguthrie@uis.edu

Required Texts

Addams, J. (1910). Excerpts from *Twenty Years at Hull House*. (Provided Online)

Astin, H. & Astin, A.W. (2000). *Leadership Reconsidered: Engaging Higher Education in Social Change*. W.K. Kellogg Foundation. (Provided Online)

Carnegie, Andrew. (1889). Excerpts from *The Gospel of Wealth*. (Provided Online)

Naylor, Gloria. (1982). *The Women of Brewster Place*. New York: Penguin.

Wren, J.T. (1995). *The Leader's Companion: Insights on Leadership Through the Ages*. New York: The Free Press

Course Requirements and Grading

Students are required to work through online units, as well as complete 60 hours of community service while completing assignments. Students will (1) complete readings as assigned, (2) develop an action plan for their service work, (3) keep a journal of reflections on their readings and service work, (4) participate in online discussions, (5) write two reflective essays, (6) complete a service project they have created, and (7) write a final reflection paper at the end of the semester.

Course Requirements and Grading

The traditional scale of grading will be used.

A >92
A- 90-92
B+ 87-89
B 83-86
B- 80-82
C+ 77-79
C 73-76
C- 70-72
D 60-69
F <60

Service Action Plan- 10%

The action plan is due on XXX; however, if you would like feedback prior to turning in the action plan- e-mail me! The service action plan has two parts, an outline of the proposed service project and an outline of personal learning objectives. The outline of the proposed service project should include: 1) description of project and agency working with; 2) reason why this particular project and agency was selected; and 3) the agency coordinator (who was contacted) including telephone number and e-mail. The project needs to be with an established non-profit organization. The agency contact listed will be contacted by the instructor. The personal learning objectives and what the student hopes to gain from the service experiences should also be outlined; this is the second part of the service action plan. While there are learning objectives for the course, it is important to think about what you, as the student, would like to personally accomplish over this semester. 3-4 personal learning objectives should be focused on. Examples of these personal learning objectives may include: to become more aware of advocacy opportunities for animals at the local and state level or to improve communication skills of homeless individuals by developing an interactive training course for a local shelter. The length of the action plan should be 4-5 pages, double spaced. This assignment will be evaluated on ability to effectively communicate the project and learning objectives the student wishes to achieve, as well as the quality of writing.

Service Participation towards Social Change- 15%

A total of 60 hours are required of community service for the semester in relation to the project outlined. That works out to be just under 4 hours per week either in an action or advocacy capacity (for example, either working at a homeless shelter to collect books and hosting a reading club or advocating for teen mothers at a local government level for a specific organization). The student needs to start an e-mail conversation with the instructor to describe what project they will be working on by the second week of course. At midterm time, XXX, your service tracking sheet will need to be turned in. The final service tracking hours sheet and a 1-2 page self-evaluation of service participation is due to the instructor on the last day of summer semester, XXX. The instructor will work with the student and agency coordinator to assign the grade. This grade will be determined on the total number of hours served and interaction with agency contact and staff, as well as the progress of the proposed project.

Reading Responses/ Discussion Board- 15%

The readings are important to this course and fully understanding the complex nature of leadership and social change. Students are expected to critically digest the reading material and reflect on service experiences through online discussions. The instructor will pose specific questions about each unit and each student is expected to respond. Each student is expected to respond to each posed question at least once and respond to another student's posting at least once, each unit will have more than one posed question. The expectation is that this will be a discussion, not just posting your opinion and that is it. Discussion board for each unit will close down at 5:00 pm on the date it is to be completed. You will not be able to go back and answer after that time. This will be evaluated by the number of times responded, quality of responses in regards to thought process, posing thought provoking questions and effective communication of thoughts.

Reflection Journal- 15%

There will be a journal assignment aimed at exploring the sociological implications of issues arising with service experiences. The first 10 journal entries are due on XXX. The second 10 journal entries are due XXX. The student is expected to incorporate readings and service experiences in these reflection entries. Service experiences should contain "fact" and student's own review and critique of performance. A minimum of 20 entries are needed for this reflection journal that is equivalent to one entry every 3 hours of service. Length of each entry should be 1-2 page double space typewritten. Journal entries should outline what happened in 2-3 sentences and then what you learned through the experience should be focused on. Refer to the first unit reflection information for more detailed information on reflection. This assignment will be evaluated on fulfilling the number and length of entries required, as well as the ability to incorporate weekly readings with service experiences. For example, if only 90% of the 20 required entries (which is 18 entries) are completed as outlined (1-2 pages in length, discusses situations and your thoughts, etc), a grade of A- would be assigned for this portion of the course grade.

Addams and Carnegie Reflective Essay- 10%

This essay is due on XXX. This assignment will be a reflective essay on how Addams and Carnegie differed in purpose and methods of social change. To fulfill the requirements of this essay, you will need to answer these questions:

* How do Addams and Carnegie differ as social change agents?
* How do these two individuals help you understand how social change can happen in various forms and for various reasons?
* How do Addams and Carnegie relate to the social change you are making in your community service project?

This paper needs to be 3-4 pages, double spaced, 1 inch margins, 12 pt. font. This assignment will be evaluated on the ability to follow required format, answer questions, critically analyze the assigned reading material and to effectively communicate reflection and relation to own service experience.

The Women of Brewster Place Reflective Essay- 10%

This essay is due on XXX. This assignment will be a reflective essay describing how any two women from the book showed leadership and service to the community in any form. Please discuss how these two women you have chosen to focus on demonstrate leadership and how they create social change. Make sure that you discuss how this relates to your experience with your community service project. It needs to be 3-4 pages, double spaced, 1 inch margins, 12 pt. font. This assignment will be evaluated on the ability to follow required format, critically analyze the assigned reading material and to effectively communicate reflection and relation to own service experience.

Final Action Project Reflection Paper- 25%

The final paper will be a reflection of the student's service project. This final project is due on XXX. This paper needs to be 7-8 pages, double spaced.

In the final paper, students are responsible for answering:

* What was the project?
* How did you attempt to implement the project?
* What could have been done differently? What worked well? What did you learn from the experience?
* How does this experience connect with the readings done throughout the semester? Does it affirm, challenge, illustrate the concepts and theories presented? **The student needs to directly connect the readings that are relevant to the project and provide examples from the experiences at the site**

- How were your personal learning objectives accomplished?
- What is your personal definition of leadership?
- What is your personal definition of social change? Do you feel the service you provided some form of social change and why?

This assignment will be evaluated on the ability to critically reflect and analyze the coursework and service experiences and communicate these thoughts through the final paper.

Unit Topics

Unit 1: Course Introduction
Unit 2: Critical Thinking for Leadership in Democracy
    Wren Ch. 1: The Cry for Leadership
    Wren Ch 41: Leadership and Democracy
        Service Action Plan Due
Unit 3: The Power of One -Historical Models of Leadership
    Wren Ch. 21: Beyond the Charismatic Leader: Leadership and Organizational Change
    Wren Ch. 24: Leadership: Do Traits Matter?
    Wren Ch. 32: Situational Leadership
    Wren Ch. 36: The Historical & Contemporary Contexts of Leadership: A Conceptual Model
    Wren Ch. 43: Martin Luther King, Jr.- Charismatic Leadership in a Mass Struggle
Unit 4: Ethical Leadership
    Wren Ch 61: Moral Leadership
    Wren Ch. 64: Universal Human Values. Finding an Ethical Common Ground
        1st 10 Reflection Journal Entries Due
        Updated Tracking Hour Sheet Due
Unit 5: Methods of Social Change and Community Organizing
    Carnegie, Andrew. (1889). The Gospel of Wealth. Provided online
    Adams, Jane.(1910).Excerpts from Twenty Years at Hull House. Provided online
        Reflective Essay on Carnegie and Addams Due
Unit 6: Community/Political Leadership
    Astin & Astin, Social Change Model of Leadership Development (p. 29-74)
    Wren Ch 4: Servant Leadership
    Naylor: The Women of Brewster Place Reading Done
        Reflective Essay on The Women of Brewster Place Due
Unit 7: Understanding Yourself and Others for Social Change
    Wren Ch. 3: Defining a Citizen Leader
    Wren Ch. 29: Leaders and Followers are the People in this Relationship
First Day of Finals:
    Final Tracking Hours Sheet Due
    Self-Evaluation on Service Participation Due
    Final Action Project Reflection Paper Due
2nd 10 Reflection Journal Entries Due

Chapter 4
Classrooms Without Walls:
Teaching Together in Second Life

Lesley A. Withers
Central Michigan University, USA

Lynnette G. Leonard
University of Nebraska at Omaha, USA

John C. Sherblom
University of Maine, USA

EXECUTIVE SUMMARY

Second Life—an online, three-dimensional, virtual world—offers educators and students the opportunity to enter a virtual classroom, participate in synchronous online discussion and decision making, and engage in group projects with teams of students located in geographically distant universities. The free basic account and portability of the program provides a cost effective way to offer students an enriched educational experience. The visual three-dimensional nature of the space and the ability to engage in either texted or voiced synchronous communication add to the user's sense of social presence, giving educational experiences in Second Life a set of communication characteristics unique among computer-mediated communication contexts. The present case study examines the communication challenges and achievements of a collaborative classroom group project in which students from three different, geographically dispersed universities worked together and responded to each other's work to reach a group outcome. Technological and communication concerns are addressed and recommendations are made for motivating students in ways that prepare them to become involved with and focused on achieving the group project goals.

CASE BACKGROUND: THE COMPUTER-MEDIATED CLASSROOM

Imagine a classroom without walls—a classroom free from physical constraints and limitations. What kinds of learning opportunities would such a classroom offer? Johnston (1992) asked educators to imagine such a learning environment; one in which students participate both in- and outside of class, shy students feel comfortable and participate as much as others, discussions occur whenever most convenient and with people anywhere in the world, all from the comfort of a student's home. Although computer-mediated communication (CMC) was

DOI: 10.4018/978-1-61520-863-0.ch004

still in its infancy in 1992, Johnston predicted that online discussion would open a new world of educational opportunities for students.

Today, the future Johnston (1992) imagined has become a virtual reality, with evidence to support her prediction that online discussion and collaboration between geographically distant students offers advantages for student learning. Interacting via online chat with students who attend universities geographically distant from their own challenges students in ways not often available in the standard "real-life" classroom course provided by a single university. This interactive experience and the attendant communication challenges involved better prepare students for the organizational work life of the 21st century.

In general, the CMC literature indicates that CMC use can enhance class discussion and offer students a wealth of opportunities for learning and collaboration that would be difficult and costly to achieve in other ways. Online collaborative group participation stimulates student learning; increases student participation, cognitive effort, critical thinking, vigorous debate, positive team building, and dynamic group problem solving; and helps develop an awareness of a connection to a larger global community (Gaimster, 2007; Schrire, 2004, 2006; Urbanovich, 2009; Vess, 2005). Students feel better prepared and more willing to express their thoughts online, take responsibility for their participation in the classroom, and engage the course materials and educational learning process in deeper and more beneficial ways (Urbanovich, 2009; Vess, 2005; Wood & Fassett, 2003). Collaborative online discussion often increases the quality of student work and produces a "combined collaborative achievement [that] considerably surpasses the simple sum of individual contributions" (Kanev, Kimura, & Orr, 2009, p. 59).

Further, the educational literature provides evidence that online discussion, both asynchronous and synchronous, facilitates classroom learning despite its limitations. Synchronous CMC chat environments, similar to Second Life, have been shown to be useful for office hours, decision-making, brainstorming, and community building (Branon & Essex, 2001). Wood and Fassett (2003) argue that learning through a CMC context empowers students and imbues them with a renewed sense of responsibility for participation in the classroom in a way that creatively transcends traditional classroom power and social norms, affords students an opportunity to renegotiate their classroom social positions with one another and the perceived role of the teacher, and to reconsider the classroom and educational learning process. Vess (2005) reports that students in the CMC context exhibit greater interactivity and cognitive effort and are more inclined to continue a discussion thread, contribute more than is required to the discussion, pursue original sources for support of their positions, and engage in vigorous debate; while students in similar face-to-face discussions tend to respond to the instructor's questions, but not to each other. Schrire (2004, 2006) argues that the networked conferencing model provided by the CMC medium facilitates online collaborative learning in a way that de-emphasizes the instructor as an authority and increases student active participation in the learning process. Students engage in conversation and develop a collaborative process that plays an important part in individual student learning and facilitates higher levels of cognitive performance in such critical thinking skills as analysis, synthesis, evaluation, and integration of ideas and positions. Gaimster (2007) describes the influence of CMC for developing a positive team-building environment and an engagement that promotes dynamic interactive learning. Thus, CMC provides students with a way to work collaboratively to solve problems and reflect on the strengths and weaknesses of their solutions. Vess (2005) reports that students in an online course demonstrate collaborative learning and make contributions that are more cognitively elaborated than students in comparable face-to-face classroom situations. In addition, many students indicate that their online postings make them feel more comfortable in subsequent face-to-face classroom discussions. Students feel "better prepared and more familiar with the material, and since they have already publicly expressed their thoughts online and successfully defended" these thoughts, students are more willing to discuss them in the face-to-face classroom (Vess, 2005, p. 361).

Although online class discussion offers students exciting opportunities for collaboration and learning, introducing a new technology into the classroom can also pose challenges for instructors and students alike. Online collaborative group projects require more planning to effectively manage and organize the many complex components involved. Faculty members must try to anticipate and plan for the many potential issues that can arise in the course of classroom projects, sometimes only to discover that the significant challenges are those they did not foresee.

Challenges are posed by technology use, as well as by the management and organization of online collaborative group projects. Concerns with the use of technology include the need for increased technical skills and student training requirements, student apprehension about the use of technology, and the functional limitations of the technology itself. These limitations include getting students online, difficulty moderating large conversations, a lack of student reflection time, and the intimidation of the medium for poor typists (Hines & Pearl, 2004). Benoit, Benoit, Milyo, and Hansen (2006) report that student difficulty using the technology early in a course leads to a great deal of frustration and reduction in the overall satisfaction with the course. Students often experience anxiety about using computers for their coursework, and whether it is described as techno-stress, techno-anxiety, or techno-phobia, they often do not feel competent using new communication technologies that are unfamiliar to them (Scott & Timmerman, 2005). Their degree of writing apprehension can also make using text-based CMC technology difficult (Wrench & Punyanunt-Carter, 2007). Computer

anxiety and writing apprehension reduce their communication competence in a way that can lead to ineffective text-based computer-mediated collaboration. Group coherence and consensus in decision making can be reduced when speaker turn-taking and listening roles are ignored or when messages are addressed to the group and receive little response, as is sometimes the case in CMC discussions (Cornelius & Boos, 2003). In addition, CMC groups can become less task oriented, experience less cohesion and less group satisfaction, and make less concise and unambiguous decisions when these group processes break down (Cornelius & Boos, 2003). Explicit training in the use of the technology, communication expectations and processes, and group communication functions, can reduce computer anxiety, writing apprehension, and group communication difficulties, and create more conversational coherence and flow in the group process.

For educators, the aim is to design a course that uses technology to develop educational opportunities while balancing them against the challenges the technology poses for instructors and students. This issue is salient not only for educators, but for anyone who seeks to use the capabilities of CMC for training and development, work group collaboration, or other educational purposes with a global workforce or group whose members are geographically separated. Although our present focus is on computer-mediated communication among students from three geographically distant universities engaged in online group discussion and collaboration in Second Life, the opportunities and challenges we discuss are those faced by anyone using similar technologies for group task collaboration in the contexts of business, research, training and development, or other educational processes.

The present case study explores the opportunities and challenges posed by the creation, implementation, and evaluation of a collaborative online group project using Second Life technology. The issues and concerns raised in this chapter can help educators and others who plan to use online group task collaboration in projects that maximize the potential outcomes while minimizing the potential costs of such endeavors.

SETTING THE STAGE: EDUCATION IN SECOND LIFE

What is Second Life?

Linden Labs created Second Life (SL) as a three-dimensional online virtual world in which users create avatars (called "residents") to explore, interact with other residents, learn, recreate, and shop with the local currency called Linden Dollars (http://secondlife.com/whatis/). In March 2010, almost 1.5 million users had logged on within the last 60 days and it is common to find between 65,000 and 85,000 users from around the world simultaneously logged into Second Life.

Visually, Second Life appears similar to a massively multiplayer online role-playing game (MMORPG), with realistic appearing graphics that allow users to immerse themselves in the virtual environment. However, unlike MMORPGs, Second Life has no implicit conflict to resolve or end goal to attain (Appel, 2006). Instead, users interact with one another in virtual space with the interpersonal goals of meeting new people, socializing with friends, being entertained, and escaping from their realities, all in a customized virtual environment of their own choosing and making.

However, Second Life is a platform for more than just play. In the last few years, many colleges and universities from around the world have created virtual classrooms in which students and educators can meet, interact, and learn (Graves, 2008). As one of the few virtual worlds that offer a free basic account, these teaching and learning environments and opportunities in Second Life have gained many educators' attention. And currently, many institutions of higher education use

Second Life for some form of educational activity (http://edudirectory.secondlife.com/). Second Life's unique immersive online educational environment provides an example of how current Internet technologies have evolved into media that highlight interaction on more levels than textual. Second Life and other persistent virtual worlds provide unique opportunities for both students and professors to experience the education potential of virtual worlds for online discussion.

Online Discussion Options in Second Life

Users communicate in Second Life through synchronous text (similar to online chat or instant messaging) or through a voice-enabled online chat (similar to voice over Internet protocol [VoIP] services such as Skype™). However, unlike instant messaging and VoIP, Second Life adds a visual element of being able to see avatars in a three-dimensional environment during the discussion. "Through avatars, users embody themselves… making the virtual environment and the variety of phenomena it fosters real" (Taylor, 2002, pp. 40-41). These visual representations of bodies help users develop users' sense of social presence—to feel present to themselves and others as they interact online (Taylor, 2002). Second Life's synchronous online discussion options include local chat, group chat, and instant messaging, and asynchronous communication occurs through the use of presentation slides, notecards, and chat logging options.

Local chat, in both text and voice, is an open, public form of synchronous communication, and the conversational default of most Second Life users. Any resident within a specific range can read or hear the conversation. Much like a face-to-face conversation on the street or in a coffee shop, conversational sound comes across more clearly as one moves closer to the person communicating. A communicator can adjust the range for local text chat by shouting (widening the range) or whispering (narrowing the range). A second synchronous communication option is group chat, in which only members of a particular group can read or hear the group's conversation. Unlike local chat, members of the group can be anywhere in Second Life and still chat with each other. A third option for synchronous conversation is private instant messaging between two residents; in this form of Second Life communication, no other residents can read the conversation. With all three of the textual forms of synchronous communication, the text appears and scrolls upward on the screen or in a separate chat window.

Several types of asynchronous communication are useful to groups, as well. Slides can be uploaded as images; notecards and notices can be created within Second Life; and the text of local, individual, or group chats can be saved and reviewed later. Slides created outside of Second Life with programs such as Microsoft's PowerPoint can be uploaded as image files and presented on screens in Second Life. Anyone within viewing range can see the slides as they advance on the screen. A notecard, which is a small text file that allows for longer messages with some formatting options, can be created and given to an individual resident or sent to the group as a notice. Notices, short group messages that also allow for attaching a notecard or inventory item, stay on a group information window for 14 days and all group members can read them by checking the group's private notice board. Once the notecard is posted via notice, group members can access the information whenever they choose. These communication options allow groups to hold meetings, make decisions, and undertake other group activities. They also provide groups with the ability to create, record, reflect on, and archive information to be reviewed at a later time.

Individuals can save the text of local, individual, and group chats for future reference. These files can be saved directly to the hard drive of the computer used to log in to the program once the recording option is checked in the communication

tab of Second Life's preferences menu. Another option for recording text chat is to highlight the text and use the copy/paste feature to insert the text into a word processing document for future reference. This option allows for a record of the conversation to exist outside of the Second Life program and can provide group members with the opportunity to reflect on the group's conversations.

CASE DESCRIPTION: INTEGRATING COURSES IN SECOND LIFE

In the fall of 2007, two instructors at two geographically distant Midwestern U.S. universities began to plan how they could collaboratively teach a three to six week course segment in Second Life during the Spring 2008 semester[i]. Although each taught a different communication course – computer mediated communication and advanced interpersonal communication – the two courses overlapped in their CMC content. Despite the differences in time zones between the two locations, the courses were scheduled for the same days and times. The course syllabi and content were coordinated so that over a period of a few weeks, students from these two universities, separated by approximately a thousand miles, were trained to use the Second Life program and to complete a series of individual and dyadic tasks designed to reinforce the training lessons.

In the Fall 2008 semester, a third course located at a Northeastern U.S. university was added to this collaboration and the instructors of the three classes at three different, geographically distanced U.S. universities initiated a more involved collaborative class project. The two classes from the Midwestern universities (class sizes of 29 students and 14 students) completed the training together, meeting at the same time and communicating through Second Life. Students from each university were assigned to one of eight groups of five or six students apiece and asked to collaborate to develop a realistic proposal for helping a "real life" non-profit organization meet one of its goals through the use of Second Life. Students researched charitable organizations and together, selected one organization for the project and used Second Life for their group decision-making processes.

The 20 students enrolled in the third class held at the mid-sized Northeastern university met and trained separately. Then students from this class were assigned to feedback groups that met and interacted with the students from the other two universities in Second Life. The feedback groups researched the same non-profit organizations, developed a set of criteria for evaluating the effectiveness of the group proposals, and provided asynchronous, evaluative feedback to the groups on their proposals according to the criteria. Then, upon the completion of the project, the proposal groups and representatives from each of the feedback groups met in the Second Life classroom as a focus group to reflect on the Second Life communication process.

Managing this complex project in a collaborative online teaching and learning environment required the instructors to meet throughout each stage of the project: before the project began, during the group meeting process, and for the assessment of the outcomes after the submission of the group proposal. The instructors met weekly in Second Life to provide this project coordination.

The Online Collaborative Group Project

The group project required students working in virtual groups to meet and collaborate in Second Life. The groups were in charge of assigning group roles and tasks for each member. For every meeting, the groups were required to create agendas and keep record of the minutes. The goal for each group was to create a written proposal for assisting a non-profit organization through some use of Second Life. This proposal required them to research a non-profit organization; describe its

goals, multiple audiences, and needs; develop a plan to assist the organization; and develop a rationale explaining the ways in which this proposal meets the organization's objectives.

Prior to beginning the group collaboration, each student was assigned to a Second Life project group, and the instructors joined each group, as well. Second Life groups provide group member access to group instant messaging and notice capabilities. As a member of the group, the instructor could participate by asking questions, sharing information, and keeping track of the group progress. Students identified and researched three non-profit organizations before their first group meeting and brought relevant ideas and suggestions about different non-profit organizations to that meeting.

From their first group meeting to the project's completion, the collaborative project involved four main steps. First, groups met, volunteered for group roles, and selected and researched a non-profit organization. Students turned on chat logging options in Second Life and volunteered for group roles and responsibilities (that is, group liaison, record keeper). Second, groups planned the proposal centered on the non-profit organization and posted the group agenda, minutes, and chat logs to group notices so all members would have copies. Third, groups developed a proposal that included descriptions of a non-profit organization's goals, audience, and needs; the group's plan for assisting the non-profit organization; and a rationale explaining how this plan met the organization's need. Proposals included plans for developing public relations, fundraising, and organizational outreach, complete with realistic timelines, planned events, and budgets. Fourth, upon completing the proposal, students wrote individual analysis papers in which they described their experiences, reflected upon those experiences, conceptualized what was learned, and articulated how that was put into action in their group problem-solving, decision-making, and collaborating processes in Second Life.

TECHNOLOGY USE: OPPORTUNITIES AND CHALLENGES

The Second Life program provided opportunities for the groups to collaborate across geographical distance and facilitated the fulfillment of the course objectives. However, any new communication technology poses challenges that students and instructors must overcome. The opportunities and challenges posed by Second Life include the technological requirements for getting started; the complex, interactive user interface; and capabilities for online discussion.

Technological Requirements for Getting Started

An advantage of using the Second Life program is the cost; any adult can register for a free basic account (teens have access to a separate "teen grid"). To begin, users (residents) must register for a Second Life account at http://www.secondlife.com and select a starter avatar (the virtual representation of the user within the virtual world). In the registration process, users create a first name, then select from a predetermined list of possible last names. This process takes only a few minutes, depending on how long one contemplates the naming possibilities and the availability of one's preferred name. Once the account is registered, the user must officially activate the account by responding to an email message sent from Linden Labs to the email address provided during registration. Once fully registered, the options for modifying the starter avatar and creating objects are almost limitless.

There are a few technology concerns to address when getting started. First, there is a limit to how many accounts can be established at one time from a single ISP address, making it difficult to register an entire class at one time from one location. Second, once an account has been established, locating a computer on a college campus that can access the program can be a challenge. Many campus labs have strict security programs that do not allow students to download the program onto lab computers and campus wireless connections may not be adequate to support the use of the program. Third, although many computers run the program without problems, there can be some difficulty with some computer video or graphics cards and other component compatibility for running the Second Life program. Finally, required updates to the program sometimes force users to download the newest version of the program. This process can be time consuming if the campus requires IT professionals to supervise or conduct the download or its installation.

There are multiple ways in which one can use Second Life as an educational space. First, instructors can simply use the Second Life program to explore topics relevant to course objectives. With this approach, only minimal set-up time is required to identify Second Life locations to revisit as a class. Second, it may be possible to find educators willing to share their Second Life classrooms at little or no cost to other instructors. Joining a Second Life educators group or listserv is key to locating these opportunities. Third, instructors can purchase land for educational purposes. Purchasing land can be expensive and may require university approval (see http://secondlifegrid.net/gs/buy-land). However, many universities have already purchased land for their instructors' use. Fourth, instructors can rent land from Second Life or the New Media Consortium (NMC, http://www.nmc.org). NMC is an international non-profit organization whose hundreds of learning-focused institutions have committed to exploring new technologies for education, research, and creative endeavors. NMC leases space in Second Life to its educators and educational institutions for as little as $100.00 a year, depending on size (for actual prices, see http://virtualworlds.nmc.org/docs/services.pdf). Leased space comes with some basic support from NMC and access to a few common areas, including an amphitheater.

Those who lease or purchase land can sculpt their land to suit their needs and construct buildings on the land. NMC offers free or low-cost buildings and other classroom objects and additional educational items can be found at one of the "freebie" spots in Second Life. Instructors can also learn to create their own objects in Second Life from the many free tutorials available for online. In addition to the NMC, many other resources are available to help instructors use Second Life, including the Second Life Grid for Education (http://secondlifegrid.net/slfe/education-use-virtual-world), the Second Life Education Wiki (http://www.simteach.com/wiki/index.php?title=Second_Life_Education_Wiki), and the Second Life Educators listserv (https://lists.secondlife.com/cgi-bin/mailman/listinfo/educators). Depending on the interests and needs of the instructor, a functional Second Life classroom space can be borrowed immediately or created within a few hours. More elaborate classrooms and campuses can take more time to build.

Complex, Interactive User Interface

Second Life's user interface offers opportunities and challenges for online discussion. Instructors can use the Second Life interface to create a virtual classroom environment that is similar to physical space. In this instructional environment, instructors and students often rely on shared behavioral norms built up through years of classroom experience to organize the implicit meanings of classroom spatial configurations, the educational experience, and rules for when to speak, where to sit, and when it is appropriate to enter and leave the classroom space. The three-dimensional look of the virtual classroom space can invoke classroom norms, expectations about appropriate classroom behavior, interpersonal and group communication expectations, and the implicit meaning structures for an educational environment. In this way, Second Life provides

instructors and students with an environment that takes advantage of shared real-world social norms, manners, and conversational rules. Second Life also facilitates certain types of communication, such as the use of either voice or text messaging, synchronous and asynchronous interaction, and easily recorded conversational histories, that can enhance the learning experience, but that are not typically part of the traditional, "real-world," classroom contexts (Nesson & Nesson, 2008).

Once the user enters Second Life, there are many options for interacting with and creating the environment. The Second Life environment is filled with three-dimensional objects such as trees, buildings, vehicles, and toys. These objects have physical properties, meaning that the user must maneuver the avatar around the objects by walking, running, flying, opening doors, sitting in chairs, and using other furniture. The view of the user can be altered with camera controls and the movements of the avatar can be animated and posed. This level of interactivity with one's environment is often fascinating to new users, adding to the unique immersive possibilities of the program. For example, rather than lecturing about the history of ancient Rome, an instructor could recreate the locations and events of interest, allowing students to explore that environment and experience history in a way that would be impossible or impractical in the physical classroom or through other CMC technologies.

However, Second Life's numerous advantages must be weighed against the inevitable challenges that educators face when incorporating a complex new technology into the classroom experience. These challenges are not insurmountable, but can be daunting to educators and others who seek to use technology for group task collaboration. Second Life's user interface has a fairly steep learning curve; the program's interface is logical, but not necessarily intuitive. With its many choices and capabilities, users often need an hour or more of training before they become comfortable with the basics of Second Life's navigation, communication, and avatar customization options. In addition, the very level of user-environment interactivity that provides the amazing immersive capabilities of the Second Life program can also be distracting in the context of a virtual classroom. With the ability to click on so many other objects and avatars, there is much that can compete with the instructor for a student's attention. For example, if the screen on which the educators display their presentation slides is not locked, students can click through the slides at will, causing confusion. Although students are often excited about trying Second Life, they may approach the program more as a game than as an environment for learning. Instructions may be missed or ignored in favor of editing one's avatar appearance during class or experimenting with other Second Life features, such as flying, dancing, using gestures, or instant messaging the instructor. Without advance planning and preparation, an instructor may face a classroom in which student avatars flip through the instructor's presentation slides, fly through the classroom space, add and remove clothing and hair from their avatars, and simultaneously instant message the instructor with the expectation of a personal and immediate response. Thus, appropriate communication and behavior rules must be articulated and enforced to maintain a productive classroom environment.

Capabilities for Online Discussion

As previously mentioned, Second Life offers many options for online discussion, including synchronous text and voice communication in local chat, group chat, and private instant messaging. The online collaborative group project incorporated synchronous text communication and asynchronous communication. Each form of communication in Second Life is useful for online discussion, but each poses its own unique communication challenges for users, as well.

Synchronous Communication

For those located in close proximity within Second Life, local chat is fast, convenient, public, and less prone to lag (delays in displaying the typed text of the chat due to technical transmission problems) than are other forms of communication. Individuals, small groups, and large crowds can use local chat to communicate with one another. However, given that any resident nearby can read the conversation, local text chat is not always the best way to communicate sensitive personal or group information, and it does require the avatars to be together in the same virtual space.

The use of group chat frees users to communicate more privately and across virtual distances within Second Life. Group chats only allow members of the group to read or hear and respond to each other's messages. Group chat can be particularly useful for group meetings when members need to be in different parts of Second Life or when they want to maintain their privacy in a busy area. However, at busy times, group chat is more apt to suffer from lag than other forms of Second Life communication. The number of people in the group chat can increase lag, and each member of the group may not experience the same amount of lag at the same time. Hence, a lag in text chat requires members to pay careful attention to the flow of the group conversation. Lag is especially detrimental when messages are delayed for a long period of time or appear out of sequence. A lack of quick response by a lagged group member may be perceived as disinterest in the group conversation, and the lagged member may feel frustrated and ignored.

Private instant messaging is another private form of Second Life communication. It works well for dyadic conversational pairs and is less prone to lag than group chat. This method of communication can be very useful when groups break into smaller work units to complete smaller tasks. However, since Second Life instant messaging is limited to two users, it is not useful for communicating with the whole group; instead, it is sometimes used to share backchannel comments between two group members about the larger group discussion and, as such, may become distracting.

For all three of the textual forms of synchronous communication, residents can log or record the chat for future reference. It is also possible to review the history of the conversation during the chat. These features can be useful for brainstorming, decision-making, and problem solving processes. However, the scrolling messages require users to monitor the screen or chat window with some vigilance. Even a quick glance away from the screen can result in missing someone's message. This point is especially salient for group chat, when multiple users exchange messages rapidly. Although users can look at the chat history to find a missed message, they do so at the risk of missing new incoming messages while they search.

Asynchronous Communication

For asynchronous forms of communication in Second Life, presentation slides can be effective for posting information to be read by a large number of people, and unlike group chat, the information remains visible on the presentation slides indefinitely. However, lag can delay both the slides' resolution (clarity and readability) and the progression between slides.

Notecards can be created, easily shared between group members, and archived for later review. These simple text documents can contain a large amount of information. For these reasons, they are especially useful for recording group minutes and agenda. However, group members must remember that, if posted to the group's notice page, notecards expire after 14 days. Therefore, group members should take a copy of the group's notecards when posted via group notice and archive them in their own inventory for later reference. In addition, groups are limited to 200 notices per group each day, and may be constrained by that

limit if group notice is their primary form of Second Life communication. Finally, the formatting and editing options for notecards are limited.

Two Technological Concerns

Whether using synchronous or asynchronous forms of communication, there are two technological concerns that can disrupt any form of online discussion in Second Life. First, Linden Labs occasionally institutes rolling restarts of the program to fix errors or to update the system. A restart can disrupt a class if some of the students are in a different region of the program or if, as class members log on, they are "bumped" or relocated to different regions. Second, when lag disrupts the flow of the online discussion, the technology can slow or disrupt the online discussion. In the worst lag situations, the program can freeze, ending the discussion completely. Lag can affect voice chat, as well, through static interference, by clipping the voice feature, or causing the voice to cut in and out. Occasionally, lag can lead to the voice chat feature disengaging, which effectively silences a group member or requires the group to switch to text chat.

OUTCOMES AND REFLECTIONS

Upon completion of the project, students identified both opportunities and challenges in online discussion and group collaboration in Second Life. With the use of Second Life technology, and despite members' physical geographic separation, collaborative groups were successful in meeting; negotiating roles; creating and sharing group agenda, minutes, and proposals; critiquing the proposals; and providing feedback about the process and technology. The Second Life medium, however, requires actively engaged, motivated communicators who can multi-task, cope with having to type text messages instead of talk, and handle the frustrations associated with computer

Table 1. Summary of students' feedback about Second Life

Second Life (SL) Opportunities	Second Life (SL) Challenges
Students report that SL: • Is advantageous for online discussion compared to email or text messaging • Facilitates creativity and collaborative brainstorming with a task orientation • Helps users to stay on task • Allows users to remain professional in their interactions • Helps users to provide honest, less emotional criticism • Promotes enjoyment and excitement for learning • Allows for reflection on course concepts • Provides an experience they appreciate	Students report that, in SL, it is more difficult to: • Avoid being misunderstood • Make a point in group discussion • Avoid distractions • Work through disagreements to reach a group consensus • Avoid being perceived as harsh or critical • Develop the socio-emotional aspects of group discussion • Get to know other participants personally • Manage initial anxiety and concern for working with new technology

lag. In general, students indicated that they prefer face-to-face group interactions that provide more nonverbal cues for interpreting the other's meaning; however, they saw a great advantage to using Second Life for group collaboration over using email or text messaging systems. They reported that, in their Second Life group discussion, it is easier to be misunderstood and more difficult to make a point in group discussion, easier to get distracted by other aspects of Second Life, more difficult to work through disagreements and reach a group consensus, easier to provide honest less emotional criticism, more difficult to avoid being perceived as harsh, easier to be creative and engage in collaborative brainstorming with a task orientation, more difficult to develop the socio-emotional aspects of group talk, easier to stay on task and remain professional in their interactions, and more difficult to get to know the other participants personally.

In addition, some students seemed anxious at first about any project involving Second Life, especially those less comfortable with using new technology. Some expressed a concern that they would not be able to complete graded course assignments and a fear that they would "fail Second Life." Emphasizing participation in the group activity and their ability to reflect on the experience, rather than technological skills, as the basis for evaluation helped to alleviate their fears. By the end of the first Second Life project, students

reflected back on the project and indicated their enjoyment, learning, excitement, and appreciation for this experience.

The instructors met–weekly in Second Life and a few times face-to-face–to share their reflections on the current state of the project and to plan for the next step. They concluded that, although the challenges can be daunting, they do not outweigh the excitement and opportunity offered by integrating Second Life into the classroom. Through reframing and modifying aspects of the project, many of the challenges were overcome or better understood for what they really are: learning opportunities.

SOLUTIONS AND RECOMMENDATIONS

To adapt to the challenges posed by the technology, the instructors modified the Second Life course segment in several ways. They required students to register for Second Life in advance of the first integrated class meeting, send their avatar names to their instructor, and complete the Second Life Orientation Island training. This modification avoided the restrictions on the number of avatars that can be registered from one ISP address at a time. The change also meant that students did not spend class time registering their accounts and had at least initially experimented with moving their avatars in Second Life prior to the first integrated class meeting. Having the avatars' names in advance allowed the instructors to invite each avatar to a class group prior to the first integrated class meeting, as well. That way, when students logged into Second Life for class, they immediately received their invitation to join the class group. Upon accepting the invitation, a teleport request could be sent via group notice, bringing all students' avatars directly to the virtual classroom.

To address the technology concerns about program access in computer labs, required program upgrades, and the need for IT administrator access to install upgrades, students were shown how to download the Second Life program and install it not onto the lab computers, but onto a portable flash drive. Once installed, these flash drives could be used on any computer with Broadband or faster connections, allowing students to take their Second Life access with them wherever they went; save their settings, photos, and chat logs; and perform program upgrades when necessary.

After reflecting on the somewhat chaotic first integrated class session in Second Life, the instructors recognized the futility of attempting lecture or discussion before giving students the chance to experiment with the new, complex, and interactive user interface. Thinking back to their own first days with avatars, they remembered the excitement of interacting with the environment, feeling compelled to change one's "newbie" appearance, and being curious about Second Life's unique features, such as flying. Rather than trying to rein students in, the instructors chose to embrace the chaos and allowed students the chance to explore and experiment in a structured way. Instead of attempting lecture or discussion during the first integrated class session, students were introduced to Second Life with a "boot camp" training session. This training involved immediately teleporting them to a location with interactive screens instructing them about how to successfully navigate Second Life and experi-

ment with its features. In this training experience, students satisfied their curiosity about the new environment and compulsion to try new features as much as they liked, learning how to use Second Life at the same time. Students then received a homework assignment that required them to incorporate lessons learned from "boot camp," reinforcing the key skills they would need.

Some challenges remained; even after being forewarned to send their instructors instant messages only if necessary during the first integrated class session, many students could not resist the temptation to share their reactions to Second Life with their instructors in this way. Rather than being deterred, the instructors reframed these challenges as a part of the excitement of the new environment. By incorporating structured activities (e.g., individual trivia hunts, paired scavenger hunts) with students' natural curiosity about the Second Life environment, students became familiar with the technology relatively quickly, recognizing its strengths and limitations in the process. Although the first integrated class session was often a little chaotic, students typically settled into their tasks by the second class session in Second Life.

Groups were informed about lag and how to best avoid it. If an area in Second Life was particularly crowded and lag occurred, students were encouraged to find a less active area of Second Life in which to meet. If the lag persisted, the instructors suggested a switch from the more lag-prone group chat to the more reliable local chat, although doing so required all members of the group to be in the same area. These options significantly reduced the lag groups experienced. Using asynchronous methods as a backup, such as recording the chat to a log, helped to ensure that all members had a transcript of the conversation afterward.

As for the course management challenges posed by integrating students from geographically distant universities, there was considerable planning prior to the start of the class to maintain consistency across the courses and establish clear pedagogical objectives for the collaborative project. Even with the best planning and preparation, unexpected challenges sometimes occurred. The instructors' weekly meetings in Second Life—before, during, and after the group project—helped to coordinate the assignments, tasks, and responsibilities as well as address issues that arose from students' interactions and discussions.

Through a process of trial-and-error, the instructors found ways to adapt to the challenges posed by the technology. By modifying the project to better fit the technology, the instructors were able to reframe the challenges as learning moments rather than aggravations. The lessons learned would likely apply to any task-based online collaboration in virtual worlds.

Lessons Learned in the Virtual Classroom

- *Lesson One*: Be prepared for apprehension and exuberance. Second Life is a whole new world, especially for those who have little prior experience with online games or other Web 2.0 technologies. Prior to the first class session in Second Life, discuss expectations with students. Explain what they can expect to see, feel, and do (for example, Second Life can be a little overwhelming at first, and Second Life has adult content). Discuss strategies for avoiding a negative experience (for example, teach students how to report abuse, stay with the class, create a safe or default avatar appearance, and teleport back to the classroom if lost, stuck, offended, or overwhelmed). Discuss expectations of student behavior, as well (that is, remaining online and on-task for the entire class period, obeying the Second Life terms of service, setting classroom norms). For the first class session in Second Life, remain calm, and accept some level of chaos as a normal part of integrating new technology into

the class (Leonard, Withers, & Sherblom, 2009).

- *Lesson Two*: Explain the pedagogical reasons for using the technology. It is possible to be swept up in the hype and excitement surrounding programs such as Second Life. Without a clear pedagogical reason for its use, the project can be perceived as just another chance to play with new technology; novelty alone is not a reason to implement the technology. Bringing students into Second Life only to attempt to recreate a physical classroom, lecture-based class format means all of the work of integrating technology without the innovative benefits it can offer. Second Life is best used for virtual "hands-on" opportunities for unique experiences–such as collaboration with geographically distant others, exploring immersive simulations, and role-playing–that would not be possible or practical in the traditional physical classroom. In addition, keep in mind that students already apprehensive about using technology can become concerned about how they will be evaluated. Avoid these challenges by having sound reasons for implementing the technology, clearly explaining those reasons and how the use of this program fulfills the course objectives, and providing clear grading criteria for the activities and assignments related to the technology use (Leonard, Withers, & Sherblom, 2009).

- *Lesson Three*: Skip the lecture on the first day; go to an interactive "boot camp" for orientation. Despite the considerable hyping of the millennial generation's technological savvy, they cannot be dropped into the virtual world and told simply to "get to work." Outside of the fairly steep learning curve with the Second Life interface, most have not used this type of technology in an educational setting or for the completion of a structured, collaborative group project.

Students need instruction on the basics of using Second Life (e.g., basic movement, camera views, and communicating; Leonard, Withers, & Sherblom, 2009) and a chance to experiment before they will be ready to focus on work. The "boot camp" orientation embraces students' curiosity about the new, interactive environment while ensuring that they learn the skills they need to successfully use the technology. Then, by the time they are required to engage the group project, students are ready to focus their attention on the activity and capable of meeting the communication demands within Second Life's technological constraints.

Perspective for the Future

Not only is it important to prepare student expectations, train for the technology, and explain the pedagogical reasons for its use; ultimately, students often want to know how their lessons will translate to marketable career skills. It is not enough to explain the popularity of virtual worlds; we must look ahead to the future use of virtual worlds in professional and personal endeavors.

As major global businesses such as IBM adopt the use of virtual worlds for collaboration, the predictions that seemed distant and far-fetched when Johnston made them back in 1992 are becoming a virtual reality. We have entered the information age, and with it, face new opportunities and challenges. New technologies will continue to emerge. To be prepared for the future means not only developing a particular skill with current technology, but also a set of skills for approaching new technology. These skills involve being able to reframe the challenges of new technologies as learning opportunities and embrace them. Teaching students today how to communicate in professional ways through the use of technology, how to handle the uncertainty that accompanies the adoption of a new technology, and how to utilize its strengths while overcoming its limitations, prepares them to be lifelong learners, ready to face the new technologies of the future.

REFERENCES

Appel, J. (2006, November 10). 'Second Life' develops educational following. eSchool News. Retrieved March 28, 2009 from http://www.eschoolnews.com/news/top-news/index.cfm?i=42030&CFID=3738571&CFTOKEN=82301560.

Benoit, P. J., Benoit, W. L., Milyo, J., & Hansen, G. J. (2006). *The effects of traditional vs. web-assisted instruction on student learning and satisfaction*. Columbia, MO: The Graduate School, University of Missouri.

Branon, R. F., & Essex, C. (2001). Synchronous and asynchronous communication tools in distance education: A survey of instructors. *TechTrends, 45*, 36–42. doi:10.1007/BF02763377

Cornelius, C., & Boos, M. (2003). Enhancing mutual understanding in synchronous computer-mediated communication by training. *Communication Research, 30*, 47–177. doi:10.1177/0093650202250874

Gaimster, J. (2007). Reflections on Interactions in virtual worlds and their implication for learning art and design. Art. *Design & Communication in Higher Education, 6*(3), 187–199. doi:10.1386/adch.6.3.187_1

Hines, R. A., & Pearl, C. E. (2004). Increasing interaction in Web-based instruction: Using synchronous chats and asynchronous discussions. *Rural Special Education Quarterly, 23*, 33–36.

Johnston, V. L. (1992). *Towards a global classroom: Using computer-mediated communications at UAA*. Anchorage, AK: University of Alaska Anchorage Vocational Teacher Education Research Project. (ERIC Document Reproduction Service No. ED356759). Retrieved March 15, 2009, from FirstSearch ERIC database.

Kanev, K., Kimura, S., & Orr, T. (2009). A framework for collaborative learning in dynamic group environments. *International Journal of Distance Education Technologies, 7*(1), 58–77.

Leonard, L. G., Withers, L. A., & Sherblom, J. C. (2009). Three universities--one classroom: Collaborative teaching in Second Life. In N. Edick & G. J. de Vreede (Eds.), *Advances in collaboration science research: The Center for Collaboration Sciences third research seminar* (pp. 29–36). Omaha, NE: The Center for Collaboration Science, University of Nebraska at Omaha.

Nesson, R., & Nesson, C. (2008). The case for education in virtual worlds. *Space and Culture, 11*(3), 273–284. doi:10.1177/1206331208319149

Schrire, S. (2004). Interaction and cognition in asynchronous computer conferencing. *Instructional Science, 32*, 475–502. doi:10.1007/s11251-004-2518-7

Schrire, S. (2006). Knowledge building in asynchronous discussion groups: Going beyond quantitative analysis. *Computers & Education, 46*(1), 49–70. doi:10.1016/j.compedu.2005.04.006

Scott, C. R., & Timmerman, C. E. (2005). Relating computer, communication, and computer-mediated communication apprehensions to new communication technology use in the workplace. *Communication Research, 32*, 683–725. doi:10.1177/0093650205281054

Taylor, T. L. (2002). Living digitally: Embodiment in virtual worlds. In R. Schroeder (Ed.), *The social life of avatars: Presence and interaction in shared virtual environments* (pp. 40–62). London: Springer.

Urbanovich, J. (2009, February). *Online course advantages*. Paper presented at the Western States Communication Association Conference, Phoenix, AZ.

Vess, D. (2005). Asynchronous discussion and communication patterns in online and hybrid history courses. *Communication Education, 54*(4), 355–364. doi:10.1080/03634520500442210

Wood, A. F., & Fassett, D. L. (2003). Remote control: Identity, power, and technology in the communication classroom. *Communication Education, 52*(3/4), 286–296. doi:10.1080/0363452032000156253

Wrench, J. S., & Punyanunt-Carter, N. M. (2007). The relationship between computer-mediated-communication competence, apprehension, self-efficacy, perceived confidence, and social presence. *The Southern Communication Journal, 72*(4), 355–378.

ADDITIONAL READING

Antonijevic, S. (2008). From text to gesture online: A microethnographic analysis of nonverbal communication in the Second Life virtual environment. *Information Communication and Society, 11*(2), 221–238. doi:10.1080/13691180801937290

Bell, L., & Trueman, R. B. (2008). *Virtual worlds, real libraries: Librarians and educators in Second Life and other multi-user virtual environments*. Medford, NJ: Information Today.

De Lucia, A., Francese, R., Passero, I., & Tortora, G. (2009). Development and evaluation of a virtual campus on Second Life: The case of Second DMI. *Computers & Education, 52*, 220–233. doi:10.1016/j.compedu.2008.08.001

Gillen, J. (2009). Literacy practices in Schome Park: A virtual literacy ethnography. *Journal of Research in Reading, 32*(1), 57–74. doi:10.1111/j.1467-9817.2008.01381.x

Graves, L. (2008). A Second Life for Higher Ed: A virtual world offers new opportunities for teaching. *U.S. News & World Report, 144*(2), 49-50.

Harrison, R. (2009). Excavating Second Life: Cyber-archaeologies, heritage and virtual communities. *Journal of Material Culture, 14*(1), 75–106. doi:10.1177/1359183508100009

Hrastinski, S. (2008, December). What is online learner participation? *A literature review. Computers & Education, 51*(4), 1755–1765. doi:10.1016/j.compedu.2008.05.005

Kolb, D. A. (1984). *Experiential learning experience as a source of learning and development.* Upper Saddle River, NJ: Prentice Hall.

Leonard, L. G., Withers, L. A., & Sherblom, J. C. (2010). The paradox of computer-mediated communication and identity: Peril, promise and Second Life. In J. Park & E. Abels (Eds.), *Interpersonal relations and social patterns in communication technologies: Discourse norms, language structures and cultural variables.* Hershey, PA: IGI Global.

Manghani, S. (2007). MyResearch.com: Speculations on bridging research and teaching. *Art. Design & Communication in Higher Education, 6*(2), 85–98. doi:10.1386/adch.6.2.85_1

Shankland, S. (2006, December 12). IBM to give birth to 'Second Life' business group. *CNET News.* Retrieved January 15, 2009 from http://news.cnet.com/2100-1014_3-6143175.html.

Sherblom, J. C., Withers, L. A., & Leonard, L. G. (2009). Communication challenges and opportunities for educators using Second Life. In C. Wankel & J. Kingsley (Eds.), *Higher education in virtual worlds: Teaching and learning in Second Life* (pp. 29–46). Bingley, UK: Emerald.

Stewart, W. (2009). Settle down avatars; classes are under way. *Times Educational Supplement, 4822*, 8.

Thompson-Hayes, M., Gibson, D., Scott, A., & Webb, L. (2009). Professorial collaborations via CMC: Interactional dialectics. *Computers in Human Behavior, 25*(1), 208–216. doi:10.1016/j.chb.2008.09.003

KEY TERMS AND DEFINITIONS

Asynchronous Communication: A message exchange that does not require all of the communicators to be present at the same time and is not time synchronized (such as email, blogs, online discussion posts, text messages).

Avatar: An interactive, virtual representation of the user within a virtual world.

Computer-Mediated Communication (CMC): An exchange of messages through the use of multiple computers sharing a network.

Online Collaborative Group Project: A project in which a group of users work together in order to achieve the group's goal.

Online Discussion: Communication about a particular topic by multiple users facilitated by the use of networked computers.

Second Life (SL): An online, three-dimensional virtual world in which users create avatars and interact with each other.

Synchronous Communication: A message exchange that requires all communicators to be present at the same time and occurs in "real-time" (such as instant messages, online chats, telephone conversations).

Virtual World: An online environment in which users, represented on screen or through avatars, interact with other users.

ENDNOTES

i   This research was sponsored in part by a grant from the Center for Collaboration Science at the University of Nebraska at Omaha.

Chapter 5
Online Discussion in Engineering Education:
Student Responses and Learning Outcomes

Stuart Palmer
Deakin University, Australia

Dale Holt
Deakin University, Australia

EXECUTIVE SUMMARY

A ubiquitous and widely used feature of online learning environments is the asynchronous discussion board. This chapter presents a case study of the introduction and evaluation of student use of an online discussion in an engineering management study unit. We introduced an assessable assignment task based on student use of an online discussion, in response to falling student unit evaluation results after we initially moved the unit to wholly online delivery mode. Both quantitative and qualitative unit evaluation data suggest that students perceive value in the online discussion activities. A regression analysis based on discussion usage data suggests that students derived significant learning outcome benefit toward their final unit grade from making reflective postings in the online discussion.

BACKGROUND

Dialogue is considered to be an essential element of human learning, particularly for distance education (Gorsky & Caspi, 2005). It includes interactions between students and teachers, exchanges between students, interactions between students and others not directly involved in their learning processes and dialogue with oneself in the form of reflective thought (Webb, Jones, Barker, & van Schaik, 2004). With the advent of online technologies in teaching and learning, particularly in distance education, the use of online discussion forums is now a widespread medium for learning dialogue. Online discussion can be synchronous through the use of real-time chat tools, but many examples of online discussions documented in the literature present the use of asynchronous discussion. That is, where students post new and follow-up messages to an electronic bulletin-board at the times that suit them, and not necessarily at the same time that other

DOI: 10.4018/978-1-61520-863-0.ch005

students are accessing the discussion system. The claimed benefits of online asynchronous discussion forums include:

- The time between postings for reflective thought that might lead to more considered responses than those possible in face-to-face situations (Garrison, Anderson, & Archer, 1999);
- For off-campus students, two-way communication can be enhanced, reducing student isolation and making possible dialogue with other students (Kirkwood & Price, 2005);
- The convenience of choice of place and time to learners (Cotton & Yorke, 2006);
- The creation of a sense of community (Davies & Graff, 2005);
- The development of skills for working in virtual teams (Conaway, Easton, & Schmidt, 2005);
- Increased student completion rates from increased peer interaction and support (Wozniak, 2005); and
- Increased student control, ability for students to express their own ideas without interruption, the possibility to learn from the collectively created content, the creation of a permanent record of one's thoughts, the creation of a reusable instructional tool that models expected answers and discussion use, and they create a valuable archive of material for investigation and research (Hara, Bonk, & Angeli, 2000).

Although there is wide agreement that participation in online asynchronous discussions can enhance student learning, and significant work has been done characterizing, and theorizing on the nature of student communications in online discussions, it has also been identified that there is a need to investigate the impact on student course performance of participation in online discussions (Hara et al., 2000). Stacey & Rice (2002) conducted a combined quantitative and qualitative analysis of the online discussion postings of education students studying by distance education in Australia. It was found that those students achieving the highest final unit grade also had the highest frequency of posting, and that lower achieving students were less active online. Although, the authors do not claim these findings as conclusive evidence of the effect of online participation on learning outcomes (as measured by marked assessment activities) (Stacey & Rice, 2002). In a quantitative analysis of two online discussions in the UK involving 543 computing students, it was found that both the number of student accesses of the system and the number of student postings to the system were significant predictors of variance in final mark (in one case) and variance in final grade (in the other) (Webb et al., 2004). Davies & Graff (2005) conducted a quantitative analysis of online discussion usage involving 122 UK business students based on what percentage of all online system accesses related to usage of the online communication system. It was found that students achieving high or medium passing grades were significantly more active in the discussion area than students achieving a low passing grade, and in turn, students achieving a low passing grade were significantly more active than students who failed (Davies & Graff, 2005).

It is noted that although the literature suggests a correlation between increased interaction and increased learning, there is limited research to understand the impact of different types of postings on learning outcomes (as measured by unit final grade) (Conaway et al., 2005). Simply encouraging students to get more involved in online discussions may not necessarily lead to better learning outcomes – there is a need to understand what are the 'salient factors' in online interaction that might enhance learning (Davies & Graff, 2005). One debated factor is whether student participation in online discussions should be optional or mandatory. It has been noted that some learning theories suggest that user motives largely determine how students engage with learning activities; intrinsically motivated learners will invest high levels of cognitive effort regardless of any associated rewards, whereas extrinsically motivated learners may be enticed to participate by gaining unit marks, but their engagement may be instrumental and shallow (Kuk, 2003). Although there is evidence that online discussion interaction carried out on a voluntary basis may lead to better learning outcomes (as measured by unit final grade) (Weisskirch & Milburn, 2003), a pragmatic approach suggests that discussion contribution is likely to be low unless there is some compulsion to participate (Graham & Scarborough, 2001). Students have many competing demands on their time, and if their use of online learning tools is optional, the perceived benefits of participation will need to outweigh the perceived efforts of using the system. In this case, for some students, there may be benefits in providing extrinsic motivators for students to learn and use the system (Garland & Noyes, 2004).

Another form of optional engagement with online discussion forums is 'lurking', where students enrolled in a discussion do not make postings, rather they simply read the postings of others. Online system may not detect these lurkers, and the question remains, are these lurkers learning or not? (Hara et al., 2000) There is some evidence that both active participation (posting) and passive participation (lurking) may be beneficial to online discussion users (Webb et al., 2004). A final, but important question about student learning and participation in online discussions relates to the often observed correlation between student participation (number of postings, assessed quality of posting, etc.) and learning outcomes (student final unit mark/grade, etc.). It is often presumed that this relationship is causative, and not simply the result of more able and/or motivated students engaging more deeply with the online discussion than less able students (Cotton & Yorke, 2006). Is it possible that the students with the best results in

a unit would have done well in the unit, regardless of whether we employ an online discussion or not?

SETTING THE STAGE

The location of the case study presented here is an Australian university that is a major provider of distance and online education. In addition, it teaches on-campus at multiple campuses located in different cities in the State of Victoria. Initially, the University saw itself as a major distance education provider, with some degree of separation between its teaching methods and materials used for on-campus teaching as opposed to off-campus teaching. The use of distance education methodologies and materials for both student cohorts gathered momentum in the early to mid-1990s under the strategic umbrella of flexible teaching and learning, and with a growing 'technological imperative' (Holt & Thompson, 1995) for the use of online systems for learning delivery and communication. In more recent times the University implemented institution-wide online teaching and learning systems to provide opportunities to bring together all students in the one learning community. Such inclusively designed online learning environments attempt to provide all students, irrespective of their official mode of enrolment and location, with equal access to learning resources and channels of communication with their teachers, fellow students, and academic and administrative support services. Pragmatically, many universities now confront the need to provide more flexible, time- and/or place- independent study pathways in the face of growing trends towards increasing part-time employment and student mobility. It would seem that even traditional, school-leaver campus-based student cohorts are taking on the characteristics of their mature-aged, in-employment, off-campus counterparts. This is happening to such an extent that we might argue that many students now seem to be having the distance-type learning experience to one degree or another.

Online learning environments (OLEs) have been a feature of educational landscape at the University since the early 1990s. Starting first with a range of different systems used in different academic departments of the university, and primarily used for particular courses, units of study or functions, the university gradually moved toward centralization through the implementation of a corporately supported learning management system (LMS). Iterating through a number of commercial LMSs, the university eventually settled on the WebCT LMS in 2003. The new LMS was trialed in 2003, and fully implemented in 2004. Concurrently, the university introduced policies requiring academic departments to migrate all OLE activity to the centrally supported LMS. University policy identified three classifications of online units: Basic Online (administrative support for unit); Extended Online (at least one component of teaching in the unit occurs online); and, Wholly Online (all of the teaching of a unit occurs online), with these categories being analogous to those employed more widely in the sector (Browne, Jenkins, & Walker, 2006). The original definition for being 'wholly online' was:

- All content online (either commercial print-based textbooks or commercial e-texts could be used as supplementary material);
- All communication and interaction with students online;
- Assignment submission and feedback online (with examinations moving online when the University was administratively ready); and
- Each unit having at least one session of interactive communication (synchronous, asynchronous, or both) between teacher and students online at least weekly or as established at the beginning of the course.

Such interactive sessions were to have an assessable component where appropriate. From 2004, all students enrolled in undergraduate courses at the University had to undertake at least one unit wholly online, with few exemptions given. Institutional-level research into student use and perceptions of elements of the OLE at the University revealed that, after accessing unit learning materials and administrative information, the next highest OLE element usage is use of the online discussion function (Palmer & Holt, in print), highlighting the importance of online discussions generally at the University.

CASE DESCRIPTION

Technology Use

The School of Engineering at the University has had an eventful history. Inherited from an antecedent Institute of Technology, it was closed in the 1980s and then reborn in the 1990s. Its rebirth saw a School committed to a different type of curriculum and to flexible delivery for its on- and off-campus and offshore students (Holt & Thompson, 1995). At the time of the case study presented here, the School offered a four year Bachelor of Engineering (BE) and three year Bachelor of Technology (BTech) at undergraduate level. The delivery modes of these programs include on-campus, off-campus and off-shore. These programs include the second-year, second-semester engineering management / professional practice study unit SEB221 Managing Industrial Organizations. This unit consists of four modules:

1. Systems Concepts for Engineers and Technologists;
2. Managing People in Organizations;
3. Manufacturing and the Environment; and
4. Occupational Health and Safety.

Managing Industrial Organizations is a good example of the variety of students within the School. All students study this unit, unless granted exemption due to prior studies or if the student is able to prove they already have the required unit outcome competencies due to work experiences. In 2004, the last time face-to-face teaching occurred, there were 175 students enrolled in this unit. There were 74 on-campus students (a mix of full-time and part-time students), 46 off-campus students (some full time but mostly part-time students), 50 full-time students studying at a tertiary institution in Malaysia that is a partner of the School, and 5 part-time students in Singapore who receive some local support. Of the 46 off-campus students, most were working full time, usually in an engineering-related occupation, and might live interstate or overseas. The age range in 2004 for students in this unit was 19 years to approximately 50 years (the part-time off-campus option is very appealing to mature age students). The average age was in the mid 20s. Prior to 2005, on-campus students had access to weekly classroom lectures, and off-campus were provided with printed study guides, with on-campus students generally purchasing the printed study guides as well. All students had access to an online area providing basic resources, including an optional asynchronous discussion forum and the capacity for academic staff to post 'announcements' to all class members. The unit assessment regime consisted of two assignments each worth 25 percent of the unit marks and an end-of-semester examination worth 50 percent of the unit marks.

In 2005, this unit was converted to 'wholly online' delivery mode, where all teaching of the unit occurred online (Holt & Challis, 2007). A CD-ROM version of the study materials replaced the printed study guides, enhanced with interactive/animated diagrams and video material. Up to this time, the first author had academic responsibility for the Managing People in Organizations module, and was not responsible for unit overall. We made no change to the assessment regime for the initial wholly online delivery.

At the end of 2005, due to staffing changes, the first author assumed full responsibility for the entirety of SEB221, and a review of the wholly online delivery strategy for the unit was undertaken. The University's policy and procedure for 'Online Technologies in Courses and Units' requires that wholly online units be, "… designed to help students to develop their skills in communicating and collaborating in an online environment…" (Holt & Challis, 2007). Although the inclusion of an optional general online discussion area may have met the 'letter of the law' for the wholly online unit policy, we considered it inadequate as a means for genuinely developing student online communication and collaboration skills. For 2006, we took 10% of the unit marks from the final examination and dedicated these to a formally assessed assignment activity based around the online discussion area. We retained all other unit assessment items. The following is a summary of the assignment instructions given to students.

This assignment requires you to both reflect on your studies and to constructively engage with the wholly online environment used in this unit. You are required to post reflections on the course material and to comment on the postings made by other students during the semester. You have two types of task in this assignment.

Task 1: *Reflect on the course material you have studied in the current week. Identify what you think is the most important topic, access the online system for this unit, open the Assignment 1 forum area for the appropriate week, select 'Compose Message' and post a few paragraphs on your selected topic that explain why you think it is important.*

Task 2: *Review some of the Assignment 1 posts made by other students and select one to comment on. With that message open select 'Reply' and post a follow-up to the original message. You may add* *your own additional thoughts/reasons for why that topic is important, you may wish to contribute an example related to that topic from your own experience, or something else.*

You need to make at least five postings for each type of task given above, i.e., at least ten postings in total, five of type one and five of type two. You should make only one of each type of posting in a given week. Only the best posting for either task type in a given week will be marked. If your postings demonstrate constructive and thoughtful reflection, you will be awarded up to 1 mark per posting, up to a maximum of 10 marks in total for the assignment. You can make more than five postings for each type of task to maximize your mark for Assignment 1. Please use your own thought/ words, do not simply reproduce the course notes. Please note that the forum areas will not remain open for posting all semester, i.e., it will not be possible to complete all your postings late in the semester.

In summary, students are asked to make at least five 'new' postings reflecting on the course material, with up to one mark awarded for each of the five 'best' new posts, and, to make at least five 'follow-up' postings reflecting on the prior posts of their peers, with up to one mark awarded for each of the five 'best' follow-ups. Student participation in the online discussion is 'mandatory' in the sense that marks are assigned to participation. As noted previously, the literature suggests that some form of extrinsic motivation is required to ensure a high level of student discussion participation. A weighting of 10% was chosen for discussion participation – this figure is noted in case studies elsewhere in the literature (Graham & Scarborough, 2001; Hara et al., 2000). It was felt that this weighting would provide incentive for most students to participate, while at the same time not compromising the unit assessment regime should there be unforeseen implementation issues with this initial trial of the asynchronous discussion

assignment. Strategies to promote a high level of participation in online discussions include requiring a specific number of postings per assignment and/or per week (Conaway et al., 2005). In this case, we combine both these strategies. It has been found that a key element in the effective use of computer conferencing is 'intentional design' of the online environment (Harasim, 1991). Intentional design includes designating conferences (online discussion areas) according to the nature of the task (formal or informal), the duration of the task (one week, whole semester, etc.), size of the group (plenary, small group, etc.), etc. We created separate weekly discussion spaces to structure the formal student assignment postings. This permits us to progressively reveal newer discussion areas, and to progressively set older areas as read-only as the semester progresses. We maintained a separate informal area for general unit discussion and questions. As noted, the assignment-related discussion areas did not remain open all semester, to encourage students to engage with the unit material in a timely manner across the semester. Due to the nature of the assignment task, all of the discussion areas are open to all students – there is no separate small-group discussions employed.

Evidence of Student Perceptions of the Online Discussion from Evaluation Data

For many years, the University has conducted a student evaluation of teaching and units (SETU) survey at the completion of every offering of every unit. Although the question items included in the survey instrument have varied over time, there is a set of questions common to all survey instruments, creating a longitudinal student evaluation data set. An 18 item survey was used prior to semester 2 2006. In 2006, the survey was simplified to include a 'core' of nine questions, which could be supplemented with optional questions relating to particular unit-related aspects, such as tutorials, laboratory work, workshops, etc. The student evaluation of teaching and units survey asks students to indicate their level of agreement with the question items on a six-point scale with the labels and corresponding numerical values of 1/strongly disagree, 2/disagree, 3/neutral, 4/ agree and 5/strongly agree. A 'NA' (not applicable) point is also included to allow students to validly respond to an item that does not apply to them in the unit under evaluation. Based on the mean student responses for the 18 survey items for SEB221 over the period 2003-2005, the question items below had a markedly different result in 2005 following the offering of SEB221 in wholly online mode for the first time:

1. The teaching staff of this unit stimulated my interest in further learning.
2. The teaching staff of this unit motivated me to do my best work.
5. This unit was well taught.
6. I had a clear idea of what was expected of me in this unit.
17. I would recommend this unit to other students.

18. The use of on-line technologies in this unit enhanced my learning experience.

The numbers indicated refer to the question item numbers in the pre-semester 2, 2006 survey instrument. Of the question items selected, only questions 5, 17 and 18 have identical or very similar questions included in the semester 2, 2006 and current survey instrument. The survey results provide one quantitative source of data on which to evaluate the student response to SEB221 moving to wholly online mode.

Figure 1 shows the mean student responses to the six survey question items identified previously, for SEB221 for the period 2003-2005 and, where possible, for 2006. The number of respondents and response rate for the student evaluation of teaching and units survey are also given. For 2006, the first author, as unit chair, had access to the complete survey data set, and included 90 percent confidence intervals for the 2006 survey data, based on the t distribution.

When converted to wholly online mode in 2005, except for question item 18, all other reported survey items for SEB221 suffered a significant

Figure 1. Mean student responses for a sub-set of student evaluation of teaching and units (SETU) question items for SEB221 for 2003-2006

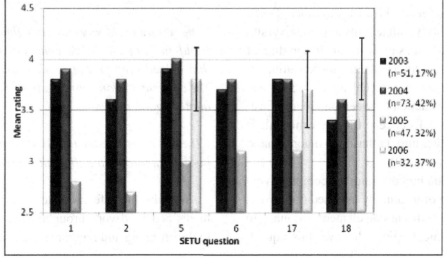

decline in mean student rating. Items 1 and 2 relate to staff/student interaction, and might reasonably suffer in a mode of delivery that eliminates all face-to-face contact. However, prior to 2005 there were many off-campus students enrolled in SEB221, and the average difference in rating between on- and off-campus students for question items 1 and 2 was about 0.3 less for off-campus students compared to on-campus students – there appears to be something more than just lack of contact with academic staff at play here.

Even though the assessment regime remained unchanged in 2005 when the unit moved to wholly online mode, the 2005 survey results for question item 6 suggest that students were less clear about what was required of them. The survey items considered overall measures of student satisfaction with the unit, question items 5 and 17, both dropped significantly with the move to wholly online delivery. Finally, question item 18, asking students about the learning value of online technologies used in the unit, remained about the same in 2005, even though significant effort and resources were invested in the re-development of the unit materials for delivery in the wholly online mode. On the face of it, given that the unit material and assessment remained ostensibly the same over 2003-2005, the principal factor associated with the decline in mean student survey ratings appears to be the change to wholly online mode of delivery. Experience with a large number of such mandatory wholly online units at the University would suggest that a significant decline in student evaluation of teaching and units survey ratings is a common experience. A (negative) discrepancy in student satisfaction between online and face-to-face modes of delivery for the same unit is noted in the literature (Johnson, Aragon, Shaik, & Palma-Rivas, 2000).

For the 2006 unit offering, the comparatively minor change of a formally assessed (i.e. marks attached) online discussion element was made to the unit assessment regime. However, this require-

ment for regular active and reflective engagement with the unit material, with the associated online environment and with other students appears to have had a beneficial impact on student evaluation of the unit (Richardson & Swan, 2003). It is known that students respond strategically to assessment tasks – they are more likely to complete activities that are directly associated with assessment (James, McInnis, & Devlin, 2002). Based on the survey questions items common to the pre- and post-2006 period, the overall student satisfaction with the unit, as measured by the mean survey rating for question items 5 and 17, returned to approximately the same levels as prior to the introduction of wholly online delivery. Further, the response to survey question item 18 increased significantly, indicating that students evaluated the re-jigged online environment as positively contributing to their learning experience in the unit.

In addition to the numerical scale items included in the student evaluation of teaching and units survey, students are also invited to contribute open-ended comments under the headings of 'What were the best aspects of your unit?' and 'What aspects of your unit were most in need of improvement?' In 2006, although no comments relating to the online discussion elements of the unit were noted under the 'needs improvement' heading, the following two contributions were recorded under the 'best aspects' heading:

"The ability to do work in your time when you could fit it in and have constant assignments that helped keep you up to date and informed. The communication between students online was another good aspect."

"The fact that the exam is only 40% which means hard work throughout the unit is rewarded."

We take the references to 'constant assignments' and 'hard work throughout the unit' to relate to the on-going and regular requirement to make postings to the online discussion. Additionally, the aspect of 'communication between students' is explicitly identified as valuable.

Evidence of Contribution of Online Discussion to Student Learning Outcomes

Student participation in online discussions can be analyzed in quantitative terms (number of postings, length of postings, number of messages read, etc.), qualitative terms (does the posting exhibit cognitive/social/teaching presence?, does the posting exhibit knowledge/comprehension/application/ analysis?, is the posting on task/off task?, etc.) or some combination of quantitative and qualitative. Quantitative analysis can be performed quickly using system data, but may not yield a complete picture of student engagement in the discussion (Hara et al., 2000). However, qualitative analysis requires the examination of every student posting to classify the content, consuming significant time and is subject to variation in message content classification by different assessors (Cotton & Yorke, 2006).

At the commencement of the semester, we made an initial model posting of the type expected, to seed the discussion and provide an exemplar to students. During the semester, we assessed student postings on an on-going basis according to the published criteria. Both in initial and follow-up postings, we asked students to discuss unit content, hence assessment of the postings is primarily on the basis of the quality/evidence of cognitive presence.

Following the completion of the semester, the following sources provided data on the student demographics and usage of the online discussion area:

- Student age (whole years at the end of semester);
- Student gender (male or female);

- Student normal mode of study (on-campus or off-campus);
- Student course of study (BTech, BE or other);
- Student prior general academic performance (measured at the University by the Weighted Average Mark);
- The total number of discussion messages read (or at least opened) by the student;
- The total number of new/initial discussion postings made by the student;
- The total number of follow-up/reply discussion postings made by the student; and
- The final unit mark obtained by the student for SEB221.

Analysis of the collected data permitted the compilation of the following information:

- Descriptive statistics on the use of the discussion areas;
- Visualization of the patterns of usage of the discussion areas;
- Investigation of correlation (Pearson's linear correlation coefficient) between data variable pairs; and
- Multivariate linear regression to find the significant independent variables contributing to the dependent variable 'final unit mark'.

The number of students completing the unit (still officially enrolled at the end of the semester) was 86. The total number of assessable messages posted was 645. The average number of words per posting was 290. Figure 2 shows the distribution of assessable student postings across the semester.

There is a general downward trend in discussion posting until week 8, after which the number of remaining weeks in the semester equals the number of posts required from a student to maximize their possible mark. After week 8 the general trend picks up again slightly, perhaps indicating a belated ef-

Figure 2. Distribution of assessable student postings across the semester

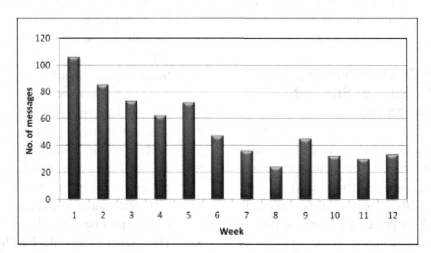

Figure 3. Ranked distribution of total new/initial postings made by students

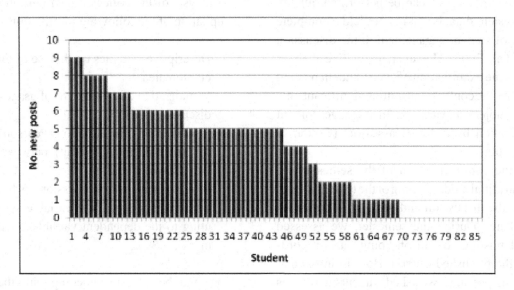

fort by those students who hadn't actively engaged with the discussion assignment task previously. Figure 3 shows the ranked distribution of total new/initial postings made by students.

The mean number of new postings is 3.8, with a standard deviation of 2.8. The median and modal number is 5, and the range is 0 to 9. Figure 4 shows the ranked distribution of total follow-up/reply postings made by students.

The mean number of follow-up postings is 3.7, with a standard deviation of 5.4. The median

number is 3.5, the modal number is 0, and the range is 0 to 47. It is well known that students take a strategic approach to study, and the learning activities they engage most fully with are those most clearly associated with what will be assessed (James et al., 2002). Even though marks were attached to students' contribution to the online discussion as an overt indicator that participation was considered important, and disregarding students with a final mark of zero for the unit, 16.7% of students made no new/initial postings

Figure 4. Ranked distribution of total follow-up/reply postings made by students

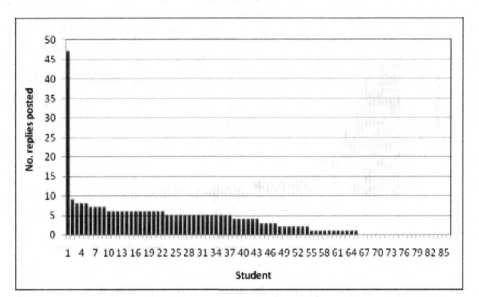

and 11.9% of students made no follow-up/reply postings. A similar rate of students forgoing assessment worth 10% based on participation in an online asynchronous discussion task is noted in the literature (Graham & Scarborough, 2001). Figures 3 and 4 suggest that even those students who did engage with the assignment task only tended to do the minimum required (one new post and one reply post per week, up to a maximum of ten combined) to qualify for the assignment marks on offer. This type of minimum student engagement in an assessable online discussion activity is reported elsewhere (Hara et al., 2000), and reinforces the idea that students are busy, and extrinsic motivation is likely to be necessary to encourage even a basic level of participation in online discussion activities. Figure 5 shows the ranked distribution of total number of messages read by students – technically, the LMS records the number of messages 'opened' by students, but this was taken as a proxy measure of number of messages 'read' by students.

The mean number of messages read is 149.6, with a standard deviation of 201.7. The median number is 63.5, the modal number is 669, and the range is 0 to 669. Note that the figure of 669 is higher than the figure of 645 assessable messages given above, as it includes some messages posted by students who commenced but did not complete the unit, but that were never-the-less read by the completing students. Interestingly, the modal number of messages read is also the maximum number, indicating that a significant proportion of students read every single discussion posting.

We devised a method for visualizing the message posting profile of all students together as a group. We compute a ranking factor for each student, based on weighting postings early in the semester higher, and postings later in the semester lower. We use this factor to rank order all students from highest to lowest. Figure 6 shows the rank ordered profile of new/initial postings made by students across the semester.

We observe four relatively distinct discussion new posting profiles, with approximately equal proportions of students in each. Students 1-21 (21 students, 24.4%) made their required five (or so) posts, commencing at week one, and then generally left the discussion space. Students 22-44 (23 students, 26.7%) commenced their posts in week

Figure 5. Ranked distribution of total number of messages read by students

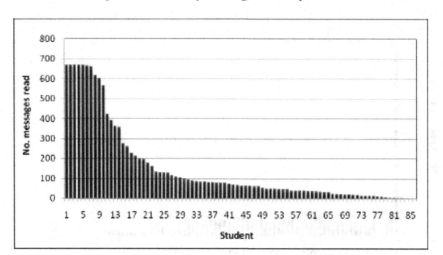

Figure 6. Rank ordered profile of new postings by students across the semester

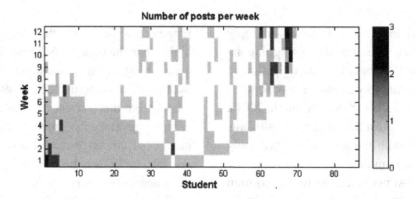

one and then had a range of posting profiles, typically not continuous, re-entering the discussion space at various points over the twelve weeks. Students 45-69 (25 students, 29.1%) commenced their posts some time after week one and then had a range of posting profiles, typically not continuous, with students who commenced their posting late in the twelve week period exhibiting more intense posting in an attempt to meet the assignment criteria of making five new posts in total. Students 70-86 (17 students, 19.8%) made no postings at all during the twelve week period.

Two significant correlations are observed; final unit mark and weighted average mark ($r =$ +0.43, $p < 4 \times 10^{-5}$), and final unit mark and total number of new postings ($r = +0.49$, $p < 2 \times 10^{-6}$). Inspection of variable pair scatter plots reveals that the relationship between final unit mark and number of new postings plateaus after five new postings. After the data range for the number of new postings is limited to five or less, the correlation is ($r = +0.59$, $p < 4 \times 10^{-9}$). As might be expected, a correlation is observed between previous general academic performance (as measured by the student's weighted average mark), and final unit result in SEB221. The observed correlation between total number of new postings and final unit mark is strongest for number of new posts between zero and five. This is not surprising as, although we allow students to make multiple new postings per week, we only take the single 'best' new posting result as the mark for the week. Although both weighted average mark and number of new posts appear to have a positive correlation with final unit mark, they do not have a significant correlation with each other ($r = +0.23$, $p > 0.033$), suggesting that they are not significantly multicollinear with the final unit result, and that both contribute independently and positively to the final unit mark.

Following removal of three data items with an unknown (not BE or BTech) course of study and four data items for students with a final unit mark of zero (did not complete unit but did not officially withdraw their enrolment), multivariate linear regression analysis is conducted, with final unit mark as the dependent variable. We initially introduce all other known variables as independent variables, and we perform step-wise regression until all remaining variables are significant. Table 1 shows the coefficients of the regression model and their significance.

An Analysis of Variance test suggests that the regression model is significant ($F_{78} = 47.29$, $p < 5 \times 10^{-14}$), though the model predicts only 55.4% of the variation in final unit mark ($R^2 = 0.554$). The regression residuals are approximately normally distributed. The model explains only just over half of the variation observed in the final unit mark, hence there exist other factors with a significant influence on final unit mark that were not available in the data collected for this analysis. The results of the regression analysis support the results of the data pair correlation analysis that both the

number of new postings and weighted average mark contribute significantly and independently to final unit mark. Based on the marking scheme of 'up to 1 mark per posting', it would be expected, all other things being equal, that posting one new message would add approximately one mark to the final unit result. Instead, the regression analysis indicates that there is a significant benefit (up to three marks per new posting) beyond the notionally allocated marks for new postings. This suggests that the work that students complete in preparing their new discussion postings engages them with the unit material and assists them in the completion of other assessable tasks for the unit.

None of the student demographic characteristics (age, gender, mode of study and course of study) are found to be significantly correlated with levels of participation in the discussion (messages read, new postings and reply postings), suggesting that all students are able to participate in the online discussion exercise on a generally equal basis. It has been proposed that the ways in which students engage with online asynchronous discussions will influence the learning outcomes achieved (Cotton & Yorke, 2006). We used the four types of student engagement with the discussion space identified in Figure 6 as a grouping variable and entered this into the multiple regression analysis, but it was not found to be a significant contributor to final units result.

CURRENT CHALLENGES

Although the introduction of a formally assessed online discussion appears to have a positive effect

Table 1. Multivariate linear regression model for dependant variable 'final unit mark'

Variable	Coefficient	Standard error	Beta	Significance
No. new posts (≤ 5)	3.05	0.47	0.50	$p < 1 \times 10^{-8}$
Weighted average mark	0.51	0.08	0.48	$p < 3 \times 10^{-8}$
Constant	28.17	5.50	-	$p < 3 \times 10^{-6}$

on student engagement with, overall perception of, and learning outcomes from an engineering study unit, a number of questions/issues remain. The regression analysis performed here identifies the explanatory factors contributing to only just over half of the variation observed in the final unit mark. Although active participation in the online discussion is a significant contributor to a student's final unit mark, what are the other factors not included in the data analysis that also contribute to unit learning outcomes? Although the qualitative feedback comments relating to the unit examined here are limited in number and scope, a larger institution-level survey of students at the University regarding their experiences of learning in wholly online units (Palmer & Holt, 2009) may shed some light on this question. This survey elicited more than 300 written responses from students to the question, "In what ways, if at all, has studying this unit online influenced your approach to learning?" An initial analysis of this qualitative data has been performed (Holt & Palmer, 2007), but a more focused analysis may help understand the full value students find in wholly online study generally, and the use of online discussions in particular.

The case presented here focuses particularly on the use of an online discussion. Both within the tools/features provided by LMSs, and via stand-alone applications that can extend LMS functionality, there is a rapidly expanding suite of e-learning technologies available to educators. An important question arises regarding the best ways in which elements from the range of technologies can be organized and combined into online learning systems to improve learning (Gibbs & Gosper, 2006). What combination of e-learning technologies, chosen from the available portfolio, creates the greatest potential educational value in a given teaching and learning context? A more recent development in the open source arena are "social software" applications, such as blogs, wikis and social networking sites, which have as

their essence the collaborative collection, ordering and interpretation of user-created content. These software systems provide new tools inherently aligned to the collaborative and reflective activities underpinning the online discussion application documented here. They offer an emerging and interesting option for the further development of online discussion activities in education.

SOLUTIONS AND RECOMMENDATIONS

As part of an institutional requirement that all undergraduate programs contain at least one 'wholly online' unit of study, we converted an existing unit in the engineering program to wholly online delivery in 2005. Initial results from student unit evaluation data indicated that students were significantly less satisfied with many elements of the unit after the move to wholly online delivery. In response to this result, we made some strategic changes to the assessment requirements for the unit in 2006. Using existing student evaluation data sources, we undertook a quantitative investigation to determine how students had responded to these changes to the unit mode of delivery and subsequent assessment changes. Based on student evaluation of teaching and units survey data collected systematically by the University, simply translating existing print-based study resources into electronic/online format, retaining the same assessment regime and dropping all face-to-face contact with academic staff appeared to lead to a significant decline in mean student ratings for a number of survey questions items. This finding suggests that simply performing a 'direct conversion' of an existing unit for wholly online delivery may not produce the optimal result for student satisfaction and learning.

By making a minor change to the unit assessment in 2006 to incorporate a formally assessed activity that requires students to regularly reflect on the course material and participate in an online discussion area, student evaluation of teaching and units survey item ratings common across the period 2003-2006 show a recovery to their prior levels. Additionally, the item relating to the value of online technologies in student learning actually rose significantly. These findings suggest that careful thought, but not necessarily major changes, may be required to avoid student disillusionment and to maximize student learning outcomes when moving an existing unit to wholly online delivery format. Although we qualitatively observed that student participation in unit online discussions increased significantly compared to previous unit offerings, following the introduction of a formally assessed online discussion task, we undertook a quantitative examination to investigate the impact of the students' participation in the online discussion on their final unit results.

We observed that, although many students read a significant number of discussion postings, generally, the posting of new and reply messages occur at the minimum level required to qualify for the assignment marks. Based on new postings to the online discussion, we observed four distinct patterns of posting. Based on correlation and multiple regression analysis, we observed a significant relation between two measured variables and a student's final unit mark – their weighted average mark (used as a proxy measure for general prior academic ability) and the number of new postings that they make to the online discussion. In addition, these two variables are not significantly correlated with each other, and are both significant in the regression model obtained, suggesting that both contribute independently to the final unit mark. Although we shouldn't interpret it literally as the 'formula' that determines a student's final unit mark, the regression model explains more than half of the observed variation in final unit mark. Additionally, it does suggest that the influence of active participation in the online discussion assignment through the posting of reflective contributions based on the course material makes approximately the same contribution to a student's final unit mark as their general prior academic ability. Further, the regression model indicates that each new posting contributes three times as much to the final unit mark as its nominal assessment value of 'up to 1 mark per posting' otherwise indicates. This suggests that the work in preparing their new discussion postings engages students with the unit material and assists them in the completion of a range of assessable tasks for the unit. However, although active contribution to the online discussion in the form of new posts is a significant factor in the final unit mark, simply reading the posts of other students is not. The number of postings read is not significantly correlated with the final unit mark, suggesting that passive 'lurking' in this online discussion does not significantly contribute to student learning outcomes (as measured by final unit mark).

REFERENCES

Browne, T., Jenkins, M., & Walker, R. (2006). A longitudinal perspective regarding the use of VLEs by higher education institutions in the United Kingdom. *Interactive Learning Environments*, *14*(2), 177–192. doi:10.1080/10494820600852795

Conaway, R. N., Easton, S. S., & Schmidt, W. V. (2005). Strategies for Enhancing Student Interaction and Immediacy in Online Courses. *Business Communication Quarterly*, *68*(1), 23–35. doi:10.1177/1080569904273300

Cotton, D., & Yorke, J. (2006, 3-6 December). *Analysing online discussions: What are students learning?* Paper presented at the 23rd annual ascilite conference: Who's learning? Whose technology? Sydney.

Davies, J., & Graff, M. (2005). Performance in e-learning: online participation and student grades. *British Journal of Educational Technology, 36*(4), 657–663. doi:10.1111/j.1467-8535.2005.00542.x

Garland, K., & Noyes, J. (2004). The effects of mandatory and optional use on students' ratings of a computer-based learning package. *British Journal of Educational Technology, 35*(3), 263–273. doi:10.1111/j.0007-1013.2004.00388.x

Garrison, D. R., Anderson, T., & Archer, W. (1999). Critical Inquiry in a Text-Based Environment: Computer Conferencing in Higher Education. *The Internet and Higher Education, 2*(2/3), 87–105. doi:10.1016/S1096-7516(00)00016-6

Gibbs, D., & Gosper, M. (2006). The upside-down-world of e-learning. *Journal of Learning Design, 1*(2), 46–54.

Gorsky, P., & Caspi, A. (2005). Dialogue: a theoretical framework for distance education instructional systems. *British Journal of Educational Technology, 36*(2), 137–144. doi:10.1111/j.1467-8535.2005.00448.x

Graham, M., & Scarborough, H. (2001). Enhancing the learning environment for distance education students. *Distance Education, 22*(2), 232–244. doi:10.1080/0158791010220204

Hara, N., Bonk, C. J., & Angeli, C. (2000). Content analysis of online discussion in an applied educational psychology course. *Instructional Science, 28*(2), 115–152. doi:10.1023/A:1003764722829

Harasim, L. (1991, 8-11 January). *Designs & tools to augment collaborative learning in computerized conferencing systems.* Paper presented at the Twenty-Fourth Annual Hawaii International Conference on System Sciences, Kauai, Hawaii.

Holt, D. M., & Challis, D. J. (2007). From policy to practice: one university's experience of implementing strategic change through wholly online teaching and learning. *Australasian Journal of Educational Technology, 23*(1), 110–131.

Holt, D. M., & Palmer, S. (2007, 2-5 December). *Staff exercising 'choice'; students exercising 'choice': Wholly online learning at an Australian university.* Paper presented at the 24th Annual Conference of the Australasian Society for Computers in Learning in Tertiary Education, Singapore.

Holt, D. M., & Thompson, D. J. (1995). Responding to the technological imperative: The experience of one open and distance education institution. *Distance Education: An International Journal, 16*(1), 43–64. doi:10.1080/0158791950160105

James, R., McInnis, C., & Devlin, M. (2002). *Assessing Learning in Australian Universities.* Melbourne, Australia: Centre for the Study of Higher Education and The Australian Universities Teaching Committee.

Johnson, S. D., Aragon, S. R., Shaik, N., & Palma-Rivas, N. (2000). Comparative Analysis of Learner Satisfaction and Learning Outcomes in Online and Face-to-Face Learning Environments. *Journal of Interactive Learning Research, 11*(1), 29–49.

Kirkwood, A., & Price, L. (2005). Learners and learning in the twenty-first century: what do we know about students' attitudes towards and experiences of information and communication technologies that will help us design courses? *Studies in Higher Education, 30*(3), 257–274. doi:10.1080/03075070500095689

Kuk, G. (2003, 9-11 April). *E-Learning Hubs: Affordance, Motivation and Learning Outcomes.* Paper presented at the UK Higher Education Academy Business Education Support Team Subject Centre Conference 2003, Brighton.

Palmer, S., & Holt, D. (2009). Examining student satisfaction with wholly online learning. *Journal of Computer Assisted Learning, 25*(2), 101–113. doi:10.1111/j.1365-2729.2008.00294.x

Palmer, S., & Holt, D. (in press). Students' Perceptions of the Value of the Elements of an Online Learning Environment: Looking Back in Moving Forward. *Interactive Learning Environments.*

Richardson, J. C., & Swan, K. (2003). Examining Social Presence in Online Courses in Relation to Students' Perceived Learning and Satisfaction. *Journal of Asynchronous Learning Networks, 7*(1), 68–88.

Stacey, E., & Rice, M. (2002). Evaluating an online learning environment. *Australian Journal of Educational Technology, 18*(3), 323–340.

Webb, E., Jones, A., Barker, P., & van Schaik, P. (2004). Using e-learning dialogues in higher education. *Innovations in Education and Teaching International, 41*(1), 93–103. doi:10.1080/1470329032000172748

Weisskirch, R. S., & Milburn, S. S. (2003). Virtual discussion: Understanding college students' electronic bulletin board use. *The Internet and Higher Education, 6*(3), 215–225. doi:10.1016/S1096-7516(03)00042-3

Wozniak, H. (2005). Online discussions: Improving the quality of the student experience. Retrieved 19 December, 2008, from http://www.odlaa.org/events/2005conf/ref/ODLAA2005Wozniak.pdf

KEY TERMS AND DEFINITIONS

Engineering Education: Those university-level programs leading to the award of a qualification recognized as adequate/appropriate for graduate membership of the national engineering professional body, and normally granting the holder the right to begin professional practice as an engineer.

Assignment: A summatively assessed activity in a university education program undertaken by students for credit/marks in a specific unit of study.

Learning Management System (LMS): A system designed for the delivery, tracking and management of education and/or training. Such systems typically use the Internet for the online delivery of learning programs, provide tools for management online assessment and offer various forms on online collaboration and communication. Historically, LMSs have been commercial software packages, but an array of open-source systems is now available.

Online Learning Environment (OLE): A system designed specifically to support online teaching and learning (as distinct from an LMS – though the distinction is becoming harder to define). An OLE may include an LMS as a foundation, with additional tools for supporting online teaching and learning provided in parallel. An OLE (however constituted) might provide the following features/tools: online assessment, communication tools, uploading of content, peer assessment, student group administration, questionnaires, wikis and blogs. Although originally aimed at supporting distance education students, OLEs are now commonly used to support on-campus enrolled students as well, in a form education known as blended learning.

Learning Outcome: The knowledge and/or skills and/or abilities that students have attained as a result of their involvement in a particular set of educational experiences. Learning outcomes are typically summatively assessed through a range of assignment activities which contribute to a final mark in a unit of study.

Asynchronous Discussion: An online discussion forum that does not require all participants to be present (physically and/or virtually) at the same time. Contributors can post a message that can be read/responded to by another participant at a different time. Conversations and an online community can develop over time.

Student Evaluation of Teaching (SET): In its most general form, this includes any method used to obtain feedback from students regarding their perceptions of their teaching/learning experiences. Commonly, this will include an end of semester/term survey of students to quantitatively assess their perceptions of unit content and/or teacher performance.

Chapter 6
B-Log on Social Change and Educational Reform:
The Case of a University Class in Greece

Eleni Sideri
University of Thessaly, Greece

EXECUTIVE SUMMARY

The use of blogs as a teaching method is something new for the Greek education. The financial and structural problems of the latter however, have not yet permitted the application of new technologies to be fully explored despite the intentions of different parties, like the political authorities or the academics. This chapter will argue that blogs could enhance class interaction without replacing face to face communication. Their use could play a positive role in an education system burdened by the gradual increase of its student population, restricted funding and infrastructural problems. In this framework, blogs could act as an arena that encourages critical dialogue and assessment regarding courses, educators and students. The author's personal engagement in blogging as part of her teaching methods coincided with a major social and political unrest in Greece, conditions that affected the ways students related to their blogs as a form of communication. This chapter will examine how blogs could play a role in the democratization of the assessment methods by enhancing classroom's dynamics and the interaction between educators and students. It will also consider how blogs would contribute to the engagement of both students and educators with social and political critical thinking. Finally, this chapter will discuss how blogging could result in the formation of more active citizens.

ORGANIZATION BACKGROUND

New technologies evangelized the coming of a new era in the context of human communication. However, neo-luddites soon started to express their

DOI: 10.4018/978-1-61520-863-0.ch006

scepticism in regards the impact of this type of communication on human relations. For example, impersonalization and de-humanization are often debated as symptoms of online communication in comparison to face to face interaction (Jonscher, 1999). The arguments of neo-luddites against a developing technological fascism often concern the formation of a homogenous, undifferentiated global culture where hegemonic trends would prevail. An example of the latter could be the gradual dominance of English in online communication (Yiannakopoulos, 2005). As it will be discussed in this chapter, the linguistic predominance of English in cyber land (cyber-English) does not necessarily preclude linguistic variety and the vivacity of national languages. Using Greeklish, for instance, is indicative of such a reaction. Another issue raised by the neo-luddites is the alleged decay of social relations that could lead to human isolation and unpredicted anti-social behaviour. However, online social networks, such as the Facebook, My Space, Hi5 are thriving and in this way, they extend or act as alternative channels to face-to-face social networks. In this context, Freire's (1977) belief that human fear of technology is not a new thing could be a starting point. As he suggests, technology since the invention of the wheel forces mankind to face new dilemmas concerning the products of its civilization and its limits.

The author's interest in online communication started earlier in her career with an online ethnography of a female chat room in order to study language, gender and identity (Sideri, 2000). However, the research concerning opportunities that internet could open for class communication emerged gradually with teaching. This interest was motivated by the department of History, Archaeology and Social Anthropology, University of Thessaly (http://www.uth.gr), which encourages the development of news courses related to new technologies. In fact, there is a special category of such courses in the program of the department called NT (New Technologies). The latter could be selected by the students of all three directions (History, Archaeology or Social Anthropology). The aim of NT is to introduce or enhance students' technological skills and knowledge. All the courses, presented in this chapter belong to this category. As a result, the author started to incorporate new technologies in the organization

of her lectures since the first year of teaching. For example, films or Power Point Presentations of the lectures were engaged on a weekly basis. Students were to find these materials online, together with the syllabus of the course on the educator's web page. The use of such methods, as it is often argued (Solomon & Shcrum, 2007; Richardson, 2008), makes the life in the classroom more creative.

Nevertheless, the introduction of new technologies in Higher Education often takes an instrumental character which rather increases the control and the workload of academics burdening their professional life with the logistics of the departments and holding them responsible for various managerial aspects of their institutions. This criticism is well-founded and was partly one the reasons for the massive mobilizations in the Greek universities during the period 2006-2007. However, it is the author's conviction that the use of new technologies as part of the academic repertoire of teaching methods could raise civic awareness by offering more channels of communications within the classroom. In this way, a stronger barrier against the instrumetalization of knowledge could be formed.

At the same time, blogs were introduced in the Greek public life. For example the demonstrations after the massive forest destruction in South Greece in 2007 were organized after the initiative of various bloggers. As a result, several of the most active bloggers either individual or groups, such as, the G700 (http://g700.blogspot.com/), a group of young bloggers whose salary does not surpass the 700 Euros, were invited to participate in a public discussion organized by a Greek channel, SKAI TV (http://www.skai.gr), during the last election campaign (2007). Nevertheless, solid evidences regarding the use of blogs and its impact on the Greek society are still limited. Blogs are not broadly used within the academic departments with the exception of media studies. The use of educational blogging in Greece, especially in Higher Education, is still in experimental stages and it is usually introduced as part of the instructor's academic interests or research. On the contrary, there is an increase of educational blogging in primary and secondary education with encouraging results that support further its use (Pappa, 2009; Tzortzakis, 2009). The reason for this difference should be studied further. Nevertheless, some initial thoughts would be the more systematic introduction of new technologies in the context of elementary and secondary education curricula, funding, smaller classes with a standard number of pupils and teachers' training. In contrast, there is scarce information about the use and the results of weblogs in Higher Education. However, whenever blogs are introduced in the universities, the feedback is encouraging.

For example, Dr Koulouktsis from the University of Ioannina used blogs as a way for his students to assess their course. The results could be found online (http://slografeiou.blogspot.com/), where one has the opportunity to read these students' positive reaction to blogs as a mode of assessment. One of the first books on blogging that was published in Greek (Andriotakis, 2007, p. 78-80) underlines in a small chapter dedicated to educational blogging that the latter has the potential to pave the way to a more direct communication between educators and students, but also between the members of these two groups. Moreover, Andriotakis proposes blog's use in the assessment of students, for example, as an incentive for publication of their best works. However, he does not lose the opportunity to express some critical points regarding the manipulations of blogs by business involved in academic research in order to promote their ideas or products, the difficulties of protecting the young bloggers and their work from anonymous attacks or plagiarism. But which aspect of blogging could be such an asset for education?

As Downes (2004) argues, blogging is not about writing. The latter comes as the end of an adventure. The main thing is helping our students to discover ideas, people, communities and networks of collaboration, to develop and learn to accept constructive criticism to each other, to structure arguments and the know-how to be involved in a dialogue. It is, therefore, this side of blogging that is possible to generate the conditions for more participatory methods, collaborative work and collective production of knowledge. In this way, blogging could help academics de-hierachize and democratize education by creating more active students/citizens coming closer to the ideal of Freire's (2001) emancipatory pedagogy. This aim often becomes distant in the Greek system of Higher Education because of a variety of problems, such as, limited funding, large number of students, infrastructural problems, and limited staff. As a result, there is not enough time to develop personal relations and to closely supervise the graduate students. Furthermore, the above hindrances cultivate the conditions for lecture-type courses which do not always allow class debates and discussion- groups. Could blogging go beyond these problems and create the space for the development of critical thinking, collaborative knowledge and re-personalization of education?

SETTING THE STAGE

The first step in order to test these questions was a new course, Cyberspace and Diasporic Media (http://elenasideri.blogspot.com/2008_03_01_archive.html).Coming from the field of diasporas and having taught a seminar on the diasporic press in the Caucasus to a group of young Greek origin Georgian journalists, the author decided to develop a course regarding the functions of the diasporic media within the new mediascapes. The course was interested in examining the ways online media contribute to the ways we conceive communities and especially, diasporic communities. It approached theoretical definitions of diasporas, questions of research methods within virtual reality, memory and online communities, refugee media, online families and sexualities, religious communities, mediatised discourses on the formation of public/private spheres in the age digitalization. The class consisted of a group of twenty people who were in an advanced or the last stage of their studies, social anthropologists in their majority but also, few historians.

Since new technologies and media were a major part of this course, the author believed that blogging could be a way to familiarize students with the subject. Furthermore, the course would lead to the introduction of more flexible system of assessment than that of final exams or writing papers. As a result, a mixed form of assessment based on multi-tasking was applied. On the one hand, students had to write a comparative essay regarding the experience of two diasporas, which they had to submit in the end of the semester. On the other hand, they had a weekly online activity. A blog, Diasporization (http://www.elenasideri. zoomshare.com/7.shtml), was created, where students had to answer online a specific question or develop further an ethnographic case that we had previously discussed in class.

The project, as described above, was based on the philosophy of "assigned blogging," a term coined by Will Richardson, the author of Blogs, Wikis, Podcasts, and Other Powerful Web Tools for Classrooms (2008), in order to describe a form of blogging controlled from above (as cited in Glogowski, 2009). In this category of blogging, students' postings are generated by specific discussions, questions or assignments that instructors give them. In this way, we open the door to innovation on the one hand, but on the other hand, we do not seem to lose control and authority. In this case, as Downes puts it (2004), we should wonder one thing: what happens when a free medium such as blogging interacts with the restrictions of the educational system? This is one of the central questions I will try to tackle here, as it goes to the heart of the question regarding democratization of teaching methods. Richardson (as cited in Downes, 2004, p. 24) is adamant about it. Assigned-blogging cannot be blogging

since it replaces free criticism, opinion analysis and conversation with restrictive thematology, controlled language style (formal/informal) and perpetuates classroom hierarchy structures. Using blogging in this way restrains the dynamics of the medium, which in other way, could contribute to engage students in discovering or creating their own material out of their experience with technology (Beal, 2002). However, I believe that even in the case of assigned blogging, one could not control the responses, the variety of ideas and approaches that might rise from a fixed, controlled "from-above," question or project.

Every week a question or an argument related to the topic of the week was posted. It was expected that the students would take this point and discuss it further according to their weekly readings. In other words, the use of the class' blog was quite "conservative," as it was the first time that the author applied blogging in her teaching methods and she had certain reservations because of various impediments: not all the students had access to a PC or a laptop, they had different levels of experience with new technologies, the number of the students attending the class varied each week, with a core group of 8-10 people participating more actively.

The first weeks of the course, two problems emerged. First, the structure of the course presupposed that all students had attended at least, the introductory course in new technologies offered by the department. This, however, was not the case. Although all students were excited with this form of communication, many of them were quite puzzled with the technicalities (how could they do the postings, should they write in Greek or in Greeklish?). Extra hours, both in class and in the instructor's office, were dedicated to these issues in order to overcome the problems. Secondly, another issue was that students seemed reluctant to offer innovative answers. Instead, they simply reproduced the class discussions without pushing the argument further or illustrating additional

Figure 1. Aims of this blog, diasporization, 10/10/2007. The blog was created by the author

engagement with the readings. It took a long discussion to partly solve this attitude together with more detailed guidelines in regards the answering of every week's question. Despite these two problems, students' comments in the end of the semester that they feel free to express themselves and the fact that they considered the class' blog as a way for them to engage in a more personalized manner with the course were encouraging. This was made possible with a new course, Anthropology of Electronic Media.

CASE DESCRIPTION

Anthropology of media was developed in 1980s/1990s in order to examine media as social practices within the context of political, economic and social changes of the interlinked global and local environments. Furthermore, anthropology of media studies how media respond and take part within these transformations (Ginsburg, Abu-Lughod &Larkin, 2005). In this framework, my course had the intention to familiarize students with the formation of global media and their complex mediascapes considering the consequences on nation-states, public/private space, gender, and minority issues. The aims of the course were:

- To make students aware of the problems of representation in media
- To help them critically assess media techniques and methods
- To introduce them to the theoretical and methodological challenges of anthropology of media

- To contribute to an empirical experience of these issues through blogging.

Previous experience with blogging made clear two things. Firstly, the course should start from the basic, introducing blogging to students, helping them with all the technical issues, for example, opening an account or making postings. Secondly, the structure of the course should let more initiatives to students in terms of how they would organize their blog or research. In this way, they could develop more immediate and experiential ideas of the issues the course tackled and they could develop multiple skills in theoretical, methodological and finally, technological terms. Giving more initiatives to students meant that they would become active partners not only in the process of teaching, but also in the actual production of knowledge, as they would take part in the choice of the subjects examined in the class as well as in the blogs. Furthermore, they would practice every week a small-scale, online, ethnography of media.

Before the beginning of the course, the author created a special blog for the course and her class, where students could find (http://iakaanthropologyofmedia.blogspot.com/):

1. The syllabus (printed and electronic references, in Greek and in English),
2. Guidelines for blogging,
3. The logistics of the course and details about the coursework,
4. Extra material, such as, links to local, alternative and international media, websites, articles and projects regarding anthropology of media, online documentaries related to

media mainly from video.google.com, such as, the Control Room by Noujaim, (2004) or Manufacturing Consent by Achbar, & Wintock (1992).

One could also find videos from events related to the course, for example, a lecture given by Dan Gillmor, the author of Citizens and New Media (2008), to a Greek media conference in October 2008. When students created their own blogs, the latter were added in the blogroll of the site. In this way, an online space where the class could "meet," was created. This space went beyond the ordinary, regimented spaces of interaction that students and educators usually have at their disposal in order to communicate with each other, such as the lab or the office.

Technology Concerns

One central problem that had to be tackled was the uneven experience that students had regarding not only blogging, but also new technologies in general. The groups consisted of 19 students. In the lab there were several computers using Windows XP and having all the known browsers, although Mozilla and Explorer were the most popular. Furthermore special programs for film processing and recordings could be found in a couple of the computers. Additionally, there were some laptops, two projectors, a television set with video and a DVD player. Besides this lab, the department owns an IT department with a larger number of personal computers, which was used when the students had to do individual work during the session and their number exceeded that of the computers found in the lab. The blogs were opened with Blogger. Students had the opportunity to choose another platform for their blogs, but they found Blogger simpler, especially those who did not have any previous experience. Two of the students had already their own blogs, which they did not mind to use for the purpose of this class. Opening an account caused many

unexpected technical problems, for example, the system crashed because of overload and time was lost because of misspellings. In our second meeting, most of the students had already opened the account without any extra help and had created a blog of their own. Few of them used office hours for further consultation. Additionally, during the classes, students that faced technical problems and overcame them, provided consultation and technical support to others that faced similar one. Similarly, more advanced in new technologies students helped weaker colleagues.

The entire process of solving technical problems more than an impediment became in the end, a more experiential way to transmit knowledge in the classroom, which could raise interesting issues concerning the introduction of new technologies to education and its results. As Barrett argued (1992), new technologies are not new only because of their novel nature, the knowledge the latter produces and its application, but also and often more importantly, because of the ways this knowledge is constructed. It is practiced and mediated. In other words, after centuries during which the West had developed and privileged textualized knowledge (textbooks), new technologies seem to bring back older forms of learning, where collaboration and practice become prominent. This form of transmission of practical knowledge results in the case of this class into reshaping the relations of the students (students become educators to other students), the ties among them were reinforced and created an atmosphere of collaboration.

Management and Organizational Concerns

In the beginning, students were not aware that their blogs could be accessed by a potentially wider audience. After the author raised this point to them, they started to look into various ways for making their blogs appealing, such as, adding hyperlinks, photographs or videos. It was fascinating to watch how each student's blog became more personal, following her/his aesthetic criteria, interests and hobbies. In this way, the impersonal virtual space became a personal place of expression for each one of them. They all chose pre-prepared templates from Blogger, playing with the colours and with various widgets offered by the provider. The majority, despite of gender, selected colours that were in fashion, for instance, light green, blue and pink (the latter was more popular among female students). Similarly, the majority of students used widgets, such as calendars, weather forecasts, photographs from the National Geographic and they included links to their classmates' blogs and other media sites.

These links created a space of intellectual proximity, a space where students could unravel social relations and networks of collaboration which provide the background for the construction of knowledge in a less restricted and controlled environment than their classroom. As Jenkins (2006) postulates, these spaces are highly productive in the sense that they call for a more active participation on the behalf of students and encourage the expansion of the existing classroom networks. They could be seen as more informal and thus, less regimented places of interaction and learning. In this sense, the formation of these e-spaces represents what Castells (2000) defines as "network society," a society whose forms of communication unravel in relation to the nature of the medium. In other words, socio-cultural ties and interests are shaped through or/and because of the electronic nature of the medium.

Furthermore, these links shaped a space of interaction between the class participants themselves, the class and different professional worlds (anthropology of media and new media sites), redefining the borders between virtual and real spaces of learning, online and face-to-face communication. These spaces were also strengthened and extended with the hyperlinks found in students' postings, which referred to articles, YouTube videos, television shows and news bulletins. These links provided extra support to students' analyses.

But, they also seem to widen the resources which these students are accustomed to refer to in order to organize their research beyond the more orthodox academic space resulting to the initiation of a dialogue between the academic and more socially open sources. The blurring of such boundaries (virtual/real, academic/non-academic) resulted as well to the more informal communication between the students of this class and the author in a number of different ways. For example, many students during the course opened an account on the Facebook or other online social networks and invited the author to join their group. They also communicated with her via emails or texting her for issues not strictly related to their coursework. For example, they felt encouraged to inform her about an interesting article or a site participating in this way, to the construction of the course itself and the knowledge produced.

The subjects of their postings escalated from more closed to completely free topics in the last weeks, so that the author could follow their progress, intervene in terms of technical issues and provide feedback to their writing wherever was necessary. For example, in the first weeks, students had assigned topics, such as, to write a summary of one of the articles from the week's reading list or to carry out specific projects. For instance, in week 4, students had to pinpoint to the ways ideas about the Greek nation are reproduced by analyzing the Greek Law on Media. The escalation in the orientation of the topics (from more controlled to free one) followed the syllabus. The first weeks (week 2-4) focused on more theoretical issues of communication and media theory (the Frankfurt School and the Birmingham School, methods of Anthropology of Media, nation-states and press history). Then, later weeks (week 5-11) had more the form of media observation and analysis starting with the role of media in conflict, media contribution to globalization, mediatic genres and language, gender and media, media and transnational communities, alternative media and new media. The final week before the

Figure 2. Homepage of IAKA anthropology of media guidelines for the final presentation. On the right, the class blogroll. The blog was created by the author

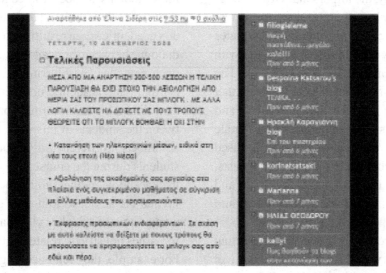

presentations was dedicated to the transformations caused by new technologies in the public and private spheres, but it was cancelled because of the political and social unrest in Greece that kept Greek universities closed.

Another interesting point was the language students used. Many felt comfortable to use Greeklish, as they often do when they chat online. The attempt to Romanize the Greek alphabet has a long history (Treliga, 2007, pp.117-118). The technological limitations in the Computer Mediated Communication contributed to the spread of Greeklish, although there has not been yet a standardized style of transcription (http://el.wikipedia.org/wiki/Greeklish). The latter could be either phonetic, orthographic or a combination of the two, which is the most frequent case. But even those who opted for standard Greek, they used it in a more informal way than the one used in academic papers, making references to their personal experience. For example in the case below, the female student who writes on alternative media, she uses Greeklish in order to introduce the topic and outline the structure.

Aftin tin vdomada skopos einai na katanoisoume ton tropo leitourgeias ton enallaktikon meson kai ton skopo auton. Arxika tha kano mia mikri anafora sta eidi ton enallaktikon meson kai stin sinexeia tha kano logo gia ena sigkekrimeno. Prota ap'ola iparxei to politismiko jamming (culture jamming), enas polemos pliroforion kai i texni tou sok. (2008, http://stelayahoogr.blogspot.com/2008/12/enallaktika-mesa.html)

The style lies between formal/informal language. For instance, she uses first person plural (na katanoisoume), indication of a formal academic language, but then she shifts to first person singular (tha kano), example of informal writing. The author agrees with Treliga (2007, pp. 133-134) that Greeklish does not necessarily indicate formal or informal style, but it is a question of digital understanding and convenience. However, it is the unconventional character of the medium that allows this language shift. This blurring of boundaries between formal/informal languages continued. In later weeks students felt more comfortable to exchange witty critical comments related to their postings or to upload funny photographs and sketches.

Students also started to develop their own "specialization," for example, several female students concentrated on gender issues. The blogger GerogiaKarra did a research concerning gender presentation in the Greek news bulletins (http://georgiakarra.blogspot.com/). Some other students used to get inspiration from subjects concerning their hometown and its media. For instance, the blogger Gertsi, whose blog was voted by his classmate as the best of the course, presented the cultural life of Volos with emphasis on environmental issues (http://tsibloulis.blogspot.com/). There were, though, some drawbacks. For example, students seemed more reluctant to read the printed material and bibliographies, unless they were asked to do so, since online material was easier to be accessed. Another factor was the fact that material about the issues the course examined in Greek language was quite limited and students did not feel comfortable to depend only on English language sources. In order to overcome this drawback, the author provided photocopies of important articles, so that all students could work with them in class in collaboration with each other and the author, minimizing in this way, any language problem.

The assignments of later weeks forced students to work on the main subject/framework of the week without, though, enforcing any thematic constraint on them by a more specific question. A group of three persons was entitled to organize the research scope of the class acting as "editors." In this way, they could experience how different filters, in their case different personal stances and interests, work in the context of media. They had to particularize the general subject by either defining specific questions, for instance, if the general topic was media in conflict, they had to provide more specific directives for the class such as, the role of media in the war in Iraq, representations of this war in different media or countries. This group was responsible to announce and explain the topics to their classmates, but the latter was free to choose which type of media would study

in their research, for example, press or television. The groups had to read and assess the work of their classmates and to present their assessment each week in class. In this way, each student apart from the author's feedback had also another one from his/her classmates.

In the last week, each student had to make an overall presentation of their blogging experience by answering three questions:

- How does blogging contribute or not to your understanding of (new) media?
- Assess blogging as a teaching/assessment method in comparison to other used within academia.
- Are you going to use blogs further in your personal or professional life?

Then, the author organized group presentations (three persons in each group) based on students' answers (similarities or interesting contradictions) and the dynamics that students had developed with each other in class. In the presentation, students were encouraged to defend their position and have a debate with their classmates regarding blogging.

In terms of course organization, the author had to consider how the method of assessment could put in question the traditional asymmetries of power and class hierarchies. Students had to create their own blogs and gradually, through their own online research and engagement with the course bibliography, to develop their own analysis and questions related to the general topics of the week. Furthermore they were encouraged to start an online dialogue with their co-students, for example, by leaving comments to each other. The author was also posting comments every week to each student's blogs drawing their attention to their performance, so that each one of them could have an immediate feedback of his/her progress. In general, their assessment was done in three steps:

1. 50% blogging
2. 30% participation in class

3. 20% final presentation of their experience of the course

In this way the overall assessment was multi-level and multi-directional:

A. *Formal Assessment*
   ◦ Educator to class through the official marking system
   ◦ Educator to individual students through comments to each student's blogs and in office consultation
   ◦ Educator to class making comments for their overall weekly performance in the beginning of each session.
B. *Informal Assessment*
   ◦ Students Groups (in charge of weekly presentations) to individual student work
   ◦ Class to groups providing feedback about the teamwork and collaboration
   ◦ Student to student by commenting to each other blogs
C. *Students Assessment to Educator*
   ◦ Mid-term assessment from individual students to educator with a de-briefing of how the course goes

Assessment Forms

Although at first, some students seemed reluctant to assess publically their colleagues, they soon changed their minds. In cases of friends, they translated assessment as betrayal of their relation. Nevertheless, this reaction was a good example of how hierarchy and authority are rooted and sustained in classrooms. Interpreting assessment as something that "teachers do," students silently accepted and reproduced the existing power structures. In this context, friendship was considered as a barrier against the authority of their teacher, whereas the assessment of their fellow students/friends was a sign of collaboration with this authority. It took a lot of persistence and the contribution of more mature students who were involved professionally in education to act as mediators in order to persuade the sceptics. All these various forms of assessment made students responsible for 1. their improvement, 2. their colleagues' performance 3. the improvement of the course itself. In this way, assessment was not a technique of control from above, but a multidirectional procedure that involved everybody. As a result, the final marking of students' performance reflected in a more holistic way their improvement and progress.

Encouraging was also the students' own evaluation of their experience with blogging. Maguirenancy states in her blog that the way "the course was structured contributed to the strengthening of the class ties and we got to know each other through collaboration" (2008, http://maguirenancy.blogspot.com, authors' translation from Greek). Similarly, Panagoyahoogr underlines that,

"The technical help I received from my classmates was crucial and their blogs became a source both of information and inspiration for my own work. In the last weeks when the universities were closed, we had the opportunity to communicate through our blogs", (2008, http://panagovayahoogr.blogspot. com/, authors' translation from Greek).

Acknowledging the positive side of blogging, though, does not mean that students underestimate face-to-face communication or the fact that blogging could not solve the problems of quality and infrastructure of the system of education in Greece. For example, Papakimon expresses in his evaluation his reservations regarding the quality of postings. In other words, he puts in question the amount of time spent for research and writing these postings every week (2009, http://papakimon.blogspot.com/2009/01/blog.html).

To what extent could blogs, apart from acquainting students with new technologies and media critique become a means of civic emancipation for students? Cope and Kalantzis (2006)

argued that, in order for education to respond to the challenges of our inter-connected world should aim at developing multiliteracies. In other words, instead of having an educational system aiming at developing traditional skills (reading/writing) and transmitting a certain type of knowledge (theoretical, scientific or more technical), to try to amplify not only the skills of our students, but their ability to grasp the underlying social-political interconnections that construct and represent what reality is. For this reason, the aforementioned writers suggest that multiliteracies should be the real focus of our education.

- By examining and comprehending a variety of discourses (social, political, economic)
- By using a multiplicity of "texts" (writing, image, audio), as medium of learning

This new design and reorientation of education will provide students the necessary skills in order to face the changes firstly, in global economy such as cross-cultural working places and flexible forms of employment, secondly, in public space, such as multicultural societies, post-national forms of membership, and finally, in their personal social life, such as multiple and culturally plural social spaces of interaction. As students' assessment illustrated the reinforcement of their ties in the classroom and the opportunities to discuss their thoughts about the social reality in Greece were considered as important as any other learning aspect of the course and it was attributed to the space that their blogs created. The connection between new technologies, blogging in particular, and the development of social skills was tested in the most challenging way in the last weeks of the semester when political unrest started in Greece after an incident of police brutality and excess of power. That period tested the ways blogs could refresh communication between educators and students.

CURRENT CHALLENGES

To what degree could blogs evolve to a new platform of communication and interaction between not only teachers and students or among students themselves, but also and more importantly, between universities and society? As H. Jenkins (2006, p. 9) underlined, "participatory culture is reworking the rules by which school, cultural expression, civic life, and work operate". These multiple connections of education with society form part of the agenda of multi-literacy so that the latter could help students meet the complex economic, political and social challenges of modern world. In other words, the need is one: to see students not as individuals, but as citizens both of specific and global communities. What role could blogs play in this context? Blogs represent, as it is often argued, a form of individual expression encouraged by the age of neo-liberal capitalism where collective forms of reaction are frequently considered as a threat. Nevertheless, this expression often aims at thinking loud and it seems to make a public contribution, however minimal, to social thinking.

Hence, blogging appears to bridge the individual to the social, offering an opportunity for the transformation of individuals to citizens through the emergence of a space of reflection. The emergence of "social individuals," a term launched by Hall (as cited in Lipman, 2005, p.319), however, could not be entirely attributed to new technologies. What blogging has succeeded in the case this chapter discusses is to provide a space that the class considered less controlled and more familiar to their needs and forms of expression. This space, though, took an unexpected significance last December in Greece. The social unrest that was evolved into political riots in certain cases in Athens in December 2008 provided the context to test the ways blogging could become a mode of mediation between classroom and society.

The riots followed almost instantly the murder of a young boy (15 years old) in Athens after a verbal dispute with two policemen. The reactions were immediate and continuous. It included massive demonstrations in all cities and even small villages of Greece, street fights between various groups of demonstrators and police forces, vandalization in the centre of Athens and other major cities. The universities closed down, as the Ministry of Education decided to announce three-day mourning. However, after this period, the student assemblies in many universities, University of Thessaly included, decided to continue the closing down of the faculties, at least, until the Christmas Holidays. The death of the young boy was a shock for the entire Greek society and increased the civil resentment against state corruption, economic recession and police disability. The contribution of new technologies to the organization of these demonstrations was enormous. Most of the demonstrations, street happenings and performances were organized through online social platforms, such as the Twitter or Facebook and mobile technology. The events were recorded and uploaded on the web. More and more people preferred online media for their information instead of traditional media which were not trusted and were considered prejudiced. On the contrary, Indy media and blogs gradually become one of the most important sources of information.

There were several researches that came out since then in order to postulate the various dimensions of the uprise ("Synchrona Themata," 2008; Economides& Monastiriotis, 2009). Most of the scientists agree that the riots of December was the signifier of diverse causes and processes that need to be unpacked within the social, political and economic semiotics of Greece and the wider economic and social context of late capitalism as well as the particular traditions of resistance. The other common theme in the analyses is the role of new technologies to the organisation and mobilization of the youth. However, there is another aspect that emerged in the discussions trying to interpret the events. This aspect stresses the fact that any kind of framing concerning these riots should

take into account the fact that there was neither a centre of organization nor a specific demand. In this way, it is extremely difficult to describe these events in their totality. Their language and form of expression point out to fragmentation and disorder. According to "Synchrona Themata" (2008, pp. 7-8) putting disorder at the centre of any study regarding December's events compels us to rethink both social regimes and conceptual frameworks generated. It also turns our attention to the language of description and how the latter organizes or fails to do so social solidarities. In this context, new forms of communication should be looked for. Blogging could become one of them.

In this framework, the author would like to examine briefly how December events had an impact on her class. By accident, the task of that week was to choose and develop a free subject. Students had to work independently and make a small research on a topic of their interest and then, to develop it in their blogs. Some reactions in the beginning of that week provided food for thought. Several students found "free subject" difficult. What should they write about? What was appropriate for coursework? Taking for granted that these reactions did not resulted from the fact that students lacked interests, the author realized that they might be the outcome of the novelty of the request in combination with internalized conceptions of what coursework should be and who could authorize it. Accustomed to work in a more structured and from the above directed environment, students felt rather insecure with such a project. In addition, since academia seems to be at a distance from the "real world," their extra-curriculum activities, interests or worries do not seem relevant to their academic work.

Nevertheless, the overwhelming event of that week seemed to have broken the ice. This was made obvious from the decision of ten of the 19 students to write about these events and to comment on each other's postings, opening in this way, the space for a dialogue between them and me, the class and society. Their opinion on the events varied, as it was expected. Some of them condemned the vandalization, but they were supportive of the general demand for change, others accepted the government's discourse about security and order, and finally, few others were sympathetic with a more radical action against the government. Some postings commented on the ways media represented the events underlining their frustration. All of them were disillusioned. They could feel the dead-end, but they could not discern a way out of the crisis. Blogging was a way to make public the feelings of distress and the disillusion that Greek citizens felt in those days.

Reading the postings of this class makes us realize to what degree their language expressed that frustration regarding the social and political situation in Greece. Their sentences are sharp, often interrupted with ellipses or question marks. The emotional tone is complemented with multiple exclamation or question marks and when prosaic, academic language seems to fail them, they turn to poetry, although the latter is often considered as a non academic language.

Θα 'ρθουν μέρες Days will come

άγριες μέρες Wild days

Που οι αλήθειες Where truths

θα σκίζουν σαν σφαίρες will be sharp like bullets

Και οι νίκες and the victories

άγιες νίκες sacred victories

Σαν μαχαίρια like knives

Θα βγουν απ τις θήκες will be pulled out from their cases

(2008, http://papakimon.blogspot.com/, author's translation from Greek)

(...)και όσο μιλάμε ο ουρανός σκουραίνει, τα σύννεφα μαυρίζουν και μια ματαιότητα απλώνεται πάνω από τις κουβέντες...

μια παιδική καρδιά είναι αναντικατάστατη,

η σιωπή είναι καλύτερο πένθος..

το σύστημα είναι από μέσα σάπιο και αλλάζει μόνο με τη καρδιά μας..

(...) and while we are talking, the sky goes darker, the clouds get blackened and vanity is spread above us like a blanket...

the heart of a child cannot be replaced,

silence is the best mourning...

the system is rotten from the inside and it can be changed only within our heart.

(2008, http://veradimopoulou.blogspot.com/2008/12/blog-post.html, authors translation from Greek)

Blog as a space of reflection was used by many Greeks in order to unpack the meaning and the subjectivities that the riots tried to constitute and communicate. As Gavriilidis (2009, pp.15-16) argued, the riots in Athens had everything to do with communication both because of the use of new technologies in order to spread news regarding demonstrations, as well as their performative and enunciative power, as a form of reaction. In this context, online communication was considered to be less restrictive by the State mechanisms. At the same time, it was viewed as more immediate, creative and evasive than face-to-face communication. Thus, blogging seemed to be more appropriate to articulate the fragmented, multi-directional and unstructured voices of the riots. As a result, students were more motivated to express themselves online than in the traditional academic channels of interaction. Of course, we should not forget the fact that there were nine other students that remained disengaged from this form of communication, and this is also significant. Does their silence present a sign of scepticism regarding new technologies? Or did they feel that blogging was not a way to respond to that social crisis? Further research regarding blogging, the Greek youth and the communities of bloggers emerging should study these questions. The experience of blogging in this class illustrated that highly controversial issues, which are debated both in society and in particular, within students' circles can and should become part of their education. In the case examined in this chapter, blogging could be considered as the needle that sews together different and separated until now fields of experience and knowledge both for students and educators.

SOLUTIONS AND RECOMMENDATIONS

One of the first issues discussed in this chapter was how to overcome the problem of uneven levels of familiarization with new technologies in our class.

Turning this problem to an asset could be the solution. More advanced students could play the role of tutors for weaker students strengthening in this way the ties among them. As the above case has indicated students collaborated with each in order to solve technical issues. This strengthened the class ties but it also bridged the gap between individual learning, which is often the case in big and competitive classes that lack a more collaborative form of knowledge.

Overcoming traditional power structures within the context of the classroom was another serious issue. Innovations in terms of assessment or coursework were met with reservations by the students, an indication of mistrust and internalization of the well established hierarchy and authority in the classroom,. Nevertheless, it would be a mistake to consider these reservations as a passive accep-

tance. Open discussion and confrontation of these reservations in class could have a positive impact. It is not a bad idea to address the targets and the expectations of the course inviting students for their contribution in the improvement of the latter. The introduction of blogging in the course led to the examination in practice of how online communication could prompt student's active participation in the construction of the course, its assessment and the production of knowledge. A multi-level and multi-directional form of assessment played a crucial role in bridging the inequalities and developing confidence and relations of trust.

Blogging appeared to encourage a more informal style of communication in class that, according to students' opinions, strengthened their ties and collaboration. However, it does not guarantee quality work, provided the tight deadlines under which students of this class had to work in order to respond to the challenges of the course, the unconventional and very diverse-sources they had to evaluate.

Students should understand that a more informal style of communication does not mean less responsible or demanding work in their part. Monitoring their postings and providing feedback each week on their writings contributed to the idea that their work is taken seriously and is evaluated in the same manner. In addition to that, more conventional material, such as important printed material, should be used in order to supplement and instigate further research. Comparing various sources creates a better interaction between them, which could help students acquire a deeper understanding of their subject and train them at evaluating diverse sources.

Another question that emerged from the above case concerned the question whether blogging guarantees the emergence of civic awareness and democratization within class communication.

The introduction of blogging in a university class in Greece has shown that new technologies are not a panacea. Structural reform in the education system is necessary. However, blogs could be an extra tool for educators who, because of the hectic schedules and the work overload, expect the transformation of their students to socially engaged individuals and citizens to be a long-term result of education. Civic awareness and democratization should be incorporated both in the theoretical preparation and the teaching methods of each course if we want a real transformation.

REFERENCES

Achbar, M., & Wintock, P. (1992*). Manufacturing consent: Noam Chomsky and media....* Retrieved November 5, 2008, from http://video.google.com/videoplay?docid=- 5631882395226827730.

Andriotakis, M. (2007). *Blog. Idisis apo to diko sou domatio* [Blog. News from your own room]. Athens: Nefeli.

Barrett, E. (Ed.). (1992). *Sociomedia, multimedia, hypermedia and the social construction of knowledge*. Massachusetts: MIT Press.

Beal, M. (2002). Teaching with technology: Construction at work. In Loyd, L. (Ed.), *Teaching with technology: Rethinking tradition* (pp. 27–132). Medford, NJ: Information Today Inc.

Castells, M. (2000). *The rise of the network society*. Oxford, UK: Blackwell.

Churchill, D. (2009). Educational applications of Web 2.0: Using blogs to support teaching and learning. *British Journal of Educational Technology, 40*(1), 179–183. doi:10.1111/j.1467-8535.2008.00865.x

Cope, B., & Kalantzis, M. (2006). A pedagogy of multiliteracies. Designing social futures. In Cope, B., & Kalantzis, M. (Eds.), *Multiliteracies. Literacy learning and design of social futures* (pp. 9–37). London: Routledge.

Demopoulou, V. (2008, December 18). *Mia prosopiki eksomologisi* [A personal confession]. Message posted to http://veradimopoulou.blogspot.com/

Downes, S. (2004). Educational Blogging. *Educause Review* 39(5), 14-26. Retrieved December 3, 2008, from http://www.educause.edu/EDUCAUSE+Review/EDUCAUSEReviewMagazineVolu. me39/EducationalBlogging/157920

Freire, P. (1977). *Politistiki Drasi gia tin kataktasi tis eleftherias* [Cultural Action for the acquisition of freedom]. Athens: Kastaniotis.

Freire, P. (2001). *Pedagogy of Freedom: Ethics, Democracy, and Civic Courage*. Lanham: Rowman & Littlefield Publishers, Inc.

Gavriilidis, A. (2008). Greek Riots 2008-A mobile Tiananmen. In S, Economides & V. Monastiriotis (Eds.), The return of street politics? Essays on the December riots in Greece (15-21). London: The Hellenic Observatory-LSE.

Georgiakarra. (2008, December 12) Anaparastasis gynekon mesa apo ta kentrika deltia idiseon tou Star ke tou Mega. [Representations of women in the central news bulletins of Star and Mega channels]. Message posted to http://georgiakarra. blogspot.com/

Gertsi. (2008). *Yerasimos Tsibloulis-Gertsi. Yia to perivallon, tin ekpedefsi, ton politismo ke tin kinoniki anthropologia.* [Yerasimos Tsibloulis-Gertsi. For the environment, education, culture and social anthropology]. Retrieved March 1, 2009, from http://tsibloulis.blogspot.com/

Gillmor, D. (2008, October). *Citizens and New Media*. Paper presented at the conference of Aristotle University of Thessaloniki on Participatory Journalism. Retrieved December 20, 2009, from http://www.blogchannel.gr/2009/04/dan-gillmor-auth/

Ginsburg, F. D., Abu-Lughod, L., & Larkin, B. (2005). Introduction. In Ginsburg, F. D., Abu-Lughod, L., & Larkin, B. (Eds.), *Media worlds. Anthropology on a new terrain* (pp. 1–36). Berkeley: University of California Press.

Glogowski, K. (2009, January 16). Teaching how to learn. Message posted to http://www.teachandlearn.ca/blog/2009/01/16/teaching-how-to-learn/

Greeklish. (n.d.) Retrieved February 3, 2009 from http://el.wikipedia.org/wiki/Greeklish

Jenkins, H. (2006). *Confronting the challenges of participatory culture: Media education for the 21ˢᵗ century*. Chicago: The MacArthur Foundation. Retrieved January 25, 2009, from http://digital-learning.macfound.org/atf/cf/%7B7E45C7E0-A3E0-4B89-AC9C- E807E1B0AE4E%7D/JENKINS_WHITE_PAPER.PDF

Jonscher, C. (1999). *The evolution of wired Life: From the alphabet to the soul-catcher chip—How information technologies change our world*. Hoboken: Wiley.

Koukloutsis, I. (2009, April 7). Anonimi i eponimi kritiki. Message posted to http://slografeiou.blogspot.com/2009/04/blog-post.html#comments

Lipman, E. (2005). Educational ethnography and the politics of globalization, war, and resistance. *Anthropology & Education Quarterly, 36*(4), 315–328. doi:10.1525/aeq.2005.36.4.315

Maguirenancy. (2008, December 17). To blog mou. [My blog]. Message posted to http://maguirenancy.blogspot.com/

Noujaim, J. (2004). *Control Room*. Retrieved November 22, 2008, from http://video.google.com/videoplay?docid=-5468579280837866970

Panagovayahoogr. (2008, December 18). Aksiologisi tou prosopikou mou blog. [Assessment of my personal blog]. Message posted to http://panagovayahoogr.blogspot.com/

Papakimon. (2008, December 11). *I via einai i mami tis istorias* [Violence is the midwife of history].Message posted to http://papakimon.blogspot.com/

Papakimon. (2009, January 7). Aksiologisi blog. [Assessment of blog]. Message posted to http://papakimon.blogspot.com/

Pappa, M. (2009). *Analisi simetokhikotitas se diadiktiaki kinotita mathisi: moodle*. [Analysis of participation in an internet learning community: moodle]. Unpublished PhD Dissertation, University of Piraeus, Piraeus.

Richardson, W. (2008). *Blogs, wikis, podcasts, and other powerful web tools for classrooms*. Thousand Oaks, CA: Corwin Press.

Sideri, E. (2000). *The women's voices in the internet*. Paper presented at the 1st Interdisciplinary Conference on Gender Ethics/ the Ethics of Gender, Leeds: University of Leeds.

Sideri, E. (2007). *Diasporization*. University of Thessaly. Retrieved 2 June, 2009 from http://www.elenasideri.zoomshare.com/7.shtml.

Sideri, E. (2008). *Anthropology of electronic media*. Retrieved 2 June, 2009, from http://iakaanthropologyofmedia.blogspot.com/

Slatin, J. M. (1992). Is there a class in this text? Creating knowledge in the electronic classroom. In Barrett, E. (Ed.), *Sociomedia, multimedia, hypermedia and the social construction of knowledge* (pp. 2–51). Massachusetts: MIT Press.

Solomon, G., & Schrum, L. (2007). *Web 2.0: New tools, new schools*. Washington, DC: International Society for Technology in Education.

Stelayahoogr. (2008, December 19). *Ta teleftea gegonota ke pos parousiazonte sta mme*. [The last events and their representation in the media]. Message posted to http://stelayahoogr.blogspot.com/

Synchrona Themata (2008). Fakelos #griots-Tekmiria. I "atakti skepsi" os gnostiki proklisi, i apopira katanoisis enanti tou apotropiasmou ke tis eksidikefsis [File#griots-Evidences. The "disordered thought" as an attempt to understanding, instead of dismay and idealization], 103, 6-26.

Tzortzakis, I. (2009). *Aksiopiisi web.2 ergalion sti skholiki ekpedefsi.* [Use of web.2 tools at schools]. Unpublished Master Dissertation, University of Piraeus, Piraeus.

Yiannakopoulos, K. I. (2005). *Ikonikes kinotites. Mia kinoniologiki prosegisi tou diadiktiou* [Virtual communities. A sociological approach of internet]. Athens: Papazisi.

ADDITIONAL READING

Camilleri, M., Ford, P., Leja, H., & Sollars, V. (Eds.). (2007). *Blogs: web journals in language education*. Graz: European Centre for Modern Languages.

Forte, M. (2008, May 10). Academic blogs: Purposes and benefits? Message posted to http://openanthropology.wordpress.com/2008/05/10/academic-blogs-purposes-and- benefits/

Forte, M. (2008, May 19). The craft of the online anthropologists: the new medium is the message. Message posted to http://openanthropology.wordpress.com/2008/05/19/the-craft-of-the-online-anthropologist-the-new-medium-is-the-message/

Forte, M. (2008, October 17). Digitize this book!: The politics of new media, or why we need open access now. Message posted to http://openanthropology.wordpress.com/2008/10/17/digitize-this-book-the-politics- of-new-media-or-why-we-need-open-access-now/

Gillmor, D. (2004). *We the media*. Retrieved June 3, 2009, from http://wethemedia.oreilly.com/

Gillmor, D. (2009). Mediactive. Creating a user's guide to media in a networked age Retrieved May 11, 2009, from http://mediactive.com/

Green, T. G., Brown, A., & Robinson, L. (2008). *Making the most of the web in your classroom: a teacher's guide to blogs, podcasts, wikis, pages and sites*. Thousand Oaks, CA: Crowin Press.

Hendron, J. G. (2008). *RSS for educators: Blogs, newsfeeds, podcasts, and wikis in classrooms*. Washington: International Society for Technology in Education.

Journal of Computer Mediated Communication. (2007). *12*(4). Retrieved May 3, 2009 from, http://jcmc.indiana.edu/

Lankshear, C. (2001). *Cut, paste, publish: The production and consumption of zines*. Retrieved September 12, 2008, from http://www.geocities.com/c.lankshear/zines.html

Lankshear, C., & Knobel, M. (2003). *Do-it-yourself broadcasting: Weblogs in a knowledge. society*. Retrieved August 28, 2008, from http://www.geocities.com/c.lankshear/blog2003.html

Lankshear, C., & Knobel, M. (2006, April). *Blogging as participation: The active sociality of a new literacy*. Paper presented at the American Educational Research Association Annual Meeting, San Francisco. Retrieved September 2, 2008, from www.geocities.com/c.lankshear/bloggingparticipation.pdf

Lessing, L. (2003). *The future of ideas*. New York: Random House USA Inc.

Nackerud, S., & Scaletta, K. (2008). Blogging in the Academy. *New Directions for Student Services*, *124*, 71–87. doi:10.1002/ss.296

Pionteck, J., & Pionteck, J. (2008). *Blogs, wikis, and podcasts, Oh, My!: electronic media in the classroom*. Huntington Beach, CA: Shell Education Publisher.

Rushkoff, D. (2003). *Open source democracy: how online communication is changing offline politics*. London: Demos.

Saka, E. (2008). *Blogging as a research tool for ethnographic fieldwork*. Retrieved October 5, 2008, from http://www.media-anthropology.net/saka_blogging.pdf

Samson, D. (2001). *Classrooms without faces: A synchronous online teaching experience*. Retrieved April 5, 2009 from, http://www.nmc.teiher.gr/activities/NHIE%202001/papers/E10_138.doc.

SYNC.GR. (2008). *O khartis tis ellinikis blogospheras* [The map of the Greek blogosphere]. Retrieved January 12, 2009, from http://blogs.sync.gr/survey2008/

Voyagis, G., Ksenos, M., & Hatzilakos, M. (2001). *Ebeiries apo ta pilotika virtual rooms* [Experiences from the pilot-virtual rooms]. Retrieved August 2, 2008, from http://nefeli.dsmc.eap.gr/ojs-2.1.1/index.php/HOUJOI/article/viewFile/3/2

VPRC. (2008). I politiki kultura ton blogs [The political culture of blogs]. *Greek Monthly Review*, *47*(112), 2–34.

KEY TERMS AND DEFINITIONS

Blog (Weblog): Virtual space of expression belonging to a person or to a group of people. Blogs vary in content. There are blogs used as diaries, news platforms, fora. Educational blogs are used as a tool of creating a more interactive space within the classroom environment.

Greeklish: A Romanized transcription of the Greek alphabet.

Emancipatory Pedagogy: A term used by the Brazilian educator, Paulo Freire who considered that the aim of education should not be only the transmission of knowledge and skills, but also, the development of citizen awareness.

Mediascape: A term launched by Arjun Appadurai (1990) in order to illustrate the fluidity created between the spaces produced by global media.

Multiliteracies: A term coined by the New London Group in order to point out the need to amplify the aims of educational literacy so that they could face the complexities of modern world. Among these complexities we find, cultural, economic and social interconnection, new technologies and media, linguistic diversity.

Neo-Luddites: People that approach technology with scepticism and a critical examination of its impact following the legacy of Luddites, a group that was active in the 19th century and fought against the results of the Industrial Revolution.

Chapter 7
'De–Coupling Groups in Space and Time':
Evaluating New Forms of Social Dialogue for Learning

Kevin Burden
The University of Hull, UK

Simon Atkinson
Massey University, New Zealand

EXECUTIVE SUMMARY

Prior to the Web, we had hundreds of years of experience with broadcast media, from printing presses to radio and TV. Prior to email, we had hundreds of years experience with personal media – the telegraph, the telephone. But outside the Internet, we had almost nothing that supported conversation among many people at once. The radical change was de-coupling groups in space and time. To get a conversation going around a conference table or campfire, you need to gather everyone in the same place at the same moment. By undoing those restrictions, the Internet has ushered in a host of new social patterns, from the mailing list to the chat room to the weblog. (Shirky, 2003)

INTRODUCTION

Removing the barriers of space and time, whilst still enabling individuals to converse in groups, promises to transform our practices and understanding of social dialogue. Technologies have evolved sufficiently to make these aspirations a reality, and educational technologists and researchers alike are actively seeking to identify the implications of such changes for society. Both are interested in identifying the unique feature sets and characteristics of

particular technologies to identify what added value they represent for the learning experience. Nowhere is this more apparent, at the present time, than in respect to Web 2.0 technologies (McLoughlin & Lee, 2007; Mejias, 2005).

There is a need to explore further the processes of identifying and measuring the added value that might be represented by the technological opportunities or affordances of specific technologies. The intention of this chapter is to explore, through the examination of a specific Web 2.0 application (VoiceThread), the opportunities for evaluating systematically the

DOI: 10.4018/978-1-61520-863-0.ch007

pedagogical affordances of emerging technologies, and to illustrate the possibilities of applying the Digital Artifacts for Learner Engagement framework (DiAL-e) to that task. The DiAL-e framework was developed as part of a project sponsored by the Joint Information Services Committee (JISC) in the UK to identify a range of opportunities for the development of activities with which to engage students in meaningful and challenging tasks using digital resources, rather than focus on content or the transmission of the information contained in those resources alone (Burden & Atkinson 2008). Although initially designed as a tool to facilitate and support the design of learning activities, the authors have also begun to recognize the framework's potential as an evaluative tool in a number of different contexts. This potential of the framework to act as an evaluative tool in discriminating between the various affordances of a single Web 2.0 technology, a conversation-sharing tool called VoiceThread (http://voicethread.com/), is described here.

Theoretical Context

In examining a particular technological tool, one is exploring a changing landscape, but through a single lens. The potential for technologies to change the social practices, behaviors and sociocultural expectations of their users is not the primary focus of this chapter, but it is necessary to outline the contextual factors and socio-cultural perspectives of the authors in order to understand the main thrust of the argument.

Research indicates there is a paucity of 'digital literacy' amongst teaching staff across the educational sectors that has a significant impact on learners (Jones, 2004). The varying levels of e-literacy have had a real impact on technology adoption, on learner performance, expectations and behavior, but they are poorly understood. As a result, it remains unusual to see genuinely interdisciplinary research teams undertaking a critical analysis of the phenomena that make up

the 'Internet'. Interdisciplinarity is essential if the true value of specialist social science traditions, investigative models and theoretical approaches are to shed useful light on these emerging questions. The theoretical context for the DiAl-e framework's use as a 'lens' for assessing the potential of any given communication technology is one that spans the range of communications theories, as applied to mass communications and interpersonal communication.

In other work, the authors have suggested the need to evaluate emerging technologies from the broadest possible theoretical perspectives. They posit that, to understand the impact of new communications technologies, one does well to recognize the insights afforded from sociology, social anthropology, semiotics, and communications studies (Atkinson & Burden, 2007). A holistic and socio-culturally aware approach to technology is advised. Cole and Derry argue for a reconceptualisation of technology and intelligence, contending that the two are indivisible, and also that the definition of technology needs to be broadened, to include not only 'tools' commonly defined as technology, but also the nature of deployment, or the action of the tool use itself, in a given social context (Cole & Derry, 2005). This rich vein of research theory in the tradition of the Cultural-Historical Activity Theorists (Engestrom, Miettinen, & Punamaki, 1999) suggests that any consideration of technology should regard technology as 'social milieu' as well as 'tools'. This is a step beyond the territory of the 'Social construction of technology', with its roots in the work of Bruno Latour, which argues that technology is not so much a determinate of human action, but that, rather, human actions serve to shape technology. Cole suggests that technologies should be envisaged as forms of tool-mediated social practice developing Piaget's notion that intelligence is the process of adaptation to the conditions of life.

In addition to these 'social cultural-historical' assertions it is also possible to draw significance from 'critical theorists' and refer to early communications and media meta-studies, such as Innis' space-time considerations. In his seminal social history of communication media, *The Bias of Communication* (Innis, 1951) Innis proposes that relative stability of cultures depends on the balance and proportion of their media. Innis asks three basic questions:

- How do specific communication technologies operate?
- On what social assumptions are they founded or created?
- What power structures do they imply or facilitate?

Social change can be examined, according to Innis, through an examination of the development of a given communication media, which identifies a relative bias between the organization and control of information. Since societies are concerned with their self-preservation over time and their extension in space, it is fruitful to identify different affordances of time-based or space-based media.

Time-biased media, chosen for their enduring qualities, might include such things as stone tablets. Durable, but difficult to transport, they do not support territorial expansion. Innis argues these media suggest endurance based on ceremony, ritual, the sacred, and the moral. He takes speech and oral traditions as time-biased media. By contrast, space-based media are transportable over large distances and facilitate physical expansion of empire over space. These media give primacy to distance reached over longevity. Radio and paper are easily transported, but might both be considered to have a relatively short lifespan.

It is an interesting reflection of the apparent threat to established news media and publishing 'empires', represented by Web 2.0 technologies and the rise of the 'prosumer', that Innis suggested social change emerges from the activities of 'new media' producers on the periphery who seek to undermine the dominant centre. The example often cited being that of the threat to the Latin based liturgy of the Christian Church on parchment from vernacular writings on paper. Notably Innis regarded oral communication, speech, as time-based because of the relative stability required for community face-to-face interaction. Oral traditions create recognizable lineages of transmission, often enforcing authority networks and justifying particular individual's authority to speak. Dialogue is a culturally bound concept.

Personal and Societal Communication in Space and Time

The emergence of Internet-related research studies have given rise to attempts at addressing the apparent contradictions inherent in earlier mass-communications studies unable to cope with the global reach of the Internet and its immediate personal context. The differences in scale are addressed, to a large degree, in 'loose web' theory, which identifies the inter-related technologies that make up the Internet and, whilst acknowledging the difficulties of conceptualizing the web as a whole, suggests that the sum total of communication produced through these associated means can be identified, and its internal and external impacts studied (Burnett & Marshall, 2003)

Cultural Production Thesis seeks to explore the difference in scale of individual engagement with the means of cultural production between the twentieth century's television and radio mass media participation, essentially a passive activity, and the mass cultural participation of the Internet (Burnett & Marshall, 2003). Early forms of the Cultural Production Thesis, which predate the onset of mass blogging and the majority of online social networking tools, still fails, however, to recognize the quantum leap from participation in mass Internet communications to the mass cultural production of content. The expectation that the web can, and will, impact on society is part of the technological determinist approach. This approach has developed in the disciplines of computer science in both cybernetics and artificial intelligence and helps to define the Internet as a living organism or an evolutionary system.

These meta-level considerations of space and time orientated communications, and attempts to reassess the mass-communications landscape for its evolutionary and organic nature, do not negate the need to consider the individual. Each individual engaged in a dialogue with another individual, or media resource, can be said to have an identifiable transactional distance with that other party. Coined by Michael G. Moore in the 1980s, the term 'transactional distance', refers to the cognitive space between teachers, and/or content, and the learner or learning peers in a distance education setting. The argument in subsequent adult education theory being that the transactional distance decreases with dialogue and increases with structure (Moore, 1993, p.37). In a face-to-face context this implies that a teaching space with high levels of interaction and less predefined structure will be more engaging to learners.

In considering the work of Innis and others, one is placing the analysis of a specific technology for communication in the broader context of interpersonal human communication. Clearly, there is more that can be said about the cognitive demands of any given technology, or its ability to disturb cultural assumptions. What is significant for the analysis of the added value to learning that any technology is said to afford its users, is that we recognize the broader context in which this communicative transaction takes place.

Communication theorists can be distinguished as those who choose to focus on the content of communication and those sometimes depicted as 'medium theorists'. The medium theorists, amongst whom Innis might be considered one, but Marshall McLuhan is perhaps the most often cited, give precedence to the means of communication, rather than the content of the message. In education there has been some considerable interest in the degree to which the medium might dictate pedagogy as applied to the virtual learning environment (VLE) but relatively little attention paid to the role of the medium in much face-to-face teaching. The exception to this is perhaps the work of Richard Mayer and others on the cognitive demands of particular mediums for learning facilitation, notably the ubiquitous use of presentation software, characterized by Microsoft PowerPoint. Mayer's cognitive theory of multimedia learning (Mayer 2005(a); Mayer 2005(b); Mayer, 2009) suggests learners perform better with supportive guidance on how to process text and graphical material and when the significance of key words and concepts are clearly articulated, and this has obvious implications for the use of specific technologies.

Communication is always set in a value-laden context. Each collocutor has value assumptions about trust, truthfulness and intent. Communicating is how we feel our way in the world. To understand, therefore, the contexts in which we communicate is essential. One could, perhaps, characterize those that prioritize the content of the message as being 'channel' theorists, and those that give precedence to the medium and meta-meaning of communication, as 'process' theorists. For channel theorists, the trust necessary to effective communication is built and maintained through mediated authenticity of the communication itself. For the process theorists, the meta-communication must be trustworthy. Perhaps the clearest illustration of this difference in perspective is the application of the often misquoted work of Albert Mehrabian, which gave rise to the 'urban myth' that 93% of communication was essentially non-verbal (Mehrabian, 1981). The '7-38-55' belief system purports that body language accounts for 55% of the 'message', 38% the tonality of anything 'sounded' and just 7% to the actual content of the words. Widely espoused in the Neuro-Linguistic Programming (NLP) field, these figures somewhat misrepresent the original research which focused primarily on the enunciation of nine words, three deemed positive, three negative and three neutral (Mehrabian & Weiner,

1967). The experience of online moderators in online learning courses clearly suggests that more than 7% of the message is being transmitted, despite the evident frustrations concerning tone and inference, which even emoticons, though useful, fail to correct fully (Derks, Bos, & von Grumbkow, 2008). The rush to embrace Web 2.0 technologies suggests practitioners believe Channel theorists are right, in that trust benefits significantly from facial expression and tonal assurances.

The fields of socio-psychology and semiotics have a great deal to bring to the debate on effective Web 2.0 communications processes, and educationalists would do well to go out and seek their interdisciplinary engagement. These colleagues can make a very significant difference to our effective use of educational technologies. In the fifty years since McLuhan's suggestion that the media itself was a socially disruptive and transformative influence both on society and our individual senses (McLuhan, 1962), we continue to struggle for a perspective which unifies, or at least acknowledges, these two extremes, the personal and the societal.

What are Pedagogical Affordances?

There is considerable hype and rhetoric surrounding the debate about the potential of Web 2.0 technologies to initiate and lead educational transformation (O'Reilly, 2005). However, very few Web 2.0 technologies were originally designed as educational tools. Most Web 2.0 technologies including wikis, blogs and mashups have been appropriated by educators for pedagogical purposes. In some cases, the potential for learning is readily apparent as in the case of wikis which are frequently used for collaborative group work in educational settings. But the potential learning value of a particular technology (affordances) is not dictated solely by a particular functionality (McLoughlin & Lee, 2007). Other factors have a role to play in determining how a particular tool might facilitate a resolution to a pedagogical problem. In other words, the specific design and functionality of a particular tool or technology does not define its pedagogical usefulness. There are other important ingredients required, including the imagination and creativity of the individual user who must conceptualize problems or issues in their own environment and context.

The first challenge, then, is to encourage educators to problematize their own practice and seek solutions. To illustrate this point, McLoughlin and Lee note how blogging entails typing and editing, which are not in themselves affordances, but rather enablers of affordances that include idea sharing and interaction (McLoughlin & Lee, 2007). They identify the following categories of 'affordances' associated with Web 2.0 or social software:

- Connectivity and social rapport
- Collaborative information discovery and sharing
- Content creation
- Knowledge and information aggregation and content modification.

Other means of identifying the pedagogical affordances of social networking software also exist. Addressing specifically the needs of learners for feedback on their own learning, one might consider the affordances of given technologies to facilitate the dialogue that is so necessary to that process. In distilling a wide range of assessment research, Hatzipanagos and Warburton identify eight dimensions affecting feedback, which might arguably subsume those categories defined by McLoughlin & Lee. However, they draw particular attention to the role of power (autonomy and ownership), dialogue, timeliness, visibility, appropriateness, action, community and reflection (Hatzipanagos & Warburton, 2009). They then go on to assess a range of electronic tools available to tutors in traditional resource-based and open and distance learning contexts, including email, online quizzes, discussion lists and forums, as well as two Web 2.0 tools in blogs and wikis. They conclude that blogs and wikis provide higher levels of personalization, immediacy and accountability then other electronic assessment forms and suggest greater opportunities for reflection and self-motivation.

McLoughlin and Lee also make the crucial point that social software affordances do not, by themselves, guarantee that effective learning will occur. This requires 'careful planning and a thorough understanding of the dynamics of these affordances' (2007, p.4). The dynamics of these affordances are under researched and under theorized and the DiAL-e framework is put forward here as a contribution to this endeavor.

The Digital Artifacts for Learner Engagement Framework (DiAL-e)

The DiAL-e framework was not conceptualized or designed as a tool for evaluating technology. It is a conceptual model for designing learning engagements with digital artifacts and has been made tangible in both a paper-based form and online manifestations as a matrix populated with authentic exemplars. Ten separate learning designs are cross-referenced to various spaces enabling users to identify learning designs by context, learning activity, or a combination of both. An example can be seen at: http://213.133.67.199/JISC/index.php

Originally the result of work commissioned by the United Kingdom Joint Information Systems Committee (JISC) to support take-up of the NewsFilm Online archive (www.nfo.ac.uk), the framework emerged as a generic template for use with a wide range of different digital media resources. The authors sought to develop sound pedagogical models and exemplars for the use of digital video in post-compulsory educational contexts, but no assumptions were made about how academics might choose to work with the final archive, although it was anticipated (and subsequently borne out in field trials) that individuals would seek to sustain their 'default search position'. This 'content default', is one in which practitioners identify a content area they are interested in using, and undertake a simple search to locate artifacts relating to that content. It was anticipated practitioners would not perceive the true value of the archive or make effective use of it without the assistance of more refined strategies. These strategies make up the DiAL-e framework.

From the outset, the DiAL-e exemplars were driven by learning designs for engagement, rather than epistemological considerations alone. Whilst it was not the intention to minimize the importance of subject or discipline perspectives, it was considered important not to surrender to the prevailing ethos that 'content is king'. It was also considered important to demonstrate how a broad range of pedagogical engagements might be predicated for all students from what might superficially appear to be a purely social sciences resource.

The emergent DiAL-e framework was effectively a toolkit consisting of a matrix on two axes (see figure 1). The first is concerned with spaces for teaching and the second models for engagement. A number of different learning spaces are identified, ranging from large (e.g. lecture theatre) through to small (e.g. tutorial), and including virtual spaces (e.g. online), practical spaces (e.g. a workshop), independent spaces (e.g. the library), along with mobile learning spaces (e.g. handheld and mobile telephone devices). These are not considered mutually exclusive, rather it was deemed necessary to support academics in considering the context in which any engagement would take place.

The other axis of the DiAL-e matrix identifies ten discrete learning designs with a significant amount of overlap between them. The specific focus of each design relates to a set of activities, aimed at a particular meta-cognitive process, but these are regarded as open for re-contextualisation and repurposing. The ten learning designs, described in further detail at www.dial-e.net, are itemized on the left hand side of the matrix in Figure 1.

Figure 1. The DiAL-e framework in its simplest paper-based form. (© 2008, Burden & Atkinson. Used with permission.)

	Large	Small	Practical	Independent	Virtual	Mobile
Stimulation						
Narrative						
Collaboration						
Conceptualisation						
Inquiry						
Authoring						
Empathising						
Research						
Representations						
Figurative						

BACKGROUND TO CASE STUDY: VOICETHREAD

The background context for creating and identifying illuminating case studies around this particular Web 2.0 application is not specifically focused on the technology itself. This report does not seek to evaluate or compare a particular instance of what might be termed 'multi-modal threaded discussion' with any other comparable application. Instead, it seeks to explore *how, and why, certain forms of interpersonal communication are adopted and adapted to different contexts.*

The authors have developed and taught entirely online modules using Web 2.0 technologies and media rich artifacts (e.g. digital video, sound archives, digital texts). Some of this work relates directly to a JISC sponsored project investigating the issues of repurposing teaching resources for use in tertiary settings (The RePRODUCE project: http://www.hull.ac.uk/dial). Other aspects of this development work, shared by colleagues worldwide, are the professional interest in exploring the application and use of technology to enhance teaching and learning.

In constructing entirely online modules based around the use of Web 2.0 technologies, and focused on media rich resources, such as video archives, there is a disparities between the richness of content under consideration and the expectation that learners reflect and discuss using an entirely text-based system, the norm in most virtual learning environments. Reflection, peer review and conversation are central design elements in the DiAL-e learning strategies which frequently require students to post both personal and public reflections around their learning and the artifacts they are exploring. This encouraged the authors to seek an online tool that would enable asynchronous comments and feedback from students and tutors alike around media rich artifacts, such as video clips, images and presentations. VoiceThread appears to meet many of these requirements (http://www.voicethread.com).

VoiceThread is a quintessential Web 2.0 tool designed to facilitate collaborative group 'conversations' in online contexts (e.g. a VLE) without the need for users to download any specific software onto their computer. Like many Web 2.0 applications, the software is situated online enabling users to access their conversations from any Internet enabled machine, worldwide. It is also freely available to users although creators may consider purchasing a professional account if they wish to generate more than five VoiceThreads. The application has the ability to capture securely and hold an entire group discussion or thread on one page, making it visually clear and immediate for learners and tutors

At one level VoiceThread appears to be a typical online multimedia slide show consisting of a variety of media, which might include images, video and audio. However, it allows users far greater interactivity than online slideshows normally facilitate. Users are able to leave comments posted around the original VoiceThread presentation. These comments can take up to four forms; text, audio, video, and SMS text (only available in the USA at the present time). Depending on the hardware available (e.g. microphone or webcam) users can leave a media rich message and initiate a conversation thread which moves beyond the limitations of text-based media described above. In addition they can 'doodle' on screen whilst leaving a message which enables them to direct attention to particular features of the object which they are describing or responding to. Finally, the creator of each VoiceThread conversation has the option to turn these comments on or off at any point in time. For example, if the creator is using the VoiceThread as an assessment exercise requiring students to post their comments about the presentation, they can disable the view comments option which means comments are not visible to other users. At a later point, perhaps once all students have responded, the comments can be reactivated enabling users to see every posting, rather than just their own. In this way the tool offers a degree of moderation which may be appropriate for particular groups in certain circumstances.

As with so many of the emergent Web 2.0 technologies, VoiceThread was not designed specifically for an educational audience and it is widely used by a range of other parties including fan groups, business interest and social groups.

In terms of functionality the application includes:

- The ability to zoom in and look around a specific artifact (e.g. an image)
- Ability to leave (and easily delete) comments related to the object/object or related to other comments
- Simple navigation through pages (where more than one image is included)
- Video doodling; allows the user to write or annotate on a video (e.g. to show what might be happening)
- Use tags (i.e. meta-data) to create groups of similar VoiceThreads
- Ability to keep the thread private, public or by invitation
- Various levels of access; able to watch but not comment; see and comment; co-editors
- Comment moderation; allows the author the opportunity to see comments before they are shown publicly.

METHODOLOGY

The empirical data, which forms the basis of this case study, is drawn from an eclectic mixture of different sources rather than a single discrete data collection. Most of the examples cited here are drawn from cases in which the focus is on the use of this technology by students involved in various accredited courses through our own institutions. These include students undertaking both undergraduate and postgraduate studies and are characterized by the common theme of continuing professional development (CPD). The focus in these case studies is centered on how individuals use any given technology (in this case VoiceThread) to support their own learning and, in particular, the extent to which that technology supports an alternative to text based communication. Specifically these case studies seek to examine the following research questions:

- How is the use of technologies, such as VoiceThread, evolving our understanding of online communication?
- What specific features or affordances of VoiceThread facilitate discussion and digital conversations?

In all, data was collected from fifteen different educators. Nine of these were students on our own programmes exploring the use of VoiceThread as an alternative tool for recording and sharing their ideas and reflections. The remaining six participants are drawn from educators working outside of our own university. They responded to an open-ended request, distributed using VoiceThread itself, to share their experiences of using VoiceThread, with particular reference to the research questions identified above.

VoiceThread was itself used as a data collection tool for this case study, and although it is beyond the scope of this chapter, its potential value as a research instrument should be noted. The original VoiceThread can be located at http://voicethread.com/share/458337/. Over the course of a six-week period in April and May 2009, students and those from outside of the university were invited to contribute their experiences and opinions of VoiceThread. Participants were invited to use any of the feedback tools in VoiceThread and the precise medium they utilized is analyzed in the results/analysis section below.

The data that was supplied has been anonymised for the purposes of confidentiality. Given the relatively small sample size (fifteen participants), the data was analyzed manually rather than through the use of a software package, using the same 'grounded theory' approach which characterizes these programmes.

In addition to this data, a selection of public VoiceThread postings (http://www.voicethread.

com) for a single calendar month in January 2009 were also analyzed. A simple search on the VoiceThread website was undertaken using the search term 'January 2009', which identified twenty-two individual VoiceThreads that had been created during that calendar month. January 2009 was chosen because it was sufficiently distant from the time of writing (May 2009) to ensure users had time to post comments, but sufficiently recent for the familiarity of the technology not to have developed in such a way as to distort user behaviors. The focus of this analysis was largely quantitative, seeking to situate the comments made by our own students in a broader user context. Of particular interest were the different types of media employed by users when responding to VoiceThread objects. These range from traditional text based communication, through audio, video (with audio) and mobile telephone (currently available only in the USA). A relatively straightforward analysis sought to establish the nature of the original postings or VoiceThreads, and the subsequent responses from users. These were analyzed in terms of (a) the media which was employed, and (b) the frequency of replies received for each VoiceThread, giving the results as outlined in Table 1.

ANALYSIS OF RESULTS

How Is the Use of Technologies Like VoiceThread Evolving Our Understanding of Online Communication?

Although a tool like VoiceThread offers the potential for an entirely non-text based form of communication, user groups are not homogenous in their adoption of this approach, and use the tool with a mixture of traditional and non-traditional media and approaches. One respondent commented that VoiceThread is '…not an alternative to text but an additional way of communicating',

Figure 2. VoiceThread screen shot with four comments. (© 2009, Kevin Burden. Used with permission-subject to approval.)

and a few doubted that VoiceThread would surpass technologies such as SMS or e-mail. Interestingly, they appear to focus more on the traditional text-based features of the application, rather than those features, such as audio commenting, that set it apart from text-based communication tools.

The analysis undertaken on the public threads suggests that tools like VoiceThread are currently challenging conceptualizations of online communication but they are not yet radically altering the substantive nature of such communications. Although a majority of the user comments sampled were non-text based (56%), a substantial minority (44%) still commented using text alone. These statistics, and the data collected from our own users, suggest users are cautious about abandoning their traditional text-based tools in favor of entirely audio or video and audio based communications. A large proportion were beginning to explore the opportunities afforded through audio comments, which might suggest this proportion will grow and move on to employ, in addition, video based communications, once they become more familiar and confident with the technology.

The concept of 'identity' in online contexts is also something many of the respondents commented on, making the point that text-based communication affords a certain degree of anonymity as far as 'identity' is concerned, but audio – and to an even greater extent, video – forms of communication begin to remove some of this.

Being one pupil in a class of thirty-two can sometimes lead to anonymity and pupils who never get the chance to be expressive or to build up their own identity. These tools can allow that, but can also do the opposite. You can become a small part in a bigger crowd with these tools but I do agree that they do give the pupils a chance to expand their horizons. (Nigerian educator)

The issues of veracity and identity are closely linked in this sense, and tools such as VoiceThread begin to explore these dimensions of online space

Table 1. Analysis of mode of response for VoiceThreads resulting from 'January 2009' search term

Number of Voice-Threads analyzed	Number of viewings	Total number of comments by viewers	Number of subsequent comments by viewers		
			Video based	Audio based	Text based
22	2,208	366	24 (7%)	166 (49%)	146 (44%)
			56%		44%

Mean average number of comments per VoiceThread: 15 (max = 459; min = 0)

in ways which may become increasingly common in the future (Atkinson & Burden, 2007).

What Specific Features or Affordances of VoiceThread Facilitate Discussion and Digital Conversations?

A number of the respondents commented on the warmth and sense of engagement created by an audio posting in VoiceThread, compared to a traditional text-based communication.

The ability to hear or see someone discussing the point in hand, in my view, makes it warmer than reading a page of comments posted by people. Those people who don't enjoy reading can still engage with the content. (A UK based Technology Teacher)

In certain educational settings, such as early years, special educational needs, or English as a second language (ESL), the audio and video features were identified as particularly valuable, enabling greater inclusivity and understanding compared to online text-based communications.

To make my work with the children truly inclusive, instructions and commentary need to be negotiated in audio or video. Naturally some of the children can negotiate text, but it is much more spontaneous and valuable to have the children make oral responses. (Australian ESL teacher)

Inclusivity also extends to the application's ability to support a number of parallel, but not always related, conversational threads within the same VoiceThread. In a traditional face-to-face classroom, conversations can be dominated by the most outspoken or confident pupils, or indeed by the teacher. This effectively curtails further participation and limits the richness of the conversation. With VoiceThread there are fewer limits, either temporal or spatial. Pupils can answer when they are ready and no one pupil is privileged over another. This theme was echoed in a number of the responses collected:

Directed questions to selected pupils can cut down on that [domination by other pupils], but you can sometimes see the relief of the other pupils when they are not selected to answer a question. A tool like this [VoiceThread] will allow them to go away, think about the topic and then post their own views, or respond to others views without that 'public pressure' of being in a classroom with their peers. (English teacher in the UK)

DISCUSSION

The responses of users to the specific possibilities of an emerging technology are bound by expectation, assumption and convention. The metaphors educators use to describe their use, or expectation, of a particular technology are conditioned by their existing practice. Increasingly educators are faced with an ever expanding array of web based social networking applications which promise to solve a multitude of problems and concerns. But what questions need to be asked when faced with these choices? Some of the questions might be at a philosophical level and others are very practical.

In this respect some 'external' criteria for the evaluation of technologies, based on understanding of their pedagogical affordances, would be beneficial. Three possible approaches are outlined below.

One evaluation methodology might be to apply McLoughlin and Lee's definition of the term affordances, namely 'the activities or practices that the function of a technology enables the user to perform' (McLoughlin & Lee, 2007), to this specific media sharing technology named Voice-Thread. Table 2 illustrates the various functional attributes of VoiceThread and, alongside them, the pedagogical 'affordances', which they enable.

From this analysis, it is apparent that the functionality of this particular application (left-hand column) does not translate directly into an affordance with pedagogical significance (right-hand column). In some cases, there is no obvious or apparent pedagogical use for the functionality of the tool. In other cases, the pedagogical affordance will only be apparent under certain specific conditions and contexts. For example, the comment moderation function will enable a teacher to make comments invisible to other users until such a point as s/he wishes to reveal them. In the context of an examination class, in which the teacher does not wish individual comments to be influenced by 'group-think', this may be very useful. Therefore, this suggests the particular affordance, deployed towards a specific pedagogical goal, is the product of the dynamic between context, software functionality and social setting.

A second approach might be appropriate to evaluate a given tool for a specific dimension of the learning experience. One could, for example, apply the criteria established by Hatzipanagos and Warburton with reference to Web 2.0 applications for formative feedback and assessment to Voice-Thread (Hatzipanagos & Warburton, 2009).

Given the enthusiasm that Hatzipanagos and Warburton show for blogs and wikis, it is not surprising perhaps that a tool such as VoiceThread

appears to fulfill most of their criteria for effective feedback support. VoiceThread can be both a dialogue tool between individuals and a group interaction space. In its dialogic form, it affords a degree of privacy for learner feedback and reflection, much like a journal or private blog. In its group form, it allows for simultaneous peer-to-peer support and reflection, as well as that with the teacher. The ability to make multiple comments and responses to any number of others is similar to the functionality achieved in most online forums. The degree to which feedback can be linked directly to assessment criteria or intended learning outcomes will depend on the degree to which the VoiceThread has been designed to reflect those aspects. Where VoiceThread offers particular advantages for feedback is the opportunity for learners to see their 'comments' juxtaposed so immediately with that of their peers. There remains a degree of asynchronicity, as each response, whether audio, text or video can only be viewed sequentially. Truly simultaneous video, audio and text applications are emerging, as the capacity of domestic computer processing allows for the development of collaborative communication and editing as 'hosted conversation' within web browsers, such as Google's Wave (Google 2009).

Kirschner and others make the important point that affordances alone do not guarantee effective learning (Kirschner, 2002). The integration of any tool into the learning process must ensure that it provides the learner with something they want and need. This brings us to the third possible approach to exploring the affordances of any given technology. This approach focuses on the actions or activities of the learner themselves in using a tool, ensuring that functionality is related to an understanding of the dynamics between functionality and learning context and learning design. The DiAL-e framework adds value to this dynamic of identifying pedagogical affordances in Web 2.0 technologies. The DiAL-e approach examines with a much greater degree of granularity, where the affordances for a particular technology are at their

Table 2. Technical features of VoiceThread and their affordances, after McLoughlin and Lee (2007)

Features of the technology	Affordances
Ability to zoom in and out of the specific artifact itself (e.g. an image)	Concentrate or focus learner attention on specific aspects of the artifact
Ability to post asynchronous comments related to the artifact: e.g. Written responses to an artifact Audio comments Video comments	Learners and teachers can provide feedback about a media object (e.g. a video) at a granular level, attached to specific aspects or points of the object itself Opportunity for formative feedback on media related work prior to formal assessment
Ability to post handwritten annotation on the artifact (e.g. a video or image)	Learners and teachers can identify specific temporal or spatial aspects of the artifacts and isolate these features for increased attention or concentration
Ability to post asynchronous comments related to other comments	Communities of learners can see and respond to the cumulative postings and 'collective wisdom'
Artifact (i.e. the subject of the discussion) can be made accessible online	Learners are able to receive feedback and comments from a global audience, easily and quickly – instant feedback possible
Ability to invite groups and keep the thread private, public or a mixture	The 'learning conversation' can be managed by the teacher or learner to ensure it is open to the appropriate audience
Comment moderation (i.e. the teacher can decide if other comments are seen by those posting their own notes)	This feature enables the teacher to decide whether to let learners see (and possibly be influenced by) other comments or whether to keep them all private until everybody has posted returns. This might be desirable in certain circumstances (e.g. tests)
Full discussion captured on one single page	The entire learning conversation can be visualized in one diagram, one a single page, rather than stretching (often discontinuously) though a long text-based thread.

strongest. This is shown in Table 4, which illustrates the pedagogical affordances for VoiceThread against each of the DiAL-e learning designs, by providing more insights and examples linked to pedagogically sound engagements. Although an application such as VoiceThread could be used in a wide variety of different educational contexts, the DiAL-e framework provides an additional level of filtering to specify, at a more practical level, the match with genuine learning opportunities.

FROM THEORY TO PRACTICE

The speed at which Web 2.0 technologies emerge, are deployed and replaced by others, provides little time to reflect on their contribution or impact. The duality described by Innis of time-based and space-based media (Innis, 1951) appears meaningless in the contemporary networked environment. If Innis saw speech, and the richness of oral traditions, as typifying the prioritization of the longevity (time) of the message over its geographical reach (space), does a VoiceThread audio conversation conform to time-based assumptions? If the theory of transactional distance was reformulated in the light of teleconferencing (Moore, 1993) because "compared to broadcast, recorded or correspondence media, learner-instructor interaction by teleconference is more dialogic and less structured', must it again be reconsidered in the light of the new structures offered by so many highly dialogic Web 2.0 applications?

Adult education theories have suggested that the transactional distance decreases with dialogue and increases with structure. In a face-to-face context, this implies that a teaching space with high levels of interaction and less predefined structure will be more engaging to learners. Online, we now have access to tools that offer multiple channels for dialogue and offer variants on structure.

Table 3. Affordances of VoiceThread as seen through Hatzipanagos and Warburton's matrix (Hatzipanagos and Warburton 2009)

Dimension	Identified attributes of feedback	Pedagogical affordances of VoiceThread
Power (autonomy and ownership)	Support management of learning Improve levels of confidence Increase responsibility and autonomy	VoiceThreads can be assigned to specific groups Contributors can decide whether to submit text, audio or visual responses
Dialogue	Ensuring sufficiently frequent and detailed feedback Supporting peer/teacher dialogue Allowing learner response to feedback Support questioning Sharing assessment criteria	Teacher can provide unlimited responses within conversation Anyone can comment on any part of Thread, their own, another's or teacher posting Assessment can be posted and negotiated within a Thread
Timeliness	Quantity and timeliness of feedback – feedback is prompt	Feedback can be provided at any time, in 'real-time'
Visibility	Ability to discern learners needs Establishing prior knowledge Identification of unintended learning outcomes	Teacher can identify not only individual responses (comprehension) but also trends within cohorts, establishing internal 'norms' where appropriate.
Appropriateness	Feedback is understandable to learners Feedback is linked to outcomes Feedback is linked to assessment criteria Feedback focused on learning not marks	Feedback can be tailored to individual response and shared or be a collective response. Specific outcomes and criteria can be addressed is shared conversation is structured appropriately. This is a learning design issue.
Action	Feedback is received and acted upon by learners Task-performance-feedback cycles are facilitated Feedback helps learners to set goals.	In a one-to-one VoiceThread the response mechanism will be evident.
Community	Support for learning communities Support for peer assessment	VoiceThreads are strong visible communities where each individual is identifiable
Reflection	Encourage reflection on the work Compare actual performance with standards set and action taken to mitigate differences Provide information to teacher to help shape teaching (reflection-in-action/reflection-on-action) Develop skills in self-awareness	The ability to review a VoiceThread (they can be downloaded in movie formats and replayed) allows individual responses to be isolated. Careful review of this resource by teachers should be part of the design process.

In the rush to adapt and adopt technologies for educational purposes, much of our theoretical understanding has been put to one side. A more considered, theoretically grounded, consideration of the pedagogical affordances of emerging technologies is required.

CONCLUSION

The affordances of a specific technology (Web 2.0 or any other) do not stand alone from other considerations, such as the social and cultural settings in which the learning is situated. Initial experiences with VoiceThread and other similar Web 2.0 applications strongly underline the importance of sound planning, imagination and creativity on the part of the teacher in designing meaningful learning experiences with these technologies. Affordances can be so broad and general, as to be almost meaningless in terms of planning specific learning experiences. Investigations using the DiAL-e framework as an evaluative tool, suggest it has considerable scope and potential in assisting educators to identify which specific affordances might have value and in which contexts. In our ongoing study, we are now moving to consider the impact and importance of space (the other axis of the DiAL-e framework) as another variable against which to consider af-

Table 4. The affordances of Voice-Thread as seen through the DiAL-e framework

Applicable DiAL-e learning designs	Pedagogical affordances available through VoiceThread
Stimulus activities (designed to engage or motivate learners)	Posting a video clip to VoiceThread without the sound, or soundtrack without the movie, and asking learners to post comments with their reflections about what might be happening or what might be missing - **'top and tail'** exercise
Narrative or story-telling (understanding the nature of story and story-teller)	Shared writing (or speaking). The teacher posts an initial image, comment or video in the artifact window and learners construct a shared narrative around the object adding to each comment that is made.
Collaborative (working in groups to construct knowledge)	Using VoiceThread to host the initial stages of an experiment (e.g. a video with voice over) and asking learners to undertake the experiment themselves and post their observation/data collections to this thread. Or – as a survey instrument – to collect opinions: post the clip and invite learners to use their phone/text to comment on the piece
Conceptual (developing higher order thinking skills: e.g. hypothesizing, analysis)	**Predict, observe and evaluate design**: Using a stimulating video clip or single image, learners are asked to predict what will happen next; i.e. to make a hypothesis. After learners have left their prediction in the form of responses, the teacher uploads a new artifact showing the next stage allowing learners to refine their original prediction. **Analysis:** Using the zoom tool, learners are able to focus in on a particular aspect of an image or diagram. Ask students to analyze and give feedback on differing parts of the image
Empathy (encouraging learners to see the world from alternate perspectives)	By carefully selecting a suitable piece of media, learners could be asked to undertake a series of different roles, posting to VoiceThread perspectives they find difficult or with which they personally disagree
Representational	Learners deconstruct an image or moving image text and leave postings around the artifact that build up to give a more complete view of how this piece of media has been constructed and what it really represents

fordances of particular technologies. These two variables – space and learning design – promise to provide educators with a valuable instrument through which to gauge the potential value of a new technology, such as VoiceThread. To ask not what the tool can do, but what their students can do with the tool.

REFERENCES

Atkinson, S., & Burden, K. (2007). Virtuality, veracity and values: Exploring between virtual and real worlds using the 3V model. In *ICT: Providing choices for learners and learning.* Presented at the Proceedings ascilite, Singapore. Retrieved August 27, 2009, from http://www.ascilite.org. au/conferences/singapore07/procs/atkinson.pdf.

Burden, K., & Atkinson, A. (2008). Beyond content: Developing transferable learning designs with digital video Archives, In *Proceedings of ED-MEDIA, Vienna 2008 conference*: http://www.editlib.org/index.cfm?fuseaction=Reader. ViewAbstract&paper_id=28949

Burnett, R., & Marshall, P. D. (2003). *Web theory*. London: Routledge.

Cole, M., & Derry, J. (2005). We Have Met Technology and it is Us. In *Intelligence and technology: Impact of tools on the nature and development of human abilities*. Mahwah, NJ: Lawrence Erlbaum Associates.

Derks, D., Bos, A. E. R., & von Grumbkow, J. (2008). Emoticons and online message interpretation. *Social Science Computer Review*, 26(3), 379–388. doi:10.1177/0894439307311611

Engestrom, Y., Miettinen, R., & Punamaki, R. (Eds.). (1999). *Perspectives on Activity Theory*. Cambridge: Cambridge University Press.

Google. (2009, May 28, 2009). *Google Wave Developer Preview at Google I/O2009*. Retrieved May 28, from http://www.youtube.com/watch?v=v_UyVmITiYQ.

Hatzipanagos, S., & Warburton, S. (2009). Feedback as dialogue: Exploring the links between formative assessment and social software in distance learning. *Learning, Media and Technology, 34*(1), 45–59. doi:10.1080/17439880902759919

Innis, H. A. (1951). *The Bias of Communication*. Toronto: University of Toronto Press.

Jones, A. (2004). *A review of the research literature on barriers to the uptake of ICT by teachers*. Coventry: Becta.

Kirschner, P. (2002). Can we support CSCL? Educational, social and technological affordances for learning. In P. Kirschner (Ed.), Three worlds of CSCL: Can we support CSCL (pp. 7-47). Heerlen: Open University of the Netherlands.

Mayer, R. E. (2005a). Cognitive Theory of Multimedia Learning. In Mayer, R. E. (Ed.), *The Cambridge handbook of multimedia learning* (pp. 31–48). New York: Cambridge University Press.

Mayer, R. E. (2005b). Principles of multimedia learning based on social cues. In Mayer, R. E. (Ed.), *The Cambridge handbook of multimedia learning* (pp. 201–212). New York: Cambridge University Press.

Mayer, R. E. (2009). *Multimedia Learning*. New York: Cambridge University Press.

McLoughlin, C., & Lee, M. (2007). Social software and participatory learning: Pedagogical choices with technology affordances in the Web 2.0 era. In *ICT: Providing choices for learners and learning*. Presented at the Ascilite Conference, Singapore. Retrieved from http://www.ascilite.org.au/conferences/singapore07/procs/mcloughlin.pdf

McLuhan, M. (1962). *The Gutenberg galaxy*. Toronto: University of Toronto Press.

Mehrabian, A. (1981). *Silent messages: Implicit communication of emotions and attitudes*. Belmont: Wadsworth Publishing Company.

Mehrabian, A., & Weiner, M. (1967). Decoding of inconsistent communications. *Journal of Personality and Social Psychology, 6*, 109–114. doi:10.1037/h0024532

Mejias, U. (2005, August 26). Social Software Affordances: Course Syllabus. *Social software affordances; blog for course offered at teacher college, Columbia University during Fall 2005*. Retrieved August 27, 2009, from http://ssa05.blogspot.com/2005/08/course-syllabus.html

Moore, M. G. (1993). Theory of transactional distance. In Keegan, D. (Ed.), *Theoretical Principles of Distance Education*. New York: Routledge.

O'Reilly, T. (2005, September 30). *What Is Web 2.0? Design Patterns and Business Models for the Next Generation of Software*. Retrieved August 28, 2009, from http://oreilly.com/web2/archive/what-is-web-20.html.

Shirky, C. (2003, March 9). Social Software and the Politics of Groups. *Clay Shirky's Writings About the Internet*. Retrieved August 27, 2009, from http://www.shirky.com/writings/group_politics.html.

KEY TERMS AND DEFINITIONS

Affordances: The features or capabilities which a particular technology can enable for the purpose of teaching or learning (i.e. for pedagogical purposes).

DiAL-e: The Digital Artefacts for Learner Engagement Framework (see above).

Engagement: The process of motivating and stimulating learners to undertake challenging and engaging cognitive tasks.

E-Literacy: The specific information processing and meaning-making abilities associated with those able to maximize the benefits of emergent digital technologies typified by the emergence of web based applications and Web 2.0 technologies.

Multi-Modal: The blend of visual, aural and tactile activity involved in a learning experience to varying degrees. Individuals with different learning preferences seek to blend input channels to optimize learning potential.

Transactional Distance: Defining the structure of learning and nature of dialogue in the distance education experience. Originated by Michael Moore the theory suggests physical distance is less of an obstacle to successful learning than learning design and support.

Personalization: The opportunity to structure learning experiences to allow individuals to make personal choices of timing, structure, sequencing and media to optimize their experience.

Socio-Cultural: Elements of technology and learning that require conscious situating in their broader social and cultural contexts. The terms 'cultural' and 'historical' are often used interchangeably on the understanding that 'culture' has an inevitable historical character and that 'history' occurs through the experience of a defined cultural milieu.

Section 2
Language and Communication Processes

Chapter 8
Towards More Productive Online Discussions:
Social Presence and the Development of Interpersonal Relations

Benjamin Kehrwald
Massey University, New Zealand

EXECUTIVE SUMMARY

This chapter deals with a case study into social presence in text-based online learning at the postgraduate level. The case seeks to address questions related to the social dynamics of online learning environments through a study of learner experiences with social presence. The case highlights the role and function of social presence in the development of interpersonal relations and the effects of those relations on social processes in online learning environments. The findings identify a set of social-relational mechanisms and a progression of relational states which promote understanding of social processes in text-based online environments.

INTRODUCTION

This chapter seeks to both promote understanding of social presence in text-based online learning environments and respond to the apparent paradox in the experiences of online learners with the cultivation of rich, productive relationships in text-only environments. It contributes to the growing body of knowledge of technology-mediated social processes by referencing a wider study into social presence in text-based online learning environments. More specifically, this chapter highlights findings related to the role and function of social presence and the progressive development of relations between social actors in text-based online learning environments. It addresses two key questions that confront online educators: (a) *How does social presence aid in the development of relations between actors in online learning environments?* and (b) *How is this beneficial to online discussion and interaction?* Finally, this chapter seeks to extend these findings to provide practical suggestions for online teaching which may improve the productivity of online discussions.

DOI: 10.4018/978-1-61520-863-0.ch008

BACKGROUND

Concomitant with the emergence of Web 2.0, recent research in online learning has focused less on learning about technology itself and focused more on what learners do to learn with and through technology. Of particular interest to educators is the study of interpersonal interaction (Beuchot & Bullen, 2005; LaPointe & Gunawardena, 2004) and related social processes such as the development of relational connections (Kreijns, Kirschner, Jochems, & Van Buuren, 2004), productive collaboration (Kobbe et al., 2007; Murphy, 2004) and the development of community in online environments (Bruckman, 2004; Preece, 2001; Schwen & Hara, 2004), including learner experiences with these processes (Kehrwald, 2008; Levy, 2006; Thorpe & Godwin, 2006).

Gunawardena (1995) points out that communicative failures in online environments occur much more often at the social than at the technical level. Despite the emergence of rich media communication tools, interactions between participants in online education are predominantly text-based. The relative leanness of the textual medium limits the sociability of these environments and creates conditions which make communication in this medium potentially difficult. These limiting conditions include the lack of contextual information; significant social and psychological distance between actors created by the media (Dron, 2007); and imbalances in the sender-receiver relationship due to a lack of synchronous two-way interaction (Riva, 2002).

Paradoxically, some participants in text-based online environments cite overwhelmingly positive experiences with online learning (Rheingold, 1993; Walther, 1992). They refer to connection, depth of interactive exchanges and quality of interaction which surpass their previous experiences with other delivery modes, including face-to-face education. They cite the quality of their technology mediated relationships as indications of the power of this medium and its ability to connect people (Baym, 1998; Turkle, 1995). This experience suggests that technology mediated learning can be rich, rewarding, and indeed humane. The question that follows is: *How is this positive outcome possible given the apparent limitations of the textual medium?*

A growing body of literature suggests that part of the answer lies in understanding online social presence and its role in online learning environments (see Gunawardena, 1995; Gunawardena & Zittle, 1996; Rourke, Anderson, Garrison, & Archer, 2001; Walther, 1992). Short, Williams and Christie (1976), the genitors of social presence theory, defined social presence as "the degree of salience of the other person in a mediated interaction and the consequent salience of the interpersonal interaction" (p. 65). Whilst the term social presence was originally used to describe the qualities of media and their respective abilities to create the illusion of non-mediation (Daft, Lengel, & Trevino, 1987; Short et al., 1976), users of virtual environments, including online learners, have appropriated the term to describe the combination of skills and abilities which allow them to achieve, in Short et al's terms, salient interpersonal interactions. More contemporary and emergent definitions of social presence describe individuals' abilities to perceive others through their mediated interactions (Collins & Murphy, 1997); the degree of "tangibility and proximity" of others within a communicative situation (McLeod, Baron, & Marti, 1997); participants' abilities to project themselves both socially and emotionally in a community (Rourke et al., 2001) and an individual's ability to demonstrate his or her state of being in a virtual environment and so signal his or her availability for interpersonal transactions (Kehrwald, 2008). As a result of experience with and increased attention to online communication, the concept of social presence in online environments has come to be viewed as much complex than originally understood.

SETTING THE STAGE

The research design employed a collective case study methodology. The collective case consisted of four individual cases, each based on a single instance of a wholly online postgraduate course in Education. For each case, a group of 3-6 respondents was recruited from the cohort of enrolled students. Within each case, information was collected using a dialogical process which functioned as an extended interview over several weeks. This dialogical process included a questionnaire, a preliminary interview, an exploratory focus group discussion, a secondary interview and a final confirmatory focus group discussion. The aim of this process was to help respondents identify, explicate and examine experience-based heuristic knowledge of the nature, role and function of social presence in mediated social processes, and then construct shared understandings of these phenomena within the respondent groups.

CASE DESCRIPTION

This study was conducted in the online postgraduate programs in education at a regional Australian university. This site was considered ideal for the study because (a) the university had an established reputation as a provider of distance and online programs and had a functional support infrastructure for online learning in place (b) the program under study was offered wholly online (c) individual courses within the program included a number of characteristics which describe good practice in contemporary networked (online) courses (see, for example, Steeples, Jones, & Goodyear, 2002) and (d) it was anticipated that the courses under study would provide learners with experiences with the phenomena of interest to the study. Indeed, courses were selected for the study based on the extent to which they were likely to produce learner experiences of interest to this study. Generally, these courses employed constructivist pedagogical approaches, a learner-centric process orientation, high levels of interaction between participants as part of the course design, extensive use of CMC tools and a significant portion of the course content that was generated by course participants over the term of study.

The use of technology in the case sites was built around text-based communications tools commonly found in commercial learning management systems. Asynchronous online discussion was the dominant form of communication between participants in the courses. This was supplemented by personal email and a limited amount of synchronous text-based "chat" in instant messengers or virtual classroom facilities. Participants indicated that they had little or no non-textual communication with other participants. Notably, each of the four cases which comprise the collective case employed a different course design and used the communications tools in different ways within the broad framework of "online discussion." For example, in at least two of the courses, learners were asked to work in small groups (of up to five learners) on explicitly collaborative learning tasks. In at least one of the cases, learners formed medium sized groups (6-12 learners) according to their professional contexts and worked mostly within this group as opposed to within the "whole class" framework. In all of the courses, there was some whole-group discussion, some of which was structured and some of which was unstructured. One result of these various structures was that the respondents in the study were likely to have had a variety of different experiences with online discussion from one-on-one communication to small and medium sized group work to whole class discussions. Also, while each individual instance of a course was considered a case for this study, it was acknowledged that each respondent drew from his or her entire body of experience with online learning, not just the course in question.

Respondents were all students enrolled in the respective courses. They were all mature aged (adult) learners who were in-service educators

161

in a variety of contexts throughout Australasia, Europe and North America. Whenever possible, more experienced learners were selected from the volunteer pool due to the richness of their personal experience and the wealth of their accumulated knowledge with the phenomena in question. In total, 20 respondents participated across the four case studies. All but one respondent had been involved with multiple online courses and the most experienced had been involved with eight courses.

Analysis

Analysis of data was thematic with the identification of units of meaning (i.e., themes) which emerged repeatedly or regularly in the data set and indicated common threads of meaning which extend through the data. Consistent with Sowden and Keeves (1988), the general analytical process involved multiple phases of data reduction; display and examination; conclusion drawing and verification at the conclusion of the following: (a) each phase of the dialogical process, (b) each case, and (c) of all collection. Themes emerging from each phase within the dialogical process were used to inform interview questions and discussion topics in future phases. As preliminary findings were constructed for each case, they were reflected back to respondents for confirmation (or otherwise). Thus, the quality of findings was enhanced by a combination of methodological and interpretive rigor which emphasized the authenticity of conclusions and confirmed progressively constructed findings through respondent validation and multiple forms of triangulation.

CURRENT CHALLENGES FACING THE ORGANIZATION

The dialogical process and iterative analysis produced findings in the form of key themes which represent the socially constructed synthesis of learner experiences. The key themes presented

here relate specifically to the focus of this paper, namely, (a) the identification of relational mechanisms which operate to affect relations between social actors (b) the progressive development of relations between social actors in text-based online learning environments and (c) the role of social presence in the development of relations.

Relational Mechanisms

Findings indicate that individuals gather information about the state of relations between themselves and others through the reading of social presence cues. In this study, exploration of participant experiences with social presence led to the identification of six of social-relational mechanisms which operate as a result of information provided in social presence cues and affect the experience of interactive, collaborative online learning. These mechanisms include *commonality and like-mindedness, trust, feelings of safety, respect, rapport* and *interdependence*.

Commonality and Like-Mindedness

Commonality refers to something shared between individuals, i.e., something that is held *in common*. This was manifest in the data as "mutuality" and things "shared" such as common interests, common background (e.g., professional situation, educational history, family situation, location/shared cultural location), shared problems, common aspirations, and shared purposes/goals. Implied in commonality is the notion of reciprocity, i.e., that both parties are involved in the relation-- that it is mutual. However, findings indicate that this is not always the case. In some instances, the identification of points of commonality provides an entrée to such reciprocity. Respondents described their experiences this way:

Kevin: Connecting starts by finding commonalities, geographic, experiences, professional things, etc. You get a few positive comments and there's suddenly a connection that wasn't there before, it's a sort of currency.

Nora: By reading through the information, you have a sense of who the person is-where they are from, what their educational background or area of expertise is, their interests, etc. all of which helps you to identify with them and perhaps feel you share a connection or common interest with.

In this way, commonality is seen as an important genesis point for other social-relational mechanisms. Commonality is a precursor to establishing connection and identification of an existing relation between individuals. A sense of connection was seen as an aid to meaning making as it helped create context for the comments of others, helped individuals make informed assumptions about the context and meaning of others' statements and promoted interaction which fuelled further operation of these social-relational mechanisms.

Andy: By working in a small group of 'school teachers,' I felt that, right from the beginning, I was clearly identifiable as belonging to a particular educational sector.

I have felt much more comfortable sharing experiences and comments about my job than I would have if I felt that others reading them were university people- tutors, lecturers, etc. I know very little about that sector so I suppose I hold them in a certain amount of awe.

As a result of feeling more comfortable in this smaller 'schoolies' group, I think my 'personal social presence' or online persona has become more obvious or 'out there.' This is probably through being more willing to make personal comments, jokes or asides.

Commonality was also linked with the notion of group cohesion. In particular, findings highlight

the notion of shared purpose and indicate that shared purpose was, in the experience of these respondents, the most important factor in creating a sense of cohesion and productive collaborative activity in group situations. Shared purpose promotes a sense of 'groupness' and seen as a defining characteristic of group formation and group membership. Notably, shared purpose describes not only specific task-oriented activity, but also more general notions of purposeful learning activity. As participants in formal education, the respondents assumed that others in the learning environment shared their overarching purpose of learning.

Feelings of Safety and the Creation of a Safe Environment

Another key relational condition highlighted in the findings is the creation of an environment which is safe in the sense that it fosters feelings of trust and promotes interpersonal interaction. This is important for creating a stable, secure environment for basic communication, interpersonal interaction and critical discourse. This notion was described by respondents in terms of comfort, confidence, safety, diminished risk and, in particular, trust.

Kevin: Engagement and connection come about because the individuals involved feel safe enough to disclose personal things about themselves such as anxiety about the process of learning, about being 'good enough' in the situation, not wanting to feel silly or stupid. It's no different than in face-to-face situations, I think you learn most from those with whom you engage and connect with at more than a superficial level.

Nora: If the goal is one of shared experiences, learning from others or collaborative work, you must feel safe within the environment in order to 'put yourself out there' with respect to anything-ideas, concerns, questions, answers....If you are expecting feedback from others, its important to know who they are... what experience they have had, in order for you to evaluate their response.

A safe environment is one in which there is a generally positive atmosphere in which participants felt safe from rebuke, ridicule or other negative behaviors. It is populated by other participants whose behavior is respectful and non-threatening. There are both tacit and explicit links between this notion of safety and rapport, respect and trust. A safe environment supports interaction by increasing participants' willingness to 'put themselves at risk' through personal disclosure, testing of ideas, seeking clarification and admitting lack of understanding. Notably, respondents repeatedly referred to negative experiences in emphasizing the need for a safe environment. Negative feelings identified included embarrassment, exclusion, a sense of being offended, dismissal, lack of respect and being ignored.

The creation of a safe environment includes a variety of conditions: facilitator modeling, shared norms of behavior, a sense of connection within the group, development of rapport and a general sense of positive relations between participants. However, findings include some ambivalence about the need for safety and suggested that over time (and through experience) online participants develop a "thick skin" and worry less about the feelings/responses/reactions of other participants in the environment. This may suggest that with increasing amounts of experience with CMC comes increased tolerance for ambiguity and potentially inflammatory statements by others.

Trust

Trust is an essential part of a productive online learning environment. Consistent with Tanis and Postmes (2005), findings indicate that trust includes both "trustworthiness" and "trusting behavior". Trustworthiness is a precondition of trusting behavior in most cases and is a subjective construct which varies from one participant to

another. Some respondents in this study indicated assumptions of trustworthiness in their learning peers; others indicated that trust had to be "earned".

Trust was described by respondents with three "C's":

1. *Confidence* in the other party, including confidence that the others would not act in a negative or unfriendly way as well as confidence that the other party can help, i.e., "has something I need," will provide an appropriate response, or help me in some way.
2. *Comfort* in interacting with others including putting themselves at risk through idea sharing, personal disclosure, etc. This idea is related to the creation of a safe environment.
3. *Courage* to "have a go" and participate actively in discussions and other interpersonal transactions. This also includes the courage to respond honestly and openly in ongoing dialogues.

Beneficial outcomes of trusting behavior include the ability to be honest and open in interpersonal transactions as well as "deeper" conversations with more critical idea sharing about and analysis of the ideas in question.

Frank: I trust someone in an online course to be honestly trying to learn along with me. Interacting with them solidifies this feeling I have. That is a stronger feeling of trust, I guess. If I am working in a group with them it is more important to me that I trust them to do what they said they would do.

Notably, trust promotes the development of interdependent relationships. Implications of these findings include the point that trust may be built and sustained incrementally, over time. Therefore supportive structures and supportive facilitation in online learning environments need to include a basis for trusting behaviors and provide opportunities for the development of trust through the demonstration of trustworthiness (as it relates to confidence in the other parties), comfort in the online environment and the exhibition of trusting behaviors in a willingness to participate in ongoing activities.

Respect

Respect is a positive relational condition between people which includes notions of trust and admiration. It is a highly subjective construct and no clear criteria for respect were evident in the data. Much like trust, individuals have very personal ideas about the development of respect and how it is conveyed. Likewise, the actions of others in a relation are interpreted very subjectively as respectful or not. Findings indicate a pattern in which instances of respect (positive) are cited when the respondent has respect for another (from me to you, I respect him), while instances of a lack of respect are indicated the other way around, e.g., he didn't respect me.

In terms of the benefits, respect provides a basis for connection between individuals, particularly in the absence of a sense of commonality. While participants may not like one another, they can still respect one another and that may provide a basis for ongoing productive relations. Likewise, respect may contribute to a sense of interdependence and facilitate collaborative activity, particularly when there is a strong task-orientation (shared purpose).

Rapport

Rapport is a positive relational condition in which there is mutuality of trust and respect. Thus, rapport is clearly related to these other social-relational mechanisms. It is based on notions of commonality and shared purpose and may develop out of necessity in task-related activity.

Rich: I think trust and rapport is important. I think generally people will interact better if they feel comfortable. For example, as a teacher I make

sure I am open and approachable. [As a student] I find that if I am unclear about something small, I will not bother clearing it up if I feel as though I am bothering people. But if I have developed relationships with the community based on a good rapport... I will interact more. Even if it is something small.

Positive results of rapport included willingness to put oneself at risk in discussions, willingness to offer critique or take critical positions, willingness to make personal disclosures and enhanced feelings of "closeness" to other individuals. Respondents repeatedly referred to notions of "honesty," "trust" and "openness" when discussing experiences with rapport in online interactions. They cited a number of negative examples of behaviors which undermined and/or prevented rapport from developing, particularly where these behaviors were interpreted as indicating a lack of respect.

These points suggest that while rapport represents a highly desirable relational state, it is a result of advanced levels of relational activity, dependent upon other relational states as pre-conditions of establishing rapport. There were no clear indications of how this might be fostered and so this is an area for further study.

Interdependence

Interdependence refers to the notion that learners both support others and need support from other learners. It manifests itself as explicit or implicit acknowledgement of the reciprocal relationships between individuals in the online learning environment. Examples include: recognizing how the contributions of individuals contribute to a collaborative effort, a sense of commitment to "the team" or "the group" or the "greater good" and expressions which indicate that there is inherent value in collaborative activity based on reciprocal commitment to a shared purpose.

Interdependence is related to the following:

1. *Commonality* in terms of shared purpose, common views and the notion that "we're all in this together." Some respondents indicated that commonality formed the basis for group formation and identification of "like minded" others who might have similar goals (shared purpose). There is an explicit recognition of the contributions others can make to personal learning, often identified through difference.

2. *Trust* in the sense that, because the other parties are experienced only in mediated interactions, they must seem "trustworthy" and trust must be given for interdependent relationships to develop. The link here to social presence is evident.

3. *Specific identifiable personal characteristics* including skills, attitudes, beliefs, abilities and more which allow for individuals to be assigned (or sought out) for particular tasks. This is related to the notion of "division of labor" and creating a functional "whole" from a given set of "parts" in collaborative work.

4. A sense of both *commitment to* the group and *accountability within* the group. Notably, there is a potential conflict between commitment to collaborative processes and pervasive assumptions about the individual nature of study (and learning) in formal education. Likewise, there is some conflict about levels of accountability to the group. Some online learners viewed this as necessary, while others could not reconcile group orientation with expectations of individual learning processes.

However, responses also indicated some conflict over the notion of interdependence and differing expectations of interdependent relationships. To some degree, this may be related to expectations of individual work, one-to-one support from the facilitator and negative previous experience with collaborative work. Some respondents expressed frustration with collaborative work while others expressed frustration with differing levels of commitment between individuals with regards to collaborative work.

Overall, a clear understanding of interdependence has not emerged from these data, but there are indications that it is an important concept in social support insofar as that is related to "networks of support," collaborative and community work situations and supportive relationship building. Further research is need into learner experiences and expectations with regard to interdependence as it relates to collaborative activity and the development of community.

Social Presence and the Progressive Development of Relations

The findings indicate that relations between individuals develop progressively from a point of first contact. In this initial encounter there is a form of communication in which one party sends and the other party receives information. The sender establishes a social presence and the receiver is made aware of the presence of the sender as an "other" party in the environment. The receiver forms an impression of the sender as real and present which encompasses such attributes as personality, background, and attitude. The receiver uses this information for two main purposes. The first purpose is to create a context for the other party's comments and so make meaning of them. This includes the recognition of the sender as a known party in the environment. The second purpose is to make informed decisions about the other party's availability and willingness to engage in ongoing transactions.

Relations between individuals develop over time based on the number of interactions and transactions between them, the intensity of those interactions and the working of the social-relational mechanism within those transactions. As the total number of transactions between individuals increases, the combination of social

Table 1. The progressive development of relational states

Progression of relations	Relational mechanisms at work
Me-other relations	Empathy Respect Admiration
Mutuality	Commonality Connection Likemindedness
Feelings of safety	Freedom from risk Comfort with others Confidence in others
Trust	Trustworthiness Trusting behaviors Willingness to put oneself at risk
Production	Group cohesion Rapport Interdependence

presence cues and social-relational mechanisms contributes to the overall development of the relationship. Individuals continue to cultivate a social presence which is read and interpreted by others, affecting their relationships. Likewise, a variety of social-relational mechanisms are called into play as individuals develop respect for one another's opinions, identify points of commonality, develop closeness and begin to trust one another. What emerges is a developing sense of history which contributes to the sense of the overall quality of the relationship. For some relationships, this quality is characterized as deep, meaningful, close, or intimate. For others, the relationship is more shallow, limited, temporary, or superficial.

Beginning with social presence as the basis for participant-other relations, findings indicate five main types of relational mechanisms which follow a developmental progression. These include (a) those which form a basis for "me-other" (one way) relations; (b) those which form a basis for mutuality, reciprocity or a shared-ness in the relation; (c) those which contribute to feelings of safety and the development of a risk-free environment; (d) those which promote feelings of trust, including informing decisions about trustworthiness of

other participants, and lead to the exhibition of trusting behaviors; and (e) those which lead to production in the completion of collaborative work (see also Murphy, 2004). These social-relational mechanisms work in concert with social presence to influence the development of relationships.

Notably, the stages in this progression are not discrete. Rather, they are relative positions. Relations are emergent and dynamic. They are in a state of constant flux--sometimes developing, sometimes waning. Table 1 illustrates these progressive stages and the relational mechanisms at work.

Basis for Me-Other Relations

Once social presence is established, participants' decisions about whether and how to respond to one another are influenced by basic feelings of relation between the parties. Social-relational mechanisms which operate here include: (a) empathy, related to attribution of sameness between participants, at least with regards to the person receiving the empathy being seen as the same as the empathizer; (b) respect, which is the acknowledged value of another party or their attributes; and (c) admiration, which not only is acknowledged value but also includes a desire to be like the other party.

For each of these relational-mechanisms to exist, a participant must acknowledge the existence of another as a real person (as previously established through social presence) and relate the other party's situation to that participant's own. These mechanisms form the basis for ongoing relations between the two parties. Notably, the relations are largely undeveloped at this stage as interaction may be limited to one-way communicative exchanges.

Basis for Mutuality

When communication becomes two-way, there is opportunity to develop mutuality, or sharedness in the relation. This sharedness is an important precondition for the development of more advanced relations between parties. Mutuality is built upon the identification of points of commonality, feelings of familiarity and a sense of "like-mindedness." This sense of mutuality is sometimes described as a sense of connection, which explicitly acknowledges the relation between individuals. These relational mechanisms contribute to a sense of reciprocity in the relation which opens the door to ongoing transactions between the parties.

Creation of a Risk-Free Environment

To build upon mutuality and create sustained interaction, participants need to feel that the social environment is relatively safe. In the data, these feelings of safety are often characterized by notions of "comfort" combined with either a "freedom from risk" or a willingness to put oneself at risk because of a decision to trust fellow participants. Generally, these behaviors result in greater numbers of interactions between individuals and a greater depth or intensity in the interactions which take place. Results from the study indicate that these social-relational mechanisms facilitate "deep" interactions which move beyond "safe," superficial interactions into more provocative or less safe interactions. The point is not to coddle learners, but to promote interactions which get beyond virtual small talk to the heart of critical discourse and higher order thinking. As the relations between individuals become more intimate and closeness develops, participants engage in greater personal disclosure and hypothesizing as they delve more deeply into the issues at hand.

Promotion of Trust

The relational mechanisms identified above have a cumulative effect as they promote the development of trust by informing decisions about the trustworthiness of the other party (Tanis & Postmes, 2005). In particular, these decisions are influenced by feelings of safety or freedom from risk in the learning environment mentioned above. Together, these feelings contribute to an individual's willingness to exhibit trusting behaviors which include personal disclosure, openness and a willingness to put him/herself at risk. When these feelings of trust are characteristic of relations within a group, there are higher levels of group cohesion and feelings of closeness.

Production

Production is one of the common goals of collaborative online learning. Learners are meant to acquire knowledge and skills through the processes related to the processes of producing particular artifacts. However, given the degrees of interaction involved in collaborative work and the complexities of the relations within dynamic collaborative groups, it is ambitious, perhaps even unrealistic, to assume collaborative production as an outcome of task assignment.

Findings in this study indicate that when the ability, opportunity and motivation exist for the full development of positive relations, rapport develops between individuals and high degrees of cohesion exist within groups. Interactions may be frequent and intense. The conditions promote the development of collaborative activity in which participants share responsibility and activity in order to create shared products. They also create the potential for the development of a sense of community, including the interdependent relationships that exist between community members and the explicitly shared purposes of members.

Notably, the development of interpersonal relations requires a combination of time and a certain level of intensity in interaction to achieve. Relations do not develop instantly and they require attention in order to be cultivated and maintained. Cultivating productive relations within the limited timeframe of a unit of study remains one of the challenges for online learning in formal education.

CONCLUSION

It is useful to return to the questions posed in the introduction to frame a conclusion for this chapter in order to draw the ideas above into a set of conclusions:

1. *How does social presence aid in the development of relations between actors in online learning environments?*
2. *How is this beneficial to online discussion and interaction?*
3. *How can this information be used by online teachers to improve online discussions?*

The preceding discussion of relational mechanisms and the development of interpersonal relations indicate a role for social presence in the development of interpersonal relations as part of social processes involving interpersonal interaction in technology mediated environments. While some researchers highlight the operation of computer-mediated communications tools as social networks (e.g., Wellman, 1997), the extent to which users of these tools are evident to one another as social actors or experience these tools as social media is not clear. The findings highlight that the participants in text-based online learning environments experience others in the environments as "real" people, that is, human beings with all of the characteristics thereof, but also that different individuals are socially present in differing degrees (see also Kehrwald, 2008). The degree to which an individual is seen to be socially present is defined, at least partly, by the relations between individual social actors. Notably, the relationship between social presence and relations is reciprocal. Just as the state of the relation between actors affects the interpretation of messages, the social presence cues provide information which informs understanding of the state of the relation. Affective, interactive and cohesive social presence cues provide information about the extent to which the other party is willing

to interact, available for immediate and ongoing interaction and committed to social activity within a group (Rourke et al., 2001).

The findings of this study indicate that there is a complementary relationship between social presence and interpersonal relations and that these concepts are also closely related to interpersonal interaction in online environments. The relationship between social presence and interpersonal relations has important effects on the social dynamics of online environments and so there are implications for both (a) the promotion of interpersonal interaction and (b) the support of interactive social processes in online learning environments

The Promotion of Interpersonal Interaction

The relationship between social presence, interpersonal relations and interactions lends insight into the promotion and sustenance of interaction in online environments. Social presence and interpersonal interaction are interdependent: Social presence cannot exist without visible demonstrations of presence and ongoing interaction is a key part of the development of presence. Ongoing interaction is facilitated by positive social presence. Interactions in the form of communicative exchanges (e.g., in online discussion) provide opportunities for the transmission of the cues which are the manifestation of an individual's social presence. Once social presence is established, relations can develop. The same cues which demonstrate social presence can indicate the state of relations between social actors. Together, social presence and relations can promote ongoing interaction in at least three ways: by participants signaling their availability for interaction, by participants indicating their willingness for ongoing interaction and by participants cultivating a positive social presence which makes them attractive as potential interactive partners. Awareness of the operation of social presence and its relationship to the development of interpersonal relations and the promotion of interaction informs design and facilitation activities which seek to leverage interaction as part of learning processes. Potentially, there are further implications for (a) the construction of messages to promote ongoing interaction, (b) the design of purposeful interactive tasks, (c) the education of learners with regard to the role of social presence, (d) the facilitation of interactive processes, and (e) the study of interpersonal relations in time-limited contexts such as most formal education situations.

It is useful to consider practical examples to highlight these points. Starting from the beginning of an online course, the establishment of social presence provides a basis for interaction between individuals and a genesis point for the development of relations between them. In online courses, this is commonly done in a dedicated discussion space for personal introductions and "getting to know you" activities. However, the inclusion of such spaces for personal introductions does not ensure either the establishment of social presence or interpersonal interaction. Online learners must have the ability, opportunity and motivation to interact (Kehrwald, 2008). Unfortunately, many novice online learners do not come to online learning environments with the skills to establish and cultivate an online social presence. Therefore, such activities should be carefully structured to (a) provide experiences from which learners can learn to both convey a social presence and read the presence of others, and (b) not only create opportunities for individuals to demonstrate their social presence, but also generate some form of interpersonal interaction that provides a basis for the development of relations between individuals, and (c) motivate learners to establish and cultivate a positive social presence.

In terms of helping learners read social presence cues, facilitators should model appropriate social presence through their own introductions and ongoing interaction. Moreover, they should draw on experienced online learners to lead and model appropriate social activity. These models should include each of the three functional links between social presence and ongoing interaction: signals of availability for interaction (e.g., "I'll be around all week"), indications of their willingness for ongoing interaction (e.g., "Drop me a line anytime"; "I'm always happy to help"; "I look forward to hearing from you") and positive social presence which makes them attractive as potential interactive partners (e.g. giving praise, acknowledging good ideas, displaying humor).

In terms of establishing social presence, introductory activities should be structured so that they require learners to provide information which is relevant to establishing a positive presence, for example, identifiers (preferred name, nickname or identifying features), background (educational history, professional background), instances of personal disclosure (personal circumstances, interests, hobbies, motivations for study), and opportunities for personalization (writing styles, formats, the inclusion of images and other media such as an audio introduction, the development of a personal profile). The particular parameters of each introductory task should be tailored to the needs of the course or situation to elicit the necessary information to promote the establishment and cultivation of social presence.

In terms of ongoing interaction, the initial task should include a clear reason to respond to others. This may be tied to the introductions, as in the case of saying hello to old friends and welcoming new ones, or may be a separate task, as in a question/answer activity around group norms or the particulars of the course environment. A key point is that the opportunity to interaction is not sufficient. There must be some motive to interact. Learners need to see a clear benefit that is associated with their expenditure of time and effort through online interaction. For example, a possible motive is the identification of future collaborative partners. Foreshadowing collaborative work and the opportunity to self-select partners may motivate learners to invest in getting-to-know-you activities.

Ideally, the establishment of a positive social presence, the initial cycles of communication and response that form interpersonal interaction and the beginnings of relations between individuals and within the group provide a basis for ongoing development of the social mechanisms which support social learning processes. Too often, the early flush of success in online discussion and interaction gives way to the realities of finite resources and learners' inevitable rationalization of their learning activity. It is important to link this early activity in the establishment of social presence and interaction to the support of ongoing interactive social presence.

The Support of Interactive Social Processes

Returning to the point that communicative failures in online environments occur are often much more often at the social than at the technical level (Gunawardena, 1995), findings of this study inform understanding of the interpersonal relations which underpin dynamic social processes such as productive collaboration and the development of community structures. Collaboration, for example, is an essential component of contemporary online learning environments (Gunawardena & Zittle, 1996). Through collaborative endeavor, learners engage in coordinated activity, develop purposeful relationships and strive to produce, create, discover and solve problems (Murphy, 2004). Indeed much of the power of network structures which underpin online learning environments is related to the synergies created in collaborative processes. The development of relations outlined in Table 1 and the findings regarding the relationship between social presence and interpersonal relations inform understandings of collaboration. In some ways, collaboration is an extension of the interactions identified above. Collaboration requires human--human interaction. However, interaction does not guarantee collaboration. Collaboration is

built upon a combination of particular types of interaction and relational mechanisms which support the development of collaborative outcomes. The interactions which constitute collaborative activity are not spontaneous. Moreover, they do not exist in a vacuum. They are part of a web of interpersonal relationships which influence the number, frequency and intensity of interactions (Shin, 2002, 2003). The collaborative development of shared perspectives, the co-construction of meaning and the production of artifacts which represent that shared understanding (meaning) require that collaborators not only interact but also relate to one another in a way which emphasizes the sharedness of the products that emerge.

There are important practical implications of these points. Although productive collaboration is frequently a part of learning tasks, the context in which the tasks are situated is too often not well understood in terms of the social dynamics of the course, unit or program in question. There is potential for a critical mismatch between the intentions of the learning task regarding collaboration and the existence of an infrastructure to support the social activity involved in such collaboration. In the absence of an established social presence for each participant or some form of ongoing interaction within which interpersonal relations can develop, the likelihood of productive collaboration is greatly diminished. Learning designers and teachers must be mindful of the requirements of the social requirements of the tasks they set and, if necessary, include the social infrastructure required to support interactive and collaborative process. The results of this study suggest a number of practical activities to support productive collaboration. One such activity is related to the establishment of rules and processes which structure and support social activity (e.g., explicit goals in the form of objectives or outcomes for each interactive task, clear procedures for social interaction, identification of key features of "good" or "desirable" messages). A second form of support is provided by consideration of online learning environments and responsibilities of participants in the interactive or collaborative situation. Role assignments with explicit descriptions clarify participant responsibilities, help establish purpose and contribute to motivation. Clear online learning environments and responsibilities provide a basis for shared understanding of each participant's activity and also promote accountability within the social unit. A third form of support is the provision of "tools" which support the intended interaction or collaboration. These tools may include (a) particular communicative tools for particular types of interact (e.g., the use of synchronous chat for negotiation of meaning or the use of video conferencing for getting to know you activity), (b) artifacts such as frameworks, organizers or concept maps which structure activity and provide a basis for shared understanding, or (c) a language as defined by a set of terms or in a glossary that identifies a definitive basis for understanding of key concepts and eliminates unnecessary ambiguity in interactive exchanges. Together, such rules, online learning environments and tools provide an infrastructure for complex social activity (Hung & Chen, 2001, 2002).

Based on the experiences of online learners, the findings reported in this chapter highlight key features of the role and function of social presence. They also lend insight into the relationship between social presence and interaction and the development of interpersonal relations as part of ongoing interaction between participants. The chapter argues that social presence and interaction are important constituents of the development of collaborative processes in online environments. Online course designers and teachers must be mindful of the functions of social presence and interaction to support more complex social activity. They must also avoid assumptions about participants' abilities and willingness to (a) establish and maintain an online social presence (b) read and understand the social presence of others (c)

participate in ongoing interaction and (d) reach a state of productive collaboration. The findings provide insights into practical issues associated with structuring, supporting and developing complex social processes as part of online discussion.

REFERENCES

Baym, N. (1998). The emergence of online community. In Jones, S. G. (Ed.), *Cybersociety 2.0* (pp. 35–68). Thousand Oaks, CA: Sage.

Beuchot, A., & Bullen, M. (2005). Interaction and interpersonality in online discussion forums. *Distance Education*, *26*(1), 67–87. doi:10.1080/01587910500081285

Bruckman, A. (2004). Co-evolution of technological design and pedagogy in an online learning community. In Barab, S. A., Kling, R., & Gray, J. H. (Eds.), *Designing for virtual communities in the service of learning* (pp. 239–255). Cambridge, UK: Cambridge University Press.

Collins, M., & Murphy, K. L. (1997). Development of communications conventions in instructional electronic chats. *Journal of Distance Education*, *12*(1-2), 177–200.

Daft, R. L., Lengel, R. H., & Trevino, L. K. (1987). Message equivocality, media selection, and manager performance: Implications for information systems. *Management Information Systems Quarterly*, *11*(3), 354. doi:10.2307/248682

Dron, J. (2007). *Control and constraint in e-learning*. Hershey, PA: Idea Group.

Gunawardena, C. N. (1995). Social presence theory and implications for interaction and collaborative learning in computer conferences. *International Journal of Educational Telecommunications*, *1*(2/3), 147–166.

Gunawardena, C. N., & Zittle, R. (1996). An examination of teaching and learning processes in distance education and implications for designing instruction. In M. F. Beaudoin (Ed.), *Distance Education Symposium 3: Instruction* (Vol. 12, pp. 51-63). State College, PA: American Center for the Study of Distance Education.

Hung, D. W. L., & Chen, D.-T. (2001). Situated cognition, Vygotskian thought and learning from the communities of practice perspective: Implications for the design of web-based e-learning. *Educational Media International, 38*(1), 3–12. doi:10.1080/09523980110037525

Hung, D. W. L., & Chen, D.-T. (2002). Learning within the context of communities of practice: A re-conceptualization of tools, rules and online learning environments of the activity system. *Educational Media International, 39*(3&4), 247–255.

Kehrwald, B. A. (2008). Understanding social presence in text-based online learning environments. *Distance Education, 29*(1), 89–106. doi:10.1080/01587910802004860

Kobbe, L., Weinberger, A., Dillenbourg, P., Harrer, A., Hamalainen, R., & Hakkinen, P. (2007). Specifying computer-supported collaboration scripts. *International Journal of Computer-Supported Collaborative Learning, 2*(2-3), 211–224. doi:10.1007/s11412-007-9014-4

Kreijns, K., Kirschner, P. A., Jochems, W., & Van Buuren, H. (2004). Determining sociability, social space, and social presence in (a)synchronous collaborative groups. *Cyberpsychology & Behavior, 7*(2), 155–172. doi:10.1089/109493104323024429

LaPointe, D. K., & Gunawardena, C. N. (2004). Developing, testing and refining of a model to understand the relationship between peer interaction and learning outcomes in computer-mediated conferencing. *Distance Education, 25*(1), 83–106. doi:10.1080/0158791042000212477

Levy, P. (2006). "Learning a different form of communication": Experiences of networked learning and reflections on practice. *Studies in Continuing Education, 28*(3), 259–277. doi:10.1080/01580370600947512

McLeod, P. L., Baron, R. S., & Marti, M. W. (1997). The eyes have it: Minority influence in face-to-face and computer-mediated group discussion. *The Journal of Applied Psychology, 82*(5), 706–718. doi:10.1037/0021-9010.82.5.706

Murphy, E. (2004). Recognising and promoting collaboration in an online asynchronous discussion. *British Journal of Educational Technology, 35*(4), 421–431. doi:10.1111/j.0007-1013.2004.00401.x

Preece, J. (2001). Sociability and usability in online communities: determining and measuring success. *Behaviour & Information Technology, 20*(5), 347. doi:10.1080/01449290110084683

Rheingold, H. (1993). *The virtual community: Homesteading on the electronic frontier*. Reading, MA: Addison-Wesley.

Riva, G. (2002). The sociocognitive psychology of computer-mediated communication: The present and future of technology-based interactions. *Cyberpsychology & Behavior, 5*(6), 581–598. doi:10.1089/109493102321018222

Rourke, L., Anderson, T., Garrison, D. R., & Archer, W. (2001). Assessing social presence in asynchronous text-based computer conferencing. *Journal of Distance Education, 14*(2), 50–71.

Schwen, T. M., & Hara, N. (2004). Community of practice: A metaphor for online design? In Barab, S. A., Kling, R., & Gray, J. H. (Eds.), *Designing for virtual communities in the service of learning* (pp. 154–179). Cambridge: Cambridge University Press.

Shin, N. (2002). Beyond interaction: The relational construct of "transactional presence.". *Open Learning, 17*(2), 121–137. doi:10.1080/02680510220146887

Shin, N. (2003). Transactional presence as a critical predictor of success in distance learning. *Distance Education, 24*(1), 69–86. doi:10.1080/01587910303048

Short, J., Williams, E., & Christie, B. (1976). *The social psychology of communication.* New York: John Wiley & Sons.

Sowden, S., & Keeves, J. P. (1988). Analysis of evidence in humanistic studies. In Keeves, J. (Ed.), *Educational research, methodology and measurement: An international handbook* (pp. 513–526). Oxford, UK: Pergamon Press.

Steeples, C., Jones, C., & Goodyear, P. (2002). Beyond e-learning: A future for networked learning. In Steeples, C., & Jones, C. (Eds.), *Networked learning: Perspectives and issues* (pp. 323–342). London: Springer.

Tanis, M., & Postmes, T. (2005). A social identity approach to trust: Interpersonal perception, group membership and trusting behaviour. *European Journal of Social Psychology, 35*(3), 413–424. doi:10.1002/ejsp.256

Thorpe, M., & Godwin, S. (2006). Interaction and e-learning: The student experience. *Studies in Continuing Education, 28*(3), 203–221. doi:10.1080/01580370600947330

Turkle, S. (1995). *Life on the screen: Identity in the age of the Internet.* New York: Simon & Schuster.

Walther, J. (1992). Interpersonal effects in computer-mediated interaction: A relational perspective. *Communication Research, 19*(1), 52–90. doi:10.1177/009365092019001003

Wellman, B. (1997). An electronic group is virtually a social network. In Kiesler, S. (Ed.), *Culture of the internet* (pp. 179–205). Hillsdale, NJ: Lawrence Earlbaum.

KEY TERMS AND DEFINITIONS

Collaboration: Refers to productive endeavors in which the work is shared amongst a group of individuals.

Commonality: A relational condition in which something is shared by individuals, i.e., something is held "in common." In this chapter the notion of commonality is manifest as shared purpose, likemindedness, and a shared basis for understanding.

Interdependence: A relational state in which individual parties are mutually dependent upon one another, i.e., they both need and are needed by others. This is a relatively complex relational condition which is built upon a combination of commonality, trust, respect and rapport.

Interpersonal Interaction: A communicative exchange between people.

Rapport: A positive relational condition in which there is a combination of trust and respect.

Social Presence: An individual's ability to demonstrate his or her state of being in a virtual environment and so signal his or her availability for interpersonal transactions.

Chapter 9
Using Discourse Analysis to Assess Social Co–Presence in the Video Conference Environment

Kristy Beers Fägersten
Dalarna University, Sweden

EXECUTIVE SUMMARY

In this chapter, I analyze computer-mediated communication in the form of online, synchronous, professional discourse in the multimodal video conference environment with the aim of assessing social co-presence (Kang, Watt & Ala., 2008). I argue for the applicability of discourse analysis methodology by presenting extracts of video conference communication which illustrate how talk-in-interaction contributes to or threatens the three elements of social co-presence: co-presence, social richness of the medium, and interactant satisfaction. Examples of interaction illustrate how disruptions in mediation serve to threaten co-presence by isolating interlocutors, how multiple modes of communication are exploited to ground participants in a shared communicative environment thereby establishing social connectedness, and how multimodal communication allows for iconic or paralinguistic support of the discursive expression of emotional stance. The chapter concludes with feature recommendations for video conference software development from the perspective of social co-presence.

BACKGROUND TO THE CASES

Increased globalization and the subsequent dispersion of human resources in the corporate environment have resulted in significant commercial interest in video conference technology (Townsend, DeMarie & Hendrickson, 1998). In answer to the growing needs of a global economy, a number of web-based video conference technologies are currently competing on the market, for example, WebEx, iVideo, Skype, Adobe Connect, and Marratech. In April 2007, Marratech was acquired by Google. That same year, Google announced that there would be no further development of the Marratech client and server software as of July, 2009. Instead, Google is now working with the Marratech team to develop its own web-based video conferencing tools.[1]

DOI: 10.4018/978-1-61520-863-0.ch009

Ultimately, the production or further development of a successful video conference product will depend on designing features that make video conferencing an effective and satisfying form of remote communication and collaboration. The technological aspects of video conferencing, such as bandwidth requirements and audio-visual quality, are the most obvious and tacit issues to consider. However, as technology improves and enables interaction that closely approximates face-to-face communication, it is the social aspects of video conferencing, and of computer-mediated and video-mediated communication in general, which emerge as essential to providing user satisfaction and, consequently, product success.

In this chapter, I consider two cases of video conferencing via the Marratech client with the aim of assessing social co-presence (Kang, Watt & Ala, 2008). First, I review the literature on video-mediated communication, establishing the evolution of VMC as a viable alternative to face-to-face communication, particularly in the virtual workplace. Next, I present the theoretical constructs of social presence, co-presence and social co-presence, and I argue for the applicability of discourse analysis methodology in assessing social co-presence. I then present extracts of video-conference interaction, illustrating how talk-in-interaction can be analyzed to evaluate co-presence, social richness of the medium, and interactant satisfaction. The analysis is followed by a discussion and summary of how research on the ways people actually communicate through online discussion can contribute to a better understanding of social co-presence. Finally, I suggest features of video conference software which can optimize the social co-presence aspects of video-mediated communication.

VIDEO-MEDIATED COMMUNICATION

Video-mediated communication (VMC) such as video-conferencing offers users the widest variety of channels of communication, combining video with voice chat, text chat, whiteboard capabilities, and collaborative document manipulation. Video conferencing thus exemplifies a rich media environment (Daft & Lengel, 1984), allowing for a form of communication that closely approximates face-to-face interaction. For this reason, video-conferencing is increasingly being adopted in workplace settings as a viable solution to the problem of communicating with dispersed colleagues and business partners. The use of video-mediated communication technologies is therefore key to facilitating meaningful teamwork activity remotely (Morgan, 1993; Nguyen & Canny, 2007; Townsend et al., 1998).

Much of the literature on video-mediated communication reveals a tendency among researchers to highlight problematic aspects of remote interaction. Bandwidth issues (Angiolillo, Blanchard, Israelski & Mané, 1997) as well as the related distortion of audio signals or visual images (Benford, Brown, Reynard & Greenhalgh, 1996; Heath & Luff, 1991; Rutter, 1987) have been established as the primary contributing factors to a compromised interaction structure, affecting the sequencing of turns. For example, in video-mediated communication, the practices of holding or relinquishing the floor, interrupting, or other negotiations of turn-taking are impeded, such that there are generally fewer speaker turns, longer lengths of turn, and fewer interruptions than in face-to-face conversations (Cohen, 1982; Cook & Lalljee, 1972; Rutter & Stephenson, 1977). Disruptions in audio or visual transmissions render these deviating features even more salient (Cohen, 1982; Isaacs & Tang, 1994; Kraut, Fussel & Siegel, 2003; O'Conaill, Whittaker & Wilbur, 1993).

Comparisons of video-mediated communication with face-to-face interactions persist as a distinct trend in the research of video-mediated communication (O'Malley, Langton, Anderson, Doherty-Sneddon & Bruce, 1996; Reiserer, Ertl & Mandl, 2002; Sapsed, Gann, Marshall & Salter,

2005; Sellen, 1994), revealing a stance towards video-mediated interaction as an inferior or flawed alternative to 'the real thing' (Clark & Brennan, 1991; Daft & Lengel, 1984; Hauber, Regenbrecht, Hills, Cockburn & Billinghurst, 2005; Inoue, Okade & Matsushita, 1997; Kraut et al., 2003; Meier, 1998; Oviatt & Cohen, 1991; Sellen, 1994; Whittaker, 1995; Whittaker & O'Conaill, 1997). Furthermore, constant advances in information and communication technologies encourage continued comparisons as video-mediated communication becomes more sophisticated (recent examples include Cornelius & Boos, 2003; Fletcher & Major, 2006; Nguyen & Canny, 2004; van der Kleij, Lijkwan, Rasker & De Dreu, in press). The viability of video conferencing is steadily increasing, as studies establish video-mediated communication as being robust enough to accommodate workplace tasks (Fletcher & Major, 2006; McGrath & Hollingshead, 1993), support frequent and complex interactions (Reiserer et al., 2002) and, on the whole, closely approximate face-to-face interaction (O'Malley et al., 1996).

In this section, I have provided a brief review of research on video-mediated communication, highlighting its evolution as a viable alternative to face-to-face communication. In fact, with technological advancements, video-mediated communication can be expected to become increasingly rich and robust. Similarly, it can be expected that video-mediated communication will allow for an increasingly greater degree of social presence. In the next section, I distinguish between various theoretical constructs in social presence research.

SOCIAL PRESENCE, CO-PRESENCE, AND SOCIAL CO-PRESENCE

Social presence, as introduced by Short, Williams and Christie (1976), was originally defined as the "degree of salience of the other person in a mediated communication and the consequent salience of their interpersonal interactions" (p. 65). In other

words, social presence represented a theoretical model for examining "the behavioral effects of the physical presence of another human being or the thought that another human being is in position to observe" (Biocca, Harms & Burgoon, 2003, p. 460). Elaborating on the concept of salience, Bull and Rumsey (1988) included in their definition of social presence the impression that develops "when one person feels another person is 'there'" (p. 162). Similarly, Schroeder (2002) describes social presence as a sense of being there with others, de Greef & IJsselsteijn (2000) as a sense of being together, and Hauber et al. (2005) as a sense of togetherness. The juxtaposition of these definitions serves to document the evolution of the concept of social presence: whereas originally social presence featured the salience of the other as central, later interpretations and usages of the term have reflected an emphasis on the salience of the *mutual* presence of interlocutors. This development could suggest a semantically widened use of the term social presence, which has taken on attributes of co-presence. However, as Zhao (2003), for example, claims that "[c]opresence has also been called *social presence*" (p. 445, original italics), supporting this claim with references to Biocca and Harms (2002), Rice (1992), and Short et al. (1976), it may instead be a question of a conflation of terms.

Biocca et al. (2003), Nowak (2001), and Nowak and Biocca (2003) have contributed significantly to differentiating social presence and co-presence. With regards to social presence, each of their interpretations remains faithful to Short et al.'s (1976) original conceptualization, retaining the focus on the other as being perceived as present, and the ability of the medium to convey that presence. Co-presence, on the other hand, is attributed to the work of Goffman (1959, 1963), and concerns mutual awareness. According to Goffman (1959), "copresence renders persons uniquely accessible, available, and subject to one another" (p. 22). In both Nowak's (2001) and Nowak and Biocca's (2003) interpretations of Goffman's construct, the experience of co-presence among interlocutors occurs when there is mutual and active perceiving of the other; "co-presence in this sense solely refers to a psychological connection to and with another person" (Nowak & Biocca, 2003, p. 482). Biocca et al. (2003) are also explicit about the aspect of mutuality in reviewing definitions of co-presence, which "move into mutual awareness when they emphasize attention to the sensory properties of the other, especially an awareness of both user/observer and mediated other. The user is aware of the mediated other, and the other is aware of the user" (p.14).

There are two significant, fundamental differences between social presence and co-presence, the first of which is direction. The social presence construct is uni-directional, only concerning a single user's perception of the ability of the medium to render another user salient, whereas co-presence is bi-directional, referring to the ability of the users to perceive each other. The second fundamental difference between social presence and co-presence is one of measurement. While both social presence and co-presence are usually measured and subsequently evaluated according to subjective self-report measures such as semantic differentials or Likert scales (Biocca et al., 2003), the focus of measurement differs. Social presence measurements reflect the uni-directional aspect of the mediation, and serve to evaluate the ability of the medium to provide a sense of the other (Nowak, 2001). The "dual nature" of co-presence (Nowak, 2001, p. 10) requires that measurements attend to both the user's perception of the involvement of the other as well as the user's account of his/her own involvement (Goffman, 1963; Nowak, 2001).

Social co-presence was recently introduced into presence literature by Kang et al. (2008) as a response to the need for a definition of social presence which included the aspects of mutual awareness in co-presence (Biocca et al., 2003) as well as the aspect of participants' perceptions of the medium, but also accounted for an assessment of the success of the communication in terms of interactant satisfaction. Social co-presence is therefore defined as the "involvement and engagement through mutual awareness between intelligent beings who have a sense of access to the other being consciously, psychologically and emotionally, within a mediated environment perceived as capable of supporting social communication." Social co-presence is a product of three aspects of mediated communication: co-presence (mutual connectedness), social richness of medium (perceived ability of the medium to support social connectedness), and interactant satisfaction (with regards to the social and emotional accessibility between interactants) (Kang et al., 2008). Like the previous theoretical models on which it is based, social co-presence is measured according to subjective self-report techniques.

In this section, I have reviewed various theoretical constructs in social presence research. The analysis featured in this chapter is guided by the social co-presence construct (Kang et al., 2008), due to the inclusion of both social presence and co-presence measurements, as well as the recognition of the importance of assessing emotional accessibility between interactants. Furthermore, as a nascent theoretical model, social co-presence is in the process of development, and for this reason it is ideally amenable to non-experimental methodology, as proposed in the following section.

Using Discourse Analysis to Assessing Social Co-Presence

Evaluations of social presence, co-presence, and/or social co-presence allow for a dynamic assessment of a communication system, and each is particularly instrumental in establishing the importance of social aspects of interaction. Indeed, it is via the application of such social presence constructs that the significance of participants' use and perception of mediation to make a connection with other participants as well as to assert their own involvement can be viably acknowledged. Consequently, a diligent evaluation of a communication system needs to account for the ability of the medium to allow users to meaningfully connect and interact in a way that is communicatively satisfactory and socially satisfying. However, three problems with the traditional approaches to evaluating social presence, co-presence, and social co-presence can thus far be identified. First, nearly all measurements are based on self-report data (Biocca et al., 2003), forcing researchers and analysts to rely on participant introspection as their source of data (Nowak, 2001). Second, elicitation of subjective self-reports requires access to participating interlocutors, which may not always be possible outside of laboratory settings. Studies on social presence, co-presence, and social co-presence are therefore largely experimental, and thus interactions featuring authentic, spontaneous speech in naturalistic settings are rare or non-existent. The inherent non-recognition of the value of naturalistic, non-experimental settings leads to the third problem, namely, that while the aim of presence research is to provide a model for assessing interlocutor connectedness in mediated communication, it is not concerned with the actual communication at hand. Participant interaction is merely a means to an end: once the communicative event is complete, the subjective measurements can be elicited from the participants and evaluated. In effect, the linguistic value of the communication is ignored.

The use of discourse analysis methodology is proposed as an alternative heuristic to social presence methodology for revealing and discovering aspects of social co-presence in mediated interaction. In general, discourse analysis concerns the use of language at the utterance level or beyond. Within discourse analysis, language is viewed as socially embedded and reflects social structures and relationships. Analyses are therefore ideally conducted on authentic and naturally occurring speech or texts so as to capture the mutual influence of social context and language use.

The application of discourse analysis methodology would inject a linguistic perspective in social presence research, resulting in two advantages. First, social presence research would no longer be confined to experimental settings, dependent on access to participants, and evaluations of social presence would not be solely guided by the subjective methodology of participant introspection. Second, the value of naturally occurring, socially embedded communication would be recognized, such that the evaluation of social presence constructs could be grounded in actual language use.

In this section, I have outlined problems with the traditional approach to evaluating social presence. Significantly, I have proposed the use of discourse analysis methodology as an alternative heuristic, serving to complement social presence research by allowing for non-experimental studies which position socially embedded language as central to the evaluation of social co-presence.

CASE DESCRIPTION

This chapter presents two cases of video-mediated communication featuring professional workplace interactions: a conference workshop and a project staff meeting. Each of the interactions was mediated and overtly recorded using the Marratech video-conferencing platform, and each featured professional workplace discourse. Marratech offers multiparty video, voice chat, text chat (i.e., instant messaging), whiteboard capabilities and collaborative document manipulation (see Figure 1). Participants using a web camera appear in thumbnail images; the larger video window automatically features whichever participant is the current speaker. The microphone can be permanently activated or turned on only as needed; an activated microphone is indicated by the participant's name appearing in red under his or her image in the participant window. The text box can be used to send both public and private instant messages. A keyboard icon appears when a participant composes a public message, but there are no indications when participants write or send private messages. The whiteboard can be used for viewing uploaded documents, or for creating new ones. Additionally, there are a number of tools for document manipulation, such as moving, deleting, or pointing to parts of documents.

The participants in each of the interactions consented to being recorded (by one of the other participants), and no outside observers actively participated in the video conferences. During the video conferences, none of the participants were aware that the recordings would be used for research purposes; final consent was obtained when the recordings were submitted to the researcher/author. Only two personal variables for each of the participants were explicitly provided by the recording participant: country of origin (where each of the interlocutors is located during the video conference; see below), and professional status (see below). However, certain additional social-demographical information can be gleaned from the video conference recordings: each of the workshop participants is male; all but one of the participants in the staff meeting are male; the participants appear to be between 35-50 years old; English is used as the lingua franca (there are five native speakers of English). Finally, it can be assumed that all of the participants are at least minimally familiar with video conferencing or web-based communication technology: each of the workshop participants is involved in the use of web-based tools in higher education, while each of the staff meeting participants are involved in an EU project aimed at developing a web-based platform to facilitate inter-corporate cooperation.

The workshop was part of a seminar series leading up to a conference and was attended by seven participants as well as five audience members[2]. The organizer of the workshop (CW-1, a university faculty member) was located in Portugal, as were three of the six discussants (CW-2, CW-3, and CW-4, all university faculty members);

another discussant participated from the Azore Islands (CW-6, a university faculty member). The remaining two discussants participated from the US (CW-5, an IT consultant) and Sweden (CW-7, an IT sales representative). The relationships among the participants is unknown, but it can be concluded from the nature of the interaction that the workshop organizer (CW-1) knows each of the Portuguese participants (CW-2, CW-3, CW-4, CW-6).

The content of the workshop was presented via a PowerPoint presentation displayed on the whiteboard, the slides of which each featured a question pertaining to the topic of distance education. The workshop organizer led the discussion by commenting or elaborating on one question at a time, then systematically asking each of the discussants to provide his own answer or comment. To hand over a turn, the organizer called on each of the discussants by name and signalled the end of his turn by thanking him. The goal of the workshop was to present and discuss aspects of web-based/distance learning. The duration of the conference workshop was 47 minutes, 50 seconds.

The project staff meeting was conducted by PM-1, an EU-project leader located in Ireland. Two other project members were also based in Ireland, PM-2, a marketing consultant, and PM-3, language adaptations consultant. The five other project members participated from Scotland (PM-4, applications consultant), Norway, (PM-5, product evaluator), Sweden (PM-6, product developer), Germany (PM-7, female, language adaptations consultant), and Italy (PM-8, language adaptations consultant). The participants all know each other and occasionally meet face-to-face at EU-project events.

Like the workshop, the project staff meeting progressed according to a document posted on the whiteboard –in this case, a meeting agenda– and it was also led by one specific participant, who regularly called on the other participants by name to contribute to the discussion. However, while

Figure 1. Screenshot of the Marratech platform (© 2009. Marratech. Used with permission.)

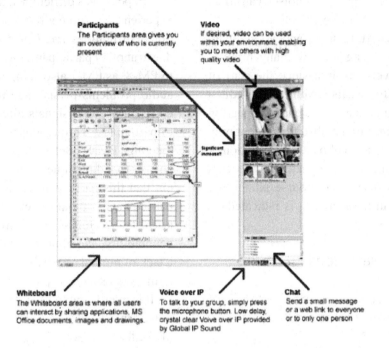

Participants
The Participants area gives you an overview of who is currently present

Video
If desired, video can be used within your environment, enabling you to meet others with high quality video

Whiteboard
The Whiteboard area is where all users can interact by sharing applications, MS Office documents, images and drawings.

Voice over IP
To talk to your group, simply press the microphone button. Low delay, crystal clear Voice over IP provided by Global IP Sound

Chat
Send a small message or a web link to everyone or to only one person

the workshop format required each discussant to answer each question, the project meeting format reflected rather a one participant per item organization. In other words, only one participant was responsible for commenting on one agenda item at a time. The goal of this particular meeting was to review and continue planning the creation and development of a web-based platform intended to facilitate cooperation between small and medium-sized EU companies. The total running time of the meeting was 57 minutes, 21 seconds.

ASSESSING SOCIAL CO-PRESENCE

In this section, extracts from the discourse of the two video conference cases are presented, illustrating the three elements of social co-presence: co-presence, social richness of the medium, and interactant satisfaction. The examples are analyzed from a perspective of socially situated language in use, and considered in terms of how they contribute to or detract from social co-presence.

Co-Presence

Included in Kang et al.'s (2008) social co-presence construct is co-presence, understood as mutual connectedness. The following examples extracted from the video conference cases illustrate how the discourse can reveal indications of or threats to co-presence, in terms of how co-presence "renders persons uniquely accessible, available, and subject to one another" (Goffman, 1959, p. 22), and whether or not "the user is aware of the mediated other, and the other is aware of the user" (Biocca et al., 2003, p.14).

In the first example, the project staff meeting (PM) has begun with the leader, PM-1, asking the participants if they will be able to attend a scheduled conference. Example 1 begins almost three minutes into the meeting, when PM-1 directs the question to PM-8, and simultaneously a muffled, static-like noise can be heard. This example includes a number of separate extracts from the discourse of the project staff meeting, each revealing how problems with mediation, such as the transmission of disruptive noises, can affect the participants' sense of co-presence.

In all examples, a time stamp appears in square brackets corresponding to how many minutes and seconds have transpired since the start of the interaction. Text chats have not been edited for spelling or grammar; voice chats (appearing in *italics*) have been transcribed for content only and therefore include no phonetic information or indications of timing. Voice chat, which occurs before or after the featured discourse extracts but is not included in the analysis, is indicated by <VOICE CHAT>.

Example 1: Project Meeting

[02.56] PM-1: *Okay, uh, PM-8, are you coming to that?*
<MUFFLED NOISE>
[02.59] PM-8: *um, I have um-uh*
[03.08]
PM-1: *There's some terrible feedback from somebody, I don't know. PM-3, you're not on twice, are you?*
[03.14]
PM-6: *Con- [.] Please continue. It was PM-2 playing with his microphone.*
[03.16] <LAUGHTER>
<VOICE CHAT>
[08.25] PM-8: *I'm having a very hard time hearing.*
<VOICE CHAT>
[16.10] PM-8: *Could you repeat that? It's very hard for me to understand.*

The discourse extracts featured in Example 1 illustrate how technical aspects of the mediation can threaten the sense of co-presence, understood as mutual awareness, accessibility, and availability, by serving to isolate the participant

who experiences difficulties. In particular, PM-8 experiences audio malfunction. The first indication of difficulties, *um, I have um-uh*, seems to be due to another participant (PM-2), and not limited to PM-8, as PM-1 also complains. However, the audio problems persist, and the inability to receive clear audio signals affects PM-8's ability to participate. Throughout the remainder of the meeting, PM-8 contributes only once more, in answer to a direct question. It should be pointed out that this participant is also one of only two participants without a web camera, which may affect the overall sense of involvement and accountability, and almost certainly contributes to a lack of mutual accessibility and, consequently, diminished social co-presence.

It is interesting to note, however, the laughter in response to PM-6's explanation of the source of feedback: *It was PM-2 playing with his microphone.* This type of meta-modal discourse, i.e., the overt attention to a particular mode of communication (in this case, the microphone), is characteristic of video conference discourse, serving to repair breakdowns and allow participants to manage their communication (Beers Fägersten et al., forthcoming). Example 1 shows that meta-modal discourse may also contribute to social co-presence by serving to remind participants of their shared communicative context. Awareness of mediation does not necessarily negatively affect co-presence (Nowak, 2001). The participants' collective laughter reflects a sympathetic recognition of this shared environment, referred to in the meta-modal discourse. Directing attention to the medium in a way that grounds the participants in their common mediated environment can therefore serve to repair or establish co-presence.

In Example 2, PM-1 discusses a case study for which PM-4 will have the responsibility of presenting at an upcoming conference. PM-1 asks PM-3 if he will be able to access certain information needed to prepare the case.

Example 2: Project Meeting

[49.57] PM-3: *No problem, yeah. No problem, will do.*
[50.01] PM-1: *Yeah, good. Okay. So, ah, yeah. Ok, will you get in contact about that?*
[50.07] PM-3: *I will, yeah.*
[50.13] PM-1: *Yeah, PM-4,*<VOICE CHAT, PM1 speaks to PM4>...
[50.14] (at this point, PM-3 can be seen removing his headset, and talking to PM-X, a non-participant sitting next to him)
[50.16-51.14] PM-4 <VOICE CHAT, answering PM1>
[51.15-52.05] PM-1 <VOICE CHAT; PM1 resumes leading the discussion>
[52.06] PM-1:...*this is why I was talking about the case study, PM-3.* (<VOICE CHAT> continues)
[52.08] (PM-3 briefly directs attention to the computer screen, then returns attention to PM-X)
[52.57] PM-1:... *What do you guys think?*
[53.00] PM-3: *PM-1* (inaudible) *say it again? Sorry, I was talking to PM-X here.*

The use of a web camera should contribute to co-presence, by virtue of the mutual awareness achieved via streaming video images of each of the participants. Moreover, the ability to view other participants and the knowledge that one is also being viewed should further establish a sense of co-presence, resulting in behavior that indicates a sense of mutual awareness and availability. However, as Example 2 illustrates, the functionality of streaming video does not reliably compel participants to remain co-present. PM-3's

behavior included marked gestures of disconnection, such as turning off the microphone, removing the headset, and engaging in conversation with a non-participant. Furthermore, by suddenly moving closer to and directing attention to his computer screen, PM-3 gave a slight indication of an awareness that PM-1 had referred to him, but no action was taken to rejoin the discussion. Not until PM-1 poses a question –after speaking for nearly two full minutes– does PM-3 mark his return to the discussion by again moving closer to his computer, putting on his headset, and then grabbing the floor by first, rather vaguely, asking what PM-1 had said, and second, apologizing and explaining his request for repetition with *"Sorry, I was talking to PM-X here."*

Much like a non-functioning mode of communication serves to isolate a participant, the deliberate non-use of one can be conceived to do the same and exploited for this purpose. By turning off the microphone and directing attention away from the screen and web camera, PM-3 isolated himself. The fact that he verbalizes what he had been doing as though he were absent and although it was visible to the other participants suggests that PM-3 does not experience a strong sense of co-presence in the video conference environment. Indeed, the mere use of a web camera does not automatically establish co-presence, as Example 2 illustrates.

Such overt disengagement as seen in Example 2 can be attributed to a number of factors, and can of course take place in non-mediated, face-to-face interaction as well. In fact, it cannot be all too uncommon that in any group meeting situation, a sub-group of participants may briefly engage in their own private, side-conversations in parallel with the main discussion. It can therefore not be reliably claimed that computer- or video-mediated interactions are *more* susceptible to such behavior of disengagement. Nevertheless, Example 2 suggests that in video-mediated communication, such deliberate disengagement is uniquely supported by the aspect of mediation. The use of several channels or modes of communication, for example, a microphone, headphones, and a web camera, raises awareness of mediation and renders the interaction non-immediate. Disengagement from the main discussion can be achieved by simply disengaging a channel or mode of communication. Thus, similar to turning away or averting one's gaze in face-to-face interaction, a video conference participant has recourse to disengagement (or, in the event of malfunction, is vulnerable to disengagement) by the disconnection of a channel. It would therefore seem that the video conference medium is *uniquely* susceptible to behaviors of presence disengagement, due to the various options of channel, or modal, disengagement.

In this section, extracts of the video conference cases were analyzed in order to assess co-presence. Two examples each illustrated how a lack of co-presence can be established according to participants' discourse and communicative behavior. The examples suggest that the greatest threat to co-presence, and ultimately social co-presence, is diminished modal capacity, such as the non-functioning or deliberate non-use of modes of communication, which serves to isolate participants, thereby compromising mutual connectedness and accessibility.

Social Richness of the Medium

In general, media richness affects the dynamics of communication (Yoo & Alavi, 2001). As Examples 1 and 2 illustrate, the deliberate disconnection or accidental malfunctioning of media resources can affect co-presence, and thus it would follow that social co-presence would be compromised as well. In contrast, access to and use of a variety of functioning media resources should contribute to social richness and ultimately social co-presence by supporting social connectedness. This hypothesis is explored in this section, where social co-presence is evaluated according to discursive indications of the social richness of the video conference medium.

The Marratech video-conferencing platform offers multiparty video, voice chat, text chat (i.e., instant messaging), whiteboard capabilities, and collaborative document manipulation. Due to the wide range of multiple and multi-user functionalities, the Marratech platform can be said to represent a high degree of media richness. In the following examples, a variety of communicative modes are exploited to mediate or complement the mediation of verbal discourse. The examples are analyzed with regards to social richness of the medium, and its ability to support interactant connectedness.

Example 3 features more extracts of the project staff meeting (PM). PM-1 has been reading aloud and commenting or eliciting comments on the agenda items, type-written and visible to all participants on the whiteboard. With the exception of the first item on the agenda, PM-1 uses the pointing tool, in conjunction with the voice chat, to direct attention to and progress through the remaining agenda items. An abridged agenda featuring a mock-up of the pointing tool is shown in Figure 2. Example 3 features two examples of this behavior from PM-1, and one example from PM-7. Simultaneous pointing and reading is indicated by underlining.

Example 3: Project Meeting

```
[05.55] PM-1: And, so, okay, the
next item on the agenda is the
dissemination and accreditation.
Maybe we can start with accredi-
tation, PM-4, because it's quick
and we can get it out of the
way?
<VOICE CHAT>
[11.04] PM-1: So, basically
what, what, what we are saying
is that, uh, the content of the
public website is to be final-
ized by the fifteenth of May.
```

[14.45] PM-7: *One quest, one question here. Is are everybody, does everyone know what to do for, eh, setting, eh, the translation of the collaboration to 100%?*

Example 3 illustrates how media richness in terms of the availability of a variety of communicative modes can contribute to social richness. First, by using the pointing tool, PM-1 establishes a visual connection with the other participants, who can see PM-1's pointer and his name on each of their own computer screens. While only two examples of this discourse behavior by PM-1 are presented in Example 3, throughout the course of the meeting, PM-1 continues to point, in underlining or circular motions, to each of the remaining agenda items as he reads or discusses them. The effect is one of repeated progress indicators on each of the participant's screens, further establishing visual connection. According to Luff and Heath (2003), social interaction is "largely accomplished in and through objects and artifacts, tools, and technologies [...]. These material resources not only feature in how people produce actions but also, and critically, in the ways in which they recognize and make sense of the actions of others" (p. 54). Equally significantly, the social richness value of this medium in terms of its ability to support social connectedness is recognized when PM-7 mimics PM-1's pointing behavior. PM-7's appropriation of PM-1's behavior suggests that it has been established as a communicative practice, and serves to reinforce their social connectedness as participants of a shared communicative environment.

Example 4 is extracted from the conference workshop (CW). The workshop organizer, CW-1, led the discussion by commenting or elaborating on one question at a time, presented in a PowerPoint document uploaded to the whiteboard. He then systematically asked one or more of the discussants to provide his own answer or comment. The discussants were called on by name, and CW-1 signaled the end of their turns by thanking them. The early establishment of this pattern of interaction was seemingly effective; as the discussants could be fairly sure of being awarded a turn, there were no overlaps and very few interruptions, each of which was performed by the organizer only. In Example 4, interruption is avoided by the use of text chat mode in parallel with voice chat. CW-5's turn has just ended, and CW-1 is introducing a new discussion point. End-of-turn time stamps are provided to indicate any overlapping between voice chat and text chat.

Example 4: Conference Workshop

[21.27] CW-1: *The next question is, what type of, um, virtual classrooms you need, and what, uh, we can do with it. We can use computer based virtual classrooms and hardware based, uh, class-, uhm, sorry, um, hardware based equipment. Um, my question is, from the mobility and interactivity point of view, can you compare it? CW-6, you have a good experience with both, I know. Uh, can you give me your opinion or can you compare both tools?* [22.10]
[22.06] CW-4: hope we will have time to discuss future of virtual classroom
[22.11] CW-6: <VOICE CHAT>
[24.41]
[24.42] CW-1: <VOICE CHAT>
[25.50]
[25.30] CW-6: that would be interesting

Figure 2. Project staff meeting agenda

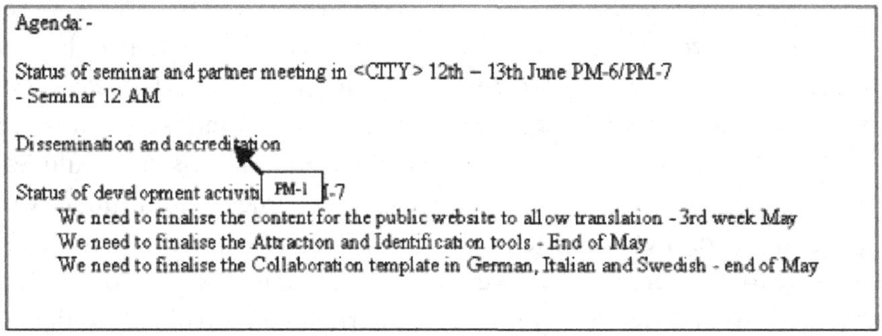

Agenda: -

Status of seminar and partner meeting in <CITY> 12th – 13th June PM-6/PM-7
- Seminar 12 AM

Dissemination and accreditation

Status of development activiti PM-1 [-7
We need to finalise the content for the public website to allow translation - 3rd week May
We need to finalise the Attraction and Identification tools - End of May
We need to finalise the Collaboration template in German, Italian and Swedish - end of May

Example 4 illustrates the use of the text chat as a supplementary mode of communication. Text chat can be used in parallel with voice chat, and Example 4 illustrates how this functionality can be exploited, for example, to make a conversational contribution without usurping the main channel of communication. Text chat thus supports social connectedness by providing participants with the possibility of engaging in parallel communication. The use of the text chat mode reflects social richness of the medium in two ways: first, CW-4 avoids threatening CW-1's face with a voiced comment, potentially disrupting CW-1's question-answer structure. Second, the hedged aspect of CW-4's comment reveals his awareness of CW-1's status of workshop leader. The pragmatic sophistication is evident: CW-4 manages to convey a particular desire, but behaviorally and discursively in a way that defers to the structure of the workshop as well as CW-1's status. Finally, CW-4's action is socially and discursively reinforced by CW-6, who not only mimics CW-4's use of text chat, but also comments positively on CW-4's contribution. In so doing, CW-6 establishes social connectedness.

In this section, social co-presence was examined from the perspective of social richness in terms of the medium's support of social connectedness. Social richness was exemplified by the use of different modes of communication in the video conference environment. The examples illustrate the dynamic social aspects of video-mediated communication, as well as how their common use serves to ground the participants in shared social behavior. Social co-presence in the video conference medium is thus proposed to be a function of social connectedness via shared behaviors which in turn suggest mutual awareness among the participants.

Interactant Satisfaction

The third element of Kang et al.'s (2008) construct of social co-presence is interactant satisfaction, which they define as "the presence of social attraction and emotional credibility between interactants." Interactant satisfaction thus refers to participants' willingness to engage in social activity and their sense of access to and evaluation of another's emotions. In the following examples, interactant satisfaction is represented by aspects of a combination of discourse and communicative behaviors which together indicate emotional credibility.

In Example 5, three participants of the conference workshop are engaged in a parallel text chat, following up on a question comparing face-to-face learning with virtual learning. CW-5 has just answered, and while CW-1 is presenting the next discussion point, CW-2 and CW-7 continue CW-5's thread.

Example 5: Conference Workshop

```
[44:41] CW-2: I agree with your
point of view. But I think that
human contact among students can
happen in the same way
[44:41] CW-2: And onn the other
end, I think it's *doable* but
not necessary immediatly
[44:42] CW-7: ☺
[44:42] CW-2: yeah
[44:42] CW-2: ☺
[44:43] CW-5: thanks
```

CW-2's contributions are directed at CW-5, who has just answered in voice chat. Although CW-2 begins his contributions with "I agree with your point of view", he in essence disagrees with CW-5, as indicated by his use of "but" twice. It is not certain at whom CW-7's smiley emoticon is directed, but it is most likely for CW-5's contribution, representing a positive attitude towards or appreciation for the comments. CW-2 is quick to appropriate its use, first acknowledging the appropriateness ("yeah"). CW-2's imitative use of the smiley emoticon is also in recognition of the positive emotive effect it can have on the potentially negative force of his contributions. Interactant satisfaction is thus clearly illustrated in this text chat both in terms of social attraction and emotional credibility, as CW-2's contributions show a willingness to engage in social activity with another (CW-5 and CW-7) and perceived/expressed appropriateness of another's emotions (CW-7's) via the use of the smiley emoticon. Finally, CW-5's acknowledgement of the positive evaluation, "thanks," represents reciprocated social attraction and emotional credibility.

The final slide of the conference workshop includes a large picture of a character from the television show "The Simpsons," Mr. Burns, with his characteristically tented hands, fingertips touching. An oval shape near his open mouth contains the words "Excelente" and "Excellent". Another oval shape in the lower left corner of the slide contains the words "Aplauso" and "Applause." Example 6 features an extract of CW-1's closing remarks, delivered as this slide was revealed, as well as the parallel text chat.

Example 6: Conference Workshop

```
[46.35] CW-1: Okay, finally
I would like an applause for
our invited and our colleagues
in there. Thank you very much
for being with us and it was
a pleasure. Uh, we overpassed
a little bit our time, but I
think it will be, it was, to to
be there.... <VOICE CHAT until
[47.50]>
[47.40] CW-4: thanks
[47.40] CW-4: a pleasure
[47.40] CW-6: nice to be here
[47.40] CW-4: nice speaking with
you
[47.41] CW-7: Bye
[47:41] CW-6: bye
[47:41] Audience1: thank you
[47:41] Audience1: very inter-
esting
[47:41] Audience2: thank you
[47:41] Audience1: thank you
CW-7
```

Significantly, as CW-1 thanks the discussants as well as the viewing audience, he repeatedly points at the words in each of the ovals, such that his pointer seems to be blinking on and off, first at 'Excelente/Excellent', and then at 'Aplauso/Applause'. This visually striking behavior in turn encourages the discussants and audience members to do the same, and for several seconds there is an intense amount of activity on the screen, as almost simultaneously a string of messages appears in the text chat box, and a frenzy of pointing activity occurs on the whiteboard. The effect is one of a silent but spontaneous and palpably enthusiastic echoing of CW-1's acknowledgements. This behavior thus reflects both access to another's emotions (appreciation, gratitude) and their evaluation as appropriate.

In this section, I have presented two examples of how interactant satisfaction in terms of the sense of social attraction and emotional credibility can be identified in the discourse and communicative behavior of the video conference participants. Alternative modes of communication were shown to enable participants to access each other's emotions and lend emotional credibility to their communication.

SUMMARY AND DISCUSSION OF THE ANALYSIS

Social presence theory has been associated with media richness theory (Daft & Lengel, 1984), exploring the idea that presence varies directly with the richness of a medium (Delfino & Manca, 2007; Hauber et al., 2006; Rice, 1993; Straub, 1994; Straub & Karahanna, 1998). Similarly, the evaluation of social co-presence includes the aspect of the social richness of a medium and its ability to "connect interactants socially" (Kang et al., 2008). In general, the more communicative cues a medium enables, the greater the degree of social presence (Yoo & Alavi, 2001) or, by extension, co-presence and social co-presence. Social co-presence would thus be a function of the richness of a medium in terms of "the communication channels it provides but also additional cues that an interface affords" (Hauber et al., 2005). The widely-held belief is that, ideally, the richness of a medium would enable communication in which interlocutors would fail to notice the medium or the mediated aspects of communication (Lombard & Ditton, 1997).

Video-mediated communication (VMC) quite possibly represents, as yet, the richest form of meditated communication and thus, by virtue of the many channels of communication available to its users, it should allow for a high degree of social co-presence. But just as the many modes of communication made available to users in the video conference environment, such as audio, visual, and text chat modes, can facilitate meaningful and dynamic interaction, they can also have the effect of emphasizing the aspect of mediation, serving as subtle –or, in the event of malfunction, obvious– reminders of the lack of shared physical space. This potentially heightened awareness raises the questions of how aspects of mediation affect interaction and, significantly, how channels of communication are exploited to overcome dispersion and achieve social co-presence. One of the fundamental properties of language and communication is creativity: people "adapt the essential features of interpersonal relationships to the changing features of available media technologies" (Palmer, 1995, p. 277). In other words, interlocutors in mediated communication will use, adapt, and adapt to the tools and modes of communication available to them in order to fulfil their communicative goals and connect with each other (Nowak, 2001). VMC is therefore fertile ground for social presence research, encouraging further investigations of the relationship between media richness and social presence, and continued examination of the unique discursive practices born of socially-embedded language use.

It is unlikely that social presence research that is based solely on experimental design and subjective self-reports can provide a reliable evaluation of social presence. In this chapter, I therefore argue that traditional social presence methodology could benefit from discourse analysis methodology, which would allow for the study of social presence constructs in non-experimental settings. The analysis of naturally occurring language in a socially embedded context is proposed as vital to a robust investigation of social co-presence. Ultimately, the application of discourse analysis methodology releases social co-presence research from experimental settings and its dependence on participant introspection. The naturally occurring language and communicative behavior of mediated interaction are positioned as central to the assessment of social co-presence as a product of linguistic indicators of the presence or absence of the defining features of social co-presence. With this chapter, I hope to encourage additional cross-disciplinary approaches to video-mediated communication and social presence research.

SOLUTIONS AND RECOMMENDATIONS

In this section, I return to the original background of the cases, namely, the imminent phasing out of the Marratech client and server software and the on-going development of a Google-brand video conference platform. Based on the interaction of the video conference cases presented in this chapter, several recommendations for software features can be offered, particularly for use in the virtual workplace environment. The Marratech platform includes a wide variety of modes of communication, such as video, voice chat, and public and private text chat. It also includes whiteboard tools and document sharing capabilities. In each of the video conference cases, it can be seen that interaction is conducted primarily via the combination of two modes of communication: voice chat (requiring microphone and speakers) and whiteboard tools, and thus the specific features of these two modes of communication are first considered.

The use of voice chat allows for interaction that closely resembles face-to-face communication by virtue of its immediacy and intimacy. In fact, it is somewhat inconceivable to conduct a virtual meeting or engage in video-mediated communication without voice chat, especially in conjunction with streaming video. Oral or textual interaction without video, in the form of traditional telecommunication or computer-mediated communication, reflect asymmetries that are less socially unsettling (Sellen, 1994) than video without oral communication. The project staff meeting case featured in this chapter included several examples of such asymmetric interaction due to non-functioning modes, suggesting that oral functionality is more important to social co-presence than video or text. Video conference software should therefore prioritize alternate oral functionalities. For example, the Marratech software features dial-up capability, allowing for participation in the video conference via a telephone.

The whiteboard and whiteboard tools were used extensively throughout the video conference interactions. According to Kraut et al. (2003), "video communication systems that provide a view of the work area are likely to be more useful in supporting situational assessment and conversational grounding" (p. 22). The data presented in this chapter support this claim, as both of the cases featured conversation that centered around documents uploaded to the whiteboard. Furthermore, on several occasions, whiteboard tools such as the pointer were used in parallel with the interaction, which was argued to contribute to co-presence by establishing visual connectedness. As participants repeat or copy such paralinguistic behavior, conversational grounding is further established. It is therefore recommended that video conference software provide shared whiteboard tools.

Finally, text chat is seen to be particularly exploited in the video conference environment, and in clearly systematic ways. Each of the interactions was quite strictly structured in terms of turn-taking, in that one participant led the interactions and designated turns by calling on participants by name. This interactional structure is not unusual in the virtual environment (see Cohen, 1982; Cook & Lalljee, 1972; Isaacs & Tang,

1994; Kraut et al., 2002; O'Conaill et al., 1993; Rutter & Stephenson, 1977; Sellen, 1994), and thus features which allow for alternative modes of communication that are not disruptive to the main channel are desirable in video conference software. The examples presented in this chapter show that the text-chat functionality is used to gain access to other participants, establishing social connectedness.

ACKNOWLEDGMENT

This research was funded by the Swedish Knowledge Foundation (*KK-Stiftelsen*, dnr 2007/0255) for the project Electronic Communication and the Need for Speed. The aim of this and other Knowledge Foundation-funded projects is to apply academic theory and analysis to professional practices for the purpose of promoting cooperation and mutual development. I would like to thank CEFAB (Sweden) for its support of this research.

REFERENCES

Angiolillo, J. S., Blanchard, H. E., Israelski, E. W., & Mané, A. (1997). Technology constraints of video-mediated communication. In Finn, K., Sellen, A., & Wilbur, S. (Eds.), *Video-mediated communication* (pp. 51–73). Mahwah, NJ: Lawrence Erlbaum Associates.

Benford, S., Brown, C., Reynard, G., & Greenhalgh, C. (1996). Shared spaces: Transportation, artificiality, and spatiality. In *Proceedings of the Conference on Computer Supported Cooperative Work* (pp. 77-86). New York: ACM Press.

Biocca, F., & Harms, C. (2002). Defining and measuring social presence: Contribution to the networked minds theory and measure. In *Proceedings of the Fifth Annual International Workshop on Presence* (pp. 7-36).

Biocca, F., Harms, C., & Burgoon, J. K. (2003). Towards a more robust theory and measure of social presence: Review and suggested criteria. Retrieved from http://www.mindlab.msu.edu/biocca/pubs/papers/2003_towards_theory_of_social_presence.pdf

Bull, P., & Rumsey, N. (1988). *The social psychology of facial appearance*. New York: Springer-Verlag.

Clark, H., & Brennan, S. (1991). Grounding in communication. In Resnick, L. B., Levine, J., & Teasley, S. (Eds.), *Perspectives on socially shared cognition* (pp. 127–149). Washington, DC: APA Press. doi:10.1037/10096-006

Cohen, K. (1982). Speaker interaction: Video teleconferences versus face-to-face meetings. In *Proceedings of Teleconferencing and Electronic Communications* (pp. 189–199). Madison, WI: University of Wisconsin Press.

Cook, M., & Lalljee, M. G. (1972). Verbal substitutes for visual signals in interaction. *Semiotics*, *3*, 212–221. doi:10.1515/semi.1972.6.3.212

Cornelius, C., & Boos, M. (2003). Enhancing mutual understanding in synchronous computer-mediated communication by training. *Communication Research*, *30*(2), 147–177. doi:10.1177/0093650202250874

Daft, R., & Lengel, R. (1984). Information richness: A new approach to managerial behavior and organization design. *Research in Organizational Behavior*, *6*, 191–233.

de Greef, P., & IJsselsteijn, W. (2000, March). *Social presence in the PhotoShare tele-application*. Paper presented at Presence 2000 - 3rd International Workshop on Presence, Delft, The Netherlands.

Delfino, M., & Manca, S. (2007). The expression of social presence through the use of figurative language in a web-based learning environment. *Computers in Human Behavior*, *23*(5), 2190–2211. doi:10.1016/j.chb.2006.03.001

Fletcher, T. D., & Major, D. A. (2006). The effects of communication modality on performance and self-ratings of teamwork components. *Journal of Computer-Mediated Communication, 11*(2), article 9. Retrieved March 3, 2009, from http://jcmc.indiana.edu/vol11/issue2/fletcher.html

Fulk, J., Schmitz, J., & Power, G. J. (1987). A social information processing model of media use in organizations. *Communication Research, 14*(5), 520–552. doi:10.1177/009365087014005005

Goffman, E. (1959). *The presentation of self in everyday life*. Garden City, New York: Anchor.

Goffman, E. (1963). *Behavior in public places: Notes on the social organization of gatherings*. New York: Free Press.

Hauber, J., Regenbrecht, H., Hills, A., Cockburn, A., & Billinghurst, M. (2005). Social presence in two- and three-dimensional videoconferencing. In. *Proceedings of ISPR, 2005*, 189–198.

Heath, C., & Luff, P. (1991). Disembodied conduct: Communication through video in a multi-media office environment. In *Proceedings of the ACM Conference on Human Factors in Computing Systems, CHI'91* (pp. 99-103). New Orleans, Louisiana.

Inoue, T., Okada, K. I., & Matsushita, Y. (1997). Integration of face-to-face and video-mediated meetings: HERMES. In *Proceedings of International Conference on Supporting Group Work* (pp. 405-414). New York: ACM Press.

Isaacs, E., & Tang, J. (1994). What video can and cannot do for collaboration: A case study. *Multimedia Systems, 2*, 63–73. doi:10.1007/BF01274181

Kang, S., Watt, J., & Ala, S. (2008, April). *Social copresence in anonymous social interactions using a mobile video telephone*. Paper presented at CHI, Florence, Italy.

Kraut, R. E., Fussell, S. R., & Siegel, J. (2003). Visual information as a conversational resource in collaborative physical tasks. *Human-Computer Interaction, 18*, 13–49. doi:10.1207/S15327051HCI1812_2

Lombard, M., & Ditton, T. (1997). At the heart of it all: The concept of presence. *Journal of Computer Communication, 3*(2). Retrieved from http://www.ascusc.org/jcmc/vol3/issue2/lombard.html.

Luff, P., & Heath, C. (2003). Fractured ecologies: Creating environments for collaboration. *Human-Computer Interaction, 18*, 51–84. doi:10.1207/S15327051HCI1812_3

McGrath, J., & Hollingshead, A. (1993). Putting the group back in group support systems: Some theoretical issues about dynamic processes in groups with technological enhancements. In Jessup, L., & Valacich, J. (Eds.), *Group support systems: New perspectives* (pp. 78–96). New York: Macmillan.

Meier, C. (1998). *In search of the virtual interaction order: investigating conduct in video-mediated work meetings*. (Arbeitspapiere „Telekooperation" Nr. 3). Institut für Soziologie, Universität Gießen. Retrieved 3 June, 2009, from http://www.uni-giessen.de/g31047

Morgan, G. (1993). *Imaginization*. London: Sage.

Nguyen, D., & Canny, J. (2004). MultiView: Spatially faithful group video conferencing. In *Proceedings of CHI 2004* (pp. 512-521). New York: ACM Press.

Nowak, K. (2001). *Defining and differentiating copresence, social presence and presence as transportation*. Paper presented at Presence, Philadelphia, PA. Available at: http://citeseerx.ist.psu.edu/viewdoc/summary?doi=10.1.1.19.5482.

Nowak, K., & Biocca, F. (2003). The effect of the agency and anthropomorphism on users' sense of telepresence, copresence, and social presence in virtual environments. *Presence (Cambridge, Mass.), 12*(5), 481–494. doi:10.1162/105474603322761289

O'Conaill, B., Whittaker, S., & Wilbur, S. (1993). Conversations over video conferences: An evaluation of the spoken aspects of video-mediated communication. *Human-Computer Interaction, 8*, 389–428. doi:10.1207/s15327051hci0804_4

O'Malley, C., Langton, S., Anderson, A., Doherty-Sneddon, G., & Bruce, V. (1996). Comparison of face-to-face and video-mediated interaction. *Interacting with Computers, 8*(2), 177–192. doi:10.1016/0953-5438(96)01027-2

Oviatt, S., & Cohen, P. (1991). Discourse structure and performance efficiency in interactive and non-interactive spoken modalities. *Computer Speech & Language, 5*, 297–326. doi:10.1016/0885-2308(91)90001-7

Palmer, M. (1995). Interpersonal communication and virtual reality: Mediating interpersonal relationships. In Biocca, F., & Levy, M. (Eds.), *Communication in the Age of Virtual Reality* (pp. 277–299). Hillsdale, New Jersey: Lawrence Erlbaum Associates.

Reiserer, M., Ertl, B., & Mandl, H. (2002). Fostering collaborative knowledge construction in desktop videoconferencing. Effects of content schemes and cooperation scripts in peer-teaching settings. In Stahl, G. (Ed.), *Computer support for collaborative learning: foundations for a CSCL community* (pp. 379–388). Mahwah, NJ: Lawrence Erlbaum Associates.

Rice, R. E. (1992). Task analyzability, use of new medium and effectiveness: A multi-site exploration of media richness. *Organization Science, 3*(4), 475–500. doi:10.1287/orsc.3.4.475

Rutter, D. R. (1987). *Communicating by telephone.* Elmsford, NY: Pergamon.

Rutter, D. R., & Stephenson, G. M. (1977). The role of visual communication in synchronizing conversation. *European Journal of Social Psychology, 2*, 29–37. doi:10.1002/ejsp.2420070104

Sapsed, J., Gann, D., Marshall, N., & Salter, A. (2005). From here to eternity?: The practice of knowledge transfer in dispersed and co-located organisations. *European Planning Studies, 13*(6), 831–851. doi:10.1080/09654310500187938

Schroeder, R. (2002). Social interaction in virtual environments: Key issues, common themes, and a framework for research. In Schroeder, R. (Ed.), *The social life of avatars: Presence and interaction in shared virtual environments* (pp. 1–18). London: Springer.

Sellen, A. (1994). Remote conversations: The effects of mediating talk with technology. *Human-Computer Interaction, 10*(4), 401–444. doi:10.1207/s15327051hci1004_2

Short, J., Williams, E., & Christie, B. (1976). *The social psychology of telecommunication.* London: John Wiley & Sons.

Straub, D., & Karahanna, E. (1998). Knowledge worker communications and recipient availability: Toward a task closure explanation of media choice. *Organization Science, 9*(2), 160–175. doi:10.1287/orsc.9.2.160

Straub, D. W. (1994). The effect of culture on IT diffusion: E-mail and FAX in Japan and the U.S. *Information Systems Research, 5*(1), 23–47. doi:10.1287/isre.5.1.23

Townsend, A., DeMarie, S., & Hendrickson, A. (1998). Virtual teams: Technology and the workplace of the future. *The Academy of Management Executive, 12*(3), 17–29.

van der Kleij, R., Lijkwan, J., Rasker, P. C., & De Dreu, C. K. W. (in press). Effects of time pressure and communication environment on team processes and outcomes in dyadic planning. *International Journal of Human-Computer Studies*. doi:.doi:10.1016/j.ijhcs.2008.11.005

Whittaker, S. (1995). Rethinking video as a technology for interpersonal communications: Theory and design implications. *International Journal of Man-Machine Studies*, *42*, 501–529.

Whittaker, S., & O'Conaill, B. (1997). The role of vision in face-to-face and mediated communication. In Finn, K. E., Sellen, A. J., & Wilbur, S. (Eds.), *Video-mediated communication: Computers, cognition, and work* (pp. 23–49). Mahwah, NJ: Lawrence Erlbaum Associates, Inc.

Yoo, Y., & Alavi, M. (2001). Media and group cohesion: Relative influences on social presence, task participation, and group consensus. *Management Information Systems Quarterly*, *25*(3), 371–390. doi:10.2307/3250922

Zhao, S. (2003). Towards a taxonomy of copresence. *Presence (Cambridge, Mass.)*, *12*(5), 445–455. doi:10.1162/105474603322761261

KEY TERMS AND DEFINITIONS

Video-mediated communication (VMC): Interpersonal interaction via the use of computers or other digital media featuring video and audio signals.

Video-Conference: Synchronous, video-mediated interaction featuring two-way video and audio signals between two or more interlocutors at different locations.

Social Presence: Attributed to Short et al (1976); refers to the salience of another in mediated communication.

Co-Presence: Attributed to Goffman (1959); refers to the mutual salience, availability, and accessibility of interlocutors.

Social Co-Presence: Attributed to Kang, et al. (2008), social co-presence refers to co-presence, social richness of the medium, and interactant satisfaction.

Social Richness of the Medium: An element of social co-presence; refers to the ability of the medium to connect interactants socially.

Interactant Satisfaction: An element of social co-presence; refers to participant satisfaction with regards to the social attraction of the medium.

ENDNOTES

[1] Information sources: http://www.marketingpilgrim.com/2007/04/google-video-conferencing.html, http://www.marketingpilgrim.com/2007/08/google-has-no-plans-to-develop-old-marratech.html, http://www.marratech.com/forum/index.php?showtopic=2106, all accessed 04 June 2009.

[2] None of the audience members actively participated or appeared on video; furthermore, their profiles and locations are unknown.

Chapter 10

Investigating the Online Interactions of a Team of Test Developers Working in a Wiki Environment

Anna Filipi
Australian Council for Educational Research, Australia

Sophie Lissonnet
Australian Council for Educational Research, Australia

EXECUTIVE SUMMARY

This chapter reports an investigation of online interactions occurring in the context of the development of a suite of foreign language tests known as the Assessment of Language Competence (ALC) (http://www. acer.edu.au/alc/). The interactions took place in a wiki environment from 2007 to 2009. The aim of the investigation was twofold. The first was to identify the features of the organization of online postings in an asynchronous online environment and to compare them with the organization of face-to-face interaction. The second was to examine how expertise is invoked in interactions centered on the vetting of test items. The chapter uses selected findings from Conversation Analysis and applies them to the postings on the wiki. Findings from the analysis include the rarity of self-repair, similarities in the organization of sequence structure and the same orientations to affiliative behavior found in conversation.

INTRODUCTION

Previous research on the features of Computer-Mediated Communication, the bulk of which comes from educational settings, has focused in a very general sense on the differences between written and spoken interaction. Because it is communication in a written mode, but interactive in its delivery even if this does not occur in real time, traditional ways and forms of communication are being challenged. Indeed Smith (2003), while noting how Computer-Mediated Communication shares similarities with both written and spoken texts, pointed out that it also has characteristics which are unique to it. For example, there is an absence or reduction of paralinguistic and nonverbal features and a greater reliance on the bald written word which can lead

DOI: 10.4018/978-1-61520-863-0.ch010

to communication breakdown and challenges for the participants as they work to understand each other (Smith, 2003). Magnan Sieloff (2008) made reference to its uniqueness when speaking of technology as reconstructing how people go about communicating with each other. Not only is there an exchange in information, but this is co-constructed so that it becomes possible to "create new meaning collaboratively in new ways and at new rhythms" (p.1).

It is this co-construction of meaning which is precisely what is at the heart of spoken interaction from the perspective of Conversation Analysis. As a field of research in its own right, Conversation Analysis has provided both a set of findings and a set of tools for investigating naturally occurring real time interactions as they unfold moment by moment. The focus is on how people take turns and how turns are organized in sequences of talk (see Drew & Heritage, 2006; ten Have, 1999). According to Mazur (2004), online interactions provide conversation analysts with a potentially rich source of naturally occurring data to investigate various forms of communication including in work and instructional contexts. While it has for decades used transcriptions of audio or video recordings as primary sources of data, nowadays, Computer-Mediated Communication logs can be used to shortcut the transcription process, so that online turn-taking and sequence organization can be studied. Though they still need minor formatting to lend themselves to Conversation Analysis, "the text logs themselves contain "naturally occurring" conversant-generated indications of some of the sociolinguistic dimensions evinced in recordings of speech. The use of emoticons … are an example of this phenomenon quite prevalent in text-based on-line conversations" (p. 1083).

It is evident that Conversation Analysis lends itself very well to the study of online interaction, both to contexts that are informal and to contexts such as the one in the current study which are institutional in character deriving as they do from the world of work.

FINDINGS FROM CONVERSATION ANALYSIS

The findings from Conversation Analysis that are of relevance to the current analysis are assessments, repair, pursuit of a response, and aspects of sequence organization.

Assessments

In conversation, it has been found that speakers display a bias towards affiliative, and therefore closely connected and supportive actions over their opposite, disaffiliative and unsupportive ones (Clayman & Heritage, 2002; Heritage, 1984; Pomerantz, 1984a). Such a bias is made manifest through structural features in conversation associated with preferred and dispreferred "turn shapes". Commonly referred to as preference organization, an example of a preferred turn is a positive response to an invitation, while a dispreferred turn is a rejection, which will be marked in some way by pauses and dysfluency (see Schegloff, 2007).

Preference organization has been studied in specific sequential contexts. One such context that is relevant to the current study is the assessment. This has been found to be pervasively present in face-to-face interaction (Pomerantz, 1984a) although it is reported as being rare in asynchronous Computer-Mediated Communication (Tanskanen, 2007). Assessments involve speakers evaluating an activity or event as they converse with one another. Structurally, in conversational terms, on the production of a first assessment, a second assessment becomes a sequentially relevant next action. Pomerantz (1984a) has argued that a preference organization for agreement over disagreement holds for assessment environments. Speakers work to achieve agreement and strive to minimize the occurrence of disagreement. However, it is not possible to always avoid disagreement (Pomerantz, 1984a).

In the current data, the core of the work that occurs involves making assessments of the test materials. This is precisely what constitutes the role of the vetter. A key analytic interest is to examine how assessments are oriented to and what happens when there is a disagreement between a writer and a vetter. In other words, how does the normal display of affiliation play out in this environment?

Repair and Pursuit of a Response

Repair is a unique conversational phenomenon, which provides an organized system for dealing with breakdown in talk. Schegloff, Jefferson and Sacks (1977) and Schegloff (1987; 1992b; 1997; 2000a) have researched the ways in which hearers and speakers adjust their talk when breakdown occurs as a result of inadequate hearing or interpretation. An important point that emerges from this research is that sources of trouble do not induce repair. Rather it is as a result of repair initiation that something in the prior talk is found to be a source of trouble in need of remedy. The initiation will lead to some kind of outcome. Either there will be a solution or abandonment. Repair sequences can be initiated by the same speaker (referred to as self-initiated) or by the next speaker (referred to as other-initiated). Corrections can also be made by the same speaker (self-repaired) or by the next speaker (other-repaired). However, there is an overwhelming preference for self-initiated self-repair in conversation (Schegloff et al., 1977). This preference has also been reported to hold true for email interaction by Tanskanen and Karhukorpi (2008) in a study of concessive repair, a particular type of repair that entails retracting overstatements or potentially challenging statements that could provoke disagreement. Tanskanen and Karhukorpi (2008) found that in email interaction concessive repair occurs in the same turn and not in the next turn as is the case in face-to-face interaction. Tanksanen and Karhukorpi maintain that this provides evidence that in Computer-Mediated Communication, participants work to achieve affiliation by taking the perspective of the other

participant. In other words, they work collaboratively to minimize conflict.

One resource that speakers can deploy as part of a broader repair strategy to facilitate communication is to pursue a response. Although not originally characterized in this way by Pomerantz (1984b), more recently in studies of very young children's talk both, Filipi (in press) and Forrester (2008) have shown that it is used as a "sequence implicated repair" phenomenon because it draws attention to the absence of an expected response.

The relevance of repair and pursuit of a response to the analysis of online interaction is obvious as they are implicated in meaning making. As noted, repair or communication breakdown has received attention particularly in studies of online interactions involving students learning a second language (Smith, 2003). Other aspects of communication such as (im)politeness and the mitigation of conflict (Graham, 2007; Harrison, 2000), concessive repair (Tanskanen & Karhukorpi, 2008) and the use of meta-pragmatic devices that focus on the communication act itself (*are you following me?*) rather than the content of the posting (Tanskanen, 2007), reveal the work that participants do to minimize actual and the potential for communication breakdown. They have all provided an increasingly rich picture of how participants co-construct meaning in online environments A focus on more general repair practices, particularly in a wiki environment, and the pursuit of a response, the focus of the current investigation, will contribute to this growing body of knowledge.

Sequence Organization

Sequence organization describes how turns at talk fit together structurally as relevant next actions to what has gone before. There are various types of sequences at the heart of this organization. One that is massively present in talk-in-interaction is the adjacency pair. This is a paired utterance composed of two turns (a first and second pair part) that "fit" together such as the question and answer pair.

While the adjacency pair can be considered a base sequence, sequences composed of a single utterance or clusters of sequences can be inserted between the first pair part and the second pair part (in which case they are not heard as an absence), or they can temporarily suspend the base sequence, as in side-sequences or asides (Jefferson, 1972). These are sequences that have nothing to do with the main business of the conversation.

All of the features just described emerge in the wiki interactions and as such provide a useful means of making comparisons between what happens in real time, face-to-face contexts and in asynchronous, online contexts.

Wikis at Work

Wiki technology is the brainchild of Ward Cunningham who wanted to create the simplest possible online database that could work. Wikis are commonly described as a collection of Web pages that anyone can edit.

According to Wood, Thoeny and Cunningham (2007), "When wikis succeed, they do so to a large degree because they meet the needs of so many different kinds of people" (p. 287). Wiki technology was chosen by the ALC team precisely because of its simplicity and ease of deployment. The team's rationale at the time of switching technology was that the team of 19 writers dispersed in a variety of locations and time zones could become operational in this environment with minimum training and technical support.

Wikis are by definition tools that support democratic participation and shared authorship. In such an environment the notion of authority and expertise is less relevant. People assume a number of roles when contributing to a wiki. They include: reader-researcher, contributor, editor, quality expert and administrator (Wood et al., 2007). In the case of the ALC, these personas are readily adopted by the writers, vetters and the

project administrators, but they are dynamic and shifting, as determined by the local environment. Such shifts have been noted by Jaques and Salmon (2006) in their research of the exchanges operating in learning groups in both face-to-face and online environments. They described several critical factors, including the physical environment and people's relative positioning, which affect group dynamics and the free flow of communication. According to Jaques and Salmon (2006), the most salient change in group dynamics occurring in online interaction (in a school or university context) was the shift of authority from student to teacher.

An interesting question for the current study is to analyze how these roles emerge, shift and are co-constructed in the interactions as writers, vetters and the project manager work together to develop the tests, and whether any group defers to the other as the authority who has the ultimate say in what passes as a final test item.

Co-Constructing Expertise

Finding new ways of working in a computer-mediated environment can be somewhat unsettling to writers and vetters. As observed during the initial training session, writers and vetters appear to operate on subtly hierarchical arrangements in face-to-face situations. Writers may create their own internal hierarchy within a language group based on personal affinities and contact, they may even agree to defer to one another, but in their interactions with vetters and the project manager they expect their status as recruited language, (inter)cultural and pedagogical experts to be deferred to, and that their knowledge and experience be consulted.

As noted, many of the studies on online interaction have occurred in educational settings and have focused on the changes in teacher-student interaction in an online environment. The ALC wiki is an example of interactions that occur in the world of work. Writers, vetters and the project manager are recruited to undertake specific tasks.

Unlike online educational settings, the risk of non-participation or disengagement is minimal. The most demanding adjustment for writers is to see their own sense of expertise being invoked as they accept or reject the vetters' assessments of their writing.

Research on workplace interaction has shown how the concurrent use of tools, instruments or graphic material, gesture and discourse form a coherent "grammar" of collaborative action (Goodwin, 1996). After observing the physical positioning and work interaction of two scientists sharing the use of a single device for two separate scientific research purposes aboard an oceanic research vessel, Goodwin (1995) concluded that human cognition is best approached as a corpus of "historically constituted and socially distributed processes including tools as well as multiple human beings situated in structurally different positions" (p. 46). A number of very basic comparisons can be drawn between Goodwin's vessel and the ALC wiki. Because of the online nature of the tools of working in a wiki environment, physical positioning matters less than status and identity positioning. Just like Goodwin's oceanic vessel, the wiki is a closed environment that forces experts from diverse disciplines to share a limited space, mitigate a range of personal and professional agendas and acknowledge each other's expertise. All these complex processes take place, often in full view of others in a rather un-buffered manner. Comments posted by vetters are sometimes received as "raw" and on occasion have been considered to be somewhat offensive. Once written, they sit in the allocated space for the duration of the writing cycle for all the team to see.

This is in sharp contrast with the more muted paneling process used for vetting items in a face-to-face environment, where speakers (usually two vetters and a writer) can interrupt each other, ask for and provide instant clarification, repair understanding immediately and use intonation and gesture as essential resources to create and display meaning.

One final issue that is pertinent to the current study of interactions in a work setting is the notion of how expertise emerges. Hall and Danby (2003) have paid particular attention to the co-construction of the expert category in professional meetings conducted in a professional educational setting. They analyzed interactions during a gathering of school and university staff intent on forming a partnership. In addition to Conversation Analysis, they also used membership category analysis (Hester & Eglin, 1997) in order to describe both people and activities as they interacted during formal meetings. Their analysis showed how participants "accomplish what might be seen as the attributes of a person belonging to the category of 'experts'" (Hall & Danby, 2004, p.4). By comparing the number of turns during the meeting, they noticed that the talk was dominated by a small number of participants, most notably the school principal and the dean of the faculty and two academic staff. The analysis showed how participants enact their everyday business through the partnership meetings and how they used words and turns to assert themselves as experts in the social worlds of education. A relevant question for the current investigation is how and when the expertise of vetters and writers is invoked through the online interactions, and like Hall and Danby's (2003) study, how roles are oriented to and shift as vetters and writers "do" the work of test development.

SETTING THE STAGE

The ALC certificate program of the Australian Council for Educational Research (ACER) (http://www.acer.edu.au/) is an annual multiple choice testing program in listening and reading comprehension for students from upper primary to senior secondary years of schooling. The tests are developed at three levels in Chinese, French, German, Indonesian, Italian and Japanese in a wiki environment. Test questions are written by a team of up to 19 writers from across Australia, all of whom are practicing teachers or curriculum writers. The writing team is supported in its work by the test development staff at ACER. The ACER based ALC team trains the writers, vets the tests and provides advice and guidance on formatting as well as on the appropriateness and range of items for the level of learning. A team of language specialists is also contracted to provide advice on the language of each test once the vetting has been completed. When a final draft is completed, the tests are trialed with a small group of schools before going to the final production stage.

Maintaining version control of the tests in a collaborative writing arrangement and providing a possibility for the team of writers (not all of whom were living in geographical proximity to each other or to the test administrators and managers), provoked the major impetus for changing processes and adopting an online collaborative workspace.

In terms of organization, the wiki is designed around spaces, each containing pages. Each language is assigned two spaces, one each for the reading and listening units which comprise a stimulus and its accompanying test questions. In order to streamline both the discussions and the vetting, each unit is developed in a separate page of the wiki duly identified by a unique unit number. Comments relevant to the development and vetting of each unit are posted at the bottom of each wiki page.

Writers can elect to receive email alerts (or subscribe to an RSS feed) to stay informed of new postings added in their language space. The test development team, including the wiki administrator, can subscribe to a "daily digest" summarizing the postings to each page made in the last 24 hours. This feature of the wiki facilitates the ALC team's effort to minimize the response time to queries and comments posted by the writers. One of the immediate consequences is that items are monitored and vetted "as we go" instead

of being batched and paneled at the end of the writing cycle. (For further details of the project, see Filipi and Lissonnet (2008)).

The interactions chosen for analysis were derived from over 2,000 postings taken from the 2008 and the 2009 test development. (Separate postings included single offerings such as "thanks".) In order to protect the identity of each member of the team, pseudonyms have been used. Other features that might reveal the identity of the team members in the transcripts have been replaced with "Target Language" as in Target Language background or Target Language country. These appear in brackets in the transcript. The transcripts themselves are formatted in italics while comments in the transcripts appear in single brackets in normal format. The postings were not edited, so some typographical errors may appear.

A Model for Online Moderation (and Student Teacher Interaction)

Working through a wiki was a new development for the test development team. In addition to the established expertise needed for the test development, it required additional skills to be developed, including a new shared set of competencies with no member of the actual writing team being more expert than the other. For this reason, Salmon's (2000) model of teaching and learning online through Computer-Mediated Communication was relevant as a way of briefly describing the key phases of interaction in the ALC wiki. Salmon's model developed from the analysis of 3000 messages posted to an online conferencing system by teachers and students enrolled in an Open University business course. It was largely devised to better understand the role teachers would have to play in their new capacity as e-moderators.

Salmon (2000) describes how the level of interactivity between participants in the Computer-Mediated Communication environment changes as the learners master specific technical skills.

Table 1. Salmon's model of online interaction and its relationship to wiki interaction as observed during test development

Description (Salmon)	Description (ALC)	Notes
Access and Motivation (Phase 1)	Set up phase and accessing the new system.	Participants check they can access the wiki from home and office. They test their password. They attend a briefing and training session. Some opposition to (or at least some reluctance to engage with) the new system is usually voiced at this point.
Online socialisation (Phase 2)	This is the phase during which participants establish online identities. They start to find others with whom to interact and play with the system.	In the case of the ALC, some of this happened during the training session and also through personal contact since some writers knew each other. This is also the phase where people get used to working differently. According to Salmon, induction is crucial and may determine future participation.
Information Exchange (Phase 3)	Participants share information about the course. They are both enthusiastic with the new system and the immediate, free-flowing information. They can also be overwhelmed by the volume of information available. Because they are still learning how to work the system, the moderator's role is to provide guidance and encouragement.	The ALC team gave rapid feedback to all requests and operated in Helpdesk mode throughout the writing phase. The team assisted writers who had trouble with accessing or navigating the system, or formatting test items.
Knowledge Construction (Phase 4)	Participants begin to interact with each other in more exposed and participative ways. During this phase they learn from others while at the same time asserting their beliefs.	Not all writers engaged in this knowledge construction with other members of the writing team preferring instead to confine this activity to engagement with the vetter only. Others were happy to engage with both vetters and other writers of the same language.
Development (Phase 5)	Participants look for more benefits from the system.	In the final phase of the ALC writing phase, writers were surveyed for feedback about working in the wiki. Some of them made comments regarding other features they would like to see implemented in the next year. This included the creation of a shared community space where writers could exchange links, tips, clipart or best practices.

For each step Salmon also describes the type of e-moderating action that is required. The table below shows each phase of the test development and the kinds of technological skills acquired by the participants. (Note: Phase 3 and 4 are described by Salmon as the phases when the level and intensity of interaction between moderator and participant peak).

The main data selected for the following analysis was generated from the Knowledge Construction phase.

CASE DESCRIPTION

General Communication on the Wiki

While the majority of the interactions and postings in the wiki were focused on the development of the tests items, there was also a small set that were germane to general administration, formal evaluations of the experience of working through a wiki and, very rarely, "socializing." Analysis begins by examining this set of interactions with the aim of drawing out the organizational features that compare with face-to-face interaction. In order to uncover these similarities and differences, a

Table 2.

Posts on the wiki
Participant stance to postings
←writing   interaction→

useful approach is to consider the stance or voice (White, 2003) of the creator of the postings first.

Postings as Written Texts

What seems to have emerged in the analysis of the postings is that some writers have taken on a more distal "writing" stance to the postings while others have adopted a more proximal, "interactionist" approach. Evidence for making this claim is the presence or absence of a response to the postings from another member of the test development team, and whether the absence is noticed and oriented to as such by, for example, pursuing a response.

As noted above, pursuit of a response is part of a speaker's conversational "tool box." It is used as an option when a speaker is faced with a response that is hearably absent (Pomerantz, 1984b). While the action of not responding offers a possible display of recipient stance, it also offers a window on speaker stance. The following posting occurred during the evaluation phase of the test development (see Development phase in the table above).

Writer: There were no "hissy fits" or strident emails. It was clear that the people at ALC appreciated the fact that many of the writers also lead busy professional lives and thus the tone and pitch of the emails and messages reminding us to move on, get things done, etc were always reasonable and polite.

Because these specific comments were elicited in a formal evaluation process, there was no reply to this posting. Writers made reference to each other's comments, but did not engage with each other. They treated them as written postings not designed to receive a response.

If all the postings were to be viewed as being on a continuum from written texts at one end to interaction at the other, then this posting would be at the writing end.

The majority of the postings, however, were more interactional. It is this set that will constitute the locus for the analysis, because one of the study's aims is to investigate how interaction is achieved in an asynchronous environment.

"Helpdesk" Postings

Postings about wiki features or how to get things done were most frequently produced in the form of the Question and Answer adjacency pair. These postings were much more conversational as a result. The example below typifies the kind of interaction in the talk about working on the wiki as opposed to talk about the items (the focus in the next sections).

Writer: I am finding it confusing to move from parent to children page. I think I am not doing it!! When I type TR I mean to be on the parent page. When I omit it I mean to be on the children page but how can I navigate between the two smoothly please??

Admin: You need to create a parent page (the translation of the text + questions) and one child page (the text in the target language) for each text. To create the parent page, you need to be in the (Target Language) home space. Check by looking at the boxes that appear at the top of the new page. They should indicate the space (Target Language) and the home page (Target Language Home). Let me know how you go.

In the absence of para- and non-linguistic features, which is a key characteristic of Computer-Mediated Communication (Smith, 2003), there is a repeat of both the exclamation and question marks that mark the writer's attitude as one of frustration. The administrator seems to be orienting to this frustration as she not only answers the question, but she also opens up the possibility for further dialogue with an instruction to get back to her. This is not taken up because the problem gets resolved.

As well as the Question and Answer format, postings were also made in the form of unsolicited comments (such as an informing about moving an item to a different page or an enthusiastic embrace of the technology which did not invite a response), general problem comments such as having posted things in the wrong place (*Sorry! I accidentally attached my grid to a wrong space and I don't know how to remove it*), which were responded to through action, and in same pair types such as thanks and return thanks as in the following example.

Writer: With my school IT staff's assistance, I was able to work on the editing bar and get all the bolding job done. Thanks for your patience, Lynn.

Vetter: And thanks for your persistence.

This example comes at the end of a long process of trying to use the wiki function to bold relevant sections as required for formatting of the items. Unlike unsolicited comments, the vetter responds verbally. Like the Question and Answer, which routinely carries structural implications for the ensuing talk, in that a question makes an answer a relevant next action (Schegloff, 2007), there appears to be a similar constraint operating in this exchange. Indeed, in conversation a normal response to a thank-you is some kind of acknowledging turn such as "you're welcome". So the question becomes to what extent is this true for the interactions in the wiki which do not occur in real time? Are the participants held accountable? And is there a pursuit of a response?

Pursuing a Response

In the postings about the test items, some writers engage in an interaction while others simply accept the assessments without comment, and sometimes the vetter is compelled to pursue an action, for example when the changes requested do not appear. This could also then be linked to the notion of expertise or roles and stance towards them which are examined in the next main section.

One important difference between face-to-face interactions and the interactions on the wiki is that the latter do not occur in real time, therefore there can be quite a time delay between the posting of a question and a response to it. There is also the potential for questions not to be answered at all because they become irrelevant or are forgotten. This is evident in the example below. However, the vetter actually pursues the suggested edits, and in doing so, makes it clear that they must be acted on.

Vetter: Where would this announcement be heard? On a community radio station? In that case wouldn't the announcer be making the announcement on the family's behalf? I don't think an address would be given would it? Replace "If you find our dog, please ring 07113579 and we will come and collect him" with "if found...", and delete "our children are crying". (Posted December 3, 2008.)

Vetter: Have changes been made? (Posted December 8, 2008.)

Writer: Julie, you are quite right. I have now changed it to be appropriate for a community radio station. (Posted December 12, 2008)

Vetter: Much more appropriate now. Thanks Melanie.

Here a series of questions are posted by the vetter which call into question the authentic like quality of the item. She then proceeds with providing a set of explicit edits she would like made. The posting lies dormant for five days at which point the vetter posts a follow-up question in the face of the absence of uptake. Noteworthy, is that the question, and therefore the pursuit, is not about whether the writer agrees or not with the suggested edits but rather whether the changes have been made. After a further time delay, the writer replies with a statement that makes evident that the vetter's pursued actions have been met. In other words, she has made the changes suggested. A final acknowledging posting by the vetter concludes the interaction and marks this as a successful completion of the pursuit. To sum up, the pursuit in this example is not of a feature of conversation such as an answer to a question, but rather of the action of editing.

Repair

Because the wiki provides an asynchronous environment, there are opportunities for participants to self-correct and to polish their postings before they are made public or to self-edit once they are posted, unlike synchronous environments and face-to-face interactions as noted by Tanskanen (2007). The self-repair is thus not made visible to the project team. Self-initiated self-repair is thus rare. Below is one of only two examples found in the corpus.

Writer: Should we mark the correct and bold the codes? (Posted at 12:01)

Sorry, I mean mark the correct answers. (Posted at 12.01)

Here the correction is made to the language form and not to the content, unlike the only other example of self-repair in the corpus. This is very rare because such slip-ups (such as omission of words or spelling errors) do occur quite often in the postings but they are not attended to because they are not essential to the meaning or can easily be retrieved from the posting as a whole.

Unlike conversation, it is therefore other-initiated self-repair or other-initiated other-repair that is more likely to occur than self-initiated self-repair in this environment, even though as noted above, they too are quite rare.

The next fragment provides an example of an other-initiated other-repair. Here the writer initiates repair on *3.10* (the test question number) which the vetter incorrectly referred to as *3.09* in the preceding posting.

Vetter: Or possibly the key for 309 is actually something like 'the pollution'

Writer: I assume you mean 3.10. I have changed the distracters and the key (made them longer). What do you think?

Vetter: Err, sorry, yes, I meant 310. The key is much more accurate, I think. Maybe another option as distractor could be

In face-to-face conversation, this kind of repair occurs in what is referred to as an insert sequence (Schegloff, 2007). As noted above, the insert is inserted into a base or main sequence of talk, and momentarily interrupts the "business" or topic of discussion. The repair similarly interrupts the discussion about the test item. However, it is dealt within the same posting. In other words, the repair is carried out directly without any confirmation check which would hand the space or floor back to the vetter to respond to. Indeed in the reply, the vetter delays answering the writer's question by building her response with an apology and a confirmation which also temporarily interrupt the discussions. Interestingly, she marks the beginning of her turn with "err" which gives it a very strong conversational flavor. Because the source of the error can easily be retrieved in the postings by the participants, there is no need to seek confirmation therefore it is possible that this kind of repair would be less common in online interaction than in face-to-face interaction. However, the other-initiated self-repair examples in the corpus are invariably about understanding the vetter's suggestions for edits to the test items. It is important to clarify the intended meaning in these postings. The following provides an example.

Writer: Not sure what you mean here... Is that what you want me to put?

Vetter: Yes Peter, that's what I meant. 'Club members' might eliminate any clumbsiness (sp).

Here the writer asks for confirmation that he has understood the vetter's suggestions which she confirms in the next posting. This provides closure to the sequence so that the discussion moves onto the next item after acceptance of the suggestion by the writer.

Socialising

Finally, there are also occasions but very rare ones, when the participants post simple messages of a social nature. Below is one example. Here the writer welcomes a new vetter on board.

Vetter: This could be presented as a pie chart–to introduce a new text type?

Writer: Hi Joanne,

Welcome on board!

Why not? Lay-out/design is really in your hands.

Daniel.

Structurally it is treated as a side-sequence (Jefferson, 1972), because the response to the question is delayed. Like the insert sequence, it suspends the base sequence where the main activity–that of a suggestion about how to present the test item–is taking place. Similarly, the main business resumes on termination of the side-sequence. The other interesting features about this posting are the conventions of the written form–the address terms and greeting–and the infrequently occurring signing-off, even though it is evident who has made this posting. The writer is treating this interaction as a kind of formal introduction.

To sum up, there are features of these postings that share structural features of face-to face-interactions, namely, basic sequence structure including paired postings such as in Question and Answer, and base, insert and side-sequences. Because of communication and its possibility to breakdown, repair is also an important and fundamental feature. However, it is not very frequent. Self-initiated self-repair in particular is rare because the postings occur in a written mode where there is an opportunity to edit before posting or to return to and retrieve relevant information which is publicly available in order to more clearly understand the meaning if required. Finally there is also evidence that participants pursue a response as is the case in face-to-face interaction, however, much more likely in the current context, is the pursuit of an action such as editing. In the next section attention turns to assessments and the discussions around the test items.

Interactions Centred on Reaction to Feedback

The following set of examples form the nucleus of the ALC team's work. Analysis has revealed three patterns: Positively received feedback, negatively received feedback, and no response to feedback. The overriding focus will be to look at how the expertise of those involved emerges.

When Reaction to Feedback is Positively Received

The following example comes at the end of quite a protracted discussion between two vetters and one writer about a particular test item which was found to be in need of editing.

Vetter: I think the issue is that the distracters aren't all the same quality; there the answers to different questions—2 are for when can entry forms be submitted and two are for how. If we take out the option of being able to enter online that makes the following possible. I think the problem is that there is too much flexibility currently offered so it makes it hard to ask an item. (Altered test question follows.)

Writer: how about (Slightly amended test question follows.)

Vetter: Great minds think alike... Yours is better though less reading and clearer. We could change by phone to by SMS then we'd have to go with on-line for B.

Writer: thank you.

Here the collaborative nature of the discussion as the writer and vetter work on improving the item to the satisfaction of both is evident. They have each contributed to this work, and they have done so in a supportive manner. In the first instance, the writer accepts the need to change the item as proffered in the vetter's assessment. Then they engage together in refining the question. This culminates in a positive assessment by the vetter directed at this collaborative effort (*great minds think alike*) and then more specifically to the writer, as is made evident in the shift to the

second person singular *yours*. In response, the writer produces a "thank-you" which ends this sequence. Here "thank-you" works both as a response to the positive assessment and as a means of closing the discussion about this particular item. In other words all changes have now been made to improve this item so that the team can move onto the next one.

When Reaction to Feedback is Negatively Received

One way of responding to a less than positive assessment is to simply ask for a suggestion. Another is to simply disagree. Yet another is to ignore it. A fourth is to produce a justification or account for the choice. In the interests of space, only the latter can be analyzed. These are the more interesting responses because in building a justification or account for the design of the original test item, the writers invoke their own claim to some kind of expertise or knowledge. For example, they may invoke their native speaker competency: "*as a* (Target Language background) *person, born and bred in* (Target Language country), *I know that this is culturally appropriate*". They may also claim having greater access to native speakers: "*I worried about the preposition to use with "in the Antarctic" so consulted 2 native speaker pedagogues whose language expertise I value most highly*". Finally they may lay claim to a greater knowledge and familiarity with the country and its practices, as in this example: "*I thought it quite reasonable to assume that all of those things might be available for hire on a tropical Island. Ever been to* (name of island)? *You can hire all of those things there*".

In the example chosen for analysis below, there are two further illustrations of how the writers invoke expertise in the face of an assessment that suggests a problem with the item.

Vetter 1: I think this is OK, but I do feel we can manage without 'because' for the distractors.

Removing it does not compromise the grammatical correctness. If someone asked me why I didn;t (sp) go to work yesterday I woudl (sp) say 'The office is too cold', definitely not 'Because the office is too cold.' Reducing the reading load is desirable.

Writer: Yes, I can drop the 'because' from the distractors, but have not done so yet. I will if you confirm your desire for it to be dropped, but I suggest you reconsider. Unlike you... if someone asked me why I didn't go to work yesterday I would DEFINITELY say "Because the office is too cold". I ALWAYS answer 'why' questions with 'because'. I cannot imagine answering a 'why' question without 'because'. Indeed, I always taught my students to study the question word and choose the appropriate response; i.e. to a 'who' question the answer is a name or a pronoun, to a 'where' question the answer is a place, to a 'why' question the answer is because.

This is a consequence of the instruction to, wherever possible, use complete questions rather than incomplete stems. Last year I would have framed this question as "Ina didn't go to school yesterday because..." but with the new instruction to use complete questions the conjunction 'because' becomes part of the answer.

As I said, I will delete them if you confirm your instruction, but it is not the way that I would answer this question.

Vetter 2: I'm happy for you to retain 'because' Peter.

In this example the vetter's suggestion to remove "because" provokes the writer's disagreement. It is built with two invocations to expert knowledge. The first is about linguistic knowledge as displayed through the comment about the preservation of grammatical correctness if "because" is removed. The second invokes test development experience as displayed through

the statement about relieving the cognitive load on the test taker as reader. In between, there is a statement about personal usage as well. This is marked by a shift in stance from the impersonal to a more personal one (marked linguistically by a shift in personal pronoun from "it" to "I" and from the passive to active construction, and then back again).

In his reply, the writer invokes his own expertise on two fronts. He lays claim to his competency as a user of the English language and recycles some of the vetter's words. Of particular note is how the vetter's "definitely", which already conveys a strong stance, is further upgraded by the writer through the use of capitalization and the accompanying "ALWAYS". He then invokes his pedagogical expertise as a teacher *(I always taught my students... This is a consequence of the instruction to, wherever possible, use complete questions rather than incomplete stems)*. This provides a mirror to the vetter's statement about strategy use (learner versus test-taker). Finally, he makes reference to the changed guidelines for writing test items which is a possible concession (though not one that emerges openly) that the repetition of "because" does jar *(Last year I would have framed this question as....but with the new instruction to use complete questions the conjunction 'because' becomes part of the answer)*. Structurally, this resembles the non-extreme concessive repair described by Tanskanen and Karhukorpi (2008) in email interactions.

Deferring to the Expertise of the Other

Clearly then there is some tension here caused by the differential experiences and knowledge bases that vetter and writer bring to the test development process. Yet, it is precisely these different kinds of expertise that are required to produce test items that will work and succeed in the test. How this is negotiated, worked on and resolved is an interesting question because it too reveals something about how the writers and vetters see their roles. In the above example, although the writer disagrees with the vetter's assessment, he opens with a statement that defers to the role of the vetter as having the last say on the item *(I can drop the 'because' from the distractors, but have not done so yet. I will if you confirm your desire for it to be dropped, but I suggest you reconsider).* This also emerges in his conclusion *(As I said, I will delete them if you confirm your instruction, but it is not the way that I would answer this question).* In opposition to this, the vetter does not directly insist on the change. It comes off more as a suggestion, albeit a fairly strong one. Interestingly, it is the second vetter who resolves the impasse–*I'm happy for you to retain 'because' Peter*–after which the discussion moves onto the next item.

The acceptance by the writers that the vetters have the final say also emerges in the absence of an agreement or disagreement, and there are copious examples in the corpus to show this. One such is where the writers make the change without providing any response or when they minimally acknowledge the vetter's suggestion (*done*). Alternatively, they may respond with a request for feedback (*How is the change now?*).

Likewise, a vetter may insist on a change. In the following example this is done by citing the set requirements (*we already have two double questions…we can't have anymore*). This works to establish the final say on the matter and therefore invokes not so much the personal expertise of the vetter, but rather the role of vetter which confers upon it the right to reject.

Writer: This is the only double question in the set. I would like to keep q11 if I can. The students at this level have learned very limited topics.

Vetter: The question is too easy. All students need to do is match. Besides, we already have two double questions in B and we can't have anymore. We are four questions short. We can have an additional question in (Target Language).

Of course, as analyzed above, the writers can also claim a right to express a desire to retain the item as they originally wrote it. However, as well as providing a reason or account for its retention in a way that is less baldly expressed, the writer also qualifies it in some way. This is evident in the example where the writer challenges the vetter on linguistic and pedagogical grounds and again in the following posting by a writer–*I prefer to leave the street name as I feel that's what she would say as her comment is about living in the same street as well as the number-but if I'm over-ruled I won't have a breakdown over it.*

Finally, there are also examples where the vetters defer to the expertise of the writers (*I am not qualified to judge, but is ('I would like')… a bit bald as a response?*), (*I can't comment on the suitability of the topic area, so please advise*), and may also explicitly acknowledge explanations proffered (*Thanks for the explanation*).

The notion of expertise is thus dynamic. It shifts as the writers and vetters defer to each other's knowledge bases as they discuss the test items one posting at a time. It is invoked when there is disagreement, when there is a need for an explanation or a decision to be made about the appropriateness of an item, and it emerges collaboratively.

SUMMARY AND CONCLUDING REMARKS

This study sought to investigate two questions. Firstly, how do the interactions in a work setting posted in an asynchronous wiki environment compare with face-to-face interactions? In terms of conversational structure, the following findings emerged.

- Self-initiated self-repair is rare because there are opportunities for the members of the wiki test development team to polish and edit their postings before they are made public. The team members also do not attend to minor spelling or other orthographic details as these do not interfere with meaning. Other-initiated self- or other-repair is also not very common but it certainly occurs more often than self-initiated self-repair. This finding is in contrast to Tanskanen and Karhukorpi's (2008) study for email exchanges and may have something to do with the setting and the explicit nature of the work being done, which is to clear up any misunderstandings which may otherwise result in a poorer test item. As in face-to-face interaction, the repair sequences momentarily interrupt the main business of the discussion until they are dealt with.

- The adjacency pair structure is also an important feature of these postings particularly the Question and Answer adjacency pair. As in conversation, the participants orient to the absence of a response, but they also pursue actions such as editing, made relevant by the work context. The presence of pursuit itself displays the orientation of the writer or vetter to the posting as interactional rather than as a more distal piece of written text.

- In terms of the organization of sequences, there are inserts and side-sequences in which the business other than the main one is dealt with before resumption of the main topic. There are also address terms to nominate recipient or addressee, as there are occasionally greetings—all features of face-to-face interaction but in contrast to face-to-face, there are also signings-off—a feature of writing.

- Finally, analysis has revealed that there is a bias towards affiliative and supportive actions as is the case in face-to-face conversation (Clayman & Heritage, 2002) despite the disagreements with assessments that sometimes arise. Participants

orient to maximising successful exchanges, which is consonant with Tanskanen and Karhukorpi's (2008) findings on concessive repair in email exchanges.

The second question was centered on the notion of expertise and how it emerged. Analysis showed that the writers enacted their roles quite differently. While all writers deferred to the vetter as having a final say in what might pass as the final draft of an item, some accepted suggestions without comment, while others disagreed by invoking their own knowledge of the language (either English or the target language), pedagogy or the culture. This was less likely to occur when the vetters implicated less of themselves (for example "I use") and used more hedging ("I wonder if", "what about"). Expertise and the role of vetter or writer were fluid and dynamic and emerged locally as they worked on the test item evaluation. They were not fixed, a finding which echoes that of Hall and Danby's (2003) for teachers and academics working together.

Taken together these findings have several implications for training. Firstly, how feedback is given and received is an important consideration. The most positive interactions were those where vetter and writer collaborated and engaged in ways that brought their different but co-constructed knowledge perspectives into play. The way that negative feedback is given is also important. Although the purpose of the team is to evaluate the test items (and therefore the work of the writers), it is important to maintain a balance and pay attention to matters of face. In this regard, as part of wiki netiquette, one writer explicitly urged the need to "keep it nice" in her evaluation. In the words of another:

Writer: I think we ALL (writers and reviewers) need to be aware of just how easy it is to 'appear' abrupt and to be offensive when adding comments to work. I think the medium lends itself to quick comments which we tap out on the keyboard and which all of us would phrase more carefully in spoken word or in other forms of written communication. I know that I responded with very sharp tongue, a number of times, to what I perceived to be offensive comments; comments which I have no doubt were intended to be constructive criticism (which is welcome) but which, because of the nature of the communication, came across (to me) as something different. I am just as guilty because of my sharp responses. I apologize.

It is also important to explicitly state the roles of each member of the team and not take it as a given that each member knows what they might be. This is particularly so because of the writers' different cultural backgrounds (and therefore different perceptions and expectations) of their own roles and roles of others as well as their degree of familiarity with, and experience in, test writing.

Lastly, as the pursuit of a response or action indicated, there could be considerable delay between the posting of a comment and a response to it, such that the comment no longer became relevant or had been forgotten. Thus, although the interactions did not occur in real time, there was a "time relevancy" in operation and the members of the team oriented to this through the conversational resource of pursuit.

In conclusion, although different from face-to-face interactions, the online wiki interactions also share some important features. As is the case in comparisons between face-to-face conversation and institutionalized interaction, where conversation is held to have a "bedrock" status (Drew & Heritage, 1992) against which other types of talk are identified, there are differences between online interactions themselves as well as between face-to-face and online interaction. What those differences are in organizational and structural terms awaits further elucidation.

REFERENCES

Cavanagh, A. (1999). Behaviour in public? Ethics in online ethnography. *Cybersociology, 6*. Retrieved June 15, 2009, from http://www.cybersociology.com/files/6_2_ethicsinonlineethnog.html

Clayman, S., & Heritage, J. (2002). *The news interview: journalists and public figures on the air*. Cambridge: Cambridge University Press. doi:10.1017/CBO9780511613623

Drew, P., & Heritage, J. (1992). Analyzing talk at work: an introduction. In Drew, P., & Heritage, J. (Eds.), *Talk at work: interaction in institutional settings* (pp. 3–65). Cambridge: Cambridge University Press.

Drew, P., & Heritage, J. (Eds.). (2006). *Conversation analysis*. London: Sage.

Filipi, A. (2009). *Toddler and parent interaction: The organisation of gaze, pointing and vocalisation*. Amsterdam, Philadelphia: John Benjamins Publishing.

Filipi, A., & Lissonnet, S. (2008, September). Using wikis to create tests. *Teacher Magazine*, 20-22.

Forrester, M. A. (2008). The emergence of self-repair: a case study of one child during the early preschool years. *Research on Language and Social Interaction, 41*(1), 99–128.

Goodwin, C. (1995). Seeing in depth. *Social Studies of Science, 25*, 237–274. doi:10.1177/030631295025002002

Goodwin, C. (1996). Transparent vision. In Ochs, E., Schegloff, E. A., & Thompson, S. A. (Eds.), *Interaction and grammar* (pp. 370–404). Cambridge: Cambridge University Press. doi:10.1017/CBO9780511620874.008

Graham, S. L. (2007). Disagreeing to agree: Conflict, (im)politeness and identity in a computer-mediated community. *Journal of Pragmatics, 3*, 742–759. doi:10.1016/j.pragma.2006.11.017

Hall, G., & Danby, S. (2003). Teachers and academics co-constructing the category of expert through meeting talk. *Proceedings of the Annual Conference of the Australian Association for Research in Education*. Retrieved June 15, 2009, from http://www.aare.edu.au/03pap/hal03027.pdf

Harrison, S. (2000). Maintaining the virtual community: use of politeness strategies in an email discussion group. In L. Pemberton & S. Shurville (Eds.), Words on the web: computer mediated communication (pp. 69-78). Exeter & Portland, OR: Intellect Books.

Heritage, J. (1984). *Garfinkel and ethnomethodology*. Cambridge: Polity Press.

Hester, S., & Eglin, P. (1997). Membership categorization analysis: an introduction. In Hester, S., & Eglin, P. (Eds.), *Culture in action: studies in membership categorization analysis* (pp. 1–23). Washington: International Institute for Ethnomethodology and University Press of America.

Jaques, D., & Salmon, G. (2006). *Learning in groups: a handbook for face-to-face and online environments*. Hoboken: Taylor & Francis.

Jefferson, G. (1972). Side sequences. In Sudnow, D. (Ed.), *Studies in social interaction* (pp. 294–338). New York: Free Press.

Magnan Sieloff, S. (Ed.). (2008). *Mediating discourse online: AILA Applied Linguistics (Series 3)*. Amsterdam, Philadelphia: John Benjamins Publishing.

Masur, J. (2004). Conversation analysis for educational technologists: theoretical and methodological issues for researching the structures, processes and meaning of on-line talk. In Jonassen, D. (Ed.), *Handbook of research for educational communications and technology* (pp. 1073–1098). New York: McMillan.

Pomerantz, A. (1984a). Agreeing and disagreeing with assessments: some features of preferred/dispreferred turn shapes. In Maxwell Atkinson, J., & Heritage, J. (Eds.), *Structures of social action: studies in conversation analysis* (pp. 57–101). Cambridge: Cambridge University Press.

Pomerantz, A. (1984b). Pursuing a response. In Maxwell Atkinson, J., & Heritage, J. (Eds.), *Structures of social action: studies in conversation analysis* (pp. 152–163). Cambridge: Cambridge University Press.

Salmon, G. (2000). *E-moderating: the key to teaching and learning online*. London, New York: Routledge.

Schegloff, E. A. (1992). Repair after next turn: the last structurally provided defense of intersubjectivity in conversation. *American Journal of Sociology, 97*, 1295–1345. doi:10.1086/229903

Schegloff, E. A. (1997). Third turn repair. In Guy, G. R., Feagin, C., Schiffrin, D., & Baugh, J. (Eds.), *Towards a social science of language: papers in honor of William Labov* (*Vol. 2*, pp. 31–40). Amsterdam, Philadelphia: John Benjamins.

Schegloff, E. A. (2000). When "others" initiate repair. *Applied Linguistics, 21*(2), 205–243. doi:10.1093/applin/21.2.205

Schegloff, E. A. (2007). *Sequence organization in interaction: a primer in conversation analysis* (*Vol. 1*). Cambridge: Cambridge University Press.

Schegloff, E. A., Jefferson, G., & Sacks, H. (1977). The preference for self-correction in the organization of repair in conversation. *Language, 53*, 361–382. doi:10.2307/413107

Tanskanen, S.-K. (2007). Metapragmatic utterances in computer-mediated interaction. In Bublitz, W., & Hübler, A. (Eds.), *Metapragmatics in use* (pp. 87–106). Amsterdam, Philadelphia: John Benjamins.

Tanskanen, S.-K., & Karhukorpi, J. (2008). Concessive repair and negotiation of affiliation in e-mail discourse. *Journal of Pragmatics*, *40*, 1587–1600. doi:10.1016/j.pragma.2008.04.018

ten Have, P. (1999). *Doing conversation analysis*. London: Sage.

White, P. (2003). Beyond modality and hedging: a dialogic view of the language of intersubjective stance. *Text*, *23*, 259–284. doi:10.1515/text.2003.011

Woods, D., Thoeny, P., & Cunningham, W. (2007). *Wikis for dummies*. Hoboken: John Wiley & Sons.

KEY TERMS AND DEFINITIONS

Repair: A unique conversational phenomenon; it refers to the ways in which hearers and speakers adjust their talk when breakdown occurs as a result of inadequate hearing or interpretation.

Pursuit of an Action: A resource that speakers can deploy as part of a broader repair strategy to facilitate communication. It draws attention to the absence of an expected response or action.

Affiliation: Participants work collaboratively to minimize conflict in their interactions both online and face-to-face.

Co-Constructed Expertise: Expertise is a dynamic process which emerges as participants work together. It shifts as the writers and vetters defer to each other's knowledge bases. It is invoked when there is disagreement or a decision to be made about the appropriateness of an item, and it emerges collaboratively.

Preference Organization: Refers to the bias for speakers to support each other's actions or assess each other's actions positively. An example of a preferred turn is a positive response to an invitation, while a dispreferred turn is a rejection of an invitation.

Sequence Organization: Describes how turns at talk fit together structurally as relevant next actions to what has gone before. One type of organization that is massively present in both face-to-face and online interaction is the paired utterance or adjacency pair. Examples include the question and answer, and a greeting and return greeting.

Stance: In the wiki postings, stance refers to how participants react to them. They may take on a distal "writing" stance to the postings or a more proximal, "interactionist" stance.

Chapter 11
A Close Look at Online Collaboration:
Conversational Structure in Chat and Its Implications for Group Work

Kris M. Markman
University of Memphis, USA

EXECUTIVE SUMMARY

This chapter employs a conversation analytic approach to the study of group interaction in synchronous chat. Chat has been used in educational settings as an adjunct to traditional face-to-face classes and as part of distance learning. This case study examines how chat was used for virtual team meetings by specifically focusing on the structural features of chat conversation as they relate to various aspects of online teamwork. Chat conversations are characterized by disrupted turn adjacency and multiple conversational threads, requiring participants to adapt different strategies to maintain coherence. The advantages and disadvantages of using chat for group work are discussed, and suggestions for implementing chat in education settings are presented.

BACKGROUND

Synchronous text-based interaction, where participants are logged in to the same virtual space at the same time, can be a useful tool for enhancing traditional classes or as part of an entirely online course. Synchronous chat, as it is also called, may not have always received the same amount of attention from educators and researchers as the various forms of asynchronous online discussion tools (Johnson, 2006), but research shows that chat can be used

to enhance learning outcomes. Some research has focused on comparing chat to face-to-face discussions. For example, Strømsø, Grøttum and Lycke (2007) examined the use of chat and face-to-face discussions in problem-based learning for medical students. They found more communication, in terms of more words and more and longer utterances, in the face-to-face setting. The chat discussions featured more social interaction and more technical talk, whereas there was more focus on the case study issues in the face-to-face discussions. They did find that the chat had more initiative turns, but that these were not elaborated on as much as in

DOI: 10.4018/978-1-61520-863-0.ch011

face-to-face. Cox, Carr and Hall (2004) compared the use of chat to face-to-face discussions in a blended course, and found that the students felt the chat discussions were empowering, although sometimes frustrating, and that the chat facilitated participation in the course by giving them greater confidence than they felt in face-to-face discussions. Similarly, the use of chat as an add-on to a compressed-schedule graduate seminar was found to be useful for bridging the gap between face-to-face sessions, helping students explore ideas, and facilitating a sense of community (Schwier & Balbar, 2002). Schweir and Balbar found that the chat conversations were dynamic and energizing, although they could also be frustrating due to the speed of the interaction, rapid topic decay, and occasional technical glitches.

Johnson (2006) reviewed the recent literature comparing synchronous and asynchronous computer-based discussion in educational settings. She found that overall research suggests that synchronous chat is a viable option in education, and that it can contribute to student motivation and skill development. Johnson also noted that synchronous chat was not necessarily better than asynchronous discussions in supporting learning outcomes, although the research she reviewed suggested that synchronous discussions will produce a greater total volume of communication. On the other hand, Repman, Zinskie and Carlson (2005) pointed out a number of advantages of chat over asynchronous tools as documented in the literature, including immediacy of communication, social relationship development, effective learner-learner and faculty-learner interaction, and more active involvement in learning. Synchronous discussions have also been found to exhibit higher levels of critical reflection when compared to asynchronous discussions (Levin, He, & Robbins, 2006). Paulus and Phipps (2008) found that the synchronous chat discussions they studied contained more asking, answering, challenging and responding moves than the asynchronous discussions, although in their study both modes contained reflection moves

in the discussion. They also note that student groups reported more technical and coherence problems with the chat environment. Discussion dynamics in synchronous and asynchronous computer-mediated communication (CMC) can also vary in mixed instructor-student groups. Yukselturk and Top (2006) found that in the asynchronous mode, participants tended to ask more questions and instructors answered, whereas in the chat discussions questions were mainly asked by instructors and answered by participants. They also found differences in the levels of socio-emotional content, with asynchronous discussions containing more positive socio-emotional messages and fewer negative socio-emotional messages than the chat discussions.

Sorg and McElhinney (2000), looking at the use of synchronous chat in an Internet-based course, found that the chat discussions contributed to the students' sense of empowerment and discovery. The students' positive associations with the chat environment were derived from the additional time they had for reflection and the feedback they received from peers. However, Sorg and McElhinney found that students also expressed frustration with the text-based interactions because of the lack of audio/visual cues and the instructor's moderation style. Participation in chat discussions in online classes has also been shown to be correlated with final grades (Wang, Newlin, & Tucker, 2001), and can also support deep learning (Osman & Herring, 2007), although Osman and Herring also note that the effectiveness of chat in distance learning settings may be mitigated by language and cultural barriers.

Based on the research reviewed here, it is clear that synchronous chat discussions can enhance communication and learning outcomes in educational settings, although the specifics may vary based on the context of use. It is also important to note that there are several recurring issues in the research on chat in education, specifically student frustration with the medium due to variations in typing skills, speed of the conversation, and other coherence problems, and to the inevitable technical glitches that pop up with chat. The aim of this case study is to explore some of these issues in more detail, by taking a computer-mediated discourse analysis (CMDA) (Herring, 2004) approach to the study of chat discussions. Rather than being a specific theory or method, CMDA is an approach to the study of CMC that is grounded in the empirical observation of text-based verbal interaction. Herring notes that CMDA adapts a variety of methods, both quantitative and qualitative, from various language-focused disciplines. The data presented in this case study will be examined from a perspective derived from conversation analysis (CA). Although CA was developed in sociology as a way to document the organization of talk-in-interaction (ten Have, 1999) it has since been used by scholars in a number of different fields for different purposes. Specifically, CA-derived methods have been used since the late 1990s to further our understanding of text-based conversations.

Although CA has generally been used to examine spoken interaction, research on text-based CMC has long shown it to have conversational properties as well (Baron, 2008). Early language-focused research on CMC noted that text-based interaction exhibited features of both written and oral communication (Ferrara, Brunner, & Whittemore, 1991; Murray, 1991; Wilkins, 1991) and could be approached as a new type of textual conversation using the CA toolkit (Murray, 1989). Research on text-based conversation from a conversation analytic standpoint has yielded insights into turn taking and turn organization (Garcia & Jacobs, 1998, 1999; Markman, 2006b; Panyametheekul & Herring, 2003; Simpson, 2005), interactional coherence and ambiguity reduction (Herring, 1999; Rintel, Pittam, & Mulholland, 2003), openings and closings (Markman, 2009; Rintel, Mulholland, & Pittam, 2001; Rintel & Pittam, 1997; ten Have, 2000) and repair (Schonfeldt & Golato, 2003). This case study follows this research tradition, with specific attention paid to the organization of

chat conversations and its implication for group collaboration.

CASE DESCRIPTION

The Virtual Team

This case study examines how a particular CMC channel, synchronous chat, was used as a platform for the virtual team meetings of a group of undergraduate students. The students were recruited for a summer-semester (five and one-half weeks) independent study course under the supervision of the director of the Science, Technology, and Society program at a large, public university in the southwest United States as part of the author's dissertation research (Markman, 2006a). All students were given the option to enroll in the course and not participate in the research project. The participants were told that they would be working as a virtual team to conduct research on innovative student uses of technology in and around the university. The course was structured so that instead of attending regular class meetings, the students would conduct the bulk of their work as a team using CMC tools, and they would hold virtual meetings using the Blackboard course management system.

A total of five students enrolled and elected to participate in the project. All team members were seniors preparing to graduate in either the subsequent fall or spring semesters. Table 1 shows the demographic breakdown of the team. All names have been changed to protect confidentiality.

The team held three face-to-face meetings with their instructor and the researcher at the beginning, midpoint, and end of the project. The purpose of the first meeting was to introduce the team members and orient them to the project. The supervising professor and the researcher conducted the first meeting, at which four of the five team members were present: Evan, Rebeca, Sidney, and Thadine. The second face-to-face

Table 1. Virtual team membership

Pseudonym	Sex	Major
Evan	male	sociology
I-Fang	female	advertising
Rebeca	female	English
Sidney	male	geography
Thadine	female	geography

meeting served as a status review for the project, and was conducted by the supervising professor with the researcher present. Four members were also in attendance: I-Fang, Rebeca, Sidney and Thadine. The purpose of the final face-to-face meeting was for the team to present their final project to the professor; all five team members and the researcher were present at this meeting. No recordings were made during any of the face-to-face meetings, however an informal discussion was held with three of the team members at the end of the last meeting.

The team held four virtual meetings using the collaboration tools provided on the Blackboard course management system. For the first meeting, the team used the Lecture Hall tool, which included a virtual whiteboard in addition to the chat interface, but this was found to be cumbersome by some participants because they could not resize the chat window. The subsequent three meetings were held using the Lightweight Chat interface, a feature new to Blackboard at the time these data were collected. The first, third, and fourth meetings averaged 52 minutes in length; the second meeting lasted for one hour and 18 minutes. With the exception of one member, Sidney, the team had generally equal rates of attendance in the four virtual meetings. The researcher was also present for at least part of all four virtual meetings.

Data were gathered by providing each team member with screen recording software in order to produce a video recording of each person's screen activities. Because of technical difficulties, miscommunications, and schedule conflicts, not all team members were present and recording during all virtual meetings. Meetings three and four offer the most complete data record, with screen recordings for all six participants available. The screen recording data were supplemented by the automatically-generated chat logs provided by the Blackboard system.

Following Chat Conversations

In order to discuss how the use of synchronous chat affected this team's discussion, it is first necessary to discuss the salient features of the chat interface and how they change the organization of conversation. Figure 1 shows the chat interface used in the team's second, third, and fourth meetings. Although the exact features and arrangement of chat interfaces will vary based on the software package being used, they generally share some version of the features discussed below.

Chat tools are distinguished from other synchronous CMC channels such as instant messaging primarily by the number of participants. Instant messaging tools are designed for the exchange of real-time text-based interaction by two people; chat systems allow for three or more people to share the same virtual conversational space. There are three main components of the chat interface. The left-hand pane shows the list of participants who are currently logged in to the chat room. The main box is the chat window, which displays all posts sent to the chat server in the order they were received. In the case of this interface the server also included an automatic timestamp at the end of each post, although not all chat systems include this feature. The chat server automatically included the name of the author to the left of each post (the irregular margins in the chat window are a result of obscuring the participants' real names). Below the chat window is the text entry box where individual participants type their posts.

All participants who are logged in to the chat room have access to the same information in the chat window, however, the information typed

Figure 1. Chat interface

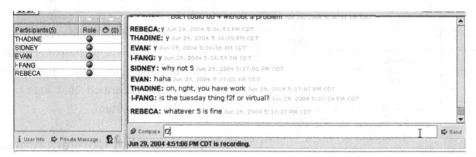

into a given participant's text entry box is only available to that person during the composition process. Pressing the enter key or clicking on "Send" sends the post to the server and thus makes it available to the rest of the group. This separation of turn composition from turn reception is one of the biggest differences between chat conversation and spoken interaction. In spoken conversations, the listener has access to the speaker's turn as it is being uttered, thereby allowing the listener to project the possible end of the speaker's turn. This allows for the sophisticated turn-taking exchange system that has been well-documented in the CA literature, whereby one person talks at a time, with little gap or overlap, and the current speaker generally selects the next (Sacks, Schegloff, & Jefferson, 1974). Instead, in chat discussion the system allows for any person to type at any time, promoting a turn allocation system of any person self-selects. Turns are composed in private, and arrive at the server all at once (as opposed to while they are being typed). In addition to separating the production from the reception of turns, the chat interface does not allow participants to choose how their turns will be placed in the chat window, thereby making it impossible to ensure that a turn will be placed adjacent to the post it is responding to. Instead, turns are posted in strict chronological order based on when they were received by the server.

As a result of the technical constraints imposed by chat technology, the flow of conversations in this medium is not regulated by the linear turn-taking exchange system present in spoken conversation. Rather, discussions in chat are additive, in that each new post contributes to the ongoing evolution of the conversation, but is not necessarily responsive to the immediately preceding post. Thus chat conversations are characterized by disrupted turn adjacency (Herring, 1999). In addition, because chat promotes any-person-self-selects turn allocation, chat discussions can, and often do, have multiple ongoing topics, or threads, of conversation. These two features of chat, disrupted turn adjacency and multiple threads, require participants to adapt new turn organization practices to restore coherence to the evolving conversation. In this case study, the team members relied primarily on threading (see also Greenfield & Subrahmanyam, 2003; Markman, 2006b; Simpson, 2005), or constructing turns so that they were sensitive to the specific topic of conversation, as their primary means of organizing turns. In addition, they sometimes used address terms to make it clear who the intended recipient was (see also Herring, 2003; Panyametheekul & Herring, 2003; Werry, 1996). Two examples will help illustrate these turn organization features.

Example 1

Example 1 takes place towards the end of the team's fourth meeting. Prior to this excerpt the team had been discussing the scheduling of various meetings, including a possible face-to-face meeting with their professor, and another meeting,

Table 2. Example 1

5:35:38	I-FANG: so when tuesday?
5:35:40	EVAN: So has everyine else...we can just meet on campus, or soemthing
5:35:48	THADINE: 5?
5:35:53	EVAN: y
5:35:57	I-FANG: i though we r meeting virtually tuesday?
5:36:15	REBECA: Can we do it earlier on Tuesday?
5:36:21	EVAN: that is fine with me
5:36:23	EVAN: 4
5:36:24	EVAN: 3
5:36:28	REBECA: how about 3?
5:36:29	I-FANG: i can meet on campus..anyday 2:30 to 6
5:36:40	EVAN: Thadine?
5:36:40	THADINE: I can't do 3. Class til 3:45
5:36:49	EVAN: how bout 4
5:36:51	THADINE: but i could do 4 without a problem

either virtual or face-to-face, to go over their final presentation before turning it in. A full transcript of this example based on the screen recording data is included in Appendix A. The left column of the example indicates the server's time stamp.

Example 1 illustrates the disrupted turn adjacency in chat caused by the inability to monitor the ongoing composition of others' turns. Prior to this excerpt Evan has proposed Tuesday as a possible time for a face-to-face meeting. I-Fang's follow-up, posted at 5:35:38, is separated by five other turns from the post it is referring to. For the participants in the chat, there appears to be a lull in the conversation after I-Fang's turn at 5:35:38 and Evan's turn two seconds later. In response to this lull, Thadine types a response at 5:35:47 that posts one second later. What Thadine cannot know, however, is that I-Fang is using this apparent lull to type a new turn that seeks further clarification (see Appendix A). While I-Fang is typing, both Thadine's turn at 5:35:48 and Evan's response at 5:35:53 are posted. Although I-Fang posts a question at 5:35:57, which would in its sequential placement in spoken conversation generally

call for a response (Schegloff & Sacks, 1974), she is unable to attract her teammates' attention, and a subsequent question, posted by Rebeca at 5:36:15, supplants I-Fang's request. The next rapid sequence of posts illustrates how disrupted turn adjacency also leads to redundancies in the conversation. Evan responds to Rebeca at 5:36:21, and then immediately suggests two additional meeting times, four or three o'clock. Rebeca starts typing "how about 3?" at the same time that Evan's suggestion of 4 is posted, which means that what appears in the chat to be a ratification of his suggestion of three o'clock is in fact a follow-up to Evan's first candidate meeting time. Similarly, I-Fang's turn that posts at 5:36:29 appears to be implicitly ratifying the previous suggestions. However the screen recording (see Appendix A) reveals that I-Fang began typing her turn at 5:36:05, before Rebeca began her post that led to this sequence.

In looking at Example 1 thus far, the disrupted turn adjacency of chat has produced some slight redundancies in the evolving conversation, but no fundamental misunderstandings or problems.

Table 3. Example 2

5:43:55	RESEARCHER: but the point of this project (part of it) is to work as a virtual team, remember ;)
5:43:57	EVAN: I think in general we can discuss our findings so far
5:44:05	SIDNEY: evidently you cant paste in here
5:44:13	THADINE: that's no good
5:44:24	EVAN: Our findings?
5:44:37	THADINE: yeah, discussing our findings so far seems to be a good place to start
5:44:43	I-FANG: ugh...yes yes...meeting up in person will just be a plus...we'll still have regular virtual meetings

However, the most salient structural characteristic of chat, the inability to monitor other participants' turns in progress, poses additional interactional challenges. In spoken conversation, silences have been shown to have interactional significance (Pomerantz, 1984), and in the linear turn-taking system can in fact function as turns themselves. Additionally, in the context of meetings silences can even be taken as a sign of implicit agreement (Boden, 1994). However, in chat, silences are really best understood as non-responses (Rintel et al., 2003), in that the participants lack the audio/visual cues necessary to tell if others have stopped participating (and are therefore silent), walked away from their computers, or are in the process of composing a turn. Thus non-responses in chat are inherently ambiguous, and it is left to the participants to work out the meaning of non-responses on the fly.

Example 1 demonstrates one tactic the participants used to disambiguate non-responses. After I-Fang's post at 5:36:29, Thadine begins composing a turn that is responsive to the previous suggestions about the meeting time. However, the only information available to her teammates is that she last posted at 5:35:48. Evan, noticing that Thadine has yet to respond, composes the turn "Thadine?" at 5:36:37, and thereby marks the gap since Thadine's last post as a non-response. The form that Evan uses, name + question mark, can be understood as both an invitation for Thadine to contribute to the thread and a request to Thadine to make her presence in the chat known. As it

happens, Thadine finishes typing at the same time that Evan does, and they hit enter simultaneously, resulting in both posts arriving at 5:36:40. Thus it appears in the chat transcript that Evan has called on Thadine to respond and she has answered, when in fact her turn was a response to earlier posts. This sequence also illustrates another phenomenon common in chat discussions known as the false adjacency pair (or phantom, see Garcia & Jacobs, 1999), whereby two posts in the chat appear to form an adjacency sequence, such as question/answer or greeting/greeting, when they were in fact typed independently of each other. Because Evan does not have access to Thadine's post in progress, he posts a further turn at 5:36:49, to which Thadine appears to respond two seconds later. In this case, the false adjacency pair serendipitously results in agreement, but this phenomenon also has the potential to cause problems or misunderstandings.

Example 2

Example 2 comes from the team's second meeting, and illustrates the importance of threading in designing turns for chat. Prior to this excerpt the team had been discussing the research the individual members had done and the different possible directions for their project as a whole. Along with that, a separate thread concerned the possibility of meeting up in person, either in addition to or in lieu of meeting face-to-face. In addition, during the time that Evan was typing his turn that posted at 5:43:57, Sidney was repeatedly trying to copy and paste some text from another website into his text-entry box. At the same time that Evan's turn posts, Sidney gives up and deletes the incorrect text from his message entry box (see the full transcript in Appendix B). He then starts a new turn expressing his frustration that gets posted at 5:44:05. At the same time that Sidney is typing, I-Fang, who had been in the middle of composing a turn related to the meeting scheduling thread, deletes her turn in progress and instead begins a new turn that is responsive to the researcher's turn at 5:43:55. Some confusion arises at 5:44:13 when Thadine responds to Sidney's most recent post. Based on the screen recordings (see Appendix B), the most likely referent for Thadine's turn "that's no good" is Sidney's complaint that he could not paste in the chat box, given that she began typing this turn four seconds after his post appeared. The substance of the post, along with its timing, makes the most likely interpretation that Thadine is offering sympathy to Sidney. However, due to the lack of a named referent, and the lack of any clear lexical links to Sidney's turn, Thadine's post allows for a possible alternative understanding, displayed by Evan at 5:44:24.

Here, the inability to precisely coordinate turns, along with the inability to monitor others' turn construction results in both disrupted turn adjacency and some confusion. As shown in the full transcript, Thadine beings typing another turn almost immediately after posting her turn at 5:44:13. This turn, which gets posted after some minor edits at 5:44:37, is clearly responsive to Evan's turn at 5:43:57. Thadine uses an agreement token, "yeah," and recycles Evan's phrase "discuss our findings so far" into "discussing our findings so far" as a way of ratifying Evan's proposal and at the same time clearly linking her turn to his. In addition, the timing of her turn construction lends further support to the conclusion that her turn at 5:44:13 was in response to Sidney, and not Evan, because she began her second turn well before Evan displayed his confusion at 5:44:24. Therefore although Thadine's turn at 5:44:37 may appear to form an adjacency pair with Evan's post

at 5:44:24, and thereby clear up his confusion, it is in fact just a serendipitous placement.

Thus, in this 48-second slice of the conversation there are three separate threads at play, as illustrated in Tables 4, 5 and 6. Shading has been used to indicate threading.

In this case study, the use of lexical repeats to indicate threading was by far the most common way of organizing turns, as illustrated by Example 2, Threads 1 and 2. Less commonly used were address terms to indicate turn organization. It is worth reiterating that the lack of either of these two elements contributed to the confusion found in Thread 3.

To review, the nature of the synchronous chat interface results in conversation that is characterized by disrupted turn adjacency, with the concordant potential for false adjacency pairs, multiple concurrent conversational topics, and ambiguous non-responses. To cope with these constraints, the team members adapted their turn construction to be sensitive to threading by including lexical and structural cues in their turns that linked them to the appropriate topic. This, along with the small size of the group, allowed them to maintain coherence with relatively infrequent use of address terms to designate specific recipients.

Using Chat for Collaboration: The Problem of Joint Attention

One consequence of the disjointed nature of chat that is particularly salient to group collaboration is that courses of action are also disrupted. From the CA standpoint, actions are built out of sequences of interaction, and these actions are revealed in the data by examining what "co-participants in the interaction took to be what was getting done, as revealed in/by the response they make to it" (Schegloff, 2007, p. 8). The difficulty with chat, for both the analyst and the participant, is that responses are often delayed, if they are present at all. The implication for group work is that creating/sustaining the joint attention necessary

Table 4. Example 2, thread 1

5:43:55	RESEARCHER: but the point of this project (part of it) is to work as a virtual team, remember ;)
5:44:43	I-FANG: ugh...yes yes...meeting up in person will just be a plus...we'll still have regular virtual meetings

Table 5. Example 2, thread 2

5:43:57	EVAN: I think in general we can discuss our findings so far
5:44:37	THADINE: yeah, discussing our findings so far seems to be a good place to start

Table 6. Example 2, thread 3

5:44:05	SIDNEY: evidently you cant paste in here
5:44:13	THADINE: that's no good
5:44:24	EVAN: Our findings?

for producing collaborative work (Boden, 1994) is more difficult to do. Participants cannot rely on the sequential implicativeness of talk, that is that one turn follows another and each turn is responsive to the immediate prior turn, as a locus for orienting their attention. Thus, it is not just that chat conversations can be difficult to follow and understand, but it may also be more difficult to coordinate actions in a group task setting. A few additional examples from the team's meetings will illustrate these coordination challenges. Screen recordings are discussed when appropriate, but full transcripts have been omitted for space considerations.

As documented in previous research on chat in educational settings, these team meetings were marked by the frequent intrusion of the technology into the conversation. This "tech talk" (Markman, 2006a) included accounts for being late or dropping out of the meeting due to technical glitches, questions about the technology (including the software used to generate the screen recordings), and expressions of frustration about the particular interface. Example 3, from the team's first meeting, illustrates how tech talk could interrupt the flow of the conversation, thereby disrupting the

action that talk sought to accomplish. Relevant turns are indicated by shading.

Example 3

Example 3 takes place towards the beginning of the meeting, and four out of the five team members have shown up to chat room. Prior to this excerpt Rebeca proposed that the meeting could start without the fifth member, Evan, and it is to her suggestion that Thadine's turn at 10:14:27 is responding. Taking advantage of the fact that the meeting discussion has not really begun, the researcher attempts to introduce the first topic, a scheduling matter, into the conversation at 10:14:45. However, the next turn to post to the chat is from Thadine, who is asking how to modify the virtual classroom display. Although the chat system allows for participants to engage in multiple conversational threads, Thadine's turn has the effect of orienting all of the team members' attention away from the researcher's scheduling message and towards Thadine's technical issue. Rebeca, I-Fang, and the researcher all join Thadine's thread, and although Sidney does not reply in this exchange, his screen recording

Table 7. Example 3

10:14:27	THADINE: Yeah, we probably should start without him.
10:14:39	SIDNEY: so what shall we talk about
10:14:45	RESEARCHER: Ok, now that most of you are here, let me ask about the meeting next week
10:14:52	THADINE: does anyone know how I can minimize the whiteboard and make our chat session larger
10:15:19	REBECA: hit the big sqaure/maximizer button
10:15:25	REBECA: square
10:15:32	RESEARCHER: Thadine,
10:15:45	RESEARCHER: It doesn't appear to change on mine
10:16:17	THADINE: Ok, thanks Researcher. I have a Mac Rebeca, so there isn't a maximizer button, but thanks for your help.
10:16:18	RESEARCHER: you used to be able to click and drag the box, but it won't let me click now
10:16:19	I-FANG: mine is disabled too..
10:16:43	THADINE: So the meeting next week?
10:16:47	RESEARCHER: they've changed the look of virtual classroom quite a bit in the new release
10:16:48	REBECA: sorry:(
10:16:54	RESEARCHER: sorry..meeting with Dr. K[......]
10:17:03	RESEARCHER: she needs to meet after 5pm
10:17:28	RESEARCHER: she just want to get a feel for how thinga are going & talk abotu research methods

indicates he is trying various buttons and tools on the chat interface, presumably to see if he can suggest a solution for Thadine. Although the issue is marked as resolved by Thadine at 10:16:17, other turns-in-progress are posted after hers, thus adding to the sequence. Thadine attempts to return the conversation to its prior track with her turn at 10:16:43, providing an opportunity for the others to reorient themselves to the researcher's turn at 10:14:45. However, the researcher is also engaged in turn composition, and it not able to reorient to the task of scheduling the meeting until 10:16:54. Thus it took two turns, one from Thadine and one from the researcher, to reorient the group to the proposed task of scheduling a meeting. It is interesting to note also that tech talk was the one topic whose presence effectively interrupted the prior talk, rather than simply adding a new concurrent thread to the conversation. It may be that because the conversations are being mediated through a technology, participants are more sensitive to technical issues than to other "interrupting" threads, and therefore more likely

to put the rest of the conversation on hold while the problems are being worked out.

The problem with coordinating actions in chat discussions is not that it is impossible, but that it may be more imprecise and take longer to accomplish, in part due to the potential for overlap and the inability to assess passive agreement through body language or silence (Boden, 1994). In the case of this team, decisions were sometimes arrived upon without any explicit consensus, but rather through the repetition and uptake of ideas by one or more team member. Explicit verbalized agreement by an individual team member was also taken as a sign of general agreement in the group.

Example 4

The excerpt in Example 4, from the team's second meeting occurs after the team has evaluated the research collected since their last meeting. They have moved on to a discussion about how to focus their project, and are specifically trying to address how many topics to pursue for more research and

Table 8. Example 4

5:46:15	EVAN: Mp3, computers and PDAs is what Rebeca said, right?
5:46:24	REBECA: Like for example: Evan studies wireless future past and present or with another member and then Me and someone else study different uses of something else?
5:46:33	EVAN: Cell phone...sorry
5:47:04	REBECA: like how useful wireless internet is for PDA's versus lap tops
5:47:05	I-FANG: so we are essentially having 2 topics?
5:47:08	THADINE: we can probably organize the research part however we want
5:47:29	EVAN: I think 3 topics and the two that produce the most information are what become the final presentation
5:47:35	REBECA: well, maybe 2 or maybe more we can work individually on things related to sum it all up at the end.
5:47:59	I-FANG: i think team work might be better
5:48:01	REBECA: We need like a general topic say, WIRELESS
5:48:04	EVAN: I think breaking it down is fine, but doing 5 distinct projects that come together at the end is too hard
5:48:09	I-FANG: wireless sounds good
5:48:16	REBECA: then we each pick areas to look at under that topic
5:48:24	SIDNEY: do we have our wireless innovator?
5:48:25	EVAN: what data do we have so far in our tree about wireless
5:48:34	THADINE: Sid and Evan have good points
5:48:42	I-FANG: i got wireless home networking

what those topics should be. After proposing that the team move on rather than collect more data (not shown), Evan moves to introduce specific candidate technologies for further study, based on the prior discussion, in his post at 5:46:15. The next turn, from Rebeca at 5:46:24, does two things: explicitly it is a proposal for a way of organizing the final project, based on assigning specific topics to specific team members. At the same time, Rebeca's turn implicitly suggests "wireless" as a possible research topic, which is then repeated in her turn at 5:47:04. The next few turns concern the matter of how many topics the team should choose, but a specific proposal for how to organize the project is not agreed upon. What happens instead is that Rebeca's turn at 5:48:01 again serves two functions: to suggest a strategy for organizing the project (a general topic), *and* to explicitly suggest a candidate topic, wireless. Interestingly, while the problem of the *number* of topics is still up in the air, Rebeca's suggestion of wireless *as* a topic is taken up by I-Fang

at 5:48:09 with an explicit agreement token, and then implicitly by Sidney at 5:48:24 and Evan at 5:48:25. That is, by asking how wireless can be used as a topic given their existing information, Evan and Sidney appear to be accepting wireless as a topic worthy of further exploration. It is also interesting to note that the ambiguity surrounding the number of topics the team will pursue allows Thadine, two minutes after this exchange, to introduce a second possible topic for their project, in this case, computer animation/computerized art. The unresolved nature of the issue of the number of topics is made clear by Evan towards the end of the meeting, nearly 20 minutes after the exchange in Example 4, when he posts "I know it is late...but we need to have a second or even third direction."

Coordinating decisions in the chat environment was aided, to an extent, by the introduction of a strategy for eliciting explicit agreement. In meeting two, the researcher, in an attempt to verify a future meeting between the team and their instructor posted the following: "Wednesday at 5pm, STS conference room (FAC 17)? Please say Y or N." The Y/N convention was subsequently used by the team for some of their own decisions, and it proved to be an effective tool. Consider the following two examples.

In Example 5, taken from the second meeting shortly after the researcher has introduced the Y/N convention to schedule a face-to-face meeting, the team members re-use this convention to quickly and clearly display their agreement to a date and time for their next virtual meeting. Example 6, from the team's fourth meeting, comes shortly after the team has used the Y/N convention to decide on a time for a face-to-face meeting to practice their presentation. However, instead of re-using that convention, the team repeats the same information several times to establish agreement. In spoken conversation repetition is commonly used as one way to show agreement. However, repetition as an agreement strategy can be a disadvantage in the chat medium, because longer turns will take more time to type, thereby increasing the potential for ambiguous non-responses. Although in Example 6 the information that was retyped was not extensive, it conveys a sense of redundancy and slightly less clarity than Example 5.

Evaluating Chat as an Online Discussion Tool

The structural features of the chat interface as described above present both advantages and disadvantages for its use as a medium for online discussion. One definite advantage illustrated by this case is that chat can be more democratic. Because most chat interfaces allow for any participant to be typing a post at any time, it is much less likely that any one member will dominate the conversation. In face-to-face or telephone-mediated settings, the general rule for spoken conversation is that one party talks at a time, and the current speaker is usually the one to cede the floor to the next speaker (Sacks et al., 1974). In group discussions, this often results in more talkative members taking the lion's share of the turns, and in extreme cases can shut out participation by quieter members. Although in chat discussions talkative group members are not prevented from taking as many turns as they want, their turns do not prevent others from contributing.

Additionally, in small group discussions such as the case study presented here, participants who have adapted their turn construction to be sensitive to threading may be able to use fewer address terms in their talk. This can help reinforce a norm

Table 9. Example 5

6:23:32	RESEARCHER: virtually?
6:23:43	THADINE: Tues?
6:23:45	REBECA: Tuesday at 5?
6:23:48	EVAN: Y
6:23:51	REBECA: y
6:23:52	THADINE: Y
6:23:59	SIDNEY: virutal you mean
6:24:05	REBECA: we'll let ifang know
6:24:16	REBECA: y
6:24:20	SIDNEY: Tuesday at 5pm Virtual meeting; Wednesday at 5pm FAC 17
6:24:27	THADINE: sounds good
6:24:27	REBECA: this whole Y or N thing works great

Table 10. Example 6

5:38:45	REBECA: ok UGL 2nd floor
5:38:52	REBECA: Tues. 5
5:38:52	EVAN: Meet in the lobby?
5:38:56	EVAN: Of the second floor
5:38:57	REBECA: sure
5:38:58	EVAN: ?
5:39:01	SIDNEY: so were meeting in the UGL 2nd floor Tuesday the 6th
5:39:07	REBECA: in the lobby
5:39:07	EVAN: Yes
5:39:09	EVAN: at 5:00
5:39:15	EVAN: In the lobby of the second gfloor
5:39:18	I-FANG: ok, all set
5:39:22	THADINE: sounds good
5:39:24	REBECA: yeah!!!!

of any-speaker-self-selects, allowing members to address the group as a whole, rather than specific individuals (Markman, 2006a). This in turn may help build a sense of community in the group chat. And by separating the composing process from the reception of turns, chat may also favor more equal participation by allowing members more time to compose and edit their thoughts. In this way, chat can be particularly beneficial for encouraging discussion by members who experience communication anxiety in face-to-face settings.

Another advantage of chat for online group discussion is that many chat systems, particularly those marketed towards the education sector, feature logging systems that allow for a persistence of conversation not possible in spoken interaction. In the case presented here, the team members frequently made use of the ongoing log kept by the chat server to review the conversation-in-progress when they entered the chat, as well as to catch up on what they missed if they ended up leaving the chat during the meeting. The students were also observed to scroll back during the meeting in order to review the conversation or pick up on a previous thread. In addition to being useful during discussion sessions, the logging feature available in some chat software also provides a valuable post-meeting record, and eliminates the need to take notes during the discussion. Rather than relying on people's memories (or handwriting), chat logs provide an exact record of the entire conversation as it unfolded.

Of course, as with any medium, there are disadvantages to chat as well. Most importantly, the feature of chat that can help equalize participation, that any person types at any time, can also be its biggest drawback, in that it can lend to chat conversations being difficult to follow. The team in this case study revealed very little in the way of coherence problems, likely because they were all fairly expert at communication via computers. For people new to synchronous CMC, however, chat conversations can be very disorienting and can take some time to get used to. One reason for this is because chat systems display turns in a linear order, thus setting up the expectation that the conversation will proceed with the same system for linear turn exchange found in spoken conversation. In addition, most chat systems do not include the type of presence awareness feature available on many instant messaging programs, wherein participants are alerted visually when their conversational partner is composing a message. This contributes to the possibility for ambiguity in chat conversations, because silence (in the form of a non-response) will not carry the same interactional relevance as it does in spoken interaction. Because chat participants cannot monitor each other's turns-in-progress, overlap and redundancies will be common, which can cause confusion and frustration for users and potentially increase the time it takes to achieve joint attention. In addition, although the team in this case study showed great sensitivity to topical threading in composing their turns, it is important to note that threading is not an inherently intuitive process, but one that must be learned as part of learning to use chat.

Finally, the usefulness of chat as an online discussion tool may be limited by the number of people participating in the chat. The team in this case study was small--with only five members plus the researcher there were never any more than six people in the chat room at any one time. The smaller number of people in the chat meant that participants could spend more time composing their turns, and could compose longer, more complicated turns. In studies of large, public chat rooms, which can have hundreds of participants, researchers have found that there is much more competition for the floor, because with so many people participating turns will scroll off the screen quickly (Herring, 1999; Werry, 1996). This generally results in shorter turns and multiple, dyadic exchanges rather than the group-oriented discussion presented here. Larger group chats will have a hard time maintaining coherence through threading alone, and will have to employ other means, such as the use of address terms (Werry, 1996).

Suggestions for Using Chat for Online Discussions

Although the material presented in the case study has to a certain extent focused on the constraints of the chat medium, and the potential problems that can arise, the intention here is not to discourage educators from using chat. On the contrary, the research amply demonstrates that, despite its potential drawbacks, chat can still be a useful tool for learning environments. Therefore, I conclude this case study with a set of suggestions for implementing chat as a discussion tool, based on the research presented above.

One important suggestion is to assess the level of CMC expertise prior to implementing chat. Even college students, who may have significant experience using other online communication channels, such as social networking sites, may be unfamiliar with chat environments and their particular turn organization characteristics. Therefore it may also be necessary and useful to set aside time to provide new users with training and an opportunity to acclimatize themselves to the chat environment before the official meetings or discussion sessions take place. Training sessions should explain threading and stress the need for users to design their turns such that the recipient or referent turn is clear.

Another suggestion is to consider using moderators or facilitators, especially for groups with people new to the chat environment and particularly in the earlier discussion sessions. Moderators can help by providing guidance in turn construction, serving as a locus for joint attention, and by paying attention to non-responding participants. Moderators should exercise restraint on their interaction as appropriate to the goals of the chat session. Employing meeting agendas or discussion outlines may also be useful, especially for non-moderated or leaderless peer groups. Agendas can facilitate smoother transitions in chat-based meetings (Markman, 2009) and also help organize joint attention by heightening the importance of agenda items. Along with this, it may also be useful to budget time for chat-based discussions or meetings more conservatively. In general, the team presented in this case was only able to get through one major decision topic per meeting, even with close to an hour spent in the chat. It is also very likely that at least some time will be spent on solving technical issues; thus a good rule of thumb would be one major topic or agenda item per discussion session. Even if the participants are skilled at following and designing turns based on threading, it will still take more time to type and read interaction than it would to converse orally. Along with this, it is important to consider the group size when deciding on discussion topics and goals. As noted above, there can be significant differences between the speed of the conversation with larger groups, and it is likely that at a certain point, discussions will branch off into multiple dyadic exchanges as opposed to true group discussions. If the goal of using chat is to promote thoughtful, reflective exchanges, then group size should be limited to 10 or fewer participants.

Finally, consider developing or encouraging the development of norms or conventions to aid in decision-making and joint attention, such as always verbalizing agreement or disagreement (such as the Y/N convention adopted buy this team). This can be done by moderators or facilitators, or be discussed as part of chat training. Keeping users aware of the need to verbalize thoughts that might go unsaid in a face-to-face setting can help reduce the ambiguity that is often inherent in chat discussions.

REFERENCES

Baron, N. S. (2008). *Always on: Language in an online and mobile world*. Oxford: Oxford University Press.

Boden, D. (1994). *The business of talk: Organizations in action*. Cambridge, MA: Polity Press.

Cox, G., Carr, T., & Hall, M. (2004). Evaluating the use of synchronous communication in two blended courses. *Journal of Computer Assisted Learning, 20*, 183–193. doi:10.1111/j.1365-2729.2004.00084.x

Ferrara, K., Brunner, H., & Whittemore, G. (1991). Interactive written discourse as an emergent register. *Written Communication, 8*(1), 8–34. doi:10.1177/0741088391008001002

Garcia, A. C., & Jacobs, J. B. (1998). The interactional organization of computer mediated communication in the college classroom. *Qualitative Sociology, 21*, 299–317. doi:10.1023/A:1022146620473

Garcia, A. C., & Jacobs, J. B. (1999). The eyes of the beholder: Understanding the turn-taking system in quasi-synchronous computer-mediated communication. *Research on Language and Social Interaction, 32*, 337–367. doi:10.1207/S15327973rls3204_2

Greenfield, P. M., & Subrahmanyam, K. (2003). Online discourse in a teen chatroom: New codes and new modes of coherence in a visual medium. *Journal of Applied Developmental Psychology, 24*, 713–738. doi:10.1016/j.appdev.2003.09.005

Herring, S. C. (1999). Interactional coherence in CMC. *Journal of Computer-Mediated Communication, 4*(4). Retrieved May 4, 2003, from http://www.ascusc.org/jcmc/vol4/issue4/herring.html

Herring, S. C. (2003). Dynamic topic analysis of synchronous chat. *New Research for New Media: Innovative Research Methodologies Symposium Working Papers and Readings* Retrieved December 30, 2006, from http://ella/slis.indiana.edu/%7Eherring/dta.htm/

Herring, S. C. (2004). Computer-mediated discourse analysis: An approach to researching online behavior. In Barab, S. A., Kling, R., & Gray, J. H. (Eds.), *Designing for virtual communities in the service of learning* (pp. 338–376). New York: Cambridge University Press.

Johnson, G. M. (2006). Synchronous and asynchronous text-based CMC in educational contexts: A review of recent research. *TechTrends: Linking Research and Practice to Improve Learning, 50*(4), 46–53.

Levin, B. B., He, Y., & Robbins, H. H. (2006). Comparative analysis of preservice teachers' reflective thinking in synchronous versus asynchronous online case discussions. *Journal of Technology and Teacher Education, 14*, 439–460.

Markman, K. M. (2006a). Computer-mediated conversation: The organization of talk in chat-based virtual team meetings. *Dissertation Abstracts Online, 67*(12A), 209. (UMI No. AAI3244348)

Markman, K. M. (2006b, November). *Following the thread: Turn organization in computer-mediated chat*. Paper presented at the Ninety-second annual meeting of the National Communication Association, San Antonio, TX.

Markman, K. M. (2009). "So what shall we talk about": Openings and closings in chat-based virtual meetings. *Journal of Business Communication, 46*, 150–170. doi:10.1177/0021943608325751

Murray, D. E. (1989). When the medium determines turns: Turn-taking in computer conversation. In Coleman, H. (Ed.), *Working with language: A multidisciplinary consideration of language use in work contexts* (pp. 319–337). Berlin: Mouton de Gruyter.

Murray, D. E. (1991). The composing process for computer conversation. *Written Communication, 8*(1), 35–55. doi:10.1177/0741088391008001003

Osman, G., & Herring, S. C. (2007). Interaction, facilitation, and deep learning in cross-cultural chat: A case study. *The Internet and Higher Education, 10*, 125–141. doi:10.1016/j.iheduc.2007.03.004

Panyametheekul, S., & Herring, S. C. (2003). Gender and turn allocation in a Thai chat room. *Journal of Computer-Mediated Communication, 9*(1). Retrieved April 3, 2004, from http://www.ascusc.org/jcmc/vol9/issue1/panya_herring.html

Paulus, T. M., & Phipps, G. (2008). Approaches to case analyses in synchronous and asynchronous environments. *Journal of Computer-Mediated Communication, 13*(2), 459-484. Retrieved June 1, 2009, from http://www3.interscience.wiley.com/cgi-bin/fulltext/119414150/HTMLSTART

Pomerantz, A. (1984). Pursuing a response. In Atkinson, J. M., & Heritage, J. (Eds.), *Structures of social action: Studies in conversation analysis* (pp. 152–163). Cambridge: Cambridge University Press.

Repman, J., Zinskie, C., & Carlson, R. D. (2005). Effective use of CMC tools in interactive online learning. *Computers in the Schools, 22*(1-2), 57–69. doi:10.1300/J025v22n01_06

Rintel, E. S., Mulholland, J., & Pittam, J. (2001). First things first: Internet Relay Chat openings. *Journal of Computer-Mediated Communication, 6*(3). Retrieved May 5, 2003, from http://www.ascusc.org/jcmc/vol6/issue3/rintel.html

Rintel, E. S., & Pittam, J. (1997). Strangers in a strange land: Interaction management on Internet Relay Chat. *Human Communication Research, 23*, 507–534. doi:10.1111/j.1468-2958.1997.tb00408.x

Rintel, E. S., Pittam, J., & Mulholland, J. (2003). Time will tell: Ambiguous non-responses on Internet relay Chat. *Electronic Journal of Communication, 13*(1). Retrieved January 13, 2004, from http://80-www.cios.org.content.lib.utexas.edu:2048getfile%5CRINTEL_V13N1

Sacks, H., Schegloff, E. A., & Jefferson, G. (1974). A simplest systematics for the organization of turn-taking for conversation. *Language, 50*, 696–735. doi:10.2307/412243

Schegloff, E. A. (2007). *Sequence organization in interaction: A primer in conversation analysis (Vol. 1)*. Cambridge: Cambridge University Press.

Schegloff, E. A., & Sacks, H. (1974). Opening up closings. In Turner, R. (Ed.), *Ethnomethodology: Selected readings* (pp. 233–264). Harmondsworth, England: Penguin Education.

Schonfeldt, J., & Golato, A. (2003). Repair in chats: A conversation analytic approach. *Research on Language and Social Interaction, 36,* 241–284. doi:10.1207/S15327973RLSI3603_02

Schwier, R. A., & Balbar, S. (2002). The interplay of content and community in synchronous and asynchronous communication: Virtual communication in a graduate seminar. *Canadian Journal of Learning and Technology, 28*(2), 21–30.

Simpson, J. (2005). Conversational floors in synchronous text-based CMC discourse. *Discourse Studies, 7,* 337–361. doi:10.1177/1461445605052190

Sorg, J. J., & McElhinney, J. H. (2000). A case study describing student experiences of learning in a context of synchronous computer-mediated communication in a distance education environment. Fort Wayne, IN: Purdue University. (ERIC Document No. ED447794)

Strømsø, H. I., Grøttum, P., & Lycke, K. H. (2007). Content and processes in problem-based learning: a comparison of computer-mediated and face-to-face communication. *Journal of Computer Assisted Learning, 23,* 271–282. doi:10.1111/j.1365-2729.2007.00221.x

ten Have, P. (1999). *Doing conversation analysis: A practical guide.* London: Sage.

ten Have, P. (2000). Computer-mediated chat: Ways of finding chat partners. *M/C: A Journal of Media and Culture, 3*(4). Retrieved May 5, 2003, from http://journal.media-culture.org.au/0008/partners.php

Wang, A. Y., Newlin, M. H., & Tucker, T. L. (2001). A discourse analysis of online classroom chats: Predictors of cyber-student performance. *Teaching of Psychology, 28,* 222–226. doi:10.1207/S15328023TOP2803_09

Werry, C. C. (1996). Linguistic and interactional features of Internet Relay Chat. In S. C. Herring (Ed.), Computer-mediated communication: Linguistic, social and cross-cultural perspectives (pp. 47-63). Amsterdam: John Benjamins.

Wilkins, H. (1991). Computer talk: Long-distance conversations by computer. *Written Communication, 8*(1), 56–78. doi:10.1177/0741088391008001004

Yukselturk, E., & Top, E. (2006). Reconsidering online course discussions: A case study. *Journal of Educational Technology Systems, 34,* 341–367. doi:10.2190/6GQ8-P7TX-VGMR-4NR4

ADDITIONAL READING

Barnes, R. (2007). Formulations and the facilitation of common agreement in meetings talk. *Text & Talk, 27,* 273–296.

Branon, R., & Essex, C. (2001). Synchronous and asynchronous communication tools in distance education. *TechTrends, 45*(1), 36–42. doi:10.1007/BF02763377

Cameron, B. A., Morgan, K., Williams, K. C., & Kostelecky, K. L. (2009). Group projects: Student perceptions of the relationship between social tasks and a sense of community in online group work. *American Journal of Distance Education, 23,* 20–33. doi:10.1080/08923640802664466

Condon, S. L., & Cech, C. G. (1996). Discourse management strategies in face-to-face and computer-mediated decision making interactions. *Electronic Journal of Communication, 6*(3). Retrieved January 13, 2004, from http://80-www.cios.org.content.lib.utexas.edu:2048/getfile%5CCONDON_V6N396

Condon, S. L., & Cech, C. G. (1996). Functional comparisons of face-to-face and computer-mediated decision making interactions. In Herring, S. C. (Ed.), *Computer-mediated communication: Linguistic, social and cross-cultural perspectives* (pp. 65–80). Amsterdam, Philadelphia: John Benjamins.

Davidson-Shivers, G. V., Muilenburg, L. Y., & Tanner, E. J. (2001). How do students participate in synchronous and asynchronous online discussions? *Journal of Educational Computing Research, 25*, 351–366. doi:10.2190/6DCH-BEN3-V7CF-QK47

Dietz-Uhler, B., & Bishop-Clark, C. (2001). The use of computer-mediated communication to enhance subsequent face-to-face discussions. *Computers in Human Behavior, 17*, 269–283. doi:10.1016/S0747-5632(01)00006-1

Flanagin, A. J., Park, H. S., & Seibold, D. R. (2004). Group performance and collaborative technology: A longitudinal and multilevel analysis of information quality, contribution equity, and members' satisfaction in computer-mediated groups. *Communication Monographs, 71*, 352–372. doi:10.1080/0363452042000299902

Havard, B., Du, J., & Xu, J. (2008). Online collaborative learning and communication media. *Journal of Interactive Learning Research, 19*(1), 37–50.

Heritage, J. (1999). Conversation Analysis at century's end: Practices of talk-in-interaction, their distributions, and their outcomes. *Research on Language and Social Interaction, 32*, 69–76. doi:10.1207/S15327973RLSI321&2_9

Herring, S. C. (1996). Linguistic and critical analysis of computer-mediated communication: Some ethical and scholarly considerations. *The Information Society, 12*, 153–168.

Hirokawa, R. Y., & Poole, M. S. (Eds.). (1996). *Communication and group decision making* (2nd ed.). Thousand Oaks, CA: Sage.

Ingram, A. L., Hathorn, L. G., & Evans, A. (2000). Beyond chat on the internet. *Computers & Education, 35*, 21–35. doi:10.1016/S0360-1315(00)00015-4

Jeong, A. (1996). The structures of group discussions in online chats. *Journal of Visual Literacy, 16*(1), 51–63.

Jeong, A. C. (2006). The effects of conversational language on group interaction and group performance in computer-supported collaborative argumentation. *Instructional Science: An International Journal of Learning and Cognition, 34*, 367–397.

Johnson, G. M., Howell, A. J., & Code, J. R. (2005). Online discussion and college student learning: Toward a model of influence. *Technology, Pedagogy and Education, 14*(1), 61–76. doi:10.1080/14759390500200193

Kangasharju, H. (2002). Alignment in disagreement: Forming oppositional alliances in committee meetings. *Journal of Pragmatics, 34*, 1447–1471. doi:10.1016/S0378-2166(02)00073-5

Palmer, S. R., & Holt, D. M. (2009). Examining student satisfaction with wholly online learning. *Journal of Computer Assisted Learning, 25*, 101–113. doi:10.1111/j.1365-2729.2008.00294.x

Park, J. (2007). Interpersonal and affective communication in synchronous online discourse. *The Library Quarterly, 77*, 133–155. doi:10.1086/517841

Pelowski, S., Frissell, L., Cabral, K., & Yu, T. (2005). So far but yet so close: Student chat room immediacy, learning, and performance in an online course. *Journal of Interactive Learning Research, 16*, 395–407.

Pfister, H.-R., & Oehl, M. (2009). The impact of goal focus, task type and group size on synchronous net-based collaborative learning discourses. *Journal of Computer Assisted Learning, 25*, 161–176. doi:10.1111/j.1365-2729.2008.00287.x

Psathas, G. (1995). *Conversation analysis: The study of talk-in-interaction*. Thousand Oaks, CA: Sage.

Sacks, H. (1992). Lectures on conversation (Vols. 1 & 2). Oxford: Blackwell.

Schegloff, E. A. (1990). On the organization of sequences as a source of "coherence" in talk-in-interaction. In B. Dorval (Ed.), Conversational organization and its development (Vol. 38, pp. 51-77). Norwood, NJ: Ablex Publishing.

Schegloff, E. A. (1995). Discourse as an interactional achievement III: The omnirelevance of action. *Research on Language and Social Interaction, 28*, 185. doi:10.1207/s15327973rlsi2803_2

Stahl, G. (2006). Supporting group cognition in an online math community: A cognitive tool for small-group referencing in text chat. *Journal of Educational Computing Research, 35*, 103–122. doi:10.2190/Q435-7611-2561-720P

Strijbos, J.-W., & Stahl, G. (2007). Methodological issues in developing a multi-dimensional coding procedure for small-group chat communication. *Learning and Instruction, 17*, 394–404. doi:10.1016/j.learninstruc.2007.03.005

Wang, C.-H. (2005). Questioning skills facilitate online synchronous discussions. *Journal of Computer Assisted Learning, 21*, 303–313. doi:10.1111/j.1365-2729.2005.00138.x

Zemel, A., & Cakir, M. P. (2007, November). *Reading's work: The mechanisms of online chat as social interaction*. Paper presented at the Ninety-third annual meeting of the National Communication Association, Chicago, IL.

Zitzen, M., & Stein, D. (2004). Chat and conversation: A case of transmedial stability? *Linguistics, 42*, 983–1021. doi:10.1515/ling.2004.035

KEY TERMS AND DEFINITIONS

Computer-Mediated Communication: Human-human conversations that take place entirely through (usually text-based) computer channels.

Chat: A platform for conducting synchronous, multi-party, text-based conversations through networked computers.

Instant Messaging: A platform for conducting synchronous, dyadic conversations through networked computers.

Conversation Analysis: A method for the collection and analysis of naturally-occurring interaction that focuses on describing micro-level characteristics of conversation.

Computer-Mediated Discourse Analysis: An empirical approach to the study of text-based verbal computer-mediated communication that combines quantitative and/or qualitative methods from several language-focused disciplines.

Disrupted Turn Adjacency: A phenomenon found in some computer-mediated communication settings whereby the normal back-and-forth exchange of turns is interrupted due to technological constraints, resulting in a conversation where turns are not presented in the correct order.

APPENDIX A

Key for Interpreting Full Transcripts

Participants' screen recordings were aligned to the time stamp provided by the chat server. Individually named columns represent that person's visible screen activities. Text is transcribed exactly as entered on the screen. The use of double strikethrough indicates deleted characters or spaces. Deleted characters are shown in reverse order, unless the entire word and/or phrase was selected and deleted in one action, in which case the deleted information is shown in normal order. Double parentheses are used for transcriber description or comments. The ↵ symbol represents hitting enter or clicking send.

Figure 2.

Example 1 Full Transcript Part 1

Chat Time	Chat Window	THADINE	EVAN	Chat Time	I-FANG	REBECA
5:35:38	I-FANG: so when tuesday?	((pause))	↵	5:35:38	((pause))	((pause))
5:35:39			((pause))	5:35:39		
5:35:40	EVAN: So has everyine else...we can just meet on campus, or soemthing			5:35:40	i though	
5:35:41				5:35:41	we	
5:35:42				5:35:42	r	
5:35:43				5:35:43	me	
5:35:44				5:35:44	eting vi	
5:35:45				5:35:45	rtul	
5:35:46				5:35:46	((pause))	
5:35:47		5? ↵		5:35:47	~~iu~~	
5:35:48	THADINE: 5?	((pause))		5:35:48	ally	
5:35:49				5:35:49	n	
5:35:50				5:35:50	~~n~~	
5:35:51				5:35:51	tuesd	
5:35:52			y↵	5:35:52	((pause))	
5:35:53	EVAN: y		((pause))	5:35:53	ay?	
5:35:54				5:35:54	((pause))	
5:35:55				5:35:55		
5:35:56				5:35:56	↵	
5:35:57	I-FANG: i though we r meeting virtually tuesday?			5:35:57	((pause))	
5:35:58				5:35:58		
5:35:59				5:35:59		
5:36:00				5:36:00		
5:36:01				5:36:01		
5:36:02				5:36:02		
5:36:03				5:36:03		
5:36:04				5:36:04		
5:36:05				5:36:05	i	I
5:36:06				5:36:06	can mee	~~I~~
5:36:07				5:36:07	t i~~e~~	Can w
5:36:08				5:36:08	o	e do i
5:36:09				5:36:09	n cam	t ea
5:36:10				5:36:10	pus	rlie
5:36:11				5:36:11	..an	r on
5:36:12				5:36:12	y d	Tu
5:36:13				5:36:13	ay	esday
5:36:14				5:36:14	((pause))	? ↵
5:36:15	REBECA: Can we do it earlier on Tuesday?			5:36:15		((pause))
5:36:16				5:36:16		
5:36:17			that is	5:36:17		
5:36:18			fine	5:36:18		
5:36:19			with	5:36:19		
5:36:20			me ↵	5:36:20	2:	

Figure 3.

Example 1 Full Transcript Part 2

Chat Time	Chat Window	THADINE	EVAN	Chat Time	I-FANG	REBECA
5:36:21	EVAN: that is fine with me		((pause))	5:36:21	30	
5:36:22			4	5:36:22	((pause))	
5:36:23	EVAN: 4		↵	5:36:23	to 6	how
5:36:24	EVAN: 3		3↵	5:36:24	((pause))	about
5:36:25			((pause))	5:36:25		3
5:36:26				5:36:26		?
5:36:27				5:36:27		↵
5:36:28	REBECA: how about 3?			5:36:28	↵	((pause))
5:36:29	I-FANG: i can meet on campus..anyday 2:30 to 6			5:36:29	((pause))	
5:36:30				5:36:30		
5:36:31		I can		5:36:31		
5:36:32		't do		5:36:32		
5:36:33		3.		5:36:33		
5:36:34		Class		5:36:34		
5:36:35		((pause))		5:36:35		
5:36:36				5:36:36		
5:36:37		til	Thad	5:36:37		
5:36:38		3:45	ine?	5:36:38		
5:36:39		↵	↵	5:36:39		
5:36:40	EVAN: Thadine?		((pause))	5:36:40		
5:36:40	THADINE: I can't do 3. Class til 3:45	((pause))		5:36:40		
5:36:41				5:36:41		
5:36:42		bu		5:36:42		
5:36:43		t i		5:36:43		
5:36:44		could		5:36:44		
5:36:45		do		5:36:45		
5:36:46		4 wi	ho	5:36:46		
5:36:47		thout	w bout	5:36:47		
5:36:48		a	4 ↵	5:36:48		
5:36:49	EVAN: how bout 4	proble	((pause))	5:36:49		
5:36:50		m ↵		5:36:50		
5:36:51	THADINE: but i could do 4 without a problem	((pause))		5:36:51		

APPENDIX B

Figure 4.

Example 2 Full Transcript

Chat Time	Chat Window	THADINE	EVAN	Chat Time	I-FANG	SIDNEY
5:43:57	EVAN: I think in general we can discuss our findings so far	((pause))	((pause))	5:43:57	((pause))	((deletes text in entry box))
5:43:58				5:43:58		
5:43:59				5:43:59		evid
5:44:00				5:44:00	~~taht erofeb~~	ently
5:44:01				5:44:01	~~team tnac~~	you can
5:44:02				5:44:02	~~os...yadir~~	t past i
5:44:03				5:44:03	~~f nretdim~~	n ~~ni~~
5:44:04				5:44:04	~~evah llew~~	=e in he
5:44:05	SIDNEY: evidently you cant paste in here			5:44:05	ugh	re↵
5:44:06				5:44:06	...ye	((pause))
5:44:07				5:44:07	((pause))	
5:44:08				5:44:08	s yes	
5:44:09		tha		5:44:09	...	
5:44:10		t'		5:44:10	but	
5:44:11		s no		5:44:11	((pause))	
5:44:12		good↵		5:44:12		
5:44:13	THADINE: that's no good	((pause))		5:44:13	mee	
5:44:14				5:44:14	t ((pause))	
5:44:15		well,		5:44:15	~~team tub~~	
5:44:16		((pause))		5:44:16	= ((pause))	
5:44:17				5:44:17	.	
5:44:18		~~,lle~~		5:44:18	meeti	
5:44:19		w		5:44:19	ng	
5:44:20		((pause))	0u	5:44:20	up in	
5:44:21		yeah,	r findong	5:44:21	pers	
5:44:22		discuss	~~gn~~oing	5:44:22	on wi	
5:44:23		ing our	s?↵	5:44:23	ll	
5:44:24	EVAN: Our findings?	fini	((pause))	5:44:24	((pause))	
5:44:25		((pause))		5:44:25		
5:44:26		~~i~~ding so		5:44:26	just be	
5:44:27		~~os~~=s		5:44:27	((pause))	
5:44:28		so far s		5:44:28		
5:44:29		eems		5:44:29		
5:44:30		t		5:44:30	a plus	
5:44:31		o be a		5:44:31	...	
5:44:32		good		5:44:32	that	
5:44:33		place		5:44:33	~~taht~~	
5:44:34		to sta		5:44:34	we	
5:44:35		rt		5:44:35	'll s	
5:44:36		↵		5:44:36	till have	
5:44:37	THADINE: yeah, discussing our findings so far seems to be a good place to start	((pause))		5:44:37	re((pause))	
5:44:38				5:44:38	gular	
5:44:39				5:44:39	v	
5:44:40				5:44:40	irtual	
5:44:41				5:44:41	meeti	
5:44:42				5:44:42	ngs↵	we n
5:44:43	I-FANG: ugh...yes yes...meeting up in person will just be a plus...we'll still have regular virtual meetings			5:44:43	((pause))	eed

Chapter 12
Online Discussion and Interaction:
The Case of Live Text Commentary

Jan Chovanec
Masaryk University, Czech Republic

EXECUTIVE SUMMARY

This contribution discusses linguistic aspects of discussion and interaction in a new genre of journalism—live text commentary—that has recently come into existence thanks to new communication technologies, most notably the Internet. Live text commentary is a professional journalistic text that is produced online contemporaneously with the event that it describes. The technology enables the text's consumers to provide instant feedback to the author, thus enhancing interpersonal interaction. Structurally, the resulting texts contain elements of discussion because readers' comments are used to co-construct the texts, while also manifesting numerous linguistic features of reader-oriented interactiveness. Live text commentary is viewed as an instance of mediated quasi-interaction. This is because the readers interact in a virtual space, discursively enacting their membership in an imaginary community, rather than participating in a real interpersonal interaction. Using material from live text commentaries of sports events, this contribution provides an analysis of such online discussion and interaction from the perspective of discourse analysis and sociolinguistics.

INTRODUCTION

While some of the chapters in this volume deal with cases of online discussion and interaction in contexts which are interactive by their very nature, e.g., chat groups, Internet forums, personal and professional blogs, etc., this chapter documents the occurrence

of interactive communication fostered by the use of modern information and communication technologies in an environment that is not inherently inclined towards discussion and interaction: Live reporting of factual events in the media. Generally speaking, the media are concerned with transmitting messages to their audiences, most typically represented by the canonical genre of news reporting (though there are other, interactive, genres, such as

DOI: 10.4018/978-1-61520-863-0.ch012

televised political debates and interviews, which are based on discussion).

This chapter focuses on one particular kind of reporting: Live text commentary, as represented by the written reporting of sports events online and in real time. While live sports reporting is an established spoken genre, online commentary is a relatively new phenomenon. The article shows how modern technology, in this case the Internet, may provide an opportunity for journalists to engage in unorthodox and innovative methods of journalism by inviting online discussion and interaction from their audiences during the process of the construction of the text.

The resulting product then integrates the functions of information-provision and interpersonal engagement in a text with a highly elaborate structure comprising two layers of narration. The description of the language and structure of live text commentary reveals that it is organized in complex thematic threads, which resemble other kinds of online interactions, e.g., chat communication. Noting the specific nature of live text commentary, this article offers a sociolinguistic explanation for this emerging genre. By relying on conversational language, dialogic structure and staged interpersonal interaction, the texts articulate the discourse participants' identity of belonging to a virtual group of sports fans.

Interaction in Mass Media Communication

In order to appreciate the interactive nature of live text commentary with all its implications and specificities, this novel genre needs to be situated in the context of mass media communication. Thus a general description of mass communication will first serve as a background against which interaction and interactivity will be discussed and several specific ways of increasing the interactivity of media texts will be noted. Then, online interaction mediated via the Internet will be considered in connection with the traditional journalistic genres

of news reporting, leading to a close discussion of live text commentary as a hybrid text type. Interactiveness and interaction in live text commentary of sports events will then be illustrated with specific examples, whose analysis will be followed by an interpretation of the social and interpersonal function of live text commentary.

Mass communication—in the most general sense—differs from interpersonal face-to-face communication in numerous respects. Most importantly, it is mediated by technology on account of the lack of any immediate physical contact between the participants. Because such communication is oriented towards an indefinite number of potential recipients rather than a specific group of addressees, it ranks as an instance of 'mediated quasi-interaction' rather than merely 'mediated interaction' (cf. Talbot, 2007). Although the mass nature of the communication seriously limits (if not blocks) direct contact between the senders of media messages and their recipients, modern ICT technologies may actually give rise to genres which go beyond this traditional limitation (as is the case with live text commentary).

Mass communication is typically described in terms of several models (for an overview, see, for instance, McQuail, 1987, Dominick, 1993, etc.). Regardless of their differences, most theorists point out the organizational—rather than the personal—origin of the message, with the journalists playing numerous roles (cf. Goffman's roles, outlined in Bell, 1991). The transmission of the messages is machine-assisted and reaches numerous recipients, who are typically unknown to each other and unknown to the source of the message. Importantly, unlike interpersonal communication, mass communication does not allow for easy or immediate feedback, which is one of its most significant differences from face-to-face or machine-mediated interpersonal communication – one that has serious implications, among others, for the linguistic shape of the message.

Although it is easy, as a result, to think of the audience as relatively passive 'recipients' of messages, this need not be so. The audience does wield significant power, if only in selecting the media sources and choosing to participate in the speech event by processing the media text. This points out the limitation of some of the transmission models of communication, based on the classic 1949 model by Shannon and Weaver that has been widely used in communication studies. According to these models, messages are transmitted unilaterally from source to receiver. This transmission is not only unidirectional (with limited feedback from the receiver), but also involves the physical 'transfer' of information rather than an attempt at understanding how meaning is arrived at. Interaction models of communication, by contrast, postulate that participants share information and try to achieve mutual understanding: That is, they have social goals since communication is fundamentally about "symbol sharing" (cf. Black & Bryant, 1995). Thus, for instance, Westley and MacLean's 1957 Conceptual Model incorporates feedback as, with increasing complexity, do other non-linear and multidimensional models used in communication studies.

Importantly, interaction models also typically contain a constructivist element. In other words, meanings are not given and merely 'transmitted' or 'extracted'. Rather, they are constructed by both addressees and addressors in a complex interplay with other, e.g., contextual, factors. This understanding of meaning has, of course, been at the core of the functional tradition in linguistics, cf., for instance, Jacobson's widely-influential model of the speech event (1960) or the socially-oriented concept of Halliday's 'meaning potential' in functional and systemic linguistics (1978).

In terms of types of discourse events, mass media communication exhibits a highly varied range of genres which are interactive to different degrees. Thus, for example, televised political debates are crucially dependent on discussion: Questions are asked, answers provided, insights shared and opinions confronted. The interaction need not necessarily involve only first-frame participants, i.e., the persons directly involved in the debate in the studio, although this is typically the case. The involvement of second-frame participants, i.e., members of the audience, is also possible, for instance by telephone. (The theory of interaction within the multi-layer participant framework has recently been studied in the field of political discourse analysis, cf. Fetzer, 2002, 2006.)

Although TV and radio phone-in programmes have been well-established platforms for media debates for a long time, audience members can nowadays also become involved in other ways: They can send text messages to the studio or email their comments which can be reacted to by the first-frame participants or shared with other viewers by means of running captions on the screen.

The reliance on discussion and interaction is somewhat more complicated in the case of genres which are not so fundamentally interpersonal. Some genres of journalism, for instance, are concerned with transmitting more-or-less factual messages that provide representations of actual events occurring in the extralinguistic reality. This is the case with such information-oriented genres as news reporting and, to a lesser extent, personalized and subjective news commentary (opinion).[1]

Yet, even in news reporting—probably the closest one can come to the most straightforward representative of the discourse type of 'information transmission'—there are conventional ways of increasing the interactive potential of a news item or a news report, i.e., its interactiveness (cf. Benwell 2001, p. 20). A common device is the use of direct citation. Written media reports have been increasingly quoting news actors, public figures and eye witnesses to describe and comment on the news stories covered. Similarly, the broadcast media increasingly rely on interactive modes to report on events. Interaction may take the form of a fictitious dialogue or the juxtaposition of the journalist in the studio and a reporter "in the field". It can likewise consist in the nature of the reporting, especially where a news actor, an opinion leader or some other stakeholder is interviewed. Visually, this multiplicity of sources of information is often accompanied by a change of camera angle, change of physical location, or the inclusion of a still image of a phoning commentator, etc. (For the interplay between the verbal and visual elements, see, e.g., Graddol, 1994.)

Regardless of the actual strategy adopted in order to increase the interpersonal potential of a media text, what is fundamentally important is the fact that the resulting text displays a multiplicity of voices: That is, it is not the verbal product of a single author. On the contrary, by yielding the floor to quotations, the author of a news report supplements his or her voice (often institutional rather than personal) with other voices, thus creating a text which is—in a Bakhtinian sense—heteroglossic (see Bakhtin, 1981). The individual voices may be involved in an implicit interaction or discussion, e.g., when they present conflicting representations.

There are also other ways of enhancing the interactivity of written or official texts, e.g., the use of features of spoken language. By using informal words, colloquial phrases, vague expressions, incomplete sentences and other phenomena typical of speech, the media may approximate to the vernacular of their audience. Fowler (1991) explicitly mentions oral modes that "bridge the discursive gap" existing between the institutional voice of the mass media, communicating in the written standard, and the individual readers, who need to be addressed on a more one-to-one basis resembling everyday face-to-face communication. Bell (1991) notes the sociolinguistic phenomenon of audience design, a strategy whereby the media accommodate to the linguistic habits of the audience by using certain salient linguistic features of the target group—features which have a high symbolic value and may be connected with the expression of personal and group identity. Fairclough (1989) describes the notion of synthetic personalization—a compensatory tendency of the media to handle members of anonymous mass audiences on a more individual and personal basis. Linguistically, this strategy accounts for the frequent use of personal pronouns, forms of address, rhetorical questions, and interpolations (insertions with explanations made for the benefit of readers).

Although these phenomena have been extensively discussed in linguistics over the past two decades, their existence has also been variously noted in earlier studies from other disciplines. The media psychologists Horton & Wohl (1956), for instance, described 'para-social interaction'—the relationship that TV viewers develop towards onscreen characters. They argued that viewers come to identify with characters on TV and, as a result, can have their own attitudes and behaviours validated by them.

It is language, of course, that plays a crucial role in the construction of such para-social interaction. There is a range of specific linguistic means and strategies used for increasing the readers' involvement in the text and establishing a sense of mock friendship (cf. Talbot, 1995, Chovanec, 2003). These are not isolated linguistic phenomena; on the contrary, they are connected with the more general trends in public discourse towards informalization (Fairclough, 1995) and infotainment, which is linguistically manifested by the presentation of often serious content in an entertaining way – this achieved by means of certain poetic devices (cf. Chovanec, 2008b). As the next section shows, however, it is modern online technologies that provide a further significant boost to some media genres, bringing real interpersonal interaction into the texts rather than mere textual interactiveness.

Aspects of Online Discussion and Interaction in the Media

All the above-mentioned strategies involve intervention in the internal structuring of printed or broadcast news stories. A less subtle—if more extraneous—way of increasing the interactive potential of a piece of news occurs in the case of online media: Most news stories are supplemented with a virtual online space, in which readers can express their comments and reactions to the relevant issue.

It is almost a truism to say that the nature of news reporting has recently undergone significant changes as a result of new technologies. As Lewis (2003, p. 99) observes, "[o]nline news style is in a state of flux: Clinging to the traditional news article genre while experimenting with hypertext." One such experiment, which has become widely adopted and has implications for the study of online interaction, is the practice in Internet versions of newspapers of including sections at the ends of articles where readers can post their comments. Internet newspapers have a significant technical advantage over their more traditional printed counterparts in that they openly encourage discussion and interaction among their readers and provide a virtual space for such communication. While an article for an online newspaper is still written by a professional journalist, the comments section opens the text up for debate by the lay audience.

Regardless of whether they are registered or unregistered users of the newspaper's online services (depending on the policy of the particular paper), the readers then have a chance to express their opinions on the relevant article, provide additional information and share their experience. What is equally important, they may also offer views diametrically different from those voiced in the article. In this way, they may express a range of opinions and articulate a hugely varied array of personal experience. Such discussion forums are very popular, although the truth value of the information may be questionable.

Unlike many online chat 'rooms', discussion forums that are appended to the text of the article do not allow a completely unchecked interaction between the readers. The forum participants should follow basic rules which the media formulate in order to regulate these discussions. The contributions are screened and offending posts may be deleted (removed) by the administrator, usually with an explanation noting that the content is abusive, offensive or violates the policies regulating the debate. Although users sometimes complain of 'censorship', opinions that are not in harmony with the editorial policy of the medium are not deleted, save for openly racist and other hate-enticing comments. The deletions are sometimes carried out by automatic software which filters out messages containing, for instance, certain taboo words. Users then typically play something of a 'cat-and-mouse' game by formally disguising what they consider to be potentially offensive words and, thus, trick the software program.

Importantly, the discussions do not revolve only around the topic of the article. They also include readers' reactions to each other's comments. In this way, the discussion may develop one or more thematic threads, with their topics having marginal or no relevance to the original subject matter of the news story to which the discussion is appended. The discussion threads then come to resemble other kinds of asynchronous computer-mediated communication (e.g., various kinds of online chat).

Based on recent technology-driven changes in the nature of online newspapers, it may be argued that such online discussion and interpersonal interaction have become a part of the 'generic structure potential' (cf. Halliday & Hasan, 1986) of online news reporting. In this sense, the genre of online news fundamentally differs from printed or broadcast news, even though a particular item of news may be identical in the printed and the online versions of a single newspaper. The interactive involvement of readers in the online debates also has an important social and political significance: Not only does it provide feedback to the media but it may also serve as a testing ground for finding out what the public thinks of a particular issue. In this sense, online discussion and interaction may, in some cases, actually be more important than the article which triggers such a debate.

Live Text Commentary and Online Sports Reporting

All the above-mentioned observations on the nature of online journalism are directly relevant for the linguistic analysis of certain forms of online sports commentary, which is unique in that it merges the provision of information with interpersonal debate. In this sense, it is a hybrid genre. It will be shown how this genre meets the traditional characteristics of spoken sports reporting and how it extends them by means of capitalizing on modern communication technologies and integrating them within the written mode.

Since online sports commentary is a specific instantiation of the more general genre of 'live text commentary', let us first briefly elaborate on the latter. Live text commentary (LTC) is a media text which is made available online simultaneously with the events which it describes—hence the attribute 'live'.[2] What is novel about this genre is the combination of the immediacy of the media coverage and the relative permanence of the online text. In other words, LTC resembles both spoken reporting—due to its relevance and temporal closeness to the events described—and written reporting in that a written text is produced as a permanent record. What is a written genre, on account of the physical medium, then draws on the spoken mode as its model (cf. Pérez-Sabater et al., 2008).

Among genres of computer-mediated communication, LTC ranks with other kinds of synchronous (or almost synchronous) communication. As a result, LTC is probably the most immediate form of written journalism because it is so closely connected to the events it describes. Thanks to this technology, the information is transmitted to the audience within the shortest possible time and benefits from the permanence of writing. (The genre's advantage can, however, also be seen as a disadvantage. An LTC may lack analytical depth as well as an external perspective, which are more likely to be present when events are described with a little more 'temporal distance'.)

The media are thus making written texts available live in real time—or with a minimal time lag necessary for the technical processing of the message (i.e., after it is typed or transformed into the electronic form in some way and posted online). This, of course, favors the reporting of *processes* rather than states. While processes develop in time, states and one-off events do not so easily allow for incremental developments, focusing as they do on the final results and implications instead. Probably the most typical example of a process that lends itself well to continued coverage is sports reporting: The events are pre-scheduled and have a limited duration, while, at the same time, there is a culmination in the form of a final result. Thanks to these elements, sports provide an ideal area for live reporting and commentary. Some media, however, occasionally use LTC to cover other events, e.g., from the sphere of politics. Recently, live text coverage included the inauguration of President Obama in the USA, the revelation of MPs' questionable expense claims in the UK, and even post-election demonstrations in Iran.[3] The advantage of this mode of reporting is that it allows for embedded links to external sources, as well as the inclusion of photographs and video material. It is not thus merely the combination of graphic and textual elements (cf. Jucker in press) that makes LTC noteworthy: It is also the hypertextual potential of this genre that is being increasingly utilized.

As suggested above, LTC draws on the model of spoken live reporting, which it merges with written genres. Jucker (2006 and in press) contrasts LTC with its model—unscripted radio commentaries—as shown in Table 1.

The iconicity of the event and narration refers to the structure of the commentary which, in Jucker's words, "to some extent at least[,] parallels the structure of the event". However, this iconicity only holds for live text commentary in general; the conversational, interaction-based type of LTC that is described in this chapter is different. According to Jucker (2006), LTC is uni-

Table 1. Features of live text commentary (Jucker in press)

	Unscripted radio commentaries	Live text commentaries
Events	Iconicity of event and narration	Iconicity of event and narration
Narration time	Narration time coextensive with real time	Narration time coextensive with real time
Fluency	Only minimal gaps	Gaps possible
Interval between individual event and its reporting	Minimal, only seconds	Between seconds and minutes
Fixity of report	Ephemeral	Permanent

directional—this means that the audience, unlike in Internet relay chat, cannot respond directly. However, LTC can also be bidirectional, as long as the medium makes provision for readers to actively participate in the interaction.

In fact, LTC covers a wide variety of forms that can be arranged on a scale depending on the interactive potential of the text. At one end, there are instances of LTC that are indeed unidirectional and iconic in Jucker's sense: These describe events as they happen and essentially satisfy the 'transmission' model of communication. On the other hand, however, there are live texts that are co-constructed by the audience and, as a consequence, cover a much wider range of issues than a mere description of events. Such conversational live texts are closer to the 'interaction' model.

Conversational live texts are the preferred type of LTC in the British Internet daily *The Guardian*, where they are referred to as minute-by-minute match reports.[4] Research based on a substantial sample of texts published online from 2006-2009 has shown that these texts are significantly more complex than they might appear at first sight and are far from simple descriptions of events on the pitch (cf. Chovanec, 2006, 2008a,b,c).

The main novelty of these live texts resides in the fact that the audience reading them in real time can respond electronically by emailing the journalist. The journalist reads the readers' emailed contributions at the same time as he watches the match and provides the online report of what is happening in the field. Those comments which the journalist finds interesting or worthy of further comment are cited in the text of his/her sports commentary. In turn, these comments are reacted to by both the journalist and other readers in their subsequent emails. The pattern can be illustrated with the following example:

(1)   **57 min:** Simunic is catapulted into the air after a challenge with Kazim-Richards, but he's OK, somehow.

59 min: It's gone rather quiet at the old Ernst Happel, suggesting the fans are either very nervous or very bored. In the interests of good humour on a Friday evening, I'll plump for the former. But I'm lying to myself. And all of you.

61 min: Kazim-Richards is replaced by Ugur Boral. "I've been contemplating the possibility of this scenario," writes Patrick Hardy. "Suppose Croatia had 13 players with a previous booking, and all of them receive a yellow card on the ongoing game, including the substitutes. Would Croatia be forced to field a 10 man field for their next game? Surely this is not permitted, so how would this sort out?" I think they probably would you know. Anyone got any ideas?

63 min: Olic has the ball in the net, but the linesman, clearly aware of whose fantasy team the striker features in, raises his flag.

64 min: "I hope you have not run afoul of any bad puns regarding those pictures," writes Bill Ceccotti. Don't go there, Bill, you don't know where it will end.

65 min: Kranjcar off, Petric on. A vaguely attacking move from Bilic. "James Murray Spangler invented the electric vaccuum, then sold his patent to Hoover out of poverty," says the knowledgeable James Wells. Now Hoover is a verb (on your side of the Atlantic at least) and Spangler is unknown. See, even in inventing the small club's talent is poached by the big teams." I'll see if I can slip 'Spanglering' in at some point, if someone can give me a definition. (Croatia vs. Turkey, EURO 2008, 20 June 2008)

Structurally, the text is organized along two narrative layers (Chovanec 2008c). The first layer, referred to here as 'primary', is the actual sports commentary, i.e., the journalist's description of, and elaboration on the game, including any speculations and background information. The utterances forming this layer are printed in ordinary print in the example above. By contrast, the second layer, labeled as 'secondary', consists of the exchanges between the discourse participants, i.e., the citations from readers' emails and the journalist's comments on these emails. The utterances belonging to this layer are underlined. It should be noted that the choice of the attributes 'primary' and 'secondary' does not necessarily reflect the relative importance of the narrative layers. In fact, the secondary (or 'gossip') layer may be the more important one: in that case, the 'primary' layer of match description merely provides the background against which the gossip is performed.

The exchanges in the secondary layer are very conversational. The interaction between the participants is pseudo-dialogical, because their discussion and the juxtaposition of their voices are staged: Though based on real email-mediated interactions, the final product is really the outcome of the journalist's authoring practices. A linguistic analysis shows numerous interactive features that can, in conjunction with the nature of the topics discussed and the character of the interaction, help to classify this layer as an instance of 'gossip'— more specifically as 'male gossip' (see below).

The two layers can be contrasted as follows:

Table 2 indicates that the two layers are structured differently. While the primary layer progresses in the form of posts following a time line, the secondary layer is not sequenced in a similar temporal manner. It revolves around topics that are discussed by the journalist and his audience in their emails. Such online conversation (cf. North, 2007) sometimes leads to the development of several discussion threads, which are, in the case of online chat, also referred to as conversational threads (cf. North, 2006, 2007). The topics are not developed in a linear way but parallel to one another: Such polyphonic topics also occur in spontaneous conversations (cf. Chafe, 1997), and their concurrent elaboration places serious demands on the readers' abilities to interpret many of the utterances as coherent. The assignment of coherence is conditioned by the recipients' awareness of the existence of the two layers of narration and the non-sequentiality of posts related to individual topics (cf. Chovanec, 2009).

Features of Real and Simulated Discussion and Interaction in Live Text Commentary

As the above description of some of the features of live text commentary has indicated, it is a genre of mass media communication that reaches a mutually anonymous audience which has a chance to become actively and individually involved in a mediated discussion of various issues. In other words, the texts provide for real online interaction between members of a virtual community. From the linguistic perspective, the texts contain numerous forms and utilize frequent strategies that foster both the texts' interactiveness (i.e., the

Table 2. The two layers of narration in conversational live text reports

	Primary layer	Secondary layer
Event	Iconicity of event and narration	Non-iconicity of event and narration
Topicality	Topical	Topical/timeless
Information	Description of event	(Male) gossip
Interaction	Interactiveness of forms	(Based on) real interaction and discussion
Function	Information provision	Entertainment, social bonding
Structure	Temporal framework	Topic framework (if any)
Textual organization	Temporal-based posts	(Potential) thematic threads

suggestion of spoken interaction by foregrounding the presence of the reader—cf. Benwell 2001, p. 20) and real interaction.

It will be best to illustrate some of the typical interactive phenomena with examples:

(2) **Preamble**:... Mind you, Chelsea's offensive verve was offset by defensive sloppiness on Saturday so, despite Thierry Henry's absence, the chances of Barca scoring an away goal have got to be decent. My hardly-earned money's on 3-1 to the home team. And yours? Why? (Chelsea-Barcelona 2009)

Linguistically, this example, taken from the very opening of a sports commentary, contains several examples of synthetic personalization, i.e., the strategy of relating to the mass audience on a seemingly personal, one-to-one basis. This includes direct address to the readers and use of personal pronouns (*Mind you*), as well as questions for the audience (*And yours? Why?*). Such interactive openings are the rule rather than the exception in conversational live text commentary. Very often, the opening lines of the journalists' texts contain instances of verbal humor,[5] which serves to trigger the readers' recognition of the non-serious mode of presentation and indicates that other humorous and non-serious comments are possible.

Similar interactive linguistic elements tend to be deployed at the end of the commentary, cf.:

(3) Thanks for tuning in. And for your very many emails, some of which were good. Please call again. Bye. (Chelsea-Barcelona 2009)

In this example, the journalist in fact addresses the audience directly four times, performing several speech acts (thanking; evaluating—possibly in a joking manner; inviting or requesting; and closing the speech event). This is a written text, yet, interestingly, the author uses several lexical units which indicate his dependence on other genres as models for the live text commentary. 'Tuning in' is usually used in connection with radio broadcasts (in fact, the sequence of several appeals to the audience imitates the closing of radio programs), while 'call again' metaphorically relexicalizes the event as a personal, face-to-face encounter, in which the discourse participants share their physical presence.

Should these forms then be really counted as instances of synthetic personalization? Undoubtedly yes, since they are identical with the strategies which are conventionally used, for instance, in magazines and advertising. Yet, they significantly differ from them in that questions such as those described in example (2) and direct appeals to the audience as in example (3) do, in fact, open and close real interaction. Since the online medium and the synchronous nature of the production and consumption of the text make it possible for readers to email their reactions in real time, the questions in (2) are meant as genuine—not fake—invitations to the readers to become actively involved. Rather than linguistic traces of a verbal interaction that is synthetic, i.e., not real and only pretended, they are genuine conversational utterances, though made by means of the mass media to a wide, mutually anonymous and spatially dispersed audiences.

Questions such as *And yours? Why?*, when uttered in casual spoken conversation, are clear indicators that the speaker is yielding the floor, i.e., they indicate what conversation analysts call a transition relevance point (cf. Liddicoat, 2007). Questions—except for rhetorical questions and some types of echo and tag questions—are devices whereby one speaker selects the next speaker, who is drawn into the interaction because he or she is understood to be required to verbally reciprocate in the form of a reply.

However, are speakers really selected in the case of live text commentary and do these questions really count as transition relevance points? The answer needs to be in the affirmative: Yes, the written text can be approached from the perspective of conversational turn-taking, albeit it does not rely on this system of conversation management to the same degree as genuine conversation. This is because there is real interaction, with individual members of the mutually anonymous audience deciding for themselves when to take the floor by means of writing an email to the sports commentator. At that point, real interaction, though mediated by technology, occurs between a particular reader and the commentator. Still, that interaction is hidden from the other discourse participants: It will become public only once (or if) the commentator chooses to include a particular reader's reaction in his text, as in the following example:

(4) **13 mins:** "While you are by far my favorite of the Guardian MBM'ers,"[6] smarms Marc Howlett, who knows how to get published. "Your analysis cannot quite match the magnificence of that goal. Echoes of Zidane,

2002?" Considerably better, I reckon. (Chelsea-Barcelona 2009)

This example indicates that the inclusion of a citation from a reader's email is considered as prestigious. 'Getting quoted' means that one's comment was chosen from among numerous other comments sent in by other readers, whose contributions were not, at a given point of the commentary, deemed by the journalist to be more interesting, humorous, absurd, etc. Clearly, the commentator performs the function of the gate-keeper because he neither yields the floor to an open discussion nor allows completely free interaction (as in the case of online chat, where all contributions appear on the screen unless they are meant as private conversations). Instead, he retains the power of selecting the next contributor whose emailed utterance may fit his purposes best. Needless to add, the commentator has a dual social function, acting not only as a gate-keeper but also as an agenda-setter (cf. Chovanec, 2006, p. 28), because it is he who introduces topics for discussion. He is in control of the topics, even if they are voiced through the citations of his readers, because his readers do not have unlimited access to the text, only in a form that is sanctioned and controlled by the commentator. The text of the commentary, although ultimately heteroglossic and interactive, is a monologic enterprise created singlehandedly by a commentator, using citations from select readers in a way reminiscent of a person putting together pieces of a puzzle.

As example (4) shows, the places where the floor is yielded to the voice of a reader are also locations which have a high interactive potential, in that the two voices are juxtaposed. There can be a discussion between the reader and the commentator, who typically adds his own comment to the readers' utterance. This is the case with the reporting clause '... *smarms Marc Howlett, who knows how to get published*' in the above example. Not only does it provide an attribution to the citation, thereby pointing out the switch of voices, but it also makes explicit the commentator's evaluative stance on the content of the utterance and the motives of the contributor (cf. the choice of the disapproving verb '*smarms*' and the mildly critical '*who knows how to get published*', which seemingly alludes to the commentator's vanity).

Because the accessed voice of the reader is cited when and how it suits the commentator, the interaction between the two discourse participants is semi-authentic: It stands on the verge of real and staged interaction. It is partly real because the reader's utterance comes from an email and is therefore original and authentic. At the same time, it is partly staged because the citation is supplemented—or interrupted—by the journalist's comment, which fictionalizes the actual verbal encounter.

The juxtaposition of voices—and thus the interaction between them—often has a competitive nature. Since the journalist is in charge of the formation of the text and the way the readers' comments are incorporated into it, he typically provides a further comment on the accessed voices of the readers. His comments are clearly places where, from the perspective of conversation analysis, he claims the floor again. In example (4), the journalist negatively comments on the reader's 'smarming'. When the reader dismisses the commentator's analysis of the key event ('*Your analysis cannot quite match the magnificence of that goal*'), the journalist counters by self-praise ('*Considerably better, I reckon*'), pointing out the misguided perception of the reader.

These quasi-dialogical interactions are far from diplomatic; it is typically the commentator who threatens the pragmatic face of individual readers, commenting on the quality of their contributions. So there is an implicit criticism contained in the utterance in example (3) ('*Thanks for... your very many emails, some of which were good*') which implies, without stating it openly, that some emails were actually the opposite. At other times, the commentator may lash out with open criticism and even hurl ridicule at a reader, as in the following exchange:

(5) **51 mins** "Are you a fan of the great Forrest team of the mid 90s?" says Richard Beniston. "Two references to Collymore and the mighty Des "Bruno" Lyttle in a minute by minute during the World Cup Final indicates you have some love for Frank Clarke's boys." And the mis-spelling of Frank Clark suggest you don't, Richard. (France vs. Italy, Football World Championship Final 2006)

The criticism can be more playful, though. The reaction of the commentator—who always has the advantage of having the last word—can come in the form a disagreement that functions as a witty repartee, as in the following example:

(6) **PEEEEEEEEEEEP!!!!!!!!!!!** That's it! This tournament is one co-host down. "Is it true that the Swiss manager is actually the famous American actor Jack Lemmon," writes Tim Finnerty. I don't think the Swiss have a manager anymore, Tim. (Switzerland vs. Turkey, EURO 2008)

These examples serve as ideal illustrations of the pseudo-dialogic structure of these commentaries which draw on real online interaction between the discourse participants.

Interpreting Online Interaction from a Social Perspective

As hinted above, however, these conversational exchanges are not antagonistic, although they may emphasize differences rather than smooth them out. They are not interactions which are genuinely hostile; on the contrary, the mock hostility makes the interactions more dynamic and contributes to a greater enjoyment of the commentary. The elements of conflict and competitiveness are the commonly accepted prerequisites for verbal interaction in this text type, with the participants being aware that the journalist—as the gate-keeper—always has the upper hand.

The interaction between the accessed voices and the commentator can be interpreted as an instance of a verbal contest (Chovanec, 2006). It has a certain prototypical structure consisting of a sequence of moves by the discourse participants—first comes a citation from a reader's email, followed by the commentator's retort, which may be simultaneously critical and humorous. These two moves are potentially preceded or followed by a first-layer descriptive comment about the sports match (cf. example 6, where the conversational exchange is appended to a statement about the end of the match). Elements of verbal contest can be found on several levels: Not only in the joking interaction between the juxtaposed voices of the readers and the commentator, but also between the readers themselves (who strive to beat the others and get quoted), and even between various journalists (because the commentator produces his live text report on the basis of a TV broadcast and often quotes and ridicules his professional colleagues).

Similar staged verbal hostility, which highlights potential conflict rather than cooperation, has been documented by linguists from other contexts. Labov (1997[1972]), for example, noted the practice of 'playing dozens' among young African Americans, where the participants take turns in inventing highly offensive remarks about each other's family members. What matters is linguistic creativity and the ability to play with the code, despite the often vulgar content of the utterances. Importantly, in interpersonal interactions, humor often serves as a resource for mitigating conflict (cf. Norrick & Spitz, 2008) and is connected with conversational joking (Norrick, 1994, 2004).

Such linguistic practices have an interesting social function: They are actions through which the participants assert their group identity and establish a symbolic position within the group. The role of humor is crucial here: Word play,

punning, joking, etc., are clear indications that the communication is in a non-serious, i.e., playful, mode and that any potential verbal aggression does not count as an act of hostility. In fact, the ability to join in and construct humor is a very positive social skill, which is also important in live text commentaries. The joint construction of humor in online environments (cf. North, 2007, Chovanec, in press), whereby people 'play along', is an important strategy for increasing the involvement and interaction between the participants, as well as for developing coherence within discussion threads. This is because humor functions phatically—it "keeps topics 'in play' over a period of time, through the network of cohesive ties that it tends to develop" (North, 2007, p. 553).

The humorous and competitive interactions in online match reports can also be explained from a gender perspective, as an instance of 'male gossip'. It has been argued that competitiveness is a typical feature of male discourse (while female discourse is, in contrast, characterized more by co-operation, cf. Coates, 1988). The role of gender in sports reporting is also noted by Kuo (2003, p. 480), who claims, following Johnson and Finlay (1997), that gossip "is also used by men to create solidarity within their own gender group".

In their analysis of genres of casual conversation, Eggins and Slade (1997, p. 278) define gossip as a specific genre which "involves the pejorative judgment of the absent other" and serves several social functions, e.g., to establish and reinforce group membership and to act as a form of social control (Eggins & Slade, 1997, p. 283). (Humor, in any case, functions in a similar way – as a means of establishing and confirming group boundaries, since it marks off insiders from outsiders, cf. North, 2007, p. 551, and Norrick, 2004.) Needless to say, pejorative talk about others—footballers, coaches, other readers and commentators—underlies much of the discussion between the discourse participants in LTCs. In the broadest sense, male gossip (or 'banter') is "a means of affirming group solidarity and an unofficial channel for information" (Benwell, 2001, p. 21). Benwell, who sets out to identify the discourse style of men's lifestyle magazines, notes that in magazines, "the tone or style is almost entirely consistent: Ironic, humorous, anti-heroic, and explicitly interpersonal, emulating the processes of social male bonding" (Benwell, 2001, p. 20). In this respect, live text commentary is very similar: Its discourse style can likewise be described in terms of frequent humor, male gossip and language play as elements that, according to Benwell, make up "masculine styles of discourse".

This necessarily leads one to consider the genre of live text commentary in the broader terms of identity politics and identity construction. The particular linguistic and narrative structures that result in online discussion and interaction may then be seen as contributing to the formation of one's personal and group identity. In the case of live text commentary, this view is supported by the function of sports reporting in general "as a form of male bonding" (Kuo, 2003, p. 481). However, because the audience of computer-mediated communication is anonymous, the identity of most participants is only virtual, i.e., it is identity that "happens to occur online" (Benwell & Stokoe, 2006, p. 245). Similarly, the group of sports fans is not a real-life assembly of individuals who know each other but a virtual community that is brought together thanks to the interactive properties of computer-mediated communication (CMC).

As noted above, social cohesion within the group is realized in three ways. First, it is realized on the level of language (i.e., forms and structures that are conversational, informal, humorous or motivated by synthetic personalization, which is essentially a matter of presentation—style); secondly, on the level of the structure of the text/genre (i.e., the pseudo-dialogical exchanges, heteroglossia, as well as real online discussion and interaction between members of a virtual community); and thirdly, on the level of cognition (i.e., the nature of the information that is communicated, which is a matter of representation—content). The vir-

tual community is constructed by its participants through their reliance on a certain assumed degree of background knowledge.

This can again be very briefly illustrated through the example (4) above, where the reader makes the following comment: '*Your analysis cannot quite match the magnificence of that goal. Echoes of Zidane, 2002?*' The reference to the name of the famous French football player Zinedine Zidane and the year 2002 is exactly such a test of common shared knowledge: Members of the virtual group will enhance their sense of belonging to the group if they are able to understand the reference. Some of them may even follow up such comments in their own contributions, thereby developing the conversational discussion thread on a side topic. By contrast, the inability to understand several such comments which rely on knowledge assumed to be shared by sports fans, may have the contrary effect: Some readers may become alienated. Since the text becomes rather incoherent for them, they may come to feel that they are outsiders and stop reading. In this way, they may choose to discontinue their participation in the live text commentary as well as in the virtual group of sports fans, because they may no longer feel part of the community. The assumed background knowledge thus operates as an in-group marker.

CONCLUSION

This chapter has argued that the media landscape has undergone significant change as a result of recent developments in communication technology. Online journalism, for instance, has led to new patterns of news presentation which allow for active involvement by readers in discussions on relevant news items as well as other related (and unrelated) issues. While news reporting and online discussions are two distinct genres that are structurally brought together—but still kept formally apart on the newspapers' web pages—the new genre of live text commentary frequently merges the presentation of information with a simultaneous, coordinated discussion between the readers and the author of the text.

The texts of a live text commentary integrate online discussion and allow for real, though mediated and non-spontaneous, interaction. As has been shown by an analysis of an extensive set of live text commentaries from the area of sports reporting, the texts are organized on two narrative layers: The primary layer and the secondary layer. While the former consists of the journalist's description of events, the latter is essentially a discussion forum coordinated by the journalist, in which readers air their comments on the game as well as on quite unrelated topics. Within such a 'gossip layer', conversational threads develop over significant stretches of intervening text, with readers reacting to both one another's and the commentator's comments.

Linguistically, the online interaction in live text commentaries can be documented by the existence of pseudo-dialogical exchanges, the juxtaposition and mixing of different voices and the strategies of synthetic personalization. The language adopted is informal, colloquial, conversational, often displaying humor and creativity. At the same time, however, the nature of the interaction between the participants is competitive, because they try to outdo each other linguistically.

From a sociolinguistic perspective, the linguistic strategies increase the involvement of the readers. Their online interactions bear evidence of features which allow the interaction to be classified as an instance of 'male gossip'. The group of sports fans engage—both actively and passively— in discursive practices whereby they articulate their sense of belonging to an imaginary group.

Not only is the group a virtual community; it is also a temporal grouping. This means that it only exists for the duration of the live text commentary, although some of its mutually anonymous members may be brought together in the same online space on the occasion of some other match. There is evidence to show that, in these online interactions, there are some 'regulars' as well as 'newbies'. In this case, the group may develop a shared history and their subsequent online interactions and discussions may refer to previous occasions of the group members participating in the consumption and co-construction of a live text report.

Clearly, live text commentaries provide a fascinating area in which to document how virtual identity is enacted, pseudo-dialogic interactions sustained, and discussion threads cooperatively developed. For this reason, it seems a very promising field for multidisciplinary research – that is, research not only from a linguistic perspective, but also from the perspectives of media studies, journalism, sociology, identity theory, and others.

SOURCES

The text uses material from the following live text commentaries (minute-by-minute match reports) from guardian.co.uk; the online version of the British daily newspaper the Guardian – full texts are available online at http://www.guardian.co.uk/football/

- Chelsea vs. Barcelona, 2009 Champions League Semi-Final
- France vs. Italy, 2006 Football World Championship Final
- Switzerland vs. Turkey, 2008 European Football Championship
- Croatia vs. Turkey, 2008 European Football Championship

REFERENCES

Bakhtin, M. M. (1981). *The Dialogic Imagination: Four Essays* (Holquist, M., Ed.). Austin, London: University of Texas Press.

Bell, A. (1991). *The Language of News Media*. Oxford: Blackwell.

Benwell, B. (2001). Male Gossip and Language Play in the Letters Pages of Men's Lifestyle Magazines. *Journal of Popular Culture, 34*(4), 19–33. doi:10.1111/j.0022-3840.2001.3404_19.x

Benwell, B., & Stokoe, E. (2006). *Discourse and Identity*. Edinburgh: Edinburgh University Press.

Black, J., & Bryant, J. (1995). *Introduction to Media Communication* (4th ed.). Brown and Benchmark.

Chafe, W. (1997). Polyphonic topic development. In Givón, T. (Ed.), *Conversation. Cognitive, Communicative and Social Perspectives* (pp. 41–53). Amsterdam, Philadelphia: John Benjamins Publishing Company.

Chovanec, J. (2003). The mixing of modes as a means of resolving the tension between involvement and detachment in news headlines. *Brno Studies in English, 29*, 51–66.

Chovanec, J. (2006). Competitive verbal interaction in online minute-by-minute match reports. *Brno Studies in English 32*, 23-35. Retrieved from http://www.phil.muni.cz/wkaa/w-publikace/bse-plone-verze>\

Chovanec, J. (2008a). Enacting an imaginary community: Infotainment in on-line minute-by-minute sports commentaries. In Lavric, E., Pisek, G., Skinner, A., & Stadler, W. (Eds.), *The Linguistics of Football* (pp. 255–268). Tübingen: Gunter Narr Verlag.

Chovanec, J. (2008b). Focus on form: Foregrounding devices in football reporting. *Discourse & Communication, 2*(3), 219–243. doi:10.1177/1750481308091908

Chovanec, J. (2008c). Narrative structures in online sports commentaries. A presentation given at the 9th ESSE conference in Aarhus, Denmark.

Chovanec, J. (2009). "Call Doc Singh!": Textual structure and making sense of live text sports commentaries. In Dontcheva-Navratilova, O., & Povolná, R. (Eds.), *Cohesion and Coherence is Spoken and Written Discourse* (pp. 124–137). Newcastle upon Tyne: Cambridge Scholars Publishing.

Chovanec, J. (in press). Joint construction of humour in quasi-conversational interaction. In Kwiatkowska, A., & Dżereń-Głowacka, S. (Eds.), *Humour. Theories, Applications, Practices, 2 (2): Making Sense of Humour. Piotrków Trybunalski: Naukowe Wydawnictwo Piotrkowskie*.

Coates, J. (1988). Gossip revisited: language in all-female groups. In Coates, J., & Cameron, D. (Eds.), *Women in Their Speech Communities, New Perspectives on Language and Sex* (pp. 94–122). London, New York: Longman.

Dominick, J. R. (1993). *The Dynamics of Mass Communication* (4th ed.). New York: McGraw-Hill, Inc.

Eggins, S., & Slade, D. (1997). *Analysing Casual Conversation*. London, New York: Continuum.

Fairclough, N. (1989). *Language and Power*. London, New York: Longman.

Fairclough, N. (1995). *Media Discourse*. London: Hodder Arnold.

Fetzer, A. (2002). Put bluntly, you have something of a credibility problem. In Chilton, P., & Schäffner, C. (Eds.), *Politics as Text and Talk: Analytic Approaches to Political Discourse* (pp. 173–201). Amsterdam, Philadelphia: John Benjamins.

Fetzer, A. (2006). "Minister, we will see how the public judges you." Media references in political interviews. *Journal of Pragmatics, 38*, 180–195. doi:10.1016/j.pragma.2005.06.017

Fowler, R. (1991). *Language in the News*. London, New York: Routledge.

Graddol, D. (1994). The visual accomplishment of factuality. In Graddol, D., & Boyd-Barrett, O. (Eds.), *Media Texts: Authors and Readers* (pp. 136–157). Maidenhead: Open University Press.

Halliday, M. A. K. (1978). *Language as Social Semiotic*. London: Edward Arnold.

Halliday, M. A. K., & Hasan, R. (1986). *Language, Context and Text. Aspects of Language in a Social-Semiotic Perspective*. Oxford: Oxford University Press.

Horton, D., & Wohl, R. (1956). Mass Communication and Para-social Interaction. *Psychiatry, 19*, 215–229.

Jacobson, R. (1960). Closing statement: linguistics and poetics. In T. A. Sebeok (Ed.), Style in Language (pp. 350-77). Cambridge, MA: the MIT Press.

Johnson, S., & Finlay, F. (1997). Do Men Gossip? An Analysis of Football Talk on Television. In Meinhof, U. H., & Johnson, S. (Eds.), *Language and Masculinity* (pp. 130–143). Oxford: Blackwell.

Jucker, A. H. (2006). Live text commentaries. Read about it while it happens. In: J. K. Androutsopoulos, J. Runkehl, P. Schlobinski & T. Siever (Eds.), *Neuere Entwicklungen in der linguistischen Internetforschung. Zweites internationales Symposium zur gegenwärtigen linguistischen Forschung über computervermittelte Kommunikation. Universität Hannover, 4.-6. Oktober 2004* (Germanistische Linguistik 186-187) (pp. 113-131). Hildesheim: Georg Olms.

Jucker, A. H. (in press). "Beckham knocks it deep": Live text commentaries on the Internet as real-time narratives.

Kuo, S.-H. (2003). Involvement vs detachment: gender differences in the use of personal pronouns in televised sports in Taiwan. *Discourse Studies, 5*(4), 479–494. doi:10.1177/14614456030054002

Labov, W. (1997). Rules for Ritual Insults. In Coupland, N., & Jaworski, A. (Eds.), *Sociolinguistics: A Reader and Coursebook* (pp. 472–486). London: Macmillan. (Original work published 1972)

Lewis, D. M. (2003). Online news: a new genre? In Aitchison, J., & Lewis, D. M. (Eds.), *New Media Language* (pp. 95–104). London, New York: Routledge.

McQuail, D. (1987). *Mass Communication Theory* (2nd ed.). London: Sage Publications Ltd.

Norrick, N. R. (1994). Involvement and joking in conversation. *Journal of Pragmatics, 22*, 409–430. doi:10.1016/0378-2166(94)90117-1

Norrick, N. R. (2004). Issues in conversational joking. *Journal of Pragmatics, 35*, 1333–1359. doi:10.1016/S0378-2166(02)00180-7

Norrick, N. R., & Spitz, A. (2008). Humor as a resource for mitigating conflict in interaction. *Journal of Pragmatics, 40*, 1661–1686. doi:10.1016/j.pragma.2007.12.001

North, S. (2006). Making connections with new technologies. In Maybin, J., & Swann, J. (Eds.), *The Art of English: Everyday Creativity* (pp. 209–260). London: The Open University.

North, S. (2007). 'The Voices, the Voices': Creativity in Online Conversation. *Applied Linguistics, 28*(4), 538–555. doi:10.1093/applin/amm042

Pérez-Sabater, C., Peña-Martínez, G., Turney, E., & Montero-Fleta, B. (2008). A Spoken Genre Gets Written: Online Football Commentaries in English, French, and Spanish. *Written Communication, 25*(2), 235–261. doi:10.1177/0741088307313174

Schudson, M. (1978). *Discovering the News. A Social History of American Newspapers*. Basic-Books.

Shannon, C. E., & Weaver, W. (1949). *A Mathematical Model of Communication*. Urbana, IL: University of Illinois Press.

Talbot, M. (1995). A Synthetic Sisterhood. In Hall, K., & Bucholz, M. (Eds.), *Gender Articulated. Language and the Socially Constructed Self* (pp. 143–165). London, New York: Routledge.

Talbot, M. (2007). *Media Discourse. Representation and Interaction*. Edinburgh: Edinburgh University Press.

KEY TERMS AND DEFINITIONS

Audience Design: A term in sociolinguistics (introduced by Allan Bell) used to refer to speakers' accommodation of style (style-shifting) towards that of their audience, mainly in order to express intimacy and solidarity. It is a stylistic variation used by speakers for strategic purposes to fit particular types of audiences.

First Frame and Second Frame: Terms used to describe the existence of a multi-layered framework for the involvement of participants in mass-media speech events. This framework distinguishes public participants, who enter into face-to-face interaction in the studio, from private participants, whose intervention in the first-frame interaction is rather limited (cf. Anita Fetzer, 2002).

Heteroglossia: A term (introduced by the literary scholar Mikhail Bakhtin) used mainly in literary theory to describe the existence of several voices in a text, i.e., "another's speech in another's language". As a result of heteroglossia, even monologic texts may assume dialogic qualities/properties.

Interactiveness: A term used to describe the property of texts that strive to increase the readers' engagement by employing various linguistic strategies and rhetorical devices, such as synthetic personalization, heteroglossia, humor, the use of direct speech (authentic or stylized), the reliance on background knowledge and shared assumptions, etc. In this sense, these phenomena may re-create some characteristics of face-to-face interactions. Also known as 'interactivity'.

Quasi-Interaction: A term used to identify a type of interaction that is not an actual interaction because the interactants do not share their physical co-presence and do not alternate their roles as speaker and hearer. It differs from both face-to-face interaction (e.g., a personal conversation) and mediated interaction (e.g., a telephone conversation) in that an indefinite number of recipients is involved and the engagement is one-way and monological (cf. Mary Talbot, 2007). Also known as 'simulated interaction'.

Synthetic Personalization: A term in discourse analysis (introduced by the critical linguist Norman Fairclough) used to refer to the strategies that writers use when constructing their texts so that members of the mass audience have the impression of being treated as individuals. The strategies are widely used in, for instance, lifestyle magazines, and include direct address, imperatives, interpolation, informality, etc.

ENDNOTES

[1] Cf. the traditional distinction between 'hard news' and 'commentary', where the former refers to the disinterested presentation of 'facts' in the idealistic tradition of journalistic objectivity about real-world events (cf. Schudson, 1978), and the latter allows personalized presentation and evaluative assessment of events, whose coverage is tinged with the subjective perspective of the journalist. This distinction is also underlined by the differential treatment of authorship: While the author of 'hard news' is usually rather backgrounded (although newspapers sometimes include the name of the journalist), authorial attribution is crucial in the case of commentary.

[2] There is no commonly agreed name for this genre. From among the few studies dealing with the phenomenon, Jucker (2006) refers

to it as 'live text commentary'. Pérez-Sabater (2008) deal with it more specifically as 'online football commentary'; similarly Chovanec (2008a) uses the names 'live or online match report' and 'minute-by-minute (commentary)', which are semi-official labels used by some newspapers.

3   Cf. <http://www.guardian.co.uk/news/blog/2009/jun/20/iran-unrest>, retrieved on June 21, 2009.

4   This is the case with sports which are structured according to a time frame. The reporting of some other sports which are organized differently may go under different names, e.g 'over-by-over' in the case of cricket.

5   Increasingly, visual humor is also used in the form of digitally touched-up/modified photographs, often in the form of 'visual puns'.

6   The word *MBM'er* is an ad-hoc coinage by the reader. It is an agent noun formed through derivation from the commonly accepted acronym *MBM*, i.e., *minute-by-minute*, used for sports live text commentary (or, more precisely, online soccer commentary) in the British newspaper *The Guardian*.

Chapter 13

Online Interpersonal Interactions Utilizing an Extremely Limited Communication Interface

Terri Toles Patkin
Eastern Connecticut State University, USA

EXECUTIVE SUMMARY

This research examines the influence of a very limited communication interface on interactions within an online backgammon game context. The ways in which four factors controlled by the player (level of play, language selected, use of the preloaded chat interface, and game play) influence interaction are described. The ability of players to engage in impression management and express social presence within such a limited communication environment is considered in both positive and negative game contexts.

INTRODUCTION

I learned to play backgammon in college. My circle of friends included a small group of backgammon fanatics; they were demons at strategy and speed play. Soon, I invested in a modest imitation leather set and joined them at every opportunity – the dining hall, in the dorms, on a mountaintop during an ecology club hike. We didn't play for money, but simply reveled in the thrill of the game.

After college, no one in my life particularly shared my interest in moving little brown and white buttons around inside a box. I taught friends and family the basics, but Monopoly, Tetris, and computer-based role-playing games seemed to be a bigger draw. So I was thrilled when my new computer came pre-loaded with Internet Backgammon. I don't know why I had never sought out an online backgammon game before, but now I discovered fellow travelers available at the click of the mouse. I was ready to play; I was ready to re-enter the board game camaraderie I remembered of old.

Not pausing to read the instructions, I eagerly clicked on play and began my journey. All the old rules were still there in the mists of memory, and all my favorite rolls still came quickly to my fingers. 5-3 to the home board. Double sixes to cover the bar points. Take a risk with a 2-3 instead of playing it safe and moving 5 spaces to an already-covered

DOI: 10.4018/978-1-61520-863-0.ch013

point. Keep a pair in the back board and turn the game around at the last moment.

Eventually, I realized that I was indeed playing with people from around the world and that they were somehow ranked. The terse info box informed me that I was competing against "*Expert, English*" or "*Intermediate, Turkish*" or "*Beginner, Spanish.*" I felt oh-so-cosmopolitan as I imagined a sophisticated Frenchman or brooding Norwegian responding to my moves. I was part of something larger than myself. The global village was real.

Some of these people even talked to me. That is to say, messages from "Brown" or "White" appeared in a space below the board. It took me a while to notice this, as my early collegiate training had emphasized focusing solely on the board and not wasting game time with idle conversation.

One day, I surfaced from the competition long enough to explore the interface on my computer. Lo and behold! I could set my own ranking. Modestly, I moved myself up from the default "Beginner" to the more experienced "Intermediate," never dreaming that within a week I would redefine myself as an internet backgammon "Expert."

At the higher level, the game changed. The slower, more deliberate play of the Beginner was replaced by a faster paced, more aggressive game worthy of an Expert. No quarter was given, no mistakes were made (at least by the other side; I found myself desperately clicking the mouse to take back an ill-considered move on more than one occasion). This tougher playing field reminded me of my college days, but with one important difference. In those days, a tough game or match would end with smiles and joking threats to "get even next time." These games simply ended in defeat...when they ended at all. Sometimes the other player would disappear in what I could only assume was a huff after I took his piece; other times my opponent left the game abruptly for no reason that I could see.

I began to take note of each player's self-identification and check my own stereotypes.

With such a limited communication interface, one quickly leaps to a social decision based on any available information, no matter how limited. I found myself categorizing other players based on their game play as well as the conversations we held. The very limited nature of the available communication interface is the point of the research; communication within such a highly-constrained environment requires far greater creativity on the part of the participants than a simple free-form instant messaging interface. This paper explores communication in such interactions through an autoethnographic analysis of a yearlong journey playing online backgammon. In all instances, I played as "Expert, English" and responded to conversational overtures made by other players, but did not initiate conversations myself.

CONSTRUCTION OF THE PLAY FRAME

The social order is often reflected in play. Play is free (i.e. not obligatory), separated in time and space, noninstrumental, governed by rules yet with an unpredictable outcome, voluntary, and fictive (Caillois, 1979; Huizinga, 1950). Signs mark the beginning and end of playfulness: overt invitations to play and/or the simple commencement of play activity signal the onset of the play frame (Glenn and Knapp, 1987; Goffman, 1974). Play and games offer important reflections of the societies in which they are situated and play communities may become permanent even outside of the game context. "Contests in skill, strength and perseverance have...always occupied an important place in every culture, either in connection with ritual or simply for fun and festivity" (Huizinga, 1950, p. 195). Games are recreational activities characterized by organized play, competition, two or more sides, criteria for determining the winner and agreed-upon rules. As games satisfy no survival needs nor provide any direct environmental or physical benefit to the society, their expressive nature is plain. Games may model various cultural activities or social interactions. Games provide exercises in mastery: games of strategy related to mastery of the social system, games of physical skill associated with mastery of the self and environment, and games of chance linked with mastery of the supernatural (Roberts, Arth and Bush, 1959). Games consist of four types, according to Caillois (1979): competition (agôn), chance (alea), simulation (mimicry) and vertigo (ilinx), as well as combinations of those types. Games and play clarify cultural forms that have become so familiar that their meaning is lost or obscured as we conduct the familiar routines of everyday life. Indeed, it has been proposed that culture itself evolved from play (Caillois, 1979; Huizinga, 1950).

Geertz (1972) asserts that the expressive nature of play and games is important on two levels, the structure of the temperament of the individual (psychological structures) and the temper of the society (sociocultural ones). He utilizes the concept of "deep play" to indicate that some play may on the surface appear irrational, but at a deep symbolic level articulates social meaning. Two levels of symbolic communication are at play during a game: symbols that regulate the activity as such and are indispensable to it, and symbols that arise as a result of the inclusion of play in a larger metasystem. Along with the play itself is transmitted a message simply saying "this is play," which is mutually perceived by the players and which distinguishes play from other social forms it may resemble. Play simultaneously equates and discriminates map and territory. On a primary level, one plays the game in all seriousness, as though it "counted," but on a secondary level, the player is aware of the fundamental unreality of the activity. Play is integral to culture; any attempt to define play is to simultaneously define culture (Ehrmann, 1968; Saraf, 1977).

THE LIMITED COMMUNICATION INTERFACE

Communication in this particular online backgammon game venue is extremely limited. Four types of personal information may contribute to impression formation: Level, Language, Chat Interface, and Game Play. The first two, Level and Language, function primarily to establish role expectations before the start of a game, while the others, Chat Interface and Game Play, influence impression management throughout the course of a game or match.

Level of Play

Each player self-selects a level of play from a pull-down menu. Choices are limited to beginner, intermediate, or expert. Since the default setting for first-time use of the program is beginner, one may assume that a player with a self-rating of intermediate or expert is familiar with both the game of backgammon and the game interface. Occasionally, a player may select a level as a communicative tool: "expert" expresses a high level of self-confidence while "intermediate" may communicate a more modest evaluation of one's own capabilities. There is, of course, no guarantee that the game strategy performed during actual play will correspond with the self-selected level.

Language Selected

The language to which the user's computer is set automatically appears as the language for chat. Several languages have been encountered in the course of this research, including Arabic, Chinese, Czech, Danish, Dutch, English, French, German, Greek, Hebrew, Japanese, Korean, Norwegian, Portuguese, Russian, Spanish, Swedish, and Turkish. However, the chat interface automatically translates the comments into the language of each player, making the language choice less of a communication barrier. Language does, however, serve to partially identify the player; a casual amateur is unlikely to reset their computer to a different language merely to participate in a short entertainment with no real-world consequences. In most cases, it is probably safe to take for granted that *"Expert, Swedish"* is in fact Swedish or at least playing from a computer based in Sweden. Language appears in conjunction with level, so that the interface offers combination information, e.g. *"Expert, Chinese,"* or *"Intermediate, French,"* or *"Beginner, English."*

Chat Interface

Direct communication with the other player may only be conducted through MSN's limited chat function in which users may select remarks from a menu of 27 short comments. The comments merely appear in random order in a pull down list. When the player clicks on the preferred comment, the automatically translated message appears in the opponent's comment box (i.e. each player sees the statement in whatever language has been set as the default on that computer). Categories of comments include:

- Greetings: Hello, Good luck!
- Farewells: Goodbye, I'm going to play at zone.com, I have to go now
- Positive Comments on Game Play: Nice try, Good job, Good game, ☺, Nice roll, Nice move, It was luck
- Negative Comments on Game Play: Oops, ☹, Uh-oh, Not again, Ouch!
- Interactional Comments: It's your turn, I'm thinking, Are you still there?, Play again?, Thank you, You're welcome, Be right back…, OK, I'm back.
- General Comments: Yes, No

Anecdotal evidence indicates that most players use chat sparingly, when it is used at all. Many

games consist of a simple play transaction with no supplementary communication by the players. After an especially close or hard-fought game, a terse "Good game" might be sent. "Play again?" is rarely used, because the system automatically sets up a new game and the intent to play again can be communicated simply by rolling the dice and beginning afresh. On rare occasions, a player who must leave in the middle of a game may elect to send a message prior to disconnecting, but the general practice does not include communication. A few players do attempt to use chat to simulate a real-world game, starting with "Hello" and commenting on each roll, but this does not appear to be a popular option.

One option players have is to turn chat on or off. A player who turns chat off from the default on setting cannot send messages and cannot see any comments sent by the other player. In fact, the player with chat off can only receive messages that the other player has toggled chat to on or off during the game. It is unusual for players to change the chat setting in the course of a game.

Game Play

To some extent, each player evaluates the opponent's style of play as communicative. Backgammon is inherently competitive, but a player may select a move that is especially aggressive, risky, or merciful to the opponent. Choosing to attack multiple pieces while leaving one's own checkers at risk is considered aggressive, for example, while other moves, such as piling several pieces on one point of the board, are intrinsically safe but perhaps boring. And some moves are just so foolish that one marvels at the choices made by the opposing player. Game play functions analogously to nonverbal communication in a face-to-face setting: it comprises by far the largest proportion of meaningful interaction, yet it is often not acknowledged explicitly as an important element of communication.

Together all four factors combine to provide a dynamic, if limited, communication interface during a game of online backgammon. Level and Language influence choice of game partner, while Chat and Game Play shape player attributions during the course of the game. All may establish markers of interactional status within the limited communication infrastructure. Sometimes the conversation mimics the structure of a real-world conversation, with greetings and farewells sandwiching commentary on the game, as illustrated by this conversation between "Expert, Turkish" (white) and "Expert, English" (brown).

White> Hello

White> Good luck!

Brown> Hello

White> ☺

White> ☺

White> Play again?

Brown> Sorry, I have to go now

Brown> Good game

White ☺

At other times, the players may provide a running commentary on their own moves and those of their opponent, noting that a particular move was lucky or saying "goodbye" as they remove the opponent's checker from the board.

White> It was luck

Brown> Nice move

Brown> Good job

Brown> Hello

Brown> Goodbye

White> ☺

Brown> Good job

Brown> You're welcome

White> Nice move

Brown> Nice try

White> Thank you

Brown> Good job

The conversation is not always reciprocal. Periodically, one player may use the chat function at high speed. If the opponent is not as facile with chat or has little to contribute to the conversation, it may become a lopsided interaction.

White> It's your turn

White> Uh oh...

White> Nice move

White> Uh oh...

Chat may set the stage for identity construction, as well. A friendly "hello" or "good luck" may augur a positive game experience, while a negative initial remark may have the opposite effect. The anonymity of the game interface creates a challenging environment for interaction. The very nature of the limited communication interface of online backgammon conceals nearly all clues to identity outside of the game context. The gender, age, race, etc. of one's opponent remains a mystery.

One method of checking for concealed identity involves expectancy violation. Players anticipate that a self-described "expert" player would be able to quickly and accurately determine appropriate moves in a given situation, whereas a beginner might be likely to make tentative or badly chosen moves. Clearly, there is no way to ensure that the player's self-description is accurate. I strongly suspect at least one player of being an expert hiding behind a *Beginner* label because this player's game play is that of an expert in terms of both speed and strategy, belying the choice of descriptor. Experts will often decline to play with someone labeled as a beginner, choosing instead to search for an opponent until another expert player appears.

Aggressive Game Play may also be used to ascertain a player's identity. While players remain anonymous, certain trademark moves may identify a player as unique. For example, a player may consistently move either the lower or higher number in the dice roll first, may take the top piece or bottom piece from a board point, or may have a particular game play style (such as leaving many single pieces, or blots) early in the game. The force of habit makes these stylistic choices difficult for a player to abandon at will.

Players may utilize chat to restrain aggressive moves. Because there are so few sanctions, players whose position takes a turn for the worse more often than not exit abruptly in the middle of the game. However, the use of chat can provide a tenuous social connection that can, on occasion, discourage such behavior. In this conversation, Brown explicitly uses chat to indicate that departure from the game represents a friendly exit rather than being motivated by the course of the game.

White> Uh oh...

Brown> ☺

White> Nice roll

White> ☺

Brown> Oops!

White> ☺

White> Good game

White> Ouch!

White> Ouch!

Brown> It was luck

White> Good job

White> It was luck

White> It was luck

White> Not again!

White> ☺

Brown> Good game

White> Yes

White> It was luck

Brown> Sorry, I have to go now

The Chat function can assist with smooth completion of the game, but there is no long-term connection beyond a single match. Some players like to begin with a pleasant "Hello" and make a comment or two about game play, ending with a "Good game" or "Good Job." Sometimes, a player will enter "Be right back", which reassures me when it appears that a move is taking a great deal of time. A player who turns chat off in the middle of the game or who toggles the switch between on and off is clearly communicating something negative about the opponent. Chat may also be used to disarm the opponent:

White> Goodbye

White> Oops

White> Hello

Brown> ☺

Brown> Hello

The aggressiveness of White's play took me by surprise after this innocent-seeming greeting sequence. What began as a friendly game with someone I initially perceived to be less familiar with the game interface evolved into a hard-fought, almost hostile, battle that ended with neither player using the Chat interface at all.

I have played more than one game with a player who has created a stigmatized condition for himself and then redeemed his reputation by the end of the game. The Chat function is turned off, but the player opens the game play with aggressive and highly questionable moves. If my response reveals a competent and competitive counter-strategy or luck is running on my side, often this opponent will alter his strategy to an aggressive but more intelligent game. If, however, my response reveals weakness, the player will make moves so absurd that I am tempted to leave the game in frustration – he makes a mockery of the rules. Additionally, the doubling cube may be used as communication here: a double at the start of the game holds very different psychological meaning than one offered at a critical turning point of the game. Rejection of the double offer leads to automatic resignation, so it becomes an important force in communicating dominance.

Additionally, language choice has the potential to trigger pre-existing stereotypes among players. Cultural forces might cause *Expert, Greek* to feel more competitive towards *Expert, Turkish* than towards *Expert, Japanese*, for instance. One supposes that personal prejudices could come into play here: a player who does not like members of a particular ethnic group could well stereotype and stigmatize another player with that identification just as they might in a nonmediated setting.

There are no long-term relationships in this particular online setting, at least none that are overt. Since the chat comments disappear after each new encounter, there is no way to tell if the player is indeed the same person after a game reset. This conversation appears to offer confirmation of continuing player identity:

White> Are you still there?

White> Hello

Brown> Okay, I'm back

On the other hand, the following conversation took place in rapid fire when I (Brown) innocently began a game and was apparently mistaken for someone who had recently irritated *Expert, English*, writing as White:

White> Good game

White> Nice try

White> Are you still there?

Brown> No

White> Nice try

White> Goodbye

White> Good job

White> Goodbye

White> Are you still there?

White> Good job

White> Are you still there?

White> Good job

White> Are you still there?

White> Good job

White> Are you still there?

White> Goodbye

White> Good job

White> Good job

White> Good job

White> Good job

White> Good job

White> Good job

White> Good job

White> Good job

White> Are you still there?

White> Are you still there?

White> Are you still there?

White> Are you still there?

White> Are you still there?

White> Not again!

White> Nice try

White> Goodbye

Despite my ineffective effort to communicate that I was not, in fact, "still there," because I had just joined the game, White continues to interact as if I have caused some sort of injury in a previous game. It is likely that another player with my description had behaved in an unsportsmanlike manner, probably exiting from the game when White had an assured victory. Since the only infor-mation White has for forming an impression of me as an opponent is evidently identical to that of the previous player (level=expert, language=English, chat=on), s/he makes the assumption that I am that person. Because White leaves the game after this logorrheic invective, I am not given the opportu-nity to demonstrate through either game play or chat that I am not in fact the previous opponent, and find myself feeling frustrated and unjustly accused in response.

Occasionally, a player (usually "*Expert, English*" in my experience) uses the chat function to distract their opponent by sending a continual stream of messages not necessarily related to the game at hand. (This more often happens on weekend evenings than at other times.) When the opponent responds by disabling chat at his end, the distracter responds by clicking chat functionality on and off rapidly, causing a similarly distracting stream of information in the chat box. In cases such as this, I find myself wishing that the limited communication interface carried sanctions for bad behavior. Some players quit games after a poor initial roll, others do so after a risky move backfires. On more than a few occasions, I have been playing a hard-fought match and losing for much of the game. At some point – often close to the finish but sometimes early in the game – my canny strategy (or more often, the luck of the dice) causes a reversal in fortune. My opponent has certain victory snatched away as my piece dashes around the board while their piece sits impotent on the bar. At this point, more often than not, the other person – sometimes me, honesty compels me to admit – quits the game, leaving in what I can only presume is a huff, taking their pieces and going home like a small, spoiled child who doesn't get to have his way in the neighborhood ball game. Ludus interruptus.

Anecdotal evidence shows that this behavior is most common among those defining themselves as Experts. Since the system keeps no statistics and each game or match is played as a unique competition, there is no fear of long-term repercussion to one's ranking as a player. Perhaps the psychological trauma caused by the dissonance of being an Expert who loses a game could explain the departure?

Similarly, rewards for good behavior are not transferred beyond the immediate interaction. There is a small reciprocity debt that can be incurred during a backgammon game. For example, suppose I have a choice between taking your piece or another, equally effective, move that leaves your piece in safety. Choosing the latter may cause you to feel a debt of gratitude towards me and behave similarly when in a parallel situation later in the game, although this response has considerably less strength than it might in a face-to-face interaction. Analogously, a player who eschews the mid-game exit and plays through to the end of a losing game incurs my gratitude for his good sportsmanship. Perhaps I will remain online and play another game with this person, maybe even a full match, out of respect for the display of grit in the face of sure defeat, even though I really meant to turn back to my work after a short break.

Consider the following interaction between Brown (*Expert, German*) and White (*Expert, English*). Brown initially had chat turned off, but turned it on at the beginning of a second game. The players are well-matched in terms of skill, but White had won the hard-fought match due to many lucky double rolls. The course of the second game creates peril for Brown and ultimately for the game itself.

Brown> ☹

White> It was luck

[White rolls doubles]

Brown> Not again!

[Brown is forced into an unfortunate move by a bad roll]

Brown> You're welcome

[Several more doubles are rolled by White in the course of the game]

Brown> Not again!

Brown> Not again!

Brown> Not again!

Brown> Not again!

Brown> Not again!

Brown> ☹

White> ☺

Brown> Not again!

Brown> ☹

Brown> Not again!

Brown> ☹

Brown> Not again!

Brown> ☹

Brown> Not again!

Brown> ☹

Brown> Not again!

[Brown has clearly lost the match with only a few moves to go. Brown turns chat off. White has no way to communicate. Brown neither moves nor closes out of the window for almost an hour.]

One feature of the backgammon interface is the ability to formally resign the game. If the situation appears hopeless, a player may select a resignation option. It feels marginally better than simply losing after playing out the useless moves. But sometimes, my opponent rejects the offer to resign, perhaps because I did not offer enough points, perhaps because the person feels that the offer is premature and wants to play out the game anyway. However, there is no barrier to the original player simply quitting the game after offering to resign, leaving both parties aggravated and unfulfilled. This, of course, results in a threat not only to the game itself, but to the play frame itself.

LIMITED COMMUNICATION, UNLIMITED MEANING

Despite the limited communication interface available in online backgammon – or perhaps because of it – the attribution and assignment of identity has strong potential to occur. That a backgammon player utilizes the very limited information available in the first seconds of an online game – speed of the initial roll, the descriptors of expertise and language, the first moves of an anonymous opponent, perhaps the selection of a preloaded comment – speaks to our ability to draw detailed and complicated information from a highly limited and largely irrelevant data set. That a player can make attributions about an opponent's personality based on little more than the movement of a few virtual checkers is truly astonishing. It also raises the question of what happens in the process of impression management when more complicated inputs – such as gender, age and race – appear in face to face communication. With judgments of identity flourishing in such a limited communication interface, how do we cope with its exponential appearance in other contexts?

Even minimal communication is better than none at all. The occasional moment of shared emotion as my opponent chats "It was luck" and I respond with a smiley emoticon is a pale reflection of authentic communication, no matter how strong the social presence of the other player. I miss those golden college days when sharing a laugh over my backgammon board was as much a part of my identity as my black turtleneck and expensive British cigarettes. Backgammon is now part of my virtual identity, not my physical identity, but I'm happy to have even the shadow of the game flickering on my screen.

REFERENCES

Caillois, R. (1979). *Man, Play and Games*. New York: Schocken Books.

Ehrmann, J. (1968). Homo Ludens Revisited. In Ehrmann, J. (Ed.), *Game, Play, Literature* (pp. 31–57). Boston: Beacon Press.

Geertz, C. (1972). Deep play: notes on the Balinese cockfight. *Daedalus*, *101*(1), 1–37.

Glenn, P. J., & Knapp, M. L. (1987). The interactive framing of play in adult conversations. *Communication Quarterly*, *35*(1), 48–66.

Goffman, E. (1974). *Frame Analysis: An Essay on the Organization of Experience*. New York: Harper and Row.

Huizinga, J. (1950). *Homo Ludens: A Study of the Play Element in Culture*. Boston: Beacon Press.

Roberts, J. M., Arth, M. J., & Bush, R. R. (1959). Games in culture. *American Anthropologist*, *61*(4), 597–605. doi:10.1525/aa.1959.61.4.02a00050

Saraf, M. J. (1977). Semiotic signs in sport activity. *International Review of Sport Sociology*, *12*(2), 89–102. doi:10.1177/101269027701200206

KEY TERMS AND DEFINITIONS

Attribution: How people make perceptual judgments about the causes of other people's behaviors.

Communication Barrier: Obstacles to successful sharing of meaning between participants in an interaction.

Impression Management: Process through which individuals attempt to control the perceptions that others have of them in interaction.

Interactional Status: Hierarchy of prestige and social roles in an interaction.

Nonverbal Communication: Sending and receiving messages without the use of words, e.g. through gestures or facial expressions.

Reciprocity: Expectation of in-kind positive or negative responses by others in an interaction.

Social Presence: Awareness of the other person in a mediated interaction.

Stereotype: Standardized, simplified perception of members of a social group.

Stigmatized: Marked by a flaw in physical or social identity.

Chapter 14
Democratic Deliberation in Online Consultation Forums:
A Case Study of the Casino Debate in Singapore

Kevin Y. Wang
University of Minnesota-Twin Cities, USA

EXECUTIVE SUMMARY

This chapter examines the extent to which the Internet can represent a place for negotiation, consensus building, and civic participation using Singapore's online consultation portal and the debate over the decision to build the nation's first casino resort as a case study. The structural design of the consultation portal and the entire content of a discussion thread with 508 posts were analyzed with a conceptual framework drawn from previous studies of democratic deliberation. Findings suggest that while the forum reflects some criteria for deliberation, the lack of transparency and government participation raises the question over the quality of the discourse and overall effectiveness of this online medium. Current challenges, recommendations, and directions for future research and development are discussed.

BACKGROUND

The rapid diffusion of information communication technologies (ICTs) over the last two decades has brought changes to the political landscape throughout the world. It has been noted that the Internet's unique technological properties, such as interactivity, immediacy, connectivity, point-to-point and non-hierarchical modes of communication, low cost to users, and accessibility across national boundaries (Barber, Mattson, & Peterson, 1997),

will reduce the distance and barriers between voters and politicians, and consequently facilitate a more direct citizen involvement in the political process (Agre, 2002). One of the many ways that such civic engagement can be seen is through the discussion of political issues *online* – in chatrooms, message boards, blogs, social media sites, and other types of web-based forums.

Although many previous studies of online political talk have noted that the Web provides a meeting place for people from different social, cultural and political backgrounds to form communities, build social relationships, share opinions, and discuss

DOI: 10.4018/978-1-61520-863-0.ch014

issues with one another (Baym, 1995; Rheingold, 1993; Wellman, 1999), others have observed that, rather than facilitating diversity, people tend to interact with users who share similar interests and values (Van Alstyne & Brynjolfsson, 1996) and hear the echoes of their own voices (Sunstein, 2001). Whether the Internet can truly represent a public sphere for negotiation, consensus building, and democratic deliberation remains to be seen, but the conditions in which online discussion may or may not flourish, and the criteria used to evaluate its outcomes are key to answering this question.

This chapter addresses these issues through the lens of a case study that explores the structure and the content of an online discussion thread in Singapore's online consultation forum. As the high-tech hub of Southeast Asia, Singapore is known for its adoption and development of information communication technologies in the private and public sectors. Recent studies indicate that Internet penetration rate in Singapore has reached 67.4%, with more than three million users (Internet World Stats, 2009). Singapore's electronic government scheme and the overall e-readiness have also consistently received high praises from benchmark reports (e.g., Economist Intelligence Unit, 2008; West, 2007). While these achievements are remarkable, Singapore is also known for its censorship and control over the Internet, a practice that has long attracted criticism domestically and abroad (e.g., Amnesty International, 2004; Gomez, 2000). The juxtaposition between the freedom afforded by technological advancement and the restrictions imposed by government regulation therefore makes Singapore a unique case.

In 2005, the Singapore government proposed plans to develop two casino-based entertainment resorts in an effort to stimulate its tourism industry. The decision to build the nation's first casino generated a vibrant debate among Singaporeans over whether the government should abandon its long held position against legalized gambling. In the months leading up to the final announcement, the government solicited views and feedback on the subject matter from the public through various communication channels, including several online discussion threads in its online consultation portal. By examining the effectiveness, or lack thereof, of this online medium to encourage public discussion and facilitate deliberation, this case study hopes to contribute to our understandings of online discussions in a political context and also to the broader conversation about the promise of the Internet as a public sphere.

SETTING THE STAGE

Online Consultation and Relevant Research

Online consultation, a term that refers to the government's use of web-based technologies to seek policy suggestion and feedback from the public, is an emerging trend in electronic government research and practice. The Organisation for Economic Co-operation and Development (OECD) defined online consultation as, "A two-way relation in which citizens provide feedback to government. It is based on the prior definition by government of the issue on which citizens' views are being sought and requires the provision of information" (OECD, 2001, p. 5). In other words, the government identifies the issues for consultation, sets the questions and manages the process, while citizens are invited to contribute their views and opinions through web-enabled applications.

From the government's perspective, online consultation represents one of the many communication *channels* that, in addition to other traditional means, are used to reach out to the public. From the citizen's perspective, it may be seen as an online meeting *place* where people interact with one another to express their opinions or discuss public policy issues. However, online consultation differs significantly from other online fora, such as blogs, bulletin boards, or social networking sites, in the sense that it is considered to be an official mechanism of the state and not merely a platform for social interaction. As such, the practice of online consultation is often guided by legislations that establish the implementation process or require the outcome of the consultation to be analyzed, archived, and relayed back to the policy circuit. Many countries around the world (e.g., Canada, Sweden, The Netherlands, United Kingdom, and the United States) have developed different forms of online consultation, varying along the lines of online public hearings, online town hall meetings, online guest or panel Q&A, live multimedia events, public comment forums, and online focus groups (Clift, 2004).

As a relatively new phenomenon, previous studies of online consultations have initially emerged from the government circle with a focus on the development of procedural guidelines and policies for implementation (Macintosh & Whyte, 2003; Poland, 2001). With online consultation and other similar e-government practices gaining popularity in recent years, a steady stream of scholarly research on citizen participation in policy making has also emerged. For example, Coleman and Gøtze (2001) argued that various forms of online public engagement platforms would strengthen the quality of representative democracy by creating opportunities for mutual learning between citizens and their representatives. Macintosh, Robson, Smith, and Whyte (2003) noted that increased level of civic participation may be particularly true among young people, who are often more comfortable with new communication technologies. Although the democratic and participatory potential of online consultation and related practices are widely recognized (e.g., Chadwick, 2003; Coglianese, 2005; Fountain, 2001; Shulman, Schlosberg, Zavestoski, & Courard-Hauri, 2003), there is also a general consensus on several areas of concerns.

For instance, Stephens, McCusker, O'Donnell, Newman, and Fagan (2006) found a culture of cynicism exists among citizens with respect to state/administration initiated consultation pro-cesses. This lack of trust in the authenticity of the process raises the question of whether the online consultation process can truly be effective. As Coleman (2004) suggested, "For online consultations to be seen as more than a gesture, there must be tangible evidence that [government officials] are interacting with the public and taking views online contributors into account in their deliberations" (p. 20). In addition, Noveck (2005) observed that in order to increase the level of participation, the design of the online platforms must facilitate and convey a sense of community to the participants. Finally, Whyte and Macintosh (2001) pointed out that the design of public consultation systems should promote shared awareness of activity and identity among users, while creating a sense of transparency in the consultation as well as the decision-making processes.

All of these issues indicate that, while online consultation represents a promising public practice and a rich subject for scholarly inquiry, more interdisciplinary dialogue and research is needed to develop guidelines for conducting consultation, identify criteria for evaluation and assessment, and design appropriate technological platforms that would facilitate citizen interaction and participation.

Theoretical Issue: Criteria for Democratic Deliberation

The idea that policy decisions should emerge from a dialogue involving citizens and their elected officials is the fundamental premise behind online consultation practices, and is also one of the central tenants of representative democracy. Many scholars (e.g., Cohen, 1989; Habermas, 1984; Rawls, 1971) have argued that a healthy democratic system requires not just conversation about political issues, but a unique process of "deliberation" that is significantly different from daily conversation. In the words of John Elster (1998), this is a collective process that requires "the participation of all who will be affected by

Table 1. Criteria for democratic deliberation

Criteria	Definition
Autonomy	The deliberation and the participants must be free from manipulation of political/economic power.
Transparency	The process should be visible from outside, and contributions should be fed to the policy making circuit by formal mechanisms.
Equality of access	Every person affected by the validity claims under consideration is equally entitled to participate.
Privacy and trust	Privacy and anonymity of the participants must be protected to encourage candid discussion and the level of trust.
Enlightened understanding	Participants must have a good understanding of issues being discussed in order to make sound judgment.
Reflexivity	Participants must critically examine their cultural values, assumptions, and interests, as well as the larger social context.
Mutuality	Participants must attempt to understand the argument from the other's perspective. This requires a commitment to an ongoing dialogue with difference in which participants respectfully listen to each other.

the decision of their representatives, and includes the decision making by means of arguments offer by and to participants who are committed to the values of rationality and impartiality" (p. 8).

Dahlberg (2001), drawing heavily from Habermas' earlier work on communicative action, constructed a model that specifies the criteria for democratic deliberation as: (a) being autonomous from economic and political manipulation; (b) demonstrating rational reasoning, rather than dogmatic assertions; (c) examining the issue with reflexivity to the larger social context; (d) demonstrating a commitment to mutual dialogue with respect; (e) displaying sincerity, with each participant making an effort to understand all relevant information; and (f) showing inclusion and equality toward all participants. Habermas was not alone in advocating specific criteria for this deliberative process. Barber (1984), in presenting his case for a "strong" democracy, also argued that a "strong political talk" should involve: (a) an articulation of interests; (b) persuasion; (c) agenda setting; (d) affiliation and affection; (e) mutuality; (f) self-expression; (g) re-formulation and re-conceptualization; and (h) community-building. Similarly, Dahl (1991) noted that effective participation, equality, enlightened understanding and control of agenda are the requirements for deliberation.

Although the specific terminology used by these scholars may differ, the central tenets overlap with one another to describe the ideal condition in which an informed citizenry can actively participate in the formation of public policy decisions through a process of democratic deliberation. The key criteria for democratic deliberation as described in previous literature can be summarized in Table 1.

Research Questions

If one were to accept that the goal of online consultation is to gather citizen feedback on public policy issues through dialogues and conversations, and that such interaction among citizens and their elected officials is at the heart of democratic governance, then the abovementioned criteria for democratic deliberation provide a framework for evaluating online consultation practices. Therefore, the broader question for the case study was: to what extent does Singapore's online consultation forum reflect the ideals of democratic deliberation?

More specifically, this larger issue could be further divided into two research questions that explore both *structural* and *content* perspectives. Here, "structure" referred to the design of the online platform, the guidelines for discussion, and the other characteristics of the online consulta-

Table 2. Research question 1 and criteria for democratic deliberation

Research Question #1: To what extent does the *structure* of Singapore's online consultation reflect the ideals of democratic deliberation?	
Sub-Questions:	Criteria for Democratic Deliberation Measured:
What is the degree of administrative control on the online consultation forums?	Autonomy
What is the level of transparency in the management of the online consultation forum?	Transparency
What are the criteria for participating in the online consultation forum?	Equality of access
How are the issues of privacy and anonymity handled on the online consultation forum?	Privacy and trust
What kind of background information of the issues discussed in the online consultation forum does the government provide?	Enlightened understanding

tion practice that may create an environment to facilitate or impede democratic deliberation. For example, whether there were barriers to participate in consultation process might be an indicator the degree of equal access. Likewise, the extent to which background information of the policy issue being discussed was provided in the discussion forum might also signal whether an enlightened understanding of the subject matter could possibly be achieved.[1] Table 2 shows Research Question 1 and the criteria for democratic deliberation measured from the structural standpoint:

On the other hand, the "content" perspective referred to the actual posts and opinions expressed by participants in the discussion. For example, the type of arguments and the sources that users relied on to make their claims might reflect the level of reflexivity demonstrated by the users. Further, whether the interaction led to a sustained debate among participants, as seen in the frequency and diversity of participation, might indicate the level of mutuality in the discussion forum. Table 3 shows Research Question 2 and the criteria

for democratic deliberation measured from the content point of view.

CASE DESCRIPTION

Online Consultation in Singapore

In Singapore, the practice of online consultation is administered by the Feedback Unit, an office set up in 1985 to solicit citizen feedback on public policy issues in order to help the government shape and fine-tune its policy decisions. Key operations of the Feedback Unit range from hosting dialogue sessions, tea sessions, or public forums, to publishing two publications, *Policy Digest* and *Feedback News*, that aim to help Singaporeans to understand the rationale behind these policies (Feedback Unit, 2005). The online consultation portal (http://www.feedback.gov.sg) was launched in March 1997 to reach out to Internet-savvy and younger Singaporeans. As seen in Figure 1, the portal includes several feedback mechanisms

Table 3. Research question 2 and criteria for democratic deliberation

Research Question #2: To what extent does the *content* of Singapore's online consultation reflect the ideals of democratic deliberation?	
Sub-Questions:	Criteria for Democratic Deliberation Measured:
What kinds of opinions are expressed? What is the level of flaming?	Reflexivity
What is the frequency of participation? What is the level of diversity among participants?	Mutuality

such as: online consultation papers on different policy topics, online polls, an online discussion forum, policy digests that provide relevant background information, a general feedback/reply area, a specific comment section for cutting red tape and government waste, and a separate section on integrated casino resort. In addition, the portal features a calendar of events, a newsroom for media relations, and an area where selected official responses to citizen feedbacks are posted.

The Debate over Legalized Gambling

In Singapore, a debate involving government officials, political parties, religious groups, industry lobbyists, and concerned citizens took place after the government announced in April 2005[2] its plan to build two casino-based Integrated Resorts (IRs) – and thereby effectively legalized gambling in the country. While the Singapore government had for many years opposed the establishment of casinos for fear of creating social ills in the country, the decision to change the long-standing policy against casinos was primarily based on the economic benefits that integrated resorts might bring. It was projected that the two Integrated Resorts would boost Singapore's tourism industry, while creating about 35,000 jobs directly or indirectly (Ministry of Trade and Industry, 2005). On the other hand, opponents of legalized gambling cited the potential negative impacts on individuals or the society at large. Concerns about social order, public corruption, gambling addiction, and moral values were noted by several social and religious groups as reasons for opposition to the government plan (Au, 2004; Chia, 2004; Teo, 2004).

To address these potential social issues associated with legalized gambling, the Singapore government proposed a set of social safeguards that included: "a minimum age requirement, a membership system for Singapore residents, self-exclusion programs, guidelines on credit extension, voluntary loss limits, advertising guidelines and patron education" (Ministry of Trade and Industry, 2004,

para. 3). At the same time, citizen feedback was solicited via the online consultation portal. The data for the present study was drawn from one such discussion entitled, "Social Safeguards for Integrated Resort with Casino Gaming," with a total of 508 posts between December 30, 2004 and April 24, 2005. The discussion thread was content analyzed in its entirety.

Structure of the Discussion Forum

As described previously, the criteria for democratic deliberation were used as a framework to explore both the structure of the discussion forum and online consultation portal, as well as the content of the discussion itself. First, the degree of administrative control that the government had over the discussion forum symbolizes the level of autonomy – or whether the consultation forum was free from manipulation of political and economic power. The Singapore forum was free from commercial influences as it clearly prohibited any direct selling, advertisement, or promotional messages. However, since the online consultation portal represents a subset of a larger government apparatus, it cannot be totally free from administrative control. Although prior approval was not a requirement for posting, government administrators had the right to remove posts that were deemed irrelevant to or inappropriate for the topic of discussion, and had taken such action against several participants' posts. The removal of these posts raised questions over the impartiality of the discussion, and such concern was expressed by many. For instance, one participant wrote:

Dear Webmaster, I am re-submitting my post after a little tweaking? Hope you can allow it this time since I have taken out a few things I thought which might have incurred your honorable wrath? I had also emailed you privately but got no reply. Please let me know where I am wrong so I can improve? (User comment, 2005)

Figure 1. Singapore's online consultation portal. This screenshot was taken in June 2005 (© 2005, Government of Singapore. Used with permission.)

Second, the level of transparency is another important criterion of democratic deliberation, as determined by whether the management of the consultation forum was visible from outside, and whether the contributions were fed to the policy making circuit. In this respect, the consultation portal clearly fell short of providing adequate information that allowed users and the public to understand the operations of the online platform, as well as the online consultation process in general. For example, while the website had clearly stated "Terms of Use" that described different guidelines ranging from the protection of intellectual property rights to many other important issues regarding proper usage, the government could change the general practices of the consultation portal in its sole discretion without notice (Feedback Unit, 2005). In addition, the consultation portal did not present adequate information that explained the consultation process (e.g., how are the posts handled/followed up), or the similarity of and differences between feedback channels available on the consultation portal. For the discussion forum, the government offered a brief netiquette guideline that prohibited defamatory statement,

name-calling, obscene, vulgar, sexually-oriented, hateful, or threatening messages. The website, however, did not provide a clear definition of what content would be considered "irrelevant" or "inappropriate" that might warrant a post's removal.

Another area where the level of transparency can be evaluated is whether government officials respond to or participate in the consultation process. While official responses were posted in a general area, government officials did not participate in specific discussion fora, which invariably provoked questions from the users. For instance:

Hi people at Feedback Unit, Really... if you would be so kind as to post a note to say "Hi", I think we would feel less strongly that you're not capturing our opinions...In fact, I feel that if *consultation* is to be done effectively, someone from the government should be here probing us with questions and counter-arguments. Feedback can be one way, but to really call it consultation, there should be two way exchanges...That will really help in breaking the perception of an un-listening government. (User comment, 2005)

While participation from government officials was lacking, general contact information for the Feedback Unit, including its mailing address, phone or fax number, and email address, was listed on the website. A detailed staff listing or directory was not available.

Third, equal participation is another aspect of democratic deliberation. For the online consultation portal in Singapore, participation appeared to be open and without restrictions based upon citizenship, age, or gender. The website only made minimal technical recommendations with regards to web browsers, and mentioned nothing about Internet connection speed or other hardware requirements. The consultation portal also stated that the content of the website is accessible for the hearing and vision impaired. An evaluation of the portal using "WAVE 3.0 Accessibility Tool," proprietary software that assesses the level of web-accessibility using industry and government guidelines, confirmed that the website was compatible to various accessibility standards.[3]

In addition, the issues of privacy and anonymity are important factors in online discussion, as they would influence the degree of trust and dictate the level of participation. In this regard, the consultation forum offered an environment that protected privacy and anonymity. A privacy policy was found on the consultation portal, which stated that the government does not capture personally identifiable data if users were only browsing the website. However, when users were participating in the activities offered by the site, such as sending feedback or posting messages in the discussion forum, the government claimed that it could collect personal data and share them with relevant government entities. Although users had the option of creating an account – thereby transmitting personal information – to the Feedback Unit, there was no required registration process before participating in the forum. Therefore, it is unclear what and how personal data were gathered when users did not voluntarily provide them. Further, posts were displayed in the discussion thread without identifiable information, such as e-mail addresses or IP addresses, which could be used to track a user's geographical location. Only a screen-name chosen by the user and the date and time of the post were shown alongside the actual message. In other words, citizens could decide to remain totally anonymous when participating in the discussion fora.

Finally, for democratic deliberation to be successful, participants of the discussion must also have an enlightened understanding of the issues being discussed in order to make a meaningful judgment. Since it was not possible to assess individual participants' level of knowledge by simply examining the content of the posts, enlightened understanding could only be explored structurally, by looking at whether the background information of the issues being discussed was provided on the portal. Since the Singapore government defines the topic of discussion in the online consultation practice, it should follow that the government would present any relevant information, such as statistics, official statements, or white papers, for participants to peruse. However, Singapore's online consultation portal failed to provide adequate information in this regard. For the particular discussion thread analyzed by this case study, the government offered only a short introduction to the topic of discussion, and an external link to the Ministry of Trade and Industry website that outlined the social safeguards for casino gaming. No other information or additional links to relevant government offices were found.

Content of the Discussion

In terms of the content of the discussion itself, the frequency of posts and interactions among users are key indicators of the mutuality and diversity of the discourse. This discussion thread had a total of 508 posts contributed by 165 uniquely identifiable users and 30 anonymous users. The average word count for each post was 220, suggesting that participants did put in some efforts to their posts, while the longest post was 1579 words. Posts were skewed toward the latter end of the four-month period specified by the government, perhaps reflecting the gradual buildup of public opinion and increased media coverage throughout the consultation period.

It is worth noting that, although there were 165 uniquely identifiable users, the discourse was dominated by a small number of active participants. For instance, five users contributed 32% of the total posts, and four other users each contributed 10 or more posts. In contrast, there were 112 users with only a single post. In other words, the level of participation in this particular discussion forum may not be characterized as broad and diverse. Further, among the 508 posts, 347 were identified "new posts" while only 141 were considered to be in "response" to other participants, indicating that there was not a sustained engagement among the participants. Overall, these statistics indicate that a sense of mutuality was somewhat lacking in the consultation forum. Finally, there was very little evidence of flaming, defined here as exchanges that involve personal attacks, insults, or hostile provocations, perhaps due to the fact that government administrators were removing potentially objectionable messages from the forum.

In terms of content, a small portion of the discussion (53 posts) was identified as irrelevant to the topic of discussion. Although a great majority (465 posts) did touch upon the general issue of integrated casino resorts, only 90 posts commented specifically on question of social safeguards, which was the main subject for consultation. Here is an example of a post that focused on the issue at hand:

I understand and support cabinet's decision of proceeding with the IR with casino. I agree that safeguards are quite necessary to address any negative social impacts. I would like to add a couple of points on the present safeguards: (a) introduce a new subject named "To be a wise gambler - Gambling education" into our educa-tion system at secondary level or incorporate it into social studies; and (b) increase the taxation on the profit from gambling. Whereas we always talk about losing money from gambling, I believe some of gamblers could be luck enough to make profits in a short term. So the government should impose a higher tax on this part of income. (User comment, 2005)

To explore signs of reflexivity – that is, the participants' ability to critically examine the issue at hand beyond their personal experiences or circumstances – each post was qualitatively analyzed to identify any source of reference, as well as the viewpoint that upon which the argument was based. The analysis revealed that, when expressing their opinions, the great majority of the post (417 out of 508) referenced personal anecdotes and beliefs as the basis of the claims. Of the 91 posts that did draw from other sources, 32 referenced other participants' comments, 30 referenced the media, 27 used a combination of both media and user, and only two posts referred to government material provided on the consultation portal. The large number of posts that relied on personal sources indicates that participants rarely go out of their ways to retrieve other information to support their arguments.

However, as for the viewpoints and perspectives expressed in the discourse, 360 out of 508 posts were identified as going beyond personal interests and belief and connecting issue to the society at large. Among them, 52% argued from a moral and social standpoint, 23% referred to the commercial and economic issues behind the casino plan, while 25% used a combination of both. As discussed previously, opponents of the casino resort argued that gambling, like many other controversial issues such as prostitution or drug use, are matters of morality that would create more social problems when legalized. This argument was highly contested by many participants. For example:

Prostitution is wrong, is a sin. Who are we to judge? Why is it a sin? Always? If it is a matter of life and death, if it is part of a culture (as we know that some places do condone it), can we say that? Are you going to banish all 'prostitutes' to hellfire? Gambling is a sin? Can it be a game? Can it be fun? It is the addiction that comes from compulsion that and how we try to feed that compulsion that brings on the woes of addiction. And that can come about with any activity. Gambling is so addictive because of the money factor, and the adrenalin that come about with the thought of making money the easy way. (User comment, 2005)

Other participants went a step further to criticize whether the Singapore government's reversal on its longstanding position against legalized gambling is consistent with other government policies, and to question whether the economic growth promised by the casino resorts may truly be realized:

Upfront, it looks like the introduction of Casino will create some 10,000 job vacancy, however, has it been assessed how many percent of these jobs could be filled by fellow Singaporeans and attribute to the reduction in local unemployment rate? Will it require even more foreign workers to fill the vacancy and introduce further social or management problems? Current government plans to develop Singapore into educational hub, cultural center, health care center, sports center are all in the line of ethical and healthy society. However, will the introduction of casino contradict with the above initiatives? (User comment, 2005)

These posts, along with other similar ones in the forum, reflect the complexity behind the casino plan, and demonstrate that many participants were able to consider the issue from multiple perspectives.

Finally, the tone of the post was analyzed to identify whether the message expresses a pro or anti-government stance. Given Singapore's record of media censorship, it was particularly relevant to see if strict government regulation over media content and information had any negative effect on people's willingness to articulate their true opinions toward public policy. Interestingly, 13% (68 posts) of the total messages expressed a clear "pro-government" position that either supported the creation of casino resorts in Singapore or approved the government's scheme for social safeguard. In contrast, 20% (100 posts) had an "anti-government" stance and opposed the government proposal for casino gambling. Although the vast majority of the posts in the discussion thread could not be clearly identified as falling into either category, a sense of cynicism over the authenticity of the consultation process and the government's seriousness in gathering citizen feedback was widespread. For instance, one participant remarked:

All along I already expected it. No matter what we common citizens say, if the Government say they are going to do it, they will do it. You can talk about the pros and cons until pigs fly. THEY DO NOT CARE, NEITHER DO THEY LISTEN. No wonder youths today could not care less about politics. They are very smart, they know there is no point talking so much because their views will never be taken into consideration. They might as well spend their time doing things which are so much more fun while they are still in the prime of youth. (User comment, 2005)

CURRENT CHALLENGES IN SINGAPORE'S ONLINE CONSULTATION FORUM

The results of the content analysis, as described above, illustrate the extent to which Singapore's online consultation forum reflected the various elements of a democratic deliberation. Structurally, the forum created an environment where equal participation, privacy, and anonymity were protected. The participants of the forum also showed some signs of reflexivity by examining the casino plan from multiple perspectives beyond personal interests. Based on the findings, it is reasonable to conclude that the online consultation forum in Singapore may have the potential to become a place for civic engagement and consensus building. However, such an ideal cannot be realized without addressing a number of issues that prevent an open and productive dialogue from occurring.

The first issue facing Singapore's online consultation forum is that the discourse in the discussion forum appeared to be fragmented from both structural and substantive standpoints. Structurally, it was difficult for viewers or other participants in the discussion thread to follow a specific line of reasoning or debate because the website only displayed 25 posts per page in reverse chronological order. For example, when users replied to one another, the original post to which he or she was responding to did not appear side-by-side, or could even be located on the same page because it was posted at an earlier time. This technical limitation created confusion and misunderstanding that eventually resulted in a lack of *sustained* discussion on the subject matter. In addition, the high number (121) of single post authors also indicates that ongoing discussion among participants was rare. The effort by government administrators to remove inappropriate or irrelevant content further increased the severity of this problem, as several authors responded to posts that had been deleted, making it difficult for others to follow the conversation.

Content-wise, with less than 20% of the posts (90 out of 508) specifically commenting on the topic set out by the government for discussion, it can be argued that the discussion failed to achieve its original purpose. In addition, while many participants did go beyond their personal interests and concerns to consider the issue in light of the larger society, the majority relied solely on personal anecdotes and beliefs as the basis of their opinions. Although drawing from one's own

values or experiences is natural in interpersonal conversation, for the results of online consultation to be taken more seriously by elected officials or policy makers, the participants of these online discussions can also utilize other sources, such as media reports, government statements, or relevant websites, to build their arguments with more objective and credible evidence. This ability to approach an issue critically from multiple angles with diverse viewpoints is central to the idea of reflexivity in democratic deliberation, but it was not fully seen in the case of Singapore's online consultation forum.

The second issue that stems from the findings of this case study is that many participants had strong reservations about the government's intention to listen to and consult with the public on this particular issue. As noted previously, the sentiment of distrust and resignation were vividly expressed in many posts. Here is another example:

I think it has already been decided long ago that the casino WILL be built regardless of what we say. I suspect they purposely started a so-called "debate" just to hype it up, to get people interested, to get people to talk about it…if that was what they intended, they have succeeded…thanks to us! (User comment, 2005)

Although this study is limited by its methodological approach and cannot measure the true attitudes or beliefs behind these posts, the existence of such cynicism is not a particular surprise, given Singapore's history of one-party rule. However, it does suggest that many Singapore citizens may still remain unconvinced of the actual usefulness of the online consultation practice. It also serves as a reminder that the content of interpersonal discussion, whether online or offline, is shaped and influenced by the larger social and cultural context.

In addition, the level of government participation may be another factor that contributed the issue of distrust. As described previously, there was neither elected official nor moderator presence in the discussion forum, which led many users to believe that civic consultation is just another "formality" that the government had to go through in order to "legitimize" their policy decision, which was believed to have already been finalized. The lack of transparency on how citizen feedback is gathered and reported also cast doubt on the entire consultation process. In other words, if the purpose of the consultation portal is to engage in a deliberative policy-making process with citizens, then the government must also demonstrate its ability to follow the criteria of democratic deliberation as part of this exchange. In the case of Singapore, it is clear that the government failed to create an environment in which a sense of transparency, authenticity, and trust was established and conveyed to users of the online consultation portal.

It is important to point out that the descriptions of the issues associated with the online consultation forum only reflect what the portal looked like at the time of data collection in 2005. The particular website examined by this case study is no longer available today. Instead, a new online consultation portal (http://www.reach.gov.sg) has been launched to include features that address, to a certain extent, some of the issues discussed in this chapter. In the current online discussion forum, for example, users can quote or incorporate others' comments in their entirety in their responses, thereby making the conversation easier to follow. The issues or topics for discussion are still being defined by the government; however, a separate section now allows users to start their own discussion threads on matters of concern. Government participation in these online forums remains extremely limited, although there are instances of administrator responding directly to user inquiries or comments. Finally, the website also suggests that feedback posted on the discussion forum is compiled into summary reports that are then transmitted to the Cabinet and other government agencies every month. Figure 2 is a screenshot of the current online consultation portal:

Figure 2. Singapore's current online consultation portal. This screenshot was taken in June 2009 (© 2009, Government of Singapore. Used with permission.)

SOLUTIONS AND RECOMMENDATIONS

To summarize, this chapter describes a case study that explores the extent to which Singapore's online consultation forum reflected the ideals of democratic deliberation by examining the *structure* or the portal as well as the *content* of a discussion thread using a framework of democratic deliberation. Data collected suggest that while the consultation portal provided an environment that ensured privacy, anonymity, and equal participation, the forum suffered from ambiguous administrative intervention characterized by the removal of posts, as well as a lack of information both in terms of guidelines to the consultation process and the background information of the topics being discussed. Further, analysis of the posts suggests that while the participation was not extremely broad and diverse, participants were able to make constructive comments on the issues of casino gaming and social safeguarding from a variety of social, moral, and economic perspectives. However, in making their arguments, participants rarely referenced sources other than their own experiences and values.

As discussed earlier, the online discussion forum faced two important challenges: (a) inadequate technical design contributed to the structural and substantive fragmentation of the discourse; and (b) the lack of government participation and transparency in the consultation process resulted in a culture of cynicism and distrust among participants toward the authenticity and usefulness of the discussion. These issues must be addressed in order for the online discussion forum and the practice of online consultation in general to fully live up to its democratic potential. To that end, several recommendations can be made to improve the effectiveness of online discussion.

First, as the Singapore case illustrates, the technical interface of the online platform influences the way people interact with one another as well as the discourse itself. This observation has also been noted by many empirical investigations (e.g., Linna

Jensen, 2003; Morison & Newman, 2001; Wilhelm, 2000; Wright, 2005; Wright & Street, 2007). With the advent of new technologies and the growing popularity of social media, the importance of designing a web environment that facilitates social interaction has also led to emergence of several research areas in recent years. For example, works on discourse architecture, defined as the design and implementation of technology base and features that structure computer-mediated communication (Jones & Rafaeli, 2000) may help create online platforms that support collaboration and community building. Similarly, research on the analysis of Very Large-Scale Conversation, which refers to large scale, network-based, and public dialogue like the one in the Singapore case, represents effort to develop techniques for identifying conversational structure and the forces that shape it (Sack, 2005). The advance in these research areas is likely to be important for online consultation and other related e-democratic practices. In addition, with the massive amount of information being generated through citizen interaction and feedback, the development of knowledge and information management systems are also essential.

Second, the fragmented content and the sense of distrust seen in the Singapore case also suggest that moderator presence and government participation is likely to increase the effectiveness of online discussion. As Kearns, Bend, and Stern (2002) noted, moderators can keep citizen engagement focused and ensure the process adds value to all parties involved. In the same vein, Wilhelm (2000) also argued that moderators could contribute to the success of political discussion forums because "a skilled and trusted facilitator is often necessary to manage the forum and to create order out of potential chaos" (p. 140). In addition, since goal of online consultation is to promote and strengthen the interaction between citizens and policy makers, government participation in the process is therefore crucial. Finally, Coleman (2004) observed, "For online consultations to be seen as more than a gesture, there must be tangible evidence that [elected officials] are interacting with the public and taking views of online contributors into account in their deliberations" (p. 20). Integrating various forms of moderation, as well as increasing the level of government participation, is likely to address many of the issues seen in the Singapore case.

As for the future scholarly research on the practice of online consultation, a more systematic investigation into the different stakeholders involved in the process may shed light on when, how, and why online consultation may be most effectively implemented. For instance, user demographic information can be gathered to construct a more representative picture of public opinion, and participants can be surveyed for their experiences and attitudes toward the practice. Experimental methods can be employed to test different technical deigns and their impact on usability, online collaboration, and interactivity. Content analysis of the discourse being generated through different online media may be used to evaluate the value and quality of these policy discussions. Interviews with elected officials and legislators could be valuable for understanding how the consultation practice may contribute to the decision-making process, and comparative studies can be conducted to analyze the lessons and experiences learned from different parts of the world. All of these potential research areas suggest that a mixed and multi-method approach is perhaps most appropriate for examining a complex and interdisciplinary subject such as online consultation. Finally, applying the abovementioned methods to study different stages of the process (e.g., pre-consultation, consultation, and post-consultation) may also generate useful insights.

REFERENCES

Agre, P. (2002). Real-time politics: The Internet and the political process. *The Information Society*, *18*(5), 311–331. doi:10.1080/01972240290075174

Amnesty International. (2004). *Country summary: Singapore*. Retrieved May 20, 2005, from http://www.amnestyusa.org/countries/singapore/document.do?id=ar&yr=2005

Associated Press. (2005). *Singapore delays launching casino tender*. Retrieved June 20, 2005, from http://www.forbes.com/associatedpress/feeds/ap/2005/06/16/ap2095993.html

Au, A. (2004, November 11). Casino decision: A bigger question looms. *The Strait Times*. Retrieved August 4, 2009, from http://www.wildsingapore.com/sos/media/041111-2.htm

Barber, B. R. (1984). *Strong democracy: Participatory politics for a new age*. Berkeley, CA: University of California Press.

Barber, B. R., Mattson, K., & Peterson, J. (1997). *The state of 'electronically enhanced democracy': A survey of the Internet*. New Brunswick, NJ: Walt Whitman Center.

Baym, N. K. (1995). The emergence of community in computer-mediated communication. In Jones, S. (Ed.), *Cybersociety* (pp. 138–163). Newbury Park, CA: Sage.

Chadwick, A. (2003). Bringing e-democracy back in: Why it matters for future research on e-governance. *Social Science Computer Review*, *21*(4), 443–455. doi:10.1177/0894439303256372

Cheney, S. (2007, May 22). Marina Bay Sands project on track for completion by 2009. *Channel News Asia*. Retrieved November 11, 2007, from http://www.channelnewsasia.com/stories/singaporelocalnews/view/277767/1/.html

Chia, S. (2004, November 26). Sizing up the casino critic. *The Strait Times*. Retrieved August 4, 2009, from http://www.wildsingapore.com/sos/media/041126-3.htm

Clift, S. (2004). *Online consultations and events - top ten tips for government and civic hosts*. Retrieved November 20, 2004, from http://www.publicus.net

Coglianese, C. (2005). The Internet and Citizen Participation in Rulemaking. *I/S: A Journal of Law and Policy for the Information Society, 1*(1). Retrieved May 2, 2009, from http://www.is-journal.org/V01I01/I-S,%20V01-I01-P033,%20 Coglianese.pdf

Cohen, J. (1989). Deliberative democracy and democratic legitimacy. In Hamlin, A., & Pettit, P. (Eds.), *The good polity* (pp. 17–34). Oxford, UK: Blackwell.

Coleman, S. (2004). Connecting parliament to the public via the Internet: Two case studies of online consultations. *Information Communication and Society, 7*(1), 1–22. doi:10.1080/1369118042000208870

Coleman, S., & Gøtze, J. (2001). *Bowling together: Online public engagement in policy deliberation*. London, UK: Hansard Society.

Dahl, R. A. (1991). *Democracy and its critics*. New Haven, CT: Yale University Press.

Dahlberg, L. (2001). Computer-mediated communication and the public sphere: A critical analysis. *Journal of Computer Mediated Communication, 7*(1). Retrieved December 20, 2005, from http://jcmc.indiana.edu/vol7/issue1/dahlberg.html

Economist Intelligence Unit. (2008). *E-readiness rankings 2008: Maintaining momentum*. Retrieved August 10, 2009, from http://graphics.eiu.com/upload/ibm_ereadiness_2008.pdf

Elster, J. (1998). *Deliberative democracy*. Cambridge, UK: Cambridge University Press.

Feedback Unit. (2005). *Government consultation portal*. Retrieved January 10, 2005, from http://www.feedback.gov.sg

Fountain, J. (2001). *Building the virtual state: Information technology and institutional change*. Washington, DC: Brookings Institution Press.

Gomez, J. (2000). *Self-censorship: Singapore's shame*. Singapore: Think Centre.

Grossman, L. (1996). *The electronic republic: Reshaping democracy in the information age*. New York: Viking.

Habermas, J. (1984). *The theory of communicative action, volume one. Reason and the rationalization of society*. Boston: Beacon Press.

Internet World Stats. (2009). *Asia Internet usage stats and population statistics*. Retrieved August 14, 2009 from http://www.internetworldstats.com/stats3.htm

Jones, Q., & Rafaeli, S. (2000). Time to split, virtually: "Discourse architecture" and "community building" as means to creating vibrant virtual publics. *Electronic Markets: The International Journal of Electronic Commerce and Business Media, 10*(4), 214–223.

Kearns, I., Bend, J., & Stern, B. (2002). *E-participation in local government*. London, UK: Institute for Public Policy Research.

Linaa Jensen, J. (2003). Public spheres on the Internet: Anarchic or government sponsored – a comparison. *Scandinavian Political Studies, 26*(4), 349–374. doi:10.1111/j.1467-9477.2003.00093.x

Macintosh, A., Robson, E., Smith, E., & Whyte, A. (2003). Electronic democracy and young people. *Social Science Computer Review, 21*(1), 43–54. doi:10.1177/0894439302238970

Macintosh, A., & Whyte, A. (2002). An evaluation framework for e-consultations? Paper presented at the International Association for Official Statistics conference, London, UK.

Ministry of Trade and Industry. (2004). Social Safeguards For Integrated Resort With Casino Gaming. Singapore: Ministry of Trade and Industry. Retrieved June 20, 2005, from http://app.mcys.gov.sg/web/corp_press_story.asp?szMod=corp&szSubMod=press&qid=674

Ministry of Trade and Industry. (2005). Proposal to develop integrated resorts. Singapore: Ministry of Trade and Industry. Retrieved August 20, 2009, from http://app.mti.gov.sg/data/pages/606/doc/Ministerial%20Statement%20-%20PM%2018apr05.pdf

Morison, J., & Newman, D. R. (2001). On-line citizenship: Consultation and participation in New Labour's Britain and beyond. *International Review of Law Computers & Technology, 15*(2), 171–194. doi:10.1080/13600860120070501

Noveck, B. S. (2005). The future of citizen participation in the electronic state. *I/S: A Journal of Law and Policy for the Information Society, 1*(1). Retrieved April 28, 2009, from http://www.is-journal.org/V01I01/I-S,%20V01-I01-P001,%20Noveck.pdf

Organisation for Economic Co-operation and Development. (2001). *Engaging Citizens in Policy Making: Information, Consultation, and Public Participation*. Paris: OECD.

Poland, P. (2001). *Online consultation in GOL-IN countries: Initiatives to foster e-democracy*. Amsterdam, The Netherlands: Ministry of the Interior and Kingdom Relations.

Rash, W. (1997). *Politics on the Net: Wiring the political process*. New York: W.H. Freeman.

Rawls, J. (1971). *A theory of justice*. Cambridge, MA: Harvard University Press.

Rheingold, H. (1993). *The virtual community: Homesteading on the electronic frontier*. Reading, MA: Addison Wesley.

Sack, W. (2005). Discourse architecture and very large-scale conversation. In Latham, R., & Sassen, S. (Eds.), *Digital formations: IT and new architectures in the global realm* (pp. 242–282). Princeton, NJ: Princeton University Press.

Shulman, S., Schlosberg, D., Zavestoski, S., & Courard-Hauri, D. (n.d.). Electronic rulemaking: New frontiers in public participation. *Social Science Computer Review, 21*(2), 162–178. doi:10.1177/0894439303021002003

Stephens, S., McCusker, P., O'Donnell, D., Newman, D., & Fagan, G. (2006). On the road from consultation cynicism to energizing e-consultation. *The Electronic. Journal of E-Government, 4*(2), 87–94.

Sunstein, C. (2001). *Republic.com*. Princeton, NJ: Princeton University Press.

Teo, J. (2004, November 26). Anti-casino groups keep up the fight. *The Strait Times*. Retrieved August 4, 2009, from http://www.wildsingapore.com/sos/media/041117-1.htm

Thatcher, J., Waddell, C., Henry, S., Swierenga, S., Urban, M., & Burks, M. (2003). *Constructing accessible web sites*. San Francisco, CA: Apress.

Van Alstyne, M., & Brynjolfsson, E. (1996). *Electronic communities: Global village or cyberbalkans?* Paper presented at the 17th International Conference on Information Systems, Cleveland, OH.

Wellman, B. (1999). *Networks in the global village: Life in contemporary communities*. Boulder, CO: Westview Press.

West, D. (2007). *Global E-Government 2007*. Providence, RI: Center for Public Policy, Brown University. Retrieved August 20, 2009, from http://www.insidepolitics.org/egovt07int.pdf

Whyte, A., & Macintosh, A. (2001). Transparency and teledemocracy: Issues from an "e-consultation." *Journal of Information Science, 27*(4), 187–198.

Wilhelm, A. (2000). *Democracy in the digital age: Challenges to political life in cyberspace*. New York: Routledge.

Wright, S. (2005). Design matters: The political efficacy of government-run discussion forums. In Oates, S., Owen, D., & Gibson, R. (Eds.), *The Internet and politics: Citizens, voters, and activists* (pp. 80–99). London, UK: Routledge.

Wright, S., & Street, J. (2007). Democracy, deliberation and design: The case of online discussion forums. *New Media & Society*, 9(5), 849–869. doi:10.1177/1461444807081230

ADDITIONAL READING

Barber, B. R. (1984). *Strong democracy: Participatory politics for a new age*. Berkeley, CA: University of California Press.

Carlitz, R. D., & Gunn, R. W. (2002). Online rulemaking: A step toward e-governance. *Government Information Quarterly*, 19, 389–405. doi:10.1016/S0740-624X(02)00118-1

Chadwick, A. (2003). Bringing e-democracy back in: Why it matters for future research on e-governance. *Social Science Computer Review*, 21(4), 443–455. doi:10.1177/0894439303256372

Coleman, S. (2004). Connecting parliament to the public via the Internet: Two case studies of online consultations. *Information Communication and Society*, 7(1), 1–22. doi:10.1080/1369118042000208870

Coleman, S., & Gøtze, J. (2003). Bowling together: Online public engagement in policy deliberation. Available from: http://bowlingtogether.net

Dahlberg, L. (2007). Rethinking the fragmentation of the cyberpublic: From consensus to contestation. *New Media & Society*, 9(5), 827–847. doi:10.1177/1461444807081228

Dryzek, J. S. (2002). *Deliberative democracy and beyond*. Oxford, UK: Oxford University Press. doi:10.1093/019925043X.001.0001

Janssen, D., & Kies, R. (2005). Online forums and deliberative democracy. *Acta Politica*, 40, 317–335. doi:10.1057/palgrave.ap.5500115

Jones, Q., & Rafaeli, S. (2000). Time to split, virtually: 'Discourse architecture' and "community building" as means to creating vibrant virtual publics. *Electronic Markets: The International Journal of Electronic Commerce and Business Media*, 10(4), 214–223.

Kearns, I., Bend, J., & Stern, B. (2002). *E-participation in local government*. London, UK: Institute for Public Policy Research.

Lazer, D., & Mayer-Schönberger, V. (2007). *Governance and information technology: From electronic government to information government*. Cambridge, MA: MIT Press.

Macintosh, A., Robson, E., Smith, E., & Whyte, A. (2003). Electronic democracy and young people. *Social Science Computer Review*, 21(1), 43–54. doi:10.1177/0894439302238970

McCusker, P., O'Donnell, D., Stephens, S., & Logue, A. M. (2005). Consultation cynicism: Whither e-consultation. In *Proceedings of European Conference on E-Government, Antwerp, Belgium.*

Morison, J., & Newman, D. R. (2001). On-line citizenship: Consultation and participation in New Labour's Britain and beyond. *International Review of Law Computers & Technology*, 15(2), 171–194. doi:10.1080/13600860120070501

Noveck, B. S. (2005). The future of citizen participation in the electronic state. *I/S: A Journal of Law and Policy for the Information Society*, 1(1). Retrieved from http://www.is-journal.org/V01I01/I-S,%20V01-I01-P001,%20Noveck.pdf

OECD. (2001). *Citizens as partners: Information, consultation and public participation, in policymaking*. Paris: OECD.

OECD. (2003). *Promise and problems of e-democracy: Challenges of online citizen engagement.* Paris: OECD.

Sack, W. (2005). Discourse architecture and very large-scale conversation. In R. Lathamand S. Sassen (Ed.), Digital formations: IT and new architectures in the global realm (pp. 242-82). Princeton, NJ: Princeton University Press.

Schlosberg, D., Zavestoski, S., & Shulman, S. W. (2007). Democracy and e-rulemaking: Web-based technologies, participation, and the potential for deliberation. *Journal of Information Technology & Politics, 4*(1). Retrieved from http://www.jitp.net/files/v004001/JITP4-1_Democracy_and_E-Rulemaking_Schlosberg_%20Zavestoski_Shulman.pdf.

Stephens, S., McCusker, P., O'Donnell, D., Newman, D., & Fagan, G. (2006). On the road from consultation cynicism to energizing e-consultation. *Electronic. Journal of E-Government, 4*(2), 87–94. Retrieved from http://www.ejeg.com/volume-4/vol4-iss2/v4-i2-art6.htm.

Stromer-Galley, J. (2003). Diversity of political conversation on the Internet: Users' perspectives. *Journal of Computer-Mediated Communication, 8*(3). Retrieved from http://jcmc.indiana.edu/vol8/issue3/stromergalley.html.

Whyte, A., & Macintosh, A. (2001). Transparency and teledemocracy: Issues from an 'e-consultation.'. *Journal of Information Science, 27*(4), 187–198.

Wilhelm, A. (2000). *Democracy in the digital age: Challenges to political life in cyberspace.* London, UK: Routledge.

Wright, S., & Street, J. (2007). Democracy, deliberation and design: The case of online discussion forums. *New Media & Society, 9*(5), 849–869. doi:10.1177/1461444807081230

KEY TERMS AND DEFINITIONS

Online Consultation: Use of web-based technologies by government agencies to seek policy suggestion and feedback from the public. It is based on the prior definition by government of the issue on which citizens' views are being sought and requires the provision of information.

Democratic Deliberation: A process of collective decision that requires the participation of all who will be affected by the decision of their representatives, and includes the decision making by means of arguments offer by and to participants who are committed to the values of rationality and impartiality.

Autonomy: The participants and the online consultation process itself must be free from the manipulation or influence of external political or economic powers in order to maintain a sense of objectivity.

Transparency: The management of the online consultation process should be visible from outside, with clearly defined guidelines and information about how the feedbacks are gathered and relayed back to the policy makers.

Equality of Access: Every person affected by the issues being discussed in the online consultation process should be equally entitled to participate and provide their views.

Privacy and Trust: The online consultation process must protect the privacy and anonymity of the participants in order to facilitate a sense of trust and encourage candid discussions.

Enlightened Understanding: Participants of online consultation should have a good understanding of the issues in order to make sound judgment and meaningful contribution to the dialogue. To facilitate such understanding, the government must provide sufficient background information of the issues on which citizens' views are being sought.

Reflexivity: Participants of online consultation should critically examine the issues in relation to their cultural values, assumptions, and interests, as well as the larger social context.

Mutuality: Participants of online consultation should attempt to understand the issue or the argument from multiple perspectives. This requires a commitment to an ongoing dialogue and to listen and engage with each other.

ENDNOTES

[1] The methodological limitation of content analysis prevented the study from measuring enlightened understanding at the individual level. Instead, the study focused on whether or not an environment that could facilitate enlightened understanding was created.

[2] Singapore announced that it would defer issuing formal requests for proposals for its two casino resorts until the third quarter of 2005 (Associated Press, 2005). Bids were solicited and announced in 2006 and the resorts are to be completed in 2009 (Cheney, 2007).

[3] Including Web Content Accessibility Guidelines (WCAG) and Section 508 standards of the US Rehabilitation Act. For more on website accessibility, see: Thatcher, J., Waddell, C., Henry, S., Swierenga, S., Urban, M., Burks, M., Regan, M., & Bohman, P. (2003). *Constructing accessible web sites*. San Francisco, CA: Apress.

Chapter 15
What We Do Online Everyday:
Constructing Electronic Biographies, Constructing Ourselves

Judith C. Lapadat
University of Northern British Columbia, Canada

Maureen L. Atkinson
University of Northern British Columbia, Canada

Willow I. Brown
University of Northern British Columbia, Canada

EXECUTIVE SUMMARY

This chapter addresses the collaborative participatory nature of online interactivity within the range of social networking spaces afforded by Web 2.0 (O'Reilly, 2005). Each individual, through his or her situated usage patterns and choices, creates a unique digital fingerprint or electronic biography. Using a multiple case study method including children and youth ranging in age from five to fifteen years of age, the authors examined children's online interactivity through their electronic biographies. This case report focuses on the children's experiences of online interaction as a seamless component of their literacy (Thomas, 2007) and presents a profile of each young person that characterizes his or her unique online fingerprint. The findings provide insight into how children learn online interactivity, and their communities of practice at different stages of development. Their roles ranged from passive surfer-viewer-seekers to interactive discussant-displayer-players. Infrequently, some youth showed proactive leadership as host-builder-creators. The experiences of these young people provide practical evidence of the transformation of literacy; for them, the Internet serves as an information resource, a collaborative medium, and a design environment (Lapadat, Atkinson, & Brown, 2009). Narrative plays a key role online, especially in the construction of identity. The results of this study have implications for educators, parents, social scientists, and policy makers, and in particular, raise concerns about the commodification of childhood and how commercial interests have shaped sites used by children.

DOI: 10.4018/978-1-61520-863-0.ch015

BACKGROUND

This chapter addresses the transition from a notion of discussion or computer-mediated communication to a broader theoretical conception of online interactivity in the range of online spaces now afforded by the collaborative participatory nature of Web 2.0. Much of the early research on online discussion was related to text-based applications that first became available for common use, including email, synchronous chat, forums (especially in online courses), and listserves. These applications shaped the nature of online discussion and interaction by their affordances. As new mediums and modalities initially are conceptualized using familiar theoretical frameworks and practical applications, the first wave of researchers wrote about online discussion as contrasted with face-to-face spoken communication contexts and written language conventions. Themes included concerns about the impoverished communication context offered by chat and email (Herring, 1999; Honeycutt, 2001), the emerging notion of interactive written discourse (Ferrara, Brunner, & Whittemore, 1991; Lapadat, 2002), a focus on community formation (Conrad, 2005; Haythornthwaite, Kazmer, Robins, & Shoemaker, 2000; Rovai, 2001), and strategies for how to design online discussion forums to create effective learning environments (Kanuka, 2005; Lapadat, 2007).

The rapid development of new technological tools and environments for human interaction and creative expression, as well as people's day-to-day applications or *situated use*[1] of online communication, is radically transforming basic human activities and institutions around the globe—schooling, politics, art, commerce, entertainment, and friendship, for example. For young people growing up digital, it is not a matter of whether to use online communication modalities nor it is a question of which is better. Rather, online discussion and interaction are an integrated part of their everyday social lives (Thomas, 2007). They move easily between mediums, often using multiple media simultaneously, and combining face-to-face communication with online modalities in the moment or sequentially. The Internet's most recent direction of development as a creative, collaborative, distributed commons, has accelerated the pace of change and generated broad enthusiasm for and uptake of virtual participation via social networking. The very notions of discussion and interaction have changed.

The broad focus of our research is the transformation of literacy itself (Bolter, 2001; Cruickshank, 2004), and the challenge this presents to schools (Merchant, 2007; Weigel, James, & Gardner, 2009). What does it now mean to be literate? What are the literacy practices of children and adolescents? Specifically, how do they "read," express themselves, interact with others, and construct or reconstruct online environments through their technologically mediated interactions, and do these environments, in turn, shape them?

The authors propose that each individual, through his or her situated usage patterns and choices, creates a unique digital fingerprint or electronic biography (Lapadat, 2008). This presents a paradox. In a global online world in which English is becoming the common language, Japanese artistic traditions such as anime the visual currency, fantasy films and their related role playing games a common interactive environment, and blogging and identity play typical pastimes, nevertheless each individual creates his or her own unique path. In today's world, children interact online by playing collaborative role playing games in teams with people they have never met from any place in the world, write and publish fan fiction, or shop online for products that integrate their online and offline play and social interaction. Our focus is to examine children's online interactivity using the concept of electronic biography, within the broader framework of the transformation of literacy.

SETTING THE STAGE

This chapter presents a multiple case study including children and youth ranging in age from five to fifteen years of age. Specifically, we focus on their experiences of online interaction as a seamless component of their literacy, and we construct a profile of each young person characterizing his or her unique online fingerprint.

Our research program involves an examination of the role of traditional print literacies, the ability to read and write print texts, within the multimodal literacies (Kress & Jewitt, 2003) of today's electronic society as lived and experienced by children at home and at school. The broad scope of the research includes mapping children's everyday literacy tools and practices (Barton, 1994), examining teachers' and parents' perceptions of the relationships between print literacy and multimodal literacies, and describing and developing initiatives for bridging gaps between home and school practices, and for children with diverse experiences and access (Merchant, 2007).

This case study examines how children use computer-mediated communication as a tool to master semiotic domains, for entertainment, for learning, for social interaction, and for other aims. Each individual, through situated usage patterns, creates his or her own electronic biography, which depends on access, affordances of the medium, personal/social values, and the *hybridity*[2] of online communities (Nilan & Feixa, 2006; Feixa & Nilan, 2006). By documenting the particular lived experiences of youths' technologically mediated literacies, we profile the changing nature of literacy practices within a conception of wider social change.

CASE DESCRIPTION AND METHOD

Specifically, this electronic biographies study has involved documenting and comparing children and youths' daily practices of using electronically mediated literacies. In the study, we employed a multiple case study design. Eight children or youth and their parents were recruited from a northern rural community in Canada using the principle of maximum variation. The young people ranged in age from five to fifteen years of age, and included boys and girls of aboriginal and non-aboriginal backgrounds, who varied in access to and experience with computer use, as well as in family circumstances, socio-economic status, and school achievement level.

Data were collected through interviews of the young people and their parents in their homes. As well, we asked participants to show us examples of their typical literacy materials and literate activities, both those that were print-based and those that were technologically mediated. The interviews and the observations were recorded using a digital video camera. The method used for the observation portion was that of a *video tour*, which essentially was a walk around the home while the participant pointed out literacy materials and electronic technologies present there and described how he or she used them. During moments when the participant pointed to or demonstrated a technological device (e.g., game system) or literacy object (e.g., bookshelf), the researcher used the digital video recorder to document the device/object. Following the interview and video tour, the participants went on to provide an extended demonstration to the researcher of several current examples of their computer usage.

CASE PROFILES

This section introduces each of the participants via a case profile. Each child or adolescent is referred to by his or her self-selected pseudonym. All but one of the interviews included the young person and his or her mother. MKL, who does not live with her parents, participated in the interview one-on-one with the signed consent of her parents. Several of the mothers contributed to the interview while choosing to remain off-camera, but Bob's, GP's, and Charlie Brown's mothers placed themselves with their child within the camera frame. One session involved an interview of siblings, Seahorse and Tabbi, along with their mother.[3] Interviews were conducted by the second author, following the interview guidelines and video tour protocol designed by the first author. As the research was conducted in a small community, all of the parents were known to the second author and two were close acquaintances.

Tabbi and Seahorse

The two youngest participants, sisters aged five and seven, both are Caucasian and attend a Francophone school in a small northern community in Canada. Although the interview of siblings was unique within this study, the sisters provided insights into the dynamics of how family relationships can impact use of technology in the home as both of these girls often share information, and play together between systems. The code names chosen by these girls have come from Internet sources as they both are fond of *Webkinz* animals. They proudly displayed their stuffed toy animals to the researcher, a tabby cat and a seahorse, and chose to be known as "Tabbi" and "Seahorse," their names for their adopted stuffed toy *Webkinz* and their virtual counterparts. *Webkinz World* (http://www.webkinz.com/us_en/) is an online site for young children. By purchasing (adopting) a *Webkinz* stuffed toy, owners gain access to the site for one year, and their toy is their avatar on the site. The website includes a house for the pet that can be decorated by the child by purchasing furniture using virtual cash (similar to the popular adult simulation game, *The Sims*). Other players' characters can visit the house, and there is a limited (safe) form of chat. As well there are contests, quizzes, and both individual and multiplayer games on the site. Children earn virtual cash by participating in them.

Tabbi is the youngest participant in the study at age five and is in Kindergarten. Although she said that she is not learning to read yet, she proudly showed off her non-technologically-mediated literacy materials, such as sticker books and journal notebooks where she wrote words that her sister and parents have encouraged her to print. She uses pencils, pens and markers to copy words from books, and from what others have written for her. She also adds graphics and colours to this text with stamp pads and stickers. She described how she matched the shape, colour, and action of stickers to the appropriate page in her *My Little Pony* sticker book.

Seahorse, seven years old and in second grade, says that she likes to read signs. Even though the language of instruction at her school is exclusively French, Seahorse is able to sound out English words, and she demonstrated this by sounding out and reading the label on a bottled water container. She likes books about natural sciences and history, as well as wildlife pictures.

The girls' parents chose not to have any television (TV) service after they moved to a rural location six months ago. They watch films on digital videodisks (DVDs) and have several computers in the household with high-speed Internet access. Seahorse said that she has her own digital camera with which she takes pictures and then views them on the computer. She explained how she hooked up the camera to the computer and uploaded the images. When asked to describe her other uses of computers, Seahorse said that she liked to look at pictures of animals on the Internet, and proceeded to demonstrate. While online, Seahorse typed in the word "Seahorse," clicked on images, and up came several digital photos of the marine animal. She said, "See? They are very, very cute." She then added that they were an endangered species. When asked how came to know these things, she said, "I looked online about seahorses. And, also, my mom told me about seahorses too."

Tabbi demonstrated accessing the Internet, logging into to a favorite website, *PBS Kids* (http://pbskids.org/), and showing how to play two or three preschool games that featured the character of Curious George. On one game, for example, she had to listen to audio instructions, select the appropriate number of fruit for George to juggle, then click to see if she had performed the task correctly. George juggled the fruit, and up-tempo music played if she had done it correctly. Tabbi wiggled her body in time with the music, clearly enjoying it.

At this point in the interview, both sisters were on the Internet on separate computers in two different rooms, talking back and forth. When asked about this later in a follow-up discussion, the girls' mother explained:

The girls sometimes "play" with each other over the Internet. Specifically, they use the Webkinz website to invite each other's pets over to play at one another's houses. Seahorse always helps Tabbi to make the connection. Sometimes she calls out to her and gives her instructions and sometimes she will physically go over and guide Tabbi through the steps. They don't use the chat features together nor have they played games against each other. However, they do send each other virtual gifts through Webkinz post. I help Tabbi pick a message to go along with her gift by reading out loud the various messages to choose from. Seahorse can do this by herself now. (Seahorse & Tabbi's mother, follow-up email)

She commented that the girls were early users of computers, with Seahorse having started at about age of three and Tabbi having started even younger at age two and a half.

Ronald

Ronald is a seven year-old Caucasian boy in a regular second grade primary class. He is the youngest child in his family, with two older siblings. Ronald's mother said that Ronald was born in December, which has had an impact on his readiness for reading and writing at school. She said that he has participated in a reading enhancement program and there has been a marked improvement.

In demonstrating his non-technological literacy materials, Ronald showed a great interest in the books that he had signed out from the public library. He shared several story picture books by author and illustrator Jan Brett, as well as oversized *Star Wars* themed books with maps, and schematics of the ships and planets featured in the movies. When asked what he liked about each, he commented he liked the little pictures in the sidebars of the books because he could see "what came next" in the story. He also explained that the *Star Wars* books had pull out sections that he liked, and showed the researcher pages of starship schematics and maps. When asked if he read the text or was more interested in the pictures and schematics, he said he looked at the pictures. His mother added that they have repeatedly taken these same books out of the library, month after month, and that Ronald has not grown tired of them.

The family subscribes to cable television and watches films on DVD on a wide screen TV. As well, they have an older desktop computer that is used by the children and their mother for games and word processing. There is also a notebook computer that Ronald's father uses at home for work purposes.

Ronald has an older sister who is ten and a brother aged thirteen, and sometimes these older siblings help him out with computer games or other aspects of technology. For example, Ronald's brother borrowed a copy of the computer game *Stronghold* from a friend, and introduced Ronald to it. This is a real-time strategy game based on medieval times, with a primary objective of military conquest and a secondary aspect of economic development through building communities or strongholds. Ronald's interest is in the building functions, whereby players construct a town or landscape using maps, and components like stonewalls, towers, castles, huts, doors, gates, and moats. When asked about what other activities he did on the computer, Ronald said he did "reading games" (*Reader Rabbit*, a drill and practice game for early readers), racing games (on the Internet), and building games such as *Heroes of Might and Magic III* (http://www.heroesofmightandmagic. com/heroes3/), a fantasy world strategy game that also involves maps, building, military campaigns, along with magic, and which can be playing individually or with other networked players.

When it came time to demonstrate some of his online activities, Ronald went to the *Miniclips* website (http://www.miniclip.com/games/) and demonstrated a few games. There are about 500 games on *Miniclips* and he when he was making his selections, he verbally identified the different games he liked to play as he scrolled through the game icons. He then selected a game, *Cheese Dreams*, in which the objective was to have the cheese character complete an obstacle course. As the cheese careened through the course, Ronald began to vocalize and move his body as if he were the cheese character.

Later he inserted a game on compact disk (CD) that his family owned, Disney's *Toy Story Two Activity Centre,* in order to demonstrate it. His mother reported that the family had removed many of the larger games from the hard drive since they take up so much memory, including this one. She helped Ronald reload the program.

Charlie Brown

Charlie Brown is a ten year-old boy of First Nations (aboriginal) background whose literacy activities focus around cartoon characters and Lego. He chose his pseudonym based on the main character in Charles Shultz's *Peanuts* cartoon series. Charlie Brown has a sister who is 8 years older than him, not living in the household. He attends a public elementary school, and is in a grade 5/6 split class. Charlie's Brown's mother also was present for the interview and used the code name "Lucy," another *Peanuts* character.

Cartoon characters seem to have played a big part in Charlie Brown's early reading. As well as enjoying books in the *Peanuts* series, he said he liked the cartoon *Little Lulu*. This interest seems to have come from his mother, who has decorated the kitchen with her own paintings and line drawings of *Peanuts* characters. Charlie Brown now has progressed to reading small chapter books in the *Geronimo Stilton* series. The main character, Geronimo Stilton, is a mouse who runs a newspaper, and the illustrations are cartoon-like. Charlie Brown said he liked these books, particularly Geronimo, because "he's funny." When asked where he got his copy of the Geronimo books from, Charlie said "the bookstore in the mall." His mother said that she tends to buy books for her son if he shows an interest in them. As well, some of these books are not available at the library.

Writing at school is mostly "low tech," although his mother said that she was surprised to find them in the computing lab one time working on creating power point presentations. Charlie Brown said that they do use *MS Word* at school for writing reports sometimes. Also, he volunteered the fact that his class was "writing a book about autism." Pointing to the publisher's trademark on the Geronimo Stilton book in front of him, he said that they (Scholastic) were having a competition to publish the work of classroom students. Charlie Brown said that a fellow student in his class has autism and they were writing this book about him. He indicated that it was a class project; the students in the class were giving the teacher ideas and she was writing them down.

At home, Charlie Brown's mother said that he has been using the computer less this year than he did previously, and certainly less than his older sister. She said that last year he was playing games on the computer, including online chess, but this year he is focused only on Lego—ordering Lego products, that is. When Charlie Brown demonstrated the Lego website (http://www.lego. com/en-US/default.aspx) on his mother's laptop computer, the researcher asked him if he played the games and if he was going to demonstrate them. Charlie Brown replied that he did not play the games, but only looked at the products so that he could order them. His mother confirmed they have ordered several different sets of Lego online over time. She reported that once Charlie selected more than $600 worth of items for purchase. Of course they didn't get it all, she said, but they did spend about $200 on that occasion. When it comes to books and other constructive play items like Lego, his mother said that she supports his interests as much as possible, within reason.

Emma

Emma, age eleven at the time of the interview and twelve in follow-up conversations, is enrolled in a French Immersion program at school and is an avid reader. The family is Caucasian. Emma's mother detailed Emma's early interest in reading and writing from the time she was three or so. Emma's mother said that she ("Mary") was working on her Master's thesis when Emma was a preschooler, so Emma was exposed to her mother spending much time word processing. She said that little Emma would imitate her on the keyboard and say, "I'm working on my thesis." Emma's father works in media communications, so reading, writing, and researching continue to be part of Emma's daily surroundings.

Emma enjoys fiction, teen magazines, newspapers, and other nonfiction print materials. For writing she had several things in progress in low-tech form, including a journal, a novel, and note-writing to friends. She said, "I am always reading and or writing something!" She is not a casual reader, but plows through books giving them her entire focus. She also described varied outside activities, such as school sports teams, music classes, and school band.

Technologically, Emma had just begun to develop proficiency in using her digital audio player (MP3) that she won through a library summer reading program. Emma and her mother talked about how they had to wait several weeks until a family friend visited and showed Emma how to download music and other files from the Internet to play on her MP3. When asked about the library and catalogues, Emma said that she knew how to access library website from home to renew her library books and access her own account information. At the time of the interview, Emma did not have an email account, but was in negotiation with her mother to get one.

A major theme during the interview was Emma's newly developing Internet use, her mother's reservations about it, and how both she and her parents are learning together through the process. Emma's mother said that when Emma was younger and watching a favorite TV show, her mother could just go about her own business. Now that Emma is on the Internet, there is actually more engagement between them. Emma shares websites and information with her mother, seeking permission, but also to find out new strategies for accessing information and making sense of the complex information. Emma drives the process by going to these websites, and then Mary, who monitors Emma's use, learns about and provides the context for the information. Emma explained that she and her mother had reviewed together a Government of Canada website that promotes Internet safety for children. They downloaded a pledge sheet for both of them to sign, stating that Emma promised to practice safe Internet use, and to protect privacy and identifying information. The pledge sheet was posted on the wall beside the home computer.

Emma demonstrated a few websites such as *Club Penguin* (http://www.clubpenguin.com/), and mentioned participating on *Webkinz World* with her adoption certificates. She plays solo games on these sites, but is not interested in multiplayer game functions. Emma also demonstrated a translation website that her teacher had shown them for language arts school work. *Babel Fish* is a free interactive online function provided by Yahoo (http://babelfish.yahoo.com/). When asked if it was more beneficial than a straight English/ French dictionary, she said that it was more useful since this translation program can translate phrases as well. She accesses it from home to complete homework assignments.

Emma showed how she goes online to the websites of authors that she likes in order to find out about other books they have written and to participate in book discussion forums. Later in the session, she showed the researcher the books and magazines that she was currently reading that she had obtained from the public and school libraries, then went to her personal bookshelf and pulled out an armload of favorite books from her own collection. Her mother mentioned the interplay between the printed text in Emma's magazines and her use of Internet sites. For example, often Emma will read an article and then go to the magazine's website to vote on a particular topic. Emma's mother said this was "a whole new level of activity for Emma in technology," that could potentially become an obsession. Mary mentioned a recent occasion when Emma had become quite upset because she had not been able to get online to cast a vote for that day. On the other hand, Mary said that Emma was learning new ways of accessing information, and finding out about what her peers in far away places were thinking and talking about, such as during the American presidential election.

Throughout the interview and video tour, Emma, her mother, and the researcher conversed about literacy and technology, the place of both in Emma's life, and the rapidly changing nature of her engagement with technology and her literacy practices. Mary's reservations about the nature and value of online interaction provided a counterpoint to Emma's enthusiastic demonstration. A few weeks after this interview, Emma obtained her own email account, which she reported that she uses to send images that she has downloaded to close friends. She also has become a news-feed subscriber, she said, because she "likes politics" and wants to keep up to date on topical news and media stories.

GP

GP is a thirteen year-old girl, the daughter of "Ruby," a single parent of Indo-Canadian background. GP's older brother lives with her father in another community. GP is very busy with artistic endeavors, including four types of dance classes, voice and music lessons, and the school band. She also is an honor roll student in her eighth grade class at the local junior high school. There is little time in her life for anything but homework, school, and the above activities, so even though they have a television, it is rarely used.

GP has always loved to read. Her mother said that GP was reading chapter books by age eight, and that she currently enjoys fiction, including the popular *Artemis Fowl* books by author Eian Colfer, and the *Inkheart* series. GP said that she takes books out of the library for research as well. GP mentioned that she does less handwriting now that she is on the keyboard more. She says that she is not very fast with the keyboard but likes researching.

Technologically, GP does not use computers much at school because of access issues. GP and Ruby both explained that often the computers there do not work, and when functioning, they are in use by other students for their projects or for gaming. GP said it was "very stressful" to be under time pressures to have assignments that were due, and not being able to get the work completed because of the under-supported technology at school. She said it was much easier to do the work at home, including research. On the differences between technology at home and at school GP and Ruby said:

Ruby: I think at home, the differences at home,...

GP: It's more relaxed (smiles)

Ruby: (laughs) The technology is available, and it's functioning. I think that's —

GP: At school, the computers are usually broken, and the, any ones that are working are all being hogged by other kids. (GP transcript)

When asked to describe how she researched on the Internet, GP said that she often has gone to *Wikipedia* (http://www.wikipedia.org/) because most of the articles and information there is true. She said that she generally judges websites by whether they look professional, as she believes this indicates whether they are more likely to have accurate information.

As for using the Internet for recreation, GP said that she used to go onto *Webkinz World* but that there was something wrong with her account. It seems that her account probably had expired. GP said that she has an email account that she uses with friends and family, but that she did not engage in online interactive gaming or networking, mostly because she did not have time. GP also had an iPod and said that she liked to download music. Her mother did not want her to demonstrate this use of the computer, expressing the concern that such downloading might be illegal.

GP said that she enjoyed *Miniclips* (http://www.miniclip.com/games/en/), a free online game site, especially the puzzle challenge games. For the researcher, she demonstrated a task-orientated game in which the character, a medieval thug, collected taxes from the peasants for the king by bashing them on the head.

The family also owns some computer games. GP demonstrated how to create a character in *The Sims* (original, deluxe edition). She commented that she liked to create characters—where they live, what they look like, what kind of job, they have, whether they have kids—as that is what made it fun. When asked if the characters she created were similar to herself she said, "Not really. I just like to create crazy characters." She demonstrated how to change the character's personality traits and joked with her mother about how this changed the astrological sign. She went on to explain that in the game, players choose and design a home,

a neighbourhood, and their character's life, and have to spend money to pay for and furnish the character's house. GP did not participate in the online *Sims* forum or virtual shopping.

Bob

Bob, aged thirteen at the initial interview and fourteen in follow-up conversations, participated in the interview along with his mother, who is a writer. The family is Caucasian. Bob and his mother described Bob's early technology use and his continuing interest in storytelling, initially using print modalities, and recently via digital movie making. They discussed the technology differences they have observed between home and school contexts.

Bob always has enjoyed drawing characters and cartoons. Even as a preschooler he would draw characters in some sort of sequence, often with a humorous storyline. As he grew older, the drawings became more elaborate in detail, but retained a sense of fantasy and fun. Bob began to experiment with writing stories as well as illustrating them. Three years ago when he was ten, Bob wrote a small chapter book titled *Supers R Us* and gave it to his friends as a Christmas gift. With some assistance from his mother, Bob typed the manuscript himself, did the layout, and printed off the copies.

In terms of his reading interests, Bob said he found the ancient civilizations of interest in school, but for leisure reading he prefers science fiction and fantasy. One of his current favorites is the *Halo* series, best-selling science fiction novels based on the first-person shooter *Halo* trilogy of video games (http://halo.xbox.com/). He said that he continues to write stories in fantasy and science fiction genres, but as a personal interest rather than for school. Although he used to write by hand, he said that now he almost exclusively writes on his laptop computer.

Bob has a digital video camera, an Xbox 360 game system, and his own Toshiba laptop. He described how he engages in interactive online role-playing games while communicating with other players as they collaborate as a team on quests, using *Xbox LIVE* (http://www.xbox.com/en-US/live). Bob talked about communication in *Halo 3*, explaining to the researcher that you can have players from all over the world online talking and discussing the game they are playing over headset microphones. Bob did not demonstrate this but said that the game allows you to select a country or zone so that everyone can understand each other's language. Many players choose not to use the headset, he added.

Bob went on to describe how he has extended the gaming environment for his own creative purposes by creating *machinimas*, animated cinematic narratives. To do this, he designs virtual action figures and scripts them to act out short action sequences or story episodes using the landscape of the game. He said that he likes using the *Halo 3* game environment for this, since there is a function that allows multiple camera angles and different points of view. As well as creating and sequencing scenes to produce a narrative, he knows how to incorporate scene transitions, voiceovers, text titles and credits, and background music.

Bob's mother pointed out that Bob's graphic story composition and storytelling has undergone a developmental progression from writing his own print-based graphic novels and sharing them with friends, to digital movie making. Bob's mother said that Bob used to host movie events during which his friends would come over to their home and act out scenes while he filmed them. Other early efforts were stop-action movies that he made with three-dimensional (3D) characters such as dinosaurs or Lego figures, often on zombie themes. On the topic of Lego kits and bionicles (a Lego toy featuring part-robot, part-organic creatures in a fantasy universe), Bob, his mother, and the researcher discussed how these products are interrelated with the marketing of online games and books. Clearly, the link between Internet sites and consumable products was a factor for Bob and

his mother. Both of them engage in online play as well as in purchasing the related toys, games, and books, and going to see the movie.

As noted, Bob's current interest is in making digital movies through the creation of machinimas. In fact, he has taken this form of technologically mediated interaction a step beyond the design of narrative cinematic episodes. He now posts his machinimas online on sites such as *YouTube* (http://www.youtube.com/), where he credits others, such as his father, who have contributed to his productions by providing character voices and so forth. When posting on *YouTube*, Bob provides written descriptions and contextual information about his piece, and participates in and responds to critique in the comments forum. For example, here is the description that he provided to accompany his third *YouTube* video: "My third bot montage, with the bots on casual, this time featuring assistance from loccust15, an Xbox live friend. I know that I am a noob, I openly accept that fact, so don't waste your time telling me." His "bot" videos that we viewed presented violent images of shooting and blood.

MKL

MKL is a fifteen year-old tenth grade student at a local alternative high school, and identified herself as a person of Métis heritage. She lives independently with a roommate in a townhouse close to her school and works part-time as a retail clerk. MKL moved into town from her parents' home because she found its rural location too isolating. Much of the interview focused on MKL's views about the negative aspects of Internet use.

MKL explained that when she lived with her parents, who are technology experts, she was online all the time. She especially enjoyed gaming using *Xbox LIVE*, and was a top scorer in some first person shooter games (games in which the player views the action from the point of view of a character shooting a weapon). As an active person with varied interests, including reading, drawing, stenciling, photography, writing, taking guitar lessons, and taking care of her horse, MKL became concerned about the amount of time she "wasted" on the Internet. MKL said having a horse was very important to her, and provided real life experience that kept her grounded during that time. MKL described gamers as lacking social skills:

If I hadn't had my horses I wouldn't have had any-thing. I would have been like every other gamer almost. You know – very shy, keeps to themselves. Not very sociable at all. That is how most gamers are because they don't have friends. They have their Xbox or their computer. And they just live in their own mind, unless they get on the game, like Xbox or PlayStation 3 where you can do live games with other people but, er, you're not with them. You're talking with them, and playing with them.... And that is the only socializing they get. (MKL transcript)

When she moved into town with her parents' support, MKL decided not to have Internet service installed, even though her parents offered to pay for it. She explained:

Yeah, it was cause I could see that I was really addicted to the computer. Cause I researched so much, and I enjoyed researching. You know, and going on the Internet and finding out anything I really wanted to know. But I saw that I'd do that all the time. Or I'd be watching TV.

MKL added that Internet use took up too much of her time: "But now that I am living on my own, I find that I use my time a lot better. And, now that I have been away from the computer and my *Xbox LIVE* for quite some time, I enjoy it, and I don't really want to go back to it." She has a notebook computer that she uses offline for writing and schoolwork, and said there were lots of places like wireless coffee shops or the public library where she could access the Internet if she needed to.

MKL also expressed concerns about confi-dentiality, identity, and Internet privacy. As a former user of the social networking site *Face-book* (http://www.facebook.com/), she said that a year ago, one of her friends hacked into her page and started adding comments and posts without MKL's permission. MKL now is cautious about using social networking sites, and is protective of her information, particularly pictures.

The alternative school that MKL attends provides individual learner support as each student works independently at his or her own pace through modules. MKL reported that the computers available at school often did not work, but the personal support and instruction given by teachers was excellent.

Although she no longer is playing games online, MKL still enjoys gaming as an offline pastime. What she presently plays most is the music band simulation game, *Rock Band* (http://www.rockband.com/). She said that she received it from her parents as a Christmas gift and that her mother sometimes plays it with her when she visits. To demonstrate how to play the game, MKL connected a console to her TV set, then plugged in the peripheral (controller), modelled after an electric guitar. Rather than strings, the *Rock Band* guitar has colour-coded keys between the frets. The *Rock Band* visuals, resembling a music video, and the music began, and different colour-coded notes and chords streamed by on a "note highway." The task for the player was to hit the right keys (and chords) at the correct time.

MKL began the game, explaining how she was playing it, and also described how some of her friends choose to sit down to play it rather than standing up. As she sat down, placing the guitar on her lap and playing, she said that it was a fun challenge, and it was great because it was music that she likes. She added: "I like technology. I think it's great–just at limits. For anyone, like–even adults. There really has to be a limit.... [You] just have to learn to control yourself."

Summary of Cases

The eight young people profiled above come from ordinary families residing in a city of less than 15,000 in a relatively isolated geographic area of Canada. Fiber optic cables reached this community only twelve years ago and residential high-speed Internet access has been available for less than ten years. Although one characteristic that the participants share is that they belong to families that value education highly, in most other ways these children and teens constitute a fairly representative cross-section of young people in the community. On the whole, they are not early adopters or extreme users. Yet each of them is active online, and each presents a unique pattern of computer usage and Internet interactivity.

KEY INSIGHTS AND CHALLENGES

In this section, we discuss key insights relating to these eight young people and their patterns of online discussion and interaction. This multiple case study, including children ranging in age from five to fifteen years, provides a glimpse into how children learn online interactivity, and their communities of practice at different stages of development. The experiences presented by the eight young people and their parents point to the changing nature of literacy, including the role that the Internet plays for them in terms of its importance as an information resource, as a space for collaboration with peers and for exploring and representing their identity, and as a resource and outlet for creativity. These case profiles also affirm the enduring importance of narrative for young people and raise cautions about commodification in the lives of children and adolescents. Finally, that each profile is so different suggests a need to reconceptualize the relationship between individuality, learning, and online interactivity. The discussion that follows elaborates the notion of electronic biography and

how this concept relates to a theory of learning in technologically mediated environments. These findings have implications for educators, parents, social scientists, and policy makers.

Literacy and How it is Changing

In the contemporary electronic world, the traditional modalities of communication—speech, print, gesture, and pictures—have lost their boundaries. Supported by the affordances of Web 2.0, children and adolescents are using technologically mediated communication to combine writing, talk, and visual images as multimodal hybrids (Kress & Jewitt, 2003). Moreover, these technological platforms support dynamic, not just static, representations. Rather than print literacy becoming obsolete, it is undergoing a process of transformation (Bolter, 2001; Thomas, 2007; Williams, 2008). Reading and writing are multimodally embedded and situated in children's lived experiences differently than in the past.

In our case interviews, some parents reported that their children began to use computers and go online as young as two and a half or three years of age, long before they were reading print text. Activities involving technologically mediated communication are a part of their everyday lives, and many of their experiences of print text, both reading and producing it, have been learned in an electronic, multimodal context. Thomas writes: "For children who are immersed in media from their earliest memories, life on the screen is an everyday natural process—they know no other way of being" (2007, p. 167).

Tabbi's mother's description of how she helps her five-year-old daughter select a print message to send through *Webkinz Post*, seven-year-old Seahorse's demonstration of how she employs both text and images to conduct online information searches, and seven-year-old Ronald's fluent visual literacy as he selects favorite online games via their icons, are all examples of the multimodality of these young children's literacy.

The activities of children a few years older, like twelve-year-old Emma with her author websites and newsfeeds, and fourteen-year-old Bob who writes, illustrates, produces, and publishes hybrid stories/films are indicative of some directions of the development of youths' literacies.

These findings counter concerns expressed by some teachers and media reporters that online pursuits distract children from becoming literate. Rather, we have observed that these eight young people embrace the net as a vast literacy resource, and that they seem to be differently, more multimodally literate than past generations. Many adolescents in particular are heavy users of the Internet, and it may be that their interests are driving the direction of technological change with respect to online interactivity. This is so, whether or not local schools and educators adopt computer technologies and online interactivity in their teaching. From the reports of these eight young people, it seems that much of their learning has taken place outside of the school context. Teachers and schools risk becoming irrelevant as the gap between contemporary social technological practices and the school curriculum widens (Weigel, James, & Gardner, 2009).

Information Resource

Perhaps the first use of the Internet that comes to most teachers' minds is its utility an information resource. In these data, there was ample evidence that each of these children used the Internet for this purpose. MKL, GP, and Emma, in particular, spoke of doing research online. Emma demonstrated how she used online resources for French translation and went to the websites of her favorite authors to source other books that they had written and to find out what they currently were working on. GP used the Internet to do research for homework assignments, and had developed strategies for determining which websites were more credible. MKL noted that she had spent hours researching topics of interest on the Internet, and Seahorse

demonstrated how she did online searches, using the word "seahorse."

Co-Construction and Collaboration

The online environments in which these young people participate are potentially global in scope. Typically, these children approached Internet use as a social occasion, and often engaged their parents, siblings, and friends in their endeavors. A surprise to us was the extent to which each of these young people looked to their parents for guidance, help, and co-participation—unlike the more common portrayal of Internet users as alienated loners. (MKL's description of her self-identified Internet addiction, however, presents a counterpoint.) Bob's father created the voice for a character in Bob's machinima, and his mother had watched the theme-related movies with him. MKL's parents supported her technological choices, and played video games with her. Charlie Brown and his mother shopped online together. Emma and her mother negotiated practices of safe Internet use on an ongoing basis, and for Tabbi and Seahorse, online interaction simply extended the rich literacy environment of the home.

Some examples of online collaboration and interaction extended beyond face-to-face interaction in the home or the immediate circle of friends, especially as reported by the adolescent participants. Emma engaged in online voting, a basic risk-free type of interaction. Bob and MKL both were experienced players of online multiplayer games involving communication and collaborative problem solving with unknown others in team-based quests. Bob recently had made himself visible within the global machinima community by posting his machinimas on *YouTube*, and MKL was a former *Facebook* social networking site aficionado.

Digital environments are mutually interactive and dynamic. The young people we studied are growing up digital in the age of Web 2.0, the web platform designed around core features that include an "architecture of participation" (O'Reilly, 2005, p. 1), and "trusting users as co-developers, harnessing collective intelligence,... [and] the perpetual beta" (O'Reilly, p. 5). Ohler (2008) describes Web 2.0 as "the current evolutionary status of the Internet as a distributed, collaborative, participatory commons" (p. 4). Richardson (2008) calls it the Read/Write Web. As individuals affiliate with particular communities and choose to engage in particular Internet-based activities, the interactive discursive environment shapes who they are becoming, and they, in turn, recursively shape the online environments and communities in which they participate (Gee, 2009; Schmidt, 2007). Roles may be passive—as a surfer-viewer-seeker, interactive—as a discussant-displayer-player, or allow for proactive leadership—as a host-builder-creator.

Creating, Building, and Designing

Through the participatory architecture of Web 2.0, the vast environment of the Internet—its spaces, resources, and tools—are constantly under development by the users themselves. Our young people made use of design elements within electronic games and activities. GP designed characters and houses in *The Sims*, and she, Emma, Seahorse, and Tabbi all had designed houses in *Webkinz World*. Ronald enjoyed designing castles and medieval communities in games such as *Stronghold*, and Charlie Brown went online to research Lego construction designs and purchase Lego products. Both MKL and Bob had designed characters for multiplayer role-playing games, and MKL had designed a *Facebook* page.

To the extent that our participants have created or designed within existing utilities or social networking sites on the Internet, they are taking on an interactive public role as discussant-displayer-player. Bob, however, has taken this one step further. He is becoming a host-builder-creator, in that he has created new works, his machinima videos, and posted them online for

viewing and critique. When many users of the Internet engage in similar uses, communities of interest spring up. Adolescents and young adults tend to be heavy users of the Internet and we speculate that the development of online sites, resources, communities, and affordances currently is being driven to a significant degree by their interests. The machinima community, with its membership of mostly youthful gamers, is a good example of this. The fantasy fan fiction communities described by Thomas (2007) are another example.

Role of Narrative

Several of the young people in our study described themselves as "writers," including MKL, Bob, and Emma. MKL, now that she no longer goes online much, said that she uses her notebook computer for writing. In addition, she writes songs, an activity that is linked to her interest in the electronic game *Rock Band*. Bob both reads and writes fantasy and science fiction. Much of his interview focused on his development as an illustrator, writer, and film maker across modalities and media, with story or narrative at the central core of each interest. Emma keeps a journal and has a novel in progress. Although she relies on a low-tech medium for her writing at present, she uses the Internet to support her reading interests in both fiction and nonfiction genres. It will be interesting to see whether she begins to turn to online writing communities or to blogging as she and her mother become more comfortable with her use of the online environment. Charlie Brown was the only participant to mention sustained school-based writing in an electronic environment. He described a collaborative whole-class writing project that his teacher initiated in response to a publisher's contest.

In recent years, a number of prominent researchers have noted the re-emergence of narrative as a central approach to meaning making in our time. The use of narrative cuts across work and leisure, theory and practice. Storying now is recognized as a fundamental way of thinking (Bruner, 1986), of conducting research (Chase, 2005), of understanding personal identity (Burgos, 1989; Bruner, 2001), of transmitting culture, of communicating, of teaching (Ohler, 2008), and of entertaining ourselves. It is interesting, considering all the uses to which computers can be put, that popular usage has put the creating, presenting, and viewing of narratives, and especially personal identity stories, front and center in the new global participatory commons.

Identity

Many researchers and media commentators have commented on the way in which the World Wide Web has become a vast public playground for the presentation and exploration of identity. One obvious manifestation is the explosion in the popularity of blogging (Huffaker & Calvert, 2005). Another is the widespread engagement in various kinds of role-playing games (Thomas, 2007).

The notion of identity itself is complex and multi-faceted. On the one hand, it refers to that enduring something that makes a person uniquely oneself. It is the sum of one's life story, or personal biography of experiences. In another sense it is relational, marking those people, communities, or cultures with which one affiliates (Buckingham, 2008). Yet identity also is layered, and shifts depending on context and circumstance (Lapadat, Bryant, et al., 2009). For adolescents, the developmental aspects of identity are particularly salient; youth culture, along with the formation, social processes, politics, and subjectivity of identity, all have been widely researched (Buckingham, 2008). Weber and Mitchell (2008) point out that as today's "techno-tots" grow up, they seek answers to their identity questions through digital media. The Internet provides an audience of peers to reflect and affirm their identity productions, they say; it is through interacting with technologies and other youth online "that identities are

constructed, deconstructed, shaped, tested, and experienced" (p. 27).

In these data, there were fascinating aspects of identity being played out digitally, even with the youngest participants. Ronald, engrossed in a game of moving a cheese ball along an obstacle course, unconsciously began to move his body and vocalize in high-pitched squeals, as if he were the cheese ball character bouncing along. Tabbi and Seahorse both identified closely with their *Webkinz* stuffed toys to the extent of choosing their toys' names as their pseudonyms for this study. In a multiple layering of identity meanings, "Seahorse" signified a seven year-old girl, her stuffed toy, her avatar on *Webkinz World*, and a marine animal that our young participant described as "endangered" and "very, very cute." When playing online, the children posted messages, played, and furnished their virtual homes in character as their avatars.

Each of the adolescents in the study had enjoyed role-playing games. GP demonstrated *The Sims*, a game that explicitly focuses on role exploration. Bob and MKL both had created and played the roles of their characters in multiplayer online team quest games. Outside of the game context, we traced the evolution of Bob's construction of his new identity as a member of the online machinima community. In the text that accompanied each video that he posted, he was careful to identity himself as a beginner ("It was my first try;" "If you feel like saying that I suck, I'm ready to accept that;" "I know that I'm a noob."). He also described every flaw in each production and explicitly asked for suggestions about how to improve his efforts, further positioning himself as a novice. Fifteen year-old MKL's self-designation as an Internet addict and gamer also presented an interesting construction of identity. Almost her entire interview focused on this topic, and on her recent attempts to reconstruct her identity differently by according technological pursuits a smaller role in her day-to-day activities.

Commodification and Commercialization

As a participatory commons, the Internet is more than an open space for individuals to pursue their interests. It also is a prime resource for commercial industries to market their products and research consumer trends. Youth have considerable spending power, and even young children influence their parents' purchasing choices. Youth often present their identities by the brands that they consume—the brand name clothing they wear, the brand of bicycle they ride, and the type of game system they own. There is increasing concern that childhood is being commodified not only through blatant website ads, but also through increasingly subtle immersive marketing practices, in which commercial products and consumption activities are build into child-focused edutainment sites. Willett (2008) writes: "Compared with television, online advertising is seen by marketers as more effective in terms of cost, impact and measurability. The interactive nature of many forms of online advertising assures marketers that children are engaging with a promotion" (p. 53).

In these data, we found many examples of consumer marketing embedded in the Internet activities of our participants. The *Webkinz World* example is interesting, because in order to get an account, and thus gain access to the most appealing activities on the site, children had to purchase a product—a *Webkinz* toy. When their account expired after a year, they had to buy a subscription or purchase another toy to maintain an account. However, *Webkinz* animals are not just any toy, but actually function as the child's avatar, or virtual identity while on the site. Thus, in a sense, these children were purchasing an identity, and that identity was affiliated with a product. Furthermore, one of the prime activities available to the children in character as their avatar was to purchase virtual products for their *Webkinz* pet. They were being socialized into how

to be a consumer, and what was available for them to choose from were virtual versions of *Webkinz* products, which could also be purchased in real stores with real dollars. A considerable part of the site is devoted to parents, and the main thrust of the parent section markets the value of the site as a "safe" place for their children to play and learn.

CONCLUSION

Through the profiles presented here of these eight young people, it is clear that each of them has created a unique digital fingerprint—essentially an electronic biography. No one child's usage choices and patterns mirror those of another. The choices they have made reflect their interests as well as the opportunities that have been available to them. But also, the choices they have made and their situated use of online interaction shapes their social world, their expression of identity, and their learning opportunities. And they, in turn, shape those with whom they interact and the evolving nature of the medium.

We have observed that the digital medium and these young people's uses of it have become integrated into both their daily praxis and their identity (Thomas, 2007). Digital environments are more than a tool for work and for school in the daily lives of young people. They provide a forum for exploring, displaying, and playing with facets of identity. Also, significantly, through the Internet activities in which they choose to engage, young people are both revealed and constructed as social entities.

Young people's situated uses, roles, and identities constructed interactively in virtual environments can no longer be fully constrained by adults in authority such as teachers and parents, discounted as fringe or optional pastimes, seen as subordinate to face-to-face "real-world" engagement, or summarized in generalities. Ready or not, their digital lives and selves have become a facet of who our young people are, and how they are embracing digital communication to connect globally and reshape the world.

NOTE

This research was supported in part by Standard Research Grant #410-2004-1647 from the Social Sciences and Humanities Research Council of Canada.

REFERENCES

Barton, D. (1994). *Literacy: An introduction to the ecology of written language*. London: Blackwell.

Bolter, D. (2001). *Writing space: Computers, hypertext, and the remediation of print* (2nd ed.). Mahwah, NJ: Lawrence Erlbaum.

Bruner, J. (1986). *Actual minds, possible worlds*. Cambridge, MA: Harvard University Press.

Bruner, J. (2001). Self-making and world-making. In Brockmeier, J., & Cargbaugh, D. (Eds.), *Narrative and identity: Studies in autobiography, self, and culture* (pp. 25–37). Netherlands: John Benjamins.

Buckingham, D. (2008). Introducing identity. In Buckingham, D. (Ed.), *Youth, identity, and digital media* (pp. 1–22). Cambridge, MA: The MIT Press.

Burgos, M. (1989). Life stories, narrativity, and the search for the self. [Récits de vie]. *Life Stories*, *5*, 27–38.

Chase, S. E. (2005). Narrative inquiry: Multiple lenses, approaches, voices. In Denzin, N. K., & Lincoln, Y. S. (Eds.), *The Sage handbook of qualitative research* (3rd ed., pp. 651–679). Thousand Oaks, CA: Sage.

Conrad, D. (2005). Building and maintaining community in cohort-based online learning [Electronic version]. *Journal of Distance Education*, *20*(1), 1–20.

Cruickshank, K. (2004). Literacy in multilingual contexts: Change in teenagers' reading and writing. *Language and Education*, *18*(6), 459–473. doi:10.1080/09500780408666895

Feixa, C., & Nilan, P. (2006). Postscript: Global youth and transnationalism: The next generation. In Nilan, P., & Feixa, C. (Eds.), *Global youth?: Hybrid identities, plural worlds* (pp. 205–212). New York: Routledge.

Ferrara, K., Brunner, H., & Whittemore, G. (1991). Interactive written discourse as an emergent register. *Written Communication*, *8*(1), 8–34. doi:10.1177/0741088391008001002

Gee, J. P. (2009). Digital media and learning as an emerging field, Part I: How we got here. *International Journal of Learning and Media*, *1*(2), 13-21. Retrieved July 22, 2009 from http://www.mitpressjournals.org/doi/abs/10.1162/ijlm.2009.0011

Haythornthwaite, C., Kazmer, M., Robins, J., & Shoemaker, S. (2000). Community development among distance learners: Temporal and technological dimensions. *Journal of Computer Mediated Communication*, *6*(1). Retrieved February 14, 2001, from http://www.ascusc.org/jcmc/vol6/issue1/haythornthwaite.html.

Herring, S. (1999). Interactional coherence in CMC. *Journal of Computer-Mediated Communication*, *4*(4). Retrieved March 1, 2001, from http://www.ascusc.org/jcmc/vol4/issue4/herring.html

Honeycutt, L. (2001). Comparing e-mail and synchronous conferencing in online peer response [Electronic version]. *Written Communication*, *18*(1), 26–60. doi:10.1177/0741088301018001002

Huffaker, D. A., & Calvert, S. L. (2005). Gender, identity, and language use in teenage blogs. *Journal of Computer-Mediated Communication, 10*(2), article 1. Retrieved October 2, 2008 from http://jcmc.indiana.edu/vol10/issue2/huffaker.html

Kanuka, H. (2005). An exploration into facilitating higher levels of learning in a text-based internet learning environment using diverse instructional strategies. *Journal of Computer-Mediated Communication, 10*(3), article 8. Retrieved January 11, 2006 from http://jcmc.indiana.edu/vol10/issue3/kanuka.html.

Kress, G., & Jewitt, C. (2003). Introduction. In Jewitt, C., & Kress, G. (Eds.), *Multimodal literacy* (pp. 1–18). New York: Peter Lang.

Lapadat, J. C. (2002). Written interaction: A key component in online learning. *Journal of Computer-Mediated Communication, 7*(4). Retrieved August 19, 2002, from http://www.ascusc.org/jcmc/vol7/issue4/lapadat.html

Lapadat, J. C. (2007). Discourse devices used to establish community, increase coherence, and negotiate agreement in an online university course. *Journal of Distance Education, 21*(3), 59–92.

Lapadat, J. C. (2008, May). *Libratory technologies: Using multimodal literacies to connect, reframe, and build communities from the bottom up.* Paper presented at the Fourth International Congress of Qualitative Inquiry, Urbana-Champaign, IL: University of Illinois. Abstract retrieved May 11, 2008, from www.icqi.org.

Lapadat, J. C., Atkinson, M. L., & Brown, W. I. (2009). The electronic lives of teens: Negotiating access, producing digital narratives, and recovering from Internet addiction. In *E-Learn: World Conference on E-Learning in Corporate, Government, Healthcare, & Higher Education Proceedings* (pp. 2807-2816). Retrieved November 5, 2009, from: http://EdITLib.org

Lapadat, J. C., Bryant, L., Burrows, M., Greenlees, S., Hill, A. S., & Alexander, J. (2009). An identity montage using collaborative autobiography: Eighteen ways to bend the light. *International Review of Qualitative Research, 1*(4), 495–520.

Merchant, G. (2007). Writing the future in the digital age [Electronic version]. *Literacy, 41*(3), 118–128. doi:10.1111/j.1467-9345.2007.00469.x

Nilan, P., & Feixa, C. (2006). Introduction: Youth hybridity and plural worlds. In Nilan, P., & Feixa, C. (Eds.), *Global youth?: Hybrid identities, plural worlds* (pp. 1–13). New York: Routledge.

O'Reilly, T. (2005, September). What is Web 2.0: Design patterns and business models for the next generation of software. Retrieved June 23, 2009 from http://oreilly.com/pub/a/web2/archive/what-is-web-20.html?page=1

Ohler, J. (2008). *Digital storytelling in the classroom.* Thousand Oaks, CA: Corwin Press.

Richardson, W. (2008). *Blogs, wikis, podcasts, and other powerful web tools for classrooms* (2nd ed.). Thousand Oaks, CA: Corwin Press.

Rovai, A. P. (2001). Building classroom community at a distance: A case study [Electronic version]. *Educational Technology Research and Development, 49*(4), 33–48. doi:10.1007/BF02504946

Schmidt, J. (2007). Blogging practices: An analytical framework [Electronic version]. *Journal of Computer-Mediated Communication, 12*, 1409–1427. doi:10.1111/j.1083-6101.2007.00379.x

Thomas, A. (2007). *Youth online: Identity and literacy in the digital age.* New York: Peter Lang.

Weber, S., & Mitchell, C. (2008). Imaging, keyboarding, and posting identities: Young people and new media technologies. In Buckingham, D. (Ed.), *Youth, identity, and digital media* (pp. 25–47). Cambridge, MA: The MIT Press.

Weigel, M., James, C., & Gardner, H. (2009). Learning: Peering backward and looking forward in the digital era. *International Journal of Learning and Media, 1*(1), 1-18. Retrieved July 22, 2009 from: http://www.mitpressjournals.org/doi/abs/10.1162/ijlm.2009.0005

Willett, R. (2008). Consumer citizens online: Structure, agency, and gender in online participation. In Buckingham, D. (Ed.), *Youth, identity, and digital media* (pp. 49–69). Cambridge, MA: The MIT Press.

Williams, B. T. (2008). "Tomorrow will not be like today": Literacy and identity in a world of multiliteracies [Electronic version]. *Journal of Adolescent & Adult Literacy, 51*(8), 682–686. doi:10.1598/JAAL.51.8.7

KEYWORDS AND DEFINITIONS

Digital: Data technology that employs discrete values, as contrasted with analog, or continuous systems. In this chapter, we use the term descriptively to refer to interactive devices, media, environments, and social processes that have arisen through the combining and sharing of digital data.

Electronic Biography: Each person, by making specific online usage choices, over time creates a unique digital-social fingerprint, or personal online history.

Identity: A person's enduring sense of self, the way he or she represents or performs that self for others, and the cluster of social relationships and group memberships that characterize who he or she is.

Multimodal Literacies: An expansion and reconception of the nature of literacy. Literacy is seen as a process that incorporates a combination of expressive modes, including written text, spoken language, and visual images. Multimodal literacies largely have arisen within technologically mediated environments, and contrast with traditional modality of print literacy.

Online Interaction: Human communication that takes place virtually, through the range of online environments available on the Internet, and particularly via the World Wide Web.

Social Networks: The structure of social relationships. Social networks characteristically are represented as a web consisting of nodes (individuals) and bonds (types of relationships). In this chapter, we use the term to refer to the communicative history and links that develop between people through online communication and interaction.

Technologically Mediated Literacy: Literate activity that occurs through the use of computers. Technologically mediated literacy includes reading and writing in digital or electronic environments, as well as the manipulation and combination of expressive modalities, communicative interaction over time, and facility with using the technical tools and social processes involved in computer-mediated communication.

Youth: People, less than eighteen years of age, who are not accorded the full rights and responsibilities of adulthood.

ENDNOTES

[1] Situated use refers to practical applications or ways of doing things within specific social or physical contexts.

[2] Hybridity arises as a result of blending expressive modalities across boundaries, and is defined as the creation of new, blended genres with enhanced creative or interactive potential.

[3] The self-selected pseudonyms of the two girls, which were their usual screen names, have been modified to protect their anonymity.

Section 3
Support

Chapter 16
"There's Always Hope:"
Content, Participants, and Dynamics of Discussions in a Lung Cancer Internet Support Group

Tamar Ginossar
University of New Mexico, USA

EXECUTIVE SUMMARY

The Internet has changed the ways in which many people cope with illnesses, by allowing for conversations between similar others that transcend traditional barriers of time and place. Despite the revolutionary potential of Internet support groups, little is known about the ebb and flow of discussion in these groups. This chapter describes online discussion in a Lung Cancer Internet Support Group. Methods include quantitative and qualitative analysis of email messages posted to this group during one month. The results reveal (a) the content of the discussion, (b) participants in the discussion, (c) topics that elicited discussion and (d) themes and messages that were "silenced." The implications of these findings to patients and their family members, to scholars, and to health practitioners are discussed.

INTRODUCTION

[last month] I joined this virtual family. After intro, I requested the experience of people as to what if anything to do next after successful sleeve lobectomy on right lung. The overwhelming response was to do something beyond just close monitoring. I am to begin some empirical chemo treatments...I am thankful for your pushing me to do something. Also I find that I am hooked to reading the [list's] mail

every day. Let us keep up the good work Gratefully in His Hands, Charles.[a]

The above Email message of an elderly cancer patient to a Lung Cancer Internet Support Group was one of over a million email messages posted annually to groups on one server alone. As this quote demonstrates, online discussion in these support groups have the potential to impact not only the degree to which patients and their family members feel emotionally supported by similar others, but also their treatment decisions. Despite the magni-

DOI: 10.4018/978-1-61520-863-0.ch016

tude of this revolutionary use of communication media, research on health online discussion from a communication perspective is limited. Therefore, the complicated ways in which communication is enacted in health online discussions are largely unknown. This gap in the literature is surprising in view of over two decades of research on computer-mediated communication.

With the rapid diffusion of computer-mediated communication in the 1990s, researchers often expressed concerns about the impact of this technology on communication. Specifically, they viewed this communication as inherently impersonal and hostile in nature due to lack of nonverbal cues (Walther, Anderson, & Park, 1994). Conversely, according to social information processing perspective (Walther, 1992; 1996; Walther, et al., 1994; Walther & Burgoon, 1992), people experience the same uncertainty and affinity needs regardless of the communication medium they utilize, and adapt their communication to meet these needs in accordance with the communication medium they are using. Therefore, computer-mediated communication is unlikely to exert uniform effects. Instead, it is important to examine the social context, including the content of communication, the communicators, and the nature of social relations between communicators (Shedletsky & Aitken, 2004; Spears & Lea, 1994; Walther, 1996).

Whereas researchers of online discussion in areas such as education (e.g., Aitken & Shedletsky, 2002; Hara, Bonk & Angeli, 2000) are increasingly heeding the call to examine the circumstances that influence this communication (Walther, 1996), the characteristics of health online discussions are largely unknown. Previous research focused on perspectives and needs of these groups' participants (Wright, 1999; 2000; 2002), or on the content of communication (Ginossar, 2008; Klemm, Reppert, & Visich, 1998; Klemm, Hurst, Dearholt, & Trone, 1999; Sharf, 1997). However, these studies did not examine the dynamics in these discussions. In particular, it is unknown how factors such as the different categories of content identified (e.g., information and emotional support) influence the discussion. For example, are there types of messages that elicit more responses than others? What are the differences in responses to different messages?

Therefore, this chapter examines the dynamics of online discussion in a Lung cancer Internet support group. The need for this examination is supported by the potential of this new peer-to-peer media to change the nature of health communication through online discussion. It is also consistent with the call to examine specific contexts and circumstances of online communication, rather than assume uniformity of technological effects on communication (Walther, 1996). In addition, this analysis will enhance the knowledge of the communicative needs of lung cancer patients and their family members who participate in online groups, needs that are currently underexplored. Understanding these needs and their manifestation in online discussions' dynamics will allow lay persons to cope better with having cancer, and to health care providers and health information professionals to help them in coping.

LITERATURE REVIEW

Face-to-Face (FTF) Support Groups

Support groups are an important mean by which Americans change their health behaviors. The leading reason for participation in such groups is having an illness. Although the distribution of groups according to diagnosis is unknown, cancer patients exhibit the highest overall tendency to participate in support groups (Davison, Pennebaker & Dickerson, 2000). The stories shared in support groups are considered to carry the weight of shared experience, the emotional potency of common suffering, and to provide an avenue for social learning (Rappaport, 1993). The content of communication in discussions in FTF support groups typically included emotional support and informational support exchanged. Interestingly, cancer patients expressed virtually no negative emotions in these forums (Davison, et al.,et al., 2000).

Internet Support Groups

Unlike FTF support groups, online groups are not temporally or geographically constrained. Health-related online support groups extend individuals' social networks by bringing together people who cope with similar challenges but are typically parted by geographical distances. Most of the research on communication in online support groups extended previous theories of communicating social support FTF (e.g., Braithwaite, Waldron, & Finn, 1999; Warisse Turner, Grube, & Meyers, 2001; Weinberg, Schmale, Uken & Wessel, 1996; Wright, 1999; 2000; 2002). These studies concluded that the dimensions of social support were similar to FTF support groups (Braithwaite et al., 1999), that participation was associated with similar beneficial effects (Weinberg, et al., 1996) and that an increased use of online cancer support groups is associated with less satisfaction with provision of social support by face-to-face social networks (Warisse Turner et al., 2001; Wright 2000). Moreover, research of the content of communication in these groups consistently reported (a) health information and (b) emotional support exchange in online support groups (Braithwaite, et al., 1999; Klemm, et al., 1998; Klemm et al., 1999; Sharf, 1997; Warisse Turner, et al., 2001; Weinberg, et al., 1996; White, 2000; Wright 2000). Some studies also indicated (c) advocacy-related messages in breast cancer group. Additionally, one study documented a small number of conflict-related messages in two groups (Author, 2008). However, the content of these messages, their role in the overall online discussion in these groups, and their impact on the discussion

as evident in the number and content of responses that they received were not examined.

THE CONTEXT

Every year more men and women die of lung cancer than of any other type of cancer, but communication in lung cancer online support groups is typically overlooked. Research focused predominantly on communication in breast and prostate cancer support groups (e.g., Klemm, et al., 1998; Klemm et al., 1999; Sharf, 1997; White, 2000). Each type of cancer involves differences in prognoses, in treatment options, and in survival rates. These differences might lead to specific communication needs of individuals with different types of cancer and consequently to differences in the content of the Email messages that they post. In addition, members of computer-mediated groups form specific communication norms (Postmes, Spears, & Lea, 2000) that affect the content of communication. Finally, cancer in general, and lung cancer in particular, are associated with stigma. Previous research indicated that having stigmatic illnesses is associated with increased use of the Internet and Internet support groups (Davison & Pennebaker, 2000). Therefore, it is important to expand the scope of research of online support groups and to examine communication in Lung cancer Internet support groups. Moreover, because lung cancer is not gender-specific this exploration facilitates understanding of online discussions of both men and women.

RESEARCH QUESTIONS

The following questions guided this research about online discussion in lung cancer Internet support group:

1. What is the content of online discussion in this group?
2. Who participates in online discussion in this group?
3. What are the topics that elicit online discussion in this group?
4. What are the topics that are ignored, or silenced in this group's online discussion?

METHODS

A triangulation of methods was utilized in the study described in this chapter. First, as part of a larger study (Ginossar, 2008), a quantitative content analysis was utilized to answer the first and second research questions about the content and participants in the discussion. This content analysis utilized seven categories of email messages (see Table 1) identified in previous literature and in a thematic qualitative analysis of messages that were not included in the current sample. Independent coders coded the email messages based on this framework. In addition, they analyzed the gender of the authors of emails and whether they were patients or family members of patients. Inter-coder reliability was calculated using Scott's pi. Inter-coder reliability was 0.87 for content, 0.99 for gender and 0.99 for role as patients/family members.

The sample of the quantitative content analysis included 668 email messages that the current author received as a subscriber to the group during one month and were saved and printed. The group, or list as member refer to it, is one of over a hundred lists hosted on a server of a non-profit organization, which was located using a link from the National Cancer Institute's Website. In contrast with many health-related websites that are short-lived (McMillan, 2001), this organization's website is consistent and prominent among users. Moreover, it prohibits commercial postings and therefore allows for an analysis of the content of

communication of people who cope with cancer, rather than commercial parties that "spam" other similar groups. The lung cancer list was chosen because of the prevalence of this type of cancer, the fact that it is not gender-specific, and because it had over 400 subscribers. This popularity suggested that it met its users' needs, and allowed for an analysis of communication between a large number of participants.

The initial analysis revealed that each e-mail message in this online group is typically short and conveys one major idea that the sender of the message wanted to express. Therefore, the unit of analysis was an e-mail message. In contrast to using smaller units of analysis, it allowed coders to interpret the overall intent and meaning of email senders and avoided giving more weight to lengthier email messages.

To answer the third and fourth research questions, the analysis included utilization of tools available on the website's archive to examine the number of emails' authors who participated in the discussion, and to examine the different threads (email messages that were posted in response to one email message) in the discussion during the observed month. A qualitative, constant-comparative analysis (Glaser & Strauss, 1967) of the email messages in the sample focused on understanding the dynamics of the discussion. First, it included a line-by-line analysis of each of the email messages in the threads that had five or more emails (i.e., emails that received at least four responses), and their themes. Then, it referred to the relationship between different themes. Finally, the current author organized these themes into larger categories that typically captured the content of more than one thread and noted an overarching theme that explained online discussion in all these email messages. Validation of these findings included contrasting them with observations of the communication in this group that the author conducted for over a year.

FINDINGS

Quantitative Content Analysis

The Content of the Online Discussion: Email Messages Posted

The most prevalent category of email messages was answering questions (30%). These messages were sent in response to questions, which constituted the second most prevalent category (17%). Therefore, each question received an average of almost two answers (1.76). In addition, the discussion included frequent announcements, in which members shared information not as response to questions (13%). Hence, exchange of health information constituted half of the online discussion, as measured by number of email messages. In contrast, exchange of emotional support only, without information provision or seeking, constituted only 12% of the discussion (See Table 1).

Participation of Men and Women in the Online Discussion

The analysis revealed that women participated more than men in this online discussion. Women posted 84% of the email messages, compared with 15% of email messages that men sent. Men and women who participated in the discussion differed in their contribution to this online discussion in two ways. First, women who participated in this online discussion were twice as likely as men to exchange only emotional support, without specific information. Conversely, men tended to provide more answers to questions that other participants posted. There were no gender differences in asking questions, announcing information, discussing conflicts and political and advocacy issues, or other topics.

Participation of Family Members and Patients in the Online Discussion

More family members (72%) than patients (28%) participated in the online discussion. There was no statistically significant difference between the proportion of male family members and female family members in participation in the discussion. Family members differed significantly from patients in their patterns of participation in the online discussion. Family members posted questions at a rate twice as high as patients, whereas patients focused on exchange of emotional support, and answered questions more than family members ($U= 22834.500$, $Z= 2.529$, $p<.01$). However, patients and family members did not differ in announcing information in a statistically significant way ($p=.93$). Similarly, differences between family members and patients in participating in conflicts and discussing political and advocacy-related issues did not reach statistical significance.

The Dynamics of Online Discussion

Number of Participants

During the examined month, 697 emails were saved in the list's archive. They were written by 151 individuals, for or an average of 4.61 emails per participant. The highest number of emails per participant ($n=41; 39$) was posted by two of the group's moderators. The most active participants, as measured by the number of email messages posted, included 21 members who contributed more than 10 email messages each during the month examined in this sample. Only one of these frequent contributors focused most of her emails on one topic, and the others responded to different topics. The other 130 participants in the discussion posted only a few emails, with 41 individuals posting only one email.

Qualitative Content Analysis

The qualitative analysis of the email messages revealed an overarching theme of "maintaining hope." Members participated in the list to maintain hope, and communicated this motivation both explicitly and implicitly. Members joined the group in order to find information about treatment that would offer them hope, and at times were very explicit about their need for hopeful messages. For example, a daughter of a recently diagnosed patient ended her email writing: "Any words of wisdom, hope, advice would be appreciated." Another wrote: "I'm hoping that you can offer me some of the knowledge and hope that you all so clearly have." Members also explained their continuous participation in the attempt to maintain hope. They expressed appreciation for other members who provided them with hopeful information and personal stories "So happy to hear such good news! It gives all of us hope! My Dad has defied the odds too!"

The meaning of hope for many participants was "beating the odds" of the negative survival statistics of lung cancer by "fighting the good fight." This included pursuing aggressive medical treatment, and not alternative medicine, or palliative care. Many participants discussed their belief that losing hope is the worst thing that can happen to a patient. They often felt that physicians failed to give them hope. They objected to physicians' statistics about survival, stating that the medical establishment "sometimes plays God.... When people are told that there is no hope, they generally give up and that is what helps to generate these dismal statistics." Moreover, "good doctors" were those who were able to communicate hope. One family member wrote: "I just cannot put my trust in someone who obviously has no hope."

In addition to many positive exchanges of information, these beliefs also led to offensive messages and conflicts between members. For instance, when a member described her mother's death, she received the following reply: "the sad thing Jenis that you, your mother and the whole family went in this thing with a defeatist attitude. Giving up brings death much quicker." Whereas some objected this message, others supported it. For example, one person wrote: "unless one has the will to fight the disease and has hope that one can give it a good fight - Marlo is right that giving up brings death much quicker."

The online discussion also included implicit expressions of the importance of hope. Analysis of email messages that received many responses (threads), indicated that both messages that increased hope, and messages that threatened it received much attention, as manifested in the number of responses. Whereas responses to hopeful messages were enthusiastic and supportive, email messages that threatened hope received mixed responses, often leading to overt conflicts and offensive comments. In addition, members who participated in the online discussion "silenced" topics that they considered to be unhelpful for maintaining hope. This "silencing" is evident in members ignoring certain topics when some members tried to raise them. The following is a description of the threads of the online discussion, and an analysis of their major themes, as well as the content of "silenced" topics.

Topics of the Discussion's "Threads"

During the month included in the sample, 377 different threads were saved in the list's archive. Of these threads, 19 threads included five or more messages and were therefore chosen for further analysis. The analysis of the content of discussion in these threads revealed that controversies that often led to conflicts comprised the most prevalent topic that elicited the largest numbers of responses.

Conflict Regarding Smokers' Responsibility for Having Cancer

The largest category, measured by both the number of related threads and the number of email messages, included 71 email messages that comprised six threads. They included conflicts between group members on whether cancer patients who smoked were to blame for their illness. Like other conflict-related threads in this online discussion, these online conflicts began with a member expressing a strong opinion and anger about a controversial issue, followed by other members supporting or rejecting this opinion. For example, Rena wrote:

I just had an extremely aggravating conversation with a woman who I've considered to be my best friend up until now [...] her comment was that [...] she has no sympathy for people who get it [lung cancer] and started smoking recently (since the surgeon general declared it hazardous, I guess).

Following two email messages supporting her, Susan responded:

It seemed to me that [the] friend was making a simple statement that sometimes we bring things on ourselves by our own actions [...] While I do not have cancer I do have an incurable disease. I am not out fighting for money for research for it. Would I like a cure, sure, but it was a result of my own actions. I would rather see money go to funding something that is out of a person's control. [...] People don't want to change, they want someone to come and clean up after them or come and fix what they did.

In response, members posted 12 emails in which they objected the idea that lung cancer patients are to blame for their illness. Susan, the member who blamed lung cancer patients for smoking posted two more email messages defending her position, but the member who initially supported her posted an apologetic email message, stating that she did not really blamed patients for their illness, whether they smoked or not.

Another thread began with Keren posting the following email:

people who continue to smoke after being diagnosed with lung cancer must have a death wish. I can't even comprehend. Why even seek treatment. and how about all the innocent people inhaling that pollution. I liken it to an Aids patient having unprotected sex. Sorry to vent but I am truly flabbergasted in the complete stupidity

In response, Heather wrote:

I hope I read this post wrong, because I can't even begin to comprehend that someone would come to a lung cancer support board and make such a vitriolic, verbal attack on those of us who are struggling against both the disease and the addiction that may have brought us to this point. I stopped smoking before I was diagnosed with lung cancer. And so far I've managed to stay clean. But some days it is a struggle not to give in to the urge to light up....... I'm not a stupid person. I'm an addict.

In this conflict, members discussed the addictive nature of smoking and how to best support smokers in trying to quit. Members who were smokers shared their difficulties, and some family members of smokers expressed their frustration, or their understanding of the difficulties in quitting smoking.

This conflict also led to a debate about the group's boundaries. Some view these conflicts as allowing members to "vent," whereas others perceived them as offensive. Finally, Mary, one of the moderators posted an email calling to end the debate:

To criticize or imply stupidity because someone continues to smoke is NOT support, so I suggest that we drop the subject and get on to the business at hand, which is providing love and support to help those dealing with lung cancer, either their own or that of a loved one.

Following this email, Keren, the person who posted the first email in the thread asked to be removed from the list. It should be noted that she posted the request, thus making it public, whereas the procedure to unsubscribe is technical and is done off the list. In response, a new thread emerged, of members calling her to stay. In addition to regreats over Keren's decision to leave the group and calls for her to stay, these messages revealed, members' perceptions of the role of conflicts in the list, and how they viewed participation and group dynamics of discussion and interaction. For example, one member wrote:

I second Eric's sentiment about not leaving the list. AND... I'm a smoker and my father has [lung] and Kidney cancer. I feel terrible guilt and am trying on a daily, minute by minute basis to stop smoking... and I'm proud to say that I've cut down by 50% in the past 2 weeks (with a lot of work)! A lot of the debate on the list has helped me to continue my personal struggle, however, I still need to do this at my own pace or I may set myself up for failure, which would be worse than not trying at all. Anyway, you stimulated a conversation that we all needed to have, no matter how uncomfortable it is for everyone involved. You came to the list to give and receive support, just like the rest of us. I hope that you'll stay with us and continue to give and gain insight that is so much needed in the face of this horrible disease.

Robin stated:

I hope you're not leaving the list because there has been some disagreement about the smoking issues. While I might disagree with you at times - I enjoy learning about your opinions. A good debate is sometimes the best way to learn all the various aspects of an issue. And quite often it's the person with the minority opinion that we learn the most from.

End of Life Treatment Decisions

The second most prevalent category centered on decisions to choose palliative care over aggressive medical treatment. It consisted of five different threads with a total of 47 email messages. The following is a quote from the first email in one of these threads, in which Mathew expressed frustration over family members and other persons who judged him for "giving up" because he opted for hospice care rather than continue with chemotherapy. His words illustrate the different considerations that are involved in this difficult decision.

Why is it that when someone with advanced cancer decides that rather than continue with chemotherapy, which is making them more sick than the cancer, decides to stop the chemo and have more quality of life and enjoy that time with their loved ones that people assume that you have given up and quit fighting the beast? I have recently joined Hospice and have had several people look at me funny and then ask why I have given up? I don't feel that I have given up at all but have made the right choice for me and my family at this point in my treatment. It really pisses me off that people assume things.

Mathew's email received five responses, all but the first one were very short, and all were supportive of him making the decisions that are right for him. The first reply was lengthier, and included the author's own thoughts about her mortality and treatment decisions. She also wrote:

Yes, indeed I think that time will come... when the treatment is not increasing the quality of my life then for heaven's sake why would I keep taking it... There are some folks that will hang on to life no matter how bad the quality is... Don't know if it is fear of dying or just that they want to live forever... The funny thing is............ we are all mortal beings... Which means that we will all die... None of us will be able to pick our time and I don't think any time is going to be perfect...

Other Themes

The third category included threads of email messages that discussed advocacy-related topics. This category included a total of 26 email messages posted to three threads. The fourth category included three threads with a total of 21 email messages that related to symptoms. One of them was burping, and the other two related to brain mets (when cancer spreads to the brain). These threads began with a question about a patient, which received answers from multiple individuals. A fifth category with two threads related to specific treatment procedure included a total of 16 email messages. Finally, three threads that constituted independent categories included a thread of discussion about a particular member's updates of his surgery (16 email messages), a discussion about the uncertainty of prognosis (8 email messages), and a discussion on whether cancer patients should avoid coffee (6 email messages).

"Silenced" Topics in the Online Discussion

The analysis further revealed two topics that were largely absent from the online discussion, and were silenced when individuals attempted to address them.

Social-Emotional Concerns

The majority of group members who participated in the online discussion focused on information exchange and not on the emotional aspects of coping with this devastating illness. The online discussion typically included expressions of encouragements, mentioning of prayers, acknowledging the difficulties in coping and other forms of verbal emotional support. However, these expressions were usually embedded in email messages that centered on the exchange of information about treatment, etiology of symptoms, etc. For example, even a message titled "need support...husband has brain mets," a title that implied a need for emotional support, in fact presented some treatment-related questions to the group. All the respondents to this email addressed these questions. Not even one person in this thread provided only emotional support. For example, one email stated:

If they have only seen one spot... size of dime... why are they not considering stereo or gamma knife radiation? Isn't that a consideration? I've talked to a few caregivers whom's loved ones have had WBR and some stated they and their love one would not recommend it. Others stated it was worth it... I'm also looking for some answers and a discussion on this topic of what to do for brain mets

Alternative Medicine

Whereas focus on emotional support only was largely marginalized in this online discussion, the topic of alternative therapies for cancer and its management was practically absent from it. Only five messages were posted requesting information about alternative therapies, and the group largely ignored them. In one, a member tried to suggest sharing kefir fungus, which he found to be helpful for improving health. Following a private email from the list moderator, he posted a clarification about his intent and his claims: "my posting was in no way meant to present the magic cure everyone is waiting for." In another email, titled "Is this another candidate for a quackwatch," a member requested input about a certain dubious claim for therapy. She received one reply that opened with the statement: "In a word - yes!" In another message, a woman asked about alternative treatment for her father, after the physicians said there was no chemotherapy that could help him: "What I'm wondering is...Has anyone tried any pharmaceuticals or herbs that can be purchased in Europe or Mexico? Has anyone had any measurable success?" She received three replies, all questioning the physicians' decision not to use chemotherapy. No one addressed her question about the alternative therapies' effectiveness. One of them wrote:

Why no chemo? Have you gotten a second opinion? I don't know why doctors tell people "time" factors----everyone is different. Just look at some of the people on this list. If the doctors were right they would have been gone long ago. Hang in there and don't give up. There is always hope

Another woman who posted a question about members' experience with certain chemotherapy and with homoeopathy received a response from a member that argued: "It won't matter what kind of 'drug' or 'herbs' or 'homeopathic medicine,' she receives as long as she is adding fuel to the fire. Small Cell Lung Cancer IS linked to cigarette smoke either directly or second-hand." The moderator posted another response, in which she shared her experience with her husband that did not quit smoking, and added: "I am not real big on alternative medicine. Just make sure that her onc is aware of each and every vitamin and supplement that she takes, since some can react adversely with some of the chemo agents." Finally, a member posted an email that received no responses, titled: "alternative medicine." She wrote: "I personally have no interest in this practice, but [...] thought some of you may be interested. They claim to collaborate with universities, educators, and other experts. So for what it is worth."

DISCUSSION

The purpose of this chapter was to describe online discussion in Lung Cancer Internet support group. In particular, the research illustrated in this chapter was motivated by an interest in understanding the content of the discussion, its participants, and its dynamics. The findings indicate that online discussion in this group is largely motivated by

participants' need to "keep up the hope." The analysis of the specific content of each message revealed that this online discussion centered on information exchange, predominantly of medical and treatment-related concerns. Exchange of emotional support only was less frequent than email messages that embedded emotional support in information exchange. Less frequent topics in this online discussion included advocacy-related issues, conflicts between group members and email messages classified as "other."

The analysis further revealed that women participated in the discussion to a much larger extent than men, that family members participated more than patients, and that there were some gender differences, and differences between family members and patients in how they participated in the discussion. Moreover, a relatively large number of individuals participated in the discussion.

The dynamics of the online discussion were further clarified by analyzing threads of email messages that received higher than average responses. Analysis of these threads pointed to the importance of conflicts in the discussion in the group. Although the overall number of conflict-related email messages was relatively low in comparison to the number of other email messages, they received more responses, and thus elicited more discussion. Finally, topics that were "silenced," or had limited discussion included focus on emotional support without exchange of information, and discussion of alternative therapies.

Some of these findings are consistent with previous research. In particular, studies of other online support groups, including cancer-related (Ginossar, 2008; Sharf, 1997; Wright, 2002), identified the importance of information and of emotional support exchange. However, this study is the first to focus on the dynamics of online discussion in a cancer Internet support group. Whereas the quantitative analysis revealed the major trends in the discussion and the most prevalent topics, the qualitative analysis indicated the meaning of these topics to participants. In addition, this study was the first to explore "threads" of email messages. This analysis provided further insights by highlighting the topics and type of email messages that attracted more online discussion than others. Specifically, this analysis led to an understanding that although the percentage of conflicts in the overall discussion in this group was relatively small, they elicited much discussion and emotions as evident in the number of responses they received and in their content. This insight is important, as the existence of conflicts and their impact on participants raised concerns among CMC scholars and practitioners in general, and in health-related online groups in particular.

In addition, this chapter illustrated the different dynamics in the online discussion in this specific online group, thus demonstrating the different group norms (Postmes et al., 2000) and how they are negotiated, shaped, and formed through discussion. Some of these norms included the importance of aggressive medical treatment, avoiding discussions of alternative treatments, and limiting the focus on emotional support without exchange of information. Emotional support was typically communicated in addition to exchange of information, but members seemed more comfortable discussing medical, treatment-oriented information and approaches rather than the emotional aspects of coping with this devastating illness. Two topics that were controversial were whether smokers were responsible for their illness, and the legitimacy of opting for palliative care.

Finally, all of those norms were related to the notion of "hope," which many members participating in the discussion perceived as "fighting the good fight," and opting to go through the painful medical treatment without "giving up." Therefore, email messages that strengthened this hope, like personal stories of individuals who faired better than the statistics, or the doctors' predictions, received much attention as evident in responses of other members and their enthusiasm. In contrast, messages that threatened these perceptions of hope, like opting for palliative care and other end-of-life issues, were resisted, and received strong and often offensive replies.

IMPLICATIONS

This study provides further support to the importance of peer-to-peer discussion in online health-related groups. This Importance is manifested not only in the degree to which participants might feel emotionally supported, but also on their treatment-related decision making. These findings have implications to patients, family members, health care providers, and online group moderators. First, patients and family members should be aware of the option to participate in online support groups. However, they should also be informed of potential differences and even conflicts between group members. Like any participation in discussion in a group setting, conflicts might stem from differences between members in communication practices, norms, values and perceptions. Moreover, in view of previous research indicating the importance of information for cancer patients and their families, and the comments made in the group's online discussion, such participation has the potential to help individuals in coping with cancer.

Health care providers should be informed about these online groups and inform patients and families about them. In addition, providers should talk to their patients about the content of communication in the online groups, and understand the type of information and beliefs that are exchanged in these discussions, in order to better understand their patients' needs and concerns.

Finally, this study has implications for online group moderators and others who are interested in facilitating health-related online discussions. In contrast to FTF groups, discussions in online groups such as this lung cancer group, include a larger number of participants, are not limited by meeting times and thus can take longer to unfold, and lack non-verbal cues. All of these factors make online groups potentially more difficult to moderate. It is therefore important that moderators, as well as other group members, will communicate norms about communicating conflicts. For example, in the current sample, it was not clear what constituted offensive messages, versus members' right to "vent," or for one to express herself. The moderators chose to end certain controversial discussions, but their criteria for doing so were not communicated in the online discussion, and many members disagreed with their actions.

LIMITATIONS AND FUTURE RESEARCH

The methodological choices made in this research are not without limitations. First, this chapter focused on only one group, during one month of discussion. Future studies should examine discussions in other online groups, to learn about the content, norms, dynamics, and participants in a wide variety of online health-related groups, and expand the time frame examined to explore potential changes over time. Another limitation is inherent to Internet research and online groups, which is the difficulty to access the "lurkers," or those who do not actively participate in the discussion, but read the messages. It is therefore important for future studies to go beyond analysis of messages and recruit participants in different ways. Finally, this study cannot establish the effects of the discussion on participants. Future studies should examine the effects of messages on patients and on their family members.

Currently, a few questions are left unanswered. For example, why did certain norms develop in this group, and what are the effects on those who do not share them? Why do members in this group view hope as possible only via medical treatment? Do other members have different perceptions, and choose not to talk about them, or do individuals who use alternative therapies leave the group when they realize it is not an acceptable topic in

the discourse? Also, it is unknown whether other norms would have elicited "better" discussion.

REFERENCES

Aitken, J. E. & Shedletsky, L. J. (2002). Using Electronic Discussion to Teach Communication Courses. *Communication Education, 51, 3* 325-331.

Albrecht, T. L., & Adelman, M. B. (Eds.). (1987). *Communicating social support*. Newbury Park, CA: Sage.

Braithwaite, D. O., Waldron, V. R., & Finn, J. (1999). Communication of social support in computer-mediated groups for people with disabilities. *Health Communication, 11*, 123–151. PubMeddoi:10.1207/s15327027hc1102_2

Davison, K. P., Pennebaker, J. W., & Dickerson, S. S. (2000). Who talks? The social psychology of illness support groups. *American Psychologist, 55*, 205-217.

Ginossar, T. (2008). Online Participation: A Content Analysis of Differences in Utilization of Two Online Cancer Communities by Men and Women, Patients and Family Members. *Health Communication, 23*(1), 1–12.

Glaser, B. G., & Strauss, A. (1967). *The discovery of grounded theory: Strategies for qualitative research*. Chicago: Aldine.

Hara, N., Bonk, C. J., & Angeli, C. (2000). Content analysis of online discussion in an applied educational psychology course. *Instructional Science, 28*, 115–152. doi:10.1023/A:1003764722829

Klemm, P., Hurst, M., Dearholt, S. L., & Trone, S. R. (1999). Cyber solace: Gender differences on Internet cancer support groups. *Computers in Nursing, 17*, 65–72.

Klemm, P., Reppert, K., & Visich, L. (1998). A nontraditional cancer support group: The Internet. *Computers in Nursing, 16*, 31–36.

McMillan, S. J. (2001). Survival of the fittest online: A longitudinal study of health-related web sites. *Journal of Computer-Mediated Communication, 6*(3).

Postmes, T., Spears, R., & Lea, M. (2000). The formation of group norms in computer-mediated communication. *Health Communication Research, 26*, 341–372. doi:10.1111/j.1468-2958.2000.tb00761.x

Rappaport, J. (1993). Narrative studies, personal stories, and identity transformation in the mutual help context. *The Journal of Applied Behavioral Science, 29*, 239–256. doi:10.1177/0021886393292007

Sharf, B. F. (1997). Communicating breast cancer on-line: Support and empowerment on the Internet. *Women & Health, 26*, 65–84. PubMed doi:10.1300/J013v26n01_05

Shedletsky, L. J., & Aitken, J. E. (2004). *Human communication on the Internet*. Boston, MA: Allyn & Bacon/Longman.

Spears, R., & Lea, M. (1994). Panacea or panopticon? The hidden power in computer-mediated communication. *Communication Research, 21*, 427–459. doi:10.1177/009365094021004001

Walther, J. B. (1992). Interpersonal effects in computer mediated interaction: A relational perspective. *Communication Research, 19*, 52–90. doi:10.1177/009365092019001003

Walther, J. B., Anderson, & Park, J. (1994). Interpersonal effects in computer mediated interaction: A meta analysis of social and antisocial communication. *Communication Research, 21*, 460–487. doi:10.1177/009365094021004002

Walther, J. B. (1996). Computer-mediated communication: Impersonal, interpersonal, and hyperpersonal interaction. *Communication Research, 23*, 1–43. doi:10.1177/009365096023001001

Walther, J. B., & Burgoon, J. K. (1992). Relational communication in computer-mediated interaction. *Human Communication Research, 19*, 50–88. doi:10.1111/j.1468-2958.1992.tb00295.x

Warisse Turner, J., Grube, J. A., & Meyers, J. (2001). Developing an optimal match within online communities: An exploration of CMC support community and traditional support. *The Journal of Communication, 51*, 231–251. doi:10.1111/j.1460-2466.2001.tb02879.x

Weinberg, N., Schmale, J., Uken, J., & Wessel, K. (1996). On-line help: Cancer patients participate in a computer-mediated support group. *Health & Social Work, 21*(1), 24–29. PubMed

White, D. M. (2000). Questioning behavior on a consumer health electronic list. *The Library Quarterly, 70*, 302–334. doi:10.1086/603195

Wood, J. (2009). *Everyday encounters*. Boston, MA: Wadsworth.

Wright, K. (1999). Computer-mediated support groups: An examination of relationships among social support, perceived stress, and coping strategies. *Communication Quarterly, 47*, 402–414.

Wright, K. (2002). Social support within an online cancer community: An assessment of emotionally support, perceptions of advantages and disadvantages, and motives for using the community from a communication perspective. *Journal of Applied Communication, 30*, 195–209. doi:10.1080/00909880216586

Wright, K. B. (2000). Perceptions of on-line support providers: An examination of perceived homophily, source credibility, communication and social support within on-line support groups. *Communication Quarterly, 48*, 44–59.

ADDITIONAL READING

Braithwaite, D. O., Waldron, V. R., & Finn, J. (1999). Communication of social support in computer-mediated groups for people with disabilities. *Health Communication, 11*, 123–151. PubMeddoi:10.1207/s15327027hc1102_2

Postmes, T., Spears, R., & Lea, M. (2000). The formation of group norms in computer-mediated communication. *Health Communication Research, 26*, 341–372. doi:10.1111/j.1468-2958.2000. tb00761.x

Sharf, B. F. (1997). Communicating breast cancer on-line: Support and empowerment on the Internet. *Women & Health, 26*, 65–84. doi:10.1300/J013v26n01_05

Walther, J. B., Anderson, & Park, D. (1994). Interpersonal effects in computer mediated interaction: A meta analysis of social and antisocial communication. *Communication Research, 21*, 460–487. doi:10.1177/009365094021004002

Walther, J. B., & Burgoon, J. K. (1992). Relational communication in computer-mediated interaction. *Human Communication Research, 19*, 50–88. doi:10.1111/j.1468-2958.1992.tb00295.x

Warisse Turner, J., Grube, J. A., & Meyers, J. (2001). Developing an optimal match within online communities: An exploration of CMC support community and traditional support. *The Journal of Communication, 51*, 231–251. doi:10.1111/j.1460-2466.2001.tb02879.x

Wright, K. (2002). Social support within an online cancer community: An assessment of emotionally support, perceptions of advantages and disadvantages, and motives for using the community from a communication perspective. *Journal of Applied Communication, 30*, 195–209. doi:10.1080/00909880216586

KEY TERMS AND DEFINITIONS

Cancer Communication: Relates to seeking and providing information and other types of social support exchanges about cancer prevention, treatment, and the experience of having cancer. Cancer communication can occur in professional medical setting among health care professionals and researchers, in patient-provider communication, between cancer patients and family members, as part of daily interactions between individuals who do not have cancer, and in the mass media.

Cancer Support Groups: Are comprised of patients and family members who meet with the goal of coping with having cancer through communicating about the experience. These groups are part of the movement to facilitate coping with difficult life events and illnesses thorough social support that is communicated in group setting. Some of these groups are moderated by lay persons, and some by professionals, such as mental health experts. Face to face cancer support groups meet in medical or community-setting at designated times, and the number of participants is limited by time, place, and other constrains. These groups have been shown to be beneficial to participants. Although minorities and individuals with lower social economic status benefit from participation, they usually do not have access to them and the majority of participants are White, middle class women.

Conflict: Involves tensions between goals, preferences, or decisions that individuals feel that they need to reconcile. According to Wood (2009), to have a conflict two perceptions have to exist; the perception that one's concerns are at odds with another person, and the perception that these differences should be resolved.

Health Information Seeking: The purposeful search for information about well-being, prevention of illnesses, and coping with illnesses. Information seeking about illness management includes information that could aid in treatment and end-of-life decisions.

Internet/Online Support Groups: Like face-to face groups, online groups aim to use social support in facilitating coping. In contrast to face-to-face groups, participants communicate using computer-mediated communication. These technologies largely removed the traditional barriers of time and place encounter by participants of face to face support groups. Many of the online groups are open to the public, and allow individuals to join them free of charge. Other Internet groups serve a limited group of specific health consumers, such as members of certain Health Management Organizations, and are not open to other users. Millions of individuals are thought to participate in online support groups, but the exact numbers are unknown.

Lung Cancer: Lung cancer is a disease of uncontrolled cell growth in tissues of the lung that can spread to other tissues beyond the lungs (metastasis). The main types of lung cancer are *small cell lung carcinoma* and *non-small cell lung carcinoma*. The most common cause of lung cancer is long-term exposure to tobacco smoke, but not all cancer patients were smokers. Symptoms include shortness of breath, prolonged cough, coughing up blood, and weight loss. Possible treatments include surgery, chemotherapy, and radiotherapy. With treatment, the five-year survival rate is 14%. The World Health Organization estimated that about 1.3 million of people die from lung cancer each year, making it the leading cause of cancer-related death in both men and women.

Social Support: The exchange of social support includes verbal and nonverbal communication "that reduces uncertainty about the situation, the self, the other, or the relationship (Albrecht & Adelman, 1987 p. 19). Although different dimensions of social support were conceptualized by different scholars (Braithwaite et al., 1999), types of social support generally include instrumental/tangible (e.g., provide a meal), informational (e.g., give advice), and emotional/esteem (e.g., give reassurance). The extent of social support that individuals have, their perceptions of social support available to them, as well as their provision of social support to others are related to better coping outcomes, including better health and well-being.

ENDNOTE

[a]   To maintain their authenticity, all the quotations of email messages are provided in their original wording. All the names of participants used are pseudonyms.

APPENDIX

Differences in distribution of Email messages according to authors' role as family member/patient was significantly different than expected by chance $\chi 2$ (1, N=657)= 5.716, p<.005.

Table 1. Content of online discussion in lung ICSG

Category	Description of Email Messages	Example	N	%
Asking Questions	Questions to other members and requesting information (mostly medical-information)	Any information or resources you can supply for people at our stage will be appreciated	113	17
Answering questions	Provision of information in response to questions posted previously	A second opinion at a major cancer center is essential before making any important treatment decision, and certainly before deciding not to treat at all.	200	30
Sharing/announcing information	Provision of information as announcement to share with the group (not as reply to questions)	Here is a link I found for information about radiofrequency ablation.	87	13
Exchanging eotional support only	Provision or request for emotional support, e.g., encouragement and prayers, no information exchange	I am so happy for you!! May you continue to dodge the chemotherapy till a cure becomes available!!!!!!	78	12
Political/advocacy	Calls for political action and discussions of advocacy-related issues	There is going to be a BIG ACS rally, walk, luminary ceremony etc in Cheshire in June	60	9
Conflict	Participating in conflicts with other group members	People who continue to smoke after being diagnosed with lung cancer must have a death wish[…]why even seek treatment […] i am truley flabergasted in the complete stupidity.	39	6
Other	Content that was not captured in the categories above	If you do it next year, I'll try to figure out a way to come also. After all, I'm a displaced New Yorker	91	13

To maintain the authenticity of participants' speech, quotes from email messages are presented without changes for spelling and grammar.

Table 2. Participation in online discussion in lung ICSG by gender and role as a patient or family member

Content	Gender				Role			
	Male		Female		Patient		Family Member	
	N	%	N	%	N	%	N	%
Information Reply	31	32	67	33	67	33	57	22
Information Seeking	14	15	23	12	23	12	**75**	**30**
Unsolicited Information	9	9	21	11	21	11	**27**	**11**
Emotional Support	9	9	39	19	39	19	**20**	**8**
Conflict	10	10	21	10	21	10	**19**	**7**
Advocacy	6	6	11	5	11	5	**18**	**7**
Other	18	19	20	10	20	10	**37**	**15**
Total	97	**100**	202	**100**	202	**100**	253	100

Note. Differences in distribution of Email messages according to authors' gender were significantly different than expected by chance $\chi 2$ (1, N=657) =326, p<. 001

Statistically significant differences between patients and family members included information reply, U= 22834.500, Z= 2.529, p<.05; information seeking, U= 20887.500, Z= 4.702, p<.001; and emotional support U=22639.500, Z= 3.593, p<.001. Differences in other categories were not statistically significant.

Table 3. Participation in lung ICSG discussion by gender and relationship to patient

Gender	Role			
	Patient		Family Member	
	N	*%*	*N*	*%*
Male	33	54	31	46
Female	167	44	216	56

Note: Differences between participation of male and female as family members versus patients in the discussion were not statistically significant, p=.24

Chapter 17
Change Talk at iVillage.com

Jolane Flanigan
University of Massachusetts Amherst, USA

EXECUTIVE SUMMARY

With the growing number of women going online, women-centered Internet sites have become more abundant. This case focuses on social support offered by relationship message board members at iVillage.com, a popular and pioneering site for women. Findings suggest that community members promote a form of individualism that reflects a dominant United States (US) cultural understanding of self. Read against research that suggests US females tend to have a more relational than individual sense of self, the promotion of an individual self may be an unhelpful aspect of the social support given on the relationship boards.

ORGANIZATION BACKGROUND

Established in 1995, iVillage.com is currently the most successful Internet site designed for women. The majority (75%) of the over four million monthly U.S. American visitors are female (quantcase.com "US Demographics"). Site photographs and advertisements feature women and content focuses on what are traditionally thought of as women's concerns: pregnancy and parenting, beauty and style, home and garden, food and recipes, health and diet, and celebrity gossip and entertainment. Site

DOI: 10.4018/978-1-61520-863-0.ch017

visitors can click through pages of articles, expert advice, and discussions that change daily, if not hourly. Community members—and iVillage.com emphasizes being a community for women—can upload pictures to the site, comment on blogs and engage in community message board discussions.

With the increasing numbers of women accessing the Internet, sites focused on serving the needs and interests of women, such as iVillage.com, should be evaluated for emergent and on-going women-centered communication practices. With the popularity and the success of iVillage.com message boards—a 2009 Alexa.com report states that its message board traffic is second only to its health pages—iVillage.com provides an opportunity to observe a rich array of conversations. While iVillage.com hosts over 1,000 message boards, some with experts available to answer questions and others with members facilitating discussions, the focus here is on the 100 boards that pertain to relationships. These boards include discussions about issues relating to such topics as men, dating, love, marriage, and infidelity. As in other online communities (Ridings & Gefen, 2004; Rodgers & Chen, 2005), relationship message board members request and provide both social support (e.g., I am sorry that you are having to go through this.) and, less often, information (e.g., hypertext links to articles or books).

This case study evaluates the extent to which the social support given on iVillage.com relationship message boards can be considered helpful to women. While work in gender and computer-mediated communication focuses on explicating how gender is communicated, read, and altered in online communication, this case study takes a different approach. Focusing on messages surrounding relationship troubles, this case explicates a cultural discourse that structures computer-mediated communication on the boards. Findings suggest that norms surrounding troubles talk on these boards are premised on a notion of self that celebrates independence and sanctions dependence. This dominant cultural discourse under-privileges people, typically women, who see relationships with others as an integral part of their definition of self. In the context of social support given on an online community dedicated to the needs of women, this finding makes more complex the evaluation of computer-mediated social support.

SETTING THE STAGE

The Internet has held many exciting possibilities for gender and communication research. As a medium of communication, the Internet provides for gender ambiguity and anonymity by rendering invisible many of the social cues that mark gender—such as one's physical appearance and the tone of one's voice. Thus, computer-mediated communication presents users with an opportunity to adopt different gender identities and styles of communicating than they do offline. For this reason, computer-mediated communication has been studied for its potential to liberate women from off-line gender roles and identities, for the resources people utilize to establish online gender identities, as well as for the fluidity and the play of gender in computer-mediated communication.

Early work on gender in computer-mediated communication offered support for the Internet's liberatory potential. Graddol and Swan's (1989) study of a text-based university conferencing system suggested that qualities of computer-mediated communication inherent in the system facilitated more equal participation between men and women with varied social statuses. Specifically, they pointed to the general invisibility of status markers (including gender), the flattened hierarchical structure, and the public nature of communication as key equalizing characteristics. However, the optimism of their findings was tempered by research that indicated computer-mediated communication was not a panacea for gender-based oppression and marginalization. Kramarae and Taylor (1991) identified three issues that disadvantage women online: (a) men controlled topic selection and monopolized the talk (see also Herring, 1993), (b) sexism and sexual harassment silenced women's participation (see also Bruckman, 1993; Herring, 1999), and (c) the more masculine style of communicating on the Internet (e.g., assertiveness and flaming) hampered women's participation (see also Crowston and Kammerer, 1998). As the early optimism faded with the findings that gender inequalities found in face-to-face interaction were also present online, research began to analyze the resources people utilized to communicate and read gender in computer-mediated communication as well as the fluidity of gender online.

While people have varied in their sensitivity to online gender cues (Lee, 2007b), gender and computer-mediated communication work has made clear that gender is communicated and read by Internet users. Online resources that convey gender have included gender revealing language (e.g., usernames, pronouns, and social identities such as wife or son) and visual cues (e.g., photographs and cartoon pictures). In the absence of this type of information, people have gendered others by attending to stereotypical conversational topics and content—for example, women talk about fashion and men talk about sports (Herring & Martinson, 2004). Research has found that online gendered language styles, similar to those found in face-to-face communication, are generally the most accurate indicator of a person's gender (Herring, 2003) and that people who do not attend to language style tend to make errors when assigning others to a gender category (cf. Lee, 2007a; Herring & Martinson, 2004; Nowak, 2003).

Even though awareness of gendered language styles proven helpful in assigning people to a gender category, online language styles should not be understood as a binary. While some work in gender and computer-mediated communication has tended to reify a rigid gender binary by gendering people according to the sexing of their bodies—thus people categorized as males were understood to be masculine and females feminine—more recent work has uprooted gender from its grounding in this sex-gender binary (see Bing & Bergvall, 1996; Rodino, 1997; c.f. Cameron, 1998). This work has demonstrated that both men and women alter their language styles in computer-mediated communication (van Doorn et al., 2007; Herring, 2003; Thomson, 2006). Thus, women have adopted a more masculine, aggressive style (see Rellstab, 2007) and men have adopted a more feminine, emotionally expressive style (Wolf, 2000). Furthermore, research that treats gender as a binary has tended to imply that all women, regardless of coming from different backgrounds, share a feminine style and all men, regardless of

differing backgrounds, share a masculine style. However, as Brown (1997) has argued, not all women (or men) have the same gender—there are important race and class differences among them. In sum, current work in gender as language style has begun to treat femininity and masculinity as more fluid than the sex-gender binary implies. According to this work, gender can be understood as existing along a continuum with the degree of masculinity or femininity expressed being mutable and related to both a person's background and the context in which one is communicating (Thomson, 2006).

The aforementioned research has established online gender fluidity in relation to language styles, but research has also found that Internet users treat gender fluidly by assuming gender identities that are either ambiguous or incongruous with their biological sex. For example, Danet (1998) has described methods utilized by people in synchronous online communication to create and play with gender. Participants have used gender- specific, neutral, or ambiguous pronouns and nicknames ("nicks") in the creation of characters whose genders differed from users' offline genders. The likelihood of an Internet user passing as a gender other than one's offline gender has depended in large part on how successfully people utilize the resources discussed above. Some textual transgender-users have not comported to expected gender-specific communication styles, or they have presented in hyper-stereotypical ways and were thus found suspect. While the most common gender switching has been for men to present as women in order to solicit sexualized attention from others, presumably heterosexual men (Herring, 2003); women have adopted a masculine gender identity not to garner attention, but to achieve or maintain social status and a sense of empowerment (Flanagin et al., 2002).

Over the past twenty years, research in gender and computer-mediated communication has yielded a rich understanding of the opportunities and limitations of the Internet for women. While the Internet has not leveled gender inequalities and neutralized male dominance found in face-to-face communication, online resources have proven to be advantageous for women. For example, gender anonymity has been utilized by women to maintain and establish greater online social power. Future gender and computer-mediated communication research can further an understanding of not only gender inequalities found online, but also the benefits of computer-mediated communication for women. As the work cited above suggests, this research would strive to treat gender not as a binary, but as fluid. Gender is not only a dynamic aspect of a person, but there is also variability among those who occupy the same sex-gender category.

One way of researching gender inequalities online while attending to the fluidity of gender is to first assess dominant ways of communicating and then consider the types of people and gender roles that are more or less privileged by these ways of communicating. This approach is consistent with Bem's (1993) emphasis on doing feminist work that moves away from a focus on studying gender differences towards a focus on analyzing social institutions that function to privilege males by rendering "a definition of males and male experience as a neutral standard or norm" (p. 2). The following section of this study presents a dominant form of socially supportive communication on iVillage.com relationship message boards. Later, the social support offered by message board members is assessed for its potential helpfulness for help-seeking members.

CASE DESCRIPTION AND ANALYSIS

Research indicates that people tend to seek computer-mediated social support when the support they receive offline is or periodically becomes insufficient (Turner et al., 2001). iVillage.com relationship message boards offer women access to an online community that is dedicated to providing social support. Unlike some public spaces on the Internet, communication on iVillage.com boards is both polite and safe for members—women do not have to negotiate sexual harassment, flaming is not present, and new members are welcomed to the boards by moderators and, sometimes, other members. As an asynchronous form of computer-mediated communication, the relationship boards also offer members, as Hample (2008) suggests, around-the-clock access to a community of people from a range of time zones. This is not to say that messages have immediate responses, but that one does not have to wait to begin the process of communicating about relationship troubles as one may have to do in order to talk face-to-face with a friend or family member.

Aside from the increased access to social support, women may find it easier to self-disclose their troubles in computer-mediated communication rather than in face-to-face communication. Research on computer-mediated self-disclosure suggests that self-disclosure happens at a higher rate in computer-mediated communication than in face-to-face communication because the medium provides for increased anonymity (Joinson, 2001)—both in terms of a member being anonymous to others and others being anonymous to that member. In general, anonymity on the relationship boards exists on a spectrum. New members tend to post messages with relative anonymity by using only a username and not disclosing personal information that is not relevant to their relationship issue. Longer-term members, however, often have pictures of themselves (presumably) below their username as well as pictures of friends and family members with captions and quotes as their signatures. Even though anonymity can be reduced as members communicate on the boards and more becomes known about their beliefs, values, and histories, a new member would have to page through archived threads to access this type of information.

While the vast majority of iVillage.com posters on the relationship boards are women—identifiable by their use of gender specific language (wife, mother), self-identification (as a woman), or picture—there are members who are identifiable as men. There are no significant gender differences between women and men in terms of who provides or seeks support and information—both women and men fulfill these roles proportionate to their overall numbers. Most help-seeking messages are written by new members or members who post infrequently, and most responders to these messages are regular participants. These regulars provide continuity and a feeling of community by commenting on members' former posts (from as long as 6 months prior), asking about others' relationships or family members' health, and sending well-wishes when tragedies strike. In order to explicate a dominant way of communicating on these boards, this study treats iVillage.com relationship message board posts as cultural communication that conveys messages about who people are and how they should talk with and relate to others.

Hymes' (1962, 1972, 1974) approach to the study of communication argues that a person cannot become a competent speaker of a language if one does not pay attention to the ways language is used in everyday social interaction. Attending to the patterned use of communication, researchers learn the rules of what is appropriate communication in particular contexts. Take, for example, the ways students are encouraged to communicate in classrooms. Traditionally, desks are arranged in rows and students are required to raise their hand in order to be called on by a teacher and gain the right to speak. In some contemporary classrooms, however, desks are arranged in a circle and students are encouraged to engage in a fluid conversation with their peers rather than to speak only to the teacher.

Beyond understanding the rules for communicating, researchers who attend to the structure of communication, the systematic way people communicate, also gain access to cultural systems of meaning. Here, it is important to clarify that cultural meaning does not indicate a dictionary meaning of a word, but a range of cultural understandings about actions, the nature of people, and how they relate and emote. Returning to the above example and noting how communication is structured in each of the classroom contexts reveals underlying beliefs about students and teachers as well as the value placed on different types of knowledge. In the hierarchical traditional classroom, a learned teacher controls the flow of conversation. In the circular contemporary classroom, both the students and the teacher share the communication floor. The former communication format is premised on a belief that an authoritarian teacher is the best vehicle for the dissemination of valuable knowledge he or she has gained through focused study. The latter is premised on a belief that an egalitarian classroom leaves room for students' experience-based knowledge that is in and of itself valuable. In this way and as Carbaugh (1995) has summarized, cultural communication researchers assume "that everywhere there is communication, a system is at work; that everywhere there is a communication system, there is cultural meaning and social organizations" (p. 272).

One method of doing communication research focused on explicating cultural systems of meaning is to focus attention on the use of key symbols—defined by Carbaugh (1988a) as symbols that are mutually intelligible, deeply felt, and widely accessible to the people who use them. With this focus, the researcher observes, records, and analyzes the ways people employ not only the focal key symbol, but also other key symbols that co-occur with or substitute for it. After establishing an understanding of how key symbols are used, cultural norms can be formulated and an interpretive analysis can be performed to expose the cultural beliefs and values on which these norms are premised. For example, Hall and Valde (1995) have treated "brown-nosing" as a key cultural symbol. Analyses of the social uses of "brown-nosing" revealed culturally meaningful notions of how a person should communicate in an organization (be genuine, straightforward and concerned about the organizational needs) and what a person whose actions have been termed "brown-nosing" should do (remedial work to regain positive social standing).

For this case study, change—chosen for its prominence and cultural force—was treated as a key cultural symbol. Hymes' (1972) SPEAKING framework was used to code instances of iVillage. com relationship message board communication that utilized change as a key cultural symbol. A descriptive account of change talk was rendered by attending to the following components: (S) the psychological *scene*, (P) the *participants*, (E) the *ends* or outcomes, (A) the *act* sequence or pattern of communication, (K) the *key* or manner in which members communicate, (I) *instrumentalities* of communication such as speech register, (N) the interpretive or interactional *norms*, and (G) the *genre*—such as information-seeking versus support-seeking communication. Coded data, generated primarily during, but not limited to a six month period, was analyzed to explicate norms active in change talk that structured the form of communication surrounding change. With an understanding of the basic form of change talk and the norms active in it, an interpretive analysis was performed. This analysis asked, as Carbaugh (2007) has: "What needs to be presumed, or understood, in order for this kind of communication practice to be intelligible here" (p. 172).

Most generally, change talk is enacted when a person asks a relationship partner to alter her or his behaviors, beliefs, or values. On the iVillage. com relationship message boards, there are three ways that change comes into conversation: The member who starts a thread can (a) post a message that requests advice on how to change her or his relationship partner, or (b) post a message that describes how her or his relationship partner is requesting change, or (c) members will hear change in a post and reply using change explicitly. Change was sought for a variety of reasons including issues pertaining to sharing housework, paying bills, taking care of dependents, engaging

in or not engaging in activities (socializing, drinking, viewing online pornography), dishonesty, physical appearance, and general ways of being (e.g., being shy, being too social). Describing and interpreting the ways that members communicate on the boards reveals a proscribed way of communicating during relationship troubles talk. This proscription on change talk, premised on cultural notions of self, organizes how members talk about their relationship troubles. Findings suggest that change talk is constrained by cultural notions of self and moderated by two additional key cultural symbols: *compromise* and *understanding*.

Conceptualizations of the Individual Self in Change Talk

Audible in communication surrounding change talk are understandings of people as having unique, individual selves that should be celebrated. These cultural notions of self are consistent with a prominent U.S. American discourse discussed by Carbaugh (1988b). Carbaugh (1988b) argues that there are three dimensions of meaning that U.S. Americans utilize to distinguish between being one's *self* (culturally valued) and adhering to social roles (culturally devalued)—independent-dependent, aware-unaware, and communicative-closed—where the first term in each set corresponds to being one's self and the second term corresponds to adhering to social roles. Change talk pivots on the independent-dependent continuum where a person is thought to have a unique core, knowable to others, that is generally consistent through time and social environment. Within an interpersonal context of relationship troubles talk where social roles (wife/husband, dating partners) are in tension with cultural notions of self, change talk is heard as violating a mandate to celebrate a unique self. More specifically, to celebrate self means that troubled relationship partners who engage in change talk should be encouraged to focus on their identity as an independent person and not on their identity as a relationship partner. Those who accept their and their partners' selves are valorized as independent and those who do not are demonized as dependent.

There are two primary ways that the conceptualization of a person as independent structures change talk: If one celebrates one's self, one would not require change. And, if one celebrates another's self, one would not ask them to change. While often co-occurring in online posts, taking each of these conceptualizations of self appreciation in turn will aid in an understanding of how cultural meanings associated with self are operating to proscribe communication that requests or requires change.

Celebrating One's Self

In the following message board extract, Tess is responding to a newlywed woman whose husband defied her request to not socialize with a particular group of his friends. The newlywed frames her husband's choice to go to a bar with his friends as an upsetting and unloving betrayal and her relationship as necessary for her financial stability. Tess dismisses the newlywed's request for advice on how to change her husband. Tess's prescription is as follows:

You need to define happiness, success, and security by your own standards and definitions.... You need to create a lifestyle for yourself in which you're happy, successful, and secure as an individual, independent of another's assistance. Then you'll be able to have a relationship of mutual benefit.

Tess reframes the newlywed's situation as an occasion where change talk is a distraction from her actualizing both a good relationship and a happy, secure, and successful life as an individual. Instead of asking her husband for change, the newlywed would be able to have a mutually beneficial relationship only when she begins to focus on and take responsibility for her own livelihood and happiness. This view expresses the importance of

relationship partners achieving happiness in their own right, without needing or wanting a partner to fulfill their wishes and needs. Devalued here are efforts made to invite a relationship partner to make one happy. In short, if there is occasion to desire or expect change, then the problem does not lie with one's partner, it lies with one's self.

Those who do not focus on self and who instead ask for change are seen as insecure and dependent. Switchback's response to the newlywed highlights this point:

You won't tolerate him being who he is. You have to control, manipulate, and maintain the environment in which he interacts because you see him as the path to success, security, and happiness. You are insecure as an individual.... You've got to love and accept yourself... before you can accept that he loves [sic] you, as you are. For you don't love him 'as he is' but 'how you require him to be'—and can't accept and appreciate his love (if it is genuine) as a result.

Because the newlywed's post focuses on changing her husband's behavior and not on herself—for example, finding a better job—she is understood as being dependent on him for her success, security, and happiness. Dependent people, members suggest, need to practice independence in order to move from controlling their spouses into truly loving and appreciating who they uniquely are. Being an independent person makes it possible to love both self and other in a balanced way. Being dependent on another indicates a fundamental limitation to one's ability to act lovingly towards both oneself and others.

Focusing on one's self in relationship troubles talk means that one is creating a happy, successful life independent of a relationship. When members post messages focused on changing their relationship partners' selves, a typical form of social support given is that the poster needs to focus on his or her self and not on the issue originally raised in the post. Of utmost importance is the celebration of one's individual and autonomous self and rendered invisible is the presence of a relational self. When members do offer social support that seeks to help the original poster work out issues, their efforts are to problem-solve ways of achieving an understanding that facilitates compromise. Understanding and compromise are two additional key symbols that will be discussed below.

Celebrating the Other's Self

Celebrating another's self reflects the focus on independence described above and adds another component of self—a core that is knowable and that generally does not change. Posters who desire change in their relationship partners are refocused by other members who maintain that knowledge of one's partner offers two options: accept the partner or leave the relationship. The following extract was taken from a thread begun by natalie2000. In a lengthy post, natalie2000 tells the story of her 12-year marriage to her fire-fighter husband who spends much of his time away from his family working and volunteering at the fire station. Additional troubles include her husband having an online emotional affair—a computer-mediated relationship that provides emotional support and nurturing but that does not have a sexual component—and having an aloof relationship with his wife and kids. Quoting natalie2000, jasmine writes:

"When do I stop blaming myself for his shortcomings, or am I just being selfish for wanting a husband to come home and spend time with his family?"

It is not selfish to want a partner who works hard alongside you and comes home every night. But that is not what you chose. Do your kids the favor that your mother did not do for you. Teach them that if they choose a narcissitic [sic], selfish, man's-man who rushes into danger daily in order to earn accolades - that that is what they will get.

The man does not change after marriage, suddenly becoming a giving, punctual, attentive husband and good father. He remains the self-centered thrill seeker.

Your husband will pay attention to people who suck up to him big time and stroke his big ego. He wants worshipers, not a loving wife who expects to receive as well as give. He wants compliments, not constructive criticisms. To make the world go around, it DOES take all kinds. His kind has a place in our world. But no woman should marry a man like yours, unless she truly is just an adoring worshiper who will never ask for any reciprocation. (Yes, I believe these ladies do exist. Be glad you are not one of them.)

Jasmine's frame of natalie2000's situation as the product of a choice she made when she married her husband emphasizes that natalie2000 knew, because core aspects of self do not change, what type of man she was marrying. Importantly, her husband is not vilified, but rather his self is celebrated, for even a selfish partner who needs accolades and attention has a place in this world. As described above, jasmine's refocusing of natalie2000's attention—away from changing her husband towards accepting who her husband is—emphasizes independence and individualism.

Knowing a relationship partner means that a person is aware of the aspects of a partner that constitute her or his self—the constellation of values, beliefs and behaviors that are immutable aspects of an individual's core. If in the process of coming to know a relationship partner, a problem arises and change is sought, members' social support takes the form of suggesting two avenues of action: either accept that the problem will not go away or leave the relationship. As X explains, "You are with someone unconditionally, not with them to change them. If you do not like their behavior, then get out…or deal with the undesired behavior and stil [sic] love them." Because change is not culturally supported, ending a relationship becomes a way to celebrate a partner's self. "He's a good person," Toni states, "who deserves to find someone who's as content and happy with who and what he is—as he is himself, as evidenced by his lack of desire for improvement except at your prompting, urging and requirement." In this example, strugglingone is encouraged to end her relationship because she is not able to appreciate her partner's self.

In sum, to be a good relationship partner is to appreciate one's and another's self. Relationship partners demonstrate that they do not appreciate their partners by asking for or requiring change, which suggests they are not only not celebrating their partner's self, but, as stated above, one is not celebrating one's self. The proscription on change talk is premised on a belief that relationship partners are first and foremost autonomous individuals who have knowable and stable core aspects that constitute the essence of a person. There are two basic norms within change talk: (a) no one should require change where change suggests altering a self and (b) if change is desired, one should strive to assuage the felt need for change either by ending the relationship or working to become a more independent person. Within this system of communication, members seeking help and support are evaluated according to their adherence to these norms. If, for example, members ask for advice on how to solicit change from their partners, they will likely be told they are insecure, dependent, and controlling—all negative evaluations. Returning to the example of the newlywed, we hear switchback chastising her because she is heard as being insecure and dependent. This evaluation comes because the newlywed "won't tolerate [her husband] being who he is" because she sees him "as the path to success, security, and happiness." While alternative responses are imaginable, switchback's response is consistent with others who hear in a request for advice on how to change a partner not an opportunity to, for example, commiserate about social disadvantages women face in the workplace that erode their

earning potentials, but as an opportunity to help the person actualize a more independent life so as to achieve both security and happiness.

Alternatives to Change: Understanding and Compromise

Relationship troubles talk that does not expect change focuses on communicating to achieve an understanding of the issues in order to arrive at a workable compromise. By juxtaposing understanding with compromise, we arrive at an appreciation of a prescribed form for communication that occurs when there is a felt need for change. The following exchange begins with Emily, a self-identified introvert, seeking advice on how to help her boyfriend understand that, while she tried, she no longer wants to socialize with his friends.

From Emily:

I did talk to my boyfriend about the problem. He was so sweet and everything. But I guess he just didn't understand…! I told him that being introvert is just me. I can never change to what he wants and he just says its alright it just takes time. But its not time that I need, its his understanding I need that I do not even wish to change myself so drastically. That is just not me.

From brokenup:

"It just takes time." Did he mean that in regards to you changing/adapting yourself to him and his liking? Ummmmm, I don't think so buddy! Have you made a true effort to tell him there is a problem and you want change/compromise? Sounds like you at least did part of that from your last post in confronting him. Either that, or he is totally oblivious and in a cloud somewhere. If that is the case, explain clearly and precisely that "it is not the TIME you are looking for, but the UNDERSTANDING that is necessary for this relationship to survive." Compromise does come

hand in hand with that, but never compromise yourself for someone else's beliefs.

This extract illustrates that compromise can occur in a relationship if an understanding that facilitates a voluntary altering of one's behavior is present, but no one should compromise who they are (i.e., one's self) for the sake of another or a relationship. Here, compromise, as when Emily agreed to go out with her boyfriend's friends, is a voluntary altering of a non-core aspect of a self in the context of relationship troubles. When a compromise begins to impinge on one's self the compromise begins to take on the characteristics of change and, as has been noted, one should not attempt to change who they fundamentally are for another.

A culturally intelligible way of relating these terms could thus be stated: Understanding seeks to invite validation and support from another through communication that explains an impinged upon or hurt aspect of one's self. Understanding can therefore facilitate compromise; however, neither understanding nor compromise is heard as requiring change. In sum, social support given on the relationship boards suggests a general communication form people should enact when an issue arises that brings about a desire for change. Accordingly, people should (a) work toward an understanding of one's self and the relationship partner's self, (b) invite compromise when this understanding is not enough to assuage the desire for change, and (c) if the compromise is ineffectual or begins to inhibit one's self, end the communication pertaining to this particular desire for change either by accepting that no change will happen or by exiting the relationship. Underpinning the meaning, form and function of these key symbols are notions of self as an indelible part of a unique individual, which is changeable only when that individual believes an alteration is in her or his best interest.

CURRENT CHALLENGES: VALUING INDEPENDENCE AT IVILLAGE.COM

The focus of this study has been on assessing the extent to which social support provided on iVillage.com message boards can be beneficial for women. To this end, data was generated by attending to change as a key cultural symbol and a dominant way of communicating in relationship troubles talk was explicated. Now, the focus turns to assessing the findings of this case study in terms of what types of people are more or less privileged by the proscription on change talk and emphasis on independence. Here, Cross and Madson's (1997) work is used to bring gender into view.

Cross and Madson (1997) offer a compelling argument for rethinking gender differences. They suggest that gender differences can best be understood as differences in independent and interdependent self-construals, people's senses of who they are as well as how they should feel and relate to others. People with an independent self-construal are more focused on their "internal traits, skills, and attributes" while "group memberships, roles, and relationships are less important for self-definition" (Cross and Madson, 1997, p. 7). People with an interdependent self-construal view relationships as "integral parts of [a] person's very being" where their "thoughts, feelings, and wishes may be interpreted and understood in light of the thoughts, feelings, and behaviors of close others" (Cross and Madson, 1997, p. 7).

From a gender perspective, self-construals can explain variations found among people who share the same sex category as well as incongruities in biological sex and gender. There are many factors, such a person's membership in collectivist cultures, that influence one's self-construal and mitigate the effects of gender socialization. For example, African-American, Asian-American, and Latin-American people living in the United States are influenced by their socialization in communities that promote interdependent senses of self. In this way, Cross and Madson (1997) are careful not to reduce men and women to their sex-gender identity. However, they also identify trends that mark differences between males and females. Existing research reviewed by Cross and Madson (1997) suggests that women "tend to develop an interdependent self-construal, whereas men tend to develop an independent self-construal" (p. 22).

Utilizing the concept of self-construals provides an interpretive lens through which to view change talk findings. Communication surrounding change talk on iVillage.com message boards reflects a dominant U.S. American conceptualization of self as independent, unique, and stable across time and place. In the midst of communication about relationship troubles, the promotion of a self as primarily independent can be understood as privileging those who are socialized to have an independent sense of self and under-privileging those who have an interdependent sense of self. For members seeking support—and it is these members who engage in change talk—whose sense of self emphasizes connection to others, the emphasis on independence can be experienced as antithetical to how they see themselves. Indeed, members who engage in change talk may do so precisely because they emphasize interdependence rather than independence.

While Cross and Madson's (1997) work suggests that women, more so than men, may find the social support provided on the boards troubling, it is important to note that women on the relationship message boards both enact and proscribe change talk. It is not the intention of this case to reduce change talk to gender, but rather to suggest that the proscription on change talk tends to devalue an understanding of self as interdependent. An interdependent sense of self is related to gender insofar as U.S. American enculturated women tend towards this orientation. Indeed, the vast majority of members who request change on the relationship message boards are women. It is these women who are likely to be underserved by the emphasis on independence that obscures

other understandings of self—understandings that may make change talk deeply meaningful to the people who engage in it.

IVILLAGE.COM AS A WOMEN'S SITE

As discussed above, iVillage.com presents itself as an online community where women can meet and converse with others for pleasure, information, support, and advice. The message boards are the cornerstone of iVillage.com as a social community. Importantly, the boards are framed by iVillage.com and used by its members as forums to find and provide social support. As a site that provides social support, iVillage.com offers a safe, community-feeling environment.

This case has presented a dominant way of communicating on iVillage.com message boards when there was a need or desire to change a relationship partner's actions, beliefs, or values. The proscription on change talk described above is connected to a U.S. American cultural discourse described by Carbaugh (1988b) as promoting a sense of self as independent, unique, and relatively stable. In this way, the proscription on change talk is understood as not unique to iVillage.com.[1] Whereas some research suggests that online support groups may not help people move past their troubles (Wood and Smith, 2001), iVillage.com members who support others through a process of negotiating a dominant U.S. American understanding of self may in fact prove helpful.

While social support may be helpful for women, there is a down-side to the support that is given on the relationship boards. Moderators and members offering social support tend to focus on individual concerns rather than macro-level factors that may compound relationship troubles—including dominant cultural understandings of self. Remembering the newlywed's change talk described above provides a useful example. As mentioned, the newlywed stated that her husband was her means for financial stability. While members suggested that the newlywed should strive for independence, they did not engage in a discussion about macro-level obstacles for U.S. American women—especially those who are working class, women of color, or who have dependents—to earn a wage comparable to men's wages. While iVillage.com has message boards that address social issues (domestic abuse, substance abuse, work-place issues), these boards do not encourage women to consider macro-level factors that contribute to the issues communicated in their posts. Moderators and members working to provide information about relevant socio-cultural factors may shift the focus of responses to change talk from individual solutions to more community-building, albeit activist, macro-level solutions. Beyond a call for activism, this understanding may help facilitate increased sensitivity for the position in which change talkers find themselves.

REFERENCES

Alexa. (n.d.). *Traffic history for iVillage.com*. Retrieved March 25, 2009 from http://www.alexa.com/data/details/traffic_details/ivillage.com

Bem, S. L. (1993). *The lenses of gender: Transforming the debate on sexual inequality*. New Haven, CT: Yale University.

Bing, J. M., & Bergvall, V. L. (1996). The question of questions: Beyond binary thinking. In Bergvall, V. L., Bing, J. M., & Freed, A. F. (Eds.), *Rethinking language and gender research: Theory and practice* (pp. 1–30). New York: Longman.

Brown, E. B. (1997). What has happened here?: The politics of difference in women's history and feminist polities. In Nicholson, L. (Ed.), *The second wave: A reader in feminist theory* (pp. 272–287). New York: Routledge.

Bruckman, A. S. (1993). Gender swapping on the Internet. In *Proceedings of INET93*. Retrieved from http://www.mith2.umd.edu/WomensStudies/Computing/Articles+ResearchPapers/gender-swapping

Cameron, D. (1998). Gender, language, and discourse: A review essay. *Signs*, *23*(4), 945–973. doi:10.1086/495297

Carbaugh, D. (1988a). Comments on 'culture' in communication inquiry. *Communication Reports*, *1*, 38–41.

Carbaugh, D. (1988b). *Talking American: Cultural discourses on DONAHUE*. Norwood, NJ: Ablex.

Carbaugh, D. (1995). The ethnographic communication theory of Philipsen and associates. In Cushman, D., & Kovacic, B. (Eds.), *Watershed traditions in communication* (pp. 269–297). Albany, NY: SUNY.

Carbaugh, D. (2007). Cultural discourse analysis: Communication practices and intercultural encounters. *Journal of Intercultural Communication Research*, *36*(3), 167–182.. doi:10.1080/17475750701737090

Cross, S. E., & Madson, L. (1997). Models of the self: Self-construals and gender. *Psychological Bulletin*, *122*(1), 5–37. doi:10.1037/0033-2909.122.1.5

Crowston, K., & Kammerer, E. (1998). Communicative style and gender differences in computer-mediated communications. In Ebo, B. (Ed.), *Cyberghetto or cybertopia* (pp. 185–203). Westport, CT: Praeger.

Danet, B. (1998). Text as mask: Gender, play, and performance on the Internet. In Jones, S. G. (Ed.), *Cybersociety 2.0: Revisiting computer-mediated communication and community* (pp. 129–158). Thousand Oaks, CA: Sage.

Flanagin, A. J., Tiyaamornwong, V., O'Connor, J., & Seibold, D. R. (2002). Computer-mediated group work: The interaction of member sex and anonymity. *Communication Research, 29*, 66–93.. doi:10.1177/0093650202029001004

Graddol, D., & Swan, J. (1989). *Gender Voices*. Cambridge, MA: Basil Blackwell.

Hall, B. J., & Valde, K. (1995). Brown-nosing as a cultural category in American organizational life. *Research on Language and Social Interaction, 28*(4), 391–419. doi:10.1207/s15327973rlsi2804_3

Hample, D. (2008). Issue forum: Can we enhance people's lives? *Communication Monographs, 75*(4), 319–350.. doi:10.1080/03637750802524269

Herring, S. C. (1993). Gender and democracy in computer-mediated communication. *Electronic Journal of Communication, 3*(2). Retrieved from http://www.cios.org/www/ejcmain.htm

Herring, S. C. (1999). The Rhetorical dynamics of ender harassment on-line. *The Information Society, 15*, 151–167. doi:10.1080/019722499128466

Herring, S. C. (2003). Gender and power in online communication. In Holmes, J., & Meyerhoff, M. (Eds.), *The handbook of language and gender* (pp. 202–228). Malden, MA: Blackwell. doi:10.1002/9780470756942.ch9

Herring, S. C., & Martinson, A. (2004). Assessing gender authenticity in computer-mediated language use: Evidence from an identity game. *Journal of Language and Social Psychology, 23*, 424–446.. doi:10.1177/0261927X04269586

Hymes, D. (1962). The ethnography of speaking. In Gladwin, T., & Sturtevant, W. (Eds.), *Anthropology and human behavior* (pp. 13–53). Washington, D.C.: Anthropological Society of Washington.

Hymes, D. (1972). Models of the interaction of language and social life. In Gumperz, J., & Hymes, D. (Eds.), *Directions in sociolinguistics: The ethnography of communication* (pp. 35–71). New York: Holt, Rinehart, and Winston.

Hymes, D. (1974). *Foundations in sociolinguistics: An ethnographic approach*. Philadelphia: University of Pennsylvania Press.

Ivy, D., & Backlund, P. (2000). *Exploring genderspeak: Personal effectiveness in gender communication* (2nd ed.). Boston, MA: McGraw-Hill.

"jasmine" (pseudo.). (2009, May, 15). Emotionally neglected, is it time? [Advice given to a married woman]. Retrieved from http://messageboards.ivillage.com/iv-rlshouldista

Joinson, A. N. (2001). Self-disclosure in computer-mediated communication: The role of self-awareness and visual anonymity. *European Journal of Social Psychology, 31*, 177–192. doi:10.1002/ejsp.36

Kramarae, C., & Taylor, H. J. (1991). Women and men on electronic networks: A conversation or a monologue? In Taylor, H. J., Kramarae, C., & Ebben, M. (Eds.), *Women, information technology, and scholarship* (pp. 52–61). Urbana, Champaign: Center for Advanced Study, University of Illinois.

Lee, E. (2007a). Effects of gendered language on gender stereotyping in computer-mediated communication: The moderating role of depersonalization and gender-role orientation. *Human Communication Research, 33*(4), 515–535.. doi:10.1111/j.1468-2958.2007.00310.x

Lee, E. (2007b). Wired for gender: Experientiality and gender-stereotyping in computer-mediated communication. *Media Psychology, 10*, 182–210. doi:.doi:10.1080/15213260701375595

Nowak, K. L. (2003). Sex categorization in computer mediated communication (CMC): Exploring the utopian promise. *Media Psychology*, *5*, 83–103. doi:10.1207/S1532785XMEP0501_4

Quantcast. *Summary*. Retrieved May 4, 2009 from http://www.quantcast.com/ivillage.com

Rellstab, D. H. (2007). Staging gender online: Gender plays in Swiss internet relay chats. *Discourse & Society*, *18*(6), 765–787.. doi:10.1177/0957926507082195

Ridings, C. M., & Gefen, D. (2004). Virtual community attraction: Why people hang out online. *Journal of Computer-Mediated Communication*, *10*(1). Retrieved from http://jcmc.indiana.edu/index.html.

Rodgers, S., & Chen, Q. (2005). Internet community group participation: Psychosocial benefits for women with breast cancer. *Journal of Computer-Mediated Communication*, *10*(4). Retrieved from http://jcmc.indiana.edu/index.html.

Rodino, M. (1997). Breaking out of binaries: Reconceptualizing gender and its relationship to language in computer-mediated communication. *Journal of Computer-Mediated Communication*, *3*(3). doi:.doi:10.1111/j.1083-6101.1997.tb00074.x

"Switchback" (pseudo.). (2004, April). Help [Advice given to a woman who seeks help with her husband's upsetting behaviors.] Retrieved from http://messageboards.ivillage.com/ relationshipproblems

"Tess" (pseudo.). (2004, April). Help [Advice given to a woman who seeks help with her husband's upsetting behaviors.] Retrieved from http://messageboards.ivillage.com/ relationshipproblems

Thomson, R. (2006). The effect of topic of discussion on gendered language in computer-mediated communication discussion. *Journal of Language and Social Psychology*, *25*, 167–178.. doi:10.1177/0261927X06286452

"Toni" (pseudo.). (2004, May). My bf wont listen [Advice given to a woman whose boyfriend spends too much time socializing with friends]. Retrieved from http://messageboards.ivillage.com/relationshipproblems

Turner, J. W., Grube, J. A., & Meyers, J. (2001). Developing an optimal match within online communities: An exploration of CMC support communities and traditional support. *The Journal of Communication*, *51*(2), 231–251. doi:10.1111/j.1460-2466.2001.tb02879.x

Van Doorn, N., van Zoonen, L., & Wyatt, S. (2007). Writing from experience: Presentations of gender identity on weblogs. *European Journal of Women's Studies*, *14*(2), 143–159.. doi:10.1177/1350506807075819

Wolf, A. (2000). Emotional expression online: Gender differences in emoticon use. *Cyberpsychology & Behavior*, *3*(5), 827–833. doi:10.1089/10949310050191809

Wood, A. F., & Smith, M. J. (2001). *Online communication: Linking technology, identity, and culture*. Mahwah, NJ: Lawrence Erlbaum.

"X" (pseudo.) (2004, April). My husband wont help out [Advice given to a married woman whose husband does not help clean or take care of the children]. Retrieved from http://messageboards.ivillage.com/relationshipproblems

KEY TERMS AND DEFINITIONS

Anonymity: In computer-mediated communication, the ability of a person to be unknown to others and others' abilities to be unknown to that person. Anonymity has been linked to both greater gender play and increased self-disclosure online.

Change Talk: Communication on iVillage. com relationship message boards that focuses on altering a relationship partner's behaviors, beliefs, or values.

Emotional Affair: A relationship that offers emotional support and nurturing but does not have a sexual component. Communication in the relationship can be either face-to-face or mediated through technologies such as computers and telephones.

Gender Binary: A term used to describe a common view of gender in which gender is correlated to biological sex and exists in two opposing and complementary forms: feminine and masculine.

Self: A culturally variable sense of the constitution of a person. A US American understanding of self defines people as being individuals who have a unique, knowable and stable core or essence.

Self-Construal: A person's understanding of who they are that influences how she or he relates to others.

Social Support: The help given to others in order to ameliorate an issue or crisis in their lives. In online communities, social support is largely comprised of emotional, informational, and problem-solving support given to members of the community. In face-to-face interactions, social support can include these types of support as well as physical (e.g., hugs) and material (e.g., money) support.

ENDNOTES

[1] While proscriptions on change talk may under-privilege some female members, it is important to take a broader perspective when assessing iVillage.com as a women's site. The extent to which this finding taps into a dominant U.S. American understanding of self is best highlighted by reference to the textbook, *Exploring Genderspeak: Personal effectiveness in gender communication* (Ivy & Backlund, 2000). In a chapter on intimate relationships, the authors suggest a commonly held belief some people have is that they can change some aspect of their relational partner. This belief in and desire for changing a relational partner is, they suggest, a nonproductive tendency that should be abandoned for the more productive and caring solution to conflict surrounding a partner's behavior—acceptance. "The importance of acceptance in this type of relationship can hardly be overemphasized," they argue, for it is "within [this] acceptance that we can change to please ourselves and to improve the relationship" (Ivy & Backlund, 2000, p. 304). The extent to which this passage reflects the communication analyzed in change talk is striking.

Chapter 18

Getting on the "E" List:
Email List Use in a Community of Service Provider Organizations for People Experiencing Homelessness

Craig R. Scott
Rutgers University, USA

Laurie K. Lewis
Rutgers University, USA

Scott C. D'Urso
Marquette University, USA

EXECUTIVE SUMMARY

This case examines how a community of organizations providing service to people experiencing homelessness made use of an electronic mail list. Current economic conditions have encouraged organizations in various sectors—including nonprofits—that might normally compete for scarce resources to collaborate with one another to increase their chances of survival. One set of tools likely to be of value in such relationships includes various online discussion technologies. An examination of this community's email list use over a three-year period suggests a somewhat complex picture regarding technology use. More specifically, some issues both constrain and enable use. Additionally, seemingly basic and minimal uses of the list provided not only the greatest functionality for the users, but also led to several unanticipated consequences for those involved.

INTRODUCTION

Homelessness continues to be a complex social problem in countries such as the U.S. It impacts individuals of all ages, races, and geographic regions. The Department of Housing and Urban Development's most recent Homeless Assessment Report (2009) puts the number of persons experiencing homelessness at some point over a year-long period at approximately 1.6 million, with nearly 700,000 on a single night. Other groups estimate as many as 3.5 million people per year experience homelessness (National Law Center on Homelessness & Poverty, 2008). Evidence seems to suggest the current economic situation in this country is

DOI: 10.4018/978-1-61520-863-0.ch018

increasing the number of persons considered homeless. HUD's most recent annual report notes a clear rise in families coming directly from housed living arrangements now seeking shelters; furthermore, a recent report from the National Law Center on Homelessness and Poverty (2009) suggests foreclosures are leading to more people findings themselves homeless. Simultaneously, the number of organizations proving services to this population and the available resources to address the concern is shrinking.

Despite the significance of this social issue, scholars in general have paid relatively little attention to the organizations that must interact with one another to serve those individuals who are homeless (see North, Pollio, Perron, Eyrich, & Spitznagel for a notable exception). Miller, Scott, Stage, and Birkholt's (1995) examination of service provision and Tompkins (2009) recent book on communicating to end homelessness represent some of the only work in the field of organizational communication to touch on this issue. In terms of communication-based solutions, communication technology has been linked directly to individuals who are homeless. Schmitz, Rogers, Phillips, and Paschal (1995) described a free computer-based network system available for use by persons who were homeless—and several sizable programs have emerged in the last two decades to provide free phones and computers with Internet access to users experiencing homelessness (see Dvorak, 2009; Ramey, 2008). The project reported in this current case (called CTOSH, for Collaborative Technologies for Organizations Serving the Homeless) attempts to provide that technological solution to the organizations tasked with providing various services to individuals who find themselves homeless.

ORGANIZATION BACKGROUND

This case examines an interorganizational network of nonprofits and government agencies provid-ing service to individuals currently considered homeless in a large metropolitan area in the southwest United States. This network includes approximately 25 organizations directly or indi-rectly providing support and services to a fluid population of over 4,000 persons experiencing homelessness—including families, unaccom-panied youth, and single men and women. The community studied here is like many others with a network of agencies creating a patchwork of service provision—sometimes working in strong collaborative relationships and sometimes work-ing only with minimal awareness of one another. Despite what was sometimes a shared mission to end homelessness, the provider organizations lacked a number of tools (e.g., website, chat tools, discussion forums, collaboration tools, etc.) to help them better interact with one another.

In 2001 the first and second authors received initial grant funding to start what would later come to be called CTOSH (Collaborative Technologies for Organizations Serving the Homeless; pro-nounced "See-Tosh"). Much of the next year was spent securing additional funds, gaining necessary approvals, and conducting baseline research on the current state of collaborative engagement, interorganizational communication, and com-munication technology use within this network of service providers. Approximately 25 agencies initially signed up to participate in CTOSH. In early 2003, most organizations were given new comput-ers (which oftentimes replaced much slower and older computers), provided with connectivity to high-speed Internet (for those organizations who lacked it), trained for and initially introduced to several new communication technologies (e.g., instant messaging, NetMeeting, email list, web-site, and a hosted electronic meeting system), and offered ongoing technical support for these tools.

The CTOSH email list was established in April 2003, but did not reach its current configuration until July of that year. CTOSH provided the email list as a means for individuals within the community of service provider organizations or others interested in receiving information about that community's activities, to post and receive messages. The list was unmoderated, but open to subscribers only. Initially, the list was configured so that all replies went back to the original list as a way to facilitate community awareness; but after a series of unintended personal replies went back to all subscribers, community members requested that replies only go back to the sender (replies-to-all would still go back to the entire list). This change was made in July of 2003, with no other major changes made to the list configuration afterwards. The list was hosted by the university where the researchers were employed at the time of data collection and continues to operate as of the writing of this case.

The CTOSH project officially ended with a final round of data collection in spring and summer of 2006—four years after the initial baseline survey was conducted in this network and three years after the email list, website, and other technologies were introduced to these organizations. Those three years have been characterized by both technology use and nonuse, and thus this network of organizations provides an ideal case site in which to examine email list use and interaction.

SETTING THE STAGE: INTERORGANIZATIONAL RELATIONSHNIPS AND INFORMATION & COMMUNICATION TECHNOLOGIES (ICTS)

Interorganizational relationships comprise long and short-term linkages among pairs or multiple partner organizations. "These linkages are seen as the means by which organizations manage their dependencies on resources necessary for organizational survival" (Miller et al., 1995, p. 681). Typically, interorganizational relationships are discussed as one of a number of formal structural arrangements among organizations (including trade associations, voluntary agency federations, joint ventures, joint programs, networks, consortia, alliances, and interlocking directorates; see Barringer & Harrison, 2000; Oliver, 1990). Researchers and theorists working out of the transaction costs perspective, resource dependence theory, stakeholder theory, and institutional theory among others (Barringer & Harrison) have explored the benefits and costs of given organizations entering specific interorganizational relations (usually with one other organization). Communication scholars have also been a part of this wave of organizational scholarship on these relationships. Studies have included examination of business consortia (Browning, Beyer, & Shetler, 1995), health and human service networks (Miller et al., 1995) and public-private alliances (Heath & Sias, 1999; Keyton & Stallworth, 2003; Zoller, 2004), communication with external stakeholders by organizations (Cheney & Dionisopoulous, 1989; Levine & White, 1961; Lewis, Hamel, & Richardson, 2001; Lewis, Richardson, & Hamel, 2003), and the role of technology and technology adoption in interorganizational relationships (Flanagin, 2000; Monge, Fulk, Kalman, Flanagin, Parnassa & Rumsey, 1998).

The communities and networks of practice literature (see Iverson & McPhee, 2002; Vaast, 2004) has been particularly relevant to understanding linkages between interorganizational relationships and ICTs. Vaast concluded from case studies of two networks of practice that ICTs create an awareness of others, reaffirm joint goals, provide access to key resources and relationships, and help create a sense of identity with the broader network practices. Burt and Taylor (2000) found that the use of electronic networks enhanced opportunities for nonprofit organizations to collaborate by drawing upon other organizations for support during campaigns, responding rapidly to events as they occurred, easily drawing on expertise across the globe, and providing knowledge and support to other organizations with similar goals. Butler's (2001) resource-based model of online social structure argued these structures help create feelings of affiliation, encourage discussion and knowledge sharing, allow for information access and dissemination, and enable collective activities. Butler's analysis of a random set of online, list-based groups concluded that communication activity and list size have both positive and negative effects on the group's sustainability.

One set of tools likely to be of value in such interorganizational relationships include various new information and communication technologies (ICTs) found on the Internet. Wellman et al. (1996) suggested that computer-supported social networks foster a wide variety of cooperative work—providing a means of communication for individuals within and between organizations. Such networks are focused on information exchange, as participants have the opportunity to read, post a question or comment, and receive additional information in return. The ability to broadcast a message through this medium increases the possibility of finding the information sought and can also alter the normal distribution process of that information.

In some ways, there is no shortage of theories and perspectives about technology "use" in the literature. Beyond providing basic access to tools, a number of theories familiar to most readers have offered various technologically-deterministic (see, for example, Daft & Lengel, 1984; Davis, 1989; Short, Williams, & Christie, 1976) or more socially-deterministic (see, for example, Fulk, 1993; Fulk, Schmitz, & Steinfield, 1990; MacKenzie & Wajcman, 1999) explanations for why people use or select certain media. In response, other perspectives such as adaptive structuration (Poole & DeSanctis, 1990; 1992), the duality of technology (Orlikowski, 1992), and the mutual shaping perspective (Boczkowski, 1999) have highlighted technologies and their users as well as the mutual influence of technology use and structure. Drawing heavily on Giddens' (1984) structuration theory, these perspectives have drawn attention to the joint interactions of users and technological structures. This duality of technology,

as Orlikowski described it, demands a consideration of technological and other structures as they influence and are influenced by usage in action.

Two pieces of scholarship help provide some useful framing within this duality. First, Lievrouw (2006) discussed both diffusion of innovation and the social shaping of technology, and used them to illustrate the distinction between determination (order) and contingency (uncertainty) as "seen at several key junctures or 'moments' in new media development and use" (p. 247). These "moments" can include the origin (introduction) of new media, actors (users and other decision makers), dynamics and choices (which involves adoption and use), and consequences of use (both expected and unexpected). For each of these moments, usage issues can be understood in terms of determination and contingency, or the degree to which technology use is shaped by various structural forces and the degree to which user choices influence technology (as well as the possibility that both occur jointly). Second, Boczkowski's (1999) work on mutual shaping is relevant both for the framework it adopts, and for the nature of the technology examined. Boczkowski studied an email list community (the Argentine Mailing list, mostly for Argentine nationals living abroad) and notes various constraints, triggers, and enablements related to the technology, users, and broader structural forces. As he concluded, taking this sort of approach ideally "broadens our understanding of the technology-user relationship in CMC by examining the dynamics of mutual shaping..." (p. 104).

This duality of technology focus seemed especially appropriate in a community of service providers for individuals experiencing homelessness as they encounter various ICTs. First, the network provided a complex social structure in which decisions about use (and nonuse) were made—providing both determination and choice possibilities. Furthermore, the technologies being used in such a community were fundamentally interactive and group based (e.g., an email list), which made usage decisions more complex than for those used individually or to facilitate even one-on-one interaction. Additionally, the ongoing nature of these communities required perspectives that view media use as subject to both forces of change and stability over time. By considering moments of use ranging from first exposure through everyday use and its consequences, one can be more aware of the situations where users and technologies exert varied degrees of influence on actual technology use.

CASE STUDY: EXAMINING THE EMAIL LIST

Research Questions

This case study examines several observations related to the use and non-use of these technologies in this community of providers—focusing most heavily on an email list that in many ways served to define this network of organizations. This focus seems appropriate considering that email lists represent a familiar form of online discussion for many, as one recent survey in the workplace context noted email lists were more common than tools such as blogs, IM, group-based collaboration tools, and web-based teleconferencing (D'Urso & Pierce, 2009). Also, these email list communities "are much more like loosely-knit voluntary organizations than the tightly knit social communities highlighted in prior case studies" (Cummings, Butler, & Kraut, 2002, p. 106), which further points to the need to examine them.

More specifically, the following questions are explored:

- **RQ1:** What are reasons for email list use and nonuse?
- **RQ2:** How are these email lists used and not used in this network?
- **RQ3:** What are the consequences of use and nonuse of these email lists?

Sources of Case Data

This case study utilized four primary sources of data from various points in time. The researchers tracked email list (and web) usage via automatically recorded logs, used an on-line survey to capture self-reports of email list users, and conducted face-to-face interviews with CTOSH participants (each described below). Additionally, the authors spent numerous hours over the four years of the project in Homeless Task Force meetings, attending events related to homelessness in the area, volunteering through formal programs to serve individuals currently considered homeless, and consulting for the larger Homeless Task Force organization that helps oversee many of these organizations.

Email List and Other Log Data

Data from 36 months (August, 2003 – July, 2006) of email list usage by members of this community help answer the research questions. More specifically, archived logs indicating not only the message content (which is not the major focus here), but also number of messages, number of subscribed members, number of active posters (versus readers/lurkers), and number of replies/forwards/original messages (by person and by year) were examined. Most analysis allows for a comparison of each of three years of use, as well as changes from year to year and over the course of the full project. Although members of the CTOSH research staff were also email list subscribers and periodically sent messages to the list members, these have been excluded in the current analysis so as to maintain focus on the community of service providers.

Email List Subscriber Survey

An online survey was used to collect data from email list subscribers about their uses of the email list. The survey was posted for two weeks in late spring of 2006, and an announcement and two reminder emails were posted to the list to encourage participants to respond to the survey. Forty-four subscribers completed and submitted the survey, representing a 41% response rate. The survey first asked participants to reflect on how often they use and how often they would like to use six different sending/reading aspects of the CTOSH website and email list (the difference between current and desired use was used to create a communication adequacy score for each of these questions). Participants were also asked to rate six items related to the value of the CTOSH email list and six items related to the value of the CTOSH website. The questionnaire also asked questions related to moving conversations started on the list to other media, preferred email list providers, and the importance of nine specific types of list messages (later collapsed into five types): posting general information, requesting information, responses to requests, emphasizing identity and community, and encouraging activist engagement.

Interviews with CTOSH Participants

Near the end of the three year project, efforts were made to interview a representative from each of the agencies involved in the CTOSH project. The authors were able to conduct 21 interviews. Interview participants were asked about the general character of communication in the network, their participation in collaboration, their personal use of the CTOSH email list and website, reasons for non-use, and changes they observed in the network since the beginning of the CTOSH project. Interviews lasted between 30 minutes and 1 hour, and 120 pages of transcripts were produced from these tape-recorded interviews. Using a combination of open coding (see Emerson, Fretz, & Shaw, 1995; Owen, 1984), analytical induction (Bulmer, 1979; Huberman & Miles, 1994), and a constant comparative method of analysis (see Glaser & Strauss, 1967), the authors eventually arrived at a set of themes to help answer the research questions.

KEY FINDINGS: EXPLORING USE AND NONUSE

The results are organized here in terms of several general themes related to the three research questions: reasons for use and nonuse, how the technology is used and not used, and consequences of that use/nonuse. These themes represent key findings about this interorganizational network's use and non-use of email lists over approximately three years of this project.

Fluid Membership and Loose Boundaries

One very prominent theme related to influences on the use or nonuse of these tools concerned the ways in which the fluid membership in this network and the rather loosely defined boundaries of the network promoted and potentially discouraged use of these tools. Part of the issue here is sizable movement of people between agencies and in/out of the provider network generally. Moreover, it is difficult to know who "belongs" to this network at any given time, perhaps because social service groups are characteristically very open and somewhat averse to drawing tight boundaries around membership. Although some agencies are focused directly on addressing homelessness, other service providers are on the edge of this network in that serving individuals who are homeless is a secondary mission (for example, some agencies were focused on teen pregnancy; serving veterans; or serving illegal immigrants all of which had some portion of their client population who were considered homeless). As one interviewee noted "I'm not sure how we ended up as part of the CTOSH group, other than that we are dealing with transition planning for people who were homeless before they came to jail..." [Interview #4].

The introduction of CTOSH provided an opportunity for individuals and organizations to draw somewhat of a line around this dispersed community (e.g., those listed as CTOSH organizations on the website, those who were reached through list announcements about the task force meetings or other planning group meetings). As the email list developed over time, and individuals informally referred to "CTOSH messages / announcements" in face-to-face interactions, its function as a virtual and central information gathering place was enhanced. This ability to define the network increased desire and appropriateness of using these tools. As one former leader of the Homeless Task Force indicated, "The thing about CTOSH, if someone wants to learn about homelessness in [*city withheld*], go to the [CTOSH] website and sign on to the [CTOSH] listserv. Do those two things before coming to a meeting and acting like you know everything" [Interview #6]. Thus, the need for a marker to determine who was "in" and who was "out" of the provider network, coupled with the need to communicate in a general forum to "all of us," tended to promote the use of CTOSH tools. The email list became the way to reach others in this community, and that need to reach out encouraged ICT use. Email list users confirmed this, with 76.2% of respondents (n = 32) indicating the email list is the single most effective means they have for spreading information to others in the network (M = 4.21), and 75.0% (n = 30) indicating the email list is the most effective means they have for obtaining information from others in the network (M = 4.10).

However, the fluidity of the user network was also reflected in the list membership. Every year, at least 20 people left the list and another 20-40 new subscribers joined. In fact, over half the membership on the list at the project's end (n = 64) were not subscribed at the outset of this effort (only 50 members were there from start through finish). This sort of fluidity may also discourage use because users do not know who is "on" the email list. Occasionally, a community leader might inquire as to who was on the list and on a few occasions this information was sent to members—but for the most part, users seemed to only have a vague idea as to who received CTOSH messages (illustrated most clearly when email list members were sometimes copied on list messages).

Ownership of Tools

In a second theme related to influences of use and nonuse, analysis revealed the "ownership" of these tools and how that ownership was perceived may have affected use. Most of the participants perceived these tools to be "owned" by the research team who was responsible for CTOSH. Despite providing information at the outset of the project, inquiries were still made by some agencies near the end of the project if the computer equipment provided was really theirs to keep. This construction of who owned the tools tended to create hesitancy on the part of the participants in creating rules and norms for the use of the tools. Only in the very end of the project when it was announced the assessment phase was concluding did the providers begin to discuss on their own what these tools should be used for, how they ought to be named, and how they ought to operate. This lack of perceived internal ownership of the CTOSH tools likely contributed to a general sense of confusion about how the email list and other technology should be used. Approximately 20% of the interview participants noted a lack of certainty about appropriate use of the list. Possibly, many of the "lurkers" on this list did not post due to some uncertainty about how to post and what was acceptable to post. One interviewee noted:

Like we had a big luncheon a couple of weeks ago... now was that appropriate to send to the listserv, or no? And then, I don't remember any organization really... talking about something, like a fundraiser, or something that their own organization was doing. But, that struck me like "huh, why not?" and wouldn't that be a good thing for everyone else in homeless services to know? [Interview #8]

Another interviewee expressed desire that some rules for what to post were made clear to the list subscribers, "there is on occasion to where communication is sent through that just kind of creates noise more so than anything else. And you know I just kind of typically delete those when I see them. Maybe if people were to have some sort of standard of protocol or just education about what is appropriate to send out" [Interview #4].

However, in other ways, the ownership issue clearly encouraged use. Beyond providing access, training, technical support, and maintenance of the tools over the course of the project, the list owners also monitored subscribers to the email list and website so that they did not become a place for spam—which almost certainly enabled use by the community. In fact, when list subscribers were asked if they'd prefer to have a separate list not owned by the research university (but potentially subject to advertising), two-thirds of respondents (n = 28, 66.7%) indicated they did not want to switch to a commercial provider (M = 2.21). Thus, the owners of the technology were clearly not objective third party researchers in this project, but both directly and indirectly encouraged and discouraged use of these tools as actors in the construction of these technologies.

Time Demands and Needs for Efficiency

A third theme concerning use and nonuse of these tools relates to the real need for these providers to be efficient with use of their time. The substantial time demands and typical understaffing of those agencies involved in service provision to individuals experiencing homelessness necessitated that everyone prioritize their time carefully. As one respondent (who eventually agreed to complete the interview) described his time crunch in terms of just making time for the interview: "I'm looking at my schedule and having a hard time fitting this in. With the Katrina evacuees and the Rita evacuees… I'm just having a hard time keeping

up…" and after a long pause, "I just don't have the time" [Interview #1]. Another noted "we have two paid staff people…and the rest of our crew is volunteers… and we have days where two volunteers are out and it is two paid staff members and one volunteer, and it is all we can do to keep our head above water" [Interview 8].

These time constraints likely explain why some tools were almost never used. As one community leader shared informally, the "costs" for learning some of the CTOSH provided tools (e.g., instant messaging, NetMeeting, and electronic meeting technology) were simply too great. Although there was some training attended by agency representatives, individuals simply did not have time to really learn new tools and habits; as a result, they were not used. These constraints were even clearer as an explanation for why individuals did not post more messages to the email list. When participants were asked to estimate their current and desired frequency of use for various aspects of the CTOSH tools, using a 1-to-5 scale, participants reported a desire to send more emails to the list; across nearly every aspect of the email list participants wanted to use the tool more than they actually do.

However, the need for efficiency was also a driver for some people's use of the email list. Most members were subscribed to the list by the owners based on existing email records or individual requests; consequently, there was no cost involved and messages appeared in one's inbox. Furthermore, the email list made it possible to efficiently send messages to multiple others in the network, and to usually receive replies quickly as well. As one interviewee commented about the responsiveness of this community through CTOSH list requests for information: "what I found as a partner in CTOSH is that people want to give you information. If they've got it, I'm not going to be sitting here waiting… I'll have something that day and by the next day I'll have several more responses and that is good" [Interview #8]. Especially for busy service providers in this sort of interorganizational network, having tools that are efficient to use will encourage use.

High-Touch, Low-Tech Norm

A final theme related to the explanations for nonuse of some CTOSH tools (including the list) centered on a conception of their "business" as one that is high-touch and low-tech. As one interviewee put it, "life is about who shows up. People are just not ready for the disconnect technology creates. We are in a high touch business. A lot of what we do is consensus work; not a lot of formal voting taken" [Interview #6]. Another interviewee said, "I'm such a people person that I'd think I'd rather call someone on the phone" [Interview #8]. This respondent went on to explain, "yeah everything feels so much more grass roots and non-tech, not even low-tech, but non-tech practically... just more front-line feel I guess." Some users seemed a little apologetic that they had no interest in most of these tools, but also satisfied with doing things in the more traditional low-tech way. This strong preference served as an explanation for lack of enthusiasm about some new technologies.

Sharing of General Information

In the first of the themes about *how* tools were used, the major value of the email list was reported to be posting general information. A strong norm developed over time that the list tool should be used to post information that would be generally useful across a wide spectrum of providers and list subscribers. Although one interviewee noted "sometimes there are things that go out that don't seem quite appropriate for the whole group. When people hit respond and they really should respond to one person, and they respond to the whole CTOSH list" [Interview #5], this was quite rare (especially after the list was reconfigured four months after its inception, at users' requests, so that replies went back to the sender only). In general, email list logs note that the list averaged about

27 messages a month (slightly less than one per day), and approximately two-thirds of those were original posts. Only 12% of posts were replies to other messages (and not all of those appear to be replies to other messages on this list) and approximately 22% were items of interest forwarded from other emails. There was a real reluctance to "overwhelm" or annoy others by posting too much unwanted information, which helped sustain email list usability in some ways. But, at the same time, configuring the list not to reply-to-all may have discouraged online discussion and engagement of issues by list members—thus resulting in the tool not being used for certain types of exchange.

As further evidence of this narrow focus, questions posted on the list were nearly always responded to off-list. As one respondent indicated, "Some people might reply to it [the list posts], but a lot of the replies are just like, you know, just small conversations about what we've done and stuff. It is more announcements and things you want everybody to know. Like I said, the discussions usually happened off-line of the listserv" [Interview #6]. This was reflected in the survey data as well, where participants were asked if they had ever moved a conversation initiated on the email list to another communication medium. Participants reported taking up conversations most often via personal email (M = 3.74), followed by telephone and face-to-face conversation (M = 3.21 and 3.12). When asked what topics they discuss off-list, participants indicated this often occurs when they are seeking or providing more specific information than the general types of public information encountered on the list, as well as issues related to individual referrals or scheduling.

Reading and Lurking

In a second theme related to types of use, the analysis suggested that many participants found benefit in "lurking." Indeed, this list is like most in that there are many lurkers who are subscribed, but do not post (Rafaeli & Sudweeks, 1997; Schild & Oren, 2005). In fact, of the 50 subscribers who were on the list for the entire 3 years of this assessment, 70% were lurkers. In none of the three years were there more posters than lurkers. In one sense, this represents a type of nonuse because these members are not engaging in any reciprocation to those making posts. Lurkers are constructed as nonusers by others (both "posters" and "lurkers") because they are largely hidden to others on the list.

Yet, this form of use is not necessarily problematic and may even be construed as a beneficial form of use. In the survey, participants were asked to reflect on the frequency with which they performed different actions using the CTOSH tools, using a 1-to-5 scale. They reported reading email list messages (M = 4.16) far more often then they reporting sending emails to the list (M = 2.43). Correlations suggest reading emails on the list is correlated with participants' perceived value of the email list (r = .457, p<.01), but sending emails to the list is not. Beyond this, there may be real benefit that not all 100+ subscribers were regularly posting to the list.

Uneven Use Over Time

In a third theme related to types of use, it became clear through observations that use and nonuse varied quite a bit over time. This can be illustrated in several ways, but perhaps the clearest illustration of this variation over time is seen in the email list logs. Over the course of the three years, there is a clear growth in the number of posts, from 234 in the first year to 314 in the second year, to 438 in the third year of assessment. This growth occurs despite relatively stable membership size in terms of list subscribers (averaging 110 for the 3 years).

This use was also punctuated. For example, the periodic announcements of website spotlight articles (journalistic style feature stories on each of the agencies) would produce activity on the website that did not exist otherwise. More

directly, if less frequently, events in the annual cycle of this community (e.g., turning in major funding proposals, the homelessness Stand-down, and high profile fundraising events by major agencies) could produce email list activity. Unexpected events also triggered substantial use. Most notably, during and immediately following Hurricanes Katrina and Rita in August/September 2005, there was a necessity to publicize up to the minute information for everyone to know about evacuees, shelter space, volunteer opportunities, etc. The email list was mobilized by people in a very active way (with usage in the month of September that year up 42 posts from the same month the year before).

Redefining What It Meant to be Part of This Community

In addition to how the CTOSH tools influenced use by helping to place a boundary on this community, this defining and redefining is also seen as a somewhat surprising consequence (the last theme category) of the way members used the technology. By joining the list, having a website spotlight on the website, or being listed as a CTOSH organization on the website, individuals and their respective organizations were more likely to be perceived as legitimately "in the network." This operated on a simple level of increasing awareness of programs; as one interviewee stated, "I like the listserv stuff. I like that people get to know about our program and that I get to know other people's programs" [Interview #4]. This "connection" was evidenced in numerous other interviews that expressed that the label / filter of CTOSH created a sense of belonging among those that used the list. There was, in some cases, a reinterpretation of the community of providers as more tight-knit as a result of their communication behaviors through the list. As one interviewee noted about communication in the network since the introduction of CTOSH, "People are more connected. There is probably much more understanding of what is happening on a macro level. Before people operated more in their silos. So CTOSH has brought people together" [Interview # 5]. Another noted about the email list specifically, "It provides more cohesion to our community of service providers…" [Interview #9].

Beyond the heightened awareness and cohesion, messages through the CTOSH tools seemed to carry a special legitimacy to them that further defined who was and was not part of this group. When one interviewee was asked "when you get a message through the CTOSH list do you pay a lot of attention to it?" he responded, "yeah, because they want to help homeless people... automatically if they are on CTOSH they are... one of our brothers, one of our sisters" [Interview #5]. Another respondent further discussed using CTOSH as a way to screen email:

When I open up an email and it is from CTOSH partners, there is no question that I found it valuable. Whether it is going to work for me or not, I have a lot of respect and value for it coming through CTOSH... there are some that I definitely go "who is that?" But "who is that" comes after ... and it is a "who is that?" because I need to know who that is source is, not who I should trust. [Interview #8]

Centralizing and Decentralizing

In a second theme about consequences of use of these tools, the prominence of organizations and individuals was often exaggerated as a result of who did and did not use these tools. In some instances, already central users gained additional voice, and in other cases voice was found by those who were previously unheard. Analysis revealed the most prominent members that had been considered highly influential prior to CTOSH were likely to use these tools in a way that augmented that high profile. On the email list, for example, the most frequent posters are often already highly visible members in the community—including the

city's service coordinator for homelessness, the manager of a large client database, chairs of the Homeless Task Force, and a well-known activist for persons considered homeless. Frequent posters (those making at least one post every two months) dominate the list, with these 13 subscribers (12% of the total) accounting for 84% of all list messages in the final year of the project. In this sense, the active use of these tools by certain members and not others helps to reinforce existing structures.

There is also evidence, though, that use of the CTOSH tools enhanced the profile of organizations and individuals who had previously been perceived as more peripheral. For example, on the email list there is some indication of wider use with 52 different individuals making posts in the last year of the project. Even some of the frequent posters are neither in what would likely be considered high profile organizations nor in official capacities in this network— suggesting that there is some ability to use these tools to gain voice.

CONCLUSION AND RECOMMENDATIONS

One of the clearest issues illustrated in this case study is the mutual shaping between technology (and other structures) and patterns of technology use within a community of users. This duality was illustrated in how the use of the list and website tended to emphasize a previously non-existent or invisible boundary around this network, and in turn, how that boundary creation served a function for the community that then reified the use of the tools that had created it. The consequence of this boundary reinforcement, for some, was an experience of both "bonding" with others who shared the "inside" status as well as an increased sense of efficiency in reaching "everyone" in the network by using these tools. Ironically, since so few people really knew who the list subscribers were, and no one had really discussed the criteria for who should be included in the list and who should not, the boundary and the subsequent feelings of "we-ness" they created may not have reflected reality. Still, as one interviewee put it, "It gives me a sense of security to know that there's a network where if there's really something important I need to see I know it will cross my computer screen." This sort of faith in the completeness of this network as it was represented on the list and website was reassuring to the participants and drove them to increasingly require newcomers to learn the CTOSH information and become familiar with the CTOSH postings before being considered "literate." This is remarkable considering that email list posts were made primarily by a small number of community members who contributed whatever they deemed potentially useful information to the list at a given point in time.

Another key conclusion about the use of these tools is how strong this sense of community arose, for the most part, from fairly routine information postings that expressed very little emotionality, group identification, or lengthy prose. Just the existence of the network as it was highlighted by the postings seemed to provide that sense of community to a somewhat beleaguered group of providers too often isolated "in silos" working with overwhelming problems and poor resources. CTOSH seems to have served as a means, however mundane, to create connections. Most importantly, those connections were experienced in a shared and public way. Given the time constraints for large gatherings of these providers, this virtual gathering substituted for other in-person large-scale interactions.

Additionally, evidence suggested despite a stated necessity of "efficiency" in communication, these providers constructed themselves as technologically averse and "high touch." People proclaimed themselves too busy to learn new tools and were more likely to lurk on the list rather than actively post; yet, one of their biggest concerns was time spent (wasted) in excessive communication with others. There seemed little

recognition of sunk costs yielding some return in ultimate efficiency if appropriate tools were adopted. Rather, the explanation for one's own or others' reluctance to use tools concerned the preference for the familiarity of high-touch, face-to-face channels. This seems to be more than a powerful norm, or an outgrowth of poor technological resources. It seems to be a highly held value of these providers. This norm created a real barrier to the exploration of certain ICTS and might have encouraged those like email lists that were not overly technical in nature.

Another interesting dynamic illustrated in this case concerns the ways in which these providers, either due to lack of interest or lack of felt "permission," did not assert their own views on how the tools ought to be used and the norms for communication that applied to them. Aside from initial complaints by list subscribers about the influx of unwanted replies that came as a result of all list replies going back to the full list, providers did not offer up any opinions or suggestions as to how these tools ought be used or not used. The normative structures for the list emerged out of the actions of the most frequent posters, though few posts were procedural or reflexive about the list itself. Not until the CTOSH project was about to end did some even raise the issue of whether the "re-owned" list and website should continue with the same name (since few knew what it even stood for). Their roles with regards to these tools will now need to be reconstructed as "owners" and it will be interesting to see whether this conversation about the "rules" and norms of use of the list and website will now take place since the research team is out of the picture.

Finally, these tools ought to have opened a door to equalize participation in this network. The "smaller" voices ought to have been amplified if they chose to do so. Organizations who got no cut, or a small cut, of the federal funding pie, could have used this forum as a means to vent concerns, argue for re-prioritization, or raise their own profile among those who had more access and sway with resource holders. They did not often do this and seem to have self-censored. Again, the same inner circle of "bigger voices" that exist in this network, was replicated in the list and the broader structures off list asserted themselves strongly in use of the list—which is not that surprising in light of duality of technology arguments (Orlikowski, 1992).

These conclusions also suggest several recommendations. First, list organizers and managers should not assume they can always strategically plan lists with user goals clearly in mind; they must recognize the need for tremendous flexibility as well. An "effective" list may be constructed with certain purpose in mind, such as spurring collaboration. But this sort of planning requires a clear sense of user needs and strong user acceptance. The findings suggest that taking a more adaptive and flexible approach to the introduction and use of new technologies is likely the best course when stakeholders' needs and interests are very diverse. In this case of an email list implementation, it was likely beneficial to allow users to make the tool work for them rather than force a narrow vision of what it should do. Although unintended consequences of an innovation can crop up in any effort to introduce a new tool, these consequences may not always be bad. The organizational change and innovation literature has long noted the potential benefits of reinvention, adaptation and modification (Leonard-Barton, 1988; Lewis & Seibold, 1993; Rice & Rogers, 1980; Rogers, 1983). For some scholars this is viewed as a very positive outcome because it demonstrates that users alter the change to fit their own needs and goals.

Second, organizational leaders and savvy organizational members should recognize the power of email lists and other group discussion technologies to define and redefine community. When group boundaries become blurry, membership rolls and technology access serve as more concrete ways of deciding who is and is not part of a community. This suggests some reasonable control on list membership—not so much to exclude certain organizations or individuals, but to keep it manageable and somewhat recognizable. Knowing that the only people on the email list were those interested in homelessness issues in this metropolitan area helps to demarcate the relevant community. Related to this, knowing that key others with such interests were part of this list makes it essential that all serious stakeholders become part of the online group. Community leaders should not wrongly assume that the list creates some sort of level playing ground where all members are equal; instead, the online structure may both reinforce certain existing structures offline as well as give additional voice to some who previously had few channels for influence.

Finally, technology users and other advocates should learn from this case that sometimes basic uses of fairly simple technologies may be best. Simply sharing information on the list was what best served the community. They in fact rejected even newer ICTs that provided what were seen as unnecessary functions and that may have been too inconsistent with their high-touch culture. It is natural to emphasize the very newest of the new media as one implements advanced tools, purchases technologies, and attempts to stay relevant; yet, finding a match between user needs and available tools demands that researchers and community leaders alike continue to consider a full range of options available to organizational members. Even today, this group continues to rely heavily on the email list and shuns social network sites and other newer ICTs.

REFERENCES

Barringer, B. R., & Harrison, J. S. (2000). Walking a tightrope: Creating value through interorganizational relationships. *Journal of Management, 26*, 367–403. doi:10.1177/014920630002600302

Boczkowski, P. J. (1999). Mutual shaping of users and technologies in a national virtual community. *The Journal of Communication, 49*, 86–98. doi:10.1111/j.1460-2466.1999.tb02795.x

Browning, L. D., Beyer, J. M., & Shetler, J. C. (1995). Building cooperation in a competitive industry: Sematech and the semiconductor industry. *Academy of Management Journal, 38*, 113–151. doi:10.2307/256730

Bulmer, M. (1979). Concepts in the analysis of qualitative data. *The Sociological Review, 27*, 651–677.

Burt, E., & Taylor, J. A. (2000). Information and communication technologies: Reshaping voluntary organizations? *Nonprofit Management & Leadership, 11*, 131–144. doi:10.1002/nml.11201

Butler, B. S. (2001). Membership size, communication activity, and sustainability: A resource-based model of online social structures. *Information Systems Research, 12*, 346–365. doi:10.1287/isre.12.4.346.9703

Cheney, G., & Dionisopoulous, G. N. (1989). Public relations? No, relations with publics: A rhetorical and organizational approach to corporate communication. In Botan, C., & Hazleton, V. (Eds.), *Public relations theory* (pp. 135–157). Hillsdale, NJ: Lawrence Erlbaum.

Cummings, J. N., Butler, B., & Kraut, R. (2002). The quality of online social relationships. *Communications of the ACM, 45*(7), 103–108. doi:10.1145/514236.514242

D'Urso, S. C., & Pierce, K. M. (2009). Connected to the organization: A survey of communication technologies in the modern organizational landscape. *Communication Research Reports, 26*, 75–81. doi:10.1080/08824090802637098

Daft, R. L., & Lengel, R. H. (1984). Information richness: A new approach to managerial behavior and organization design. *Research in Organizational Behavior, 6*, 191–223.

Davis, F. D. (1989). Perceived usefulness, perceived ease of use, and user acceptance of information technology. *Management Information Systems Quarterly, 13*, 319–340. doi:10.2307/249008

Department of Housing and Urban Development. (2009). *The 2008 annual homeless assessment report to Congress.* Retrieved September 13, 2009 from http://www.hud.gov/utilities/intercept.cfm? http://www.hudhre.info/documents/4thHomeless AssessmentReport.pdf.

Dvorak, P. (2009, 30 May). On the street and on Facebook: The homeless stay wired. *Wall Street Journal.* Retrieved on September 13, 2009 from http://online.wsj.com/article/SB124363359881267523.html.

Emerson, R. M., Fretz, R. I., & Shaw, L. L. (1995). *Writing ethnographic field notes.* Chicago, IL: University of Chicago Press.

Flanagin, A. J. (2000). Social pressures on organizational website adoption. *Human Communication Research, 26*, 618–646. doi:10.1111/j.1468-2958.2000.tb00771.x

Fulk, J. (1993). Social construction of communication technology. *Academy of Management Journal, 36*, 921–950. doi:10.2307/256641

Fulk, J., Schmitz, J., & Steinfeld, C. W. (1990). A social influence model of technology use. In Fulk, J., & Steinfeld, C. (Eds.), *Organizations and communication technology* (pp. 117–140). Newbury Park, CA: Sage.

Giddens, A. (1984). *The constitution of society: Introduction of the theory of structuration.* Berkeley, CA: University of California Press.

Glaser, B. G., & Strauss, A. L. (1967). *The discovery of grounded theory: Strategies for qualitative research.* Chicago: Aldine.

Heath, R. G., & Sias, P. M. (1999). Communicating spirit in a collaborative alliance. *Journal of Applied Communication Research, 27*, 356–376. doi:10.1080/00909889909365545

Huberman, A. M., & Miles, M. B. (1994). Data management and analysis methods. In Denzin, N. K., & Lincoln, Y. S. (Eds.), *Handbook of qualitative research* (pp. 428–444). Thousand Oaks, CA: Sage.

Iverson, J. O., & McPhee, R. D. (2002). Knowledge management in communities of practice: Being true to the communicative character of knowledge. *Management Communication Quarterly, 16*, 259–266. doi:10.1177/089331802237239

Keyton, J., & Stallworth, V. (2003). On the verge of collaboration: Interaction processes versus group outcomes. In Frey, L. R. (Ed.), *Group communication in context: Studies of bona fide groups* (2nd ed., pp. 235–260). Mahwah, NJ: Erlbaum.

Leonard-Barton, D. (1988). Implementation as mutual adaptation of technology and organization. *Research Policy, 17*, 251–267. doi:10.1016/0048-7333(88)90006-6

Levine, S., & White, P. E. (1961). Exchange as a conceptual framework for the study of interorganizational relationships. *Administrative Science Quarterly, 15*, 583–601. doi:10.2307/2390622

Lewis, L. K., Hamel, S. A., & Richardson, B. K. (2001). Communicating change to nonprofit stakeholders: Models and predictors of implementers' approaches. *Management Communication Quarterly, 15*, 5–41. doi:10.1177/0893318901151001

Lewis, L. K., Richardson, B. K., & Hamel, S. A. (2003). When the stakes are communicative: The lamb's and the lion's share during nonprofit planned change. *Human Communication Research, 29*, 400–430. doi:10.1093/hcr/29.3.400

Lewis, L. K., & Seibold, D. S. (1993). Innovation modification during intraorganizational adoption. *Academy of Management Review, 2*, 322–354. doi:10.2307/258762

Lievrouw, L. A. (2006). New media design and development: Diffusion of innovations v. social shaping of technology. In Lievrouw, L. A., & Livingstone, S. (Eds.), *The handbook of new media: Updated student edition* (pp. 247–265). London: Sage.

MacKenzie, D., & Wajcman, J. (Eds.). (1999). *The social shaping of technology* (2nd ed.). Buckingham: Open University Press.

Miller, K., Scott, C. R., Stage, C., & Birkholt, M. (1995). Communication and coordination in an interorganizational system: Service provision for the urban homeless. *Communication Research, 22*, 679–699. doi:10.1177/009365095022006006

Monge, P. R., Fulk, J., Kalman, M. E., Flanagin, A. J., Parnassa, C., & Rumsey, S. (1998). Production of collective action in alliance-based interorganizational communication and information systems. *Organization Science, 9*, 411–433. doi:10.1287/orsc.9.3.411

National Law Center on Homelessness & Poverty. (2008). *2008 annual report: Changing laws, changing lives.* Retrieved on September 13, 2009 from http://www.nlchp.org/view_report.cfm?id=318.

National Law Center on Homelessness & Poverty. (2009). *2009 foreclosure survey.* Retrieved on September 13, 2009 from http://www.nlchp.org/view_report.cfm?id=310.

North, C. S., Pollio, D. E., Perron, B., Eyrich, K. M., & Spitznagel, E. L. (2005). The role of organizational characteristics in determining patterns of utilization of services for substance abuse, mental health, and shelter by homeless people. *Journal of Drug Issues, 35*, 575–591.

Oliver, C. (1990). Determinants of interorganizational relationships: Integration and future directions. *Academy of Management Review, 15,* 241–265. doi:10.2307/258156

Orlikowski, W. J. (1992). The duality of technology: Rethinking the concept of technology in organizations. *Organization Science, 3,* 398–427. doi:10.1287/orsc.3.3.398

Owen, W. F. (1984). Relational themes in interpersonal communication. *The Quarterly Journal of Speech, 70,* 274–287. doi:10.1080/00335638409383697

Poole, M. S., & DeSanctis, G. (1990). Understanding the use of group decision support systems: The theory of adaptive structuration. In Fulk, J., & Steinfeld, C. (Eds.), *Organizations and Communication Technology* (pp. 173–193). Newbury Park, CA: Sage Publications.

Poole, M. S., & DeSanctis, G. (1992). Microlevel structuration in computer-supported group decision making. *Human Communication Research, 18,* 5–49.

Rafaeli, S., & Sudweeks, F. (1997). Networked interactivity. *Journal of Computer-Mediated Communication, 4.* http://jcmc.indiana.edu/vol2/issue4/rafaeli.sudweeks.html.

Ramey, C. (2008, 29 May). Mobile phone use among homeless people. Retrieved on September 13, 2009 from http://mobileactive.org/mobiles-homeless.

Rice, R, E., & Rogers. E, M. (1980). Re-invention in the innovation process: Knowledge, creation, diffusion. *Utilization, 1,* 499–514.

Rogers, E. M. (1983). *Diffusion of innovations* (3rd ed.). New York: Free Press.

Schild, S., & Oren, K. (2005). The party line online: An oligarchy of opinion on a public affairs listserv. *Journalism and Communication Monographs, 7,* 5–47.

Schmitz, J., Rogers, E. M., Phillips, K., & Paschal, D. (1995). The public electronic network (PEN) and the Homeless in Santa Monica. *Journal of Applied Communication Research, 23,* 26–43. doi:10.1080/00909889509365412

Short, J., Williams, E., & Christie, B. (1976). *The social psychology of telecommunications.* London: Wiley.

Tompkins, P. K. (2009). *Who is my neighbor: Communicating and organizing to end homelessness.* Boulder, CO: Paradigm.

Vaast, E. (2004). O brother, where are thou? From communities to networks of practice through intranet use. *Management Communication Quarterly, 18,* 5–44. doi:10.1177/0893318904265125

Wellman, B., Salaff, J., Dimitrova, D., Garton, L., Gulia, M., & Haythornthwaite, C. (1996). Computer networks as social networks: Collaborative work, telework, and virtual community. *Annual Review of Sociology, 22,* 213–238. doi:10.1146/annurev.soc.22.1.213

Zoller, H. M. (2004). Dialogue as global issue management: Legitimizing corporate influence in the transatlantic business dialogue. *Management Communication Quarterly, 18,* 204–240. doi:10.1177/0893318904265126

KEY TERMS AND DEFINITIONS

Collaboration: Minimally, collaboration is understood to involve (a) cooperation, coordination, and exchange of resources (e.g., people, funding, information, ideas), and (b) mutual respect for individual goals and/or joint goals.

CTOSH: Collaboration Technologies for Organizations Serving the Homeless, a collaborative project between academics and health and human service providers aiming to improve the capacity of homeless service providers in the area to work cooperatively and make use of collaborative communication tools to improve efficiency and effectiveness of their interaction with one another.

E-Mail List: An electronic mail list is a collection of e-mail addresses created either by participants subscribing to a list or being enrolled as part of an organizational need. These lists facilitate regular e-mail communication among participants of the list. They are often maintained by an organization employing special software and the use of an e-mail server.

Homeless: The U.S. Department of Housing and Urban Development (HUD) defines a person or family as homeless only when he/she resides in one of the following: (a) places not meant for human habitation, such as cars, parks, sidewalks, abandoned buildings (e.g., on the street); (b) an emergency shelter, transitional housing program, or supportive housing; or (c) in any of the above places even if spending a short time (up to 30 consecutive days) in a hospital or other institution.

Nonprofit Organizations: Also known as the civil society sector, independent sector and the non-governmental sector, the generally accepted guidelines include that these are the set of entities that are organized, private, non-profit-distributing, self-governing, voluntary to some meaningful extent, and of public benefit.

Online Discussion: An asynchronous message exchange among interested parties. These discussions can occur as part of an e-mail list, through the use of an electronic discussion board, or via other networked technologies that store messages for later receipt and reply.

Technology Use: The utilization of any type of communication technology (hardware or software) on a regular basis.

User: A specific individual who chooses to employ a particular communication technology as part of ongoing communication efforts.

Chapter 19
"The Secret is Out!"
Supporting Weight Loss through Online Interaction

Laura W. Black
Ohio University, USA

Jennifer J. Bute
Ohio University, USA

Laura D. Russell
Ohio University, USA

EXECUTIVE SUMMARY

This chapter provides a case study of how social support is communicated through online interaction on a weight loss community website. The site has many features including member profiles, journals, discussion boards, exercise and food trackers, and charts to help members keep track of their weight loss efforts. Members set goals, write journal entries, comment on one another's journals, upload photos, join groups and challenges, and discuss concerns issues related to diet, exercise, lifestyle changes, and other issues in their lives. Through analyzing journal entries and discussion forum comments, we discern how members demonstrate and respond to social support with one another. We also investigate the ways in which features of the online interaction and social networking help people communicate support. This study offers implications for facilitators or web designers who want to create online spaces that foster supportive communication, particularly related to health concerns.

BACKGROUND OF THE CASE

"I was laid up due to my heart issues and was afraid to eat anything. I literally felt that one more bite of something with fat in it and I could die. My doctor suggested the South Beach diet to me because of my heart issues. While researching online I saw the

Today show say that FatSecret was one of 5 websites that could change your life! Like a sign from above I logged on immediately. Right away I saw recipes and ideas and tips for my specific plan. I met other people following the same plan. It was incredible. I met people who have lost weight, some who were well along their way and others just like me...just starting out along the journey! I could gripe, cry, whine, vent and ask away. There was a lot of asking

DOI: 10.4018/978-1-61520-863-0.ch019

when I started here and I always found answers. FatSecret people were my comfort, my hope and my confidants." --FatSecret member who lost 45 pounds

Obesity is a major health concern in contemporary U.S. society as the number of people who are obese has increased substantially over the past twenty years. Recent health research has found that three out of every five Americans is considered overweight or obese (Strum & Wells, 2001). Moreover, obesity has been linked to many chronic health concerns such as heart problems, joint pain, diabetes, limited mobility, cancer, and a host of other ailments. Health researchers have warned that obesity should be considered an "epidemic" in the U.S., and that it has a greater impact on Americans' chronic health concerns and medical expenditures than regular smoking, problem drinking, or poverty (Strum & Wells, 2001).

As the problem of obesity has become more widely recognized and accepted, many people have sought social support from others to help them manage their weight. Some of these people have turned to online communities where they can ask questions, discuss their concerns, and connect with other people engaging in weight loss efforts similar to their own. Online communities exist when groups of people gather around some common purpose or activity and use computer-mediated communication as one of their primary means of social interaction (cf. Baym, 2000; Rheingold, 2000; Smith & Kollock, 1999). Rheingold notes that the mediated interaction in online communities occurs over time and involves "sufficient human feeling, to form webs of personal relationships in cyberspace" (1999, p. xx). In the case of online communities devoted to health issues, people build relationships through computer-mediated interaction related to their health and well being. In this way, these interactions become the social fabric of the online community.

One of these online communities can be found on the website FatSecret, which is the focus of this case study. FatSecret is a relatively new online community, beginning in 2006. The site combines attributes of a general online support group, such as discussion boards and journals, with features of more popular social networking sites such as Facebook. FatSecret's goal, as described on their website, is to be:

a new online diet, nutrition and weight loss community that harnesses the collective contributions of our members to generate practical and motivating information so that you can make better decisions to achieve your goals.... FatSecret evolved from the idea that the most abundant and highly valuable source of information on diet, nutrition and weight management is the sum of the views, performances, achievements and recommendations of individuals that make up the broader community. We've tried to create an easy to use system that gathers, stores and sorts the input of members of the FatSecret community to provide quality information and useful recommendations so that we can all benefit. (FatSecret website, "About Us")

Since its inception in 2006 FatSecret has undergone substantial growth with thousands of active members participating on the site. As the title of this chapter implies, one of their mottos is "The Secret is Out!" The website's innovative combination of user-generated content, visual presentation of personal information, social networking, and online interaction may be the secret of its success. The site has been highlighted by both online and traditional news media, including a feature on the Today Show and inclusion in *Time Magazine's* top 50 websites of 2007.

SETTING THE STAGE

In recent years, the substantial increase of online support groups and communities focusing on health-related issues has offered Internet users a new tool for coping with their health concerns (Rains & Young, 2009; White & Dorman, 2001; Wright & Bell, 2003). Such groups have provided individuals with a network that can supplement or replace traditional sources of support (e.g., health care providers, family members, friends) by offering online anonymity, access to diverse sources of information, contact with similar others, and a sense of community (Wright & Bell, 2003). These benefits, though, have not come without challenges, such as a lack of visual and aural cues (White & Dorman, 2001).

Online groups can be particularly appealing to those dealing with a potentially stigmatizing condition (Goldsmith & Brashers, 2008; Wright & Bell, 2003), including people who are obese or overweight. "It has been said that obese persons are the last acceptable targets of discrimination" (Puhl & Brownell, 2001, p. 788). Indeed, people who are overweight have reported mistreatment and discrimination in employment, education, and health care (Falkner et al., 1999; Puhl & Brownell, 2001).

Online forums can provide a lower risk means of seeking support for those who want to lose weight but are concerned about the ongoing discrimination and social stigma they might face. Rather than presenting an overtly visible and discrediting stigma to others (King, Hebl, & Heatherton, 2005) by discussing their weight struggles in face-to-face settings, individuals with Internet access can elicit and provide social support in relative privacy while maintaining their anonymity. In fact, the anonymity offered by online interactions has been cited as a major advantage by users of Internet support groups who struggle with stigmatized conditions. Such anonymity is linked to what Walther (1996, 2008, 2009) calls "hyperpersonal" communication, which is a type of interaction that involves a high level of emotion and affection and is more personal than we might expect to encounter in similar face-to-face settings. As reviews of online support groups demonstrate, computer-mediated support can mitigate social

stigma and enhance levels of comfort in disclosing intimate details and exchanging social support (Wright & Bell, 2003; Rains & Young, 2009).

Social support, including access to and participation in online support groups and interventions, has been identified as an important and effective element in successful weight loss (Elfhag & Rossner, 2005; Krukowski, Harvey-Berino, Ashikaga, Thomas, & Micco, 2008; Tate, Wing, & Winett, 2001; Verheijdden, Bakx, van Weel, Koelen, & van Staveren, 2005). For example, Elfhad and Rossner's (2005) examination of factors associated with weight loss maintenance revealed that social support assisted people who were working to maintain a healthy weight. Internet-based support via a weight control website can be especially effective in promoting weight loss and maintenance, particularly if the site includes features like progress charts, journals, and community bulletin boards (Krukowski et al., 2008). In one study, participants' use of progress charts and journals was found to predict weight loss, and participation in social support through online chats was the best predictor of weight maintenance (Krukowski et al., 2008). Thus, particular features of online groups can provide members with opportunities to communicate with one another and communicate the social support that is an essential part of members' weight loss efforts. Although both scholars and practitioners have recognized that social support is important in promoting weight loss and is a vital function of online communities, very little research has investigated the ways in which the varied formats for online interaction assist or inhibit members as they provide social support for one another.

Social support can be defined in a number of ways (Goldsmith, 2004); it is not a single, unified construct but rather "an umbrella term for providing a sense of reassurance, validation, and acceptance, the sharing of needed resources and assistance, and connecting or integrating structurally within a web of ties in a supportive network (Albrecht & Goldsmith, 2003, p. 265). As communication scholars, we follow Goldsmith's (2004) lead in conceptualizing social support as *enacted support*, otherwise understood as "what individuals say and do to help one another" (p. 13). Supportive interactions can include a wide array of topics and supportive resources, including expressions of encouragement or validation, advice or feedback about behaviors, sharing of information, and offers of tangible assistance (Albrecht & Goldsmith 2003; Goldsmith, 2004). We wish to emphasize that social support is a communicative phenomenon. This conceptualization assumes that "support occurs through the process of conversations in which meanings are inferred and conclusions are drawn by both parties" (Goldsmith & Brashers, 2008, p. 321). Understanding social support as enacted support, rather than perceived support, draws attention to how support happens in everyday interactions and commands a focus on the form, style, content, and sequence of talk (Goldsmith, 2004). In other words, we are interested not in whether individuals perceive that they can access support when they need it, but rather, in how they communicate and co-construct supportive interactions. Thus, communication processes take center stage as the phenomenon of interest. Although both face-to-face and online support groups provide opportunities for supportive exchanges, online groups offer scholars the ability to capture how such interactions unfold (White & Dorman, 2001).

We also recognize that providing and receiving social support can pose dilemmas for involved parties (Goldsmith, 2004; Goldsmith, Lindholm, & Bute, 2006). Interactants might seek ways of offering and receiving information and advice, for instance, without infringing on or compromising autonomy. Both seekers and providers of support might feel that incessant talk about an issue, particularly a health-related concern, means dwelling on that issue in an unproductive way (Goldsmith, Lindholm, & Bute, 2006). Though we acknowledge that social support is a complex process that is not always positive in nature, our goal in this chapter is not to explore such dilemmas per se but to understand how technological features of online groups facilitate or deter the communication of social support. We observe that one of the characteristics that makes FatSecret successful as an online community is the social support that members communicate to one another. The focus of our case study is to *better understand how people communicate social support in their online interactions about weight loss in this community*. In particular, we examine the FatSecret community to compare the social support communicated in two kinds of online interaction: discussion forums and responses to members' journal entries. In so doing, we discuss how features of these formats foster or constrain members' expressions of social support for one another.

CASE DESCRIPTION

In this section we provide information about site design, particularly by emphasizing the features of the FatSecret site that promote group interaction. The features described below enable members to present information about themselves and interact with other members. Although the site includes several components designed to help members track and visualize their progress toward their weight loss goals, the prominent features of the site are those that enable interaction.[1]

Features that Present Personal Information

The first set of technological features consists of the *personal profile* and related information that each member creates when he or she joins the FatSecret community. A member's personal profile, such as the one included in Figure 1, functions as the central location for all of the personal information a member enters into the website. The profile includes the person's FatSecret name, information about which diet he or she is fol-

Figure 1. Fat Secret member profile

lowing, the starting weight and goal, and a brief biographical statement. Some members choose to post a profile picture, either a photograph or other image that he or she selects. The profile page serves as a centralized location for all of a member's personal information and activity.

The member profile page includes several visual indicators of a member's experience with weight loss. One of the most prominent features is a weight history chart that indicates the member's progress toward his or her weight goal. The chart, which is displayed below the member's personal information and photo, is populated with data points that track the member's weight over the time period since the member's involvement in the FatSecret community. The chart is a line graph that provides a horizontal line near the top, representing the member's starting weight, and another horizontal line near the bottom, which

represents the member's goal weight. Members record their own weight when they choose, and these weigh-in values populate their weight history chart. Additionally, members can track their daily exercise and food intake by entering information into a personal log. A brief summary of this food and exercise log is evident on the right side of the member's profile page next to the weight history chart. Website users can click on this summary to access the member's complete food and exercise log.

The profile page also provides access to the members' journal entries. Each FatSecret member has the ability to journal about his or her experience, and a brief summary of these journal entries is evident on the upper right side of the member's profile page, above his or her food and exercise log. A member's full journal can be viewed publicly by clicking on the summary. A sample

Figure 2. Sample journal entry with comments

journal entry is displayed in Figure 2. From our initial observations of the FatSecret community we noticed that many members regularly document their experiences in their journals and, as such, the journals could be seen as a dominant feature of the site.

In addition to including a member's personal information (i.e., photo, bio, weight history chart, food/exercise log, and journal), the profile page is also a member's entry point into the community. Although profiles and other information are viewable by the public, only members who have joined the community and created a profile are able to participate in FatSecret's social networking features. For example, as Figure 1 demonstrates, the profile page includes a list of the member's "buddies," who are other FatSecret members with

whom the person has connected. The site offers a request system for buddies, which is similar to other social networking sites. Once members are linked together as buddies they can send private messages to one another and easily keep track of each other's journal entries and other activity on the site.

Features that Foster Interaction

From our observations of the website, we notice that one of the primary ways that members engage in online interaction is through *commenting on each other's journal entries*. As Figure 2 illustrates, the comments are displayed below the journal entry. Any member can comment on another's journal entry, although we notice that members

Figure 3. Example My FatSecret page

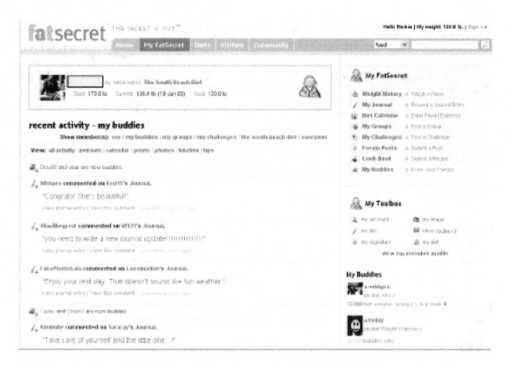

tend to form groups of buddies who consistently comment on each other's journal entries. In our initial experience with the community we noticed that there was a great deal of social support in the comments to journal entries.

Members also communicate with each other through participating in *discussion forums*, joining *groups or challenges*, or posting *recipes or diet tips*. These interactive features of the FatSecret community are accessible to members through their "My FatSecret" page, which is analogous to a member's "Home" page in Facebook or other social networking sites. An example of a My FatSecret page is shown in Figure 3.

This page provides an abbreviated version of a member's personal profile information and displays updates on other members' activities on the site. The prominent feature of the My FatSecret page is the personally-tailored compilation of other people's activities on the site. A FatSecret member can select whose recent activity (everyone, just

buddies, people who follow a particular diet, etc.) and what kind of activity (either all activity or just journal entries) he or she wants to observe. In Figure 3, for example, the member has selected to see all recent activity, but only by her buddies. Viewing this activity feed gives the member an opportunity to engage in interaction with others by commenting on their journal entries, responding to a post in a discussion forum, or rating and commenting on a recipe or diet tip.

In our observations of the site, we noticed that a great deal of interaction occurred in the *Discussion Forums*. As the example presented in Figure 4 demonstrates, discussions typically begin with a member posting a question, comment, or request for advice on some topic. Any FatSecret member can respond, and some forums involve lengthy discussions of a wide range of topics related to nutrition, health, and weight. Like journal entries and comments, the discussions seem to be a very common way FatSecret members choose to in-

Figure 4. Example discussion forum

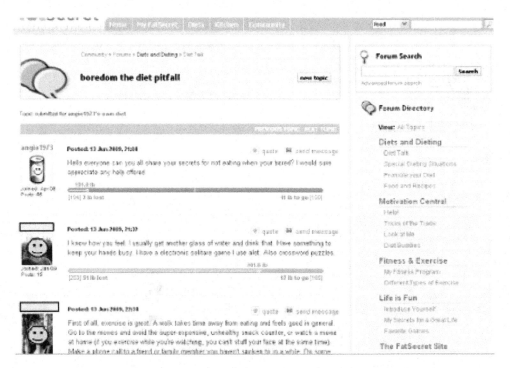

teract with one another. Our initial observations lead us to believe that many discussion forums involve social support.

Participants who post to the discussion forum are identified by their FatSecret name, a thumbnail image of their profile picture, and a "ticker" at the bottom of their post, which indicates how much weight they have lost toward their goal. These tickers are colorful bars that look a bit like thermometers, and the color of the ticker depends on the percentage of weight a member has lost toward his or her target weight. Members who have made only minimal progress toward their goal have tickers that are red, and further levels of success lead to tickers that are orange, yellow, green, and finally blue. These tickers were not originally part of the FatSecret design, but were developed in response to members using tickers available from other organizations or creating other ways to visually display their progress.

Members also can join *Groups and Challenges*, which connect them with others who share some similar characteristics or goals. Groups tend to be organized around characteristics such as "30s with 25 to 50 pounds to lose" and serve as a gathering place for members with shared attributes to discuss aspects of their weight loss efforts. A specific kind of group is a "Challenge," in which members organize into teams and participate in a sort of competition with other teams to accomplish certain goals (such as exercise for 30 minutes every day, or try to lose ten pounds by a pre-set date). These groups and challenges were officially developed in 2007 after members started to informally organize themselves. Currently, any member can create a group or challenge and invite others to join. These groups and challenges are closed to outsiders so that only those FatSecret members who are participating in the group or challenge can see and respond to information posted there.

Finally, members can interact with one another through posting and commenting on *Diet Tips and Recipes*. Although there are many recipes and diet tips posted, only some have ratings and comments associated with them. As such, FatSecret members do not seem to treat the recipes and diet tips as an opportunity for interactive communication.

Summary

As is evident from the site design features, FatSecret members communicate information about themselves in their personal profile and interact through a variety of social networking features. Through all of these forms of interaction, members engage in various communication processes. Individuals chronicle the mundane choices they make related to food and diet, they confess straying from their plan, they vent about frustrations, they celebrate their progress, and they talk about other aspects of their lives. Members also participate in reciprocating supportive communication with their "buddies" and others on the site. Because social support is such an important factor in helping people achieve success in their weight-loss efforts, we believe that it is important to uncover the features of the FatSecret site that enable supportive online interaction.

In our initial observations of the community, we find that most of the social support is evidenced in people's comments to one another's journal entries and in the discussion forums. Although there ostensibly could be social support enacted through the other information-sharing formats (such as posting recipes and diet tips), most of the supportive interaction is evident in the discussion forums and journals. For this reason, we turn our attention to analyzing examples of these two types of online interaction to discern how social support is communicated.

COMMUNICATING SOCIAL SUPPORT THROUGH ONLINE INTERACTION

Our goals in this section are to describe how social support is communicated through online interaction and examine the similarities and differences in the communication of social support appearing in FatSecret's online journal and discussion forum formats. The online journals and discussion forums are available for use by all registered members of the site. Nonmembers can view the journals and forums, though they do not have access to post responses. To better understand the communication of social support and the ways that particular formats of the site enable and constrain support processes, we examined features of both the journals and the discussion forums by analyzing a sample of journal entries and discussion threads.

For our analysis, we concentrated our focus on four points of comparison between the journal and discussion forum formats: (a) the style and format of the original posting, (b) the nature of the social support communicated by other members in their responses to the original posting, (c) the extent to which the support process is characterized by dyadic or group dynamics, and (d) the advantages and disadvantages of the technological attributes of each format in terms of facilitating the communication of social support. Through this examination we explain how the journal and discussion forum features of FatSecret serve different functions in facilitating engagement in social support interactions.

Style and Format of the Original Posting

Attention to the ways in which social support is elicited by members is crucial for understanding how support processes unfold in online contexts. To understand how supportive exchanges are initiated, we explored the style and format of the original postings in members' journals and in discussion forum threads. We suggest that the ways in which FatSecret members solicit and offer social support are shaped by the particular formats they choose to use on the site.

In general, journal entries tend to follow a diary-like format in which the poster reflects on current events, articulates affirmations, or makes motivational statements directed toward him or herself. For example, in one journal entry a member mused about an appointment with her physician during which she found out that, despite her best efforts to maintain a healthy weight, she was pre-diabetic and had high cholesterol. Reflecting on the frustration of appearing to be physically fit while suffering from unseen health conditions, she stated:

From now on when someone looks at me and wonders why I am in the sugar free aisle or someone thinks I'm nuts for telling them I can't indulge in even one ice cream cone because I "look fit," I'm going to pull out my lab results.[2]

Although journal postings typically resemble diary entries, it is clear that journal posters are aware that other members will read and respond to their postings (in contrast to diary entries, which are not usually intended for a public audience). Some members explicitly address the reading audience in their entries by asking questions or expressing supportive wishes to the group. Moreover, journal entries do not often include straightforward requests for social support, perhaps because members find value in simply reflecting on and expressing their experiences. Even so, members who read the entries infer the need for support and respond accordingly. Thus, online journals are similar to blogs in that they are personal diaries that have an intended audience other than the self.

In contrast, original postings in discussion forums tend to include more direct requests for support (e.g., validation, information, advice) than journal entries, though the request's level

of explicitness can still vary. For instance, one member posted a request to a South Beach diet forum in which she asked for feedback on her diet: "I would really appreciate it if someone who has been through phase 1 would look at my food intake and tell me if I'm doing everything right." While not all posts are direct requests for advice, members might interpret them as such. Another posting to the South Beach diet forum featured a woman with a question regarding the link between oral contraceptives and weight gain:

Has anyone noticed their weight loss slows, stops, or they actually gain from taking birth control pills? I tried to pinpoint exactly when I stopped losing weight and started gaining even with dieting and it was when I started the pills again... anyone heard of this???

Although this member's query could be interpreted as a call for advice (e.g., what should I do?), the posting could simply be a request for experience swapping or validation (e.g., is this just me, or does this happen to you, too). The implicit intentions and ambiguity behind support seeking, therefore, elicit a variety of different responses. For instance, some members reply by providing an account of similar personal experiences as a way to validate the questions d or concerns of the initial poster. In other cases, people offer advice for answering questions by providing expertise, references, or lay perspectives. These various responses exemplify how social support functions as a complex process shaped through the ways people express personal identity, recognition of others, and a variety of knowledge claims. Social support, therefore, is contextually defined in and through the communication in which it is embodied.

Nature of Support Communicated by Members

The diverse formats (journal or discussion forum) seem to elicit different forms of social support from members who respond to original postings. These differences appear to be related to the manner in which the original post is framed.

As previously noted, journals do not typically include direct requests for social support, but do entail highly personal reflections and self-affirmations. Subsequently, members who post responses to journal entries tend to focus their supportive messages on validating the journaler's emotions and experiences. In our analysis, we found that *validation* appeared to be the key function of every comment from other members. Validation appeared in a variety of forms including how members identified with others through their personal experiences, expressed general understanding and encouragement, conveyed understanding through venting, provided information or instruction, and showed agreement and support for decision making. For example, in response to one member's bad news from her physician, another member shared her own personal experience:

Come sit over here. I have the same three conditions and take meds for all. It drives me batty. I am glad you doctor has a diet for you. My doctor just pushes pills. I tried to get off the cholesterol med after I lost 20 lbs but it did not work.

Others responded to the same entry with more general words of encouragement, such as, "Hang in there chica...you're going to get through this with flying colors!! **hugs to you**" Such responses indicate members' attempts to validate and console the needs of the journaler. In addition, the content of the support expressed was frequently focused on encouraging others to maintain strength and control with their diets. As we observed, there were repeated times when people would compliment others' strength as a way of providing encouragement. Further, such encouragement would often be followed by a supporter sharing a personal experience of his or her own. Or, others simply

posted encouraging words to convey that they were "thinking about" the journaler.

Based on the style and tone of journal entries and the content of members' responses, it seems that a primary goal of journalers is to receive validation and confirmation from others. Therefore, they post their journals publicly to receive confirmation that their experiences are meaningful, valid, and recognized.

The need for validation seems to be understood by others responding, given the supportive, encouraging, and relating comments provided in response to the journaler. In this way, social support in the context of online journals tends to focus largely on the person authoring the journal, particularly in how responders focus on validating the emotions or experiences of that individual. Discussion forums, however, feature divergent ways of communicating social support, and responses to discussion postings tend to focus less on personal aspects of the member who submitted the original post. In fact, the nature of support in responses to discussion forum posts varies widely. In particular, responses tend to be more focused on the post itself rather than aspects of the "poster."

Reponses to the discussion forum member who asked others to review her recent food intake generally focused on instrumental or informational support, such as "Nuts can be a downfall, if we're not careful. Be sure that they are raw, little to no salt and measured out to a nice small portion. Chewing then thoroughly will help soak up the satisfying taste, too." Others combine some instrumental advice with words of encouragement: "ITs just 12 more days if u look at it... so stick with it... Lots of water. U can do IT I know we all can."

In other cases, some members responded to forum threads without directly addressing the original posting. In the response to the request for an evaluation of food intake, one person simply wrote,

This is what i am eating... Eggs(lots of eggs) Tuna (bought the chicken of the sea fro costco)Come

nuts to munch on just 1 oz 2 times a day. lots of salade, chicken (grilled, curry) Extrra lean ham rolled in mozerella cheese sticks.) thisis what i have eatedn orthe last 2 days... I have bought Hummus to eat with celery sticks...

Though this response could be interpreted as experience swapping or indirect advice, at no point does the member personally address the original poster. In contrast, addressing the original poster directly seemed to be the norm in response to journal entries.

In comparison to journal threads, discussion threads are also more likely to feature responses that diverge from the topic of the original post. In the thread on oral contraceptives, for example, several members engaged in a debate about the pros and cons of natural family planning without addressing or involving the member who posted the original question. Such tangential discussions seem to be rare in journal-centered comments.

Although the nature of support expressed in discussion forums tends to differ from support offered in response to journals, using personal testimony as a form of evidence appears to be a common and widely accepted practice in both formats. Recall the member who shared her own health challenges in response to another member's reflection on disappointing news from her physician. Likewise, responses to the discussion post on oral contraception also resulted in experience swapping through testimony. One member wrote, "I gained initially, about 5 pounds when I first started the pill. I noticed an increase in appetite almost immediatly. It did even out over time, and i lost the weight after about six months without dieting." Thus, personal experience serves as a recurrent form of evidence used to legitimize support sought and offered throughout this online community in both the discussion and journal formats.

Dyadic and Group Oriented Interaction

Social support on the FatSecret website is communicatively shaped through *individual, dyadic* and *group* dynamics. In both the journals and forums, members share personal reflections as well as offer opinions and raise questions to others. The interactive opportunities of this online context allow participants to create a collective community with others. Binding the relationships among members is the reciprocal process of seeking and providing support. Whether sharing a personal story or explicitly requesting support, members are aware that their voice is shared with an audience. Further, this audience is unique in that members hold a common interest in losing weight. Therefore, FatSecret hosts a communicative context wherein common interests and social support promote a sense of interdependence. Such interdependence governs the structure of this online community as it is not the individual, but rather, the collective activity that constitutes the essence of this social support group.

Despite the collective image of this social community, the progression of group discussion is seemingly fragmented. Particularly in the forum threads, participants not only respond to initial posts, but also to subsequent responses. As evident in a discussion about a specific diet plan, members respond to the initial post while also referring to others in the discussion. This was demonstrated in a controversial discussion about the effects birth control has on weight loss:

Kelly[3]: *I think as women..we can use hormones, PMS, the fact that our bodies don't have the metabolism that mens bodies do, child bearing, all as a reason to gain weight. We can all sit here and cry about how being a woman makes it soooo hard to lose weight. Is it true? Well sure. Is it doomed sentence? No.*

JulieB: *Kelly, every woman is different and while you were able to lose the weight, a different woman could have been doing everything that you did and not lose an ounce.*

Kelly: *Julie, you CAN see results in your situation. What I am saying is a simple fact though that a lot of people do use these as excuses.*

As these members explicitly call out one another in discussion, they draw attention to points of disagreement and explore the topic at hand in further depth. At the same time, however, other participants of the same thread either continue to comment on the initial post or implicitly direct their replies to others' responses. While members may be cognizant that all group participants see their posts, the intended audience for each response is frequently ambiguous. This ambiguity is reduced in the journal format where members tend to direct most of their responses to the journaler. Still, even appearing in the journals are responses with an unclear audience. Therefore, a sporadic flux between dyadic and group interactions occurs in both forums and journals.

With the given formats for communicating on FatSecret, *dialogic moments* (Cissna & Anderson, 1998) infrequently emerge throughout topic discussions. That is, we notice that many times the communication is one-way in that members are posting comments, but these comments are not directly responded to by the journaler or the person who began the forum topic. Yet, there are moments where FatSecret members seem to engage in a back-and-forth interaction where both people are fully engaged in and open to one another. At times, the initial poster will follow up with a comment to a particular respondent, thus demonstrating what Weick (1979) identified as a *double interact*. For a double interact to take place, a statement, response to a statement, and feedback to the response must be present. The interconnection between each of these steps constitutes an interactive process through which relationships are established and sense making occurs. In the current context, members reciprocating continual responses with one another demonstrate attempts to deepen discussion and create new ways of understanding weight loss experiences. Therefore, in discussions where double interacts emerge, members take part in a process that may lead to a dialogical construction of meaning.

At the same time, however, double interacts between specific persons in a thread may function as exclusionary forces that disrupt the flow of whole group discussions. For instance, as two members in a thread begin to move into a deeper exchange of opinions with one another, others may become confused as to whether they should respond to the persisting interaction or to the initial post. The dispersed nature of responses and dyadic interactions complicates the progression of discussion, particularly because it creates difficulty in discerning to whom each comment is directed. The fluctuation between members commenting on initial posts and members engaging in dyadic interactions, therefore, creates a disunity that slows the progress of discussing topics in depth. While this disunity is present in the journal entires, fragmented interactions are most apparent in the discussion forums.

Advantages and Disadvantages

The distinctive features of the journal and forum discussion formats legitimize why both are necessary for the social support processes taking shape on FatSecret. The journals offer opportunity for individuals to reflect personally on their experiences while sharing their thoughts openly with others. This space provides members opportunities to share not simply issues concerning weight loss, but also other aspects of their lives that give meaning to who they are as individuals. The presence of a group audience provides journalers with a context conditioned for receiving validation, encouragement, and other supportive responses. While the nature of journal discussions tends to be dyadic, respondents participate collectively in an effort to create a supportive environment. The sense of interdependence is, therefore, evidenced in how members respond similarly by providing personal experiences and encouraging statements to ultimately validate the feelings and support needs of journalers. For instance, one journaler wrote about her nervousness about an upcoming surgery. Members, in turn, responded by expressing care and concern:

Jimmy: *Wow, I turn my head for one minute and look what happens. Surgery too? Take care Fruity and have yourself a really good Easter.*

CookieNo: *Thinking of you and all good thoughts and prayers for surgery. Also I know how hard it was for you to type that weight in and I'm so proud of you for being brave. You WILL get it off and more to boot when you're feeling better-first things first!!*

To show recognition of and appreciation for others' support, the journaler responded after returning to the site a few days after her surgery:

Fruity: *I'm back home and going back to sleep... thanks everyone for your prayers and wishes... things went great today and in two weeks we get the results from the lab...thanks again...*

This example illustrates the dynamic unfolding of social support, a process through which a journaler writes about a particular personal experience, receives encouragement in response to that experience, and in turn, expresses a thanks for others' responses.

Whereas journals provide a space for more personal relationships to evolve, the forums offer participants opportunities to engage in more topical discussions related to weight-loss issues in general, typically with a larger group of members. While support is provided throughout forum discussions, responses tend to include more informational instructions than encouraging statements. In addition, because the focus of forum discussions tends to be on the topic rather than the person presenting the topic, members will challenge and disagree with one another about weight-loss concerns. Through disagreement, a number of different perspectives may surface with regard to a particular issue that allows for deeper meaning and/or more holistic understanding to take shape among the weight-loss community. This type of interaction was exemplified in the previously mentioned birth control discussion where members disagreed with and challenged one another's perspectives.

Both the journal and forum formats provide advantages to support-providing processes. First, these online features have lasting quality and serve as permanent records to which users can refer back at later points in time. A journaler, for instance, can turn back to previous entries and read the supportive comments of others at any given moment. Related to time, a second advantage is that the online availability of these features provides around-the-clock access to a social support context. Members can seek and/or provide support at the convenience of their personal schedules. Third, the combination of journal and discussion forum outlets fosters a broad spectrum of dyadic and group interactions. Participants on the website have opportunity to develop interpersonal relationships while also becoming involved in building a supportive community with many others. FatSecret, therefore, promotes the support of individuals while also encouraging broader support for a cause: weight loss.

IMPLICATIONS AND CONCLUSION

FatSecret combines iconic features of online support groups, such as discussion forums, with social networking features that allow members to connect with others who are undergoing similar challenges. The wide range of ways that members can participate in the FatSecret community seems to be one of the secrets of its success. In particular, we find that the journal entries and discussion forums are particularly rich sites of online discussion and social support.

While the journals and forums offer promising advantages for providing support, there are also evident complications. In particular, because of the linear display of responses, it is sometimes difficult to determine who is responding to whom. Unless explicit names are mentioned in responses, it is often challenging to interpret if posts are intended for the initial poster, a particular respondent, or the group as a whole. This ambiguity complicates participants' abilities to build upon one another's contributions and slows the progression of discussion. Therefore, a considerable number of responses are needed to move a topic into greater depth. Consequently, numerous responses can further complicate the flow of discussion and inhibit deeper sense making from occurring. Such observations lead us to a key question: *How can communicative formats for online support groups be structured in a way that promotes a clearer direction for in-depth discussion?*

The aforementioned question problematizes the organization of communication for online communities. A potential possibility for structuring FatSecret is exemplified in a current model developed by Microsoft for *Windows Live Q&A* (http://home.live.com). This site has a comment feature for each initial post and each subsequent response. Therefore, if responders wish to address the initial post, they simply reply to the thread. However, if one would like to comment on a previous respondent, she or he can do so by selecting the comment option for a particular response. Comments remain hidden unless members intentionally select an expand key to make the comments present. This method of organizing responses and subsequent comments helps focus the discussion on the central topic presented in the initial post. The option to branch off into other discussions about particular responses enables

members to engage in deeper interactions about particular ideas and better distinguishes who is addressing whom. Therefore, the Live Q&A format may serve as a potential option for online social support sites.

In addition, the observations we offer in this case study may have a few implications for the design of online support groups as a whole. We found that journal entries and discussion forums facilitate the exchange of social support in different ways. Whereas online journaling allows members to get more personalized support through receiving others' validating responses, discussion forums allow members to engage in conversation about a wider range of topics that encourage social support in the form of information or advice (e.g., suggestions for specific foods to eat or modifications to particular diet plans). Because support on the FatSecret site is communicated in different ways through the journal and discussion forum formats, we would encourage organizers and site designers of FatSecret and other online support communities to continue offering multiple interactive features that facilitate communication among group members. Doing so allows users to connect with a network of similar others in a manner that suits their comfort level. For instance, users who do not wish to initiate discussion of a particular issue with a larger number of users might find the journal option a more suitable format. Other users seeking feedback about a specific issue, such as asking members following the same diet plan to review a recent food log, might find the discussion forum more useful. Or the same individual might utilize both the journal and the discussion forum options, depending of their interactional goals and their own experiences in using these formats. Whatever the case, offering multifaceted features provides group members with a wide range of options when it comes to communicating social support.

REFERENCES

Albrecht, T. L., & Goldsmith, D. J. (2003). Social support, social networks, and health. In Thompson, T. L., Dorsey, A. M., Miller, K. I., & Parrot, R. (Eds.), *Handbook of health communication* (pp. 263–284). Mahwah, NJ: Erlbaum.

Baym, N. K. (2000). *Tune in, log on: soaps, fandom, and online community*. Thousand Oaks, CA: Sage Publications.

Cissna, K. N., & Anderson, R. (1998). Theorizing about dialogic moments: The Buber-Rogers position and postmodern themes. *Communication Theory*, *8*, 63–104. doi:10.1111/j.1468-2885.1998.tb00211.x

Elfhag, K., & Rossner, S. (2005). Who succeeds in maintaining weight loss? A conceptual review of factors associated with weight loss maintenance and weight regain. *Obesity Reviews*, *6*, 67–85. doi:10.1111/j.1467-789X.2005.00170.x

Falkner, N. H., French, S. A., Jeffrey, R. W., Neumark-Sztainer, D., Sherwood, N. E., & Morton, N. (1999). Mistreatment due to weight: Prevalence and sources of perceived mistreatment in women and men. *Obesity Research*, *7*, 572–576.

Goldsmith, D. J. (2004). *Communicating social support*. Cambridge: Cambridge University Press. doi:10.1017/CBO9780511606984

Goldsmith, D. J., & Brashers, D. E. (2008). Communication matters: Developing and testing social support interventions. *Communication Monographs*, *75*, 320–330.

Goldsmith, D. J., Lindholm, K. A., & Bute, J. J. (2006). Dilemmas of talking about lifestyle changes among couples coping with a cardiac event. *Social Science & Medicine*, *63*, 2079–2090. doi:10.1016/j.socscimed.2006.05.005

King, E. B., Hebl, M. R., & Heatherton, T. F. (2005). Theories of stigma: Limitations and need directions. In Brownell, K. D., Puhl, R. M., Schwartz, M. B., & Rudd, L. (Eds.), *Weight bias: Nature, consequences, and remedies* (pp. 109–120). New York: Guilford Press.

Krukowski, R. A., Harvey-Berino, J., Ashikaga, T., Thomas, C. S., & Micco, N. (2008). Internet-based weight control: The relationship between web features and weight loss. *Telemedicine and E-Health*, *14*, 775–782. doi:10.1089/tmj.2007.0132

Puhl, R., & Brownell, K. D. (2001). Bias, discrimination, and obesity. *Obesity Research*, *9*, 788–805. doi:10.1038/oby.2001.108

Rains, S. A., & Young, V. (2009). A meta-analysis of research on formal computer-mediated support groups: Examining group characteristics and health outcomes. *Human Communication Research*, *35*, 309–336. doi:10.1111/j.1468-2958.2009.01353.x

Rheingold, H. (2000). *The Virtual Community: Homesteading on the Electronic Frontier*. London: MIT Press.

Smith, M., & Kollock, P. (Eds.). (1999). *Communities in cyberspace: Perspective on new forms of social organization*. London: Routledge.

Strum, R., & Wells, K. B. (2001). Does obesity contribute as much to morbidity as poverty or smoking? *Public Health*, *115*, 229–295. doi:10.1016/S0033-3506(01)00449-8

Tate, D. F., Wing, R. R., & Winett, R. A. (2001). Using Internet technology to deliver a behavioral weight loss program. *Journal of the American Medical Association*, *285*, 1172–1177. doi:10.1001/jama.285.9.1172

Verheijdden, M. W., Bakx, J. C., van Weel, C., Koelen, M. A., & van Staveren, W. A. (2005). Role of social support in lifestyle-focused weight management interventions. *European Journal of Clinical Nutrition, 59*, S179–S186. doi:10.1038/sj.ejcn.1602194

Walther, J. B. (1996). Computer-mediated communication: Impersonal, interpersonal, and hyperpersonal interaction. *Communication Research, 23*, 3–43. doi:10.1177/009365096023001001

Walther, J. B. (2008). Social information processing theory. In Baxter, L. A., & Braithwaite, D. O. (Eds.), *Engaging theories in interpersonal communication: Multiple perspectives* (pp. 391–404). Thousand Oaks, CA: Sage.

Walther, J. B. (2009). Computer-mediated communication and virtual groups: Applications to interethnic conflict. *Journal of Applied Communication Research, 37*, 225–238. doi:10.1080/00909880903025937

Weick, K. (1979). *The social psychology of organizing* (2nd ed.). Reading, MA: Addison-Wesley Publishing Company.

White, M., & Dorman, S. M. (2001). Receiving social support online: Implications for health education. *Health Education Research, 16*, 693–707. doi:10.1093/her/16.6.693

Wright, K. B., & Bell, S. B. (2003). Health-related support groups on the Internet: Linking empirical findings to social support and computer-mediated communication theory. *Journal of Health Psychology, 8*, 1359–1053. doi:10.1177/1359105303008001429

KEY TERMS AND DEFINITIONS

Discussion Forums: Interactive feature of the FatSecret website that involves discussions structured around an initial post made by one of the members. Discussion forums are titled by the person who makes the initial post. The initial post to a discussion forum is usually not directed to any particular other person, and discussions are open to any member of the online community.

Obesity and Overweight: Obese and overweight are terms used to describe ranges of weight that are heavier than what is considered healthy compared to the individual's height. The Center for Disease Control and Prevention describes how obesity and overweight are calculated based on body mass index.

Online Community: A community of people with shared interests or goals who use computer-mediated communication as one of the primary means of interaction.

Online Journals: A feature of the FatSecret website that involves individual members writing about their daily lives. Journals are individualized and can be responded to through a comment system.

Social Support: Communication that helps provide people with a sense of assurance, validation, and acceptance from others. Social support is "enacted" in interaction between people and can occur in a wide range of communicative forms and contexts.

Weight Loss: The act of decreasing one's bodyweight. For many FatSecret members, weight loss was often part of their larger effort to work toward a healthy lifestyle.

ENDNOTES

[1] As requested by the administrators of FatSecret, some images appearing in this section have been altered to protect the anonymity of FatSecret members.

[2] All quoted material is presented as it appeared in the FatSecret member's original post. We did not alter the grammar or spelling in any of the quoted material.

3   The names presented in this paper are
    pseudonyms, used to protect the anonymity
    of FatSecret members.

Compilation of References

"jasmine" (pseudo.). (2009, May, 15). Emotionally neglected, is it time? [Advice given to a married woman]. Retrieved from http://messageboards.ivillage.com/iv-rlshouldista

"Switchback" (pseudo.). (2004, April). Help [Advice given to a woman who seeks help with her husband's upsetting behaviors.] Retrieved from http://messageboards.ivillage.com/ relationshipproblems

"Tess" (pseudo.). (2004, April). Help [Advice given to a woman who seeks help with her husband's upsetting behaviors.] Retrieved from http://messageboards.ivillage.com/ relationshipproblems

"Toni" (pseudo.). (2004, May). My bf wont listen [Advice given to a woman whose boyfriend spends too much time socializing with friends]. Retrieved from http://messageboards.ivillage.com/relationshipproblems

"X" (pseudo.) (2004, April). My husband wont help out [Advice given to a married woman whose husband does not help clean or take care of the children]. Retrieved from http://messageboards.ivillage.com/relationshipproblems

Achbar, M., & Wintock, P. (1992). *Manufacturing consent: Noam Chomsky and media....* Retrieved November 5, 2008, from http://video.google.com/videoplay?docid=-5631882395226827730.

Addams, J. (1910). *Twenty years at hull house.* New York: Signet Classics.

Agre, P. (2002). Real-time politics: The Internet and the political process. *The Information Society, 18*(5), 311–331. doi:10.1080/01972240290075174

Aitken, J. E. & Shedletsky, L. J. (2002). Using Electronic Discussion to Teach Communication Courses. *Communication Education, 51, 3* 325-331.

Albrecht, T. L., & Adelman, M. B. (Eds.). (1987). Communicating social support. Newbury Park, CA: Sage.

Albrecht, T. L., & Goldsmith, D. J. (2003). Social support, social networks, and health. In Thompson, T. L., Dorsey, A. M., Miller, K. I., & Parrot, R. (Eds.), *Handbook of health communication* (pp. 263–284). Mahwah, NJ: Erlbaum.

Alexa. (n.d.). *Traffic history for iVillage.com.* Retrieved March 25, 2009 from http://www.alexa.com/data/details/traffic_details/ivillage.com

Amnesty International. (2004). *Country summary: Singapore.* Retrieved May 20, 2005, from http://www.amnestyusa.org/countries/singapore/document.do?id=ar&yr=2005

An, Y.-J., & Frick, T. (2006). Student perceptions of asynchronous computer-mediated communication in face-to-face courses. *Journal of Computer-Mediated Communication, 11*(2), 485–499. doi:10.1111/j.1083-6101.2006.00023.x

Anderson, B. (2004, June). Dimensions of learning and support in an online community [Electronic version]. *Open Learning, 19*(2), 183–190. doi:10.1080/0268051042000224770

Andriotakis, M. (2007). *Blog. Idis is apo to diko sou domatio* [Blog. News from your own room]. Athens: Nefeli.

Angiolillo, J. S., Blanchard, H. E., Israelski, E. W., & Mané, A. (1997). Technology constraints of video-mediated communication. In Finn, K., Sellen, A., & Wilbur, S. (Eds.), *Video-mediated communication* (pp. 51–73). Mahwah, NJ: Lawrence Erlbaum Associates.

Appel, J. (2006, November 10). 'Second Life' develops educational following. eSchool News. Retrieved March 28, 2009 from http://www.eschoolnews.com/news/top-news/index.cfm?i=42030&CFID=3738571&CFTOKEN=82301560.

Arbaugh, J. B. (2001). How instructor immediacy behaviors affect student satisfaction and learning in web-based courses. *Business Communication Quarterly, 64*(4), 42–54. doi:10.1177/108056990106400405

Associated Press. (2005). *Singapore delays launching casino tender.* Retrieved June 20, 2005, from http://www.forbes.com/associatedpress/feeds/ap/2005/06/16/ap2095993.html

Atkinson, S., & Burden, K. (2007). Virtuality, veracity and values: Exploring between virtual and real worlds using the 3V model. In *ICT: Providing choices for learners and learning.* Presented at the Proceedings ascilite, Singapore. Retrieved August 27, 2009, from http://www.ascilite.org.au/conferences/singapore07/procs/atkinson.pdf.

Au, A. (2004, November 11). Casino decision: A bigger question looms. *The Strait Times.* Retrieved August 4, 2009, from http://www.wildsingapore.com/sos/media/041111-2.htm

Bai, H. (2009). Facilitating students' critical thinking in online discussion: An instructor's experience. *Journal of Interactive Online Learning, 8*(2), 156–164.

Bakhtin, M. M. (1981). *The Dialogic Imagination: Four Essays* (Holquist, M., Ed.). Austin, London: University of Texas Press.

Barber, B. R. (1984). *Strong democracy: Participatory politics for a new age.* Berkeley, CA: University of California Press.

Barber, B. R., Mattson, K., & Peterson, J. (1997). *The state of 'electronically enhanced democracy': A survey of the Internet.* New Brunswick, NJ: Walt Whitman Center.

Baron, N. S. (2008). *Always on: Language in an online and mobile world.* Oxford: Oxford University Press.

Barrett, E. (Ed.). (1992). *Sociomedia, multimedia, hypermedia and the social construction of knowledge.* Massachusetts: MIT Press.

Barringer, B. R., & Harrison, J. S. (2000). Walking a tightrope: Creating value through interorganizational relationships. *Journal of Management, 26,* 367–403. doi:10.1177/014920630002600302

Barton, D. (1994). *Literacy: An introduction to the ecology of written language.* London: Blackwell.

Baxter, L. A., & Montgomery, B. M. (1996). *Relating: Dialogues and dialectics.* New York: Guilford.

Baym, N. (1998). The emergence of online community. In Jones, S. G. (Ed.), *Cybersociety 2.0* (pp. 35–68). Thousand Oaks, CA: Sage.

Baym, N. K. (1995). The emergence of community in computer-mediated communication. In Jones, S. (Ed.), *Cybersociety* (pp. 138–163). Newbury Park, CA: Sage.

Baym, N. K. (2000). *Tune in, log on: soaps, fandom, and online community.* Thousand Oaks, CA: Sage Publications.

Beal, M. (2002). Teaching with technology: Construction at work. In Loyd, L. (Ed.), *Teaching with technology: Rethinking tradition* (pp. 27–132). Medford, NJ: Information Today Inc.

Belenky, M. F., Clinchy, B. M., Goldberger, N. R., & Tarule, J. M. (1997). Women's ways of knowing: The development of self, voice, and mind (10th anniversary ed.). New York: Basic.

Bell, A. (1991). *The Language of News Media.* Oxford: Blackwell.

Bem, S. L. (1993). *The lenses of gender: Transforming the debate on sexual inequality.* New Haven, CT: Yale University.

Benford, S., Brown, C., Reynard, G., & Greenhalgh, C. (1996). Shared spaces: Transportation, artificiality, and spatiality. In *Proceedings of the Conference on Computer Supported Cooperative Work* (pp. 77-86). New York: ACM Press.

Benoit, P. J., Benoit, W., Milyo, J., & Hansen, G. (2006). *The effects of traditional vs. web-assisted instruction on student learning and satisfaction. Report published by the University of Missouri. Brookfield, S. D., & Preskill, S. (2005). Discussion as a way of teaching* (2nd ed.). San Francisco, CA: Jossey-Bass.

Benwell, B. (2001). Male Gossip and Language Play in the Letters Pages of Men's Lifestyle Magazines. *Journal of Popular Culture, 34*(4), 19–33. doi:10.1111/j.0022-3840.2001.3404_19.x

Benwell, B., & Stokoe, E. (2006). *Discourse and Identity.* Edinburgh: Edinburgh University Press.

Benyon, D., Stone, D., & Woodroffe, M. (1997). Experience with developing multimedia courseware for the World Wide Web: The need for better tools and clear pedagogy. *International Journal of Human-Computer Studies, 47,* 197–218. doi:10.1006/ijhc.1997.0126

Beuchot, A., & Bullen, M. (2005). Interaction and interpersonality in online discussion forums. *Distance Education, 26*(1), 67–87. doi:10.1080/01587910500081285

Bing, J. M., & Bergvall, V. L. (1996). The question of questions: Beyond binary thinking. In Bergvall, V. L., Bing, J. M., & Freed, A. F. (Eds.), *Rethinking language and gender research: Theory and practice* (pp. 1–30). New York: Longman.

Biocca, F., & Harms, C. (2002). Defining and measuring social presence: Contribution to the networked minds theory and measure. In *Proceedings of the Fifth Annual International Workshop on Presence* (pp. 7-36).

Biocca, F., Harms, C., & Burgoon, J. K. (2003). Towards a more robust theory and measure of social presence: Review and suggested criteria. Retrieved from http://www.mindlab.msu.edu/biocca/pubs/papers/2003_towards_theory_of_social_presence.pdf

Black, J., & Bryant, J. (1995). *Introduction to Media Communication* (4th ed.). Brown and Benchmark.

Boczkowski, P. J. (1999). Mutual shaping of users and technologies in a national virtual community. *The Journal of Communication, 49,* 86–98. doi:10.1111/j.1460-2466.1999.tb02795.x

Boden, D. (1994). *The business of talk: Organizations in action.* Cambridge, MA: Polity Press.

Bolter, D. (2001). *Writing space: Computers, hypertext, and the remediation of print* (2nd ed.). Mahwah, NJ: Lawrence Erlbaum.

Boud, D., Keogh, R., & Walker, D. (Eds.). (1985). *Reflection turning experience into learning.* London: Kogan Page.

Braithwaite, D. O., Waldron, V. R., & Finn, J. (1999). Communication of social support in computer-mediated groups for people with disabilities. Health Communication, 11, 123–151. PubMeddoi:10.1207/s15327027hc1102_2doi:10.1207/s15327027hc1102_2

Branon, R. F., & Essex, C. (2001). Synchronous and asynchronous communication tools in distance education: A survey of instructors. TechTrends, 45, 36–42. doi:10.1007/BF02763377doi:10.1007/BF02763377

Brookfield, S. D. (1987). *Developing critical thinkers: Challenging adults to explore alternative ways of thinking and acting.* San Francisco: Jossey-Bass Publishers.

Brookfield, S. D., & Preskill, S. (1999). *Discussion as a way of teaching.* San Francisco: Jossey-Bass Publishers.

Brown, E. B. (1997). What has happened here?: The politics of difference in women's history and feminist polities. In Nicholson, L. (Ed.), *The second wave: A reader in feminist theory* (pp. 272–287). New York: Routledge.

Browne, T., Jenkins, M., & Walker, R. (2006). A longitudinal perspective regarding the use of VLEs by higher education institutions in the United Kingdom. *Interactive Learning Environments, 14*(2), 177–192. doi:10.1080/10494820600852795

Browning, L. D., Beyer, J. M., & Shetler, J. C. (1995). Building cooperation in a competitive industry: Sematech and the semiconductor industry. *Academy of Management Journal, 38*, 113–151. doi:10.2307/256730

Bruckman, A. (2004). Co-evolution of technological design and pedagogy in an online learning community. In Barab, S. A., Kling, R., & Gray, J. H. (Eds.), *Designing for virtual communities in the service of learning* (pp. 239–255). Cambridge, UK: Cambridge University Press.

Bruckman, A. S. (1993). Gender swapping on the Internet. In *Proceedings of INET93*. Retrieved from http://www.mith2.umd.edu/WomensStudies/Computing/Articles+ResearchPapers/ gender-swapping

Bruner, J. (1986). *Actual minds, possible worlds*. Cambridge, MA: Harvard University Press.

Bruner, J. (2001). Self-making and world-making. In Brockmeier, J., & Cargbaugh, D. (Eds.), *Narrative and identity: Studies in autobiography, self, and culture* (pp. 25–37). Netherlands: John Benjamins.

Buckingham, D. (2008). Introducing identity. In Buckingham, D. (Ed.), *Youth, identity, and digital media* (pp. 1–22). Cambridge, MA: The MIT Press.

Bull, P., & Rumsey, N. (1988). *The social psychology of facial appearance*. New York: Springer-Verlag.

Bulmer, M. (1979). Concepts in the analysis of qualitative data. *The Sociological Review, 27*, 651–677.

Burden, K., & Atkinson, A. (2008). Beyond content: Developing transferable learning designs with digital video Archives, In *Proceedings of ED-MEDIA, Vienna 2008 conference*: http://www.editlib.org/index.cfm?fuseaction=Reader.ViewAbstract&paper_id=28949

Burgos, M. (1989). Life stories, narrativity, and the search for the self. [Récits de vie]. *Life Stories, 5*, 27–38.

Burnett, R., & Marshall, P. D. (2003). *Web theory*. London: Routledge.

Burt, E., & Taylor, J. A. (2000). Information and communication technologies: Reshaping voluntary organizations? *Nonprofit Management & Leadership, 11*, 131–144. doi:10.1002/nml.11201

Butler, B. S. (2001). Membership size, communication activity, and sustainability: A resource-based model of online social structures. *Information Systems Research, 12*, 346–365. doi:10.1287/isre.12.4.346.9703

Caillois, R. (1979). *Man, Play and Games*. New York: Schocken Books.

Cameron, D. (1998). Gender, language, and discourse: A review essay. *Signs, 23*(4), 945–973. doi:10.1086/495297

Carbaugh, D. (1988a). Comments on 'culture' in communication inquiry. *Communication Reports, 1*, 38–41.

Carbaugh, D. (1988b). *Talking American: Cultural discourses on DONAHUE*. Norwood, NJ: Ablex.

Carbaugh, D. (1995). The ethnographic communication theory of Philipsen and associates. In Cushman, D., & Kovacic, B. (Eds.), *Watershed traditions in communication* (pp. 269–297). Albany, NY: SUNY.

Carbaugh, D. (2007). Cultural discourse analysis: Communication practices and intercultural encounters. *Journal of Intercultural Communication Research, 36*(3), 167–182.. doi:10.1080/17475750701737090

Carnegie, A. (1889). *The gospel of wealth*. New York: DoubleDay.

Carrell, L. J., & Menzel, K. E. (2001). Variations in learning, motivation, and perceived immediacy between live and distance education classrooms. *Communication Education, 50*, 230–240. doi:10.1080/03634520109379250

Castells, M. (2000). *The rise of the network society*. Oxford, UK: Blackwell.

Cavanagh, A. (1999). Behaviour in public? Ethics in online ethnography. *Cybersociology, 6*. Retrieved June 15, 2009, from http://www.cybersociology.com/files/6_2_ethicsinonlineethnog.html

Cell, E. (1984). *Learning to learn from experience.* Albany, NY: State University of New York Press.

Chadwick, A. (2003). Bringing e-democracy back in: Why it matters for future research on e-governance. *Social Science Computer Review, 21*(4), 443–455. doi:10.1177/0894439303256372

Chafe, W. (1997). Polyphonic topic development. In Givón, T. (Ed.), *Conversation. Cognitive, Communicative and Social Perspectives* (pp. 41–53). Amsterdam, Philadelphia: John Benjamins Publishing Company.

Chase, S. E. (2005). Narrative inquiry: Multiple lenses, approaches, voices. In Denzin, N. K., & Lincoln, Y. S. (Eds.), *The Sage handbook of qualitative research* (3rd ed., pp. 651–679). Thousand Oaks, CA: Sage.

Cheney, G., & Dionisopoulous, G. N. (1989). Public relations? No, relations with publics: A rhetorical and organizational approach to corporate communication. In Botan, C., & Hazleton, V. (Eds.), *Public relations theory* (pp. 135–157). Hillsdale, NJ: Lawrence Erlbaum.

Cheney, S. (2007, May 22). Marina Bay Sands project on track for completion by 2009. *Channel News Asia.* Retrieved November 11, 2007, from http://www.channelnewsasia.com/stories/singaporelocalnews/view/277767/1/.html

Chia, S. (2004, November 26). Sizing up the casino critic. *The Strait Times.* Retrieved August 4, 2009, from http://www.wildsingapore.com/sos/media/041126-3.htm

Chovanec, J. (2003). The mixing of modes as a means of resolving the tension between involvement and detachment in news headlines. *Brno Studies in English, 29,* 51–66.

Chovanec, J. (2006). Competitive verbal interaction in online minute-by-minute match reports. *Brno Studies in English 32,* 23-35. Retrieved from http://www.phil.muni.cz/wkaa/w-publikace/bse-plone-verze>\

Chovanec, J. (2008a). Enacting an imaginary community: Infotainment in on-line minute-by-minute sports commentaries. In Lavric, E., Pisek, G., Skinner, A., & Stadler, W. (Eds.), *The Linguistics of Football* (pp. 255–268). Tübingen: Gunter Narr Verlag.

Chovanec, J. (2008b). Focus on form: Foregrounding devices in football reporting. *Discourse & Communication, 2*(3), 219–243. doi:10.1177/1750481308091908

Chovanec, J. (2008c). Narrative structures in online sports commentaries. A presentation given at the 9th ESSE conference in Aarhus, Denmark.

Chovanec, J. (2009). "Call Doc Singh!": Textual structure and making sense of live text sports commentaries. In Dontcheva-Navratilova, O., & Povolná, R. (Eds.), *Cohesion and Coherence is Spoken and Written Discourse* (pp. 124–137). Newcastle upon Tyne: Cambridge Scholars Publishing.

Chovanec, J. (in press). Joint construction of humour in quasi-conversational interaction. In Kwiatkowska, A., & Dżereń-Głowacka, S. (Eds.), *Humour. Theories, Applications, Practices, 2 (2): Making Sense of Humour. Piotrków Trybunalski: Naukowe Wydawnictwo Piotrkowskie.*

Churchill, D. (2009). Educational applications of Web 2.0: Using blogs to support teaching and learning. *British Journal of Educational Technology, 40*(1), 179–183. doi:10.1111/j.1467-8535.2008.00865.x

Cissna, K. N., & Anderson, R. (1998). Theorizing about dialogic moments: The Buber-Rogers position and postmodern themes. *Communication Theory, 8,* 63–104. doi:10.1111/j.1468-2885.1998.tb00211.x

Clark, H., & Brennan, S. (1991). Grounding in communication. In Resnick, L. B., Levine, J., & Teasley, S. (Eds.), *Perspectives on socially shared cognition* (pp. 127–149). Washington, DC: APA Press. doi:10.1037/10096-006

Clayman, S., & Heritage, J. (2002). *The news interview: journalists and public figures on the air.* Cambridge: Cambridge University Press. doi:10.1017/CBO9780511613623

Clift, S. (2004). *Online consultations and events - top ten tips for government and civic hosts.* Retrieved November 20, 2004, from http://www.publicus.net

Coates, J. (1988). Gossip revisited: language in all-female groups. In Coates, J., & Cameron, D. (Eds.), *Women in Their Speech Communities, New Perspectives on Language and Sex* (pp. 94–122). London, New York: Longman.

Coglianese, C. (2005). The Internet and Citizen Participation in Rulemaking. *I/S: A Journal of Law and Policy for the Information Society, 1*(1). Retrieved May 2, 2009, from http://www.is-journal.org/V01I01/I-S,%20V01-I01-P033,%20Coglianese.pdf

Cohen, J. (1960). A coefficient of agreement for nominal scales. *Educational and Psychological Measurement, 20*, 37–46. doi:10.1177/001316446002000104

Cohen, J. (1989). Deliberative democracy and democratic legitimacy. In Hamlin, A., & Pettit, P. (Eds.), *The good polity* (pp. 17–34). Oxford, UK: Blackwell.

Cohen, K. (1982). Speaker interaction: Video teleconferences versus face-to-face meetings. In *Proceedings of Teleconferencing and Electronic Communications* (pp. 189–199). Madison, WI: University of Wisconsin Press.

Cole, M., & Derry, J. (2005). We Have Met Technology and it is Us. In *Intelligence and technology: Impact of tools on the nature and development of human abilities*. Mahwah, NJ: Lawrence Erlbaum Associates.

Coleman, S. (2004). Connecting parliament to the public via the Internet: Two case studies of online consultations. *Information Communication and Society, 7*(1), 1–22. doi:10.1080/1369118042000208870

Coleman, S., & Gøtze, J. (2001). *Bowling together: Online public engagement in policy deliberation*. London, UK: Hansard Society.

Collins, M., & Murphy, K. L. (1997). Development of communications conventions in instructional electronic chats. *Journal of Distance Education, 12*(1-2), 177–200.

Collison, G., Elbaum, B., Haavind, S., & Tinker, R. (2000). *Facilitating online learning: Effective strategies for moderators*. Madison: Atwood Publishers.

Conaway, R. N., Easton, S. S., & Schmidt, W. V. (2005). Strategies for Enhancing Student Interaction and Immediacy in Online Courses. *Business Communication Quarterly, 68*(1), 23–35. doi:10.1177/1080569904273300

Conrad, D. (2005). Building and maintaining community in cohort-based online learning [Electronic version]. *Journal of Distance Education, 20*(1), 1–20.

Cook, M., & Lalljee, M. G. (1972). Verbal substitutes for visual signals in interaction. *Semiotics, 3*, 212–221. doi:10.1515/semi.1972.6.3.212

Cope, B., & Kalantzis, M. (2006). A pedagogy of multiliteracies. Designing social futures. In Cope, B., & Kalantzis, M. (Eds.), *Multiliteracies. Literacy learning and design of social futures* (pp. 9–37). London: Routledge.

Cornelius, C., & Boos, M. (2003). Enhancing mutual understanding in synchronous computer-mediated communication by training. *Communication Research, 30*(2), 147–177. doi:10.1177/0093650202250874

Cotton, D., & Yorke, J. (2006, 3-6 December). *Analysing online discussions: What are students learning?* Paper presented at the 23rd annual ascilite conference: Who's learning? Whose technology? Sydney.

Cox, G., Carr, T., & Hall, M. (2004). Evaluating the use of synchronous communication in two blended courses. *Journal of Computer Assisted Learning, 20*, 183–193. doi:10.1111/j.1365-2729.2004.00084.x

Cranton, P. (2006). *Understanding and promoting transformative learning*. San Francisco: John Wiley and Sons, Inc.

Cross, S. E., & Madson, L. (1997). Models of the self: Self-construals and gender. *Psychological Bulletin, 122*(1), 5–37. doi:10.1037/0033-2909.122.1.5

Crowston, K., & Kammerer, E. (1998). Communicative style and gender differences in computer-mediated communications. In Ebo, B. (Ed.), *Cyberghetto or cybertopia* (pp. 185–203). Westport, CT: Praeger.

Cruickshank, K. (2004). Literacy in multilingual contexts: Change in teenagers' reading and writing. *Language and Education, 18*(6), 459–473. doi:10.1080/09500780408666895

Cummings, J. N., Butler, B., & Kraut, R. (2002). The quality of online social relationships. *Communications of the ACM, 45*(7), 103–108. doi:10.1145/514236.514242

Curtis, D. D., & Lawson, M. J. (2001, February). Exploring collaborative online learning. *JALN, 5*(1), 21–34.

D'Urso, S. C., & Pierce, K. M. (2009). Connected to the organization: A survey of communication technologies in the modern organizational landscape. *Communication Research Reports, 26*, 75–81. doi:10.1080/08824090802637098

Daft, R. L., Lengel, R. H., & Trevino, L. K. (1987). Message equivocality, media selection, and manager performance: Implications for information systems. *Management Information Systems Quarterly, 11*(3), 354. doi:10.2307/248682

Daft, R., & Lengel, R. (1984). Information richness: A new approach to managerial behavior and organization design. *Research in Organizational Behavior, 6*, 191–233.

Dahl, R. A. (1991). *Democracy and its critics.* New Haven, CT: Yale University Press.

Dahlberg, L. (2001). Computer-mediated communication and the public sphere: A critical analysis. *Journal of Computer Mediated Communication, 7*(1). Retrieved December 20, 2005, from http://jcmc.indiana.edu/vol7/issue1/dahlberg.html

Danet, B. (1998). Text as mask: Gender, play, and performance on the Internet. In Jones, S. G. (Ed.), *Cybersociety 2.0: Revisiting computer-mediated communication and community* (pp. 129–158). Thousand Oaks, CA: Sage.

Daudelin, M. W. (1996). Learning from experience through reflection. *Organizational Dynamics, 24*(3), 36–48. doi:10.1016/S0090-2616(96)90004-2

Davies, J., & Graff, M. (2005). Performance in e-learning: online participation and student grades. *British Journal of Educational Technology, 36*(4), 657–663. doi:10.1111/j.1467-8535.2005.00542.x

Davis, F. D. (1989). Perceived usefulness, perceived ease of use, and user acceptance of information technology. *Management Information Systems Quarterly, 13*, 319–340. doi:10.2307/249008

Davison, K. P., Pennebaker, J. W., & Dickerson, S. S. (2000). Who talks? The social psychology of illness support groups. American Psychologist, 55, 205-217. Ginossar, T. (2008). Online Participation: A Content

Analysis of Differences in Utilization of Two Online Cancer Communities by Men and Women, Patients and Family Members. Health Communication, 23(1), 1–12.

de Greef, P., & IJsselsteijn, W. (2000, March). *Social presence in the PhotoShare tele-application.* Paper presented at Presence 2000 - 3rd International Workshop on Presence, Delft, The Netherlands.

Delfino, M., & Manca, S. (2007). The expression of social presence through the use of figurative language in a web-based learning environment. *Computers in Human Behavior, 23*(5), 2190–2211. doi:10.1016/j.chb.2006.03.001

Demopoulou, V. (2008, December 18). *Mia prosopiki eksomologisi* [A personal confession]. Message posted to http://veradimopoulou.blogspot.com/

Department of Housing and Urban Development. (2009). *The 2008 annual homeless assessment report to Congress.* Retrieved September 13, 2009 from http://www.hud.gov/utilities/intercept.cfm? http://www.hudhre.info/documents/4thHomelessAssessmentReport.pdf.

Derks, D., Bos, A. E. R., & von Grumbkow, J. (2008). Emoticons and online message interpretation. *Social Science Computer Review, 26*(3), 379–388. doi:10.1177/0894439307311611

Dewey, J. (1991). *How we think.* Buffalo, NY: Prometheus. (Original work published 1910)

Dominick, J. R. (1993). *The Dynamics of Mass Communication* (4th ed.). New York: McGraw-Hill, Inc.

Downes, S. (2004). Educational Blogging. *Educause Review* 39(5), 14-26. Retrieved December 3, 2008, from http://www.educause.edu/EDUCAUSE+Review/EDUCAUSEReviewMagazineVolu. me39/EducationalBlogging/157920

Drew, P., & Heritage, J. (1992). Analyzing talk at work: an introduction. In Drew, P., & Heritage, J. (Eds.), *Talk at work: interaction in institutional settings* (pp. 3–65). Cambridge: Cambridge University Press.

Drew, P., & Heritage, J. (Eds.). (2006). *Conversation analysis.* London: Sage.

Dron, J. (2007). *Control and constraint in e-learning.* Hershey, PA: Idea Group.

Duphorne, P. L., & Gunawardena, C. N. (2005, March). The effect of three computer conferencing designs on critical thinking skills of nursing students. *American Journal of Distance Education, 19*(1), 37–50. doi:10.1207/s15389286ajde1901_4

Dutton, J., Dutton, M., & Perry, J. (2002). How do online students differ from lecture students? *JALN, 6*(1). Retrieved from http://www.sloan-c.org/publications/jaln/v6n1/index.asp

Dvorak, P. (2009, 30 May). On the street and on Facebook: The homeless stay wired. *Wall Street Journal.* Retrieved on September 13, 2009 from http://online.wsj.com/article/SB124363359881267523.html.

Economist Intelligence Unit. (2008). *E-readiness rankings 2008: Maintaining momentum.* Retrieved August 10, 2009, from http://graphics.eiu.com/upload/ibm_ereadiness_2008.pdf

Eggins, S., & Slade, D. (1997). *Analysing Casual Conversation.* London, New York: Continuum.

Ehrmann, J. (1968). Homo Ludens Revisited. In Ehrmann, J. (Ed.), *Game, Play, Literature* (pp. 31–57). Boston: Beacon Press.

Elfhag, K., & Rossner, S. (2005). Who succeeds in maintaining weight loss? A conceptual review of factors associated with weight loss maintenance and weight regain. *Obesity Reviews, 6*, 67–85. doi:10.1111/j.1467-789X.2005.00170.x

Elster, J. (1998). *Deliberative democracy.* Cambridge, UK: Cambridge University Press.

Emerson, R. M., Fretz, R. I., & Shaw, L. L. (1995). *Writing ethnographic field notes.* Chicago, IL: University of Chicago Press.

Engestrom, Y., Miettinen, R., & Punamaki, R. (Eds.). (1999). *Perspectives on Activity Theory.* Cambridge: Cambridge University Press.

Ertmer, P. A., Richardson, J. C., Belland, B., & Camin, D. (2007). Using peer feedback to enhance the quality of student online postings: An exploratory study. *Journal of Computer-Mediated Communication, 12*, 78–99. doi:10.1111/j.1083-6101.2007.00331.x

Eyler, J., Giles, D. E., & Schmeide. (1996). *A practitioner's guide to reflection in service- learning: Student voices and reflections.* A Technical Assistance Project funded by the Corporation for National Service. Nashville, TN: Vanderbilt University.

Fahy, P. J., Crawford, G., & Ally, M. (2001). Patterns of interaction in a computer conference transcript. *International Review of Research in Open and Distance Learning, 2*(1), 1–24.

Fairclough, N. (1989). *Language and Power.* London, New York: Longman.

Fairclough, N. (1995). *Media Discourse.* London: Hodder Arnold.

Falkner, N. H., French, S. A., Jeffrey, R. W., Neumark-Sztainer, D., Sherwood, N. E., & Morton, N. (1999). Mistreatment due to weight: Prevalence and sources of perceived mistreatment in women and men. *Obesity Research, 7*, 572–576.

Feedback Unit. (2005). *Government consultation portal.* Retrieved January 10, 2005, from http://www.feedback.gov.sg

Feixa, C., & Nilan, P. (2006). Postscript: Global youth and transnationalism: The next generation. In Nilan, P., & Feixa, C. (Eds.), *Global youth?: Hybrid identities, plural worlds* (pp. 205–212). New York: Routledge.

Ferrara, K., Brunner, H., & Whittemore, G. (1991). Interactive written discourse as an emergent register. *Written Communication, 8*(1), 8–34. doi:10.1177/0741088391008001002

Fetzer, A. (2002). Put bluntly, you have something of a credibility problem. In Chilton, P., & Schäffner, C. (Eds.), *Politics as Text and Talk: Analytic Approaches to Political Discourse* (pp. 173–201). Amsterdam, Philadelphia: John Benjamins.

Fetzer, A. (2006). "Minister, we will see how the public judges you." Media references in political interviews. *Journal of Pragmatics*, *38*, 180–195. doi:10.1016/j.pragma.2005.06.017

Filipi, A. (2009). *Toddler and parent interaction: the organisation of gaze, pointing and vocalisation*. Amsterdam, Philadelphia: John Benjamins Publishing.

Filipi, A., & Lissonnet, S. (2008, September). Using wikis to create tests. *Teacher Magazine*, 20-22.

Flanagin, A. J. (2000). Social pressures on organizational website adoption. *Human Communication Research*, *26*, 618–646. doi:10.1111/j.1468-2958.2000.tb00771.x

Flanagin, A. J., Tiyaamornwong, V., O'Connor, J., & Seibold, D. R. (2002). Computer-mediated group work: The interaction of member sex and anonymity. *Communication Research*, *29*, 66–93.. doi:10.1177/0093650202029001004

Fletcher, T. D., & Major, D. A. (2006). The effects of communication modality on performance and self-ratings of teamwork components. *Journal of Computer-Mediated Communication, 11*(2), article 9. Retrieved March 3, 2009, from http://jcmc.indiana.edu/vol11/issue2/fletcher.html

Forrester, M. A. (2008). The emergence of self-repair: a case study of one child during the early preschool years. *Research on Language and Social Interaction*, *41*(1), 99–128.

Fountain, J. (2001). *Building the virtual state: Information technology and institutional change*. Washington, DC: Brookings Institution Press.

Fowler, R. (1991). *Language in the News*. London, New York: Routledge.

Fredericksen, E., Pelz, W., Pickett, A., Shea, P., & Swan, K. (2001). Student satisfaction and perceived learning with online courses: Principles and examples from the SUNY Learning Network. *Journal of Asynchronous Learning Networks, 4*(2). Retrieved March 22, 2009, from http://www.aln.org/publications/jaln/v4n2/pdf/v4n2_fredericksen.pdf

Freire, P. (1970). *Pedagogy of the oppressed* (Ramos, M. B., Trans.). New York: Herder & Herder.

Freire, P. (1977). *Politistiki Drasi gia tin kataktasi tis eleftherias* [Cultural Action for the acquisition of freedom]. Athens: Kastaniotis.

Freire, P. (2001). *Pedagogy of Freedom: Ethics, Democracy, and Civic Courage*. Lanham: Rowman & Littlefield Publishers, Inc.

Fulk, J. (1993). Social construction of communication technology. *Academy of Management Journal*, *36*, 921–950. doi:10.2307/256641

Fulk, J., Schmitz, J., & Power, G. J. (1987). A social information processing model of media use in organizations. *Communication Research*, *14*(5), 520–552. doi:10.1177/009365087014005005

Fulk, J., Schmitz, J., & Steinfeld, C. W. (1990). A social influence model of technology use. In Fulk, J., & Steinfeld, C. (Eds.), *Organizations and communication technology* (pp. 117–140). Newbury Park, CA: Sage.

Gaimster, J. (2007). Reflections on Interactions in virtual worlds and their implication for learning art and design. Art. Design & Communication in Higher Education, 6(3), 187–199. doi:10.1386/adch.6.3.187_1doi:10.1386/adch.6.3.187_1

Garcia, A. C., & Jacobs, J. B. (1998). The interactional organization of computer mediated communication in the college classroom. *Qualitative Sociology*, *21*, 299–317. doi:10.1023/A:1022146620473

Garcia, A. C., & Jacobs, J. B. (1999). The eyes of the beholder: Understanding the turn-taking system in quasi-synchronous computer-mediated communication. *Research on Language and Social Interaction*, *32*, 337–367. doi:10.1207/S15327973rls3204_2

Garland, K., & Noyes, J. (2004). The effects of mandatory and optional use on students' ratings of a computer-based learning package. *British Journal of Educational Technology*, *35*(3), 263–273. doi:10.1111/j.0007-1013.2004.00388.x

Garrison, D. R., Anderson, T., & Archer, W. (1999). Critical Inquiry in a Text-Based Environment: Computer Conferencing in Higher Education. *The Internet and*

Higher Education, 2(2/3), 87–105. doi:10.1016/S1096-7516(00)00016-6

Garrison, D. R., Anderson, T., & Archer, W. (2003). Critical thinking, cognitive presence, and computer conferencing in distance education. *American Journal of Distance Education, 15*(1), 7–23. doi:10.1080/08923640109527071

Gavriilidis, A. (2008). Greek Riots 2008-A mobile Tiananmen. In S. Economides & V. Monastiriotis (Eds.), The return of street politics? Essays on the December riots in Greece (15-21). London: The Hellenic Observatory-LSE.

Gee, J. P. (2009). Digital media and learning as an emerging field, Part I: How we got here. *International Journal of Learning and Media, 1*(2), 13-21. Retrieved July 22, 2009 from http://www.mitpressjournals.org/doi/abs/10.1162/ijlm.2009.0011

Geertz, C. (1972). Deep play: notes on the Balinese cockfight. *Daedalus, 101*(1), 1–37.

Georgiakarra. (2008, December 12) Anaparastasis gynekon mesa apo ta kentrika deltia idiseon tou Star ke tou Mega. [Representations of women in the central news bulletins of Star and Mega channels]. Message posted to http://georgiakarra.blogspot.com/

Gergen, K. (1995). Social construction and the educational process. In Steffe, L., & Gale, J. (Eds.), *Constructivism in education* (pp. 17–39). Hillsdale, NJ: Erlbaum.

Gertsi. (2008). *Yerasimos Tsibloulis-Gertsi. Yia to perivallon, tin ekpedefsi, ton politismo ke tin kinoniki anthropologia.* [Yerasimos Tsibloulis-Gertsi. For the environment, education, culture and social anthropology]. Retrieved March 1, 2009, from http://tsibloulis.blogspot.com/

Gibbs, D., & Gosper, M. (2006). The upside-down-world of e-learning. *Journal of Learning Design, 1*(2), 46–54.

Giddens, A. (1984). *The constitution of society: Introduction of the theory of structuration.* Berkeley, CA: University of California Press.

Gilbert, N., & Driscoll, M. (2002). Collaborative knowledge building: A case study. *Educational Technology*

Research and Development, 50*(1), 59-71. Retrieved June 9, 2009 from http://education.korea.ac.kr/innwoo/edu603/computers_in_education/collaborative%20knowledge%20building.pdf

Gillmor, D. (2008, October). *Citizens and New Media.* Paper presented at the conference of Aristotle University of Thessaloniki on Participatory Journalism. Retrieved December 20, 2009, from http://www.blogchannel.gr/2009/04/dan-gillmor-auth/

Ginsburg, F. D., Abu-Lughod, L., & Larkin, B. (2005). Introduction. In Ginsburg, F. D., Abu-Lughod, L., & Larkin, B. (Eds.), *Media worlds. Anthropology on a new terrain* (pp. 1–36). Berkeley: University of California Press.

Glaser, B. G., & Strauss, A. L. (1967). *The discovery of grounded theory: Strategies for qualitative research.* Chicago: Aldine.

Glenn, P. J., & Knapp, M. L. (1987). The interactive framing of play in adult conversations. *Communication Quarterly, 35*(1), 48–66.

Glogowski, K. (2009, January 16). Teaching how to learn. Message posted to http://www.teachandlearn.ca/blog/2009/01/16/teaching-how-to-learn/

Goffman, E. (1959). *The presentation of self in everyday life.* Garden City, New York: Anchor.

Goffman, E. (1963). *Behavior in public places: Notes on the social organization of gatherings.* New York: Free Press.

Goffman, E. (1974). *Frame Analysis: An Essay on the Organization of Experience.* New York: Harper and Row.

Goldsmith, D. J. (2004). *Communicating social support.* Cambridge: Cambridge University Press. doi:10.1017/CBO9780511606984

Goldsmith, D. J., & Brashers, D. E. (2008). Communication matters: Developing and testing social support interventions. *Communication Monographs, 75*, 320–330.

Goldsmith, D. J., Lindholm, K. A., & Bute, J. J. (2006). Dilemmas of talking about lifestyle changes among couples coping with a cardiac event. *Social Science & Medicine, 63*, 2079–2090. doi:10.1016/j.socscimed.2006.05.005

Gomez, J. (2000). *Self-censorship: Singapore's shame*. Singapore: Think Centre.

Goodwin, C. (1995). Seeing in depth. *Social Studies of Science, 25*, 237–274. doi:10.1177/030631295025002002

Goodwin, C. (1996). Transparent vision. In Ochs, E., Schegloff, E. A., & Thompson, S. A. (Eds.), *Interaction and grammar* (pp. 370–404). Cambridge: Cambridge University Press. doi:10.1017/CBO9780511620874.008

Google. (2009, May 28, 2009). *Google Wave Developer Preview at Google I/O2009*. Retrieved May 28, from http://www.youtube.com/watch?v=v_UyVmITiYQ.

Gorsky, P., & Caspi, A. (2005). Dialogue: a theoretical framework for distance education instructional systems. *British Journal of Educational Technology, 36*(2), 137–144. doi:10.1111/j.1467-8535.2005.00448.x

Graddol, D. (1994). The visual accomplishment of factuality. In Graddol, D., & Boyd-Barrett, O. (Eds.), *Media Texts: Authors and Readers* (pp. 136–157). Maidenhead: Open University Press.

Graddol, D., & Swan, J. (1989). *Gender Voices*. Cambridge, MA: Basil Blackwell.

Graham, M., & Scarborough, H. (2001). Enhancing the learning environment for distance education students. *Distance Education, 22*(2), 232–244. doi:10.1080/0158791010220204

Graham, S. L. (2007). Disagreeing to agree: Conflict, (im)politeness and identity in a computer-mediated community. *Journal of Pragmatics, 3*, 742–759. doi:10.1016/j.pragma.2006.11.017

Greeklish. (n.d.) Retrieved February 3, 2009 from http://el.wikipedia.org/wiki_Greeklish

Greenfield, P. M., & Subrahmanyam, K. (2003). Online discourse in a teen chatroom: New codes and new modes of coherence in a visual medium. *Journal of Applied Developmental Psychology, 24*, 713–738. doi:10.1016/j.appdev.2003.09.005

Griffin, E. (2006). *Communication: A first look at communication theory* (6th ed.). Boston: McGraw-Hill.

Grossman, L. (1996). *The electronic republic: Reshaping democracy in the information age*. New York: Viking.

Guiller, J., & Durndell, A. (2007). Students' linguistic behaviour in online discussion groups: Does gender matter? *Computers in Human Behavior, 23*, 2240–2255. doi:10.1016/j.chb.2006.03.004

Guiller, J., Durndell, A., & Ross, A. (2008). Peer interaction and critical thinking: Face-to-face or online discussion? *Learning and Instruction, 18*(2), 187–200. doi:10.1016/j.learninstruc.2007.03.001

Gunawardena, C. N. (1995). Social presence theory and implications for interaction and collaborative learning in computer conferences. *International Journal of Educational Telecommunications, 1*(2/3), 147–166.

Gunawardena, C. N., & Zittle, R. (1996). An examination of teaching and learning processes in distance education and implications for designing instruction. In M. F. Beaudoin (Ed.), *Distance Education Symposium 3: Instruction* (Vol. 12, pp. 51-63). State College, PA: American Center for the Study of Distance Education.

Guthrie, K. (2009). *Social change and leadership: An undergraduate course developed for the University of Illinois at Springfield*. Springfield, Ill.: University of Illinois at Springfield.

Habermas, J. (1984). *The theory of communicative action, volume one. Reason and the rationalization of society*. Boston: Beacon Press.

Hall, B. J., & Valde, K. (1995). Brown-nosing as a cultural category in American organizational life. *Research on Language and Social Interaction, 28*(4), 391–419. doi:10.1207/s15327973rlsi2804_3

Hall, G., & Danby, S. (2003). Teachers and academics co-constructing the category of expert through meeting talk. *Proceedings of the Annual Conference of the Australian Association for Research in Education*. Retrieved June 15, 2009, from http://www.aare.edu.au/03pap/hal03027.pdf

Hall, J. (2003, January). Assessing learning management systems. *Chief Learning Officer*. Retrieved March 15,

2009, from http://www.clomedia.com/features/2003/January/91/index.php?pt=a&aid=91&start=16797&page=6

Halliday, M. A. K. (1978). *Language as Social Semiotic*. London: Edward Arnold.

Halliday, M. A. K., & Hasan, R. (1986). *Language, Context and Text. Aspects of Language in a Social-Semiotic Perspective*. Oxford: Oxford University Press.

Hample, D. (2008). Issue forum: Can we enhance people's lives? *Communication Monographs*, *75*(4), 319–350.. doi:10.1080/03637750802524269

Hara, N., Bonk, C. J., & Angeli, C. (2000). Content analysis of online discussion in an applied educational psychology course. *Instructional Science*, *28*(2), 115–152. doi:10.1023/A:1003764722829

Harasim, L. (1991, 8-11 January). *Designs & tools to augment collaborative learning in computerized conferencing systems*. Paper presented at the Twenty-Fourth Annual Hawaii International Conference on System Sciences, Kauai, Hawaii.

Harasim, L., Hiltz, R. S., Teles, L., & Turoff, M. (1995). *Learning networks*. Cambridge: MIT Press.

Hare, A. P. (2003). Roles, relationships, and groups in organizations: Some conclusions and recommendations. *Small Group Research*, *34*, 123–154. doi:10.1177/1046496402250430

Harman, K., & Koohang, A. (2005). Discussion board: A learning object. *Interdisciplinary Journal of Knowledge and Learning Objects*, *1*, 67–77.

Harrison, S. (2000). Maintaining the virtual community: use of politeness strategies in an email discussion group. In L. Pemberton & S. Shurville (Eds.), Words on the web: computer mediated communication (pp. 69-78). Exeter & Portland, OR: Intellect Books.

Hart, J. W., Karau, S. J., Stasson, M. K., & Kerr, N. A. (2004). Achievement motivation, expected coworker performance, and collective task motivation: Working hard or hardly working? *Journal of Applied Social Psychology*, *34*, 984–1000. doi:10.1111/j.1559-1816.2004.tb02580.x

Hatzipanagos, S., & Warburton, S. (2009). Feedback as dialogue: Exploring the links between formative assessment and social software in distance learning. *Learning, Media and Technology*, *34*(1), 45–59. doi:10.1080/17439880902759919

Hauber, J., Regenbrecht, H., Hills, A., Cockburn, A., & Billinghurst, M. (2005). Social presence in two- and three-dimensional videoconferencing. In. *Proceedings of ISPR*, *2005*, 189–198.

Haythornthwaite, C., Kazmer, M., Robins, J., & Shoemaker, S. (2000). Community development among distance learners: Temporal and technological dimensions. *Journal of Computer Mediated Communication*, *6*(1). Retrieved February 14, 2001, from http://www.ascusc.org/jcmc/vol6/issue1/haythornthwaite.html.

Heath, C., & Luff, P. (1991). Disembodied conduct: Communication through video in a multi-media office environment. In *Proceedings of the ACM Conference on Human Factors in Computing Systems, CHI'91* (pp. 99-103). New Orleans, Louisiana.

Heath, R. G., & Sias, P. M. (1999). Communicating spirit in a collaborative alliance. *Journal of Applied Communication Research*, *27*, 356–376. doi:10.1080/00909889909365545

Heckman, R., & Annabi, H. (2005). A content analytic comparison of learning processes in online and face-to-face case study discussions. *Journal of Computer-Mediated Communication*, *10*(2), article 7. Retrieved from http://jcmc.indiana.edu/vol10/issue2/heckman.html

Heritage, J. (1984). *Garfinkel and ethnomethodology*. Cambridge: Polity Press.

Herring, S. (1999). Interactional coherence in CMC. *Journal of Computer-Mediated Communication*, *4*(4). Retrieved March 1, 2001, from http://www.ascusc.org/jcmc/vol4/issue4/herring.html

Herring, S. C. (1993). Gender and democracy in computer-mediated communication. *Electronic Journal of Communication*, *3*(2). Retrieved from http://www.cios.org/www/ejcmain.htm

Herring, S. C. (1999). Interactional coherence in CMC. *Journal of Computer-Mediated Communication, 4*(4). Retrieved May 4, 2003, from http://www.ascusc.org/jcmc/vol4/issue4/herring.html

Herring, S. C. (1999). The Rhetorical dynamics of ender harassment on-line. *The Information Society, 15*, 151–167. doi:10.1080/019722499128466

Herring, S. C. (2003). Dynamic topic analysis of synchronous chat. *New Research for New Media: Innovative Research Methodologies Symposium Working Papers and Readings* Retrieved December 30, 2006, from http://ella/slis.indiana.edu/%7Eherring/dta.htm/

Herring, S. C. (2003). Gender and power in online communication. In Holmes, J., & Meyerhoff, M. (Eds.), *The handbook of language and gender* (pp. 202–228). Malden, MA: Blackwell. doi:10.1002/9780470756942.ch9

Herring, S. C. (2004). Computer-mediated discourse analysis: An approach to researching online behavior. In Barab, S. A., Kling, R., & Gray, J. H. (Eds.), *Designing for virtual communities in the service of learning* (pp. 338–376). New York: Cambridge University Press.

Herring, S. C., & Martinson, A. (2004). Assessing gender authenticity in computer-mediated language use: Evidence from an identity game. *Journal of Language and Social Psychology, 23*, 424–446.. doi:10.1177/0261927X04269586

Hester, S., & Eglin, P. (1997). Membership categorization analysis: an introduction. In Hester, S., & Eglin, P. (Eds.), *Culture in action: studies in membership categorization analysis* (pp. 1–23). Washington: International Institute for Ethnomethodology and University Press of America.

Hines, R. A., & Pearl, C. E. (2004). Increasing interaction in Web-based instruction: Using synchronous chats and asynchronous discussions. Rural Special Education Quarterly, 23, 33–36.

Hoefling, T. (2003). *Working virtually: Managing people for successful virtual teams and organizations*. Sterling, VA: Stylus Publishing.

Holt, D. M., & Challis, D. J. (2007). From policy to practice: one university's experience of implementing strategic change through wholly online teaching and learning. *Australasian Journal of Educational Technology, 23*(1), 110–131.

Holt, D. M., & Palmer, S. (2007, 2-5 December). *Staff exercising 'choice'; students exercising 'choice': Wholly online learning at an Australian university.* Paper presented at the 24th Annual Conference of the Australasian Society for Computers in Learning in Tertiary Education, Singapore.

Holt, D. M., & Thompson, D. J. (1995). Responding to the technological imperative: The experience of one open and distance education institution. *Distance Education: An International Journal, 16*(1), 43–64. doi:10.1080/0158791950160105

Honeycutt, L. (2001). Comparing e-mail and synchronous conferencing in online peer response [Electronic version]. *Written Communication, 18*(1), 26–60. doi:10.1177/0741088301018001002

Horton, D., & Wohl, R. (1956). Mass Communication and Para-social Interaction. *Psychiatry, 19*, 215–229.

Houle, C. O. (1972). *The design of education*. San Francisco: Jossey-Bass Publishers.

Huang, H.-M. (2002). Towards constructivism for adult learners in online learning environments. *British Journal of Educational Technology, 33*(1), 27-37. Retrieved May 30, 2009 from http://www.speakeasydesigns.com/SDSU/student/SAGE/compsprep/Constructivism_for_Adults_Online.pdf

Huberman, A. M., & Miles, M. B. (1994). Data management and analysis methods. In Denzin, N. K., & Lincoln, Y. S. (Eds.), *Handbook of qualitative research* (pp. 428–444). Thousand Oaks, CA: Sage.

Huffaker, D. A., & Calvert, S. L. (2005). Gender, identity, and language use in teenage blogs. *Journal of Computer-Mediated Communication, 10*(2), article 1. Retrieved October 2, 2008 from http://jcmc.indiana.edu/vol10/issue2/huffaker.html

Huizinga, J. (1950). *Homo Ludens: A Study of the Play Element in Culture*. Boston: Beacon Press.

Hung, D. W. L., & Chen, D.-T. (2001). Situated cognition, Vygotskian thought and learning from the communities of practice perspective: Implications for the design of web-based e-learning. *Educational Media International, 38*(1), 3–12. doi:10.1080/09523980110037525

Hung, D. W. L., & Chen, D.-T. (2002). Learning within the context of communities of practice: A re-conceptualization of tools, rules and online learning environments of the activity system. *Educational Media International, 39*(3&4), 247–255.

Hunt, S., Simonds, C., & Simonds, B. (2007, November) Uniquely qualified, distinctively competent: Delivering 21st century skills in the Basic Course. *93rd annual convention, National Communication Association* (pp. 1-24) (AN 35506038).

Hymes, D. (1962). The ethnography of speaking. In Gladwin, T., & Sturtevant, W. (Eds.), *Anthropology and human behavior* (pp. 13–53). Washington, D.C.: Anthropological Society of Washington.

Hymes, D. (1972). Models of the interaction of language and social life. In Gumperz, J., & Hymes, D. (Eds.), *Directions in sociolinguistics: The ethnography of communication* (pp. 35–71). New York: Holt, Rinehart, and Winston.

Hymes, D. (1974). *Foundations in sociolinguistics: An ethnographic approach*. Philadelphia: University of Pennsylvania Press.

Innis, H. A. (1951). *The Bias of Communication*. Toronto: University of Toronto Press.

Inoue, T., Okada, K. I., & Matsushita, Y. (1997). Integration of face-to-face and video-mediated meetings: HERMES. In *Proceedings of International Conference on Supporting Group Work* (pp. 405-414). New York: ACM Press.

Internet World Stats. (2009). *Asia Internet usage stats and population statistics*. Retrieved August 14, 2009 from http://www.internetworldstats.com/stats3.htm

Isaacs, E., & Tang, J. (1994). What video can and cannot do for collaboration: A case study. *Multimedia Systems, 2*, 63–73. doi:10.1007/BF01274181

Iverson, J. O., & McPhee, R. D. (2002). Knowledge management in communities of practice: Being true to the communicative character of knowledge. *Management Communication Quarterly, 16*, 259–266. doi:10.1177/089331802237239

Ivy, D., & Backlund, P. (2000). *Exploring genderspeak: Personal effectiveness in gender communication* (2nd ed.). Boston, MA: McGraw-Hill.

Jacobson, R. (1960). Closing statement: linguistics and poetics. In T. A. Sebeok (Ed.), Style in Language (pp. 350-77). Cambridge, MA: the MIT Press.

James, R., McInnis, C., & Devlin, M. (2002). *Assessing Learning in Australian Universities*. Melbourne, Australia: Centre for the Study of Higher Education and The Australian Universities Teaching Committee.

Janis, I. (1982). *Groupthink: Psychological studies of policy decisions and fiascos* (2nd ed.). Boston: Houghton Mifflin.

Jaques, D., & Salmon, G. (2006). *Learning in groups: a handbook for face-to-face and online environments*. Hoboken: Taylor & Francis.

Jefferson, G. (1972). Side sequences. In Sudnow, D. (Ed.), *Studies in social interaction* (pp. 294–338). New York: Free Press.

Jenkins, H. (2006). *Confronting the challenges of participatory culture: Media education for the 21st century*. Chicago: The MacArthur Foundation. Retrieved January 25, 2009, from http://digitallearning.macfound.org/atf/cf/%7BE45C7E0-A3E0-4B89-AC9C-E807E1B0AE4E%7D/JENKINS_WHITE_PAPER.PDF

Jeong, A. C. (2003). The sequential analysis of group interaction and critical thinking in online threaded discussions. *American Journal of Distance Education, 17*, 25–43. doi:10.1207/S15389286AJDE1701_3

Johnson, G. M. (2006). Synchronous and asynchronous text-based CMC in educational contexts: A review of recent research. *TechTrends: Linking Research and Practice to Improve Learning, 50*(4), 46–53.

Johnson, S. D., Aragon, S. R., Shaik, N., & Palma-Rivas, N. (2000). Comparative Analysis of Learner Satisfaction and Learning Outcomes in Online and Face-to-Face Learning Environments. *Journal of Interactive Learning Research, 11*(1), 29–49.

Johnson, S., & Finlay, F. (1997). Do Men Gossip? An Analysis of Football Talk on Television. In Meinhof, U. H., & Johnson, S. (Eds.), *Language and Masculinity* (pp. 130–143). Oxford: Blackwell.

Johnston, V. L. (1992). *Towards a global classroom: Using computer-mediated communications at UAA.* Anchorage, AK: University of Alaska Anchorage Vocational Teacher Education Research Project. (ERIC Document Reproduction Service No. ED356759). Retrieved March 15, 2009, from FirstSearch ERIC database.

Joiner, R., & Jones, S. (2003). The effects of communication medium on argumentation and the development of critical thinking. *International Journal of Educational Research, 39*(8), 861–871. doi:10.1016/j.ijer.2004.11.008

Joinson, A. N. (2001). Self-disclosure in computer-mediated communication: The role of self-awareness and visual anonymity. *European Journal of Social Psychology, 31*, 177–192. doi:10.1002/ejsp.36

Jonassen, D., Davidson, M., Collins, M., Campbell, J., & Bannan Haag, B. (1995). Constructivism and computer-mediated communication in distance education. *American Journal of Distance Education.* Retrieved May 29, 2009 from http://www.c3l.uni-oldenburg.de/cde/media/readings/jonassen95.pdf

Jones, A. (2004). *A review of the research literature on barriers to the uptake of ICT by teachers.* Coventry: Becta.

Jones, Q., & Rafaeli, S. (2000). Time to split, virtually: 'Discourse architecture' and "community building" as means to creating vibrant virtual publics. *Electronic Markets: The International Journal of Electronic Commerce and Business Media, 10*(4), 214–223.

Jonscher, C. (1999). *The evolution of wired Life: From the alphabet to the soul-catcher chip—How information technologies change our world.* Hoboken: Wiley.

Jucker, A. H. (2006). Live text commentaries. Read about it while it happens. In: J. K. Androutsopoulos, J. Runkehl, P. Schlobinski & T. Siever (Eds.), *Neuere Entwicklungen in der linguistischen Internetforschung. Zweites internationales Symposium zur gegenwärtigen linguistischen Forschung über computervermittelte Kommunikation. Universität Hannover, 4.-6. Oktober 2004* (Germanistische Linguistik 186-187) (pp. 113-131). Hildesheim: Georg Olms.

Jucker, A. H. (in press). "Beckham knocks it deep": Live text commentaries on the Internet as real-time narratives.

Kamin, C., Glicken, A., Hall, M., Quarantillo, B., & Merenstein, G. (2001). Evaluation of electronic discussion groups as a teaching/learning strategy in an evidence-based medicine course: A pilot study. *Education for Health, 14*(1), 21–32. doi:10.1080/13576280010015380

Kanev, K., Kimura, S., & Orr, T. (2009). A framework for collaborative learning in dynamic group environments. International Journal of Distance Education Technologies, 7(1), 58–77.

Kang, S., Watt, J., & Ala, S. (2008, April). *Social copresence in anonymous social interactions using a mobile video telephone.* Paper presented at CHI, Florence, Italy.

Kanuka, H. (2005). An exploration into facilitating higher levels of learning in a text-based internet learning environment using diverse instructional strategies. *Journal of Computer-Mediated Communication, 10*(3), article 8. Retrieved January 11, 2006 from http://jcmc.indiana.edu/vol10/issue3/kanuka.html.

Kearns, I., Bend, J., & Stern, B. (2002). *E-participation in local government.* London, UK: Institute for Public Policy Research.

Kehrwald, B. A. (2008). Understanding social presence in text-based online learning environments. *Distance Education, 29*(1), 89–106. doi:10.1080/01587910802004860

Keyton, J., & Stallworth, V. (2003). On the verge of collaboration: Interaction processes versus group outcomes. In Frey, L. R. (Ed.), *Group communication in context: Studies of bona fide groups* (2nd ed., pp. 235–260). Mahwah, NJ: Erlbaum.

King, E. B., Hebl, M. R., & Heatherton, T. F. (2005). Theories of stigma: Limitations and need directions. In Brownell, K. D., Puhl, R. M., Schwartz, M. B., & Rudd, L. (Eds.), *Weight bias: Nature, consequences, and remedies* (pp. 109–120). New York: Guilford Press.

Kirkpatrick, G. (2005). Online "chat" facilities as pedagogic tools. *Active Learning in Higher Education, 6,* 145–159. doi:10.1177/1469787405054239

Kirkwood, A., & Price, L. (2005). Learners and learning in the twenty-first century: what do we know about students' attitudes towards and experiences of information and communication technologies that will help us design courses? *Studies in Higher Education, 30*(3), 257–274. doi:10.1080/03075070500095689

Kirschner, P. (2002). Can we support CSCL? Educational, social and technological affordances for learning. In P. Kirschner (Ed.), Three worlds of CSCL: Can we support CSCL (pp. 7-47). Heerlen: Open University of the Netherlands.

Klemm, P., Hurst, M., Dearholt, S. L., & Trone, S. R. (1999). Cyber solace: Gender differences on Internet cancer support groups. Computers in Nursing, 17, 65–72. PubMed

Klemm, P., Reppert, K., & Visich, L. (1998). A nontraditional cancer support group: The Internet. Computers in Nursing, 16, 31–36. PubMed

Klemm, W. R. (2002, September/October). Extending the pedagogy of threaded-topic discussions. *The Technology Source.* Retrieved November 1, 2004 from http://ts.mivu.org/default.asp?show=article&id=1015

Knowles, M. S. (1984). *The adult student: A neglected species* (3rd ed.). Houston: Gulf Publishing Company.

Kobbe, L., Weinberger, A., Dillenbourg, P., Harrer, A., Hamalainen, R., & Hakkinen, P. (2007). Specifying computer-supported collaboration scripts. *International Journal of Computer-Supported Collaborative Learning, 2*(2-3), 211–224. doi:10.1007/s11412-007-9014-4

Koukloutsis, I. (2009, April 7). Anonimi i eponimi kritiki. Message posted to http://slografeiou.blogspot.com/2009/04/blog-post.html#comments

Kramarae, C., & Taylor, H. J. (1991). Women and men on electronic networks: A conversation or a monologue? In Taylor, H. J., Kramarae, C., & Ebben, M. (Eds.), *Women, information technology, and scholarship* (pp. 52–61). Urbana, Champaign: Center for Advanced Study, University of Illinois.

Kraut, R. E., Fussell, S. R., & Siegel, J. (2003). Visual information as a conversational resource in collaborative physical tasks. *Human-Computer Interaction, 18,* 13–49. doi:10.1207/S15327051HCI1812_2

Kreijns, K., Kirschner, P. A., Jochems, W., & Van Buuren, H. (2004). Determining sociability, social space, and social presence in (a)synchronous collaborative groups. *Cyberpsychology & Behavior, 7*(2), 155–172. doi:10.1089/109493104323024429

Kress, G., & Jewitt, C. (2003). Introduction. In Jewitt, C., & Kress, G. (Eds.), *Multimodal literacy* (pp. 1–18). New York: Peter Lang.

Krukowski, R. A., Harvey-Berino, J., Ashikaga, T., Thomas, C. S., & Micco, N. (2008). Internet-based weight control: The relationship between web features and weight loss. *Telemedicine and E-Health, 14,* 775–782. doi:10.1089/tmj.2007.0132

Kuk, G. (2003, 9-11 April). *E-Learning Hubs: Affordance, Motivation and Learning Outcomes.* Paper presented at the UK Higher Education Academy Business Education Support Team Subject Centre Conference 2003, Brighton.

Kuo, S.-H. (2003). Involvement vs detachment: gender differences in the use of personal pronouns in televised sports in Taiwan. *Discourse Studies, 5*(4), 479–494. doi:10.1177/14614456030054002

Labov, W. (1997). Rules for Ritual Insults. In Coupland, N., & Jaworski, A. (Eds.), *Sociolinguistics: A Reader and Coursebook* (pp. 472–486). London: Macmillan. (Original work published 1972)

Lapadat, J. (July, 2002, July). Written interaction: A key component in online learning. *Journal of Computer Mediated Communication, 7*(4). Retrieved July 12, 2007 from http://jcmc.indiana.edu/vol7/issue4/lapadat.html

Lapadat, J. C. (2007). Discourse devices used to establish community, increase coherence, and negotiate agreement in an online university course. *Journal of Distance Education, 21*(3), 59–92.

Lapadat, J. C. (2008, May). *Libratory technologies: Using multimodal literacies to connect, reframe, and build communities from the bottom up.* Paper presented at the Fourth International Congress of Qualitative Inquiry, Urbana-Champaign, IL: University of Illinois. Abstract retrieved May 11, 2008, from www.icqi.org.

Lapadat, J. C., Atkinson, M. L., & Brown, W. I. (2009). The electronic lives of teens: Negotiating access, producing digital narratives, and recovering from Internet addiction. In *E-Learn: World Conference on E-Learning in Corporate, Government, Healthcare, & Higher Education Proceedings* (pp. 2807-2816). Retrieved November 5, 2009, from: http://EdITLib.org

Lapadat, J. C., Bryant, L., Burrows, M., Greenlees, S., Hill, A. S., & Alexander, J. (2009). An identity montage using collaborative autobiography: Eighteen ways to bend the light. *International Review of Qualitative Research, 1*(4), 495–520.

LaPointe, D. K., & Gunawardena, C. N. (2004). Developing, testing and refining of a model to understand the relationship between peer interaction and learning outcomes in computer-mediated conferencing. *Distance Education, 25*(1), 83–106. doi:10.1080/0158791042000212477

Lee, E. (2007a). Effects of gendered language on gender stereotyping in computer-mediated communication: The moderating role of depersonalization and gender-role orientation. *Human Communication Research, 33*(4), 515–535..doi:10.1111/j.1468-2958.2007.00310.x

Lee, E. (2007b). Wired for gender: Experientiality and gender-stereotyping in computer-mediated communication. *Media Psychology, 10*, 182–210. doi:. doi:10.1080/15213260701375595

Leonard, L. G., Withers, L. A., & Sherblom, J. C. (2009). Three universities--one classroom: Collaborative teaching in Second Life. In N. Edick & G. J. de Vreede (Eds.), Advances in collaboration science research: The Center for Collaboration Sciences third research seminar (pp. 29–36). Omaha, NE: The Center for Collaboration Science, University of Nebraska at Omaha.

Leonard-Barton, D. (1988). Implementation as mutual adaptation of technology and organization. *Research Policy, 17*, 251–267. doi:10.1016/0048-7333(88)90006-6

Levin, B. B., He, Y., & Robbins, H. H. (2006). Comparative analysis of preservice teachers' reflective thinking in synchronous versus asynchronous online case discussions. *Journal of Technology and Teacher Education, 14*, 439–460.

Levine, J. M., & Moreland, R. L. (1990). Progress in small group research. *Annual Review of Psychology, 41*, 585–634. doi:10.1146/annurev.ps.41.020190.003101

Levine, S. J. (2007, Spring). The online discussion board. *New Directions for Adult and Continuing Education, 113*, 67–74. doi:10.1002/ace.248

Levine, S., & White, P. E. (1961). Exchange as a conceptual framework for the study of interorganizational relationships. *Administrative Science Quarterly, 15*, 583–601. doi:10.2307/2390622

Levy, P. (2006). "Learning a different form of communication": Experiences of networked learning and reflections on practice. *Studies in Continuing Education, 28*(3), 259–277. doi:10.1080/01580370600947512

Lewis, D. M. (2003). Online news: a new genre? In Aitchison, J., & Lewis, D. M. (Eds.), *New Media Language* (pp. 95–104). London, New York: Routledge.

Lewis, L. K., & Seibold, D. S. (1993). Innovation modification during intraorganizational adoption. *Academy of Management Review, 2*, 322–354. doi:10.2307/258762

Lewis, L. K., Hamel, S. A., & Richardson, B. K. (2001). Communicating change to nonprofit stakeholders: Models and predictors of implementers' approaches. *Management Communication Quarterly, 15*, 5–41. doi:10.1177/0893318901151001

Lewis, L. K., Richardson, B. K., & Hamel, S. A. (2003). When the stakes are communicative: The lamb's and the lion's share during nonprofit planned change. *Human Communication Research, 29,* 400–430. doi:10.1093/hcr/29.3.400

Liden, R. C., Wayne, S. J., Jaworski, R. A., & Bennett, N. (2004). Social loafing: A field investigation. *Journal of Management, 30,* 285–304. doi:10.1016/j.jm.2003.02.002

Lievrouw, L. A. (2006). New media design and development: Diffusion of innovations v. social shaping of technology. In Lievrouw, L. A., & Livingstone, S. (Eds.), *The handbook of new media: Updated student edition* (pp. 247–265). London: Sage.

Light, V., Nesbitt, E., Light, P., & Burns, J. R. (2000). 'Let's you and me have a little discussion': Computer mediated campus-based university courses. *Studies in Higher Education, 25,* 85–96. doi:10.1080/030750700116037

Linaa Jensen, J. (2003). Public spheres on the Internet: Anarchic or government sponsored – a comparison. *Scandinavian Political Studies, 26*(4), 349–374. doi:10.1111/j.1467-9477.2003.00093.x

Lipman, E. (2005). Educational ethnography and the politics of globalization, war, and resistance. *Anthropology & Education Quarterly, 36*(4), 315–328. doi:10.1525/aeq.2005.36.4.315

Lombard, M., & Ditton, T. (1997). At the heart of it all: The concept of presence. *Journal of Computer Communication, 3*(2). Retrieved from http://www.ascusc.org/jcmc/vol3/issue2/lombard.html.

Luff, P., & Heath, C. (2003). Fractured ecologies: Creating environments for collaboration. *Human-Computer Interaction, 18,* 51–84. doi:10.1207/S15327051HCI1812_3

Macintosh, A., & Whyte, A. (2002). An evaluation framework for e-consultations? Paper presented at the International Association for Official Statistics conference, London, UK.

Macintosh, A., Robson, E., Smith, E., & Whyte, A. (2003). Electronic democracy and young people. *Social Science Computer Review, 21*(1), 43–54. doi:10.1177/0894439302238970

MacKenzie, D., & Wajcman, J. (Eds.). (1999). *The social shaping of technology* (2nd ed.). Buckingham: Open University Press.

Magnan Sieloff, S. (Ed.). (2008). *Mediating discourse online: AILA Applied Linguistics (Series 3).* Amsterdam, Philadelphia: John Benjamins Publishing.

Maguirenancy. (2008, December 17). To blog mou. [My blog]. Message posted to http://maguirenancy.blogspot.com/

Mandernach, B. J., Gonzales, R. M., & Garrett, A. M. (2006). An examination of online instructor presence via threaded discussion participation. *Journal of Online Learning and Teaching, 2,* 248–260.

Markel, S. (2001). Technology and education online discussion forums: It's in the response. *Online Journal of Distance Learning Administration, 4*(2). Retrieved April 10, 2009 from http://www.westga.edu/~distance/ojdla/summer42/markel42.html

Markman, K. M. (2006a). Computer-mediated conversation: The organization of talk in chat-based virtual team meetings. *Dissertation Abstracts Online, 67*(12A), 209. (UMI No. AAI3244348)

Markman, K. M. (2006b, November). *Following the thread: Turn organization in computer-mediated chat.* Paper presented at the Ninety-second annual meeting of the National Communication Association, San Antonio, TX.

Markman, K. M. (2009). "So what shall we talk about": Openings and closings in chat-based virtual meetings. *Journal of Business Communication, 46,* 150–170. doi:10.1177/0021943608325751

Marttunen, M. (1998). Electronic mail as a forum for argumentative interaction in higher education studies. *Journal of Educational Computing Research, 18*(4), 387–405. doi:10.2190/AAJK-01XK-WDMV-8M0P

Masur, J. (2004). Conversation analysis for educational technologists: theoretical and methodological issues for researching the structures, processes and meaning of online talk. In Jonassen, D. (Ed.), *Handbook of research for educational communications and technology* (pp. 1073–1098). New York: McMillan.

Mayer, R. E. (2005a). Cognitive Theory of Multimedia Learning. In Mayer, R. E. (Ed.), *The Cambridge handbook of multimedia learning* (pp. 31–48). New York: Cambridge University Press.

Mayer, R. E. (2005b). Principles of multimedia learning based on social cues. In Mayer, R. E. (Ed.), *The Cambridge handbook of multimedia learning* (pp. 201–212). New York: Cambridge University Press.

Mayer, R. E. (2009). *Multimedia Learning*. New York: Cambridge University Press.

McCarthy, M. D. (1996). *The 4MAT system: Teaching for learning with right/left mode techniques*. Barrington, IL: EXCEL Inc.

McCracken, H. (2005). *Virtual learning communities: Facilitating connected knowing. The Encyclopedia of Distance Learning* (2nd ed.). Hershey, PA: IGI Global.

McGrath, J., & Hollingshead, A. (1993). Putting the group back in group support systems: Some theoretical issues about dynamic processes in groups with technological enhancements. In Jessup, L., & Valacich, J. (Eds.), *Group support systems: New perspectives* (pp. 78–96). New York: Macmillan.

McLeod, P. L., Baron, R. S., & Marti, M. W. (1997). The eyes have it: Minority influence in face-to-face and computer-mediated group discussion. *The Journal of Applied Psychology*, *82*(5), 706–718. doi:10.1037/0021-9010.82.5.706

McLoughlin, C., & Lee, M. (2007). Social software and participatory learning: Pedagogical choices with technology affordances in the Web 2.0 era. In *ICT: Providing choices for learners and learning*. Presented at the Ascilite Conference, Singapore. Retrieved from http://www.ascilite.org.au/conferences/singapore07/procs/mcloughlin.pdf

McLuhan, M. (1962). *The Gutenberg galaxy*. Toronto: University of Toronto Press.

McMillan, S. J. (2001). Survival of the fittest online: A longitudinal study of health-related web sites. Journal of Computer-Mediated Communication, 6(3).

McQuail, D. (1987). *Mass Communication Theory* (2nd ed.). London: Sage Publications Ltd.

Mehrabian, A. (1981). *Silent messages: Implicit communication of emotions and attitudes*. Belmont: Wadsworth Publishing Company.

Mehrabian, A., & Weiner, M. (1967). Decoding of inconsistent communications. *Journal of Personality and Social Psychology*, *6*, 109–114. doi:10.1037/h0024532

Meier, C. (1998). *In search of the virtual interaction order: investigating conduct in video-mediated work meetings*. (Arbeitspapiere „Telekooperation" Nr. 3). Institut für Soziologie, Universität Gießen. Retrieved 3 June, 2009, from http://www.uni-giessen.de/g31047

Mejias, U. (2005, August 26). Social Software Affordances: Course Syllabus. *Social software affordances; blog for course offered at teacher college, Columbia University during Fall 2005*. Retrieved August 27, 2009, from http://ssa05.blogspot.com/2005/08/course-syllabus.html

Merchant, G. (2007). Writing the future in the digital age [Electronic version]. *Literacy*, *41*(3), 118–128. doi:10.1111/j.1467-9345.2007.00469.x

Merriam, S., & Cafferella, R. (1999). *Learning through adulthood*. San Francisco: Jossey-Bass Publishers.

Meyer, K. (2003a). Face-to-face versus threaded discussion: The role of time and higher-order thinking. *JALN*, *7*(3), 55–65.

Meyer, K. (2003b). The web's impact on student learning. *T.H.E. Journal*, *30*(10).

Meyer, K. A. (2002). Quality in distance education: Focus on on-line learning. *ASHE-ERIC Higher Education Report*, *29*(4).

Meyer, K. A. (2003). Face-to-face versus threaded discussions: The role of time and higher order thinking. *Journal of Asynchronous Learning Networks*, *7*(3), 55–65.

Meyers, S. (2008, Fall). Using transformative pedagogy when teaching online [Electronic version]. *College Teaching, 56*(4), 219–224. doi:10.3200/CTCH.56.4.219-224

Miller, K., Scott, C. R., Stage, C., & Birkholt, M. (1995). Communication and coordination in an inter-organizational system: Service provision for the urban homeless. *Communication Research, 22,* 679–699. doi:10.1177/009365095022006006

Ministry of Trade and Industry. (2004). Social Safeguards For Integrated Resort With Casino Gaming. Singapore: Ministry of Trade and Industry. Retrieved June 20, 2005, from http://app.mcys.gov.sg/web/corp_press_story.asp?szMod=corp&szSubMod=press&qid=674

Ministry of Trade and Industry. (2005). Proposal to develop integrated resorts. Singapore: Ministry of Trade and Industry. Retrieved August 20, 2009, from http://app.mti.gov.sg/data/pages/606/doc/Ministerial%20Statement%20-%20PM%2018apr05.pdf

Monge, P. R., Fulk, J., Kalman, M. E., Flanagin, A. J., Parnassa, C., & Rumsey, S. (1998). Production of collective action in alliance-based interorganizational communication and information systems. *Organization Science, 9,* 411–433. doi:10.1287/orsc.9.3.411

Moore, M. G. (1993). Theory of transactional distance. In Keegan, D. (Ed.), *Theoretical Principles of Distance Education.* New York: Routledge.

Morgan, G. (1993). *Imaginization.* London: Sage.

Morison, J., & Newman, D. R. (2001). On-line citizenship: Consultation and participation in New Labour's Britain and beyond. *International Review of Law Computers & Technology, 15*(2), 171–194. doi:10.1080/13600860120070501

Morreale, S., Hugenberg, L., & Worley, D. (2006). The basic communication course at U.S. colleges and universities in the 21st century: Study VII. *Communication Education, 55,* 415–437. doi:10.1080/03634520600879162

Murphy, E. (2003). Moving from theory to practice in the design of web-based learning from the perspective of constructivism, Murphy, E. (2003). *The Journal of Interactive Online Learning, 1*(4). Retrieved October 30, 2006 from http://www.ncolr.org/jiol/archives/2003/spring/4/MS02028.pdf

Murphy, E. (2004). Recognising and promoting collaboration in an online asynchronous discussion. *British Journal of Educational Technology, 35*(4), 421–431. doi:10.1111/j.0007-1013.2004.00401.x

Murray, D. E. (1989). When the medium determines turns: Turn-taking in computer conversation. In Coleman, H. (Ed.), *Working with language: A multidisciplinary consideration of language use in work contexts* (pp. 319–337). Berlin: Mouton de Gruyter.

Murray, D. E. (1991). The composing process for computer conversation. *Written Communication, 8*(1), 35–55. doi:10.1177/0741088391008001003

National Law Center on Homelessness & Poverty. (2008). *2008 annual report: Changing laws, changing lives.* Retrieved on September 13, 2009 from http://www.nlchp.org/view_report.cfm?id=318.

National Law Center on Homelessness & Poverty. (2009). *2009 foreclosure survey.* Retrieved on September 13, 2009 from http://www.nlchp.org/view_report.cfm?id=310.

Naylor, G. (1982). *The women of brewster place.* New York: Penguin.

Nesson, R., & Nesson, C. (2008). The case for education in virtual worlds. Space and Culture, 11(3), 273–284. doi:10.1177/1206331208319149doi:10.1177/1206331208319149

Newman, G., Webb, B., & Cochrane, C. (1995). A content analysis method to measure critical thinking in face-to-face and computer supported group learning. Interpersonal Computing and Technology, 3(2), 56-77. Retrieved from http://www.helsinki.fi/science/optek/1995/n2/newman.txt

Nguyen, D., & Canny, J. (2004). MultiView: Spatially faithful group video conferencing. In *Proceedings of CHI 2004* (pp. 512-521). New York: ACM Press.

Nilan, P., & Feixa, C. (2006). Introduction: Youth hybridity and plural worlds. In Nilan, P., & Feixa, C. (Eds.),

Global youth?: Hybrid identities, plural worlds (pp. 1–13). New York: Routledge.

Norrick, N. R. (1994). Involvement and joking in conversation. *Journal of Pragmatics, 22*, 409–430. doi:10.1016/0378-2166(94)90117-1

Norrick, N. R. (2004). Issues in conversational joking. *Journal of Pragmatics, 35*, 1333–1359. doi:10.1016/S0378-2166(02)00180-7

Norrick, N. R., & Spitz, A. (2008). Humor as a resource for mitigating conflict in interaction. *Journal of Pragmatics, 40*, 1661–1686. doi:10.1016/j.pragma.2007.12.001

North, C. S., Pollio, D. E., Perron, B., Eyrich, K. M., & Spitznagel, E. L. (2005). The role of organizational characteristics in determining patterns of utilization of services for substance abuse, mental health, and shelter by homeless people. *Journal of Drug Issues, 35*, 575–591.

North, S. (2006). Making connections with new technologies. In Maybin, J., & Swann, J. (Eds.), *The Art of English: Everyday Creativity* (pp. 209–260). London: The Open University.

North, S. (2007). 'The Voices, the Voices': Creativity in Online Conversation. *Applied Linguistics, 28*(4), 538–555. doi:10.1093/applin/amm042

Noujaim, J. (2004). *Control Room*. Retrieved November 22, 2008, from http://video.google.com/videoplay?docid=-5468579280837866970

Noveck, B. S. (2005). The future of citizen participation in the electronic state. *I/S: A Journal of Law and Policy for the Information Society, 1*(1). Retrieved April 28, 2009, from http://www.is-journal.org/V01I01/I-S,%20V01-I01-P001,%20Noveck.pdf

Nowak, K. (2001). *Defining and differentiating copresence, social presence and presence as transportation.* Paper presented at Presence, Philadelphia, PA. Available at: http://citeseerx.ist.psu.edu/viewdoc/summary?doi=10.1.1.19.5482.

Nowak, K. L. (2003). Sex categorization in computer mediated communication (CMC): Exploring the utopian

promise. *Media Psychology, 5*, 83–103. doi:10.1207/S1532785XMEP0501_4

Nowak, K., & Biocca, F. (2003). The effect of the agency and anthropomorphism on users' sense of telepresence, copresence, and social presence in virtual environments. *Presence (Cambridge, Mass.), 12*(5), 481–494. doi:10.1162/105474603322761289

O'Conaill, B., Whittaker, S., & Wilbur, S. (1993). Conversations over video conferences: An evaluation of the spoken aspects of video-mediated communication. *Human-Computer Interaction, 8*, 389–428. doi:10.1207/s15327051hci0804_4

O'Malley, C., Langton, S., Anderson, A., Doherty-Sneddon, G., & Bruce, V. (1996). Comparison of face-to-face and video-mediated interaction. *Interacting with Computers, 8*(2), 177–192. doi:10.1016/0953-5438(96)01027-2

O'Reilly, T. (2005, September 30). *What Is Web 2.0? Design Patterns and Business Models for the Next Generation of Software*. Retrieved August 28, 2009, from http://oreilly.com/web2/archive/what-is-web-20.html.

Ohler, J. (2008). *Digital storytelling in the classroom*. Thousand Oaks, CA: Corwin Press.

Oliver, C. (1990). Determinants of interorganizational relationships: Integration and future directions. *Academy of Management Review, 15*, 241–265. doi:10.2307/258156

Organisation for Economic Co-operation and Development. (2001). *Engaging Citizens in Policy Making: Information, Consultation, and Public Participation.* Paris: OECD.

Orlikowski, W. J. (1992). The duality of technology: Rethinking the concept of technology in organizations. *Organization Science, 3*, 398–427. doi:10.1287/orsc.3.3.398

Osman, G., & Herring, S. C. (2007). Interaction, facilitation, and deep learning in cross-cultural chat: A case study. *The Internet and Higher Education, 10*, 125–141. doi:10.1016/j.iheduc.2007.03.004

Oviatt, S., & Cohen, P. (1991). Discourse structure and performance efficiency in interactive and non-interactive spoken modalities. *Computer Speech & Language, 5,* 297–326. doi:10.1016/0885-2308(91)90001-7

Owen, W. F. (1984). Relational themes in interpersonal communication. *The Quarterly Journal of Speech, 70,* 274–287. doi:10.1080/00335638409383697

Palloff, R. M., & Pratt, K. (1999). *Building learning communities in cyberspace: Effective strategies for the online classroom.* San Francisco: Jossey-Bass Pfeiffer.

Palloff, R., & Pratt, K. (2001). *Lessons from the virtual classroom.* San Francisco: Jossey-Bass Pfeiffer.

Palmer, M. (1995). Interpersonal communication and virtual reality: Mediating interpersonal relationships. In Biocca, F., & Levy, M. (Eds.), *Communication in the Age of Virtual Reality* (pp. 277–299). Hillsdale, New Jersey: Lawrence Erlbaum Associates.

Palmer, S., & Holt, D. (2009). Examining student satisfaction with wholly online learning. *Journal of Computer Assisted Learning, 25*(2), 101–113. doi:10.1111/j.1365-2729.2008.00294.x

Palmer, S., & Holt, D. (in print). Students' Perceptions of the Value of the Elements of an Online Learning Environment: Looking Back in Moving Forward. *Interactive Learning Environments.*

Panagovayahoogr. (2008, December 18). Aksiologisi tou prosopikou mou blog. [Assessment of my personal blog]. Message posted to http://panagovayahoogr.blogspot.com/

Panyametheekul, S., & Herring, S. C. (2003). Gender and turn allocation in a Thai chat room. *Journal of Computer-Mediated Communication, 9*(1). Retrieved April 3, 2004, from http://www.ascusc.org/jcmc/vol9/issue1/panya_herring.html

Papakimon. (2008, December 11). *I via einai i mami tis istorias* [Violence is the midwife of history].Message posted to http://papakimon.blogspot.com/

Papakimon. (2009, January 7). Aksiologisi blog. [Assessment of blog]. Message posted to http://papakimon.blogspot.com/

Pappa, M. (2009). *Analisi simetokhikotitas se diadiktiaki kinotita mathisi: moodle.* [Analysis of participation in an internet learning community: moodle]. Unpublished PhD Dissertation, University of Piraeus, Piraeus.

Paulus, T. M., & Phipps, G. (2008). Approaches to case analyses in synchronous and asynchronous environments. *Journal of Computer-Mediated Communication, 13*(2), 459-484. Retrieved June 1, 2009, from http://www3.interscience.wiley.com/cgi-bin/fulltext/119414150/HTMLSTART

Pena-Shaff, J., & Nicholls, C. (2004). Analyzing student interactions and meaning construction in Computer Bulletin Board (BBS) discussions. *Computers & Education, 42,* 243–265. doi:10.1016/j.compedu.2003.08.003

Pérez-Sabater, C., Peña-Martínez, G., Turney, E., & Montero-Fleta, B. (2008). A Spoken Genre Gets Written: Online Football Commentaries in English, French, and Spanish. *Written Communication, 25*(2), 235–261. doi:10.1177/0741088307313174

Picciano, A. G. Beyond student perceptions: Issues of interaction, presence, and performance in an online course. *JALN, 6*(1). Retrieved from http://www.sloan-c.org/publications/jaln/v6n1/v6n1_picciano.asp

Poland, P. (2001). *Online consultation in GOL-IN countries: Initiatives to foster e-democracy.* Amsterdam, The Netherlands: Ministry of the Interior and Kingdom Relations.

Pomerantz, A. (1984). Pursuing a response. In Atkinson, J. M., & Heritage, J. (Eds.), *Structures of social action: Studies in conversation analysis* (pp. 152–163). Cambridge: Cambridge University Press.

Pomerantz, A. (1984a). Agreeing and disagreeing with assessments: some features of preferred/dispreferred turn shapes. In Maxwell Atkinson, J., & Heritage, J. (Eds.), *Structures of social action: studies in conversation analysis* (pp. 57–101). Cambridge: Cambridge University Press.

Pomerantz, A. (1984b). Pursuing a response. In Maxwell Atkinson, J., & Heritage, J. (Eds.), *Structures of social action: studies in conversation analysis* (pp. 152–163). Cambridge: Cambridge University Press.

Poole, M. S., & DeSanctis, G. (1990). Understanding the use of group decision support systems: The theory of adaptive structuration. In Fulk, J., & Steinfeld, C. (Eds.), *Organizations and Communication Technology* (pp. 173–193). Newbury Park, CA: Sage Publications.

Poole, M. S., & DeSanctis, G. (1992). Microlevel structuration in computer-supported group decision making. *Human Communication Research, 18*, 5–49.

Postmes, T., Spears, R., & Lea, M. (2000). The formation of group norms in computer-mediated communication. Health Communication Research, 26, 341–372. doi:10.1111/j.1468-2958.2000.tb00761.xdoi:10.1111/j.1468-2958.2000.tb00761.x

Preece, J. (2001). Sociability and usability in online communities: determining and measuring success. *Behaviour & Information Technology, 20*(5), 347. doi:10.1080/01449290110084683

Puhl, R., & Brownell, K. D. (2001). Bias, discrimination, and obesity. *Obesity Research, 9*, 788–805. doi:10.1038/oby.2001.108

Quantcast. *Summary.* Retrieved May 4, 2009 from http://www.quantcast.com/ivillage.com

Rafaeli, S., & Sudweeks, F. (1997). Networked interactivity. *Journal of Computer-Mediated Communication, 4.* http://jcmc.indiana.edu/vol2/issue4/rafaeli.sudweeks.html.

Rains, S. A., & Young, V. (2009). A meta-analysis of research on formal computer-mediated support groups: Examining group characteristics and health outcomes. *Human Communication Research, 35*, 309–336. doi:10.1111/j.1468-2958.2009.01353.x

Ramey, C. (2008, 29 May). Mobile phone use among homeless people. Retrieved on September 13, 2009 from http://mobileactive.org/mobiles-homeless.

Rappaport, J. (1993). Narrative studies, personal stories, and identity transformation in the mutual help context. The Journal of Applied Behavioral Science, 29, 239–256. doi:10.1177/0021886393292007doi:10.1177/0021886393292007

Rash, W. (1997). *Politics on the Net: Wiring the political process.* New York: W.H. Freeman.

Rawls, J. (1971). *A theory of justice.* Cambridge, MA: Harvard University Press.

Reiserer, M., Ertl, B., & Mandl, H. (2002). Fostering collaborative knowledge construction in desktop videoconferencing. Effects of content schemes and cooperation scripts in peer-teaching settings. In Stahl, G. (Ed.), *Computer support for collaborative learning: foundations for a CSCL community* (pp. 379–388). Mahwah, NJ: Lawrence Erlbaum Associates.

Rellstab, D. H. (2007). Staging gender online: Gender plays in Swiss internet relay chats. *Discourse & Society, 18*(6), 765–787..doi:10.1177/0957926507082195

Repman, J., Zinskie, C., & Carlson, R. D. (2005). Effective use of CMC tools in interactive online learning. *Computers in the Schools, 22*(1-2), 57–69. doi:10.1300/J025v22n01_06

Rheingold, H. (1993). *The virtual community: Homesteading on the electronic frontier.* Reading, MA: Addison-Wesley.

Rice, R, E., & Rogers. E, M. (1980). Re-invention in the innovation process: Knowledge, creation, diffusion. *Utilization, 1*, 499–514.

Rice, R. E. (1992). Task analyzability, use of new medium and effectiveness: A multi-site exploration of media richness. *Organization Science, 3*(4), 475–500. doi:10.1287/orsc.3.4.475

Richardson, J. C., & Swan, K. (2003). Examining Social Presence in Online Courses in Relation to Students' Perceived Learning and Satisfaction. *Journal of Asynchronous Learning Networks, 7*(1), 68–88.

Richardson, W. (2008). *Blogs, wikis, podcasts, and other powerful web tools for classrooms* (2nd ed.). Thousand Oaks, CA: Corwin Press.

Ridings, C. M., & Gefen, D. (2004). Virtual community attraction: Why people hang out online. *Journal of Computer-Mediated Communication, 10*(1). Retrieved from http://jcmc.indiana.edu/index.html.

Rintel, E. S., & Pittam, J. (1997). Strangers in a strange land: Interaction management on Internet Relay Chat. *Human Communication Research, 23*, 507–534. doi:10.1111/j.1468-2958.1997.tb00408.x

Rintel, E. S., Mulholland, J., & Pittam, J. (2001). First things first: Internet Relay Chat openings. *Journal of Computer-Mediated Communication, 6*(3). Retrieved May 5, 2003, from http://www.ascusc.org/jcmc/vol6/issue3/rintel.html

Rintel, E. S., Pittam, J., & Mulholland, J. (2003). Time will tell: Ambiguous non-responses on Internet relay Chat. *Electronic Journal of Communication, 13*(1). Retrieved January 13, 2004, from http://80-www.cios.org.content.lib.utexas.edu:2048getfile%5CRINTEL_V13N1

Riva, G. (2002). The sociocognitive psychology of computer-mediated communication: The present and future of technology-based interactions. *Cyberpsychology & Behavior, 5*(6), 581–598. doi:10.1089/109493102321018222

Roberts, J. M., Arth, M. J., & Bush, R. R. (1959). Games in culture. *American Anthropologist, 61*(4), 597–605. doi:10.1525/aa.1959.61.4.02a00050

Rodgers, S., & Chen, Q. (2005). Internet community group participation: Psychosocial benefits for women with breast cancer. *Journal of Computer-Mediated Communication, 10*(4). Retrieved from http://jcmc.indiana.edu/index.html.

Rodino, M. (1997). Breaking out of binaries: Reconceptualizing gender and its relationship to language in computer-mediated communication. *Journal of Computer-Mediated Communication, 3*(3). doi:. doi:10.1111/j.1083-6101.1997.tb00074.x

Rogers, E. M. (1983). *Diffusion of innovations* (3rd ed.). New York: Free Press.

Rourke, L., & Kanuka, H. (2007). Computer Conferencing and Distance Learning. In Bidgoli, H. (Ed.), *The Handbook of Computer Networks (Vol. 3*, pp. 831–842). Hoboken, NJ: John Wiley & Sons.

Rourke, L., Anderson, T., Garrison, D. R., & Archer, W. (2001). Assessing social presence in asynchronous text-based computer conferencing. *Journal of Distance Education, 14*(2), 50–71.

Rovai, A. (2002, April). Building a sense of community at a distance. *International Review of Research in Open and Distance Learning, 2*(1). Retrieved March 22, 2009, from http://www.irrodl.org/index.php/irrodl/article/viewArticle/79/152

Rovai, A. P. (2001). Building classroom community at a distance: A case study [Electronic version]. *Educational Technology Research and Development, 49*(4), 33–48. doi:10.1007/BF02504946

Rovai, A. P. (2007). Facilitating online discussions effectively. *The Internet and Higher Education, 10*(1), 77–88. doi:10.1016/j.iheduc.2006.10.001

Rutter, D. R. (1987). *Communicating by telephone.* Elmsford, NY: Pergamon.

Rutter, D. R., & Stephenson, G. M. (1977). The role of visual communication in synchronizing conversation. *European Journal of Social Psychology, 2*, 29–37. doi:10.1002/ejsp.2420070104

Sack, W. (2005). Discourse architecture and very large-scale conversation. In Latham, R., & Sassen, S. (Eds.), *Digital formations: IT and new architectures in the global realm* (pp. 242–282). Princeton, NJ: Princeton University Press.

Sacks, H., Schegloff, E. A., & Jefferson, G. (1974). A simplest systematics for the organization of turn-taking for conversation. *Language, 50*, 696–735. doi:10.2307/412243

Salmon, G. (2000). *E-moderating: the key to teaching and learning online.* London, New York: Routledge.

San Millan Maurino, P. (2006). Looking for critical thinking in online threaded discussions. *E-Journal of Instructional Science and Technology, 9*(2), 1–18.

Sapsed, J., Gann, D., Marshall, N., & Salter, A. (2005). From here to eternity?: The practice of knowledge transfer in dispersed and co-located organisations. *European Planning Studies, 13*(6), 831–851. doi:10.1080/09654310500187938

Saraf, M. J. (1977). Semiotic signs in sport activity. *International Review of Sport Sociology, 12*(2), 89–102. doi:10.1177/101269027701200206

Schegloff, E. A. (1992). Repair after next turn: the last structurally provided defense of intersubjectivity in conversation. *American Journal of Sociology, 97*, 1295–1345. doi:10.1086/229903

Schegloff, E. A. (1997). Third turn repair. In Guy, G. R., Feagin, C., Schiffrin, D., & Baugh, J. (Eds.), *Towards a social science of language: papers in honor of William Labov* (Vol. 2, pp. 31–40). Amsterdam, Philadelphia: John Benjamins.

Schegloff, E. A. (2000). When 'others' initiate repair. *Applied Linguistics, 21*(2), 205–243. doi:10.1093/applin/21.2.205

Schegloff, E. A. (2007). *Sequence organization in interaction: a primer in conversation analysis* (Vol. 1). Cambridge: Cambridge University Press.

Schegloff, E. A., & Sacks, H. (1974). Opening up closings. In Turner, R. (Ed.), *Ethnomethodology: Selected readings* (pp. 233–264). Harmondsworth, England: Penguin Education.

Schegloff, E. A., Jefferson, G., & Sacks, H. (1977). The preference for self-correction in the organization of repair in conversation. *Language, 53*, 361–382. doi:10.2307/413107

Schild, S., & Oren, K. (2005). The party line online: An oligarchy of opinion on a public affairs listserv. *Journalism and Communication Monographs, 7*, 5–47.

Schmidt, J. (2007). Blogging practices: An analytical framework [Electronic version]. *Journal of Computer-Mediated Communication, 12*, 1409–1427. doi:10.1111/j.1083-6101.2007.00379.x

Schmitz, J., Rogers, E. M., Phillips, K., & Paschal, D. (1995). The public electronic network (PEN) and the Homeless in Santa Monica. *Journal of Applied Communication Research, 23*, 26–43. doi:10.1080/00909889509365412

Schonfeldt, J., & Golato, A. (2003). Repair in chats: A conversation analytic approach. *Research on Language and Social Interaction, 36*, 241–284. doi:10.1207/S15327973RLSI3603_02

Schrire, S. (2004). Interaction and cognition in asynchronous computer conferencing. Instructional Science, 32, 475–502. doi:10.1007/s11251-004-2518-7doi:10.1007/s11251-004-2518-7

Schrire, S. (2006). Knowledge building in asynchronous discussion groups: Going beyond quantitative analysis. Computers & Education, 46(1), 49–70. doi:10.1016/j.compedu.2005.04.006doi:10.1016/j.compedu.2005.04.006

Schrodt, P., & Turman, P. D. (2005). The impact of instructional technology use, course design, and sex differences on students' initial perceptions of instructor credibility. *Communication Quarterly, 53*, 177–196. doi:10.1080/01463370500090399

Schrodt, P., & Witt, P. L. (2006). Students' attributions of instructor credibility as a function of students' expectations of instructional technology use and nonverbal immediacy. *Communication Education, 55*, 1–20. doi:10.1080/03634520500343335

Schroeder, R. (2002). Social interaction in virtual environments: Key issues, common themes, and a framework for research. In Schroeder, R. (Ed.), *The social life of avatars: Presence and interaction in shared virtual environments* (pp. 1–18). London: Springer.

Schudson, M. (1978). *Discovering the News. A Social History of American Newspapers*. BasicBooks.

Schwartzman, R. (2006). Virtual group problem solving in the basic communication course: Lessons for online learning. *Journal of Instructional Psychology, 33*, 3–14.

Schwartzman, R. (2007a). Electronifying oral communication: Refining the conceptual framework for online instruction. *College Student Journal, 41*, 37–50.

Schwartzman, R. (2007b). *Fundamentals of oral communication*. Dubuque, IA: Kendall/Hunt.

Schwartzman, R. (2007c). Refining the question: How can online instruction maximize opportunities for all students? *Communication Education, 56*, 113–117. doi:10.1080/03634520601009728

Schwen, T. M., & Hara, N. (2004). Community of practice: A metaphor for online design? In Barab, S. A., Kling, R., & Gray, J. H. (Eds.), *Designing for virtual communities in the service of learning* (pp. 154–179). Cambridge: Cambridge University Press.

Schwier, R. A., & Balbar, S. (2002). The interplay of content and community in synchronous and asynchronous communication: Virtual communication in a graduate seminar. *Canadian Journal of Learning and Technology, 28*(2), 21–30.

Scott, C. R., & Timmerman, C. E. (2005). Relating computer, communication, and computer-mediated communication apprehensions to new communication technology use in the workplace. Communication Research, 32, 683–725. doi:10.1177/0093650205281054d oi:10.1177/0093650205281054

Sellen, A. (1994). Remote conversations: The effects of mediating talk with technology. *Human-Computer Interaction, 10*(4), 401–444. doi:10.1207/s15327051hci1004_2

Shannon, C. E., & Weaver, W. (1949). *A Mathematical Model of Communication*. Urbana, IL: University of Illinois Press.

Sharf, B. F. (1997). Communicating breast cancer on-line: Support and empowerment on the Internet. Women & Health, 26, 65–84. PubMeddoi:10.1300/J013v26n01_05doi:10.1300/J013v26n01_05

Shea, P. (2006, February). A study of students' sense of learning community in online environments. *Journal of Asynchronous Learning Networks, 10*(1). Retrieved March 22, 2009, from http://www.sloan-c.org/publications/jaln/v10n1/v10n1_4shea_member.asp

Shedletsky, L. (2000). The online double bind: mixed messages about online teaching & scholarship. *The Maine Scholar, 13*, 163–173.

Shedletsky, L. J., & Aitken, J. E. (2001). The paradoxes of online academic work. *Communication Education, 50*, 206–217. doi:10.1080/03634520109379248

Shedletsky, L. J., & Aitken, J. E. (2004). *Human communication on the Internet*. Boston: Allyn and Bacon.

Shedletsky, L., & Aitken, J. E. (2001, July). The paradoxes of online academic work. *Communication Education, 50*(3), 206–217. doi:10.1080/03634520109379248

Shin, N. (2002). Beyond interaction: The relational construct of "transactional presence.". *Open Learning, 17*(2), 121–137. doi:10.1080/02680510220146887

Shin, N. (2003). Transactional presence as a critical predictor of success in distance learning. *Distance Education, 24*(1), 69–86. doi:10.1080/01587910303048

Shirky, C. (2003, March 9). Social Software and the Politics of Groups. *Clay Shirky's Writings About the Internet*. Retrieved August 27, 2009, from http://www.shirky.com/writings/group_politics.html.

Short, J., Williams, E., & Christie, B. (1976). *The social psychology of telecommunication*. London: John Wiley & Sons.

Shulman, S., Schlosberg, D., Zavestoski, S., & Courard-Hauri, D. (n.d.). Electronic rulemaking: New frontiers in public participation. *Social Science Computer Review, 21*(2), 162–178. doi:10.1177/0894439303021002003

Sideri, E. (2000). *The women's voices in the internet.* Paper presented at the 1st Interdisciplinary Conference on Gender Ethics/ the Ethics of Gender, Leeds: University of Leeds.

Sideri, E. (2007). *Diasporization*. University of Thessaly. Retrieved 2 June, 2009 from http://www.elenasideri.zoomshare.com/7.shtml.

Sideri, E. (2008). *Anthropology of electronic media*. Retrieved 2 June, 2009, from http://iakaanthropology-ofmedia.blogspot.com/

Simpson, J. (2005). Conversational floors in synchronous text-based CMC discourse. *Discourse Studies, 7*, 337–361. doi:10.1177/1461445605052190

Slatin, J. M. (1992). Is there a class in this text? Creating knowledge in the electronic classroom. In Barrett, E. (Ed.), *Sociomedia, multimedia, hypermedia and the social construction of knowledge* (pp. 2–51). Massachusetts: MIT Press.

Smith, M., & Kollock, P. (Eds.). (1999). *Communities in cyberspace: Perspective on new forms of social organization*. London: Routledge.

Solomon, G., & Schrum, L. (2007). *Web 2.0: New tools, new schools*. Washington, DC: International Society for Technology in Education.

Sorg, J. J., & McElhinney, J. H. (2000). A case study describing student experiences of learning in a context of synchronous computer-mediated communication in a distance education environment. Fort Wayne, IN: Purdue University. (ERIC Document No. ED447794)

Sowden, S., & Keeves, J. P. (1988). Analysis of evidence in humanistic studies. In Keeves, J. (Ed.), *Educational research, methodology and measurement: An international handbook* (pp. 513–526). Oxford, UK: Pergamon Press.

Spears, R., & Lea, M. (1994). Panacea or panopticon? The hidden power in computer-mediated communication. Communication Research, 21, 427–459. doi:10.1177/009365094021004001doi:10.1177/009365094021004001

Spiceland, J. D., & Hawkins, C. P. (2002). The impact on learning of an asynchronous course format. *JALN, 6*(1).

Stacey, E., & Rice, M. (2002). Evaluating an online learning environment. *Australian Journal of Educational Technology, 18*(3), 323–340.

Stanton, T. K., Giles, D. E., & Cruz, N. I. (1999). *Service-learning: A movement's pioneers reflect on its origins, practice, and future*. San Francisco: Jossey-Bass.

Steeples, C., Jones, C., & Goodyear, P. (2002). Beyond e-learning: A future for networked learning. In Steeples, C., & Jones, C. (Eds.), *Networked learning: Perspectives and issues* (pp. 323–342). London: Springer.

Stelayahoogr. (2008, December 19). *Ta teleftea gegonota ke pos parousiazonte sta mme*. [The last events and their representation in the media]. Message posted to http://stelayahoogr.blogspot.com/

Stephens, S., McCusker, P., O'Donnell, D., Newman, D., & Fagan, G. (2006). On the road from consultation cynicism to energizing e-consultation. *The Electronic. Journal of E-Government, 4*(2), 87–94.

Strait, J., & Sauer, T. (2004). Constructing experiential learning for online courses: The birth of e-Service. *EDUCAUSE Quarterly, 27*(1). Retrieved May 30, 2009 from http://www.educause.edu/EDUCAUSE+Quarterly/EDUCAUSEQuarterlyMagazineVolum/ConstructingExperientialLearni/157274Constructing Experiential Learning for Online Courses: The Birth of E-Service-Constructing Experiential Learning for Online Courses: The Birth of E-Service

Straub, D. W. (1994). The effect of culture on IT diffusion: E-mail and FAX in Japan and the U.S. *Information Systems Research, 5*(1), 23–47. doi:10.1287/isre.5.1.23

Straub, D., & Karahanna, E. (1998). Knowledge worker communications and recipient availability: Toward a task closure explanation of media choice. *Organization Science, 9*(2), 160–175. doi:10.1287/orsc.9.2.160

Strømsø, H. I., Grøttum, P., & Lycke, K. H. (2007). Content and processes in problem-based learning: a comparison of computer-mediated and face-to-face communication. *Journal of Computer Assisted Learning, 23*, 271–282. doi:10.1111/j.1365-2729.2007.00221.x

Strum, R., & Wells, K. B. (2001). Does obesity contribute as much to morbidity as poverty or smoking? *Public Health, 115*, 229–295. doi:10.1016/S0033-3506(01)00449-8

Sunstein, C. (2001). *Republic.com*. Princeton, NJ: Princeton University Press.

Swan, K. (2006, February). Online Collaboration: Introduction to the Special Issue. *JALN, 10*(1). Retrieved from http://www.sloan-c.org/publications/JALN/v10n1/v10n1_1swan_member.asp

Synchrona Themata (2008). Fakelos #griots-Tekmiria. I "atakti skepsi" os gnostiki proklisi, i apopira katanoisis enanti tou apotropiasmou ke tis eksidikefsis [File#griots-Evidences. The "disordered thought" as an attempt to understanding, instead of dismay and idealization], 103, 6-26.

Talbot, M. (1995). A Synthetic Sisterhood. In Hall, K., & Bucholz, M. (Eds.), *Gender Articulated. Language and the Socially Constructed Self* (pp. 143–165). London, New York: Routledge.

Talbot, M. (2007). *Media Discourse. Representation and Interaction*. Edinburgh: Edinburgh University Press.

Tanis, M., & Postmes, T. (2005). A social identity approach to trust: Interpersonal perception, group membership and trusting behaviour. *European Journal of Social Psychology*, *35*(3), 413–424. doi:10.1002/ejsp.256

Tanskanen, S.-K. (2007). Metapragmatic utterances in computer-mediated interaction. In Bublitz, W., & Hübler, A. (Eds.), *Metapragmatics in use* (pp. 87–106). Amsterdam, Philadelphia: John Benjamins.

Tanskanen, S.-K., & Karhukorpi, J. (2008). Concessive repair and negotiation of affiliation in e-mail discourse. *Journal of Pragmatics*, *40*, 1587–1600. doi:10.1016/j.pragma.2008.04.018

Tate, D. F., Wing, R. R., & Winett, R. A. (2001). Using Internet technology to deliver a behavioral weight loss program. *Journal of the American Medical Association*, *285*, 1172–1177. doi:10.1001/jama.285.9.1172

Taylor, K. (1995). Sitting beside herself: Self-Assessment and women's adult development. In *Learning Environments for Women's Adult Development* (pp. 21–28). San Francisco: Jossey-Bass Publishers.

Taylor, T. L. (2002). Living digitally: Embodiment in virtual worlds. In R. Schroeder (Ed.), The social life of avatars: Presence and interaction in shared virtual environments (pp. 40–62). London: Springer.

ten Have, P. (1999). *Doing conversation analysis*. London: Sage.

ten Have, P. (2000). Computer-mediated chat: Ways of finding chat partners. *M/C: A Journal of Media and*

Culture, 3(4). Retrieved May 5, 2003, from http://journal.media-culture.org.au/0008/partners.php

Teo, J. (2004, November 26). Anti-casino groups keep up the fight. *The Strait Times*. Retrieved August 4, 2009, from http://www.wildsingapore.com/sos/media/041117-1.htm

Thatcher, J., Waddell, C., Henry, S., Swierenga, S., Urban, M., & Burks, M. (2003). *Constructing accessible web sites*. San Francisco, CA: Apress.

Thomas, A. (2007). *Youth online: Identity and literacy in the digital age*. New York: Peter Lang.

Thompson, L., & Ku, H.-Y. (2006). A case study of online collaborative learning. *Quarterly Review of Distance Education*, *7*, 361–375.

Thomson, R. (2006). The effect of topic of discussion on gendered language in computer-mediated communication discussion. *Journal of Language and Social Psychology*, *25*, 167–178..doi:10.1177/0261927X06286452

Thorpe, M., & Godwin, S. (2006). Interaction and e-learning: The student experience. *Studies in Continuing Education*, *28*(3), 203–221. doi:10.1080/01580370600947330

Tompkins, P. K. (2009). *Who is my neighbor: Communicating and organizing to end homelessness*. Boulder, CO: Paradigm.

Tough, A. (1967). *Learning without a teacher. Educational Research Series, 3*. Toronto: Ontario Institute for Studies in Education.

Townsend, A., DeMarie, S., & Hendrickson, A. (1998). Virtual teams: Technology and the workplace of the future. *The Academy of Management Executive*, *12*(3), 17–29.

Tuckman, B. (1965). Developmental sequence in small groups. *Psychological Bulletin*, *63*, 384–399. doi:10.1037/h0022100

Turkle, S. (1995). *Life on the screen: Identity in the age of the Internet*. New York: Simon & Schuster.

Turman, P. D., & Schrodt, P. (2005). The influence of instructional technology use on students' affect: Do course designs and biological sex make a difference? *Communication Studies, 56,* 109–129. doi:10.1080/00089570500078726

Turner, J. W., Grube, J. A., & Meyers, J. (2001). Developing an optimal match within online communities: An exploration of CMC support communities and traditional support. *The Journal of Communication, 51*(2), 231–251. doi:10.1111/j.1460-2466.2001.tb02879.x

Twigg, C. A. (1999). *Improving learning and reducing costs: Redesigning large enrollment courses.* Troy, NY: Rensselaer Polytechnic Institute Center for Academic Transformation.

Tzortzakis, I. (2009). *Aksiopiisi web.2 ergalion sti skholiki ekpedefsi.* [Use of web.2 tools at schools]. Unpublished Master Dissertation, University of Piraeus, Piraeus.

Ullman, C., & Rabinowitz, M. (2004, October). Course management systems and the reinvention of instruction. *T.H.E. Journal.* Retrieved March 15, 2009, from http://thejournal.com/articles/17014

Urbanovich, J. (2009, February). *Online course advantages.* Paper presented at the Western States Communication Association Conference, Phoenix, AZ.

Vaast, E. (2004). O brother, where are thou? From communities to networks of practice through intranet use. *Management Communication Quarterly, 18,* 5–44. doi:10.1177/0893318904265125

Van Alstyne, M., & Brynjolfsson, E. (1996). *Electronic communities: Global village or cyberbalkans?* Paper presented at the 17th International Conference on Information Systems, Cleveland, OH.

Van de Pol, J. (2001, May/June). A look at course management systems. *IT Times.* Retrieved March 15, 2009 from http://ittimes.ucdavis.edu/june2001/cms.html

van der Kleij, R., Lijkwan, J., Rasker, P. C., & De Dreu, C. K. W. (in press). Effects of time pressure and communication environment on team processes and outcomes in dyadic planning. *International Journal of Human-Computer Studies.* doi:.doi:10.1016/j.ijhcs.2008.11.005

Van Doorn, N., van Zoonen, L., & Wyatt, S. (2007). Writing from experience: Presentations of gender identity on weblogs. *European Journal of Women's Studies, 14*(2), 143–159..doi:10.1177/1350506807075819

Verheijdden, M. W., Bakx, J. C., van Weel, C., Koelen, M. A., & van Staveren, W. A. (2005). Role of social support in lifestyle-focused weight management interventions. *European Journal of Clinical Nutrition, 59,* S179–S186. doi:10.1038/sj.ejcn.1602194

Vess, D. L. (2005, October). Asynchronous discussion and communication patterns in online and hybrid history courses. *Communication Education, 54*(4), 355–364. doi:10.1080/03634520500442210

Walther, J. (1992). Interpersonal effects in computer-mediated interaction: A relational perspective. *Communication Research, 19*(1), 52–90. doi:10.1177/009365092019001003

Walther, J. B. (1996). Computer-mediated communication: Impersonal, interpersonal, and hyperpersonal interaction. *Communication Research, 23,* 3–43. doi:10.1177/009365096023001001

Walther, J. B. (2008). Social information processing theory. In Baxter, L. A., & Braithwaite, D. O. (Eds.), *Engaging theories in interpersonal communication: Multiple perspectives* (pp. 391–404). Thousand Oaks, CA: Sage.

Walther, J. B. (2009). Computer-mediated communication and virtual groups: Applications to interethnic conflict. *Journal of Applied Communication Research, 37,* 225–238. doi:10.1080/00909880903025937

Walther, J. B., & Burgoon, J. K. (1992). Relational communication in computer-mediated interaction. Human Communication Research, 19, 50–88. doi:10.1111/j.1468-2958.1992.tb00295. xdoi:10.1111/j.1468-2958.1992.tb00295.x

Walther, J. B., & Parks, M. R. (2002). Cues filtered out, cues filtered in: Computer-mediated communication and relationships. In Knapp, M. L., & Daly, J. A. (Eds.), *Handbook of interpersonal communication* (pp. 529–563). Thousand Oaks, CA: Sage.

Walther, J. B., Anderson, & Park, J. (1994). Interpersonal effects in computer mediated interaction: A meta analysis of social and antisocial communication. Communication Research, 21, 460–487. doi:10.1177/009365094021004002doi:10.1177/009365094021004002

Walther, J., & Bunz, U. (2005, December). The rules of virtual groups: Trust, liking and performance in computer-mediated communication. *The Journal of Communication, 55*(4), 828–846. doi:10.1111/j.1460-2466.2005.tb03025.x

Wang, A. Y., Newlin, M. H., & Tucker, T. L. (2001). A discourse analysis of online classroom chats: Predictors of cyber-student performance. *Teaching of Psychology, 28*, 222–226. doi:10.1207/S15328023TOP2803_09

Wang, Z., Walther, J. B., Pingree, S., & Hawkins, R. P. (2008). Health information, credibility, homophily, and influence via the Internet: Web sites versus discussion groups. *Health Communication, 23*, 358–368. doi:10.1080/10410230802229738

Warisse Turner, J., Grube, J. A., & Meyers, J. (2001). Developing an optimal match within online communities: An exploration of CMC support community and traditional support. The Journal of Communication, 51, 231–251. doi:10.1111/j.1460-2466.2001.tb02879.xdoi:10.1111/j.1460-2466.2001.tb02879.x

Waterman, A. S. (1997). *Service-learning: Applications from the research*. Mahwah, NJ: Lawrence Erlbaum Associates.

Webb, E., Jones, A., Barker, P., & van Schaik, P. (2004). Using e-learning dialogues in higher education. *Innovations in Education and Teaching International, 41*(1), 93–103. doi:10.1080/1470329032000172748

Weber, S., & Mitchell, C. (2008). Imaging, keyboarding, and posting identities: Young people and new media technologies. In Buckingham, D. (Ed.), *Youth, identity, and digital media* (pp. 25–47). Cambridge, MA: The MIT Press.

Weick, K. (1979). *The social psychology of organizing* (2nd ed.). Reading, MA: Addison-Wesley Publishing Company.

Weigel, M., James, C., & Gardner, H. (2009). Learning: Peering backward and looking forward in the digital era. *International Journal of Learning and Media, 1*(1), 1-18. Retrieved July 22, 2009 from: http://www.mitpressjournals.org/doi/abs/10.1162/ijlm.2009.0005

Weinberg, N., Schmale, J., Uken, J., & Wessel, K. (1996). On-line help: Cancer patients participate in a computer-mediated support group. Health & Social Work, 21(1), 24–29. PubMed

Weisskirch, R. S., & Milburn, S. S. (2003). Virtual discussion: Understanding college students' electronic bulletin board use. *The Internet and Higher Education, 6*(3), 215–225. doi:10.1016/S1096-7516(03)00042-3

Wellman, B. (1997). An electronic group is virtually a social network. In Kiesler, S. (Ed.), *Culture of the internet* (pp. 179–205). Hillsdale, NJ: Lawrence Earlbaum.

Wellman, B. (1999). *Networks in the global village: Life in contemporary communities*. Boulder, CO: Westview Press.

Wellman, B., Salaff, J., Dimitrova, D., Garton, L., Gulia, M., & Haythornthwaite, C. (1996). Computer networks as social networks: Collaborative work, telework, and virtual community. *Annual Review of Sociology, 22*, 213–238. doi:10.1146/annurev.soc.22.1.213

Werry, C. C. (1996). Linguistic and interactional features of Internet Relay Chat. In S. C. Herring (Ed.), Computer-mediated communication: Linguistic, social and cross-cultural perspectives (pp. 47-63). Amsterdam: John Benjamins.

West, D. (2007). *Global E-Government 2007*. Providence, RI: Center for Public Policy, Brown University. Retrieved August 20, 2009, from http://www.insidepolitics.org/egovt07int.pdf

White, D. M. (2000). Questioning behavior on a consumer health electronic list. The Library Quarterly, 70, 302–334. doi:10.1086/603195doi:10.1086/603195

White, M., & Dorman, S. M. (2001). Receiving social support online: Implications for health education.

Health Education Research, 16, 693–707. doi:10.1093/her/16.6.693

White, P. (2003). Beyond modality and hedging: a dialogic view of the language of intersubjective stance. *Text, 23,* 259–284. doi:10.1515/text.2003.011

Whittaker, S. (1995). Rethinking video as a technology for interpersonal communications: Theory and design implications. *International Journal of Man-Machine Studies, 42,* 501–529.

Whittaker, S., & O'Conaill, B. (1997). The role of vision in face-to-face and mediated communication. In Finn, K. E., Sellen, A. J., & Wilbur, S. (Eds.), *Video-mediated communication: Computers, cognition, and work* (pp. 23–49). Mahwah, NJ: Lawrence Erlbaum Associates, Inc.

Whyte, A., & Macintosh, A. (2001). Transparency and teledemocracy: Issues from an 'e-consultation.'. *Journal of Information Science, 27*(4), 187–198.

Wilhelm, A. (2000). *Democracy in the digital age: Challenges to political life in cyberspace.* New York: Routledge.

Wilkins, H. (1991). Computer talk: Long-distance conversations by computer. *Written Communication, 8*(1), 56–78. doi:10.1177/0741088391008001004

Willett, R. (2008). Consumer citizens online: Structure, agency, and gender in online participation. In Buckingham, D. (Ed.), *Youth, identity, and digital media* (pp. 49–69). Cambridge, MA: The MIT Press.

Williams, B. T. (2008). "Tomorrow will not be like today": Literacy and identity in a world of multiliteracies [Electronic version]. *Journal of Adolescent & Adult Literacy, 51*(8), 682–686. doi:10.1598/JAAL.51.8.7

Wolf, A. (2000). Emotional expression online: Gender differences in emoticon use. *Cyberpsychology & Behavior, 3*(5), 827–833. doi:10.1089/10949310050191809

Wood, A. F., & Fassett, D. L. (2003). Remote control: Identity, power, and technology in the communication classroom. Communication Education, 52(3/4), 286–296. doi:10.1080/0363452032000156253d oi:10.1080/0363452032000156253

Wood, A. F., & Smith, M. J. (2001). *Online communication: Linking technology, identity, and culture.* Mahwah, NJ: Lawrence Erlbaum.

Wood, J. (2009). Everyday encounters. Boston, MA: Wadsworth.

Woods, D., Thoeny, P., & Cunningham, W. (2007). *Wikis for dummies.* Hoboken: John Wiley & Sons.

Wozniak, H. (2005). Online discussions: Improving the quality of the student experience. Retrieved 19 December, 2008, from http://www.odlaa.org/events/2005conf/ref/ODLAA2005Wozniak.pdf

Wrench, J. S., & Punyanunt-Carter, N. M. (2007). The relationship between computer-mediated-communication competence, apprehension, self-efficacy, perceived confidence, and social presence. The Southern Communication Journal, 72(4), 355–378.

Wright, K. (1999). Computer-mediated support groups: An examination of relationships among social support, perceived stress, and coping strategies. Communication Quarterly, 47, 402–414.

Wright, K. (2002). Social support within an online cancer community: An assessment of emotionally support, perceptions of advantages and disadvantages, and motives for using the community from a communication perspective. Journal of Applied Communication, 30, 195–209. doi:10.1080/00909880216586doi:10.1080/00909880216586

Wright, K. B. (2000). Perceptions of on-line support providers: An examination of perceived homophily, source credibility, communication and social support within on-line support groups. Communication Quarterly, 48, 44–59.

Wright, K. B., & Bell, S. B. (2003). Health-related support groups on the Internet: Linking empirical findings to social support and computer-mediated communication theory. *Journal of Health Psychology, 8,* 1359–1053. doi:10.1177/1359105303008001429

Wright, S. (2005). Design matters: The political efficacy of government-run discussion forums. In Oates, S., Owen, D., & Gibson, R. (Eds.), *The Internet and politics:*

Citizens, voters, and activists (pp. 80–99). London, UK: Routledge.

Wright, S., & Street, J. (2007). Democracy, deliberation and design: The case of online discussion forums. *New Media & Society, 9*(5), 849–869. doi:10.1177/1461444807081230

Yiannakopoulos, K. I. (2005). *Ikonikes kinotites. Mia kinoniologiki prosegisi tou diadiktiou* [Virtual communities. A sociological approach of internet]. Athens: Papazisi.

Yoo, Y., & Alavi, M. (2001). Media and group cohesion: Relative influences on social presence, task participation, and group consensus. *Management Information Systems Quarterly, 25*(3), 371–390. doi:10.2307/3250922

Yukselturk, E., & Top, E. (2006). Reconsidering online course discussions: A case study. *Journal of Educational Technology Systems, 34*, 341–367. doi:10.2190/6GQ8-P7TX-VGMR-4NR4

Zhao, S. (2003). Towards a taxonomy of copresence. *Presence (Cambridge, Mass.), 12*(5), 445–455. doi:10.1162/105474603322761261

Zoller, H. M. (2004). Dialogue as global issue management: Legitimizing corporate influence in the transatlantic business dialogue. *Management Communication Quarterly, 18*, 204–240. doi:10.1177/0893318904265126

About the Contributors

Leonard Shedletsky is Professor of Communication at The University of Southern Maine. He is the author of Meaning and Mind: An Intrapersonal Approach to Human Communication (1989), Human Communication on the Internet (2004, with Joan Aitken), co-editor of Intrapersonal Communication Processes (1995), as well as numerous articles and chapters. He wrote the entry, "Cognition," for the International Encyclopedia of Communication, 2008. He has been teaching since 1974. He teaches a range of courses in communication with cognition, discourse and meaning as underlying themes. He developed and taught the course "Intergenerational Communication and the Internet," in which college students mentored older adults in Internet use. He was named The Russell Chair, 2009 – 2011 in Philosophy and Education for a two-year period. The distinction carries the responsibility of presenting one or more public lectures on issues in education and/or philosophy during each of the two years. He was awarded recognition for STELLAR scholarship and teaching, University of Southern Maine (USM) 2003 and 2007. He has received a Center for Technology-Enhanced Learning Development Grant at USM (2007) to develop the course, Research Methods, for online delivery. In 2009 he received a Alfred P. Sloan Foundation grant to expand the online capacity for his department to deliver the major in communication and media studies. His resume is available at: http://www.usm.maine.edu/com/resume.html. His current research interest explores discussion online versus in the classroom. He is trying to find out what facilitates active and high quality discussion in education.

Joan E. Aitken is Professor of Communication and Leadership, at Park University. Previously, she taught at the University of Missouri-Kansas City, University of Louisiana-Lafayette, and University of Arkansas-Fayetteville. Aitken's main lines of research have been in Internet communication and communication education. She has completed 40 graduate hours as an online student and taught online courses for three universities. During her career, Aitken obtained $3.5 million in competitive grant funding, including $1.5 million as the primary grant writer, and others as a collaborative team member. She has taught internationally in Jamaica and the People's Republic of China. A former editor of the National Communication Association's Communication Teacher, Aitken has published several books and more than 50 articles and book chapters. She has co-authored or co-edited three books with her close colleague and friend, Leonard J. Shedletsky. Aitken's most recent book was coauthored with Roy M. Berko and Andrew D. Wolvin, is entitled ICOMM: Interpersonal Concepts and Competencies, and published by Rowman & Littlefield.

* * *

Maureen L. Atkinson has a background in History, Interdisciplinary Studies, and Media Studies. She currently is a researcher on a federally funded project examining technologically mediated literacies at the University of Northern British Columbia. Her research interests include identity, historical representations, and technological change in rural northern British Columbia. She has a co-authored chapter in the Proceedings of the World Conference on E-Learning in Corporate, Government, Healthcare, and Higher Education 2009, and another chapter in press in an edited book by Sarah Carter and Patricia McCormack.

Simon Atkinson is a social scientist, educational developer and strategist with specialist interests in educational technologies. His research interests focus on tertiary educations strategic response to technology driven social change, the impact of technology-enabled communication on cultural interactions and the values of academe. Current work is developing reusable learning designs to maximize engagement with digitally rich resources (DiAL-e Framework - http://www.dia-e.net). He has held a number of senior roles in higher education based e-learning as Strategic e-Learning Advisor, College of Education, Massey University, New Zealand (2008-), Acting Director of the Learning & Teaching Support Unit, Head of Centre for Learning Development and Head of eLearning, at the University of Hull, United Kingdom (2003-2008). He was project officer for the UK Open University's Academic Professional Development Programme at the Institute of Educational Technology (2001-2003). Simon was a European TEMPUS visiting expert for the Croatian National e-Learning Project – EQIBELT from 2005-2008. He presents on the web and in person on issues of foresight, planning and creative communications in higher education.

Kristy Beers Fägersten received her PhD in Linguistics from the University of Florida in 2000. She is currently an Assistant Professor at the School of Arts and Media at Dalarna University (Sweden), where she teaches courses in Applied Linguistics for the Master's Degree in English Linguistics. Kristy's research interests include sociolinguistic analyses of swearing (with particular focus on gender, race and native-speaker status), discourse analyses of media appropriation and intertextual quotation, conversation analyses of synchronous, online communication, and pragmatic analyses of multimodal, online communication. She is currently concluding a research project funded by Sweden's Knowledge Foundation (KK-Stiftelsen) on the language of the Need for Speed racing video game series.

Laura W. Black (Ph.D., University of Washington) is an assistant professor in the School of Communication Studies at Ohio University. She studies public deliberation, dialogue, and conflict in small groups. Much of her work investigates the use of personal storytelling in public forums and she is particularly interested in online citizen discussions. Her research has examined how members of online deliberative groups tell personal stories to help them manage conflicts, make arguments, and build community. Her work has appeared in Communication Theory, Human Communication Research, International Journal of Public Participation, Journal of Public Deliberation, Small Group Research, Political Communication, and several edited books.

Willow I. Brown is an Assistant Professor in the School of Education at the University of Northern British Columbia, where she coordinates a graduate program in educational leadership. Drawing on her years as a teacher leader, her academic work focuses on professional inquiry, learning community development, and instructional leadership, with recent publications in Young Children, Networks Online

Journal of Teacher Research, and Pacific Rim Studies. Her work in developing pedagogy for multimodal literacies, with Judith Lapadat and supported by the Social Sciences and Humanities Research Council of Canada, is showcased in a new online space for teacher collaboration, the Learners' Platform Network.

Kevin Burden is an education specialist with a background in history, education and technology. His research investigates how technology impacts on learning with specific reference to the use of technologies for professional learning and professional development. He is interested in the emergence of new media forms and social networking and how they can be incorporated into teaching and learning. He is currently focused on work around the framework outlined in this chapter (DiAL-e) which he has developed with his colleague and co-author, Simon Atkinson. Kevin has worked in a variety of different educational settings including schools and the university sector where he is currently responsible for post-graduate professional development (PPD) at The University of Hull. He works with teachers and other educators from across the region to explore their own professional learning through action research and other related methodologies. He is the programme director for the Advanced Certificate in Sustained Professional Development, a Teacher Development Agency (TDA) programme based in the work-place.

Jennifer J. Bute (Ph.D., University of Illinois at Urbana-Champaign) is an assistant professor in the School of Communication Studies at Ohio University. She studies communication about health in personal relationships and is particularly interested in issues related to privacy/disclosure, social support, and gender. Her recent projects include an analysis of women's communication about fertility-related norms and privacy management for women coping with infertility. Her worked has appeared in Health Communication, Human Communication Research, Communication Teacher, Qualitative Health Research, and Social Science and Medicine.

Jan Chovanec is assistant professor in the Department of English and American Studies at the Faculty of Arts, Masaryk University in Brno, Czech Republic, where he completed his doctoral thesis (2001) on the interpersonal aspects of news in English. His field is sociolinguistics and discourse analysis, mainly in the area of media discourse and legal language. He has published in linguistic journals (e.g. Discourse & Communication) and volumes (e.g. The Linguistics of Football; Language and the Law: International Outlooks; Current Directions in Political Discourse Analysis: Methodological and Critical Perspectives). His research interests include the interactive nature of discourse in media contexts, the representation of social actors, and word play. He has recently focused on the language of live text commentary. He is the editor-in-chief of the journal Brno Studies in English.

Scott C. D'Urso (Ph.D., University of Texas at Austin, 2004) is an Assistant Professor of Communication Studies at Marquette University, where he teaches courses focused on organizational and corporate communication and new communication technology. His primary research interests include organizational use of communication technologies such as e-mail, instant messaging and chat. He has published manuscripts on privacy and surveillance in the workplace, new communication technology usage, communication channel selection, crisis communication and stakeholder issues. He is currently working on several projects including digital divides in organizations, and the role of online identity creation and privacy concerns with social networking websites. Prior to a career in academia, Scott worked for several years as a multimedia specialist/manager of a multimedia production department for a government defense contractor in the Southwest.

Jolane Flanigan is a Ph.D. candidate in Communication and graduate student in Women, Gender, Sexuality Studies at The University of Massachusetts Amherst. Her research explores the ways people make gender meaningful in different contexts, through different channels of communication. Her current research on the construction of gender in an alternative living community combines an intersectional approach to gender with ethnography of communication theory and methods to examine the ways a localized gender ideology shapes communication practices, the manner in which members relate to one another, and understandings of the body and the environment. She has taught courses in interpersonal and cultural communication and currently teaches within the Women, Gender, Sexuality Program.

At the time of writing, **Anna Filipi** was a Senior Research Fellow at the Australian Council for Educational Research and Project Director for the Assessment of Language Competence certificates. Her research interests include the application of the findings and methods of Conversation Analysis to the study of language acquisition (both First and Second) and spatial language as well as her more recent interest in online interactions in a work setting. She is also interested in bilingualism and teacher education. She is currently living in Switzerland where she continues to work as a Consultant for ACER.

Tamar Ginossar received Ph.D. in health communication from the University of New Mexico, where she is now Research Assistant Professor. Her expertise and primary research interests are health communication in intercultural settings and communication technologies. In particular, her research focuses on (a) understanding processes of individuals' and communities' health information seeking and use of new communication technologies for health promotion, empowerment, and advocacy, and (b) creating culturally-appropriate community-based interventions to reduce health disparities. She published articles in different journals including Applied Communication, Communication-Education, Health Care for Women International, Health Communication, the Journal of Computer Mediated Communication, and in book chapters.

Kathy Guthrie, Ph.D. is an Assistant Professor in Educational Leadership and Policy Studies at Florida State University. In this position she coordinates the Undergraduate Certificate in Leadership Studies and teaches in the Higher Education Program. Before joining Florida State University, Dr. Guthrie served as a Clinical Assistant Professor in Experiential and Service-Learning Programs at University of Illinois at Springfield, as well as spending several years as a student affairs administrator. Dr. Guthrie's interests and areas of expertise focus on development of leadership skills and responsible citizenship in undergraduate students. Her current focus is on learning outcomes in relation to reflective teaching and learning through curricular and co-curricular pedagogies.

Dale Holt is Associate Director of the Institute of Teaching and Learning at Deakin University. Dale has focused on teaching staff members' and students' experiences of teaching and learning in higher education over his career with a special focus on flexible, online and distance education contexts. He has researched the professional development experiences of participants undertaking postgraduate management studies at a distance, undergraduate students' learning in various online and work placement settings, and the special case of teaching and learning in wholly online environments. He has had an interest in leadership and management in higher education, most notably around the design and implementation of e-learning technologies across the organization and the strategic leadership of teaching and learning centers. Dale enjoys collaborative research and evaluation projects with colleagues within Deakin and other universities. He has published in a range of journals related to distance education, educational technology and cooperative education.

Benjamin Kehrwald is an e-learning specialist currently with Massey University as Senior Lecturer, Distance and Online Education. He is involved with design, development and postgraduate teaching in e-learning, online learning, blended learning and other uses of technology in the service of education. His research interests include social learning theory, computer mediated communication, social presence and teaching and learning in higher education.

Judith C. Lapadat, Northwest Regional Chair for the University of Northern British Columbia and Professor of Education, publishes in both scholarly and literary realms. Her academic work, focused on language, literacy, technology, and qualitative research methods, most recently has been published in Qualitative Inquiry, the International Review of Qualitative Research, the Journal of Distance Education, and the Proceedings of the World Conference on E-Learning in Corporate, Government, Healthcare, and Higher Education 2009. Current interests include autoethnographic writing, and multimodal literacies in electronic environments. The latter has been funded by a three year grant awarded by the Social Sciences and Humanities Research Council of Canada.

Lynnette G. Leonard's research and teaching interests include communication and new technology. Active in Second Life (SL) since 2006, she has integrated SL into her communication classes since Spring 2007. She has been integral in the development of the University of Nebraska at Omaha (UNO) School of Communication's SL campus. She has presented on SL and education to the faculty at UNO, the Omaha Public School District, and the Lincoln Public School district. Along with Lesley Withers (in 2008) and with Withers and John Sherblom (2009), she conducted SL training workshops at the annual National Communication Association conferences. For further information on their SL project, see Leonard, L. G., Withers, L. A., & Sherblom, J. C. (2010, March). The paradox of identity and computer-mediated communication: Promise, peril, and Second Life. In J. Park & E. Abels (Eds.), Interpersonal relations and social patterns in communication technology. Hershey, PA: IGI Global Publishing.

Laurie K. Lewis (Ph.D., University of California at Santa Barbara, 1994) is an Associate Professor in Rutgers' School of Communication and Information. Her areas of expertise include organizational change, stakeholder communication, nonprofit organizations, and interorganizational collaboration. Her research has appeared in a variety of communication and management journals. Prior to her doctorate, she earned her M.A. in Communication from the University of Illinois and her B.A. from the University of Washington. She has held faculty positions at The Pennsylvania State University and The University of Texas at Austin. Dr. Lewis' research has been funded by the Microsoft Foundation, RGK Foundation, and the Veteran's Administration. She has consulted for a number of for-profit, nonprofit and governmental organizations including Habitat for Humanity, USAID, Internal Revenue Service, Austin Presbyterian Theological Seminary, Community Action Network, Frito Lay, Merrill Lynch, and Kraft Foods.

Sophie Lissonnet has a Masters in Information Management and a Masters in Indigenous Studies. She works as an indexer and digital repository officer at the Cunningham Library (Australian Council for Educational Research) in Melbourne. In 2008, she was invited by the ALC team to set up and support the ALC wiki for the purpose of test development.

Kris M. Markman (Ph.D., 2006, The University of Texas at Austin) is an Assistant Professor in the Department of Communication at the University of Memphis. She teaches classes in computer-mediated communication, new media, and broadcasting, and conducts research on people's everyday uses of new communication technologies. She is particularly interested in examining language and social interaction in online groups and communities. A former public radio professional, she is also interested in how the internet is changing the way media content is produced and distributed, particularly by amateurs and fans, and has recently begun studying independent podcasters.

Holly McCracken, M.A., is currently employed as the Director of Online Programming for the College of Liberal Arts and Sciences at the University of Illinois, Springfield where she oversees academic support provision for web-based programs, including student recruitment, outreach, and other capacity-building activities. She has previously taught at both the undergraduate level (in a variety of programs focusing on non traditional learning, including applied studies, liberal studies, and prior learning assessment) and at the graduate level (in the curricular areas of instructional design, training and performance improvement, and adult and post-secondary education) in both media-based and on ground learning environments. Additionally, McCracken is a faculty member at Capella University where she teaches web-based undergraduate and graduate courses in the areas of business and technology, and education. Her areas of professional interest include adult and post secondary education, outreach and program development and administration, and media-based instructional delivery.

Megan Morrissey graduated from the University of North Carolina at Greensboro in 2008 with an MA in Communication Studies. She is currently pursuing her PhD in Communication at the University of Colorado at Boulder. Her research interests include applied communication, critical cultural studies, women and gender studies and communication pedagogy.

Stuart Palmer is a Senior Lecturer in the Institute of Teaching and Learning at Deakin University. He is a chartered professional engineer, having practiced in consulting engineering for a decade before joining the School of Engineering at Deakin University. He lectured in the management of technology for twelve years, working with engineering students studying in on-campus, off-campus, off-shore and online modes. In 1999 he was awarded the Australasian Association for Engineering Education McGraw-Hill New Engineering Educator Award. His research interests include frequency domain image analysis and the effective use of digital/online technologies in teaching and learning. More recently, he has joined the Deakin University Institute of Teaching and Learning where he contributes to institutional research and academic professional development.

Terri Toles Patkin is Professor of Communication at Eastern Connecticut State University in Willimantic, Connecticut. Her research focuses on the boundary between interpersonal and mass communication, changes in social interaction following the introduction of new technologies, and the sociology of popular culture.

Laura D. Russell (M.A., University of Dayton) is a doctoral student in the School of Communication Studies at Ohio University. Her work draws from both organizational and health communication perspectives to examine issues concerning wellness and recovery. Her research includes studies of online social support dynamics, particularly those taking shape on Workaholics Anonymous and pro-anorexia websites.

Roy Schwartzman (Ph.D., University of Iowa) is a Professor of Communication Studies at the University of North Carolina at Greensboro. His research interests include computer-mediated communication, online teaching and learning, rhetoric of science and technology, figurative language, and Holocaust studies. He is founding co-editor of the Journal of Applied Learning in Higher Education and serves on the editorial review boards of several IT journals, including Informing Science Journal and the Journal of Information Technology Education. His research is published in many journals and anthologies, including Communication Education, College Student Journal, the Journal of Communication and Media Research, and the Journal of Instructional Psychology. He is the author of Fundamentals of Oral Communication (Kendall/Hunt).

Craig R. Scott (Ph.D., Arizona State University, 1994) is an Associate Professor of Communication and Director of the Ph.D. program in the Rutgers School of Communication & Information. His research examines communication technology use, identification, and anonymous communication in the workplace. His work related to communication technology use by organizational members has been published in Communication Monographs, Communication Research, Management Communication Quarterly, Journal of Computer-Mediated Communication, IEEE Transactions on Professional Communication, Western Journal of Communication, Communication Quarterly, Small Group Research and several current and forthcoming book chapters. He has been on the top paper panel at international, national, and regional conferences 13 different times. He currently serves on the editorial boards for Human Communication Research, Communication Monographs, and Management Communication Quarterly.

John C. Sherblom teaches undergraduate and graduate courses in communication and technology, persuasion, organizational communication, and research methods at the University of Maine. He currently teaches a course in Second Life (SL). His research interests focus on issues of identity, presence, social support, and group decision making processes in SL. He has published numerous research articles and book chapters, and is the author of a textbook on Small Group and Team Communication that is in its fifth edition. Along with Lesley Withers and Lynnette Leonard, he conducted a SL training workshop at the 2009 meeting of the National Communication Association. An example of his recent collaborative work is: Sherblom, J. C., Withers, L. A., & Leonard, L. G. (in press). Communication challenges and opportunities for educators using Second Life. In J. Kingsley & C. Wankel (Eds.), Higher education in virtual worlds: Teaching and learning in Second Life. Bingley, UK: Emerald.

Eleni Sideri graduated from Aristotle University of Thessaloniki, department of French Language and Literature where she also completed a Master Degree in Sociolinguistics. Then, she continued her postgraduate studies in Social Anthropology at the School of Oriental and African Studies(SOAS)/ University of London where she completed a PhD in Social Anthropology. Her research was focused on the memories and practices of diaspora among the Greek-speaking communities of Georgia (South

Caucasus). She taught at various departments, such as, SOAS, New York College –Skopje. She is currently teaching at the department of History, Archaeology and Social Anthropology, University of Thessaly. Her academic interests are globalization and diasporas, language and media, new technologies.

Kevin Y. Wang is a Ph.D. candidate in the School of Journalism and Mass Communication at the University of Minnesota-Twin Cities. He received his master's degree in digital media and bachelors degrees in political science and communications from the University of Washington. Kevin conducts research on the social and political implications of new communication technologies and teaches courses in new media, strategic communication, and globalization. Along with topics in online discussion, he has authored papers and articles on Web campaigning, electronic government, and virtual communities.

Lesley A. Withers publishes research on computer-mediated social support and presents at academic conferences on teaching and communication in Second Life (SL). She teaches graduate and undergraduate courses in the area of interpersonal communication, nonverbal communication, and research methods at Central Michigan University (CMU). Active in SL since 2006, she has taught multiple courses incorporating SL and engaged in research on the effects of communication apprehension, competence, and social presence on students' class participation in SL. She was a presenter in 2008 and an invited speaker in 2009 on topics related to education in SL at one of the national Lilly Conferences on College and University Teaching. She serves as chair of the SL learning community at CMU. Along with Lynnette Leonard (in 2008) and with Leonard and John Sherblom (2009), she conducted SL training workshops at the annual meetings of the National Communication Association.

Index